HUMAN RIGHTS

the essentials of...

HUMAN RIGHTS

Rhona K.M. Smith
Christien van den Anker

Hodder Arnold

A MEMBER OF THE HODDER HEADLINE GROUP

First published in Great Britain in 2005 by
Hodder Arnold, a member of the Hodder Headline Group,
338 Euston Road, London NW1 3BH

http://www.hoddereducation.com

Distributed in the United States of America by
Oxford University Press Inc.
198 Madison Avenue, New York, NY10016

The advice and information in this book are believed to be true and
accurate at the date of going to press, but neither the authors nor the publisher
can accept any legal responsibility or liability for any errors or omissions.

British Library Cataloguing in Publication Data
A catalogue record for this book is available from the British Library

Library of Congress Cataloging-in-Publication Data
A catalog record for this book is available from the Library of Congress

ISBN–10 0 340 81574 4
ISBN–13 978 0 340 81574 8

2 3 4 5 6 7 8 9 10

Hodder Headline's policy is to use papers that are natural, renewable and
recyclable products and made from wood grown in sustainable forests. The logging
and manufacturing processes are expected to conform to the environmental
regulations of the country of origin.

Typeset in 8/10pt New Baskerville by Dorchester Typesetting Group Ltd
Printed and bound in Spain

What do you think about this book? Or any other Hodder
Education title? Please send your comments to the feedback
section on www.hoddereducation.com

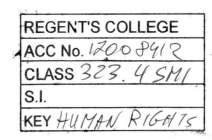

Contents

Rights and freedoms

Preface

In barely 50 years, international human rights have evolved into a distinctive branch of international law of increasing importance in global politics. The belief that individuals should not be exclusively at the mercy of their governments is so widespread it could be called a global consensus. Human rights have now become an issue that extends beyond the discipline and practice of international law. Students of politics, international relations, sociology and cultural studies are all looking at aspects of human rights. This has resulted in the flourishing of programmes of study on human rights globally. These include programmes for future lawyers as well as multidisciplinary programmes involving philosophy, politics, sociology and law.

In practice, the doctrine of human rights has become the only universal moral discourse in international politics. Despite criticism of its foundations (Western, male dominated, Enlightenment-based), its contents (the right to a holiday with pay is irrelevant in countries too poor to provide safe drinking water to their populations) and its practice (US domination of the UN; hypocrisy in requiring implementation of human rights), human rights discourse has been taken up with vigour by social movements and grassroots organisations in protest against governments as well as multinational corporations. The supposed cultural relativity of the concept of human rights is contradicted by a wide variety of groups all over the world stating their demands in terms of human rights and, increasingly, the human rights doctrine includes the perspectives of women and minority groups. In recent international law this is recognised by including separate instruments on minority rights, women's rights, children's rights and the rights of migrants.

The challenge for human rights is now to work towards more universal implementation worldwide. The trend towards establishment of national human rights institutions, the inception of the International Criminal Court and the consensus at the 1993 Vienna World Conference on Human Rights are all steps in the right direction. However, in order to make human rights a reality all over the world, the present contest over their meaning and who is to enforce them needs to take into account cultural difference and the possibility of non-Western conceptions of human dignity as a base for the implementation of human rights with support from local communities. Likewise, the hijacking of the human rights agenda as a justification for military intervention for the sake of national interests needs to be avoided.

In other words, the language of human rights is used widely, but this also makes it difficult to see whether or not it is always critical and progressive. Yet this struggle for the meaning of human rights notwithstanding, the codification in international and national law provides a basis for pressure by NGOs and grassroots campaigners. In order to make human rights more relevant the advocates need to integrate some of the criticism and the critics need to engage with the central message of the human rights discourse.

The aim of this volume is to contribute to human rights education by providing a quick way for people who are new to the human rights debate to familiarise themselves with the history of human rights, the debates over their justification, instruments, examples of specific rights and freedoms and the present state of their implementation. The breadth of expertise contained within this volume provides an insightful overview of these issues.

We have compiled a thematic table of contents which should help the reader to quickly find information on any given topic. Each contribution includes a list of further reading. In addition, words in bold cross reference directly to another entry.

Inevitably with a work like this, there are a number of other people whose assistance and support must be gratefully acknowledged. At Hodder Arnold, Liz Gooster steered the project while Liz Wilson provided substantial back-up support. Emma Dowling provided valuable administrative support. Jérémie Gilbert and Audrey Guichon kindly assisted with identifying experts on several of the topics. Finally, the contributors themselves are due an enormous thank you, particularly given the tight schedule within which we were working.

The text is accurate (as far as the contributors and editors are aware) as at 28 June 2004.

Rhona K. M. Smith and Christien van den Anker

Foreword – Mary Robinson

An essential guide such as this provides an opportunity for anyone who has an interest in human rights to become informed of the broad framework, the principles, norms and standards of international human rights. It gives perspective in noting the developments over more than half a century since the adoption of the Universal Declaration of Human Rights. It indicates the legal basis for promoting global justice and ending impunity for gross violations of human rights. It explains the value of a human rights approach to global issues such as tackling poverty and promoting sustainable development.

This guide, in short, is essential reading for all in the spirit of the Preamble to the Universal Declaration, which saw itself 'as a common standard of achievement for all peoples and all nations, to the end that every individual and every organ of society, keeping this Declaration constantly in mind, shall strive by teaching and education to promote respect for these rights and freedoms…'.

The climate of today is, of course, different and challenging. Doubts have been raised as to whether international law itself, including international human rights and humanitarian standards, will be able to deal with the challenges of our new millennium – from global diseases like HIV/AIDS to persistent challenges such as extreme poverty. From imbalances in international trade policies which impact on development in the poorest countries to violent conflicts and threats of terrorism, which are no longer confined within borders.

As states shed their power both upwards (to regional and international institutions) and downwards (through decentralisation and to private actors) how can we ensure that governments live up to their existing commitments to human rights? What safeguards are in place to provide redress and protection for citizens whose rights, for example, are violated by private security companies contracted by the state? What role will the International Criminal Court play in cases involving international actors? To whom are multinational corporations held accountable for their actions? How much reform is necessary for the appropriate international organisations to ensure equitable trade, effective development policies and the ability for states and citizens alike to take effective action when human rights have been violated or have not been progressively implemented? These are some of the important issues of our time and ones which I believe can be addressed through the principles and tools inherent in the international human rights system.

The authors whose scholarship is presented in this *Essentials of Human Rights* collectively illustrate that human rights are more relevant than ever to the most pressing global concerns – and indeed are a powerful set of standards and legal commitments which can help to bridge the vast divides in our world.

I welcome this guide as a source book and a valuable contribution to a deeper understanding of the universality of human rights and the need for constant dialogue on how to imbed human rights values in different cultures in a way which tackles discrimination and protects minorities. If we can build on these shared values, this century can, after such a difficult beginning, become one of human development and human security for all – a century of human rights and of peace.

Mary Robinson

Biographies

Feride Acar Professor Feride Acar holds a PhD from Bryn Mawr College, Pa., USA and is Professor at the Middle East Technical University, (METU), Ankara, Turkey. Her main research areas are women's human rights; women in education and academia; women and Islamist politics; social and political movements and Turkish political life. Professor Acar has been serving as member (since 1997) and chairperson (since 2003) of the UN Committee for the Elimination of Discrimination Against Women (CEDAW).

Christien van den Anker Dr Christien van den Anker is a Lecturer and acting Deputy Director at the Centre for the Study of Global Ethics at the University of Birmingham. She trained as a political theorist and is working on a theory of global justice and on the development and implementation of international norms. She currently works on two EC-funded projects: the Network of European Women's Rights (NEWR) and Releasing Indigenous Multiculturalism through Education (RIME) which focuses on combating racism in South Eastern Europe, Russia and the Caucasus. Her most recent publication is *The Political Economy of New Slavery*, Palgrave 2004.

Karin Arts Dr Karin Arts is Associate Professor in International Law and Development at the Institute of Social Studies in The Hague, The Netherlands. She published a range of writings on ACP-EU development cooperation and has advised several governmental and non-governmental organisations on the human rights and gender aspects of this relationship.

Peter R. Baehr Professor Peter R. Baehr is Professor Emeritus of Human Rights at the Universities of Leiden and Utrecht. Publications in English include: (with Leon Gordenker) *The United Nations at the End of the 1990s* (1999), *Human Rights: Universality in Practice* (2001), (with Monique Castermans-Holleman and Fred Grünfeld) *Human Rights in the Foreign Policy of the Netherlands* (2002), (with Monique Castermans-Holleman) *The Role of Human Rights in Foreign Policy* (2004).

Tae-Ung Baik Professor Tae-Ung Baik is Assistant Professor of Law at the Faculty of Law, University of British Columbia. He holds an LLB degree from the Seoul National University College of Law and studied law at Notre Dame Law School (LLM and JSD candidate). He was visiting scholar at the EALS, Harvard Law School during 2002-2003. He is writing his dissertation on problems related to the human rights system in Asia and his publications include *A War Crime against an Ally's Civilians: The No Gun Ri Massacre.*

John Baker Dr John Baker is Senior Lecturer in Equality Studies at University College Dublin. He is the author of *Arguing for Equality* (1987) and co-author of *Equality: From Theory to Action* (2004). His main areas of research are theoretical issues of equality and democracy.

Anneliese Baldaccini Anneliese Baldaccini is Human Rights Legal Officer (Asylum) at JUSTICE, the British section of the International Commission of Jurists. She has acted as a policy advisor to the UK Foreign and Commonwealth Office on preparations for the 2001 UN World Conference Against Racism and has been consultant for various human rights organisations on issues of asylum and immigration, minority rights, and non-discrimination. She is the author, amongst others, of *Providing Protection in the 21st Century – Refugee rights at the heart of UK asylum policy* (2004), a report published by the Asylum Rights Campaign in the UK.

Nicholas Bamforth Nicholas Bamforth BCL MA (Oxon) is a Fellow in Law at Queen's College. He previously taught at University College London and Cambridge, UK.

Peter Bartlett Dr Peter Bartlett is a Senior Lecturer in Law at the University of Nottingham. Following two degrees in philosophy at the University of Toronto, Peter Bartlett read law at Osgoode Hall Law School of York University, Canada. After his call to the bar in 1988, he served as Law Clerk to the Justice of the Ontario High Court and then as research associate to the Ontario Enquiry on Mental Competency. He obtained his doctorate in 1993. His major research and teaching interests lie in the areas of socio-legal history (particularly as it relates to queer studies and to mental health) and health care law (particularly mental health law).

Upendra Baxi Professor Upendra Baxi is currently engaged at Warwick University Law School. He has held various appointments in India, the USA and Australia, including Vice Chancellor of the University of Delhi. His areas of specialist interest include comparative constitutionalism, social theory of human rights, law in globalisation, science, technology and human futures. He has also prepared the People's Report on Human Rights Education.

Tristan Anne Borer Tristan Anne Borer is an Associate Professor of Government at Connecticut College in New London, Connecticut, USA. She is the author of *Challenging the State: Churches as Political Actors in South Africa: 1980-1994* (Notre Dame, IN: University of Notre Dame Press, 1998), as well as the forthcoming *Telling the Truths: Truth Telling and Peacebuilding in Post-Conflict Societies.* She has also published several articles on the South African Truth and Reconciliation Commission. She teaches courses on human rights and world politics, South African politics, women's human rights, and the politics of refugees.

Giovanni Bonello Giovanni Bonello was born in Malta and has been a judge in the European Court of Human Rights since 1998. Before that, he had been a practising lawyer, specialising in human rights litigation. He defended 170 human rights cases in the domestic courts, the European Commission of Human Rights and the European Court of Human Rights, before his appointment as judge.

Richard Bourne Richard Bourne has been Head of the Commonwealth Policy Studies Unit, University of London, since 1998. He was the first Director of the non-governmental Commonwealth Human Rights Initiative.

Bill Bowring Bill Bowring is a barrister and Professor of Human Rights and International Law at London Metropolitan University, where he is also Director of the Human Rights and Social Justice Research Institute. He is Academic Co-ordinator of the Institute's European Human Rights Advocacy Centre (EHRAC), which, in partnership with the Russian NGO 'Memorial', assists Russians in taking cases to the European Court of Human Rights. Professor Bowring has been working in Russia and the FSU generally since 1991. He is an Executive Committee Member of the Human Rights Committee of England and Wales; a Council Member of Liberty, the National Council for Civil Liberties; a Fellow of the Human Rights Centre at the University of Essex; and a Member of the Rule of Law Council of the International Helsinki Federation.

Kevin Boyle Professor Kevin Boyle is Professor of Law, University of Essex and member of the university's Human Rights Centre. He was senior advisor to the United Nations High Commissioner for Human Rights, Mary Robinson, 2001-02. He has written widely on international human rights themes, including on freedom of religion and racial discrimination. He is also a practising lawyer with extensive experience of litigation before the European Court of Human Rights.

Maria Virginia Bras Gomes Ms Bras Gomes was born in Goa (India). She presently lives and works in Lisbon. She is Head of the Department of Social Research and International Relations of the Directorate-General of Solidarity and Social Security of the Ministry for Social Security and Labour and a Member of the UN Committee of Economic Social and Cultural Rights, since January 2003.

Fernne Brennan Fernne Brennan holds BA, LLB, LLM, PG Dip, Law and PGCTLHE degrees and is a Lecturer in Law and a member of the Human Rights Centre at the University of Essex. Her current research interests focus on institutional racism, including a study of the treatment of ethnic minority women within the criminal justice system, reparations for trading in slaves, and racial and religious hate crime. She received an award from the Arts and Humanities Research Board to write a book entitled *Institutional Racism and the Law.*

Joshua Castellino Dr Joshua Castellino completed his PhD in International Law at the University of Hull, UK in 1998. He worked as a journalist in India, covering a wide range of issues including human rights, before being awarded the British Council Chevening Scholarship in 1995. He regularly publishes articles on issues related to international law and human rights, and is the author of two books: *International Law & Self-determination* (The Hague: Kluwer 2000) and *International Law & the Acquisition of Territory* (Dartmouth: Ashgate 2002, with Steve Allen).

Kathleen Cavanaugh Dr Kathleen Cavanaugh obtained her PhD in the Department of Government at the London School of Economics & Political Science and an LLM in Comparative International and Human Rights Law at Queen's University of Belfast. She is currently a Lecturer in International Law at the National University of Ireland, Galway, in the Irish Centre for Human Rights.

Christina M. Cerna Dr Christina M. Cerna is Principal Specialist in the Inter-American Commission on Human Rights and has been a member of the General Secretariat of the Organisation of American States since 1979. She has taught International Human Rights Law as an Adjunct Professor at George Washington University Law School.

Shami Chakrabarti and **Kathryn Kenny** Shami Chakrabarti is Director of Liberty. A law graduate from LSE, she practised briefly as a barrister before joining the Home Office legal department in 1995. She became Liberty's in-house counsel in September 2001 and has been Director of Liberty since September 2003. Kathryn Kenny qualified as a solicitor in 1997 and worked for five years as a litigation lawyer for a commercial firm in London. Since 2003 she has worked as a volunteer researcher and legal advisor for both Mind and Liberty.

Joseph Chan Joseph Chan is Associate Professor of the Department of Politics and Public Administration, University of Hong Kong. His research interests include Confucian political philosophy, the theory and practice of human rights in Chinese societies, liberalism and perfectionism, and civil society.

Stephen Chan Professor Stephen Chan received his PhD from the University of Chicago Divinity School and currently is an Associate Professor of Religious Studies at Seattle University, USA. He has published articles in the areas of Buddhist-Christian dialogue, Christian mysticism, and hermeneutical theory.

Simon Chesterman Simon Chesterman is Executive Director of the Institute for International Law and Justice at New York University School of Law. His books include *You, The People: The United Nations, Transitional Administration, and State-Building* (Oxford University Press, 2004) and *Just War or Just Peace? Humanitarian Intervention and International Law* (Oxford University Press, 2001).

Rebecca J. Cook Professor Rebecca Cook holds the Faculty Chair in International Human Rights, the Faculty of Law, and is cross-appointed to the Faculty of Medicine and Joint Centre for Bioethics, University of Toronto. Her most recent book, co-authored with B.M. Dickens and M.F. Fathalla, is *Reproductive Health and Human Rights* (Oxford University Press, 2003). She is a recipient of the Ludwik and Estelle Jus Memorial Human Rights Prize and is a Fellow of the Royal Society of Canada.

James Cooper James Cooper is Assistant Dean, Mission Development and Executive Director of the Center for Creative Problem Solving at California Western School of Law, San Diego. His entry is co-authored posthumously with **Janeen Kerper** who was Professor of Law at California Western School of Law and Academic Director of the Center for Creative Problem Solving. She died in January 2003.

J. Angelo Corlett Professor J. Angelo Corlett is Professor of Philosophy & Ethics at San Diego State University and the Editor-in-Chief of *The Journal of Ethics: An International Philosophical Review* (1997-present) and *Equality and Liberty: Analysing Rawls and Nozick* (1990). He is the author of over 75 articles and the following books: *Analysing Social Knowledge* (1996); *Responsibility and Punishment* (2001); *Race, Racism, and Reparations* (2003); and *Terrorism: A Philosophical Analysis* (2003); *Ethical Dimensions of Law* (2005); *Interpreting Plato's Dialogues* (2005).

François Crépeau and **Delphine Nakache** François Crépeau's posts include Professor of International Law, Faculty of Law, University of Montreal; Canada Research Chair in International Migration Law; and Scientific Director of the International Studies

Centre of the University of Montreal (CERIUM). The author gratefully acknowledges the financial support of the Fonds québécois de recherches sur la société et la culture (FQRSC), of the Social Sciences and Humanities Research Council of Canada (SSHRC) and of Valorisation-Recherche Québec (VRQ). Delphine Nakache is a Research Associate, Faculty of Law, University of Montreal and Doctoral Student, Institute of Comparative Law, McGill University.

Simone Cusack Simone Cusack (BA/LLB (Hons) Candidate, Monash University; Osgoode Hall Law School, York University 2003) interned with the Victorian State Parliament, Australia, for which she authored *Hidden Identities of a Nation: A Report on the Role of Women in Natural Resource Management* (2000). Simone also interned with the Australian Red Cross and most recently the Australian Permanent Mission for the UN Commission on Human Rights. She is currently working with Professor Rebecca Cook on *Women's Access to Justice: The Optional Protocol to the Convention on the Elimination of All Forms of Discrimination against Women* (2005).

Katerina Dalacoura Dr Katerina Dalacoura is Lecturer in International Relations at the London School of Economics and Political Science. She has previously worked at the University of Essex and at the International Institute of Strategic Studies. Her main areas of expertise are Human Rights and Democracy in the Middle East, Political Islam and Western Policies towards the Middle East. She is author of *Islam, Liberalism and Human Rights* (2003) and *Engagement or Coercion* (2003).

Scott Davidson Professor Scott Davidson is a graduate of the University of Cambridge. He has taught in law schools in England and New Zealand. He has written extensively in the field of international law and has a particular interest in human rights and the law of the sea. He is a member of the editorial and advisory boards of the International Journal of Marine and Coastal Law, the New Zealand Yearbook of International Law and the New Zealand Journal of Public and International Law. He is currently Pro Vice-Chancellor (Law) in the University of Canterbury, New Zealand.

Simon Davies Simon Davies' work in the fields of privacy, consumer rights and technology policy has spanned twenty years. He is the founder and Director of the watchdog group Privacy International (PI), and is a Visiting Fellow in the Department of Information Systems of the London School of Economics.

Marie-Bénédicte Dembour Marie-Bénédicte Dembour is a Lecturer in Law at the University of Sussex; she is also an anthropologist. Her original interests were colonialism and memory; human rights has now become her predominant field of research, with a sub-interest in migration. She has published numerous articles and co-edited *Culture and Rights: Anthropological Perspectives*. With the support of a Leverhulme Research Fellowship and the AHRB, she is currently finishing a monograph about the concept of human rights, its critiques and the European Convention.

Emma Dowling Emma Dowling (BA International Relations/MSc Global Ethics) is the outreach officer at the Centre for the Study of Global Ethics, University of Birmingham, UK. She has published in the areas of Development Ethics, Human

Rights and International Political Economy, as well as on the European and World Social Fora. She is an active campaigner with the movements for global justice and is currently preparing for a doctorate on the relationship between social movements and national and global governance institutions.

Ulrich Duchrow Ulrich Duchrow is professor of theology at Heidelberg University. He is also a representative of Kairos Europe and main inspirator of the European Ecumenical Coalition. His publications include *Alternatives to global capitalism* (1996) and *Property for people not for profit* (2004).

Tim Dunne Tim Dunne is Reader in International Relations and Head of the Department of Politics, University of Exeter, UK. He is author of *Inventing International Society* (1998) and was associate editor of the Review of International Studies from 1998-2002. He has edited six books including *Human Rights in Global Politics* (with Nicholas J. Wheeler, 1998) and *Worlds in Collision: Terror and the Future of Global Order* (with Ken Booth, 2002).

Asbjørn Eide Asbjørn Eide is Senior Fellow at the Norwegian Centre for Human Rights and Torgny Segerstedt Professor of Human Rights at the University of Gothenburg, Sweden. He was the Director of the Norwegian Institute (now Centre) of Human Rights since its inception in 1987 to 1998. He has been a member of the United Nations Sub-Commission on the Promotion and Protection of Human Rights for 20 years, Chairman of its working group on Minorities, and is a member of the Council of Europe's advisory committee on national minorities. His main publications deal with the development of the international system for the protection of human rights in general, and on economic and social rights and minority rights in particular.

Tony Evans Tony Evans is Senior Lecturer in the Department of Politics and International Relations at the University of Southampton, UK. His research interests are human rights and human dignity, globalisation, and international relations. His publications include *The Politics of Human Rights: A Global Perspective*, London: Pluto Press (2001) and *Human Rights Fifty Years On: A Reappraisal.* Manchester: Manchester University Press and New York: St. Martin's Press (1998).

Miranda Forsyth Miranda Forsyth holds an LLB/BA Hons from Melbourne and an LLM from Connecticut. She is a Lecturer in the Law School at the University of the South Pacific. She is currently writing a thesis on the issue of the relationship between customary legal systems and the state legal system in Vanuatu.

Michael Freeman Professor Michael Freeman is Research Professor in the Department of Government, University of Essex. He is author of *Human Rights: An Interdisciplinary Approach* (Polity Press, 2002), and numerous books and articles on political theory, human rights, minorities, ethnic conflict and genocide. He has lectured on human rights in more than twenty countries.

Des Gasper Des Gasper studied economics, international development and evaluation at the universities of Cambridge and East Anglia, and spent the 1980s working in Southern Africa. From 1989 he has been at the Institute of Social Studies in The Hague, specialising in public policy analysis, evaluation, argumentation analysis and develop-ment ethics. His publications include *Arguing Development Policy* (co-editor R. Apthorpe; Cass, 1996) and *The Ethics of Development* (Edinburgh University Press, 2004).

Conor Gearty Professor Conor Gearty is Rausing Director of the Centre for the Study of Human Rights and Professor of Human Rights Law at the LSE. He is also a barris-ter, practising at Matrix chambers. His most recent book is *Principles of Human Rights Adjudication* (Oxford University Press, 2004).

Nazila Ghanea Nazila Ghanea is Senior Lecturer in International Law and Human Rights at the University of London, Institute of Commonwealth Studies. Her recent publications include the monograph *Human Rights, the UN and the Bahá'ís in Iran* (The Hague: Kluwer Law, 2003); the edited collection *The Challenge of Religious Discrimination at the Dawn of the New Millennium* (Leiden: Martinus Nijhoff, 2003) and a forthcoming journal article with Human Rights Quarterly *Convergences and dispari-ties between the human rights of religious minorities and of women in the Middle East* (August 2004). Her areas of interest include minority rights, freedom of religion or belief and the UN human rights machinery. She produced a 2003 UN publication on minorities in Iran.

Jérémie Gilbert Jérémie Gilbert (Maitrise Paris X/UQAM, LLM in International Human Rights Law, Galway) received his PhD from the Irish Centre for Human Rights, Galway. He worked for the South Asia Documentation Centre in New Delhi, India and is a co-founder and project officer of the organisation Human Rights for Change (www.humanrightsforchange.org). He is a guest lecturer at the Centre for the Study of Global Ethics (University of Birmingham) and a lecturer at the Transitional Justice Institute, University of Ulster, UK. He has published on indige-nous people's rights in international law, the link between human rights and envi-ronmental protection and on self-determination. His most recent publication is 'The Blur of a Distinction: Adivasis Experience with Land Rights, Self-Rule and Autonomy' in N. Walsh and J. Castellino, *Indigenous Peoples & Human Rights Law* (Kluwer, 2004).

Mario Gomez Dr Mario Gomez holds LLB, LLM and PhD degrees and is a Program Associate with the Berghof Foundation for Conflict Studies in Colombo and a mem-ber of the Law Commission of Sri Lanka. He was previously a lecturer in law at the University of Colombo and has published in the areas of economic and social rights, women's rights, national institutions and internally displaced persons. He has been involved in human rights programs for judges, members of the armed forces and civil society activists.

Michael Goodhart Michael Goodhart teaches political theory at the University of Pittsburgh. He studies democratic and human rights theory and has just completed a book tentatively entitled *Democracy as Human Rights: Freedom and Equality in the Age of Globalization*. He is president of the American Political Science Association's human rights section.

Carol C. Gould Carol Gould is Professor of Philosophy and Government and Director of the Center for Global Ethics at George Mason University. She is the author of

Globalizing Democracy and Human Rights (Cambridge University Press, 2004) and of *Rethinking Democracy* (1988), and editor of seven books including *Cultural Identity and the Nation-State* (2001) and *Gender* (1999). She has been Fulbright Chair at the European University Institute and President of the American Society for Value Inquiry and is currently Editor of the Journal of Social Philosophy.

Francesco Grillo is Director and **Simona Milio** and **Claire O'Brien** are consultants of the Italian think-tank Vision (www.vision-forum.org).

Audrey Guichon Audrey Guichon (LLB LLM) is currently employed at the Centre for the Study of Global Ethics at the University of Birmingham. She is the researcher for the EC-funded project Network for European Women's Rights (NEWR). Before that, she worked as an intern at the International Secretariat of Amnesty International, London and at the South Asia Human Rights Documentation Centre, New Delhi.

David Hallmark David Hallmark is a practising Lawyer in the UK, with international experience working in US Courts-Martial (in the Vietnam War) and in Thailand, Indonesia and Hong Kong. He is the author *The Role of Lawyers in Developing Countries* (Lawasia 1975), and was a mission member for the International Commission of Jurists to Thailand (1978 and 1992) and Malaysia (1985). He founded the Worcester Human Rights Academy to promote understanding of the history of human rights because the body of King John, who signed the Magna Carta of 1215, lies in Worcester Cathedral and also because Worcester is the place where the English Civil War started in 1642 and finished in 1651.

Hurst Hannum Professor Hurst Hannum is Professor of International Law at The Fletcher School of Law and Diplomacy of Tufts University. He has served as a consultant to the United Nations on a number of issues and has served on the boards of several non-governmental human rights organizations. Among other publications, Professor Hannum is author of *Autonomy, Sovereignty, and Self-Determination: The Accommodation of Conflicting Rights* (revised ed. 1996), co-author of *International Human Rights: Problems of Law, Policy, and Practice* (3rd ed. 1995) and editor of *Guide to International Human Rights Practice* (4th ed. 2004).

Sirkku K. Hellsten Dr Sirkku Hellsten is Reader in Development Ethics and acting Director of the Centre of the Study for Global Ethics, University of Birmingham. She previously worked as Philosophy Programme Coordinator at the University of Dar es Salaam and as a Senior Research Fellow at the University of Helsinki. She has conducted research on various topics in development ethics and global justice focusing particularly on women's rights, health and HIV/AIDS, non-Western concepts of human rights and post-colonial theory.

Eric Herring Eric Herring is Senior Lecturer in International Politics at the University of Bristol. His entry was written with the support of a grant from the Economic and Social Research Council held jointly with Glen Rangwala.

Christof Heyns Professor Christof Heyns studied law and philosophy at the Universities of Pretoria, Yale (USA) and the Witwatersrand. He is Professor of Human Rights Law and the Director of the Centre for Human Rights at the University of Pretoria. He has served as technical consultant in respect of the repeal of discriminatory legislation during the transition in South Africa; and has done consultancies for the UN Office of the High Commissioner for Human Rights and the Organisation of African Unity. His publications include *The Impact of the UN Human Rights Treaties on the Domestic Level*, and the annual *Human Rights Law in Africa* series.

Edel Hughes Edel Hughes obtained a degree in Law and French from University College Cork and an LLM in International Human Rights Law from NUI Galway. She is currently a doctoral fellow at the Irish Centre for Human Rights, NUI Galway.

Andreas Huyssen Andreas Huyssen is the Villard Professor of German and Comparative Literature at Columbia University where he also served as founding director of the Center for Comparative Literature and Society. He is one of the founding editors of *New German Critique*. His books in English include *After the Great Divide: Modernism, Mass Culture, Postmodernism* (1986), *Twilight Memories: Marking Time in a Culture of Amnesia* (1995), and *Present Pasts: Urban Palimpsests and the Politics of Memory* (2003).

Vinodh Jaichand Vinodh Jaichand is Deputy Director of the Irish Centre for Human Rights. He has been the National Executive Director of Lawyers for Human Rights in South Africa. Prior to that he was Associate Professor and Dean at the Faculty of Law in the University of Durban-Westville. He holds a doctorate and an LLM (magna cum laude) from the University of Notre Dame. His publications include a book on *The Restitution of Land Rights in South Africa*.

Niraja Gopal Jayal Professor Niraja Gopal Jayal is Professor at the Centre for the Study of Law and Governance, Jawaharlal Nehru University, New Delhi. Her publications include *Democracy and the State: Welfare, Secularism and Development in Contemporary India* (OUP, 1999) and *Democracy in India* (ed.) (OUP, 2001). Her current research interests include citizenship, gender and governance, ethnic inequality in public institutions, and environmental political theory.

Peter Jones Professor Peter Jones is Professor of Political Philosophy at the University of Newcastle. He has written on a number of subjects, including human rights, group rights, cultural diversity, freedom of belief and expression, political equality, democracy, liberalism and toleration. His publications include *Rights* (Basingstoke: Macmillan, 1994).

Ratna Kapur Professor Ratna Kapur is Director of the Center for Feminist Legal Research, New Delhi, and Global Visiting Professor at NYU School of Law.

Jan Kavan Jan Kavan (BSc, IOM) is a Member of the Czech Parliament, Former Foreign Minister and Deputy Prime Minister of the Czech Republic and Former President of the United Nations General Assembly. Mr Kavan founded and ran the Palach Press Agency. He returned to Prague from political exile in november 1989 and was elected in June 1990 to Parliament. His academic career included a Visiting Professorship of Politics and History at Adelphi University (New York) from 1993 to 1994 and the Karl Loewenstein Fellowship in Politics and Jurisprudence at Amherst

College (Massachusetts). In June 2002 Jan Kavan was elected Deputy to the Czech Parliament where he now serves on the Foreign Affairs Committee.

Mike Kaye Mike Kaye has worked in the human rights field for nearly 15 years. This includes field work in Central America, as a policy officer for the Central America Human Rights Committee and as Parliamentary Officer for the Refugee Council. He is currently the Communications Manager for Anti-Slavery International.

David Keane David Keane is a PhD candidate and a Government of Ireland scholar at the Irish Centre for Human Rights, National University of Ireland, Galway, where his area of research is caste-based discrimination in international law. He holds an LLM in international human rights law from NUI Galway, and a BCL in Law and French from University College Cork, Ireland. He is also a founding member of the human rights organisation Human Rights for Change. He previously published 'The Environmental Causes and Consequences of Migration: A Search for the Meaning of "Environmental Refugees"', 16 *Georgetown International Environmental Law Review* (2004) p 209.

Kevin Kerrigan Kevin Kerrigan is a Principal Lecturer in Law at Northumbria University. He is also a practising solicitor with extensive experience of conducting criminal cases. His teaching and research interests are in the fields of criminal litigation and human rights. He was formerly the cases editor of the *Journal of Civil Liberties* and has written numerous articles and practitioner textbooks. Kevin was a member of the Lord Chancellor's Department Human Rights Act Walkthrough Committee and has provided numerous human rights training courses for professionals, including solicitors, police, barristers, social workers, mental health professionals and court clerks.

Miloon Kothari Miloon Kothari is the Special Rapporteur on adequate housing with the UN Commission on Human Rights. He was appointed in 2000 to this global mandate charged with monitoring, research and investigative functions to examine the right to housing and related issues, including water and sanitation, women's rights to land, housing, property and inheritance and protection against forced evictions. Kothari, an architect by training, lives in New Delhi, India and has extensive civil society experience in housing and land rights. He is currently Coordinator of the South Asian regional programme of Habitat International Coalition's Housing and Land Rights Network.

Thomas R. Lansner Thomas Lansner has taught on international media and politics at Columbia University School of International and Public Affairs since 1994. He writes regularly on international affairs, and has served as a consultant on media, elections, human rights, and democratisation issues. From 1980–1990 Mr Lansner was a correspondent in Africa and Asia for the *Observer*, the *Guardian*, and other publications.

Iain Law Dr Iain Law is a lecturer in Philosophy at the University of Birmingham. He researches and teaches in the areas of Moral and Political Philosophy. He specialises in normative ethics, especially contemporary moral theory.

Jeremy McBride Jeremy McBride is Reader in International Human Rights Law, University of Birmingham and Visiting Professor, Central European University; member, European Union Network of Independent Experts in Fundamental Rights; expert on human rights law for the Council of Europe and Organisation for Co-operation and Security in Europe; Editor, *Butterworths Human Rights Cases* and Consultant Editor, *Commonwealth Human Rights Law Digest*; co-founder and Vice-Chair of INTERIGHTS (the International Centre for the Legal Protection of Human Rights).

Sheila A. M. McLean Professor Sheila McLean is the Director of the Institute of Law and Ethics in Medicine and professor in Law at the University of Glasgow, UK. She has acted as a consultant to the World Health Organisation and the Council of Europe, and to individual states. She has published extensively in the area of medical law and is on the editorial boards of a number of national and international journals.

Sorcha MacLeod Sorcha MacLeod is a lecturer in law in the Department of Law at the University of Sheffield. She joined the department in 2001 and she teaches, researches and publishes in the areas of human rights, international law, globalisation and transnational corporations.

Chris McWilliams and **Jonathan Walton** Dr Jonathan Walton works for Glasgow Caledonian University and is Research Fellow in the Sustainability Centre in Glasgow, a multi-disciplinary research centre at the University that integrates expertise in the built and natural environment with that in the social sciences and the field of business. Dr Chris McWilliams is Lecturer in Urban Studies at Heriot-Watt University, Edinburgh, UK.

Sumi Madhok Sumi Madhok is a Senior Lecturer at the University of Plymouth, UK.

Ivan Manokha Ivan Manokha holds a PhD from Sussex University, UK and is currently lecturing on International Relations and International Political Economy at the University of Le Havre and on Business Ethics at ESSEC Business School, France. His publications include 'Modern slavery and Fair Trade products: buy one and set someone free' in C. van den Anker (ed.) *The Political Economy of New Slavery*, Palgrave, 2004: 217-234.

Christopher May Christopher May is Reader in International Political Economy at the University of the West of England (UK). His publications include *A Global Political Economy of Intellectual Property Rights: The New Enclosures?* (Routledge 2000) and *The Information Society: A Sceptical Vview* (Polity 2002) as well as numerous articles on issues connected with IPRs. As one of the series editors for the IPE Yearbook, he is currently editing a volume on *Global Corporate Power* and is also in the final stages of writing an international history of IPRs with Susan Sell.

Ann Elisabeth Mayer Dr Ann Mayer earned a PhD in Middle Eastern History from the University of Michigan in 1978; a Certificate in Islamic and Comparative Law from the School of Oriental and African Studies in 1977; and a JD from the Law School of the University of Pennsylvania in 1975. She is an Associate Professor of Legal Studies at the Wharton School of the University of Pennsylvania. She has published extensively on law in the contemporary Middle East and on resistance to international human rights law in both Muslim and Western societies.

András Miklós András Miklós is a PhD candidate at the Department of Political Science, Central European University, Budapest, Hungary. He specialises in political philosophy.

Yousry Moustafa Yousry Moustafa is a researcher and human rights activist from Egypt. He was the ED of the Egyptian Organization for Human Rights and Programs Coordinator of the Cairo Institute for Human Rights Studies. In 2003, he was appointed a human rights consultant to the Ford Foundation Cairo Office exploring the opportunity of establishing an Arab Human Rights Fund. His areas of interest are civil society, human rights and social movements in the Arab region.

Tim Mulgan Professor Tim Mulgan studied at the Universities of Otago and Oxford. He currently teaches at the University of Auckland. From June 2005, he will be Professor in Moral and Political Philosophy at St Andrews University. He is the author of *The Demands of Consequentialism* (Oxford University Press, 2001) and of a number of articles on moral and political philosophy in leading international journals.

Timothy Murithi Dr Timothy Murithi is a Programme Officer in the Programme in Peacemaking and Preventive Diplomacy at the United Nations Institute for Training and Research (UNITAR) in Geneva. He is responsible for coordinating the Regional Training Programme to Enhance Conflict Prevention and Peacebuilding in Africa. In 2003 he was a Visiting Research Fellow at the Africa Centre for Peace and Conflict Studies, in the Department of Peace Studies, at the University of Bradford, UK.

Rachel Murray Dr Rachel Murray is Lecturer in Law at the University of Bristol. She has taught previously at Birkbeck College, University of London, and Queens University Belfast where she was also Assistant Director of the Human Rights Centre. She has written widely on the African human rights system, but is also currently working on a Nuffield funded project evaluating the Northern Ireland Human Rights Commission.

Mario Novelli and **Berenice Celeyta** Mario Novelli is a writer and researcher at the Centre for Studies of Globalisation, Societies and Education based at the University of Bristol, UK, and a founding member of the Colombia Solidarity Campaign. Berenice Celeyta is the Director of the Association for Investigation and Social Action NOMADESC, a Colombian based human rights NGO. She is also the Director of the Human Rights Department of SINTRAEMCALI, a Colombian Public Service Trade Union based in Cali in the South West of Colombia.

Manfred Nowak Professor Manfred Nowak is Director of the Ludwig Boltzmann Institute of Human Rights at Vienna University, Chairperson of the European Master Programme on Human Rights and Democratisation in Venice, UN expert on enforced disappearances and adviser of the UN High Commissioner for Human Rights on poverty reduction strategies. His past positions include Director of the Netherlands Institute of Human Rights at Utrecht University, Olof Palme Visiting Professor at the

Raoul Wallenberg Institute of Human Rights and Humanitarian Law at Lund University and judge at the Human Rights Chamber for Bosnia and Herzegovina in Sarajevo.

Clémentine Olivier Clémentine Olivier is a jurist, specialised in international and comparative criminal law. She has a Diplôme d'Etudes Approfondies in Public International Law from Université de Paris II (1994), and an LLM in International Human Rights Law from the University of Essex (2000). She is currently finalising a doctoral research at the National University of Ireland (Galway). She is a Fellow of the Irish Research Council for the Humanities and Social Sciences and a member of the expert group on Draft Criminal Codes for Post Conflict Justice, at the Irish Centre for Human Rights and the United States Institute of Peace, in cooperation with the United Nations.

Dianne Otto Dr Dianne Otto teaches human rights law at the Faculty of Law, The University of Melbourne, Australia, where she is an Associate Professor. Her research focuses on examining the ways in which human rights law can be used, paradoxically, to maintain marginalization and inequality, rather than redress it. Her work is particularly concerned with the way that gender hierarchies are reproduced by human rights law, and she draws on a range of critical and postcolonial theories in order to suggest strategies to resist such replications.

John Otieno Ouko John Otieno Ouko was born in Western Kenya in 1974. He holds a Bachelor of Arts degree in Philosophy (Hons) from Urbaniana University in Italy and a Master of Arts degree in Philosophy from the University of Nairobi in Kenya. Currently he is a visiting Lecturer in Philosophy at Kenyatta University and works for the Kenya Human Rights Commission as Programme Associate.

David Ould David Ould is the Deputy Director of Anti-Slavery International. He has been closely involved with campaigning on issues of the commercial sexual exploitation of children and the use of bonded child labour in the hand knotted carpet industries of South Asia. He helped to establish ECPAT UK and Rugmark UK. The representative for Anti-Slavery International and Chair of the NGO Caucus of the Ethical Trading Initiative, a UK based group that brings together companies, trade unions and non-governmental organisations to set common standards for companies trading in the South and to work together to trial different approaches to the monitoring and verification of these standards. He is also the Treasurer of Kalayaan, a UK based NGO working in support of migrant domestic workers.

Bhikhu Parekh Professor Bhikhu Parekh is professor of political philosophy at the University of Westminster and Emeritus professor of political theory at the University of Hull. He has been a Visiting Professor at McGill, Harvard, University of Pennsylvania and the University of British Columbia, and a Centennial Professor at the LSE. He is a Fellow of the British Academy, President of the Academy of Learned Societies for the Social Sciences, a Labour Member of the House of Lords, and a recipient of the Sir Isaiah Berlin Prize for Lifetime Contribution to Political Studies. He has written extensively on Hannah Arendt, Marx, Gandhi, non-western political thought, multiculturalism and global ethics.

Jo M. Pasqualucci Dr Jo Pasqualucci is a professor at the University of South Dakota School of Law. She has an SJD in International and Comparative Law from the George Washington Law School where she studied under Judge Thomas Buergenthal and Professor Louis B. Sohn. She worked at the Inter-American Court of Human Rights while on a Fulbright in 1986–87.

Jelena Pejic Jelena Pejic is a Legal Adviser in the Legal Division of the International Committee of the Red Cross (ICRC). She is also Head of the ICRC's Project on the Reaffirmation and Development of International Humanitarian Law.

Thomas Pogge Professor Thomas Pogge received his PhD from Harvard. He is Professorial Research Fellow at the Centre for Applied Philosophy and Public Ethics at Australian National University. A member of the Norwegian Academy of Science, his research has been supported, most recently, by the John D. and Catherine T. MacArthur Foundation, the Princeton Institute for Advanced Study, All Souls College (Oxford) and the National Institutes of Health.

Rebecca Probert Rebecca Probert is a lecturer in law at the University of Warwick, specialising in family law. She previously worked as a research assistant at the Law Commission and taught at the University of Wales Aberystwyth and the University of Sussex. Her research examines the development of the law relating to marriage and cohabitation, from both an historical and a comparative perspective. She is currently writing a book on eighteenth-century marriage law.

Andrew Puddephatt Andrew Puddephatt is Director of Article 19, a major NGO focusing on freedom of expression. He is also a visiting lecturer at Westminster University, London, UK.

Oliver Richmond Oliver Richmond is a lecturer in the Department of IR, University of St. Andrews, UK. His publications include *Maintaining Order, Making Peace* (Palgrave, 2002) and *Mitigating Conflict: The Role of NGOs* (co-edited: Frank Cass, 2003). His latest monograph is entitled *The Transformation of Peace and War* (Palgrave, 2005).

Mary Robinson Mary Robinson is the Executive Director of the Ethical Globalization Initiative. She served as United Nations High Commissioner for Human Rights from 1997 to 2002 and as President of Ireland from 1990–1997. She is a founder member and Chair of the Council of Women World Leaders. Before her election as President, Mrs Robinson served as Senator, holding that office for 20 years. In 1969 she became Reid Professor of Constitutional Law at Trinity College, Dublin and now serves as Chancellor of Dublin University.

Nigel Rodley Professor Sir Nigel Rodley KBE, PhD (Essex), was the founding head of Amnesty International's legal office, at the same time as he taught part-time at the LSE (1973-90). He is Chair of the Human Rights Centre of the University of Essex, where he has taught since 1990 and is a Professor of Law. From 1993 to 2001, he served as Special Rapporteur on the question of torture for the United Nations Commission on Human Rights. Since 2001, he has been a member of the Human Rights Committee, established under the International Covenant on Civil and Political Rights. He is also a Commissioner of the International Commission of Jurists. In 1998, he was knighted for services to human rights and international law.

Deborah Rook Deborah Rook, LLB, solicitor, is a principal lecturer at the University of Northumbria. She lectures in Animal law and Property law and her publications include *Property Law and Human Rights* (Blackstone Press, 2001) and an article examining the human rights implications of a ban on hunting with dogs, *New Law Journal* (2001 151, p.372).

Colin Samson Dr Colin Samson is Senior Lecturer in Sociology and member of the Human Rights Centre at the University of Essex. He has been working with the Innu people of Northern Labrador since 1994 on projects examining the human rights implications of Canada's policies of assimilation and 'land claims.' His book, *A Way of Life That Does Not Exist: Canada and the Extinguishment of the Innu* was published in 2003 (Verso and ISER Press). Currently, he is undertaking research to document the health and other benefits of Aboriginal ways of life in the Far North.

Marília Sardenberg Marília Sardenberg was born in Brazil and is a Career Diplomat. She has been a member of the United Nations Committee on the Rights of the Child since 1993 and is the Brazilian Representative in the Working Group responsible for drafting the Convention on the Rights of the Child. She is also a founding Member of the Brazilian National Council on the Rights of Children and Adolescents.

Saskia Sassen Saskia Sassen is the Ralph Lewis Professor of Sociology at the University of Chicago, and Centennial Visiting Professor at the London School of Economics. She is currently completing her forthcoming book *Denationalization: Territory, Authority and Rights in a Global Digital Age* (Princeton University Press). She has edited one of fourteen volumes for the new UNESCO *Encyclopedia of Life-Systems*. Her most recent books are *Globalization and its Discontents* (New York: New Press 1998) and *Global Networks, Linked Cities* (New York and London: Routledge 2002). *The Global City* came out in a new fully updated edition in 2001.

William A. Schabas Professor William Schabas is director of the Irish Centre for Human Rights at the National University of Ireland, Galway, where he also holds the professorship in human rights law. A prolific author, he has also been very active on behalf of international non-governmental organizations, and served as one of three international commissioners of the Sierra Leone Truth and Reconciliation Commission.

Martin Scheinin Professor Martin Scheinin is Armfelt Professor of Constitutional and International Law and Director of the Institute for Human Rights at Åbo Akademi University, Finland (1998–), Dr iuris (1991, University of Helsinki) and Member of the Human Rights Committee (1997–2004).

Doris Schroeder Dr Doris Schroeder was educated in Germany and England in economics/management and philosophy/politics. She holds the post of Senior Lecturer in Philosophy at the Centre for Professional Ethics, Preston, England and is currently working on a book about human rights with the former Iranian President, A.H. Banisadr.

Rebecca Shah Rebecca Shah graduated with first class honours in Applied Psychology from Cardiff University. She has conducted research at the Institute of Child Health and was assistant psychologist at the National Centre for Young People with Epilepsy. She obtained an MSc in Global Ethics with distinction from Birmingham University. Her dissertation addressed the ethics of treating HIV/AIDS patients in sub-Saharan Africa. She is currently working at the UK Department for International Development contracted Governance Resource Centre at the University of Birmingham.

Dinah L. Shelton Professor Dinah Shelton is research professor of law at George Washington University School of Law. Prior to joining the GWU faculty in 2004 she directed the JSD program at Notre Dame Law School's Center for Civil and Human Rights. She has lectured at law schools throughout the world and has been a consultant to most major international organisations. She is the author of numerous books and articles, including the prize-winning books *Protecting Human Rights in the Americas* (with Thomas Buergenthal, 4th ed. 1995) and *Remedies in International Human Rights Law* (1999).

David Silbergh, **L. Chen** and **R. Greenwood** Dr Silbergh, Dr Chen and Dr Greenwood all work for Glasgow Caledonian University. They are respectively Associate Director, Research Fellow and Manager of the Sustainability Centre in Glasgow, a multi-disciplinary research centre that integrates expertise in the built and natural environment with that in the social sciences and the field of business.

Rhona K.M. Smith Dr Rhona Smith is a Principal Lecturer in Law at Northumbria University in Newcastle, UK. Her previous publications include *Textbook on International Human Rights* (OUP, 2nd edition 2004/5).

Awraham Soetendorp Awraham Soetendorp is rabbi of the Liberal Jewish Community, Amsterdam, the Netherlands.

Louise and Herbert F. Spirer Louise and Herbert Spirer are a team that has been working for over fifteen years in human rights. Ms Spirer is an independent scholar. Mr Spirer is Professor Emeritus of Operations and Information Management at the University of Connecticut and was a former Adjunct Professor of International Affairs at Columbia University.

Neil Stammers Neil Stammers is Senior Lecturer in Politics at the University of Sussex. His research interests lie in the fields of social movements, globalisation, power and human rights. He is currently writing a book on 'Social Movements and Human Rights' and editing a book on 'Global Activism/Global Media'.

Lisa Stearns Lisa Stearns has an LLB from the UK and an LLM from the US. She has taught law at Cardiff University, Wales and was Assistant Director of the Legislative Drafting Research Fund at Columbia Law School. She has worked with China and law reform issues since 1990, as a law teacher at Beijing University, then as a full-time consultant to the Beijing Office of the Ford Foundation and, since 1997, as Director of the China Programme at Oslo University's Norwegian Center for Human Rights.

Hillel Steiner Professor Hillel Steiner is Professor of Political Philosophy at the University of Manchester and a Fellow of the British Academy. He is the author of *An Essay on Rights* (1994) and co-author of *A Debate Over Rights: Philosophical Enquiries* (with Matthew Kramer and Nigel Simmonds, 1998). He is also co-editor of *The Origins of Left-Libertarianism: An Anthology of Historical Writings*, and *Left-Libertarianism and Its Critics: The Contemporary Debate* (with Peter Vallentyne, 2000). His current research includes the application of libertarian principles to global and genetic inequalities.

Shiyan Sun Dr Shiyan Sun holds an LLB, an LLM and an LLD. His positions include Research Fellow, Centre for International Law, Chinese Academy of Social Sciences; Director of Human Rights Institute, Centre for Jurisprudence of Jilin University; Visiting Professor 2003, Raoul Wallenburg Institute of Human Rights and Humanitarian Law, Lund University.

Lee Swepston Lee Swepston is chief of the Equality and Employment Branch, and Human Rights Coordinator, in the International Labour Standards Department of the International Labour Organization in Geneva. He took his legal degree at Columbia University in New York. After one year with the International Commission of Jurists, a human rights non-governmental organization in Geneva, he joined the ILO in 1973. His present responsibilities include supervision of the ILO's standards concerning equality, indigenous and tribal peoples, and employment policy issues, as well as coordination of the ILO's relations with other intergovernmental organizations concerning human rights questions. Mr Swepston is the author of a number of books and articles on international human rights and international labour standards.

Philippe Texier Philippe Texier is judge at the French Court de Cassation after having been Presiding Judge at the Court d'Appel de Paris. He is an expert member of the Committee on Economic, Social and Cultural Rights to which he has been elected and re-elected since 1987. He is also a member of the National Advisory Commission to the Prime Minister on Human Rights and has conducted numerous human rights missions in South America, Central America, Africa and Asia, as a consultant of the United Nations Centre for Human Rights or on behalf of non-governmental organisations.

Claire de Than Claire de Than is a Senior Lecturer in Law at City University, London, UK and has published academic articles and books on various areas within the fields of public law, civil liberties and international criminal law.

Thanh-Dam Truong Dr Thanh-Dam Truong is a women, gender and development specialist and senior lecturer at the Institute of Social Studies, the Hague, the Netherlands. She has pursued many areas of research in this field, including the problem of sex tourism.

Michael Urminsky Michael Urminsky is an official with the International Labour Office. His research interests centre on the interaction between business, economic relations and human rights. He holds a Graduate Degree from the University of Essex's Human Rights Centre (1996) where he also teaches on the subject of business and human rights.

Fernand de Varennes Dr Fernand de Varennes is Senior Lecturer, international law and human rights, Murdoch University, Australia, and Senior Non-resident Researcher at the European Centre for Minority Issues, Germany. Dr de Varennes is also laureate of the 2004 Linguapax Award.

Rebecca M.M. Wallace Professor Rebecca Wallace is Professor of International Human Rights Law at Robert Gordon University, Aberdeen, Scotland. She has written extensively and her publications, which include *International Law, A Student's Text* and *International Human Rights, Text and Materials,* enjoy a world wide readership. In 1994 she was the Ariel Sallows Professor in Human Rights at the University of Saskatchewan, Canada. She is a member of the English Bar as well as a part-time immigration adjudicator.

David Weissbrodt Professor David Weissbrodt has taught international human rights law at the University of Minnesota for over 25 years. He is a prominent scholar of international human rights and co-author of a major textbook on that subject; he has also published over 125 other books, monographs, and articles on human rights and other aspects of international law. Professor Weissbrodt served from 1996 to 2004 as a member of the UN Sub-Commission on the Promotion and Protection of Human Rights and as its chairperson in 2001–02.

Heather Widdows Dr Heather Widdows is a lecturer at the Centre for the Study of Global Ethics at the University of Birmingham. Her background is Systematic Theology, Moral Philosophy and Bioethics. Her current research focuses are the nature and status of moral value, communication across value frameworks and belief-systems and practical ethical issues in the global context, particularly the bioethical areas of genetic, research and reproductive ethics. She has recently been working on the philosophy of Iris Murdoch (published as *The Moral Vision of Iris Murdoch: A New Ethics*) and is now working on the topic of 'Religion, Ethics and Liberal Democracy' which is the topic of her Visiting Scholarship at the Centre of European Studies at Harvard which she will take up in 2005.

Andrew Williams, Solange Mouthaan and **Phil Shiner** Andrew Williams and Solange Mouthaan are lecturers in law at the University of Warwick and Phil Shiner is a practising solicitor at Public Interest Lawyers. All are executive members of Peacerights and were joint authors of the Report of the Inquiry into the Alleged Commission of War Crimes by Coalition Forces During the Iraq War 2003, which was submitted to the ICC in April 2004.

Shanti Williamson Shanti Williamson is a lecturer in Medical Law at the University of Glasgow, Scotland. She teaches in all areas of medical law, with a particular focus on Genetics and the Law. Her research interests lie mainly in the areas of Genetics and the Law and Law at the End of Life.

Duncan Wilson Duncan Wilson (LLB (Hons), LLM) is Coordinator of the Right to Education Project. Previously researcher to the United Nations Special Rapporteur on the right to education, he now works as Consultant with UNESCO International Bureau of Education, UNESCO and the Global Monitoring Report on Education for All.

Adrien Katherine Wing Professor Adrien Katherine Wing is the Bessie Dutton Murray Professor at the University of Iowa College of Law (USA), and she holds degrees from Princeton (AB), UCLA (MA), and Stanford Law School (JD). Author of over 70 publications, Professor Wing has taught at Iowa since 1987. Her courses include Human Rights, Law in the Muslim World, Constitutional Law, and Comparative Law.

Jane Wright Jane Wright is Professor of Law, Dean of the School of Law and a member of the Human Rights Centre at the University of Essex. Her research interests include international human rights law, minority rights, comparative law and tort law. She is author of *Tort Law and Human Rights* (Hart Publishing, 2001) as well as many articles on human rights, including minority rights.

Galina Yemelianova Galina Yemelianova is Senior Research Fellow at the Centre for Russian and East European Studies at the University of Birmingham. She has researched and published extensively in Russia and internationally on historical and contemporary ethno-political and religious issues in the Middle East and the Islamic regions of the Russian/Soviet empire and post-Soviet Russia.

Jean Ziegler Professor Jean Ziegler has been the UN Special Rapporteur on the Right to Food since his appointment by the UN Commission on Human Rights in September 2000. He is also Honorary Professor at the University of Geneva and at Paris, Sorbonne. **Sally-Anne Way** and **Christophe Golay** support his mandate through research carried out under the auspices of the Research Unit on the Right to Food based at the Graduate Institute of Development Studies, University of Geneva. For more information about the work on the right to food of the UN Special Rapporteur and the Research Unit, see www.righttofood.org

AFRICA: THE REALITY OF HUMAN RIGHTS

Promotion and protection of human rights is essential for the survival and progression of humanity. The concept of human rights has been with us for centuries and its formalisation into a distinct branch of law during the 20th century has been of utmost importance in solidifying its observance.

From the onset it is important to acknowledge that African states have been active in the ratification of, or accession to, human rights conventions. At the time of writing at least 43 African states have ratified the **INTERNATIONAL COVENANT ON CIVIL AND POLITICAL RIGHTS** (ICCPR), while 42 have ratified the **INTERNATIONAL COVENANT ON ECONOMIC, SOCIAL AND CULTURAL RIGHTS** (ICESCR). The two covenants form part of the 'international bill of human rights' that has moral and legal force and binds ratifying governments to respect and enforce the rights of their citizens. The ICCPR broadly seeks to advance and protect the rights of the people to elect their own governments, assemble freely, to be free from **TORTURE**, cruel, inhuman and degrading treatment, and to participate in political activity, among other rights. The ICESCR complements the provisions of the former covenant by promoting basic rights such as the right to **HEALTH**, **FOOD** and **EDUCATION**, the rights of workers, the right to work and the right to cultural identity.

Indeed, human rights are guaranteed in the political constitutions of almost all independent African states. The constitutions of Gabon, Nigeria, Rwanda, Burkina Faso, Cameroon, Guinea, Liberia, Malawi, Tanzania, Togo, Morocco and Cote D'Ivoire, to mention but a few, all contain lofty human rights provisions. At independence, the French-speaking African states invariably declared, in the preambles to their constitutions, adherence to the principles of democracy and human rights as defined in the Declaration of the Rights of Man and Citizen of 1789 and in the **UNIVERSAL DECLARATION OF HUMAN RIGHTS** of 1948. English-speaking African countries took similar steps.

Mano River Women's Peace Network (MARWOPNET) – West Africa Manu River Region

This network of women's organisations from Sierra Leone, Liberia and Guinea was established in May 2000 in response to the deteriorating security situation in the West African region. The network has brought an effective multidimensional, coordinated and regional approach to the struggle for human rights to restore peace and to ensure that women's voices are included at all levels of the decision-making process.

The Mano River Women's Peace Network has been active initiating projects for the demobilisation and reintegration of child soldiers; organising peace marches and public demonstrations; visiting refugee camps to distribute basic provisions and advocate for their special needs; and participating in programmes to destroy small arms. Its work to ensure gender equality in all spheres of nation building, and to teach conflict resolution and negotiation techniques was deemed likely to pay long-term dividends to future generations in the Mano River Region, hence the organisation was awarded the 2003 United Nations Prize in the Field of Human Rights.

(From www.un.org/events/humanrights/awards.html)

However, massive and systematic violations of basic human rights have continued to be committed in the independent African states, despite the throwing off of colonial rule in the 1950s and 1960s. In 1981, in response to growing human rights pressure at home and abroad, African heads of state adopted the **AFRICAN CHARTER ON HUMAN AND PEOPLES' RIGHTS** (Banjul Charter) and established an **AFRICAN COMMISSION ON HUMAN AND PEOPLES' RIGHTS** to promote, protect and interpret the human rights provisions enshrined in the charter.

Institutional protections essential for the enjoyment of human rights, such as an independent judiciary, are also constitutionally established in African countries' constitutions. The constitutions of Kenya, Ghana, Nigeria and those of many other African States contain detailed rules and procedures for the protection of human rights. The institution of the ombudsman, mandated to investigate complaints arising from administrative malpractice against individual citizens, was also created in certain countries such as Tanzania, Uganda, Senegal, Ghana and Nigeria. In 1987, Togo went further to establish an autonomous National Human Rights Commission to protect and promote human rights. Nigeria followed suit in 1995, creating a National Human Rights Commission to facilitate the country's implementation of its various treaty obligations. Uganda has also created the Ugandan Human Rights Commission while Kenya has created the Kenya National Commission on Human Rights.

Despite this express codification of human rights norms in the domestic legal systems of independent African states, unprecedented breaches of human rights have occurred repeatedly in Africa. Indeed, violence and human rights abuse exploded on the African continent in the 1990s. At least 800,000 Tutsis and moderate Hutus were systematically killed in the Rwanda genocide of 1994. Civilians were killed and tortured in conflicts between opposing forces in Somalia, Angola, Sierra Leone and recently Liberia. Political persecution of critics, political opponents, journalists and human rights activists is also common practice in many African states. Recent reports reveal that the president of Uganda, Yowari Museveni, has maintained a heavy hand over political opposition under the framework of his so-called 'no party system' of government since 1986. Ugandan security forces are torturing supporters of the political opposition and holding them in secret detention under the pretext of pursuing rebels.

Human rights organizations in Kenya reported an increase in torture and extra-judicial executions in 2004. In Rwanda there have been many human rights violations in which critics of the Rwandese government, including human rights activists and journalists, have been subjected to arbitrary arrests, ill treatment and attempted extra-judicial execution. Similar political persecution is occurring in Algeria, Zambia and many other African countries. In his final report to the African Human Rights Commission, Commissioner Ben Salem, the special Rapporteur on Extra-judicial Executions in Africa, indicted such countries as Rwanda, Burundi, Chad, Comoros and the Democratic Republic of Congo for state-sponsored extra-judicial executions and 'disappearances'.

At the moment the small gains which may have been made by a few African states with regard to civil and political rights risk being watered down by the passing of the Suppression of Terrorism Bill. Most African governments are keen on passing the bill because they are eager to go along with their 'development partners', at the cost of instituting a law that is against their citizens. In Africa in general and Kenya in particular the strongest concern about the bill is the imprecise manner in which terrorist offences are defined. In Kenya, for instance, if the bill becomes law it may lead to the death of the human rights movement because the bill gives the government a leeway to designate any movement in the country as terrorist; it will outlaw the growth of alternative politics; it will also hinder progressive democratisation in Kenya as it gives the state and its institutions draconian powers. The bill allows torture, maiming and even killing of suspects by security officers. If it becomes law in African countries this will return them to the dark ages of repression and terror. But African governments are bent on passing the bill because it will bestow on them the power to crush their opponents and critics.

Endemic state corruption also leads to systematic abuse of **SOCIAL, ECONOMIC, CULTURAL** and **ENVIRONMENTAL RIGHTS** of large majorities of people. In Nigeria, the government pervades almost every aspect of life and dominates the lucrative oil industry. In Kenya, high-ranking government officials including cabinet ministers have been involved in corrupt deals. The state and the corporate bodies often infringe on common citizens' rights. In many African countries, high-ranking government officials have stolen billions of shillings and stashed them in foreign accounts. Since the idea of an independent judiciary exists only on paper and not in practice in Africa, court orders, when they conflict with government and multinational interests, are routinely disobeyed. Such corruption has aggravated violations of the right to health, education, food, water, housing and employment, among others.

When confronted with the poor social and economic rights of their countries, African governments usually blame the World Bank/International Monetary Fund (IMF) approach to development as the factor most responsible for undermining the progressive realisation of economic and social rights in Africa. The two institutions have come up with certain conditions as means of sorting the African states' balance of payment problem. These conditions are cutbacks in state spending, such as withdrawing state subsidies on basic food items, social services, health, education and the civil service (which has led to staff lay-offs); abolition of subsidies for consumer items in areas of production such as agriculture; and control on wages and salaries for workers and decontrolled prices. These World Bank/IMF policies are unfavourable to the African economy. But even if all African debts were to be written off and the multilateral lenders' conditionality withdrawn, African citizens will not be able to realize their social and economic rights if corruption and mismanagement are not stamped out.

In summary, implementation of human rights in Africa has been and still is poor. The international procedures which Africans have been pursuing in an attempt to realise human rights have not qualified as effective substitutes for national mechanisms and measures in terms of giving effect to human rights standards. The primary responsibility of states is to the people who live under the jurisdiction. A first step would be for each African state to embark on a genuine search for the root cause of persistent human rights violations. It is from there that Africans can effectively address those issues.

Further Reading

Code, Luca (1991) *The African Charter on Human and Peoples' Rights*, Zimbabwe: Catholic Commission for Justice and Peace.

Larner, Natan (2000) *Religion, Beliefs and International Human Rights*, New York: Orbis Books.

Rupensinghe, Kumar (1998) *Human Conflict and Human Rights*, New York: UN University Press.

Shivji, Issa G (1989) *The Concept of Human Rights in Africa*, London: CODESRIA Books Series.

Contributor: John Otieno Ouko

THE AFRICAN CHARTER ON HUMAN AND PEOPLES' RIGHTS

The African Charter on Human and Peoples' Rights was adopted by the Organization of African Unity (OAU, now the African Union (AU)) in 1981, entered into force in 1986 and has been ratified by all 53 African states since 1995. The Charter was partially drafted at meetings in Banjul, The Gambia, and as a consequence it is also known as the Banjul Charter. Following in the footsteps of the European and Inter-American system, the Charter has created a regional human rights system for Africa (See: **THE AFRICAN COMMISSION AND COURT**).

The Charter of the Organization of African Unity of 1963 did not recognise the pursuit of human rights as one of the objectives of the organisation expressly, although some of the main aims of the OAU – such as the elimination of remaining instances of colonisation and apartheid – were indeed human rights objectives.

The Charter shares many features with other regional instruments. Nevertheless it has notable unique characteristics concerning the norms it recognises and also its supervisory mechanism. With regard to the norms that state parties undertake to comply with, the following may be noted:

1. The Charter recognises not only most of the universally accepted civil and political rights but also certain socio-economic rights.

The civil and political rights recognised in the Charter include the following: non-discrimination (Articles 2 and 18(3)); EQUALITY (Article 3); LIFE and personal integrity (Article 4); dignity (Article 5); freedom from SLAVERY (Article 5); freedom from cruel, inhuman or degrading treatment or punishment (Article 5); rights concerning arrest and detention (Article 6); FAIR TRIAL (Articles 7 and 25); RELIGION (Article 8); information and expression (Article 9); association (Article 10); assembly (Article 11); movement (Article 12); political participation (Article 13); and PROPERTY (Article 14).

The Charter, however, does not contain or adequately cover some of the internationally recognised civil and political rights. For example, a right to privacy or a right against forced or compulsory labour are not explicitly recognised, and the provisions covering fair trial and political participation are incomplete by international standards.

Uniquely, in the same document which recognises the civil and political rights outlined above, the following socio-economic rights are also contained: work ('the right to work under equitable and satisfactory conditions', Article 15); HEALTH (Article 16), and EDUCATION (Article 17).

In a remarkable decision, SERAC v Nigeria (2001) the Commission has held that the Charter should be understood to also include a right to housing and a right to FOOD.

2. The Charter recognises not only the individual rights mentioned above but also certain collective or GROUP RIGHTS. According to the Charter, the family has a right to be protected by the state (Article 18). 'Peoples' have the right to equality (Article 19), SELF-DETERMINATION (Article 20), to dispose of their wealth and national resources (Article 21), DEVELOPMENT (Article 22), peace and security (Article 23), and 'a general satisfactory ENVIRONMENT' (Article 24).

3. In addition to rights, the Charter includes duties. The duties recognised include those towards the family and state security and the duties to pay taxes and to promote the achievement of African unity (Article 29).

Article 27(2), which is also included under the heading 'duties', provides: 'The rights and freedoms of each individual shall be exercised with due regard to the rights of others, collective security, morality and common interest.'

Monitoring of compliance with the Charter by state parties is entrusted to the African Commission on Human and Peoples' Rights (African Commission). Operational since 1987 and based in The Gambia, the Commission consists of 11 part-time members, who meet twice a year for a two-week period, in either The Gambia or another African country. The Commission takes decisions in respect of complaints it receives from individuals about violations of the Charter by state parties (inter-state complaints are also possible but are rare); and reviews the reports which state parties are required to submit biannually. It also appoints special rapporteurs (eg in respect of prisons, extra-judicial executions, women, freedom of expression and indigenous peoples) and adopts resolutions on human rights issues. The Commission operates in terms of its Rules of Procedure (1995) and has issued Guidelines on Reporting to state parties (1989 and 1998).

When the Charter was drafted in the early 1980s, a decision was taken to create a commission without the power to take legally binding decisions. Consequently it did not follow the European and American model of the time of having a regional human rights court as well as a commission. It was argued that the traditional way of solving disputes in Africa was not through courts but through mediation and conciliation, a task for which a commission was better suited. Moreover, creating a supra-national court could have been perceived as threatening the sovereignty of newly independent states.

Two protocols to the African Charter have been adopted. The 1998 Protocol on the African Court on Human and Peoples' Rights entered into force in 2004. This provides for the creation of an African Human Rights Court to complement the jurisdiction of the Commission. The Protocol on the Court provides for the appointment of 11 judges, all of them part-time with the exception of the President of the Court. The Court will receive cases submitted by the Commission, individual states or where an additional declaration to that effect has been made by a ratifying state, cases submitted 'directly' to the Court by individuals.

The 2003 Protocol on the Rights of Women, which is not in force at the time of writing, has elaborated and extended the rights of women under the Charter.

The Commission is potentially powerful, but it is not yet a continental human rights force. Its work is not widely known and state parties routinely disregard its findings. The Commission has heard only a few hundred cases and most states do not take their reporting obligation seriously. The Commission is often criticised for the apparent lack of independence of its members and the Secretariat has been plagued by problems in its administration.

At the same time the Commission has to be credited for its creative interpretation of the African Charter, filling in the gaps in the Charter in numerous ways. The Commission has over the years carved out its own role in terms of receiving individual communications and state reports and the appointment of special rapporteurs, despite the fact that the Commission's mandate is not set out with clarity in the Charter. The Commission has elaborated the contents and expanded the scope of a number of rights recognised in the Charter.

The Commission has dealt with the question of how the rights contained in the Charter may be limited or even suspended. The Charter does not have an express general limitation clause outlining the conditions under which all the rights in the Charter may be limited. Instead, certain provisions in the Charter contain what are known as 'clawback' clauses: provisions according to which the rights in question are to be exercised 'within the law'. For example, Article 9(2) provides that 'every individual shall have the right to disseminate his opinions within the law'. Predictably, when taken to task before the Commission because of domestic laws that have allowed infringements of these rights, state parties have invoked the 'clawback clauses', and argued that the complainants had to comply with these domestic laws. The Commission has held, however, that such domestic laws have to comply with international standards. Increasingly, the Commission has used the general duty imposed by the Charter in Article

27(2), to exercise their rights within certain parameters, as a general limitation clause.

The Commission has also been required to interpret the implications of the absence of a derogation clause in the Charter. In other similar treaties such clauses define the conditions and extent to which the state is allowed to suspend rights during emergency situations. The Commission has ruled that the absence of a derogation clause means that Charter rights cannot be suspended during an emergency.

The Charter is silent on the issue of reservations by state parties. In practice, only three states have entered reservations or made deductions when they acceded to the Charter.

The Commission's creative interpretation of the Charter has served to fill numerous gaps in the Charter. However, at the same time it has led to a situation where the Charter, as interpreted by the Commission, has a meaning which in many respects differs from the apparent meaning of the text. In the long run this discrepancy undermines the rule of law and commentators have called for the Charter to be comprehensively reformed.

While the Commission suffers from resource constraints, it has developed innovative ways of drawing on and involving civil society. Commission sessions are preceded by a non-governmental organisation (NGO) forum, where human rights issues to be taken up with the Commission are discussed. Some of the more effective special rapporteurs have also received logistical as well as other support from NGOs.

Some of the other treaties with a human rights dimension adopted under the auspices of the OAU/AU and which complement the African Charter deal with refugees (1969/74) and children (1990/1999).

The African Union, in its 2001 Constitutive Act, explicitly recognises the realisation of human rights as one of its main objectives. The AU is developing the African Peer Review Mechanism (APRM) in respect of governance as part of the New Partnership for Africa's Development (NEPAD). Several sub-regional organisations in Africa, such as the South African Development Commuity (SADC) and Economic Community of West African States (ECOWAS), have also adopted human rights instruments.

The African Charter functions not in isolation but as part of a network of human rights instruments and protective mechanisms on the continent, such as the domestic and the UN regimes as well as the work of civil society. While this means that there is a much more conducive environment for the protection of human rights in Africa today than was the case 30 years ago, commentators have also warned about the proliferation of human rights mechanisms in the African Union drawing on the same resources.

The Commission created under the African Charter remains well placed to be of great value to the protection of human rights in Africa. Some of the challenges it faces include getting its own administration in order and the achievement of greater independence among commissioners. There is also an onus on state parties to take their obligations under the Charter more seriously in terms of the submission of state reports and the implementation of Commission decisions. Hopefully the large number of national human rights institutions in Africa can be mobilised to help monitor the implementation of the Charter and other international norms on the domestic level. Civil society remains obligated to promote the work of the Commission for the system to work. The way in which the relationship between the Commission and the African Human Rights Court is managed, as well as other mechanisms such as the APRM, will be crucial to the role of the Charter in the future.

WEBSITES

www.achpr.org – African Commission on Human and Peoples' Rights

www.africa-union.org – African Union

www.nepad.org – NEPAD

www.up.ac.za/chr – Centre for Human Rights, University of Pretoria

Further Reading

Evans, M. and Murray, R. (eds) (2002) *The African Charter on Human and Peoples' Rights: The system in practice, 1986–2000*, Cambridge: Cambridge University Press.

Heyns, C. (ed) (2004) *Human Rights Law in Africa*, The Hague: Martinus Nijhoff.

Mugwanya, G.W. (2003) *Human Rights in Africa: Enhancing human rights through the African regional human rights system*, Ardsley, N.Y.: Transnational Publishers.

Österdahl, I. (2002) *Implementing Human Rights in Africa – the African Commission on Human and Peoples' Rights and individual communications*, Uppsala: Iustus.

Ouguergouz, F. (2003) *The African Charter on Human and People's Rights: A comprehensive agenda for human rights*, The Hague: Kluwer Law International.

Contributor: Christof Heyns

THE AFRICAN COMMISSION AND THE COURT ON HUMAN AND PEOPLES' RIGHTS

In 1981 the Organization of African Unity (OAU), the political body for the African continent, adopted the **AFRICAN CHARTER ON HUMAN AND PEOPLES' RIGHTS**. This treaty contained a list of rights for individuals and for 'peoples'. Since then all member states of the OAU have agreed to be legally bound by the Charter.

The African Charter provided for one institution, the African Commission on Human and Peoples' Rights, to oversee implementation of the rights by states. This Commission was supposed to be independent and to have the power to promote and protect rights in the Charter by receiving reports from states every two years and having the power to examine complaints from anyone alleging that the Charter had been violated. Since it was established in 1987 the Commission, which is headquartered in The Gambia, has undertaken considerable work. It has adopted resolutions on a number of the rights in the Charter, elaborating further what they mean, as well as on a number of countries where there have been problems. It has made decisions on complaints that have come before it, finding that states have violated various rights in the Charter. Some of what are perceived as the more unusual human rights, the Commission has been willing to consider further. It has thus, for example, appointed a working group on indigenous populations/communities.

Although it is possible, therefore, to cite various successes of the Commission, it has come under considerable criticism. The

Commission, in order to operate effectively, must be independent of states. However, over the course of its history several of its 11 members have been known to have close government connections, some of them being ambassadors or holding government office whilst sitting on the Commission. This aside, in order for a body such as this to be able to carry out the required work, it must be adequately funded and resourced. This has been a consistent problem for the African Commission. From its inception it has been dogged by lack of funds from the OAU (although it has received funding from other sources) and its full-time secretariat in The Gambia is poorly staffed and resourced. This has inevitably impacted on its ability to be effective. Although the Commission has in more recent years gained increased respect from states and others for what it has done, its inability to be truly effective has been one of the reasons for calls for a court to be established.

The African Charter on Human and Peoples' Rights, unlike similar treaties in the European and Inter-American systems, did not initially provide for a court, only a commission. In the early days when an African Charter was under consideration, the idea of a court was raised, and various theories have been put forward as to why it was not adopted, including the suggestion that a judicial body was not appropriate for the African context and that a commission was sufficient. In more recent years, however, due to a feeling that the Commission was not as effective as it could be or that the African system was somehow incomplete without a court, the idea was raised again.

Prompted by NGOs – in particular Amnesty International and the International Commission of Jurists – the African Commission on Human and Peoples' Rights thus began looking at the need to establish a separate court to complement its functions. A series of meetings were held first in Cape Town in 1995, then in Nouakchott, Mauritania, in 1997, with the general agreement that a separate court should be adopted while maintaining the present commission. This reflected the previous European and existing Inter-American models. At these meetings, government experts and others worked towards drafting a Protocol to the

Amnesty International

Amnesty International (AI) is a worldwide movement of people who campaign for internationally recognised human rights. AI's vision is of a world in which every person enjoys all of the human rights enshrined in the Universal Declaration of Human Rights and other international human rights standards. It is independent of any government, political ideology, economic interest or religion. It is concerned solely with the impartial protection of human rights.

At the latest count, there were more than 1.8 million members, supporters and subscribers in over 150 countries and territories in every region of the world.

Amnesty produces an annual Amnesty International report documenting the human rights situation in hundreds of countries throughout the world.

(From www.amnesty.org)

African Charter to set up the court, namely a separate document that states would have to agree to. The document was finalised in 1998 and adopted formally by the OAU's Assembly of Heads of State and Government, although 15 states were required to agree to it for the court to actually come into force. This took a

International Commission of Jurists

The International Commission of Jurists (ICJ) was founded in 1952 and is based in Geneva.

What distinguishes the ICJ is its impartial, objective and authoritative legal approach to the protection and promotion of human rights through the rule of law. It has 60 members, all eminent jurists representing the world's differing legal traditions.

The ICJ provides legal expertise at both the international and national levels to ensure that developments in international law adhere to human rights principles and that international standards are implemented at the national level.

(See: http://www.icj.org)

number of years, but eventually, in January 2004, the court was established.

The aim of the Court, which is to be funded by the African Union, is to 'complement the protective mandate' of the Commission.

The Protocol provides for an 11-member court, composed of individual judges who should be jurists of 'high moral character and of recognised practical, judicial or academic competence and experience in the field of human and peoples' rights'. They must be nationals of African Union states but no two judges should be nationals of the same state. Judges are also required to be independent of government, although it is governments which nominate and appoint them. In the nomination and appointment process, there is the express requirement that there be 'adequate gender representation' and that 'main regions of Africa and principal legal traditions' also be reflected. Judges will generally sit for six years and can be re-elected once, their removal being by unanimous decision of the other judges and finalised by the Assembly of Heads of State and Government. Although judges hold part-time positions, a full-time registrar and staff are to be appointed by the Court. At the time of writing, a decision has yet to be made about the Court's permanent base.

The Court has the power firstly to adopt 'advisory opinions', namely to give an authoritative statement on an issue relevant to the African Charter or 'any other relevant human rights instrument'. This can be requested by African Union states, the African Union or any of its organs or 'any African organisation recognised' by the African Union. It can hear cases if they are submitted by the Commission, a state which has lodged a complaint to the Commission, a state against whom a complaint has been lodged at the Commission, a state whose citizen is the alleged victim of a violation, or African intergovernmental organisations. Individuals and NGOs can also apply directly to the Court alleging violations of rights under the Charter as long as states have agreed to be bound by the Protocol and made a separate statement that they allow the Court to hear such cases.

The Court has the power to try to reach an 'amicable settlement' between parties to the case. It can receive written and oral evidence and although its hearings are in public, it can hold private hearings if necessary. Legal representation may also be provided free 'if the interests of justice so require'. The Court can order a remedy if it finds a violation of the African Charter and this can include compensation or reparation. Judges are allowed to give separate and dissenting opinions, although the Court will give a majority decision.

It is difficult to know how the Court will function as it has yet to be established fully and judges are still to be appointed. However, the history of the African system suggests that several issues need to be considered carefully. Firstly, it is essential to give serious attention to ensuring that the judges appointed are independent from their governments and not subject to such pressure. A high-profile and inclusive nomination process involving elements of civil society at the national level can help to ensure a good quality pool of candidates.

Secondly, although the Court will exist alongside the African Commission on Human and Peoples' Rights, it is not clear how these two institutions will interact. Detailed consideration needs to be given to how this relationship will work in order to ensure efficiency when the Court actually starts operating.

Thirdly, the African human rights system has been struggling constantly with lack of financial support from the OAU, now African Union. As noted above, the African Commission on Human and Peoples' Rights has not received adequate funding from its founders (although it has received external support). If the Court is to operate effectively and if states are to show political commitment to it, they must be prepared to provide the necessary resources. As both the African Commission and the Court will be competing for funds, there needs to be close examination to ensure that they are provided to both.

Fourthly, the Protocol establishing the Court provides that its decisions will be legally binding. However, the Court is unlikely to add much to what the African Commission already does if this is not actually ensured in practice. Consideration must be given to an effective procedure to ensure that any state found in violation of human rights is checked to see whether it has complied with the decision.

Lastly, the Court is being created as part of the wider African Union in which there are numerous other organs which have some remit over human rights. Some attention must be given to how they will operate together.

WEBSITES

www.achpr.org – African Commission on Human and Peoples' Rights

www.africa-union.org – African Union Documents produced by the Organization of African Unity/African Union organs can be found on: www.iss.co.za, and more recently: www.au2003.gov.mz

Further Reading

Ankumah, E. (1996) *The African Commission on Human and Peoples' Rights. Practice and Procedures*, Martinus Nijhoff, The Hague.

Evans, M. and Murray, R. (2002) *The African Charter on Human and Peoples' Rights. The System at Work. 1986–2000*, Cambridge University Press.

Murray, R. (2000) *African Commission on Human and Peoples' Rights and International Law*, Hart Publishing.

Contributor: Rachel Murray

THE AMERICAN CONVENTION ON HUMAN RIGHTS

The American Convention on Human Rights (also known as the Pact of San José) was adopted at a special inter-governmental conference in San José, Costa Rica on 22 November 1969. In accordance with Article 74(2) the Convention entered into force on 18 July 1978 following the deposit of the 11th instrument of ratification by Grenada. The sources of inspiration for the drafters of the Convention were the non-binding American Declaration on the Rights and Duties of Man (1776), the UNIVERSAL DECLARATION OF HUMAN RIGHTS (1948), the United Nations INTERNATIONAL COVENANT ON CIVIL AND POLITICAL RIGHTS (1966) and the EUROPEAN CONVENTION ON HUMAN RIGHTS AND FUNDAMENTAL FREEDOMS (1950). The scheme, content and institutional structure of the American Convention is modelled closely on the latter instrument, but the American Convention's drafters, drawing on the experience of the European Convention, were able to avoid some of its less satisfactory elements. The inter-relationship between the American Convention and the instruments which inspired it are preserved by Article 29 which provides that the Convention is not to be interpreted as excluding or limiting the effects of the American Declaration on the Rights and Duties of Man or 'other international acts of the same nature', that is, other international human rights instruments. Two supervisory institutions are established by the Convention: the INTER-AMERICAN COMMISSION ON HUMAN RIGHTS (q.v.) and THE INTER-AMERICAN COURT OF HUMAN RIGHTS (q.v.).

The preamble to the Convention states that its purpose is 'to consolidate in this [the Western] hemisphere, within the framework of democratic institutions, a system of personal liberty and social justice based on respect for the essential rights of man'. Chapter I establishes the general obligation of the state parties to respect the rights and freedoms recognised in the Convention without discrimination and to give effect to those rights through domestic legislation or other measures. Chapter II contains a catalogue of civil and political rights which must be guaranteed to all persons. The list of rights to be protected comprises the right to juridical personality (Article 3); THE RIGHT TO LIFE (Article 4); the right to humane treatment (Article 5); FREEDOM FROM SLAVERY (Article 6); the right to personal LIBERTY (Article 7); THE RIGHT TO A FAIR TRIAL (Article 8); freedom from ex post facto laws (Article 9); the right to compensation for miscarriage of justice (Article 10); the right to privacy (Article 11); freedom of conscience and religion (Article 12); freedom of thought and expression (Article 13); the right of reply for injury by inaccurate or offensive statements or ideas disseminated to the public by a legally regulated medium of communication (Article 14); the right of assembly (Article 15); FREEDOM OF ASSOCIATION (Article 16); the rights of the family (Article 17); the right to a name; (Article 18); THE RIGHTS OF THE CHILD (Article 19); the right to nationality (Article 20); THE RIGHT TO PROPERTY; (Article 21); freedom of movement and residence (Article 22); the right to participate in government (Article 23); the right to equal protection before the law (Article 24); and the right to judicial protection (Article 25). In recognition of the relationship between rights and duties as evinced in the American Declaration on the Rights and Duties of Man, Chapter V, entitled 'Personal Responsibilities', states in its only provision (Article 32) that 'every person owes responsibilities to his family, his community and mankind' and that 'the rights of each person are limited by the rights of others, the security of all and the just demands of the general welfare in a democratic society'.

While the American Convention emphasises **CIVIL AND POLITICAL RIGHTS**, it also refers to **ECONOMIC, SOCIAL AND CULTURAL RIGHTS**. Chapter III, which contains a single provision (Article 26), commits states parties to undertake to adopt measures both nationally and through international cooperation with a view to achieving progressively the realisation of the rights implicit in the economic, social, educational, scientific and cultural standards set forth in the Organisation of American States (OAS) Charter. This obligation has been given further vigour by the subsequent adoption of the Protocol of San Salvador in 1988.

Article 31 of the American Convention provides that other rights and freedoms can be included in its system of protection via the procedures for amendment of the Convention (Article 76) and the adoption of additional protocols (Article 77). Thus, in order to promote the development of economic, social and cultural rights, the Inter-American Commission submitted a draft protocol to the OAS General Assembly in 1986. Following consultation with the member states, the Additional Protocol to the American Convention on Human Rights in the area of Economic, Social and Cultural Rights (the Protocol of San Salvador) was approved at the 18th regular session of the OAS General Assembly in San Salvador, El Salvador on 14 November 1988.

Like the American Declaration, the Protocol of San Salvador draws upon a variety of international instruments, including the United Nations International Covenant on Economic, Social and Cultural Rights, for its inspiration. The rationale for the adoption of the Protocol is contained in its preamble which notes that the different categories of rights – civil and political on the one hand and economic, social and cultural on the other – constitute, in fact, 'an indivisible whole based on the recognition of the dignity of the human person' and which thus require permanent protection and promotion if they are to be fully realised. The rights recognised in the Covenant are the right to work (Article 6); to just, equitable and satisfactory conditions of work (Article 7); trade union rights (Article 8); the right to social security (Article 9); **THE RIGHT TO HEALTH** (Article 10); the right to a healthy environment (Article 11); **THE RIGHT TO FOOD** (Article 12); **THE RIGHT TO EDUCATION** (Article 13); the right to the benefits of culture (Article 14); the right to the formation and protection of families (Article 15); the rights of children (Article 16); the protection of the elderly (Article 17); and protection of the handicapped (Article 18) (See: **DISABILITY AND HUMAN RIGHTS LAW**). In a departure from the usual mode of protection of economic, social and cultural rights, the Protocol makes the rights recognised subject to the same protection mechanisms as civil and political rights.

The Protocol to the American Convention on Human Rights to Abolish the Death Penalty was adopted at Asunción on 8 June 1990 (See: **THE RIGHT TO LIFE: THE DEATH PENALTY**). The rationale of the Protocol is to give expression to the abolitionist trend which the **INTER-AMERICAN COMMISSION ON HUMAN RIGHTS** considered to be emerging among American states. Although Article 4 of the American Convention places strict limitations on states parties' use of the death penalty so that it is applicable only to the most serious crimes, cannot be reinstated once abolished, is not to be imposed for political offences or common crimes and is not to be used against those aged under 18 or over 70 or against pregnant women, the adoption of the Additional Protocol commits states parties not to apply the death penalty in their territory or to any person subject to their jurisdiction. Abolition, however, is restricted to peacetime only since states parties might reserve the use of the death penalty in wartime for 'extremely serious crimes of a military nature' (Article 2(1)).

The American Convention (Article 27) provides for the suspension and restriction of certain rights in well-defined circumstances. Thus in time of war, public danger or other emergency threatening the independence or security of a state party it can derogate from its obligations 'for the period of time strictly required by the exigencies of the situation'. Such suspension must not be inconsistent with a state's other obligations under international law, nor must it be discriminatory. Further-more, the **INTER-AMERICAN COURT OF HUMAN RIGHTS** made it clear in its opinion in The Word 'Laws' (1986) that such suspen-sion can only be temporary. Furthermore, Article 27 itself provides that certain rights may not be subject to derogation. These are the right to juridical personality (Article 3); the right to life (Article 4); the right to humane treatment (Article 5); freedom from slavery (Article 6); freedom from ex post facto laws (Article 9); freedom of conscience and religion (Article 12); the rights of the family (Article 17); the right to a name; (Article 18); the rights of the child (Article 19); the right to nationality (Article 20); the right to participate in government (Article 23) and the judicial guarantees essential for the protection of such rights. In exercising its power to suspend cer-tain rights under Article 27, a state party must conform to the requirements of Article 30 which states that restrictions may not be applied except in accordance with laws enact-ed for reasons of general interest and in accor-dance with the purposes for which such restrictions have been established.

Notes

(1986) Advisory Opinion OC-6/86 of May 9, 1986, Restrictions to the Rights and Freedoms of the American Convention – The Word 'Laws' in Article 30, Inter-American Court of Human Rights, Series A, No 6.

Further Reading

Buergenthal, Thomas, Norris, Robert and Shelton, Dinah (1990) *Human Rights in the Americas: Selected Problems*, Kehl-am-Rhein: P. Engel Verlag. 3rd edn.

Buergenthal, Thomas (1971) 'The American Convention on Human Rights: Illusions and Hopes', *21 Buffalo Law Review*, 121.

Davidson, Scott (1997) *The Inter-American Human Rights System*, Aldershot: Dartmouth Publishing Company Ltd.

Livingstone, Stephen and Harris, David John (1998) *The Inter-American System of Human Rights*, Oxford: Oxford University Press.

Contributor: Scott Davidson

ANIMAL RIGHTS

Imagine an overcrowded lifeboat containing four humans and a dog. There is no hope of survival for any of the five unless one is thrown overboard. Who should it be – a human or the dog? Most people would say the dog, an auto-matic assumption that rests upon our belief that animals have an inferior moral status to humans. Consequently less value is placed on the life of the dog than on that of the humans. But why do animals have an inferior moral sta-tus to humans?

Philosophical debate about the moral sta-tus of animals has a long history and the theo-ries that have arisen have varied and evolved over time. Things have advanced considerably since the days when Descartes argued that animals lacked consciousness and, being incapable of suffering pain, were effectively no different to machines. If we ask why humans enjoy a superior moral status to animals, we must identify a characteristic which humans possess and animals do not. There are two such characteristics that philosophers consid-er: sentiency and autonomy. Sentiency means the capacity to experience pain and pleasure and it is now universally accepted that many animals are sentient beings. Used in this con-text, autonomy is a difficult concept to define. It includes rationality, thoughts, intentions and beliefs (See: **AUTONOMY AND HUMAN RIGHTS**).

Many people believe that animals are not autonomous and this is what distinguishes animals from humans and justifies their inferi-or moral status. The problem with relying upon a lack of autonomy as the justification for this stance is that not all humans are autonomous. There are marginal cases, for example newly born babies and some severely mentally disabled people, who may possess less ability to think rationally than some animals. Returning to the scenario of the overcrowded lifeboat, would it make any difference if one of the four humans were a newborn baby? Would the life of the dog be spared in these circum-stances? Presumably not, but explaining why the dog should be thrown overboard instead of the human has nothing to do with an absence of autonomy on the part of the dog.

It is also arguable that not all animals lack autonomy. Maybe we underestimate the mental capabilities of animals so that at least some animals, such as adult chimpanzees, bottle-nosed dolphins and even crows, could be considered to be autonomous. For example, the conceptual abilities of two crows, Betty and Abel, recently surprised scientists at Oxford University. The two birds were given a choice between using two tools, a straight wire and a hooked wire, to extract food from inside a tube. Both birds chose the hooked wire. When Abel stole Betty's hook, leaving her with only a straight wire, she pushed the tip of the wire into a crack in the tray and bent it with her beak to fashion a hook (Weir et al. (2002) 'Shaping of hooks in New Caledonian crows', *Science* 297: 981). Betty's actions showed an understanding of cause and effect and, coupled with her ability to create tools, may be evidence of autonomy.

It seems likely that some animals are autonomous, but even if we take the lowest common denominator and recognise that animals are sentient but not autonomous, questions as to their differential treatment still need to be answered. Why is it that a greater wrong is committed by inflicting pain on a human than on an animal? Why is it that thousands of monkeys and baboons are used each year in medical research experiments but humans are not? If an animal's capacity to suffer physical pain is the same as that of a human, should it not be treated equally? To argue that inflicting pain on a human is a greater moral wrong than inflicting pain on an animal on the grounds that they belong to a different species is speciesism. This is the word given to the practice of discriminating on the grounds of species membership alone. It is analogous to the concepts of 'racism' and 'sexism' in which discrimination rests on the incorrect assumption of superiority based on colour and gender respectively (See: **FREEDOM FROM DISCRIMINATION**). This does not mean that treating animals differently from humans is always wrong. In some circumstances it is justifiable to treat humans and animals differently because they have different needs. Whilst humans and animals do share needs, such as food, water and the avoidance of pain, there are other needs that some humans value highly, such as **RIGHTS TO EDUCATION, MARRIAGE** and

FREEDOM OF RELIGION. These latter needs are unlikely to hold any significance to animals. But where humans and animals have similar interests – for example, the avoidance of pain and death – why is preference given to the interests of the human? Why is the dog thrown overboard even when one of the humans on the lifeboat is a newborn baby and lacks autonomy?

The difficulties in trying to justify giving humans a superior moral status are evident, especially if the conceptual abilities of a newly born human are compared with those of an adult gorilla. If the inferior moral status of animals cannot be justified on the basis of a particular characteristic, it seems to be a case of discrimination on the grounds of species membership alone. Ultimately, the question may be whether speciesism is morally right or wrong.

There are a number of divergent bodies of theory to help understand how humans should treat animals. The two most prevalent approaches are the utilitarian and the rights theories. Utilitarianism involves determining whether action is morally right or wrong according to the consequences that flow from that action (See: **UTILITARIANISM AND HUMAN RIGHTS**). Human action is morally right if it brings about the best total consequences for everyone regardless of the individuals concerned. Peter Singer applied utilitarianism to understanding the human treatment of animals. He argued that where humans and animals have similar interests, for example the avoidance of physical pain, their interests should be counted equally. This theory sanctions harming the individual, whether a human or an animal, for the greater aggregate good and therefore conducting painful experiments on animals is justifiable if it cures a major disease. The problem is that this theory justifies harming an individual in circumstances where most people would think it is wrong to do so. For example, killing a miserable, millionaire recluse and giving all his money to charity may be for the greater good of the community, but it is nevertheless morally wrong to kill him.

The rights theory is a moral theory to explain the duties that humans owe to one another. It has also been used to understand whether humans owe any duty to animals and, if so, the nature of that duty. Tom Regan argues that all humans have inherent value as individuals above and beyond their usefulness to others. Consequently they have a right to be treated with respect and not to be treated as if they exist as resources for others. On this basis a person acts immorally if they fail to show respect for another's independent value. All humans possess inherent value equally, regardless of their sex, race, skills and intelligence. Regan believes that the rights theory can be applied to animals. He argues that some animals (specifically mammals aged one year and over) have inherent value because they are conscious beings with an individual welfare that is important to them whatever their usefulness to others. Once it is accepted that some animals have inherent value, it follows that they have a moral right to be treated in such a way that shows respect for their independent value. For Regan the fundamental wrong in how humans treat animals is the way in which we view them as our resources, existing for our benefit as if their value were reducible to their usefulness to us.

It is not suggested here that a human should be thrown from the lifeboat instead of the dog. However, we need a better understanding of why there is an automatic assumption that it should be the dog. In analysing the 'why?' it is hoped that humans will appreciate that animals have a value independent of their usefulness to us and that our treatment of animals should better reflect this recognition of their rights. The lifeboat scenario is merely a device to stimulate debate about the moral status of animals. However, the concepts that have arisen from that debate can be applied to real-life scenarios to help inform decisions concerning the future of practices in which animals suffer, such as factory farming, bear farming and whale hunting.

Further Reading

Garner, Robert (1993) *Animals, Politics and Morality*, Manchester: Manchester University Press.

Regan, Tom (1983) *The Case for Animal Rights*, London: Routledge.

Singer, Peter (1990) *Animal Liberation: A New Ethics for Our Treatment of Animals*, New York: Random House. 2nd edn.

Contributor: Deborah Rook

ASIA: THE REALITY OF HUMAN RIGHTS

In order to address the current status of human rights in Asia, due emphasis should be put on understanding the Asian perceptions of human rights. The inquhould go beyond the assessment of the implementation of universal human rights norms in the region, engaging in an open dialogue regarding the real-world context of human rights issues in Asia.

Many Asians have felt that culturally biased conceptions of human rights might be misused for political motives. Tensions between universalism and cultural relativism have emerged since the early adoptive stage of the UNIVERSAL DECLARATION OF HUMAN RIGHTS in 1948. The debate was refuelled in the 1990s when some Asian leaders, including Lee Kuan Yew of Singapore, challenged universalism arguing that Asia was flourishing because of certain Asian values. Based on the same line of argument, Asian-Pacific governments adopted the Bangkok Declaration in 1993 in the context of preparation for the Vienna World Conference, in which they strongly emphasised the principles of respect for national sovereignty and territorial integrity, as well as non-interference in the internal affairs of states and a prohibition of the use of human rights as an instrument of political pressure.

The Asian values argument seems to have been considerably weakened after the economic hardships endured by most Asian countries in the late 1990s. However, the issue of reconciling Asia's cultural particularities with universal human rights norms has not been completely resolved. A third approach to solve this problem, raised by a group of scholars, was the proposal for cross-cultural dialogues. Dialogue among different cultures is not a new concept; it was already taking place when the Universal Declaration was adopted in 1948. A number of Asian countries participated in the drafting process of the Universal Declaration of Human Rights and the active role of P.K. Chang from China has been recognized widely. P.K. Chang was a Chinese representative active in contributing to the drafting of the UDHR.

Given these antecedents, it was surprising when most Asian countries eventually agreed on the formulation in the Vienna Declaration and Program of Action adopted at the World Conference in 1993. The Declaration emphasises the universality of human rights as follows:

'All human rights are universal, indivisible and interdependent and interrelated... [I]t is the duty of States, regardless of their political, economic and cultural system, to promote and protect all human rights and fundamental freedoms.'

The adherence of the Asian countries shows therefore how far the dialogues have proceeded in the 1990s.

However, the representation of Asian voices in the human rights norm building process has been far from sufficient so far and, in many cases, political motives played a decisive role in adopting international instruments. Nevertheless, it is already an irreversible trend that more and more Asian countries participate in the human rights dialogue in one way or another. In this vein, the quote from Mary Robinson (former United Nations High Commissioner for Human Rights) that the 'main hope of harmony lies not in any imagined uniformity, but in the plurality of our identities, which cut across each other and work against sharp divisions into impenetrable civilisation camps' becomes even more meaningful.

Regardless of the grumbling of reluctant political leaders in some countries, the majority of Asian governments are gradually ratifying the international human rights treaties, although the pace is extremely slow. As of May 2004, all of the 46 Asia-Pacific countries that are members of the United Nations Economic and Social Commission for Asia and the Pacific have ratified at least one fundamental human rights treaty. The **CONVENTION ON THE RIGHTS OF THE CHILD** (CRC) was ratified by all of the countries. Half of them have ratified both the **INTERNATIONAL COVENANT ON CIVIL AND POLITICAL RIGHTS** and the **INTERNATIONAL COVENANT ON ECONOMIC, SOCIAL AND CULTURAL RIGHTS** and 35 countries have ratified the **CONVENTION ON THE ELIMINATION OF ALL FORMS OF DISCRIMINATION AGAINST WOMEN** (CEDAW) as of December 2002. The increasing ratification of international human rights treaties provides each Asian country with more flexibility in regional human rights cooperation.

The status of international treaties varies greatly from country to country. Chinese civil procedure law provides: 'If any international treaty concluded or acceded to by the People's Republic of China contains provisions differing from those found in this Law, the provisions of the international treaty shall prevail, except for those provisions to which China has declared its reservations' (See: **HUMAN RIGHTS IN CHINA**). Japanese law carries a clause saying, 'Treaties have the force of law and override statutes enacted by the Diet.' South Korean Constitutional Law Article 6 also acknowledges that treaties shall be respected as domestic laws. However, most of the Asian states do not give any priority to international treaties over domestic laws in the real interpretation of conflicting laws. The jurisprudence regarding the status of international law is in its early development stage in Asia. Nevertheless, it is clear that the ratification of international human rights treaties practically improves the human rights condition in a country.

Asia is the only remaining area that does not have either a regional commission or a regional court for the protection of human rights (See: **THE ASIAN REGIONAL HUMAN RIGHTS SYSTEM**). It is often overlooked, however, that significant changes have been made in the region during the last decade. Positive signs of the development of human rights institutions are found in various inter-governmental meetings or workshops on diverse human rights issues either on the regional level or sub-regionally to promote regional human rights cooperation. Different dimensions of human rights cooperation activities have been going on. Among them are: (1) The United Nations-sponsored Annual

Workshop on Regional Cooperation for the Promotion and Protection of Human Rights in the Asian and Pacific Region (UN workshop); (2) Asia-Pacific Forum of National Human Rights Institutions; (3) Sub-regional (ASEAN and SAARC) level meetings; and (4) NGO level international meetings.

The twelfth UN workshop was held in Doha, Qatar from 2–4 March, 2004 with 39 governments, 16 National Human Rights Institutions, 7 NGOs and other international organisations participating. The framework of four 'pillars' to support the development of regional arrangements – namely (i) national human rights plans of action, (ii) human rights education, (iii) national human rights institutions and (iv) the realization of the **RIGHT TO DEVELOPMENT** and **ECONOMIC, SOCIAL** and **CULTURAL RIGHTS** – is slowly but steadily moving towards a better regional cooperation under the principle of a 'step-by-step, building-block approach'. Another significant development is the expansion of the Asia-Pacific Forum of National Human Rights Institutions. Currently, 12 countries are members of the regional gathering and four or five more are planning to establish institutions to participate in the forum. Sub-regional organizations such as the Association of South-East Asian Nations (ASEAN) and South Asian Association for Regional Cooperation (SAARC) have also extended the commitment to the promotion of human rights in their communiqués or declarations from summit meetings.

Most importantly, the map of human rights in Asia is changing because of the active role of the NGOs, including, among others, Law Asia, the Asian Human Rights Commission, the Asia-Pacific Human Rights NGOs Facilitating Team, the Asia-Pacific Human Rights Information Center and the Working Group for an ASEAN Human Rights Mechanism. The Asian Charter of Human Rights adopted by NGOs in 1997 is frequently referred to as an important human rights document.

Even if the norms and institutions are growing rapidly in Asia, the norm-enforcing procedures are still not very strong. It would be an irony if so many meetings and inter-governmental exchanges ended up being a verbal commitment only without improving the real situation. It is of paramount importance to establish a functional mechanism to push the governments in the region towards better promotion and protection of human rights.

Human rights violations take place regularly in Asia. Amnesty International in its 2003 annual report observed extrajudicial executions/unlawful killings, disappearances, torture and ill-treatment, prisoners of conscience, detention without charge or trial, the death penalty and human rights abuses by armed opposition groups.

No country in the region is free from human rights abuses. Human Rights Watch singles out the following examples. China is criticised for Xinjiang and the 'War on Terror'; HIV/AIDS and SARS; the treatment of North Korean refugees; restrictions on the Internet and media which violate freedom of information; forced eviction; labour rights; the rights of women and girls; China's legal system; the violation of the right to self-determination and other human rights of people in Tibet; the situation in Hong Kong. Indonesia is criticised for the impunity of the Indonesian armed forces (Tentara Nasional Indonesia, TNI); the human rights violations in the province of Aceh and in Papua; the existence of political prisoners and lack of press freedom. Malaysia is criticised for arbitrary detention of alleged Islamic militants; restrictions on media freedom; lack of independence of the judiciary; and unjust treatment of refugees and migrants. Burma is criticised for having political prisoners; violating labour rights; forced relocations; censorship; the use of child soldiers; and violations of religious freedom as well as atrocities committed against ethnic minorities. India is criticised for its Prevention of Terrorism Act; its treatment of HIV/AIDS; police harassment and abuse of outreach workers; caste-based discrimination. Pakistan lacks freedom of expression; sees legal discrimination against and mistreatment of women; lacks religious freedom; engages in discrimination against religious minorities; participates in human rights violations as part of the 'War on Terror'; practises torture and arbitrary arrests of dissidents and political opponents.

Even if Asia has almost two-thirds of the world's population, the growth of human rights movements in the region has been a relatively recent phenomenon. However, the improvement in the human rights protection in the region will reshape the future of the world.

Further Reading

Christie, Kenneth and Roy, Denny (2001) *The Politics of Human Rights in East Asia*, London: Pluto Press.

de Varennes, Fernand (1998) *Asia-Pacific Human Rights Documents and Resources*, Leiden: Kluwer.

Human Rights Watch, World Report 2003 (2003) [available at http://www.hrw.org/wr2k3/]

Langlois, Anthony J (2001) *The Politics of Justice and Human Rights: South East Asia and Universalist Theory*, Cambridge: Cambridge University Press.

Contributor: Tae-Ung Baik

THE ASIAN REGIONAL HUMAN RIGHTS SYSTEM

The merits of regional systems for human rights protection are clear: they enable regions to create appropriate mechanisms whereby specific rights can be guaranteed while paying due attention to the history of that region and obeying its customs. Such a system has the significant advantage over the international system that it can focus on issues that are germane to the region – issues that can often be determined only by the people of that region – in keeping with the best democratic traditions. These regional systems, rather than obfuscating the need for an international regime, complement and provide an extra layer of protection and guarantee of human rights standards to the citizens of states that shelter under its umbrella.

It is in this context that the lack of a regional system for Asia is particularly worrisome. This conspicuous absence remains a fundamental lacuna in the umbrella of global protection and promotion of human rights standards. This is exacerbated because close to 60 per cent of the world's population live in Asia, often in circumstances of terrible poverty not unlike those in Africa. However, there have never been strong unifying factors that have fostered cooperation continent-wide. Instead Asian states have developed in isolation and competition with each other, with strong regional rivalries.

The root of the failure to create a regional system in Asia lies deeper than a mere failure of cooperation between states. Many Asian leaders have expressed scepticism of human rights as being nothing more than an agenda of Western neo-colonialism. While this charge is relatively easy to refute, based on the UNIVERSALITY of the norm of inherent human dignity, in practice it has reduced the scope for co-operation on this issue between Asian states. The use of human rights rhetoric by Western states against Asian states in international fora has further consolidated the view of human rights being a Western agenda. It can also be argued that the strategy adopted by some international NGOs, albeit motivated by a genuine desire for the promulgation of human rights standards, has been inappropriate and has served to alienate rather than gain the co-operation of states which are relatively sensitive about their sovereignty and wary of criticism stemming from standards to which they consented.

It is relatively inarguable that the human rights agenda, as expressed in much of the United Nations era, is based on western values stressing civil liberties. Typical examples of this lie in the emphasis of civil and political rights over ECONOMIC, SOCIAL and CULTURAL RIGHTS and the greater stress laid on individual rights over GROUP RIGHTS. Yet, in more recent years, as human rights regimes have themselves become more inclusive, increasing attention has been paid to these two aspects within the international system. As a result there has been a renewed emphasis on economic, social and cultural rights and the onus of protection has also been extended to group rights. However the subtle change of agenda at international level is not clearly emphasised and thus the perception reigns among many Asian states that the human rights agenda remains as it was expressed at the birth of the regime. Further, while the agenda may have modified its emphasis, this has yet to yield significant results in the protection of group rights or of economic, social and cultural rights.

Ironically, it is the acceptably vehement criticism of the international system itself that justifies and underscores the need for a regional system of rights protection in Asia. It is precisely through a regional mechanism cognisant of the cultural ethos of the region that difficulties in ideology can be overcome. Thus as long as the basic premise remains the goal of protecting the inherent dignity and worth of every human being and group of human beings, there is little to prevent Asian states from forging a system that fits closer to an Asian ethos. Rather than a rejection of human rights per se, a venture of co-operation between the states for its interpretation in an Asian context would be more progressive.

Yet, desirable as this may be in theory, in practice it is hindered by fundamental differences that exist between the different regions. It can be argued that there are at least five distinct sub-regions within the continent, in terms of geography, cultural ethos and regional identity. East Asia would consist of states such as China, Japan and the Koreas; South-East Asia, the most developed in terms of regional co-operation, would include the ten states that currently form the regional association of ASEAN, such as Indonesia, Malaysia, Vietnam and others; South Asia would inculcate the weak customs union SAARC, consisting of seven states including India, Pakistan and Bangladesh; the Middle East region would include the Arab states in Asia that are part of the Arab League; with the fifth sub-region consisting of the former Soviet states such as Azerbaijan, Turkmenistan and Kazakhstan, among others. Of course, there remain several doubts about such classification, with many states such as Afghanistan (not part of SAARC) arguably closer in ethos to one rather than another of its neighbours. In addition it could be argued that a state like Japan is more likely to fit with the ASEAN states in terms of its development rather than alongside its perpetual rival superpower China. Yet though the placing of the states in particular sub-regions may vary depending on perspective, it is clear that the emergence of any regional system of human rights protection is more likely to be successful through such an approach.

A different approach, namely that of bringing together civil society organisations to frame a charter, has had relatively little success. While the Asian Human Rights Commission was formed and is based in Hong Kong, it is difficult to see what role it is likely to play in fostering state co-operation. As a result, while an Asian Human Rights Charter was launched in 1997 after sub-regional consultations in South Asia, South-East Asia and

East Asia, its utility remains in doubt, especially in terms of the creation of a regional mechanism for the promotion of human rights that has the consent of governments.

Even assuming that geographic classification of states may theoretically provide a more effective starting point for a discussion on sub-regional systems of human rights protection, there remain fundamental difficulties with forging such a discussion. In two of the biggest sub-regions identified, the leading states – for example China and Japan in East Asia and India and Pakistan in South Asia – have historically had and continue to have extremely antagonistic relationships that make it impossible to foster cross-border discussions. These big regional rivalries are less pertinent to the other three regions, but it could be argued that in each of those regions the emphasis has been placed on different issues. Thus while in the Middle East co-operation exists between the oil-producing Arab states, economic co-operation and relative development of the ASEAN states has not necessarily hailed a new dawn for the human rights agenda. By contrast, co-operation along lines similar to those achieved in the Middle East is being fostered in the newly independent former Soviet Republics. Interestingly, these republics have also adopted relatively high standards of human rights protection in their newly framed constitutions, are increasingly looking West and may possibly accede in whole or part to the Council of Europe system (See: **CENTRAL ASIA, THE REALITY OF HUMAN RIGHTS**).

Despite the existence of regional particularities that may propel or repel a given region towards or against human rights standards, for the vast populations of Asia the larger issue of **POVERTY** reduction is the context in which the building of a human rights regime struggles. The building of any regional or sub-regional system of human rights will need to overcome the opinion that, in the quest for poverty reduction, a human rights agenda with an emphasis on civil and political rights is completely ineffective. Instead, in national discussions in many Asian states, human rights are often perceived as being a privilege that can be only invoked once states are at a suitable level of development. Until it can be proved that the human rights agenda includes economic, social and cultural rights protections, and unless key leaders can be convinced that the pursuit of poverty reduction does not require abrogation of the inherent dignity of human beings, the forging of a regional or sub-regional system for the protection of Asian human rights will remain a distant dream.

Further Reading

Bauer, Joanne R. and Bell, Daniel A. (eds) (1999) *The East Asian Challenge for Human Rights*, Cambridge, England; New York: Cambridge University Press.

De Bary, William Theodore (1998) *Asian Values and Human Rights: a Confucian Communitarian Perspective*, Cambridge, Mass.: Harvard University Press.

Jacobsen, Michael and Bruun, Ole (eds) (2000) *Human Rights and Asian Values: Contesting National Identities and Cultural Representations in Asia*, Richmond, Surrey: Curzon.

Kelly, David and Reid, Anthony (eds) (1998) *Asian Freedoms: the Idea of Freedom in East and Southeast Asia*, Cambridge: Cambridge University Press.

Meijer, Martha (ed.) (2001) *Dealing with Human Rights: Asian and Western Views on the Value of Human Rights*, Bloomfield, CT: Kumarian Press.

Welch, Jr, Claude E. and Leary, Virginia A. (eds) (1990) *Asian Perspectives on Human Rights*, Boulder: Westview Press.

Contributor: Joshua Castellino

ASSOCIATION, FREEDOM OF

Freedom of association enables individuals to come together and collectively to express, promote, pursue and even defend common interests. Respect for it by all public authorities and its assiduous exercise by all sections of society are essential both to establish a genuine democracy and to ensure that, once achieved, it remains healthy and flourishing. However, although such a democracy can be conceived of in a strictly party political sense and the formation of political parties is a significant manifestation of this freedom, it is the pursuit by persons from all sectors of a vast array of interests – such as culture, recreation, sport and

social and humanitarian assistance, to say nothing of the rights of those at work and the simple personal fulfilment of those who belong to the bodies concerned – that underpins its vitality.

The essential role played by the bodies that are the fruit of such associational activity – often termed 'non-governmental organisations' and collectively referred to as 'civil society' – is not open to question but is still not appreciated by all states at all times, not least because it entails an unambiguous commitment to democracy. Nonetheless, realising and sustaining such a commitment is an objective of paramount importance for global and regional organisations and unsurprisingly provisions guaranteeing and promoting freedom of association have readily found a place in instruments adopted by them. It is also guaranteed by many constitutions.

The principal international guarantees of this freedom are in the **UNIVERSAL DECLARATION OF HUMAN RIGHTS** (Article 20), the **INTERNATIONAL COVENANT ON CIVIL AND POLITICAL RIGHTS** (Article 22), the African Charter on Human and Peoples' Rights (Article 10), the American Convention on Human Rights (Article 16), the **EUROPEAN CONVENTION ON HUMAN RIGHTS** (Article 11), an undertaking made by states belonging to the **ORGANISATION FOR SECURITY AND CO-OPERATION IN EUROPE** (OSCE) at its Copenhagen Meeting in 1990 and the **EUROPEAN UNION CHARTER OF FUNDAMENTAL RIGHTS** (Article 12). Most of these provisions refer to the right to form and join trade unions but there are also several guarantees specifically devoted to this aspect of the freedom, notably the International Covenant on Economic, Social and Cultural Rights (Article 8), the European Social Charter (Article 5) and the Convention Concerning Freedom of Association and Protection of the Right to Organise of the International Labour Organization (See: **LABOUR RIGHTS**).

There are also instruments concerned with this freedom's enjoyment by particular sectors in society, notably children (Convention on the Rights of the Child, Article 15 and African Charter on the Rights and Welfare of the Child, Article 8), environmental campaigners

(Convention on Access to Information, Public Participation in Decision-making and Access to Justice in Environmental Matters (Aarhus Convention), Articles 1, 2 (4, 5) and 3), human rights defenders (UN Declaration on the Right and Responsibility of Individuals, Groups and Organs of Society to Promote and Protect Universally Recognised Human Rights and Fundamental Freedoms (Declaration on Human Rights Defenders) (GA Res 53/144, 9 December 1998) and undertakings made at several OSCE meetings, namely Vienna in 1989 (Questions relating to Security in Europe, paras 13.3, 13.6 and 21), Copenhagen (paras 10, 10.1–10.4, 11 and 11.2) and Budapest (Chapter VIII, para 18), judges (UN Basic Principles on the Independence of the Judiciary, Council of Europe Recommendation R(94)12 'On the Independence, Efficiency and Role of Judges' and the European Charter on the Statute for Judges), members of national minorities (Framework Convention for the Protection of National Minorities, Articles 3, 7 and 8 and the undertakings made at the OSCE meeting in Copenhagen in 1990 (para 32.2, 32.6 and 33)), migrant workers (International Convention on the Protection of the Rights of All Migrant Workers and Members of Their Families, Articles 26 and 40), refugees (Convention Relating to the Status of Refugees, Article 15) and stateless persons (Convention Relating to the Status of Stateless Persons, Article 15), as well as bodies of an international character (European Convention on the Recognition of the Legal Personality of International Non-Governmental Organisations). In addition the **COUNCIL OF EUROPE** has articulated some Fundamental Principles on the Legal Status of Non-governmental Organisations in Europe (noted by the decision of the deputies at their 837th meeting on 16 April 2003).

Associations should be able to pursue any activity which individuals alone can pursue, including a change in the law or the constitution so long as the intention is to do this only by lawful means and the outcome is not anti-democratic. Otherwise the only requirements for a grouping to be seen as an exercise of freedom of association are that it has an institutional structure and it is either not intended to be a profit-making body or, where trading activities are undertaken, does not distribute profits accruing to the membership but uses them for the pursuit of the common objectives. Nevertheless, associations can still exist to advance the interests of their members – trade unions are a prime example of this. Professional and other bodies for which membership is obligatory are not a manifestation of freedom of association but voluntary groupings within them are (for example, a bar association's human rights committee). The ability to form and join associations is enjoyed by 'everyone', meaning legal as well as natural persons but also children. Adopting some protective measures to ensure that the latter are not exploited or exposed to moral and related dangers would not be precluded so long as these lessened as a child's capacities evolved. Non-citizens are also included, even if some restrictions on their involvement in political activity may be admissible. Although the freedom to seek to join existing associations is guaranteed, this cannot be against the wishes of members unless inadmissible discrimination is involved. Some limits might also be imposed on a person's exercise of freedom of association as a criminal penalty, provided that these correspond to the nature of the offence concerned and their duration is not excessive.

Legal personality for an association which is distinct from that of its members should always be an option. Such personality does not mean that every legal capacity be enjoyed but an ability to enter into contracts, to exercise ownership rights over property and to protect rights by being able to bring and defend legal proceedings will be vital for the pursuit of an association's objectives. Other capacities that may be helpful for this purpose only cannot be derived from freedom of association; trade unions, for example, have been unable to use it to establish rights regarding collective bargaining, consultation and strikes. Nonetheless, there is increasing recognition of the need for states to establish legal and financial environments that will facilitate the work of associations. A requirement for certain types of association (e.g., religious bodies and trade unions) to take on specific legal forms for regulatory purposes or the conferment of benefits should not thereby impede the pursuit of their objectives.

Membership of an association should

never be the basis for a penalty unless it is legitimately prohibited and members should also be protected against harassment, intimidation and violence on this account. While this does not preclude such membership being found to be incompatible with responsibilities under an employment contract or other commitments, it should not be assumed that such an incompatibility necessarily exists for those employed in the public service.

While the permissibility of regulation of associational activity cannot be questioned, it ought not to be unduly cumbersome or bureaucratic and should certainly never embody an inherently hostile or oppressive attitude to the existence or activities of associations. Rather regulation should always be founded upon a full appreciation that these bodies are an essential constituent of any society committed to democracy, human rights and the rule of law. Those belonging to an association should thus be generally free to draw up their own rules and to administer their own affairs, but a state should ensure that persons are not being unduly coerced into joining or remaining a member. Furthermore, the need for accountability to members, donors and the public will justify obligations to report on activities and expenditure, as well as to have accounts audited.

Action against an association may be justified where it has not observed legal requirements, but technical failings should not have serious consequences for either the association or the individuals concerned. In most instances a requirement to rectify its affairs will be a sufficient sanction, but the imposition of civil liability and/or administrative or criminal penalties, where appropriate, should always observe the principle of proportionality. The circumstances where enforced dissolution is justified are likely to be very rare indeed, covering only situations in which the association undertook anti-constitutional activities, failed to desist from other illegal conduct after warnings and opportunities to rectify such failings or had such prolonged inactivity that it was necessary to intervene to ensure that its funds were properly applied. A well-founded basis for such a drastic action is essential but has often been found to be lacking.

Further Reading

Armstrong, P. and Rekosh, E. (eds) (2003) *Enabling Civil Society*, Budapest: PILI.

Council of Europe (1994) *Freedom of Association*, Leiden: Nijhoff.

Flauss, J. F. (ed.) (2004) *International Human Rights Law and Non Governmental Organizations*, Brussels: Bruylant.

International Labour Organisation (1998) *International Labour Standards*, 4th ed., revised, Geneva: ILO.

Contributor: Jeremy McBride

AUTONOMY AND HUMAN RIGHTS

A conceptual link between autonomy and individual rights is often conceded to with autonomy of the individual regarded as the 'foundational' right upon which all other rights are premised. In fact, it is often held that the object of human rights is to enhance the autonomy of the individual through safeguarding the security, LIBERTY and political rights of persons. As a consequence, human rights discussions are centred around two issues: first, the nature and form of legal structures, procedures and safeguards which guarantee rights of individuals; and second, the philosophy of the person who is the recipient of these rights and institutional protections. This philosophy of the person is one of moral individualism. Moral individualism allows persons not only to formulate their own conceptions of what constitutes the 'good life' but also affirms that entitlements and immunities always attach themselves to individuals and not to communities and cultures (See: GROUP RIGHTS; MINORITY RIGHTS; INDIGENOUS PEOPLES' RIGHTS). In other words, moral individualism presupposes a 'separation' of persons from their families and cultures (See: FAMILY LAW; CULTURAL RIGHTS). It is this conceptual homology of human rights with moral individualism that the detractors of the human rights discourse resist.

Many critics of universal human rights are found both within the western world and in the developing world. Within the West these include many feminist philosophers and those anti-foundational philosophers who do not subscribe to the idea that there might be a natural basis or a universal foundation for human rights (See: **FEMINIST CRITIQUES OF HUMAN RIGHTS**). Outside the western world, these critics are often regarded as supporters of what are known as the 'Asian and Islamic values'. They express a certain discomfort with the idea of the 'autonomous self', a self who is separate from the shared values of the community and the family, and argue that it is this individual-centred philosophy which has led to privileging individual and political rights over **SOCIAL** and **ECONOMIC RIGHTS** within the human rights discourse.

Some writers have commented that human rights have become the moral language of globalisation used to bring the errant third world into the 'modern' global economic framework. Human rights discourse, they argue, smacks of neo-colonialism and is uncritically Western-centric.

Feminist philosophers too have questioned the value of autonomy. Much of the feminist critique of autonomy is directed against the excessive individualism of liberal theory with its emphasis on distinctness and separateness of the subject. It has been argued that the alignment of autonomy with individualism has led to a popular conception of the autonomous person as one who is self-sufficient, self-reliant, independent and self-interest maximising (Code, 1987). Feminists have argued that not only does this privilege psychological egoism and endorse the separate and distinct interests of individuals but it also denies that the characteristics and capacities of persons are constituted in relation to others and are not 'simply caused'. The discomfort with liberal individualism has led to two main developments within feminist epistemological practice: one is the radical critique of philosophy, the other is a 'reformist' project of extending alternative understandings of philosophical concepts, including autonomy.

This seemingly widespread discomfort with the philosophical underpinnings of moral individualism often eclipses the conceptual complexity, internal differentiation and difficulty of pinning one single definition of autonomy. Autonomy originates from the Greek term *autonomia* whose etymological roots are the words *auto* (self) and *nomos* (law). While its use has been recorded in Ancient Greek times, in the religious debates in the reformation era

and in the contemporary debates on the sovereign status of modern nation states (Schneewind, 1998), it is only recently that the term has been applied to the individual. Therefore, despite its ancient roots, few writers claim it to be anything other than a modern concept. Its modern roots are traced to two distinct strands of theoretical reasoning: Kantian psychologism and utilitarian rationalism (See: **UTILITARIANISM AND HUMAN RIGHTS**). There are two ways of understanding these distinct strands. The first views the notion of autonomy as an innate quality. It includes within it two opposing views. On the 'quasi-Kantian' understanding, persons are considered inherently autonomous and are to be accorded universal respect; the second view on the other hand, conceives autonomy as a product of a particular historical and social circumstance, as something which can be developed only in certain 'ideal' conditions.

The second understanding of this distinction between Kantian ethics and utilitarian rationality is centred on the meaning of freedom itself. It debates whether autonomy is understood primarily in terms of an inner state or a quality of one's motivational structure or whether it lies in the absence of the influence of unwarranted external causation upon the individual. This distinction has come to be looked upon in recent times as the distinction between negative liberty and positive liberty, between freedom and autonomy.

The idea of autonomy has been associated with the many diverse philosophical traditions in modern times. Kantians, utilitarians, Marxists, existentialists, liberal individualists all employ a conception of autonomy. The modern meaning of autonomy has become polarised around the theories of two philosophers: Immanuel Kant and John Stuart Mill. As a consequence of their philosophical contributions, autonomy has been conceptualised in three main ways. It is upheld as a social, political and moral idea (Dworkin, 1988) and consequently there are three kinds of autonomy to which theorists refer: political autonomy, personal or individual autonomy and moral autonomy. Political autonomy is applied to states, whereas moral and personal autonomy are applied to individuals. Autonomy can be used both descriptively as well as normatively. Invoking autonomy in a normative sense is to state that persons ought to be treated according to the principles of autonomy or that they have a right to be treated as though they were autonomous. Descriptive accounts of autonomy on the other hand typically focus on the psychological or cognitive abilities required in order to be considered autonomous. Recent theorising on autonomy has introduced a further distinction between procedural and substantive accounts of autonomy. Procedural or formal accounts of autonomy do not insist that people display particular values in the choices they exercise or in their actions. Substantive accounts of autonomy, however, insist that certain values ought to be evident in people's actions. In the event of these given values being absent in their choices and actions, these persons relinquish their autonomy. It is the latter accounts, demanding the substantive presence of values, which have dominated conventional autonomy theorising.

So what do we mean when we speak of the autonomous individual and is this autonomous individual a free being? We mean at least two different things. The first is to do with what can be called an absence of coercion or negative liberty; the second are what we might call agent capacities or positive liberty. Negative liberty is to do with absence of external constraints on the behaviour and actions of individuals and positive liberty is to do with self-authorship, self-governance and exercising self-control over one's internal shortcomings and failures. The supporters of positive liberty as distinct from negative freedom argue that while liberty, power and control are important aspects of our lives, autonomy is distinct from these and not all 'interference with the voluntary character of one's action interferes with a person's ability to choose his mode of life' (Dworkin, 1988:14).

When human rights advocates speak of safeguarding people's autonomy or agency, they refer almost exclusively to negative liberty. They argue that legal safeguards for individuals are paramount if we want to empower individuals not only to take control of their life options but also to resist and overcome oppression. These safeguards must protect individuals within families and communities because very often it is these institutions that promote and legitimise oppression of their members. Individual autonomy is important not only for human rights but also for democratic institutions to function (See: **DEMOCRACY AND HUMAN RIGHTS**). A democratic electoral system, human rights proponents argue, is premised on ideas of equality and participation of all citizens. Autonomous citizens have the capacity to shape their moral outlook and life options and this necessarily includes the ability to decide on the nature of their government. In order for autonomous citizens to make informed political decisions, it is incumbent on the state to make available the social conditions necessary for individuals to author their lives in the manner they choose. Further, since matters of public policy affect the citizens' priorities, it is important that they have a say in deciding not only the identity of policy makers but also the moral ends to which these policies are put. A democratic system of government is the only one that offers citizens the right to make a choice in respect of who governs them, hence it is the only form of government which meets the needs of autonomous individuals.

In sum, there are at least three main problems with the philosophical underpinnings of autonomy which informs the thinking on human rights. The moral philosophy of the autonomous person, it is increasingly argued, is gendered, culturally particularist and constitutes a misdescription of the 'nature' of the self. Popular characterisations of autonomy as an ability to freely pursue and choose whatever one wishes premises itself on an individualist conception of the self, a self which is independent, complete and self-sufficient. Not only is the descriptive account of the autonomous person an account of the ascendant ideas of a particular historical and cultural period, it is also on account of certain individual representatives of a 'high' white, male, bourgeois culture. The third problem concerns the transposition of the particularist account of autonomy into a language of universals, of historical and culture-specific descriptions of an 'autonomous life' seeking to represent universal components and standards of individual well-being. For instance, most dominant conceptions of autonomy carry an individualist baggage and it is this 'rugged individualism' which claim a universal status for itself, whereas it is in effect a descriptive category 'centred' on a particular experience.

Further Reading

Code, Lorraine (1987) 'Second Persons' in Marsha Hanen and Kai Nelson (eds) *Science, Morality and Feminist Theory*, Calgary: University Of Calgary Press.

Dworkin, Gerald (1988) *The Theory and Practice of Autonomy*, Cambridge: Cambridge University Press.

Ignatieff, Michael (2001) *Human Rights as Politics and Idolatry*, Princeton: Princeton University Press.

Schneewind, J. B. (1998) *The Invention of Autonomy*, Cambridge: Cambridge University Press.

Van Ness, Peter (ed.) (1999) *Debating Human Rights: Critical Essays from the USA and Asia*, London and New York: Routledge.

Contributor:　　　　　　　Sumi Madhok

BIOETHICS AND HUMAN RIGHTS

Bioethics is the study of ethical issues arising in health care and the life sciences locally or globally. The distinction refers back to the foundation of ethics and one of its central questions: are there any universal moral values? Those who believe in global bioethics assume that conflicts in bioethics can be resolved cross-culturally, based on values shared across humanity. Opponents to this view assume that different cultures' moralities are so diverse that no minimal global ethics exists.

Global bioethics is still in its infancy, but two examples of expressions of 'global ethics' are prominent: first, the statements from the United Nations Millennium Summit, which regard the values of freedom, equity, solidarity, tolerance, non-violence, respect for nature and shared responsibility as essential for humankind; and second, the Declaration Toward a Global Ethics by Hans Küng on behalf of the Parliament of World Religions, which lists four commitments: to a culture of

non-violence and respect for life, to a culture of solidarity and a just economic order, to a culture of tolerance and a life of truthfulness and to a culture of equal rights and a partnership between men and women. That intercultural dialogue has led to these two formulations of global ethics bodes well for the development of global bioethics.

Global bioethics is a bold project. In its moderate form, it aims to find solutions to the dilemmas posed by modern medicine and the biological sciences through inter-cultural understanding of human obligations and opportunities. In its more ambitious form, it endeavours to cover all possible ethical problems arising with regard to life and living things on earth. Given the ambitiousness of even the moderate aim, it is unsurprising that disputes are frequent and agreements scarce. One of the most contentious issues is whether or not human rights should play an important role in global bioethics.

The Western approach to bioethics depends almost entirely on the human rights discourse that regards individuals as autonomous decision makers whose rights to well-being and fair treatment have to be respected. But can this approach be universalised?

Parties in the dispute agree that a global approach to bioethical problems is essential for the future development of human societies. However, they disagree on the values and procedures that should inform this approach. On the one hand, Hyakudai Sakamoto, the President of the Japanese Association of Bioethics as well as the Asian Bioethics Association argues that the human rights discourse is a specifically Western approach to bioethics, which should not be imposed on other parts of the world. On the other hand, it is maintained that human rights are a promising concept that can transcend religions, borders and cultures with the potential to flourish around the globe.

This divide is not easily bridged. Simplified, one could say that Western bioethics relies almost exclusively on the concepts of individualism and human rights and can often be described as anthropocentric (i.e. focused on human rather than plant or animal life). In contrast, the African world view in bioethics has been described as 'eco-bio-communitarian', implying a preference of community values over individualistic values as well as a recognition of the interdependence of all forms of life on earth. Similarly, the essence of the Asian world view in bioethics has been described as 'a holistic harmony' with a higher esteem for social over individual values and no strict dichotomy between humans and nature.

The future might lie in a middle way between the two extremes of exclusively focusing on human rights and individuals versus a focus on human obligations and communities. But finding this middle way is a challenging undertaking, one that at least requires agreement on essential cross-cultural values and principles, even if these were articulated in different terminology, ranked differently and expressed in different moral practices.

What could the human rights discourse contribute to this undertaking? Whether one calls it a human right or a human capability (See: THE CAPABILITY APPROACH AND HUMAN RIGHTS), 'life' is, above all, an individual asset. A mother who starves so that her children can live might make an invaluable community contribution, but she loses the one life she has. Similarly, 'bodily integrity and health' are individual assets. The pains of violent attacks, torture, rape, hunger, cold, disease are individual pains of separate human beings. Whatever the merits of altruism, modesty, humility and willingness for self-sacrifice, there is a need to set limits to what one human can inflict on another (through action, e.g. violence, or non-action, e.g. refusal of solidarity and beneficence). The language of human rights is well suited to express these limits.

However, despite the strength of the human rights approach to formulate constraints, the language of human rights has its limitations in global bioethics, for at least two reasons. First, 'human rights' is not a globally accepted concept and its sense is weak and foreign in many parts of the world, such as Asia. Insistence on its terminology may only strengthen the complaint of American-Eurocentrism and risk the success of harmonising different ethical systems. However, this does not mean that one cannot discuss ethical constraints on human action at all, but that these might be expressed with different principles (e.g. the Chinese 'Jen' (humaneness), 'Ci' (benevolence) or the Japanese 'Taijisokuin' (great mercy)).

Second, insisting on rights without careful consideration of equivalent obligations and those able to discharge them could be regarded as highly irresponsible. A right to health care has no meaning if nobody exists who can discharge the equivalent obligation. Non-Western value systems could be invaluable in emphasising the importance of obligations in ethical systems and filling this topic with substantive content – obligations not only with reference to other human beings but also to other living entities.

Discussions in bioethics are well suited for inter-cultural dialogue and the exploration of diverse value systems, as the following example shows. Advances in health care increasingly move medical activities beyond national borders into a global setting. The fact that bone marrow transplants with non-related donors are carried out routinely nowadays has led to international bone marrow registers to increase the chances of finding perfect tissue matches. But, of course, international co-operation in this area requires the harmonisation of legal and ethical guidelines. The procedure of individual informed consent obtained from the bone marrow donor is taken for granted in Western countries. But Japan, for instance, has a strong tradition of prioritising family consent over individual consent. Working out guidelines for international co-operation in the health care setting has, therefore, the strong potential to foster constructive dialogue. And those who believe in global bioethics as an enterprise that will help to secure the values of freedom, equity, solidarity, tolerance, non-violence, respect for nature and shared responsibility on a global scale will happily enter this dialogue. Whether this dialogue can produce an enriched version of the concept of human rights remains to be seen.

Further Reading

Benatar, Solomon, Daar, Abdallah and Singer, Peter (2003) 'Global health ethics: the rationale for mutual caring' in: *International Affairs*, vol. 79, no. 1, pp. 107–38.

Campbell, Alastair (1999) 'Presidential address: global bioethics – dream or nightmare?' in: *Bioethics*, vol. 13, no. 3/4, pp. 183–90.

Sakamoto, Hyakudai (1999) 'Towards a new "global bioethics"' in: *Bioethics*, Vol. 13, No. 3/4, pp. 191–97.

Tangwa, Godfrey (1999) 'Globalisation or Westernisation? Ethical concerns in the whole bio-business' in: *Bioethics*, vol. 13, no. 3/4, pp. 218-26.

Widdows, Heather, Dickenson, Donna and Hellsten, Sirkku (2003) 'Global bioethics' in: *New Review of Bioethics*, vol. 1, no. 1, pp. 101-16.

Contributor: Doris Schroeder

BUDDHISM AND HUMAN RIGHTS

Buddhism is remote from the two central ideas which constitute the modern discourse of human rights, namely the Western philosophy of rights and individualism. The idea of rights asserts that rights are embedded in human beings, while individualism assigns individuality as the basic category of human existence. Both ways of thinking are incongruous with the Buddhist doctrine of no-soul (*anatman*), which denies the very idea of autonomy, continuity and authenticity of the self. Nevertheless, Buddhist philosophers have

© R.K.M. Smith.

been debating the meaning and implications of *anatman* for centuries. Hence the recent appraisals of human rights issues bring Buddhist ethics to the forefront of its theoretical formulation and practical implication.

The doctrine of no-soul poses a problem internally in relation to the Buddhist teaching of reincarnation (*samsara*), for it seems that reincarnation presupposes a continuity of individual existence or consciousness. On the other hand, *anatman* also generates a dilemma in ethical issues. The very idea that a human person is not an enduring entity seems to deny both the vital role of being an ethical agent and the intrinsic worth of personhood.

Buddhist philosophers have been addressing these philosophical and ethical problems by employing several heuristic strategies to interpret the meaning of *anatman*. Firstly, *anatman* is not a meta-theory of human nature. Given the non-dualistic and non-essentialist orientation of Buddhist philosophy, it is consistent not to interpret *anatman* ontologically but more as an ontic concept. Certainly it is ironic that one can avow the doctrine of no-soul to the extent that it becomes another essentialist assertion of human beings. The Buddhist path of *anatman* holds that there is neither soul nor any essential form that constitutes a human being. 'Form is none other than emptiness; emptiness is none other than form.' Secondly, *anatman* is not the denial of self as person but denial of self as self-centredness. It is the detachment from any essentialist view of self, to search for liberation of an egoless self for service of others. Thus *anatman* becomes a form of religious practice, especially in the type of insight meditation (*vipassana*), whose aim is to reorient oneself towards the ultimate realization and compassion towards all beings. Thirdly, the goal of *anatman* is to detach from our egocentricity in order to realize the interdependence and interconnectedness of all beings, sentient and insentient. It is exactly this final stage of meditative practice that gives rise to a Buddhist formulation of human rights.

It is imperative that in examining Buddhist positions on a range of human rights issues one must constantly remind oneself that Buddhism is neither centralised nor uniform in terms of its system of belief and practice. Hence it is problematic to speak of a unitary

Buddhist view on any particular ethical issue. Nevertheless it is still justifiable, or even necessary, to describe a set of Buddhist majority views, be it Mahayana, Theravada, Tibetan or Zen, provided one can differentiate appropriately the mainstream from the sectarian views.

One of the main engagements of Buddhism in the arena of human rights is the massive and persistent involvement of Buddhist relief works. Buddhist aid organisations have carried out large-scale relief works in disaster-stricken and destitute regions over the years. The relief works are often international and inter-religious in scope and the operations are managed through efficient Western management techniques. Although many Buddhist charity organisations are still incomparable in size with the global operations of the Red Cross and the Salvation Army, Buddhist social relief is significant for its increasing scale of operation and its employment of Western modes of organisation. In utilising Western systems of communication and management in their charity works, many Buddhist groups transform themselves in their organisations and religious activities. These changes are slow but salient for they represent the encounter of Buddhism with modernity, both on the practical level of social actions and on the deeper level of ideals and values. As Buddhist groups continue to contribute their benevolent efforts locally and globally, Buddhism will come into close proximity to the global community and the vision of human rights.

The second significant focus of personal rights is the area of life issues. Buddhist ethicists increasingly have to engage in bio-medical issues such as abortion, euthanasia and prostitution. The challenge of investigating and formulating the Buddhist views on a range of life issues is similar to the case of Christianity and other world religions. The internal spectrum of views and teachings within one's faith's tradition is as diverse as the external variations among world religions. Among all Buddhist concepts of life issues, *ahimsa* as non-killing is the most recognized principle of deliberation in various ethical issues. *Ahimsa* is part of the basic Ten Precepts and is employed both in the individual and social realms. It is the major regulating principle of Buddhist ethics to sanction the sanctity of life. However, *ahimsa* is mostly applied in

the social sphere, which results in a general tendency of Buddhist pacifism against war, the death penalty and other issues of social justice. On the individual level, it is problematic to arrive at a unitary Buddhist stance on life and reproductive issues. For example, the regulating principle of *ahimsa* does not necessarily lead to a censure on the abortion debate. Many anthropological and sociological studies have been conducted on the phenomenon of abortion in Japan. The ritualization of abortion in Japan (*mizuko*) by manufacturing *jizo* statues as means of memorial for the aborted fetus is an intriguing case study of the intersection of religious practice and bio-medical issues. Another controversial case is the industrialisation of prostitution in Thailand and sex trafficking connected with its tourism industry. While it is evident that the problem in Thailand is more socio-economic than religious, it is also relevant that in Thailand Buddhism can become an instructive case study on the social implication of Buddhist sexual ethics on a national level. (However, studies have shown that it is less tourists and more the local middle class that use prostitutes in Thailand.)

Ecological concern is the subject of one of the most vibrant movements within Buddhism today. Buddhist ecology is based on the fundamental idea of interdependence and interconnectedness of all sentient and insentient beings. Buddhism contributes to the idea of human rights by including ecology in its humanitarian concern. Thus it broadens the discourse of human rights to a trans-personal level.

Another major human rights agenda is that of the rights and roles of women in world religions. Some of the older literature has presented a feminist critique of Buddhism in terms of its exclusion and subordination of women in its founding narrative, such as Gautama's abandoning his wife and child in order to search for ultimate enlightenment, and the earlier formation of sangha solely as a male monastic order. However, one can also find various emancipatory elements in Buddhist history, such as the popular female imageries of Bodhisattva and the significant involvement of nunneries in various stages and regions of East Asian Buddhism. Furthermore, the narrative theme of sex transformation as means to and sign of religious enlightenment found in *Lotus Sutra* and other relevant Buddhist scriptures continues to fascinate religious scholars. The intricate history and teachings of Buddhism on gender issues and women's rights warrant a consistent employment of hermeneutics of retrieval of its multi-faceted traditions in the context of world religions.

In the social dimension of human rights issues, contemporary Buddhism has been especially connected to the pacifist movement. The Buddhist view of most international and socio-political issues has been largely informed by its pacifist outlook. Yet the history of Buddhism's political involvement is as ambiguous and complex as that of other major world religions. Historically, the meditative skill of Zen Buddhism was utilised with martial arts for the service of imperial courts in medieval China and Japan. In the contemporary setting, the political situation of Sri Lanka continues to be a contentious spot between Hinduism and Buddhism. The exilic dispersion of the Tibetan Buddhist community continues to arouse global concern for the plight of the Tibetans.

Buddhism as a non-creedal religion has been strong in its charity works and infrequent in its advocacy and political role. But this will gradually change as Buddhist communities continue to involve themselves in the socio-political arenas of today's world. Similar to other world religions, Buddhism is resourceful in its individual and collective dimensions. The Four Nobel Truths, as the core religious avowal of Buddhism, clearly delineate the individual dimension of Buddhist belief, while the Eightfold Paths denote the communal practice of Buddhism. This combination of individual and communal dimensions forms the core principles of Buddhism and will continue to inform the socio-political praxis of Buddhist communities. The ambiguity and ever-changing situation in today's world call for a more systematic approach to socio-political issues from an informed Buddhist philosophical perspective and this will become the challenge and task for all Buddhist philosophers who are concerned for the noble cause of human rights.

Further Reading

Bloom, Irene, Martin, J.P. and Proudfoot, W.L. (eds) (1996) *Religious Diversity and Human Rights*, New York: Columbia University Press.

Collins, Steven (1994) 'What are Buddhists doing when they deny the self?' in *Religion and Practical Reason*, Frank Reynolds and David Tracy (eds), New York: SUNY Press, pp. 59–86.

Collins, Steven (1982) *Selfless Persons: Imagery and Thought in Theravada Buddhism*, Cambridge: Cambridge University Press.

Griffiths, Paul (1986) *On Being Mindless: Buddhist Meditation and the Mind-Body Problem*, Illinois: Open Court.

Rouner, Leroy (ed.) (1988) *Human Rights and the World's Religions*, Indiana: University of Notre Dame Press.

Contributor: Stephen Chan

BUSINESS AND HUMAN RIGHTS

Shell, Nike, Texaco, Calvin Klein, BP, Levi-Strauss, Donna Karan, Rio Tinto Zinc, Gap, Reebok: what do these well-known yet diverse brand names have in common? They have all been accused of abusing human rights in developing countries. An increasingly globalised world has given rise to new challenges to human rights. The human rights implications for business can arise in many different arenas, for example in relation to labour standards, environmental protection or indigenous populations. Furthermore, increasing numbers of non-governmental organisations and enhanced information technology have heightened awareness of business practices around the world. In recent years the concept of corporate social responsibility (CSR) has emerged in response to claims of corporate misconduct in a variety of areas.

CSR can mean different things to different people. For example, the World Business Council for Sustainable Development sees CSR as a voluntary initiative and defines it as 'the commitment of business to contribute to sustainable economic development, working with employees, their families, the local community and society at large to improve their quality of life' (World Business Council for Sustainable Development, 2002). Mary Robinson in her capacity as United Nations

High Commissioner for Human Rights stated that CSR encompasses mandatory regulation of corporations alongside voluntary mechanisms (United Nations High Commissioner for Human Rights, 2000). Others such as NGOs and trade unions argue that only mandatory regulation will lead to effective CSR and it is therefore necessary to establish minimum standards of conduct.

This 'voluntary versus regulation' divide can be problematic. However, in essence, CSR recognises that corporations have wider societal obligations than was perceived traditionally. Historically, the only social responsibility corporations faced was to 'increase profits' for shareholders (Friedman, 1970). However, the late 20th century witnessed a shift towards a 'stakeholder' paradigm. In other words, society has demanded that corporations become more accountable to the wider community in which they operate – to consumers, pressure groups and citizens, among others. Specifically, concern has grown about the role of business in the violation of human rights standards and about the role of transnational corporations (TNCs), companies which operate in more than one country, in particular. Allegations of human rights abuses have been made against a range of diverse companies operating across a variety of business sectors and in a range of countries. Some of these allegations have resulted in unsuccessful litigation on the basis that human rights standards form part of national laws. For example, lawsuits have been lodged in the USA against Shell Petroleum, Texaco, UNOCAL and many companies in the clothing industry.

There are numerous high-profile examples of situations where business and human rights abuses have been linked. Throughout the 1990s Shell Petroleum was consistently charged with being involved in the violation of the human rights of the Ogoni people of Nigeria. While exploiting oil resources in the region Shell was accused of involving the military in the dispersal of peaceful Ogoni protests. Texaco also fell foul of human rights standards when it was blamed for causing severe environmental degradation in the Ecuadorean rainforest over a 30-year period, thereby violating the indigenous population's right to life (See: **INDIGENOUS PEOPLE'S RIGHTS**). Clothing and sportswear manufacturers such as Gap, Donna Karan, Nike and Reebok have been accused of utilising 'sweatshop' operations in South-East Asia to manufacture their products in violation of international labour standards. In Myanmar (formerly known as Burma), energy company UNOCAL has been the focus of international protests under allegations that the military junta has been using forced labour to build the infrastructure to support the construction of the company's gas pipeline as part of the Yadana natural gas development project.

These may appear to be clear-cut examples of human rights abuses and as such fall within the ambit of international human rights instruments. The problem, however, is that

Case Study

The Social and Economic Rights Action Center and the Center for Economic and Social Rights v Nigeria

The African Commission on Human and Peoples' Rights investigated complaints surrounding the Nigerian government's involvement in the exploitation of oil reserves in Ogoniland without regard for the health or environment of the local communities.

The state oil company, Nigerian National Petroleum Company, was a majority shareholder in a consortium with Shell Petroleum Development Corporation. Disposal of toxic materials and numerous spillages resulted in serious contamination of water, soil and air, giving rise to short- and long-term health problems for local people.

The Commission found Nigeria in breach of many human rights obligations, including the right to health, rights to disposal of natural resources and rights to property. Nigeria was asked to investigate, compensate the victims and ensure environmental and social impact assessments are conducted in the future for oil development plans.

these instruments as part of the international legal system were designed to protect individuals from the excesses of the nation-state. Consequently there is an absence of internationally binding agreements governing corporate behaviour in relation to human rights. In addition, many businesses accused of misconduct have argued that they were operating within the legal parameters of the host country and as such have denied any wrongdoing. With over 60,000 TNCs plus 800,000 affiliates operating globally (UNCTAD, 2001), this lack of international regulation could be viewed as alarming. As discussed previously, there is an ongoing debate as to the merits of the 'voluntary model versus regulatory model' approaches to the problem. Many corporations have responded to vociferous criticism and pressure from NGOs, citizens and consumers and produced codes of conduct detailing employees' rights, environmental policies and other ethical standards to which they purportedly adhere (OECD, 2000).

These codes often utilise the language of human rights, in particular, the Universal Declaration on Human Rights. Not surprisingly, companies prefer self-regulation as opposed to any form of legislative control, but even such self-regulatory measures have been implemented in response to criticism of specific operational practices rather than undertaken voluntarily.

In addition to the individual corporate codes of conduct, numerous voluntary initiatives have been implemented at international, regional and national levels in an attempt to provide a measure of regulation. One of the earliest and best-known attempts to regulate business in the social sphere at the international level was the Organisation for Economic Co-operation and Development's (OECD) drafting of the Guidelines for Multinational Enterprises in 1976 (OECD, 2000). These Guidelines set out general principles of acceptable behaviour for transnational corporations in relation to labour standards and the environment and address such issues as child labour, discrimination, forced labour, environmental management systems and health and safety. It is a measure of the importance of the Guidelines and corporate governance in general that 2000 witnessed their revision by the 30 OECD member states. Nevertheless, they remain a mere 'add-

In 1999 total annual sales of most of the top 20 transnational corporations were greater than the gross domestic products of each of the states registering low human development in the same year. An important challenge to human rights originates from this increasing power and influence of the corporate sector. Clarifying the scope for the private sector's direct responsibility for human rights is an ongoing process at regional and international levels.

(UN Doc.A/58/36, 2003)

on' to national legislative provisions and corporations are encouraged to 'develop and apply effective self-regulatory practices'. In other words, the Guidelines have no independent legal effect.

In 1999 there was further international recognition of the importance of regulating TNCs when Kofi Annan, Secretary General of the UN, announced the creation of the United Nations Global Compact. The Compact consists of 'Nine Principles' to which member companies consent to adhere. Participants agree to support and respect human rights and to ensure that they are not complicit in human rights abuses. In addition to the general human rights principles, participants agree to adhere to minimum labour and environmental standards. Like the OECD Guidelines, the Global Compact is voluntary and its architects are at great pains to emphasise that it does not 'police' corporate activities. This could be regarded as the Compact's greatest failing because while there are several hundred participant companies, there is no enforcement mechanism and many observers believe transnational corporations may use it as a mere marketing tool. Yet the Compact has wide stakeholder participation and may be regarded as a good example of a cooperative approach to regulation.

The most recent United Nations initiative in the field of CSR is the Draft Norms on the Responsibility of Transnational Corporations and Other Business Enterprises (UN Doc. E/CN.4/Sub.2/2003/12 (2003)). These norms, while not legally binding, have received widespread support from NGOs such as Amnesty International and other stake-

© R.K.M.Smith

holders and this is the most detailed state-ment to date of the potential human rights obligations of TNCs. Encouragingly, there are moves afoot to implement a monitoring and compliance regime to ensure the effective implementation of the norms and it has the potential to integrate the cooperative and reg-ulatory approach to CSR, notwithstanding opposition from business organisations such as the International Chamber of Commerce and individual companies such as Shell. In April 2004, at the request of the UK and other countries, the UN Commission on Human Rights agreed to compile a report on the human rights obligations of TNCs and acknowledged the need to strengthen stan-dards. (See: Amnesty International (2004) Commission on Human Rights, 60th Session (15 March–23 April 2004) Corporate Responsibility Breakthrough, Public Statement, AI Index: IOR 41/025/2004 (Public) News Service No: 098 20 April 2004.)

Beyond international efforts to regulate the activities of TNCs, regional organisations and individual countries have a vital role to play. The European Union has been making strides in recent years towards embracing CSR, albeit adhering to the 'business case' by following the self-regulation model. As an organisation it has a powerful voice on the international stage, for example within the World Trade Organisation, and could make some valuable contributions to the implementation of CSR. There have also been unsuccessful attempts in individual coun-tries such as the United Kingdom, Norway and the USA to introduce binding CSR frameworks (e.g. UK Private Members Bill on Corporate Responsibility, Bill 145, 53/1, 12 June 2002). Australia has also attempted to introduce com-pulsory CSR without success – see the Corporate Code of Conduct Bill 2000 which proposed regulation of Australian corporations operating overseas: the Joint Statutory Committee on Corporations and Securities rejected it on 28th June 2001 on the basis that it was unnecessary and unworkable. In October 2000, US Congresswoman Cynthia McKinney introduced the Bill of 2000 (Transparency and Responsibility for US Trade Health) HR 5492. The bill sought to require US companies oper-ating abroad to disclose information about their operations, e.g. the location and address of facilities, age and gender of employees, envi-ronmental performance and labour practices, but it was never adopted. France, however, suc-cessfully implemented mandatory CSR report-ing measures in 2001 (Loi relative aux nouvelles regulations économiques, Loi 2001-420 du 15 Mai 2001).

There have been significant strides in recent years towards a workable solution to the problem of corporate misconduct. The difficulty remains, however, that the 'business case' always champions a voluntary approach to CSR. Ultimately the protection of human rights in this area will depend upon the imple-mentation and integration of mandatory CSR rules at the international, regional and national levels as well as widespread stake-holder participation. International organisa-tions, national governments, consumers, citizens, NGOs and the companies themselves all have a vital role to play in ensuring that economic development progresses in a social-ly responsible manner and businesses adhere to human rights standards.

WEBSITES

www.unglobalcompact.org

www.unhchr.ch/business.htm

Further Reading

Addo, Michael (ed.) (1999) *Human Rights Standards and the Responsibility of Transnational Corporations*, Kluwer: The Hague.

Friedman, M. (1970) 'The social responsibility of business is to increase its profits', in *New York Times*, 13 September, 1970, §6 (Magazine), at 32.

MacLeod, Sorcha and Parkinson, John (eds) (forthcoming 2004) *Corporations and Corporate Governance*, Oxford: Hart Publishing.

The OECD Guidelines for Multinational Enterprises, Revision 2000, Paris: OECD.

Tully, Stephen (ed.) (2005) *The Handbook on Corporate Legal Responsibility*, Cheltenham, UK: Edward Elgar Publishing.

United Nations Conference on Trade and Development (UNCTAD) (2001) *World Investment Report*, New York: United Nations.

United Nations High Commissioner for Human Rights (2000) *Business and Humans Rights: A Progress Report*, Geneva.

Contributor: Sorcha MacLeod

THE CAPABILITY APPROACH AND HUMAN RIGHTS

The capability approach is not to be viewed as an alternative to the human rights discourse. The human rights discourse allows for a particular moral justification and articulation to carry weight in the political and economic process. Yet, as advocates of the capability approach argue, it is this approach that should give substance to human rights.

The capability approach has gained large-scale respect in development ethics over the last decade. More recently, its main protagonists, the Indian Nobel Laureate Amartya Sen and the US philosopher and public intellectual Martha Nussbaum, have developed the approach in relation to questions of global justice and ethics, and Sen's work in particular has been used in studies such as the United Nations Human Development reports of recent years. For this reason, it needs to be evaluated in terms of its relationship with the human rights approach, which has been the most dominant discourse from within which to make moral demands for the management of human relations on a local and global scale.

Amartya Sen developed the capability approach originally out of a critique of economic utilitarianism from a Marxist-influenced perspective. His concern, to put the human being back at the core of development policies that have come to treat economic growth as an end in itself, resonated with the concerns of Martha Nussbaum, who sought to bring Aristotelian notions of human flourishing to the debate on human development. Together, they developed a theory that was geared towards assessing the real human impact of development policies with a view to establishing a framework from within which policy makers and people in developing countries themselves could bring about the necessary shift in focus that would allow for real human development to occur. Today, hundreds of scholars worldwide are working on a variety of aspects of the capability approach to refine and develop it.

The shift in focus away from economic growth, whether aggregate in terms of gross domestic product or even in terms of income per capita, is viewed as absolutely crucial to a capability analysis. In order to understand what it is that human beings really require from development policy, the language of capabilities and functionings is employed.

According to Sen and Nussbaum, the capability approach is concerned with establishing what human beings are able to really do and be in a given context, coupled with the normative commitment to promoting the conditions within which all human beings can attain the maximum human flourishing – that is, they can live the life they wish to live. A functioning is the expression of an actual activity, such as the uptake of nutritious food, whereas the capability describes the possibility for this to occur, whether due to an internal capacity or an external facilitation. More recently, Sen has replaced the notion of capability with freedom, whereas Nussbaum has refined the concept of capability to incorporate notions of basic, internal and combined capabilities. In short, capability theorists think about what functionings people have or should have the capability to exercise.

Primarily, Sen's theory can be seen as a framework for thought in assessments of standards of living and quality of life measurements, whereas Nussbaum uses capabilities to provide a basis for central constitutional principles that citizens can demand from their governments.

A crucial area within this work is the subject of how to determine what functionings are important and who should determine this by what process. Here Sen and Nussbaum are divided. Sen is reluctant to be specific about this, out of respect for the self-determination of individuals or groups within the democratic process. Nussbaum, however, takes a different stance. She seeks to determine, through a liberal approach informed by Rawlsian political liberalism and Aristotelian philosophy, that firstly, the life that humans lead must be a dignified one, worthy of living, and secondly, certain capabilities are central to this as the enabling factors and therefore stand outside of the democratic process and cannot be supplanted.

Therefore, Nussbaum adds to the approach that human flourishing is not just about achieving the life that one wants to live but must entail a notion of human dignity; what this should be, she then abstracts from a liberal position on the intrinsic worth of the individual. Much work within the capability approach has been done on the problem of adaptive preferences and the possibility of determining whether someone's choices for themselves fall short of what they really could achieve. Such obstacles may include low expectations resulting from certain life experiences, internalised low esteem or oppression, or an uncritical adherence to the teachings of the dominant culture of a community. Sen, wishing to place the responsibility for overcoming this with people themselves, again puts much emphasis on the democratic process. Nussbaum proposes a list of central capabilities and a framework from within which this freedom can actually be realised, a form of liberal democracy, thereby trying to deal with problems of power relationships.

In Nussbaum's work, basic capabilities refer to the innate equipment of individuals that is the necessary basis for developing the more advanced capability; internal capabilities are the developed states of this, the mature conditions for readiness; and combined capabilities are internal capabilities combined with suitable external conditions for the exercise of a function. It is combined capabilities that inform Nussbaum's list of central human capabilities (life, bodily health, bodily integrity, senses, imagination and thought, emotions, practical reason, affiliation, relationships with other species and control over one's environment) upon which she wishes to base her prescriptions for policy making in any given context.

In thinking about human rights, these two theorists agree that the language of rights should be the tool with which to make the moral claims that are established through the capability method; in other words, the capability approach is there to inform the content that human rights take. In short, we have a right to what we ought to have the capability to do.

In his recent work on development as freedom, Sen argues that rights must have the following characteristics, which his capability or basic freedom approach serves to clarify:

- intrinsic importance, meaning that it is not only important for the fulfilment of needs but crucial for the formulation of needs and respect for each other's pursuit
- consequential role in providing political incentives for economic security
- constructive role in genesis of values and priorities.

This position is not anti-thetical to human rights and can indeed inform the human rights debate in a useful way. The discussion then moves to asking what types of approaches would be most useful in informing how rights are to be derived, which is what Nussbaum follows up in her work. Nussbaum argues that the capability approach can overcome the philosophical disputes that underpin rights, as it articulates clearly what the motivation and goal of a particular right is. The capability approach also has the capacity to elaborate more clearly on whether a person has the ability to exercise a right or not because it has the scope to be more concrete about the circumstances in which a particular right is claimed and fulfilled:

contradiction explains itself through the character of capitalism and its historical development. In its varying forms, capitalism is an economic and social system in which competing individuals who own the means of production (capital, land and labour) as private property join in the fight of all against all to gain wealth, power and status (Hobbes). Through wage labour (in earlier times in conjunction with slave labour, which, after its official abolition in the 19th century, is increasing again, particularly in subcontracting firms of transnational corporations) the capital and land owners acquire the added value of production, traded goods and services for themselves. All human relations, not only production and trade, are mediated through money, which has become a commodity in itself. The goal of economic activity is the profit maximisation of the property owner. This is realised through contracts and competition in the market place in which the price is determined by the supply and demand of those who have buying power. By analogy with Newtonian mechanistic physics, the market is seen as a self-regulatory mechanism. The sovereign (the state) oversees the compliance with market rules to ensure that the struggle in the market does not become a physically violent one. The result: capitalist economic activity does not even intend to satisfy the needs of all human beings as real living subjects, or if it does, only as a side-effect.

This is also apparent in the basis of the modern human rights doctrine, the English Bill of Rights (1689) (See also: **THE HISTORICAL ROOTS OF HUMAN RIGHTS BEFORE THE SECOND WORLD WAR**). The bill stipulated the rights of bourgeois property owners in relation to the king and the aristocracy – non-property owners such as slaves and women were excluded. Locke was the protagonist of this approach (1690, see Duchrow and Hinkelammert 2004, p. 43). In his theory, human beings are essentially (in the state of nature) property owners – they own their freedom, goods and body (labour). It is through work and money that they aggregate wealth. Whoever violates this order should be destroyed like a wild animal or made a slave. State intervention should be limited to the protection of property rights and contracts. This meant that in the name of the human rights of property owners, the rights of

real human beings were not allowed and, in actual fact, violated. However, within the framework of the rights of property owners, Locke also introduced self-ownership as a limit on the powers of the sovereign and even a right to revolution.

The Virginia Declaration of Rights (1776) and the US Constitution and Amendments (1789/90) went one step further to speak about the 'innate rights' of all 'men' – this was the origin of civil and political human rights (inviolable status of the person, freedom and so on). It was the women's movement struggling for universal suffrage that made them more inclusive; and it was the workers' movement, during the industrial capitalist period of the 19th century, that created the conditions for the recognition of **ECONOMIC, SOCIAL** and **CULTURAL RIGHTS** (**LABOUR RIGHTS, HEALTH** and so on) of all human beings. On the initiative of the socialist and third world countries these rights were subsequently formulated in the **INTERNATIONAL COVENANT ON ECONOMIC, SOCIAL AND CULTURAL RIGHTS** (1966) on the basis of the **UNIVERSAL DECLARATION OF HUMAN RIGHTS** (1948) (complementing the civil – property – and political rights).

Of course, in the capitalist system, civil and political rights are always more prominent than economic, social and cultural rights. Nevertheless, economic, social and cultural rights are in principle justiciable and thus should be formally demanded. But the rights to private **PROPERTY**, contracts and the accumulation of wealth have always been positive law through the civil codes as well as through British common law. Since the Code Napoleon (Article 544), the right to private property has been seen as absolute (La propriete est le droit de jouir et disposer des choses de la manière la plus absolue, pourvu qu'on ne fasse un usage prohibé par les lois ou par les règlements: Property is the absolute right to utilise and possess things, provided that one does not use these things in ways that contradict the laws and statutes). Economic, social and cultural rights, on the other hand, have not even been included in all national legal systems (for example in constitutions) in the form of basic rights (the USA has not ratified the ICESCR), let alone translated it into positive law. These rights have to be fought for in line with the political forces of a country or demanded through international courts. This is not the case only within European nation states but also in relation to their former colonies (See also: **THE FUTURE OF ECONOMIC, SOCIAL AND CULTURAL RIGHTS**).

Between the 1930s and 1970s in the USA and Europe some gains were made within the capitalist system in the area of social human rights. After the demise of classical liberalism during the world economic crisis in 1929, Keynesianism (socially regulated market economy) gained extensive ground in the Western world. Many constitutions, such as the German Basic Law, stipulated that private property entails obligations to society (Article 14.2) and this was transposed into positive law by the welfare state. In the 1970s, however, the dams began to break and the existing form of capitalism began to develop into a more ferocious neo-liberalism accompanied by increasing human rights violations.

Already at the world economic conference at Bretton Woods (1944), Keynes tried to push for a socially regulated global economy, but this fell through due to intense opposition from the USA. The course was set for ever more liberalisation across national borders. Corporations and banks transnationalised and looked for the most lucrative locations worldwide, while exploiting resources and violating human rights. In particular, the USA put dictators in power wherever possible with support – or at least without much interference – from other Western powers, thereby accessing markets and resources for its own interests and crushing all political and social resistance (e.g. Persia 1953, Congo 1960, Brazil 1964, Indonesia 1965/66, Chile 1973) (See also: **LATIN AMERICA: THE REALITY OF HUMAN RIGHTS**). In these cases, it was not only economic, social and cultural rights that were violated but, massively and notoriously, civil and political rights as well. On this, Johan Galtung stated: 'Nazism in particular and fascism in general is a phenomenon that comes into being when capitalism is in crisis and is no longer capable of operating (meaning, giving an adequate return for investment) smoothly or softly' (Duchrow 1987, 117, H. Arendt, 1951, Chomsky and Herman, 1979, Gross, 1980).

At the same time, these dictators contracted national debts, thereby instigating the over-indebtedness of their countries. These foreign debts were used by Western-dominated, undemocratic institutions such as the IMF and the World Bank, with the help of structural adjustment policies (SAPs), to liberalise, privatise and deregulate the economies and societies of these countries. In this way, direct military force was replaced by the structural force of finance. The results were massive impoverishment, expropriation of national resources and increased violence between the people of these countries, now struggling bitterly for survival (See: **POVERTY AND HUMAN RIGHTS**). The worst example of this was the genocide in Rwanda (Chossudovsky 1997).

This development has intensified since the collapse of the competing system, state socialism (which in the same modern context as capitalism in its own way concentrated political and economic power and violated human rights): the neo-liberal-capitalist model has become globalised.

The decline in economic, social and cultural rights is moving increasingly from the periphery (poor countries) to the centre (rich countries). The state is allowing itself to be blackmailed by big business: tax cuts for the rich, lax treatment of tax evasion, with consequent programmes for the retrenchment of social security systems, the creation of 'jobless growth', along with the privatisation of basic public services (water, energy, transport, health and education). In this way, capital can make extensive gains while people see their quality of life deteriorate, a phenomenon which is even affecting the middle classes. Women, single parents and children suffer disproportionately. The draft Constitution for Europe is taking Europe in this same neo-liberal direction, although human rights are formally included as 'fundamental rights'. Very importantly, what is missing in the constitution is the social accountability of private property. Although the neo-liberal economic and political mainstream continues to claim that all the negative effects are temporary sacrifices for a better future ('the invisible hand of the market will lead to general prosperity'), cynical capitalism is taking over, according the **RIGHT TO LIFE** only to those who own private property and can enter into contracts, while others are excluded and can be sacrificed (Hayek, in Duchrow/ Hinkelammert, 2004, p. 69).

Beyond these social cutbacks, one can also detect a serious decline in civil and political rights as a result of the neo-liberal global order. Until recently, the USA globalised the capitalist market indirectly through military means and finance policy. Now President George W. Bush has moved towards pushing the capitalist agenda as well as his own economic and political interests by invoking the human rights regime in a propagandistic way, in open and explicit disrespect of international law. This has had dramatic consequences for human rights on an institutional level too.

The worst result is the shift from the training of torturers for dictators the USA has set up itself (for example in the School of the Americas in Panama) towards direct torture by US military and secret services in the prisons of Iraq and Afghanistan, as well as the creation of lawless camps for 'enemy fighters' in Guantanamo Bay. At the same time, more and more civil rights are being eroded in the USA itself. During military interventions, not only by the USA but also by NATO, the United Nations and international law are ignored as a matter of principle, as part of the new strategy of self-mandating, and invoked only if they serve the interests of these forces. The USA consistently rejects the **INTERNATIONAL CRIMINAL COURT**. Furthermore, profitable Western arms deliveries are still made to countries that abuse human rights (according to Amnesty International). Public police and militaristic security systems are increasingly being privatised and thereby subjected to the capitalistic logic of profit. (see www.business-humanrights.org, www.amnesty.org, link: themes-economic globalisation).

To manifest itself, capitalism used the sovereignty of the absolutist state, which then became the democratic state. Capitalism has also encroached on the state's exclusive monopoly on the use of force and international law, and increasingly on civil and even social rights. Globalised neo-liberal capitalism is now not only destroying economic, social and cultural rights, and producing chaos in societies, it is also destroying the monopoly on the use of force that is bound to civil and political rights, thereby digging the grave of all human rights and possibly even of the planet. The most dangerous articulation of this is the US strategy of pre-emptive war – in itself in breach of international law – involving

weapons of mass destruction, including nuclear weapons. As capitalism becomes ever more separated from human rights, it is facilitating its own self-destruction, on the pattern of the terrorism it helped to spawn (See also: **GLOBALISATION WITH A HUMAN FACE**).

In conclusion, no strategy to defend human rights today can start from their existence as given. Rather, any such strategy must develop from the perspective of justice, fighting for the preconditions of the very establishment of human rights, which means seeking to overcome the imperialist, neo-liberal capitalist system.

Further Reading

Arendt, Hannah (1951) *The Origin of Totalitarianism*, New York: Hartcourt Brace Jovanovich.

Chomsky, N. and Herman, E.S. (1979) *The Washington Connection and Third World Fascism: The Political Economy of Human Rights*, Boston: South End Press.

Chossudovsky, M. (1997) *The Globalisation of Poverty*, Penang/Malaysia Monro.

Duchrow, U. (1987) *Global Economy*, Geneva: WCC.

Duchrow, U. and Hinkelammert, F. (2004) *Property for People: Not for Profit*, London: ZED.

Gross, B. (1980) *Friendly Fascism: The New Face of Power in America*, Boston: South End Press.

Contributor: Ulrich Duchrow
Translated from German original by:
                                Emma Dowling

CENTRAL AND EASTERN EUROPE: THE REALITY OF HUMAN RIGHTS

During communism the human rights record of Central and Eastern Europe – Albania, the Baltic republics, Bulgaria, the former Czechoslovakia, Hungary, Poland, Romania and the former Yugoslavia – was poor, though in most Central European countries from the mid-1960s onwards human rights violations became less severe, taking the form of structural oppression rather than direct governmental violence (Sajó 1996, p. 141). Until the collapse of communism, there was no free press, freedom of conscience and the right to privacy were restricted, political rights and the right to free movement were denied. Certain important safeguards in criminal procedure were not granted. Beginning with the 1960s, communist regimes ratified some international human rights documents, such as the two **UNITED NATIONS** basic human rights covenants (See: **THE COVENANT ON CIVIL AND POLITICAL RIGHTS AND THE COVENANT ON ECONOMIC, SOCIAL AND CULTURAL RIGHTS**), but individual citizens were not given the right to submit private petitions, hence these documents remained promises on paper without implementation in actual practice.

The collapse of communism – brought about partly by popular movements demanding protection for internationally recognized human rights – brought with it significant changes in the human rights situation in the states of Central and Eastern Europe in two respects. Firstly, wide-ranging changes took place in the actual protection or securing of human rights. Most of these countries are now liberal democracies with regular, free elections. There is freedom of speech and assembly, there are no political killings, and there are procedural rules securing fair trials and criminal procedures. Secondly, perhaps the most far-reaching change regarding human rights concerned the status of rights included in constitutions. Human rights in the communist regimes – to the extent that they were enumerated in the constitutions and other legal rules of these states at all – were seen as privileges granted by the state to its citizens and not as rights individuals could enforce even against their states. For instance, the rights that had featured most prominently in all communist constitutions in the region, at least at the level of propagandistic declarations, were **SOCIAL** and **ECONOMIC**

RIGHTS. However, granting such rights was seen as conditional on the citizen's fulfilment of her obligations towards the state or the party (Halmai 1995, p. 162). By contrast, human rights in the new democracies acquired the status of genuine, enforceable rights. We can assess the remarkable improvements that took place after the collapse of communist systems in most Central and Eastern European countries from three aspects: at the level of the codification of human rights, at the level of human rights protecting institutions and at the level of actual human rights practice.

After the collapse of communism all states in Central and Eastern Europe initiated large-scale legal reforms to give protection to human rights. Measures included the repealing of laws and constitutional provisions that enabled human rights violations, rehabilitating former victims of human rights violations, and the codification of human rights (Sajó 1996, p. 144). Importantly, catalogues of human rights were included in the newly enacted or revised constitutions, and other elements of the legal system – criminal law, laws of criminal procedure and administrative procedure – were also reformed. After the end of communism, these countries ratified the **EUROPEAN CONVENTION ON HUMAN RIGHTS** and other European and international human rights documents under the auspices of, for example, the UN or the **COUNCIL OF EUROPE**. In these countries international treaties are generally regarded as superior to national law, but usually there are no enforcement mechanisms to ensure adherence to them.

As a result of these changes, the legal texts in most Central and Eastern European countries by now almost completely meet international human rights standards. Individual rights such as the **RIGHT TO LIFE**, inviolability of the person, the right to freedom of movement, freedom of conscience and religion, the right to privacy and the right to private **PROPERTY** have become legally protected. Furthermore, extensive rights relating to judicial due process have been provided with legal safeguards. Political rights, such as the right to **FREEDOM OF ASSOCIATION** or the right to form political parties, are also protected through constitutional provision and other legal means.

Finally, social, economic and **CULTURAL RIGHTS** – such as the right to work, social security, **HEALTH CARE, EDUCATION**, rest or **MINORITY RIGHTS** – have been endorsed in many of the new constitutions, although their status is often not that of enforceable rights but of constitutional aspirations. Furthermore, the demands such rights impose on the states are regarded as limited, usually confined to the provision of basic necessities.

As concerns actual human rights practice as opposed to legal texts, the trends were country-specific. In the republics of the former Yugoslavia, the human rights situation, at least temporarily, actually got worse than it was during the communist regime. Some extreme human rights violations took place in the wars following the dissolution of Yugoslavia, including genocide and ethnic cleansing, to name only the gravest. By contrast, the Baltic states and countries in Central Europe have made significant progress and the protection of human rights has become normal practice. Human rights protection was facilitated by several important institutional guarantees that were introduced during the transition from communism. Constitutional courts were set up, one of their main functions being the protection and enforcement of human rights. On the basis of the provisions of the new constitutions and their underlying principles, these courts struck down a number of laws and administrative decisions they found to violate human rights. Next, ombudsman offices have been created for the supervision of the protection of human rights, for publicising human rights problems and for establishing initiatives for solving such issues by political and judicial means.

Another important catalyst on the improvement of these countries' human rights record was their ratification of the European Convention on Human Rights, the binding jurisdiction of the **EUROPEAN COURT OF HUMAN RIGHTS** on the basis of the Convention, and individual citizens' right to submit private petitions to the Court. Ratification of and adherence to the Convention were regarded in these countries as inevitable, since it was seen as a sign of being European as well as a necessary step on the way to EU membership, possibly securing economic benefits in the long run through EU accession (Forsythe 2000, p. 113). The Court has proved effective in exercising its authority to review national decisions about and practices of human rights. Furthermore, national courts have increasingly based their decisions on the Convention, which is directly applicable in national legal systems. The human rights protecting function of the European Union is also becoming more pronounced, and since most Central and Eastern European countries have become or are becoming members of the EU, such European human rights law will have a direct influence on the national legal systems through the rulings of the European Court of Justice, the supra–national court of the EU (See: **THE EUROPEAN UNION CHARTER OF FUNDAMENTAL RIGHTS**).

Apart from domestic and EU institutional guarantees, an important role has been played in human rights protection, especially in the process of transition, by foreign policy instruments through institutions such as the **ORGANISATION FOR SECURITY AND COOPERATION IN EUROPE (OSCE)**, supervising the implementation of the Helsinki Accord, NATO, or international financial organizations, such as the IMF or the World Bank. The instruments they have employed in the protection of human rights include diplomacy (in the case of the OSCE), humanitarian military intervention (in the case of NATO) or economic incentives (as with the IMF or the World Bank).

These institutional guarantees and foreign policy instruments have helped bring about a more favourable human rights situation in the Central European countries.

Even though the human rights situation in most countries in Central and Eastern Europe is acceptable, there are problems remaining even in countries with a relatively good human rights record, such as the Czech Republic, Hungary and Poland. Perhaps the gravest and most widespread human rights violation in the region is represented by the violence and discrimination against the Roma. The Roma in many countries are victimised over issues such as access to education, employment, health care, and goods and services, or in ill-treatment by the police, from which they receive no effective legal protection (OSI 2001, p. 17). Even when candidate countries have initiated special programmes to address such problems out of eagerness to demonstrate their compliance with the political criteria of EU membership, they have often failed to establish the institutions or to provide the financial resources necessary to guarantee effective implementation (OSI 2001, p. 25).

Apart from discrimination against the Roma, and in some states against other national and linguistic minorities, there are problems with police abuse, treatment under and conditions of detention and imprisonment, ill-treatment of asylum-seekers and the mentally ill, discrimination against the disabled, violations of the right to information and the freedom of the media. These problems are partly explained by the fact that the rights culture in these countries is still relatively weak and in many cases court decisions protecting human rights are slowly implemented in actual practice or remain ineffective (Kardos 2000, p. 231). Nevertheless, individual or NGO actions are important in raising awareness about human rights problems and the need for their solution. For example, transnational and national NGOs are important in publicising abuses, monitoring developments, publishing reports and periodicals, advocating changes in government policy, providing legal aid and raising funds (Kardos 2000, p. 229). In general, people in these countries are becoming used to the human rights discourse, which was virtually non-existent in the communist era, and also to the legal protection of their human rights.

Further Reading

Forsythe, David P. (2000) *Human Rights in International Relations*, Cambridge: Cambridge University Press.

Halmai, Gábor (1995) 'The protection of human rights in Poland and Hungary' in Istvan Pogany (ed.) *Human Rights in Eastern Europe*, Aldershot: Edward Elgar.

Kardos, Gábor (2000) 'Human rights and foreign policy in Central Europe: Hungary, the Czech Republic, and Poland' in David P. Forsythe (ed.) *Human Rights and Comparative Foreign Policy*, Tokyo: The United Nations University Press.

Open Society Institute (2001) *Monitoring the EU Accession Process: Minority Protection*, Budapest: Central European University Press.

Pogany, Istvan (ed.) (1996) *Human Rights in Eastern Europe*, Aldershot: Edward Elgar.

Sajó, András (1996) 'Rights in post-communism' in Sajó András (ed.) *Western Rights? Post-Communist Application*, The Hague: Kluwer Law International.

Contributor: András Miklós

CENTRAL ASIA: THE REALITY OF HUMAN RIGHTS

After a decade of independent existence the former Soviet Central Asian republics of Kazakhstan, Kyrgyzstan, Tajikistan, Turkmenistan and Uzbekistan have made little if any progress in improving their human rights record. Rather, what has emerged is what some analysts describe as 'contested states', the key features of which are the low level of governmental legitimacy and authority, the weak capacity for governance, the supremacy of non-state affiliations and loyalties, the prevalence of violent politics and a basic disregard for the majority of their impoverished populations.

All five republics have been held together by authoritarian sultanistic regimes, characterised by the strong personal rule of the president, a system of punishments and rewards and extensive corruption. Government personnel are often chosen directly by the president to include his family, clan, friends and business associates. The president distributes both rewards and penalties with little or no external constraint. In the absence of countervailing factors, decision making is generally arbitrary and guided by expediency and calculations of self-interest and self-aggrandisement. The   extent   of   the   regimes' 'sultanisation' differs significantly. At the worst extreme is the regime of Saparmurat Niyazov in Turkmenistan, while the mildest is Askar Akayev's regime in Kyrgyzstan, with the regimes in Uzbekistan, Tajikistan and Kazakhstan somewhere in between. In all the Central Asian republics the ruling regimes suppress opposition and manifestations of dissent, although some do so more brutally than others. At the same time, they are increasingly plagued by a range of social problems such as growing under-age prostitution, human trafficking, especially to the Gulf countries, opium production, consumption and trafficking, and a burgeoning HIV/AIDS epidemic (See: **FREEDOM FROM SLAVERY; THE MIGRANT WORKERS' CONVENTION**).

Let us look at the five Central Asian republics in turn. Throughout the 1990s and the beginning of the 2000s the human rights situation in Kazakhstan has deteriorated as a result of the increasing concentration of power in the hands of President Nursultan Nazarbayev and his clan. There has been a growing mismatch between the officially proclaimed respect for civil rights and freedoms and the regime's actual intolerance of oppositional activity. Leading opposition figures, journalists and human rights advocates have faced physical attacks, harassment, detention, arbitrary or spurious criminal charges, bugging and imprisonment after unfair trials. Among the regime's recent victims have been the two leaders of the Democratic Choice Organisation, which presents a potent challenge to Nazarbayev's government. The de facto policy of 'kazakhisation' has affected Russians and other Slavs, who make up nearly half of the republic's population, as well as Uyghurs and ethnic Kazakh exiles married to non-Kazakhs, who have suffered from violation of their citizenship and discrimination in employment, housing and educational rights (See: **FREEDOM FROM DISCRIMINATION; THE RIGHT TO HOUSING; THE RIGHT TO EDUCATION**).

Kyrgyzstan was originally presented as a model of Central Asian **DEMOCRACY**, yet under President Askar Akayev it has exhibited dangerous signs of authoritarianism and disregard for human rights since the late 1990s. In the aftermath of September 11, 2001 the Kyrgyz government followed the example, albeit less ruthlessly, of its neighbour

Uzbekistan in its persecution of political opponents and alleged Islamic extremists, primarily members of Hizb-ut-Tahrir (Party of Liberation), a non-violent Islamic group that seeks to establish a Caliphate, or Islamic state, in Central Asia. In spring 2002 the authorities intensified a crackdown in response to the eruption of political unrest in southern Kyrgyzstan. Since then Islamist parties have been banned and independent mass media have been increasingly silenced through lawsuits, threats and violence. Like Kazakhstan, the republic has also witnessed human rights problems relating to increased under-age prostitution, trafficking in women, forced labour and drugs-related criminal activity (See: **LABOUR RIGHTS; ISLAM AND HUMAN RIGHTS**).

Tajikistan is the poorest and weakest Central Asian state and endured a bloody civil war in 1992 between various regional factions. Since 1994 it has been ruled by representatives of the Kulyab region under Emomali Rakhmonov. Despite nominal adherence to democratic principles and religious freedom, the government has persecuted its opponents in the north of the country as well as alleged members of Hizb-ut-Tahrir (See: **FREEDOM OF RELIGION**). Law enforcement officers have routinely tortured hundreds of detainees to obtain confessions, which have been used in trials without qualification (See: **FREEDOM FROM TORTURE**). Freedom of the press and of assembly has been restricted (See: **FREEDOM OF EXPRESSION; FREEDOM OF ASSOCIATION**). Other human rights grey areas have included the mass exploitation and enslavement of women farm workers by their male managers, mainly in the cotton fields, the beating and other abuse of women by their husbands and other male relatives, and trafficking in women and children (See: **WOMEN'S RIGHTS; CHILDREN'S RIGHTS**).

Turkmenistan under the rule of President Saparmurad Niyazov, who calls himself 'Turkmenbashi' ('Father of the Turkmens'), retains the harshest system of state control over its citizens of any of the former Soviet republics. The regime has imposed serious obstacles to travel abroad (See: freedom of movement), curtailed access to independent information (for example, the Internet) and discriminated against Turkmenistanis educated abroad. It does not tolerate any political or religious opposition. The activities of independent religious communities are banned and punishable under administrative or criminal law, while the state-sanctioned Sunni Muslim Board and the Russian Orthodox Church are closely monitored by the security services. Niyazov's government has forbidden meetings of any kind and turned torture and execution into common 'law enforcement' measures. Human rights activists are either in exile or operate largely underground. State control was tightened even more in the wake of a failed assassination attempt on the president in November 2002. Apart from this, ethnic non-Turkmens (Russians, Armenians, Azeris, Uzbeks and Kazakhs) suffer from the official policy of 'turkmenisation' which seriously restricts their access to the top political and economic positions and to higher education. In 2003 the human rights of ethnic Russians, numbering over 150,000, were further affected by Turkmenistan's cancellation of a bilateral agreement on dual citizenship with Russia.

In Uzbekistan the regime of President Islam Karimov crushed the internal democratic opposition and forced regime opponents, particularly Islamic militants (largely based in the Ferghana valley), underground. It banned opposition parties, set heavy restrictions on the press and imposed state control over mosques. Since September 11 the Karimov government, empowered by its strategic partnership with the USA, has justified its suppression of opposition and dissent in the context of the global campaign against **TERRORISM**. By mid-2004 the government had incarcerated an estimated 7000 Muslim dissidents. Torture used on detainees includes beatings, electric shock, asphyxiation, suspension from their wrists or ankles, rape and burning with cigarettes or lit newspaper. Government officials have paraded independent Muslims or their relatives in front of assembled members of their community (mahalla) and vilified them as 'traitors' or 'enemies of the state'. Police and security forces have arrested and tortured the relatives of so-called extremists, sometimes holding them hostage in police custody until the suspect turns himself over to the authorities. The official campaign against independent Muslims has been codified in legislation on

religion and religious organisations and in the country's criminal code. More than half of the government's targets have been members of Hizb-ut-Tahrir. Victims of state oppression are often charged with having links to an Islamist radical organisation, Islamic Movement of Uzbekistan (IMU), 'subversion', 'encroachment on the constitutional order' or 'anti-state activities'. In the run-up to the meeting of the European Bank for Reconstruction and Development in Tashkent in May 2003 the Karimov government made a pretence of political liberalisation. In March 2002 Islam Karimov visited US President George W. Bush in Washington and signed an ambitious agreement to uphold human rights. In early 2003 the Uzbek government adopted the strategy for national development of Uzbekistan, an important part of which involves progress in human rights. However, as soon as the meeting was over the human rights situation appeared to deteriorate even further.

In the aftermath of September 11 the governments of Uzbekistan, Kyrgyzstan and Tajikistan have been directly drawn into the new Western security arrangements by offering their land and air space for the United States to use in the anti-terrorist campaign. They have also secured increased economic and financial assistance from various international financial institutions, including the European Bank for Reconstruction and Development. The region's vital role in the US-led 'war on international terrorism' has enabled local regimes to legitimise their persistent disregard for human rights and to crack down on opposition and free media. In the current political climate the appeals of local and international human rights organisations to Central Asian governments and the international community to improve the human rights situation there have been ineffective. Meanwhile, there is an urgent need to protect human rights against counter-terrorism measures.

Further Reading

Creating Enemies of the State: Religious Persecution in Uzbekistan (2004) Human Rights Watch Report, (http://www.hrw.org/reports/2004/uzbekistan0304/2.htm)

Oliker, O. and Szayna, Thomas S. (2002) *Faultlines of conflict in Central Asia and the South Caucasus*, Santa Monica: RAND.

Rashid, A. (2002) *Jihad: The Rise of Militant Islam in Central Asia*, New Haven: Yale University Press.

Whitlock, M. (2002) *Beyond the Oxus: The Central Asians*, London: John Murray (Publishers) Ltd.

Yaacov, R. (1995) *Muslim Eurasia: Conflicting Legacies*, London: Frank Cass.

Contributor: Galina Yemelianova

CHILDREN'S RIGHTS

In the words of the 1924 Geneva Declaration on the Rights of the Child, mankind owes to the child the best it has to give. Eighty years later, this sentiment articulated by the Assembly of the League of Nations still rings true. For example, the impact of abuses of the environment today may not be fully realised until our children or grandchildren come of age. Statistical information on endangered wildlife, the depletion of the ozone layer, pollution and deforestation testify to changes wreaked to date. Many environmentalists now vocalise concerns over the quality of the planet which future generations will inherit. However, the environment is not the sole issue affecting children.

Children are recognised as having particular needs, distinct from those of adults. Inherently vulnerable, children depend on others for their well-being in a manner not matched by any other group which has been accorded protection (refugees, women, migrant workers, prisoners). The very survival of an infant is dependent on external nutritional provision. Secondary violations of human rights can thus occur – the poverty or lack of food suffered by a malnourished mother unable to produce milk or milk of sufficient quality will clearly have an impact on the health of her child should no other food sources be available. Similarly, children born to mothers suffering from HIV or other conditions which may be inherited are likely to suffer more acutely from any lack of adequate health care for the mother (for example, appropriate anti-viral drugs or pre/post-birth diagnostic tests and medical treatment may

not be provided), while in the colder regions of North America, a homeless family will struggle to ensure warmth and safety for their children. Improving the lives of parents and carers will inevitably impact on the lives of their children. Securing respect for universal rights must therefore remain a priority as the rights of children and the rights of their carers are often interdependent to a degree which precludes separation, especially during the formative years of the child's development.

Taking up the mantle of children's rights from the League of Nations, the United Nations General Assembly proclaimed its own Declaration on the Rights of the Child in 1959. An International Year of the Child followed in 1979, spurring the international community into further action to prepare a binding charter of children's rights. The resulting 1989 **CONVENTION ON THE RIGHTS OF THE CHILD** has attracted almost universal ratification. In the words of its preambular paragraphs, it is based on recognition that childhood is entitled to special care and assistance and that every child should have the opportunity to grow up in a happy, loving, understanding family atmosphere in order to ensure the full and harmonious development of the child's personality. Although the Convention and its two protocols are unique in international human rights law and perhaps represent the apex of the current international human rights movement, there is a plethora of additional instruments on children's rights. Many of these rights are codified within the Convention, others coexist with it. None has attracted the near-universal support of the United Nations Convention on the Rights of the Child. Nevertheless they should not be overlooked.

POVERTY, social exclusion, hunger and homelessness inevitably impact on children. In many households, children are the healthiest and strongest members, thus inevitably they can be made to work. **THE INTERNATIONAL LABOUR ORGANISATION** (ILO) has been concerned with limiting working hours and restricting abusive working conditions for children since its inception following the Treaty of Versailles. Many of its conventions impact on the rights of children, seeking to prevent economic exploitation. Two of the first ILO conventions

– No. 5 on Minimum Age (Industry) 1919 and No. 6 on Night Work of Young Persons (Industry) 1919 (as revised by Convention No. 90, 1948) – concerned children. Adopting its characteristic sectoral approach, a number of minimum age conventions followed for sea, agriculture, and non-industrial employment, before the current Convention No. 138 (1973) on Minimum Age. This latter instrument, along with the 1999 Convention No. 182 on the elimination of the worst forms of child labour, are two of the ILO's most fundamental conventions.

On 12 June 2004 it was the World Day against Child Labour with the emphasis on domestic labour behind closed doors. Domestic labour is a potentially abusive situation and, in extremis, children are sold into practices analagous to **SLAVERY** or are trafficked to work in exploitative industries and the sex trade. One of the principal challenges faced by the international community is the potential for abuse through the worldwide web, especially with pornography and sex tourism. The 2000 Protocol to the United Nations Convention on the Rights of the Child addresses this issue in more detail and a number of international conferences and initiatives seek to internationalise protection of children from such treatment. For example, the Organisation of American States adopted a resolution on child trafficking (OAS Doc. AG/RES.1948 (XXXIII-O/03)).

Of continuing concern is the plight of young people during armed conflict. Child soldiers, whether drawn into international or civil insurgency, are protected by the UN Convention and its other 2000 Protocol. The International Committee of the Red Cross/Red Crescent and the International Labour Organisation (Convention No. 182) both condemn the use of children in armed conflict, while the Statute of the International Criminal Court lists 'conscripting or enlisting children under the age of 15 years into armed forces or groups or using them to participate actively in the hostilities' as a war crime (Article 8(2)(e)(vii)).

Given the importance of a support network for children (particularly young ones), there is an overlap with the right to family life (See: **THE RIGHT TO MARRIAGE AND A FAMILY**). The Hague Convention on the Protection of Children and Cooperation in Respect of Intercountry Adoptions and the Hague Convention on the Civil Aspects of International Child Abduction, though lacking universal ratification, provide recourse for some parents separated from their children. Cross-country adoptions are increasing popular, with regulations focused primarily at a national level on immigration criteria and naturalisation processes. The high profile of some of these adoptions – for example the actress Angelina Jolie and her Cambodian-born son – has raised awareness of the potential for inter-state adoptions. However, many problems may arise, particularly with cultural integration and even ultimately with the demographics of the country of origin (primarily female babies are offered for adoption in China). Some countries have recently sought to tighten regulations on international adoptions, Romania being a prime recent example. A moral dilemma remains for many 'wealthy' potential parents: is adopting a child from a 'poorer' country providing a 'better' life for that child or a patronising gesture, denying a child his or her cultural heritage through a system which is open to abuse by unscrupulous adoption agencies? Which right prevails?

The importance of children is clearly recognised by the United Nations. UNICEF and UNESCO are both heavily involved in promoting the rights of children. One of the key areas in which these organisations are active is **EDUCATION**. In many respects education and human rights education is the key to the future of the human rights movement. Compulsory (and selective) education of children has been shown to protect against accidental injury by landmines and the transmission of disease through poor personal hygiene. A number of similar educational schemes are being funded globally. Educating children can also have a positive effect on the parents or carers. From a human rights perspective, much has been done to generate an awareness of children's rights among children.

Within the regional systems, only Africa has adopted a substantial tabulation of children's rights. In Africa, over half the population of many countries are children, hence the situation is often acute. In 1990, the African Charter on the Rights and Welfare of the

Child was adopted by the then OAU. It applies to all human beings below the age of 18 and echoes much of the UN Convention. Children enjoy a variety of rights, including the right to life, survival and development, the right to a name and nationality, freedom of expression, association, thought, conscience and religion, privacy, education and health care. Children are to be protected from abuse, economic and sexual exploitation, harmful traditional practices, torture, armed conflict, apartheid and trafficking. Refugees and mentally handicapped children are singled out for particular care. In keeping with the ethos of the **AFRICAN CHARTER ON HUMAN AND PEOPLES' RIGHTS**, children are also the incumbents of a series of duties. These include respecting their parents, serving the national community, preserving African cultural values and contributing towards African unity (Article 31).

While most agree that children are owed the best the world has to give, what we must ask ourselves is whether the current range of children's rights realises that standard.

WEBSITES

www.unicef.org – United Nations Children's Fund

www.unesco.org – United Nations Education, Science and Cultural Organisation

www.savethechildren.org – Save the Children international website

---

Further Reading

Cohen, Cynthia Price (2004) *Jurisprudence on the Rights of the Child*, New York: Transnational.

Fottrell, D. (2001) *Revisiting Children's Rights – 10 Years of the UN Convention on the Rights of the Child*, Leiden: Kluwer.

UNICEF, *The State of the World's Children 2004* (UNICEF, 2004, available online from www.unicef.org).

Freeman, M. (ed.) (1996) *Children's Rights – A Comparative Perspective*, Aldershot: Dartmouth.

United Nations, *Fact Sheet No. 10 (Rev. 1) The Rights of the Child*, Geneva: Office of the High Commissioner for Human Rights.

Van Bueren, Geraldine (1994) *The International Law on the Rights of the Child*, Dordrecht: Martinus Nijhoff.

Contributor: Rhona K.M. Smith

CHINA: THE REALITY OF HUMAN RIGHTS

The Supreme People's Court of China asserts that the Constitutional Right to Education can directly protect a student's legal claim. Silent guards watch idly as demonstrators chant their grievances across the street from the Great Hall of the People. These scenes would have been impossible in the first years after 4 June 1989 when the Chinese state's violent suppression of dissent splashed across international television screens. Shadows of that time linger. The Chinese authorities continue to ignore the pleas for apology and reconciliation to victims of June 4th by respected national figures such as Dr Jiang Yanyong, who helped expose the cover-up of SARS, and Professor Ding Zelin, organiser of Tiananmen Mothers. Nevertheless dramatic changes have taken place.

The picture that emerges of human rights protection in China today is a hologram. At one angle a potpourri of human rights improvements is apparent: the scope for unthreatened individual expression and behaviour has widened; living standards have increased for broad strata of the citizenry; government transparency has increased; the press is less controllable; the harshest restrictions on freedom of movement have weakened; criminal, administrative and civil law reforms have provided procedural protections and avenues of redress; experiments in local **DEMOCRACY** are being extended; **HUMAN RIGHTS EDUCATION** has been sanctioned for law students.

Cast the light from another direction and the hologram reveals persistent and tragic abuses of human rights. Criminal sanctions are used to suppress political dissent; the death penalty is widely applied (See: **THE RIGHT TO LIFE: THE DEATH PENALTY**); police have broad discretion to detain under administrative powers without due process; the state exercises various controls over information distribution; the implementation of family planning policy harshly limits rights to family life; discrimination on the basis of health status, party membership and social origin is condoned by the state; and despite constitutional guarantees, enforceable laws narrowly restrict freedoms of assembly, **ASSOCIATION** and **RELIGION**.

Only looking backwards will we be able to judge whether the improvements in human rights enforcement are part of a pragmatic, progressive, cultural and legal embrace of international human rights norms or a thin patina masking an unchanged authoritarian system that is merely willing to selectively enforce its international human rights obligations.

Several forces will largely determine how this history unfolds. The first is how the new party leadership defines its historical mission. The fourth generation leaders are committed to policies that they perceive will preserve economic growth and social stability. They see the necessity of bolstering party legitimacy in order to fulfil these goals. To the extent that policies consistent with international human rights standards serve these missions, the future of human rights in China is hopeful. Building a social security net, reducing exploitative rural taxes and tackling the challenges of a health service gutted by the dismantling of the socialist welfare state are seen as consistent with building domestic consumption. A more professionalised legal system, legal aid and a reform of the household registration system are perceived as servicing social stability. Increasing local experiments in competitive elections and improving government transparency are argued for by many branches of the state as necessary medicine to fight party corruption.

A second force is the increasing integration of China into the world community of globalised economics and multilateral politics. Human rights have become a part of the international vocabulary. Integration, therefore, exposes China to external demands that it address human rights abuses within its territory. Integration, however, also provides a means for China to stake its claim as a legitimate global power. This combination of external pressure and self-interest is propelling ratification of international human rights conventions. It has also resulted in the domestic appropriation of a human rights vocabulary, as can be seen from the Chinese White Papers

on Human Rights. China has ratified five of the seven core UN human rights treaties: the **CONVENTION ON THE ELIMINATION OF ALL FORMS OF DISCRIMINATION AGAINST WOMEN**, ratified 1981; the **CONVENTION ON THE ELIMINATION OF ALL FORMS OF RACIAL DISCRIMINATION**, ratified 1981; the Convention Against Torture, ratified 1988 (See: **FREEDOM FROM TORTURE**); the **CONVENTION ON THE RIGHTS OF THE CHILD**, ratified 1992; and the **CONVENTION ON ECONOMIC SOCIAL AND CULTURAL RIGHTS**, ratified 2001. It has signed the **CONVENTION ON CIVIL AND POLITICAL RIGHTS**. China has ratified three of eight core International Labour Organisation conventions: C100 on Discrimination, ratified 1990; C138 on child labour, ratified 1999; and C182 on child labour, ratified 2002 (See: **LABOUR RIGHTS**). Ratification of ILO C111 on employment equality is expected soon. The historical wall excluding international inspectors has also been cracked. The Special Rapporteur of the Commission on Human Rights on freedom of religion or belief visited China in 1994 and the Special Rapporteur on Education in 2003. International trade generally, and WTO membership specifically, require that China build a system of transparent law predictably applied by professional institutions.

The Chinese state is far from willing to ratify the Convention protocols that establish individual complaint procedures, however. Nor does it allow human rights Conventions to be directly applied by domestic courts (although some justices are arguing for their citation as persuasive evidence in interpretation of domestic law). Furthermore, Chinese state reports to United Nations bodies, like the reports of the Special Rapporteurs, are not widely circulated. Nevertheless, by accepting the obligations of a state party under these conventions, China must appropriate a language of human rights and expose itself to a measurement of its human rights performance based on internationally agreed indicators. It is noteworthy that the first National People's Congress under the new party leadership passed a constitutional amendment stating that 'The State respects and protects human rights' (10th NPC, March 2004).

China can be said to have entered the process that Tomas Risse describes as human rights normative socialisation. At the very least, international integration and the new constitutional amendment are tools of leverage for Chinese citizens seeking improved human rights implementation.

Chinese citizens now have access to an unprecedented flow of information. This information is another force that is likely to affect domestic demands for human rights implementation. Inconsistent efforts by Chinese authorities to control the press and the Internet are not so sweeping that they can be said to contain this escalating access. In Chinese chat rooms you can find many human rights issues being discussed, from forced evictions of migrants to constitutional reform. The web has also become a tool of organising. Hepatitis B carriers have organised a website (www.hbvhbv.com) to exchange information. Website participants recently provided evidential support to the first case establishing that laws barring civil service employment to Hepatitis B carriers are illegal employment discrimination (Zhang Xianzhu Case, Anhui Province). Nearly 10 per cent of the Chinese population are Hepatitis B carriers and have been excluded in many jurisdictions from civil service jobs. Gay and lesbian communities also have active web exchanges. This birthing ground for interest groups gives participants a new way to join international debates and gives scholars new means to both collect and distribute data.

Like Internet users, Chinese print and broadcast journalists are reigned in by authorities, but not consistently. Sometimes they are given a longer lead, especially if the authorities perceive it useful, for example to harness investigative journalist skills to the discovery and fight against corruption or consumer fraud. At other times, the lead is shortened to a stranglehold. Principled journalism in China is a precarious business. But even under restraints, Chinese journalists know far more about the outside world and China's domestic reality than they did in 1989. They also succeed in communicating far more information to their audiences. Such increases in access to information may contribute to raising human rights consciousness among the citizens.

How fast and in what vein a popular consciousness of human rights develops will, in turn, influence how rapidly Chinese authorities feel propelled to implement their international obligations. As Marina Svensson (2002) has demonstrated, although China has a history of indigenous philosophical debates on human rights that dates from at least the 1800s, many of those voices have been forgotten or buried. Today, popular consciousness of human rights is probably more influenced by Chinese traditions regarding the role of law. **CONFUCIANISM**, and later communism, both took law to be a feeble tool for the pursuit of justice: Confucianism because moral virtue was seen as the more powerful force and communism because law was deemed a tool of bourgeoisie oppression. The legalist tradition took law to be a useful tool to implement the will of leadership and to punish criminals. Thus the stress which international human rights law lays on due process protections, individual rights and the inherent dignity of the individual is not intuitive to all Chinese. The last 20 years of legal reforms, however, have built a legal system that is arguably compatible with what Professor Peerenboom (2002) has called the 'thin rule of law'. These changes have affected the rights consciousness of Chinese citizens. Development assistance programmes have also directed considerable resources to rights consciousness-building among grassroots communities as well as professionals. For all the shortcomings to which Sophia Woodman and others have pointed, such programmes have exposed a host of communities to rights awareness. An example of changing consciousness is the increasing number of cases in which individuals challenge government abuse of power via administrative law: 88,050 cases in 2003 compared with 23,000 in 1996.

One cannot speak of human rights movements in China. Chinese rights to association and assembly are limited, inter alia, by the Social Organization Law and the Public Demonstration Law. It is interesting to note, however, that China abstained but did not vote against passage of the UN Declaration on Human Rights Defenders. The content of international human rights obligations is also not yet widely understood. However, creative grassroots organising on rights-related issues is taking place despite hurdles. The party welcomes some organisational initiatives, such as the China Disabled Persons' Federation, headed by the son of Deng Xiaoping; it tolerates an increasing number; and it systematically represses those it defines as threatening to social stability and economic development, for example Falun Gong. **WOMEN'S RIGHTS**, environmental protection and consumer rights generate the most visible rights-oriented organisation. More recently, support structures for those living with HIV/Aids and Hepatitis B have surfaced. Where registration as an NGO is difficult or inadvisable, university projects and even business licences can provide shelter for these and other public interest initiatives that have the potential to effect human rights improvements.

Without an enforceable right to association, the borders of what is politically acceptable shift according to ad hoc local decision making and central policy campaigns. Clear boundaries exist, however, against any organisation that is seen to threaten the constitutional leadership of the Communist Party (Falun Gong or independent trade unions) or that is deemed to be motivated by a desire to restructure China's geographical boundaries (e.g. **MINORITY RIGHTS** organising in Tibet, or Xinjiang). The success of advocacy for human rights-related reforms and expanded human rights consciousness among ordinary citizens may well depend, therefore, on the packaging organizers design for their goals and the structures within which they work. An ability to strategically explore the parameters of acceptable challenge and organise innovatively are skills that have afforded many activists more political space than might be expected.

Finally, scholars have traditionally been the voice of social conscience in China and a crucial source of policy advice to leaders. Their future priorities in academic research and policy advice will therefore also influence China's path towards enforcement of international human rights law. Today, important arguments regarding the need to make the Constitution justiciable, how to limit the use of the death penalty, how to abolish re-education through labour and how to reintroduce the right to strike are all being debated within the party with the encouragement of scholars.

Whether the academic institutions can retain the best and the brightest despite the temptations of private sector incomes will be an important factor. A dramatic improvement in the salaries and conditions at 'key universities' is heartening. The down-side, however, as the Special Rapporteur on the Right to Education was quick to point out, is that state investment in tertiary education has been to the detriment of investment in primary and secondary education. Another concern is what choices the current generation of students will make. These students are among the first who are able to make their own career choices and who face a career bridled to market forces. Many scholars of the older generation are disappointed by the younger generation's focus on economic rewards rather than public service. The students of Tiananmen are not the role models for this generation. Nevertheless, law school students are showing an unexpectedly high interest in human rights law courses as well as legal clinic classes that provide practice in defending the disadvantaged, and in that lies promise.

The trajectory of human rights implementation in China will follow the logic of the Communist Party unless the Chinese population develops a tolerance for social disruption that is still far from apparent. At present, with the Cultural Revolution still within living memory, not only the leadership but the bulk of the population accept that social stability and economic development are preconditions for improved human rights. There is also widespread approval for harsh treatment of those whose lack of patience threatens these foundations. Chinese, generally, admire strong government. However, the costs of incrementalism may be higher than even those with patience expect. Rising expectations are being spurred both from inside and outside China. And losers in the economic reform process look to the newly privileged across an income canyon wider than that in the USA. The party is aware that it ignores the potential catalysing of dissatisfaction at its peril. Survival for the party requires tangible responses. Whether that is grounds for optimism that human rights in China will improve depends on how the hologram is tilted.

WEBSITES

www.amnesty.org, Amnesty International
www.duihua.org, Dui Hua Foundation Reports
iso.hrichina.org/iso/, Human Rights in
China Reports

www.hrw.org, Human Rights Watch Reports
www.cecc.gov/pages/annualRpt/2003annRpt
.pdf, Information Office of the State Council
of the PRC, Progress in China's Human
Rights Cause, March 2004, Beijing
US Congressional-Executive Commission on
China 2003 Annual Report
www.chinadevelopmentbrief.com, Young,
Nick, China Development Briefs

Further Reading

Edwards, Randle, Henkin, Louis and Andrew,
J. Nathan (1986) *Human Rights in
Contemporary China*, New York : Columbia
University Press.

Lee, Ta-ling and Cooper, John F. (1994) *The
Bamboo Gulag: Human Rights in the People's
Republic of China, 1991-1992*, Baltimore, Md.:
University of Maryland School of Law.

Office of the High Commissioner for Human
Rights (2004) 'The PRC and the International
Human Rights System', in *Country Profile*,
Spring.

Peerenboom, Randall (2002) *China's Long
March Toward Rule of Law*, Cambridge:
Cambridge University Press.

Svensson, Marina (2002) *Debating Human
Rights in China*, Oxford: Rowman & Littlefield
Publishers.

Contributor: Lisa Stearns

THE COMMONWEALTH OF INDEPENDENT STATES' (CIS) CONVENTION ON HUMAN RIGHTS AND FUNDAMENTAL FREEDOMS

The Commonwealth of Independent States
(CIS) was created in December 1991 by 11 of
the 15 republics of the former USSR –
Armenia, Azerbaijan, Belarus, Kazakhstan,
Kyrgyzstan, Moldova, Russia, Tajikistan,
Turkmenistan, Uzbekistan and Ukraine.
Another republic of the former Soviet Union
– Georgia – joined in December 1993. The
formation of the CIS served as a de jure recognition of the disintegration of the USSR and a
new institutional framework for political and
economic relations among the newly formed
states in the post-Soviet era. The CIS has since
developed a number of legal instruments, one
of which is the Convention on Human Rights
and Fundamental Freedoms (CHRFF). The
CHRFF was signed on 26 May 1995 by 7 of the
11 CIS member states (Armenia, Belarus,
Georgia, Kyrgyzstan, Moldova, Russia,
Tajikistan) and has since been ratified by
Russia, Tajikistan and Belarus. It entered into
force on 11 August 1998, the day the third
instrument of ratification was deposited by
Belarus (See: **THE COMMONWEALTH OF
INDEPENDENT STATES: THE REALITY OF
HUMAN RIGHTS**).

The CHRFF guarantees such political and
civil rights and liberties as the **RIGHT TO
LIFE** (Article 2), the right not to be tortured
(See: **FREEDOM FROM TORTURE**) (Article
3), **FREEDOM FROM SLAVERY** and forced
labour (Article 4), individual freedom and
personal integrity (See: **LIBERTY**) (Article
5), **THE RIGHT TO FAIR TRIAL** and equality of individuals before law (Article 6), the
right to **PRIVACY** (Article 7), freedom of
thought and religious affiliation (See: **FREE-
DOM OF RELIGION AND BELIEF**) (Article
8), **FREEDOM OF EXPRESSION** (Article 9),
FREEDOM OF ASSOCIATION (Article 10)
and **THE RIGHT TO VOTE** (Article 29). It
also provides for such **SOCIAL** and **ECO-
NOMIC RIGHTS** as the **RIGHT TO MARRY**
(Article 13), the right to work (Article 14), the
right to paid holiday and maternity leave
(Article 15), **THE RIGHT TO HEALTH**
(Article 16), the right to social welfare (Article
17), the right of ethnic minorities to speak
their languages and practise their customs
(See: **MINORITY RIGHTS**) (Article 21),
freedom of movement and migration (Article
22), the right to private **PROPERTY** (Article
26) and the right to free primary and secondary school **EDUCATION** (Article 27). To
monitor the execution of the CHRFF, the signatories created a control mechanism in the
form of a Human Rights Commission (HRC)
(Article 34).

Despite providing for such an extensive
range of human rights, the CHRFF has been
an object of international criticism, in particular by the **COUNCIL OF EUROPE** (COE), on
the grounds that the rights guaranteed by the
CHRFF diverged in some important respects

from those guaranteed by the **EUROPEAN CONVENTION ON HUMAN RIGHTS** (ECHR) and that the impartiality and credibility of the HRC as a control mechanism were in doubt. For example, if Article 2 of the ECHR clearly specifies the cases in which deprivation of life shall not be regarded as a violation of the right to life, Article 2 of the CHRFF merely refers to cases of extreme necessity provided for in the national legislation of the member states, which effectively leaves it to the discretion of the respective legislatures to fix such cases. As regards capital punishment, although the CHRFF provides that women shall not as a rule be sentenced to the death penalty and forbids the imposition of the death penalty in the case of pregnant women, as well as its imposition for crimes committed before the perpetrator reached the age of 18 (Article 2), it does not abolish the death penalty entirely, as does Protocol 6 to the ECHR. Concerning the right to liberty, if Article 5 of the ECHR clearly states the cases of lawful detention, Article 5 of the CHRFF merely requires that a person's detention be in accordance with the legislation of the member states, which are thereby free to determine an unlimited number of cases where detention is lawful. With respect to the right to fair trial, whereas Article 6 of the ECHR includes the interests of 'national security in a democratic society' among the grounds for excluding the press and the public from a trial, Article 6 of the CHRFF uses the broader term 'state secrecy' and again leaves its interpretation to the member states' discretion. In terms of the comparison of control mechanisms of the two conventions, if the ECHR sets up an impartial court of law, the Human Rights Commission established by the CHRFF is composed of representatives of the member states who are not elected but appointed by the state parties and their absolute independence and impartiality therefore cannot be guaranteed.

In addition to these legal inadequacies, the CHRFF has suffered from problems of the CIS itself which has so far served mostly as a discussion forum and has failed to adopt or implement important binding decisions. In recent years the member states have preferred to establish smaller organisations with mostly economic objectives such as customs unions or free trade areas. For example, Belarus, Kazakhstan, Kyrgyzstan, Russia and Tajikistan have created a trading bloc known as the Eurasian Economic Community, while Georgia, Ukraine, Uzbekistan, Azerbaijan and Moldova have established a similar institutional arrangement called GUUAM. As a result, the CIS has failed to address serious violations of human rights committed by the member states, in particular widespread abuses of fundamental human rights by the regime of president Nyazov in Turkmenistan, massive political repressions in Belarus practised by the government of Lukashenko and violations of human rights by the Russian troops in Chechnya.

However, despite all the above limitations, the existence of the CHRFF in itself is an important positive factor in terms of promotion and protection of human rights in the world. It may be recalled that the former USSR strongly opposed the idea of individual human rights, in particular political and civil rights, and was supported by a number of non-Western oppressive regimes, which claimed that economic development was their first priority and used this argument to continue repression of political opponents and abuses of human rights. Today, by contrast, political and civil rights are becoming a form of global norm in terms of which behaviour of individual actors (such as states or business firms) is evaluated, in terms of which they are increasingly disciplined by different actors (provided, of course, this does not interfere with the interests of the major powers of corporate bodies) and to which actors themselves increasingly tend to conform (although, for the most part, still only officially). In other words, rather than challenging the notion of human rights as a Western/capitalist concept, as many non-Western governments used to do during the cold war, they increasingly tend to adopt measures and declarations which bring them, at least officially, closer to the norm. For example, African states in the framework of the African Union (former Organisation of African Unity) have in recent years declared that promotion of individual human rights and empowerment of civil society organisations to this end constitute one of the key objectives of the organisation. The same is true as regards the Mercosur, a Latin American trading bloc, and the ASEAN

(Association of South-East Asian Nations). And, most recently, business firms have expressed similar commitments.

Thus, the CHRFF is, on the one hand, evidence of the fact that human rights are becoming a global norm in that the member states of the CIS, whose commitment to human rights is at best questionable, nevertheless felt obliged to adopt such a document, and on the other, another important contribution to the further development of human rights as a global norm. This contribution seems to be important especially given the fact that the CHRFF was signed by states that in the past comprised one of the major opponents of the notion of human rights – and particularly passive rights of individuals – the USSR. That is to say, the very existence of the CHRFF, even if only on paper, plays a significant role in the development of global consent as regards the existence and importance of human rights.

What remains to be done is to take advantage of this developing consent, that is, to ensure that human rights are not only acknowledged but also respected in practice. In the world where strong powers exist and where national interest often trumps other considerations, this is not an easy task. However, with the end of the cold war, the development of global civil society and decline in opposition to the concept of human rights around the world, the international environment is now more favourable for a better realisation of human rights. The fact that human rights is becoming a recognized norm, especially by those states that used to oppose it, makes it easier to challenge governments that abuse human rights and makes it more difficult for them to invoke such arguments as state sovereignty or economic development. The CHRFF, therefore, despite its legal and practical problems, is an important element in terms of facilitating international protection and promotion of human rights.

WEBSITES

www.cis.int, Commonwealth of Independent States

www.cis.minsk.by, Executive Committee

www.coe.int, Council of Europe

Contributor: Ivan Manokha

THE COMMONWEALTH OF INDEPENDENT STATES: THE REALITY OF HUMAN RIGHTS

The Commonwealth of Independent States has been a controversial institution since its birth in 1991. It has attempted more than once to play a role in the international protection of human rights, but with generally minimal results, which must have proved embarrassing to its leaders.

The CIS came into existence as an integral part of the dissolution of the former USSR. It was created on 8 December 1991 in Minsk, the capital of Belarus, by the leaders of three of the remaining 12 states of the USSR: Belarus, Russia and Ukraine (the three Baltic states, Estonia, Latvia and Lithuania, had already left). The Declaration and the Agreement Establishing the Commonwealth of Independent States were signed by the heads of state of the Republic of Belarus, the Russian Soviet Federative Socialist Republic and Ukraine. These were not the best-drafted documents: the Agreement contained no provision for entry into force, though this was remedied by a Protocol of 21 December 1999.

The CIS was of dubious legality from the start, since the three heads of states had not obtained the consent of the other nine Soviet republics. This was put right in part by the decisions made by 11 of the 12 republics at the Alma-Ata Summit, held in Kazakhstan on 21 December 1991. Georgia was the missing state and joined the CIS only in 1993, when President Shevardnadze came to power.

The CIS cannot be classified as a federation, since the founders explicitly stated that the Commonwealth 'is neither a state nor a supra-state entity'. It follows that the Commonwealth as such cannot be in any way treated as a legal successor to the former USSR.

In some respects the CIS resembles the British Commonwealth (See: **THE COMMONWEALTH AND HUMAN RIGHTS**) Both are the consequences of the break-up of former multinational state formations (the British Empire and the USSR). Both are associations of states, whose international legal nature is questionable. However, there are a number of sharp distinctions between the two commonwealths. Unlike the British Commonwealth, which is based on the Royal Titles Act of 1953, the legal foundation of the CIS is a set of international agreements. Unlike the unequal status of the British Commonwealth members (the sovereign of the United Kingdom remains 'Head of the Commonwealth' and some members are still dependent colonial territories), the CIS rests on the principle of sovereign equality of its members (although there are different categories of CIS membership). Further, compared with the organisational structure of the British Commonwealth (which has a Secretariat, established in 1965, that has no executive functions), the CIS has a variety of institutional mechanisms, beyond the scope of this short introduction.

The Charter of the CIS was adopted at the Minsk Summit on 22 January 1993. Only 7 of the 11 states signed the Charter – Ukraine, Turkmenistan and Moldova refrained from signing, while Azerbaijan did not intend to sign from the very beginning.

According to Article 2 of the Charter, some significant aims of the CIS are:

- cooperation in political, economic, ecological, humanitarian, cultural and other fields;
- ensuring human rights and basic freedoms in accordance with the universally recognized principles and norms of international law and the documents of the conference for security and cooperation (CSC);
- mutual legal aid and cooperation in other spheres of legal relationships;
- peaceful settlement of disputes and conflicts among the states of the Commonwealth.

As to human rights, the USSR had been an assiduous ratifier of **UNITED NATIONS** Human Rights treaties, ahead of many Western states, but had no intention that these instruments should have any domestic effect. Paradoxically, however, one of the last acts of the USSR, in October 1991, was to ratify the First Optional Protocol to the UN's **INTERNATIONAL COVENANT ON CIVIL AND POLITICAL RIGHTS (ICCPR)**. Some cases have now been taken to the UN's **HUMAN RIGHTS COMMITTEE** against Russia.

By agreement with the other members of the CIS, Russia is successor to the USSR in the UN. It has submitted periodical reports to the UN Treaty Bodies and the process of consideration of them has been greatly enlivened by the alternative ('shadow') reports prepared by the large number of active non-governmental organisations. Thus, Russia found the sessions devoted to the **CONVENTION FOR THE ELIMINATION OF ALL FORMS OF RACIAL DISCRIMINATION** (CERD) and the ICCPR, both held in 2003, to be distinctly uncomfortable.

Indeed, all states of the CIS have now ratified practically all the 'big six' UN human rights treaties and are more or less integrated into the system.

The **COUNCIL OF EUROPE** has posed considerably greater problems for the CIS. It is one of the great 'ironies of history' that the CoE, originally created as the 'ideological counterpart of NATO' and designed to prove the seriousness of its members' commitment to first-generation human rights through the establishment of the first international court able to make binding adjudications on human rights violations, has grown to include so much of the territory of its former opponent.

Thus, of the 12 states of the CIS, six – Armenia, Azerbaijan, Georgia, Moldova, Russia and Ukraine – are now members of the CoE. Belarus cannot join under its present regime, while there are many reasons, geographical and cultural, why the five Central Asian states are excluded. It should be noted, however, that Kazakhstan is eager to form a closer relationship, starting with observer status (See: **CENTRAL ASIA: THE REALITY OF HUMAN RIGHTS**).

Difficulties with the CoE came to a head in the mid-1990s when the CIS began to try to implement its human rights commitments. Firstly, on 21 October 1994 the CIS member states (with the exception of Uzbekistan and Turkmenistan) signed in Moscow the CIS Convention on Rights of Persons Belonging to National Minorities (Azerbaijan signed it subject to a reservation and Ukraine subject to its laws). The Convention has entered into force for Azerbaijan, Armenia and Belarus only. It contradicts the spirit of the CoE's Framework Convention on the Protection of National Minorities in that it not only defines national minorities, but stipulates that only citizens of its member states may be members of such minorities.

Secondly, on 26 May 1995 the **CIS CONVENTION ON HUMAN RIGHTS AND FUNDAMENTAL FREEDOMS** was opened for signature in Minsk and it entered into force on 11 August 1998. This treaty-making process collided directly with the applications by Ukraine, Russia and the three Caucasus states – Armenia, Azerbaijan and Georgia – to join the Council of Europe. Russia applied to join on 7 May 1992 and was finally accepted into membership on 28 February 1996, despite the fact that the first Chechen war (which Russia lost) had been raging and despite negative reports from the CoE's experts and Russian human rights bodies.

The existence of the CIS Convention on Human Rights was an immediate issue for the CoE when considering Russia's application for membership. It was worried that the Convention might jeopardise the effective use of the right to submit individual applications to the **EUROPEAN COURT OF HUMAN RIGHTS**. Thus, in 1995, the Parliamentary Assembly of the Council of Europe (PACE) recommended to the applicant states not to sign or ratify the CIS Convention until further research on the compatibility of the two legal instruments had been carried out. PACE conducted the research and took the view that the CIS convention offered less protection than the **EUROPEAN CONVENTION OF HUMAN RIGHTS**, both with regards to the scope of its contents and with regard to the body enforcing it. The CIS commission could not offer the guarantees of impartiality and independence offered by the ECHR, nor could its recommendations enjoy the same enforceable character as judgments issued by that court.

Thus, on 23 May 2001, by Resolution 1249, PACE confirmed the primacy and supremacy of the ECHR and its court for all member states of the CoE and resolved to:

■ recommend to those CoE member or applicant states which are also members of the CIS not to sign or ratify the CIS Convention on Human Rights;
■ recommend to those CoE member and applicant states which are also members of the CIS and have already ratified the CIS

Convention on Human Rights to issue a legally binding declaration confirming that the procedure set out in the ECHR shall not be in any way replaced or weakened through recourse to the procedure set out in the CIS Convention on Human Rights;
■ recommend that member states of the CIS and of the CoE keep their citizens informed about the difference in the legal nature of the mechanism of the ECHR and the mechanism of the CIS convention.

A more decisive put-down is hard to imagine and the CIS Convention on Human Rights has been a dead duck.

At the time of writing the future of the CIS itself was in doubt. Following President Putin's State of the Nation Address on 26 May 2004, three schools of thought emerged. The first, characterised as 'neo-imperialists', argue that Russia must, especially since the 'Rose Revolution' in Georgia, extend immediate help to the 'third tier' of unrecognised entities, such as Abkhazia, South Ossetia and the 'Predniestrovian Moldovan Republic'. The second, the 'benevolent integrationists', argue for a process of 'building in the Euro-East a unique supra–national model distinct from the one sponsored by the EU'. The third group of 'pragmatists' argue for a shift away from 'paper integration' to a strategy solidly based on bilateral relations with the various CIS countries, so that Russia becomes their 'true leader and magnet'.

On this basis, the CIS cannot have much of a future. Nor can that future have much to do with the protection of human rights.

Further Reading

Drzemczewski, Andrew Trindade, Antonio Cancado and Frowein, Jochan A. (1996) 'The CIS Convention on Human Rights' (with texts) in *Human Rights Law Journal* vol. 17, no. 3–6, pp. 157-184.

McBride, Jeremy (1995) 'A Treaty of Dubious Value: The CIS Human Rights Convention' in *Interights Bulletin*, Vol. 9, pp. 137–140.

Voitovich, Sergei A. (1993) 'The Commonwealth of Independent States: An Emerging Institutional Model' in *European Journal of International Law*, vol. 4, no. 3, p. 403.

Weiler, Jonathan (2004) *Human Rights in Russia. A Darker Side of Reform*, Boulder, Colorado: Lynne Rienner Publishers.

Contributor: Bill Bowring

THE COMMONWEALTH AND HUMAN RIGHTS

There are no special human rights exclusive to the Commonwealth. But by virtue of its history and its nature at the start of the 21st century, the Commonwealth has particular concerns and practicalities which make it a significant player in the world human rights movement.

What is the Commonwealth? Although several governments were temporarily suspended from membership of its councils in the 1990s and the Zimbabwe government withdrew in 2003, it is simplest to regard it as a grouping of 54 states which had a shared but not identical colonial history. All but Mozambique, the former Portuguese colony which joined in 1995, had directly or indirectly been part of the British Empire. They had been exposed to British customs and the English language. However, by the early years of the new century this experience was 30–50 years in the past and the great majority of citizens were probably more unaware of their Commonwealth membership than they were of their colonial history.

As an international organisation with its own Secretariat, the Commonwealth dates from 1965, the year before the UN passed both the **INTERNATIONAL COVENANT ON CIVIL AND POLITICAL RIGHTS** and the **INTERNATIONAL COVENANT ON ECONOMIC, SOCIAL AND CULTURAL RIGHTS**. In 1977, the year that the Ugandan dictator Idi Amin threatened to attend a Commonwealth summit, Commonwealth leaders condemned 'the massive violation of basic human rights' in his country. Neither the UN nor the Organisation of African Unity had spoken out in this way. Two years later, at the Lusaka summit which cleared the way for a recognised independence for Zimbabwe, the Commonwealth leaders also anathematised racism and racial prejudice.

The Ugandan atrocities, and the Commonwealth's struggle against apartheid in South Africa, led to increasing demands for a specialist section within the Commonwealth Secretariat to promote human rights. The then president of the Gambia put up a scheme for a Commonwealth Human Rights Commission, with judicial functions, in 1977. In 1985, after much discussion – in which it was clear that many governments were nervous of any investigative or judicial functions – a modest Human Rights Unit came into being in the Commonwealth Secretariat. It had limited promotional, educational and coordinating purposes, and a small budget. The situation in 2004 was not so different, although its mandate was broader and the gender section in the Secretariat has done important work for women's equality.

The politics of human rights in the Commonwealth in the 1980s were complex, with some developing countries promoting a statist right to development and some developed countries promoting an individualist rights regime as a backdoor attack on one-party and military regimes which were campaigning against apartheid in South Africa. A new element emerged in 1987, when three Commonwealth non-governmental bodies – the Commonwealth Journalists' Association, Commonwealth Trade Union Council and Commonwealth Lawyers' Association – banded together to push for a serious Commonwealth initiative for human rights.

This Commonwealth Human Rights Initiative (CHRI) is now supported by eight bodies, with a staff of up to 40 people in three capitals; it has also stimulated an important coalition of Amnesty International Sections (the Association of Commonwealth Amnesty International Sections, ACAIS) to come into existence. The existence of the CHRI, along with the impact of the fall of the Berlin Wall in 1989, helped change the stance of the Commonwealth to human rights in the 1990s.

There were two key changes. The first was at the Harare meeting of Commonwealth heads in 1991, which followed the CHRI's survey report, 'Put Our World to Rights'. Ironically, in view of what has happened more recently in Zimbabwe, the summit committed the Commonwealth to 'fundamental human rights, including equal rights and opportunities for all citizens regardless of race, colour, creed or political beliefs'. The lengthy Harare communiqué has more recently been boiled down to the Harare Principles of just and accountable government, the rule of law and fundamental human rights.

The second major change took place in 1995, when the Nigerian military dictatorship was suspended from Commonwealth membership and a Commonwealth Ministerial Action Group (CMAG) was set up, with a rotating membership of eight foreign ministers, to police the Harare Principles of the Commonwealth. Meeting two to three times each year they have in eight years overseen the suspension of Nigeria, Sierra Leone, The Gambia, Pakistan, Fiji and Zimbabwe. In most cases the governments returned to full membership, but in December 2003 the Zimbabwean government of Robert Mugabe, already suspended, withdrew from the Commonwealth entirely.

It may be asked what this CMAG process and suspension from the Commonwealth amounts to in terms of human rights. After the initial suspension of Nigeria the Commonwealth defined suspension more carefully as 'suspension of a government from the councils of the Commonwealth'. This meant that a country's political leaders could not attend meetings of heads or ministers and the relatively small multilateral aid budget applied through the Commonwealth Fund for Technical Cooperation could no longer go to a country whose government was suspended. However, links with non-governmental and civil society organisations were encouraged: a people could not be thrown out of the Commonwealth and it was recognised that in some cases the government might be a conspiracy against its people.

The effect of the Harare Declaration and of the CMAG process has been to make Commonwealth membership itself more valuable – often a guarantee for tourists and outside investors – and to link it, if only indirectly, with the state of human rights and democratic governance inside a country. Any country wishing to join the Commonwealth now has to sign up to the Harare Declaration. Because the CMAG membership is drawn from across the world it is less restricted by regional considerations in interpreting its mandate.

To begin with, CMAG was limited to dealing with countries where governments had come to power by unconstitutional means – by a military coup. However, the CHRI and other human rights bodies argued strongly that there were other types of abuse, including electoral manipulation, oppression of the media and the destruction of socio-economic rights, which should require CMAG attention. When Commonwealth heads met in Coolum, Australia, in early 2002, prior to a Zimbabwe election which Commonwealth observers were to deem unfair, it was agreed that CMAG could move beyond concerns with military coups. However, it would get involved in a country's situation only after the Secretary-General's good offices had been exhausted and regional groupings had been consulted. Following much agonising, the civilian government of Zimbabwe was suspended after a flawed presidential election in 2002. It walked out after the Abuja summit in December 2003.

Although CMAG consists of foreign ministers and does not yet have a qualified Human Rights Adviser – a case I argued for in a report from the Commonwealth Policy Studies Unit (CPSU) in October 2003 – it has, according to the testimony of a recent Deputy Secretary-General, discussed human rights issues at almost every meeting. It has taken an interest in Cameroon, for example, which was never on its list, and in the Solomon Islands, where a damaging civil war was ended in 2003 by a military intervention from Commonwealth Pacific states. The action of the Commonwealth, in banning the presence of military leaders at its meetings after 1991, led to similar action by the Organisation of African Unity (now the African Union) a few years later. Although some Commonwealth officials are still more comfortable in talking about 'Commonwealth political values', the reality is that CMAG has played and is playing a role in promoting human rights.

So what is the special Commonwealth contribution in the human rights arena and what are the main challenges in the early years of the new century? Put simply, the Commonwealth strengths are its concerns – with racism, development, democracy and the free flow of information; its processes – which turn the membership of a club of governments into some minimum guarantees for their citizens, which promote guidelines and 'best practices' rather than treaties or legally-binding requirements; and its institutions – of governments which literally and figuratively speak a common language, and a civil society world of intelligence and vitality.

But there are several challenges too. One is that the Commonwealth should take itself, and be taken by others, more seriously. John Major, UK Prime Minister in the early 1990s, said of this association: 'We must use it or lose it.' In fact, in the noisy worlds of international activity, the Commonwealth is in danger of becoming a minor player, hardly known to its own 1800 million citizens and overlooked by powers outside. Its multilateral resource – the staff and budgets available to the Commonwealth Secretariat – fell drastically between 1990 and the early years of the 21st century.

At the governmental level, in spite of enormous progress since the Harare Declaration, there is still some hesitancy about pushing an overtly human rights agenda. Some governments see this as hostile to themselves or potentially leading to the fracturing of a nation or a diversion from their own developmental efforts.

At the non-governmental level, where so much responsibility for human rights progress now lies, the danger is of a failure to bear the weight of expectation. Efforts to establish a human rights network for the Commonwealth, which go back to 1997, received a fillip in 2003 at Abuja. A two-day Human Rights Forum called on the CHRI, ACAIS and the CPSU to get together to make such a network a reality. However, it will have to overcome problems of finance, organisation and regular utilisation if it is to succeed.

Further Reading

Commonwealth Secretariat (2003) *Freedom of expression, association and assembly*, best practice handbook, London.

Duxbury, Alison (2003) 'Reviewing the Commonwealth's rights record: from recognition to realisation', *South African Journal on Human Rights*. 19(4), pp636–662.

'Human rights and poverty eradication' (2001) report by a commission chaired by Margaret Reynolds, Commonwealth Human Rights Initiative, New Delhi.

Musah, A.-F. and Thompson, N. (eds) (1999) *Over a barrel: light weapons and human rights in the Commonwealth*, Commonwealth Human Rights Initiative, New Delhi and London.

'Open sesame: looking for a right to information in the Commonwealth' (2003) report by a commission chaired by Margaret Reynolds, New Delhi.

'Put our world to rights' (1991) report by a group chaired by Flora MacDonald, Commonwealth Human Rights Initiative, London.

Contributor: Richard Bourne

CONFUCIANISM AND HUMAN RIGHTS

Confucianism as a tradition of thought began life in China more than 2500 years ago. Although its core ideas can be traced back to the teachings of Confucius (551 BC–479 BC), this tradition was never thought to be wholly created by Confucius alone. Confucius regarded himself as a person who transmitted the old tradition rather than created a new one. Nevertheless, it was Confucius who most

Confucianism

creatively interpreted the rich tradition that he had inherited, gave it a new meaning and expounded it so effectively that his views have influenced a great number of generations of Confucian thinkers. The most fundamental text in the Confucian tradition, *The Analects*, is a record of the teachings of Confucius written by his students. The other two major exponents of Confucian thought in classical times were Mencius (approx. 379 BC–289 BC) and Xunzi (approx. 340 BC–245 BC) and their works are also important texts in the tradition. Confucianism has continued to evolve ever since its inception, in part as a response to the political needs of the time (as in Han Confucianism) and in part to the challenges of other schools of thought (as in Song-Ming Confucianism). No matter what innovations were made in these later developments, however, classical Confucianism, especially the Confucius–Mencius strand, has been recognized as the canon of the tradition.

The Confucian ethical tradition is a system of human relationships based on the virtue of *ren*. The moral ideal for each individual is the attainment of *ren* – the highest and most perfect virtue. *Ren* is a human quality, an expression of humanity, which can be manifested in a wide range of dispositions from personal reflection and critical examination of one's life to respect, concern and care for others. In dealing with oneself, *ren* requires us to 'overcome the self through observing the rites' (*The Analects*, Book XII: 1). In dealing with others, *ren* asks us to practise the art of *shu* – 'do not impose on others what we ourselves do not desire' (*The Analects*, Book XII: 2), an ethics of sympathy and reciprocity similar to the Golden Rule in other traditional religions and in the Kantian tradition. In more concrete terms, the Confucian ideal of *ren* holds that people should cultivate their minds and virtues through life-long learning and participation in rituals, they should treat their family members according to the norms of filial piety and fatherly love, respect their superiors and rulers, and show a graded concern and care for all. Today, this Confucian vision of human life has not only fundamentally shaped the culture and the basic structure of Chinese societies such as mainland China, Taiwan and Hong Kong, but also penetrated deeply into their neighbouring countries, such as Korea, Japan and Singapore.

Although the Confucian cultural traditions in these countries have been considerably eroded by modernisation and the powerful forces of global **CAPITALISM**, basic Confucian values such as the importance of the family, the respect for learning and education and the emphasis on order and harmony remain significant.

One major contemporary challenge to Confucianism is that it is unfit for modern life because it does not respect human dignity and human rights. In recent years there have been important debates on the relationship between Confucianism and human rights. This is a complex issue and it raises a number of questions. Is Confucianism compatible with (or can it accept) the idea of human rights? Can it accept the specific human rights listed in the Universal Declaration of Human Rights? Let us look at these two questions in turn.

Is Confucianism compatible with the concept of human rights? Human rights are rights that people have solely by virtue of being human, irrespective of sex, race, culture, religion, nationality or social position. Some scholars argue that this concept of human rights presupposes that human beings are asocial beings with interests and rights independent of and prior to society and culture. Since Confucianism holds the contrary view that human beings are thoroughly social and cultural beings, Confucianism cannot accept this conception of human rights. This argument is, however, problematic because the concept of human rights does not imply that human beings are asocial beings. It implies only that one's cultural or social background is morally irrelevant insofar as one's entitlement to human rights is concerned. Moreover, many civil, **CULTURAL** and **SOCIAL RIGHTS** do protect human interests that are social in nature and these rights precisely presuppose that human beings are social and cultural animals.

It is also argued that the concept of human rights implies that people have rights irrespective of their social roles; but for Confucianism, moral duties or rights arise solely from social relationships, such as familial relationships and political associations. Confucian ethics, the argument goes, is a role-based ethics that precludes the ascription of duties (or rights, if any) to human individuals as such. Although Confucianism does place great emphasis on particularistic social relationships, it is, however, not a purely role-based or relation-based ethics. Mencius holds that people have a compassion and moral duty to help others in suffering even if they may not have any personal relationship with them. Confucius's golden rule, 'do not impose on others what you yourself do not desire', is also a moral principle applicable to everyone irrespective of their social roles or status. Confucianism can accept non-role-based moral claims.

Even if Confucianism is compatible with the concept of human rights, would it allow much room for rights? Some scholars argue that Confucianism as a virtue-based ethic needs no rights. For Confucians, people should be guided by the virtues appropriate to the kind of relationships within which they are situated and should act virtuously towards each other; they need not be guided by any considerations of rights. This argument shows, at the most, that in a healthy relationship in which people do act virtuously and care for each other, rights may not have much practical importance. But if the relationship breaks down or no longer holds for the parties in it, the parties may need to fall back on moral and legal rights to guide their behaviour and protect their interests. At least, rights can serve as a fallback apparatus in Confucian ethics.

Would Confucianism endorse the specific human rights listed in the **UNIVERSAL DECLARATION OF HUMAN RIGHTS**? There should not be much difficulty for Confucianism to accept personal rights such as the **RIGHT TO LIFE, FREEDOM FROM TORTURE** and **THE RIGHT TO FAIR TRIAL**. These rights serve as a fallback auxiliary apparatus to protect basic human interests, interests that Confucian ethics of ren or benevolence would certainly recognize. How about civil rights such as the **FREEDOM OF EXPRESSION** and **FREEDOM OF RELIGION**? This is a more complex issue. Confucianism would probably endorse the freedom of expression on instrumental grounds rather than on the liberal ground of individual **AUTONOMY**. The primary concern of Confucianism is the ethical development of individuals. Confucians would tend to see this freedom as a means for society to cor-

rect wrong ethical beliefs, to ensure that rulers would not abuse power or indulge in wrongdoing and to promote valuable arts and cultures in the long run. Confucianism would not endorse an oppressive moral community that stifles ethical reflection and the development of genuine ethical character.

But it seems that neither would Confucianism endorse a liberal open society that in principle permits the existence of a large number of bad ways of life and the circulation of bad ideas. Such an environment would not be conducive to ethical reflection and the development of individuals' ethical character. Confucians would not recognize that individuals have the moral right to debased speech and bad ways of life and so it would not say that the freedom of expression is absolute. Although Confucianism does not advocate oppression, it may not reject milder forms of regulation, such as the mild legal restriction of expression and an ideologically selective schooling system. Confucianism would rather favour a morally conservative environment in which liberties and their restriction are balanced in such a way as best to promote the moral good and the common good of people.

Further Reading

The Analects, translated (2000) with an introduction by D.C. Lau, Hong Kong: Chinese University Press.

Angle, Stephen (2002) *Human Rights and Chinese Thought: A Cross-Cultural Inquiry*, Cambridge: Cambridge University Press.

Chan, Joseph 'A Confucian Perspective on Human Rights for Contemporary China' in Bauer, Joanne R. and Bell, Daniel A. (eds) *The East Asian Challenge for Human Rights*, Cambridge: Cambridge University Press, p. 212–237.

Chan, Joseph (2002) 'Moral Autonomy, Civil Liberties, and Confucianism' in *Philosophy East and West*, vol. 52, no. 3, July, 281–310.

de Bary, Wm. Theodore and Weiming, Tu (eds) (1998) *Confucianism and Human Rights*, New York: Columbia University Press.

Contributor: Joseph Chan

THE CONVENTION ON THE ELIMINATION OF ALL FORMS OF DISCRIMINATION AGAINST WOMEN

Since its inception, the United Nations has been committed to equality and elimination of all forms of discrimination. Under its roof these principles have been gradually integrated into international law. The adoption of the UNIVERSAL DECLARATION OF HUMAN RIGHTS (UDHR) in 1948 set the scene for later developments which integrated the moral and ethical principles of this document into international law. Similarly, women's equality with men has been recognised as a supreme ethical responsibility of all human societies and incorporated into international law in various legal instruments.

All the central normative instruments on human rights adopted by the UN address themselves to overcoming inequalities and eliminating discrimination first and foremost. The twin INTERNATIONAL COVENANTS ON ECONOMIC, SOCIAL AND CULTURAL RIGHTS and CIVIL AND POLITICAL RIGHTS, adopted in 1966 and brought into force in 1976, both emphasise and elaborate the commitment to eliminate discrimination in the recognition, protection and promotion of all human rights. The INTERNATIONAL CONVENTION ON THE ELIMINATION OF ALL FORMS OF RACIAL DISCRIMINATION (1969) addresses a specific form of discrimination directly, while the CONVENTION ON THE RIGHTS OF THE CHILD (1990) and the International Convention on the Protection of the Rights of All Migrant Workers and Members of their Families (2003) (See: MIGRANT WORKERS' CONVENTION) establish rights for children and migrants, to be enjoyed on the basis of non-discrimination.

Targeting gender equality, the Convention on the Elimination of All Forms of Discrimination Against Women was drafted in the latter part of the 1970s and adopted by the General Assembly of the UN on 18 December 1979. It came into force in September 1981.

This Convention elaborates the standards of non-discrimination in the full spectrum of women's rights. It is the only legally binding international instrument that recognises women's equality with men in social, economic, political and cultural areas as well as the private sphere of family life and marital relations. As of May 2004, 177 states from all regions of the world are party to the Women's Convention. As such, CEDAW is the UN human rights convention that has the second highest number of ratifications after the International Convention on the Rights of the Child. The principles and provisions of CEDAW constitute the universally applicable yardstick to measure discrimination against women and gender inequality in a society.

CEDAW also has the largest number of reservations of any human rights treaty (See: DEROGATIONS AND RESERVATIONS). A good number of these reservations are entered to Articles 2 and 16, with some being stated in broad, sweeping terms. Since Article 2 constitutes the core provision of the Convention and Article 16 pertains to marriage and family matters, they are considered to delineate the spirit and essence of effective implementation of women's human rights. The Committee therefore has considered the presence of wide-scoped reservations, particularly to these articles, as highly problematic; in fact, they are considered as incompatible with the 'object and purpose' of the Convention itself. The Convention, however, does not contain a procedure for rejection of incompatible reservations other than the referral in Article 29 to the International Court of Justice of disputes between states. This article is itself the subject of many reservations.

The content and structure of CEDAW have been shaped by both the international human rights movement and the women's movement so that its unique and almost 'revolutionary' text reflects the major gains achieved by both of these movements in defining women's human rights (See: FEMINIST CRITIQUES OF HUMAN RIGHTS). Incorporated in CEDAW are such human rights principles and standards as the 'INDIVISIBILITY' and 'UNIVERSALITY' of rights as well as fundamental issues and concerns ranging from legal equality and equality in political representation and work life to, most significantly, equality in the family which constituted the agenda of the women's movement in the 20th century.

The Convention is built on the understanding that discrimination against women in any area of social, economic, political or cultural life is not an isolated incident; it is inextricably related to discrimination in others. CEDAW recognises at the outset the systemic nature of discrimination against women as stemming from the universal reality of patriarchy and foresees women's enjoyment of their human rights as contingent upon the dissolution of this institution in all its forms. This is one of the reasons why CEDAW has been called 'an innovative and ambitious' treaty.

The Convention is not based on an abstract concept of gender equality. The need for this Convention as well as its title reflects the international community's recognition that discrimination against women is a widespread reality, all forms of which are to be eradicated. Article 1 of the Convention, which contains its basic premises, provides a clear definition of discrimination against women:

'... the term "discrimination against women" shall mean any distinction, exclusion or restriction made on the basis of sex which has the effect or purpose of impairing or nullifying the recognition, enjoyment or exercise by women irrespective of their marital status, on a basis of equality of men and women, of human rights and fundamental freedoms in the political, economic, social, cultural, civil or any other field.'

As seen in this article, the Convention talks about discrimination of 'effect' and 'purpose', thus manifesting a comprehensive perception which covers both 'direct' and 'indirect' or 'intentional' and 'unintentional' forms of discrimination. The definition also makes it clear that 'any distinction, exclusion or restriction' on the basis of sex that in any way obstructs women's enjoyment of their human rights is discrimination. Article 1, by specifically referring to all women's right to full enjoyment of their human rights 'regardless of their marital status', considers different attribution of rights to 'unmarried', 'married', 'widowed' women etc. (observed in many societies) as essentially discriminatory.

This article also gives expression to the wide scope of women's human rights. The reference to 'any distinction, exclusion and action ...' ensures at the outset that discrimination against women is not seen as limited to state action but also as relevant to others.

Similarly, the article's reference to not only political, economic, social, cultural and civil areas but also 'any other field' renders the instrument responsive to any and all existing or future forms of discrimination, thereby reflecting the progressive and expansive nature of the rights foreseen in the Women's Convention.

Although in its substantive articles (Articles 1–16) CEDAW provides a comprehensive framework for conceptualising and implementing women's human rights, it states principles and guidelines as well as elaborating standards for implementation.

Article 2 of CEDAW recites, in potent language, what state parties need to do in order to ensure elimination of discrimination against women. The chapeau of this article condemns discrimination against women in all its forms and obligates states to put in place and implement policies to eliminate discrimination against women 'without delay'. It is in this article (paragraphs d and e) that state obligations that cover not only public authorities but also private persons and organisations are delineated and an obligation is spelt out to go beyond legal measures to ensure elimination of discrimination (paragraphs b and f).

De jure and *de facto* discrimination against women are both targeted in the Convention. While Article 2 (paragraph f) and Article 5 specifically call for assurances of non-discrimination of women in all legislation, including penal codes (Article 2, paragraph g), Article 5 in particular addresses legal as well as social norms, cultural practices and customary and traditional behaviour patterns that are based on and/or promote stereotyped roles as sources of discrimination against women. State parties to CEDAW are expected to identify and take measures to modify those traditions, cultural norms and practices that discriminate against women. They are to ensure that gender stereotypes are not perpetuated and/or strengthened.

In Article 3 and Article 5, the Convention sets forth grand and ambitious goals such as 'full development and advancement of women' (Article 3) and 'modify(ing) the social and cultural patterns of conduct' (Article 5). Article 4.1 of the Convention states that temporary special measures, taken to speed up *de facto* equality of women with men, are not to be considered discriminatory.

provision of the Convention has been to mean that 'affirmative action' or 'positive discrimination' measures including quotas, time-bound targets and calendars should not be considered discrimination so long as they are in place for the purpose of accelerating the achievement of substantive, *de facto* gender equality and eliminating discrimination. The Convention, however, in the same article clearly rules out the permanent maintenance of unequal and separate standards for sexes, considering them discriminatory.

In its Articles 7 to 13, the Convention takes up an array of fields – political public life (Articles 7 and 8), nationality (Article 9), education (Article 10), employment (Article 11), health (Article 12), economic social and cultural life (Article 13) – in which respect, protection and promotion of women's human rights are specifically addressed in almost programmatic fashion. Article 14, a unique feature of CEDAW, obliges state parties to respond to the need of applying the Convention's provisions specifically to rural women and spells out their rights. Article 15 of the Convention pertains to states' obligation to accord women equality with men before the law and in exercising their legal rights and Article 16 contains provisions for non-discrimination of women under family law, marital and family relations (See: **THE RIGHT TO MARRIAGE AND A FAMILY**).

The Committee on the Elimination of Discrimination Against Women, composed of 23 independent experts and established under Article 17 of the Convention, monitors the implementation of the CEDAW mainly through the consideration of reports presented by state parties. Committee members, nominated by state parties as persons of 'high moral standing and competence in the field covered by the Convention' (Article 17), are elected by secret ballot and serve in their personal capacity for four-year terms. The Convention also requires that consideration is given to equitable geographical distribution and representation of different forms of civilisation and principal legal systems in the composition of the Committee.

As in all international human rights law, the purpose of reporting is to assist governments to improve their compliance with the Convention. The initial report of a state is intended to establish the basis of existing data, to help to identify obstacles and problems in achieving compliance with the international human rights law. The subsequent reports serve to monitor the progress (or retrogression) as well as providing feedback for the government's policy.

As provided for under Article 18 of the Convention, state parties are required to present their initial report one year after ratification and every four years thereafter or whenever so demanded by the Committee. The members of the Committee also make use of any other details including country-specific information provided by UN specialised agencies and NGO 'shadow reports' during the review of state reports.

The review process starts with the pre-session working group of the Committee reading the state party's report and formulating further questions and/or raising issues of remaining concern that are communicated to the state party. Responses to these issues and questions are also taken into consideration by experts when the Committee considers the report. The consideration process hinges largely on what is termed the 'constructive dialogue' with the representatives of the state where an exchange of information, experiences and suggestions takes place in an effort to facilitate and enhance efforts for effective implementation of the Convention in the state party concerned. Following the review process, 'concluding comments' of the Committee are drafted and sent to the state party. These comments include positive points observed as well as points of concern for which specific recommendations are made by CEDAW.

The Committee also drafts General Recommendations on the basis of the examination of reports and information from state parties. These texts elaborate on how the obligations set out in the provisions of the Convention are to be interpreted and implemented. They are tools to interpret the Convention in a dynamic way. The Committee has so far produced 25 General Recommendations pertaining to various Convention articles and related matters. The Committee is also empowered to make suggestions directed at UN organs.

Article 20 of the Convention allocates the Committee a meeting time of two weeks annually. This is the shortest of all times allocated to any human rights Committee in the UN and has proven to be problematic. In the face of the large number of state parties to the Convention, the allocated time has been inadequate for review and the Committee has been granted extra time by the General Assembly. While Article 20 has still not been amended, since 1997 the Committee has been meeting for two three-week sessions annually to keep up with the workload.

The Optional Protocol to CEDAW is a relatively new instrument designed to ensure more effective implementation of the Convention. It came into force as of 21 December 2000 and had been ratified by 60 state parties as of May 2004. The Optional Protocol allows individual women and groups of individual women to complain to the Committee of violations of the rights under the Convention. The Optional Protocol also entitles the Committee to inquire of its own motion into 'grave or systematic' violations of women's human rights as provided for under CEDAW. Under the Optional Protocol there is also a provision which obligates states to protect individuals from ill-treatment or intimidation as a result of using the Protocol's provisions. While the true impact of this instrument can only be assessed in time and on the extent of its use, its adoption and entry into force has clearly improved the international legal frameworks' capacity to address the human rights concerns of women. (See: **WOMEN'S RIGHTS**).

WEBSITES

www.un.org/womenwatch/daw/cedaw/
www.un.org/womenwatch/daw/cedaw/
states.htm
www.unhchr.ch/html/menu3/b/e1cedaw.htm
www.womenstreaty.org/
www.now.org/nnt/11-95/cedaw.html
www.amnestyusa.org/cedaw/
www.unifem.org/
http://iwraw-ap.org/
www.unwatch.com/cedaw-81502.shtml
www.hrw.org/campaigns/cedaw/
www.rightsconsortium.org/resources/
assessment/CEDAWtool.pdf
www.safnet.com/cedaw/cedaw.html
www.pch.gc.ca/ddp-hrd/docs/cedaw_e.cfm
www.owc.org.mn/cedaw/

www.womenstreaty.org/why.htm
www.wildforhumanrights.org/cedaw_around_
us.html
www.eagleforum.org/topics/CEDAW/index.
shtml
www.iwrp.org/CEDAW_Impact_Study.htm
www.fafia-afai.org/Bplus5/5thcedaw.html

Further Reading

Bayefsky, A.F. (2002) *How to Complain to the UN Human Rights System,* New York: Transnational Publishers.

Byrnes, A., Connors, J. and Bik, L. (eds) (1997) 'Advancing the Human Rights of Women: Using International Human Rights Standards in Domestic Litigation', Papers and Statements from the Asia/South Pacific Regional Judicial Colloquium, 20–22 May, Hong Kong, London: Commonwealth Secreteriat.

Cook, R. (ed.) (1994) *Human Rights of Women: National and International Perspectives,* Philadelphia: University of Pennsylvania Press.

Peters, J. and Walper, A. (1995) *Women's Rights, Human Rights, International Feminist Perspectives,* London: Routledge.

Steiner, H.J. and Alston, P. (2000) *International Human Rights in Context: Law, Politics, Morals, Text and Materials* (2nd edn), Oxford: Oxford University Press.

Contributor: Feride Acar

CONVENTION ON THE ELIMINATION OF ALL FORMS OF RACIAL DISCRIMINATION, THE INTERNATIONAL (ICERD)

'Of Equality – as if it harm'd me, giving others the same chances and rights as myself – as if it were not indispensable to my own rights that others possess the same.'

Walt Whitman, 'Thought' (1860)

The movement towards international legislation to combat racial and religious discrimination began as a response to a growing number of anti-Jewish incidents that took place in the winter of 1959 and 1960, known as the 'swastika epidemic', and gained momentum through the support of developing countries. The issues of racial and religious discrimination were split, however, resulting in the Third Committee issuing two separate Resolutions, 1780 (XVII) and 1781 (XVII), calling for the preparation of draft declarations and conventions dealing separately with racial discrimination and religious intolerance. A proposal not to include any reference to specific forms of racial discrimination in the draft Convention was approved and thus a draft article on anti-Semitism was excluded. The consensus was in favour of a legal text of general scope covering all forms of racial discrimination without the necessity of listing them. On 21 December 1965, the International Convention on the Elimination of All Forms of Racial Discrimination (ICERD) was unanimously adopted by 106 votes to none. Following the vote, the representative of Ghana was prompted to say of the General Assembly that 'this was its finest hour'.

The apartheid regime in South Africa also provided an impetus for the Convention, which is reflected in the particular condemnation of racial segregation and apartheid in its Article 3. The retention of the specific reference to apartheid while other singular instances of racial discrimination such as Nazism and anti-Semitism were not named is due to apartheid being the official policy of a state member of the United Nations while other forms were outlawed in domestic law already. The post-colonial context in which the Convention was adopted, whereby a universalist treaty seeking to eliminate all forms of racial discrimination was perceived as applying only to certain countries and regimes, led to states frequently declaring in their early reports on the implementation of the Convention's provisions that no racial discrimination existed in their countries. Such assertions were vigorously opposed by the Committee on the Elimination of Racial Discrimination (CERD), the treaty body charged with monitoring the Convention.

The ICERD is restricted, according to its purpose, to race and related grounds, but covers in principle the entire legal order of a state party, as is evident from its Article 5, which has been described as 'a Bill of Rights in a nutshell'. It lists those rights, including civil and political (Article 5(c) and (d)) and economic, social and cultural rights (Article 5(e)), which must be guaranteed without distinction as to race, colour, descent or national or ethnic origin. Fundamental obligations are also detailed in Article 2(1) of the Convention, where each state party undertakes to amend laws or regulations that may have the effect of perpetuating racial discrimination and to discourage actions which tend to strengthen racial division. The dissemination of ideas based on racial superiority or hatred must be declared an offence under Article 4. It has been the subject of the largest number of reservations to the Convention because of its potential conflict with the right to freedom of expression.

The Convention offers no definition of 'race'. The term 'racial discrimination' is defined in Article 1 paragraph 1 as 'any distinction, exclusion, restriction or preference based on race, colour, descent or national or ethnic origin which has the purpose or effect of nullifying or impairing the recognition, enjoyment or exercise, on an equal footing, of human rights and fundamental freedoms'. While 'race' has been a contentious subject of anthropological and biological debate for almost two centuries, the international legal approach has consistently followed the principles first enunciated in the United Nations Educational, Scientific and Cultural Organisation's (UNESCO) Four Statements on the Race Question, the first of which appeared in 1950. The UNESCO 1950 Statement on Race held, inter alia, that 'the biological fact of "race" and the myth of "race" should be distinguished; for all practical social purposes "race" is not so much a biological phenomenon as a social myth'. Thus, while race as a biological construct has been rejected, the concept remains valid as a social construct. The ICERD therefore seeks to combat the effects of racial discrimination beyond any academic discourse on the meaning of 'race'. Article 1(4) of the Convention holds that special measures taken for the sole purpose of securing adequate advancement of certain racial or ethnic groups or individuals shall not be deemed racial discrimination provided that such measures do not lead to the maintenance of separate rights for different racial groups. Article 2(2) requires that states parties shall, when the circumstances so warrant, take special measures in the social, economic, cultural and other fields to ensure the adequate development and protection of certain racial groups.

Article 1(4) is concerned only with the point that special measures, or affirmative action, do not constitute racial discrimination. It can be seen as a theoretical provision, in that the juxtaposition of special measures with the principle of non-discrimination underpinning the Convention is justified as being necessary in order to ensure the equal enjoyment of human rights. It places no obligation on state parties to implement special measures; it holds only that such measures do not violate the non-discrimination principle. Article 2(2) is more practical in that it requires States to enact such special measures in the social, economic and cultural fields, when the circumstances so warrant: a number of states have entered reservations to this provision.

The Committee on the Elimination of Racial Discrimination was the first treaty-monitoring body created under the United Nations human rights system. Its composition and functions are outlined in Part II of the Convention. There are three procedures whereby CERD can fulfil its task of monitoring compliance with the provisions of the Convention – state reports, individual complaints and inter-state complaints. It has also developed the practice of issuing General Recommendations which serve to interpret the provisions of the Convention. Each state is required to submit a periodic report to the Committee under Article 9, with a detailed explanation of any domestic legislation that has been enacted and its effectiveness in giving substance to the protection afforded by the Convention. The inter-state procedure under article 11 has proved wholly ineffective, for no state party has initiated a proceeding against another state party. The individual complaints mechanism exists for citizens of States Parties who have made a declaration recognizing the competence of the Committee to receive such communications under Article 14.

The Committee's work has focused primarily on state reports and the issuing of General Recommendations. The processes are linked in that the General Recommendations are designed to facilitate reporting states in understanding the extent of their obligations under the Convention, as well as preventing deliberate or accidental misinterpretation of the Convention's provisions. The Committee relies on the moral weight of its pronouncements for compliance. If faced with state party intransigence, the Committee cannot compel that party to adhere to its findings. It issues concluding observations to state reports which do not have sanctions attached to them. Nevertheless, the procedure is well sustained through careful coercion, for ultimately being a party to the Convention is a matter of choice.

Uniquely, in 1993 the Committee adopted a working paper which is now the basis for its early warning procedure. These measures permit potentially inflammatory situations to be identified and monitored by the international community. For example, in August 2004 Sudan (Darfur) was mentioned (UN Doc CERD/C/65/Dec. 1).

Forty years of the ICERD have seen significant progress towards the elimination of all forms of racial discrimination. The treaty represents a legal condemnation of a practice that spans many disciplines. In the past, the law has been responsible for securing racist doctrines developed in the anthropological or biological discourses. The Convention provides a means of legal redress for the victims of racist ideologies as well as constituting a moral document that represents the international community's abhorrence of doctrines of racial superiority.

There has been, however, very little focus on the economic and social causes and effects of racial discrimination. The socio-economic disparity between identifiable populations is a reality that transcends academic debate on the meaning of race and related issues. The Convention is equipped to tackle such fundamental manifestations of latent racial discrimination – from the definition contained in Article 1(1) which includes the 'economic, social [and] cultural' elements of racial discrimination, to the provisions on special measures and the list of six economic, social and cultural rights in Article 5(e), there is a strong emphasis on social and economic rights throughout the document. An increased focus on the part of the Committee on economic and social rights may prove an effective resource in the future fight against racial discrimination.

Law must have both a positive and an ethical character if it is to be effective. Furthermore, law must be elastic in order to enable it to adapt to changing perceptions, attitudes and developments, while keeping a core minimum that can never be deviated from. The ICERD, while allowing for evolving interpretations of race, ethnicity and related concepts, recognises that the condemnation of all forms of racial discrimination is an important element of that core minimum required for the safeguarding of human dignity.

Further Reading

Banton, Michael (1987) *Racial Theories*, Cambridge: Cambridge University Press.

Lerner, Natan (1991) *Group Rights and Discrimination in International Law*, Dordrecht: Martinus Nijhoff Publishers.

Meron, Theodor (1985) 'The Meaning and Reach of the International Convention on the Elimination of All Forms of Racist Discrimination', in *American Journal of International Law*, 79, pp. 283–318.

Partsch, Karl Joseph (1992) 'The Committee on the Elimination of Racial Discrimination' in *The United Nations and Human Rights: A Critical Appraisal*, Philip Alston (ed.), Clarendon: Oxford University Press, pp. 339–368.

Schwelb, Egon (1966) 'The International Convention on the Elimination of All Forms of Racial Discrimination', *International and Comparative Law Quarterly*, 15, pp. 996–1068.

Contributor: David Keane

THE CONVENTION ON THE RIGHTS OF THE CHILD (CRC)

These are times of dramatic change. Sweeping changes are taking place in the world, driven by globalisation of the world economy, by pervasive urbanisation and by rapid technological progress. These complex factors are changing the world, the people and their relations to each other. Change may always entail great risks and challenges. It is against this background that it is fundamental to focus on the United Nations Convention on the Rights of the Child. Interestingly enough, at the beginning of a new century, there are clear perceptions of a greater sense of hope and opportunity for building up a new world.

The fact is that this globalised world has become – at least in some parts – increasingly poorer over the last two or three decades. Similarly, there is a renewed interest in and a greater concern over the role of human DEVELOPMENT in a fair and democratic society. POVERTY and human development relate closely to individuals and their right to live in harmony and freedom. In this context, children – who constitute roughly half of the present world population – cannot be ignored.

It could be surprising to associate children with the search for human development. Actually, children, in view of their vulnerability, are perhaps the most affected by the negative impact of poverty and social exclusion, of hunger and disease, of homelessness and illiteracy, of violence and exploitation, present almost everywhere today. At the same time, children may benefit most from adequate public policies geared to human development in any country. Among others, maybe these are reasons why the last two decades have witnessed an ever increasing and unprecedented worldwide concern for children, their well-being and human rights.

As a historical background for this phenomenon, it seems essential to mention two milestones which have paved the way to its very emergence: the Geneva Declaration of the Rights of the Child, adopted by the League of Nations in 1924, containing five basic principles on the rights of the child; and the Declaration of the Rights of the Child, adopted by the United Nations General Assembly on 20 November 1959, which stated that 'the child, by reason of his (sic) physical and mental immaturity, needs special safeguards and care'.

Throughout the second half of the 20th century, while society became increasingly aware of the needs of children, issues related to children gradually captured the attention of scholars and politicians, raising social awareness and creating change at all levels, finally leading to the inclusion of the concept of children's rights as a top item on the political agenda of our times. Although an emerging phenomenon of contemporary society, the concept represents the outcome of this complex evolution of past perceptions, traditions and ideas about the child and childhood, across years and centuries, in different cultures, systems and societies. This multifaceted process may be, in a way, summed up by the decision of the United Nations Commission on Human Rights to establish, in 1979, a working group which, for a period of ten years, under the chairmanship of Professor Adam Lopakta, from Poland, was responsible for drafting an international treaty on the human rights of children.

At long last, General Assembly resolution 44/25 of 20 November 1989 adopted, by consensus, the **CONVENTION ON THE RIGHTS OF THE CHILD**. It was opened for signature, ratification and accession on that same date and entered into force on 2 September 1990 (Article 49). With the record number of 192 state parties, the Convention has become the first human rights instrument to achieve universality in the United Nations system.

The Convention constitutes the major international legal reference for the promotion and protection of the rights of the child, including adolescents. As an 'umbrella' document, it encompasses civil, political, **ECONOMIC, SOCIAL** and **CULTURAL** rights of the child. Hence, it incorporates a perspective of rights into all situations in the life of a child, from birth to 18 years of age (Article 1). It calls state parties to respect and ensure those rights 'to each child within their jurisdiction, without discrimination of any kind' (Article 2). State parties have the overall obligation to undertake 'all appropriate legislative, administrative and other measures' to ensure the implementation of the rights enshrined therein (Article 4). However, the same provision states: 'With regard to economic, social and cultural rights, states parties shall undertake such measures to the maximum extent of their available resources and, where needed, within the framework of international co-operation.' Enjoyment of all rights is 'inextricably intertwined, thus reflecting the interdependence and indivisibility of human rights' (United Nations document CRC/GC/2003/5).

Four general principles capture the spirit and philosophy of the treaty: non-**DISCRIMINATION** (Article 2), best interests of the child (Article 3), right to **LIFE**, survival and development (Article 6) and right to participation (Article 12). These general principles provide the framework for all actions concerning children and adolescents. However, the Convention must be looked at in its entirety and implemented in a dynamic and holistic way: all provisions and principles focus on the child – as a subject of rights, as a citizen – entitled to participate in the decision-making process affecting his or her life, in accordance with his or her age and maturity (Article 12). This perception leads to the need for an integrated and multidisciplinary process of implementation.

The Convention ratification entails a political commitment by state parties to improve the quality of life for children, not only at the national level, through the formulation of adequate public policies taking into account the principles and provisions of the Convention, but around the world as well, as members of the international community, through active cooperation, coordination and partnership in this field. The document constitutes, actually, an effective political tool for systematically raising awareness and training and for continuous advocacy and mobilisation around the cause of children's rights. It is the only human rights instrument which contains a specific provision to ensure its dissemination, 'by appropriate and active means, to adults and children alike' (Article 42).

Although the child emerges in the Convention as a fully fledged subject of rights, he or she is always envisaged within a family environment: from the Preamble and throughout the text, great importance is attached to the role of the family. The family is referred to as 'the fundamental group of society' (Preamble). The document recognises that 'for the full and harmonious development of his or her personality', a child 'should grow up in a family environment, in an atmosphere of happiness, love and understanding' (Preamble). Family is broadly defined, including 'members of the extended family or community as provided for by local custom' (Article 5) (See: **THE RIGHT TO MARRIAGE AND A FAMILY**).

The Convention addresses different aspects of the parent–child relationship. It also focuses on children in difficult situations and/or from disadvantaged groups, such as the girl child, the child in alternative care, the child with a **DISABILITY**, the refugee child, the child from **INDIGENOUS** or **MINORITY** groups. The Convention covers everyday situations in the school environment, including aspects related to **HEALTH** and **EDUCATION**. It also addresses possible situations of risk, danger, violence, negligence, ill-treatment and **TORTURE**, sexual abuse and exploitation, child labour, abduction, sale and traffic (See: **SLAVERY**) – any situation where there could be room for a potential violation of the rights of children.

Focusing on implementation, the Convention establishes its own mechanism, the Committee on the Rights of the Child, to monitor the implementation of the treaty by states parties (Article 43(1)).

The Committee, based in Geneva, expanded its membership in 2003 to 18 experts, to be elected by state parties with due consideration to equitable regional distribution and to the principal legal systems (Article 43(2)). It monitors progress achieved and obstacles encountered on the basis of the submitted state party report and relevant information from specialised agencies, UNICEF (Article 45 (a)), other treaty bodies and international organisations, including non-governmental organisations ('other competent bodies as it may consider appropriate', Article 45 (a)) engaging in an on-going 'constructive dialogue' with governmental authorities of state parties. In the spirit of Article 45, the Committee on the Rights of the Child and UNICEF have succeeded in establishing a very positive partnership. The Committee has also built up an innovative relationship with civil society through national and international NGOs.

The Committee adopts 'Concluding Observations', including positive aspects, concerns and recommendations and calls for the observance and protection of children´s rights, as provided for by the Convention and by other international human rights instruments pertinent to children.

Realistically, it is evident that 'the situation of children in many parts of the world remains critical' (United Nations document A/Res/58/157, adopted 22 December, 2003). However, the widespread implementation of the Convention in different countries indicates 'a change in the perception of the child's place in society, a willingness to give higher political priority to children and an increasing sensitivity to the impact of governance on children and their human rights' (United Nations document CRC/GC/2003/5).

Fifteen years after its adoption, the Convention on the Rights of the Child stands out as the universal human rights treaty which has established a rights-based ethics for children, in the light of a unique change in the global perception of the child. As for the present century, the Convention will surely face complex challenges, such as its *de facto* implementation in a world threatened by increasing poverty and violence. Note that the scope of the Convention on the Rights of the Child was expanded on 25 May 2000 by the General Assembly adoption of the Optional Protocol on Children in Armed Conflicts (A/54/Res/263) and of the Optional Protocol on the Sale of Children, Child Prostitution and Child Pornography (A/54/Res/263), both opened for signature on the same date and both entered into force early in 2002. And there are still other challenges ahead for children's rights, some of the more fascinating ones include the impact from the new technologies on children and their rights.

Further Reading

Alston, Philip (2000) *The Impact of Ten Years of the Convention on the Rights of the Child: 1990–2000*, September.

Implementation Handbook for the Convention on the Rights of the Child (2002) fully revised edition prepared for UNICEF by Rachel Hodgkin and Peter Newell.

Landsdown, Gerison (2000) 'The reporting process under the Convention on the Rights of the Child' in Alston, Philip and Crawford, James (eds) *Future of UN Human Rights Treaty Monitoring*, Cambridge: Cambridge University Press, pp.113–128.

UNICEF, *The 2004 State of the World's Children, Girls' Education and Development*.

Veerman, Philip E. (1992) *The Rights of the Child and the Changing Image of Childhood*, The Netherlands: Kluwer Academic Publishers.

Contributor: Marília Sardenberg

COSMOPOLITANISM AND HUMAN RIGHTS

Cosmopolitanism is a perspective that argues in favour of a global scope of justice. It has been expressed with regard to a wide range of issues, such as global governance, conflict resolution, migration, **POVERTY** and global inequality. Cosmopolitan theories have three main common characteristics: they see the individual as the ultimate unit of moral concern, they argue for universality (all presently living human beings fall within the scope of justice) and they hold out for generality (principles should apply universally to equal cases). Short descriptions often summarise cosmopolitanism by its statement that 'the boundaries of nation-states are not the boundaries of morality' or by asking the question: 'Is it just that the place where someone happens to be born determines their access to resources?'

Within the cosmopolitan tradition, which has its roots at least as far back as Ancient Greek political thought, there are various approaches. Several different distinctions between them can be made. One possible distinction is the one between moral and political cosmopolitanism. Political cosmopolitanism is concerned with the project of global government and global governance. Moral cosmopolitanism focuses on global principles of distributive justice and duties across boundaries, independently of the political structure that governs relations between states. Another distinction within cosmopolitanism is between principled and practical cosmopolitanism. Principled cosmopolitanism advocates a global scope of justice on the basis of specific principles or justifications; practical cosmopolitanism is either based on the post-modern and post-structuralist worries about the lack of ultimate justification or it is based on a pragmatic point of view that hopes to create a larger political coalition on the basis of more minimalistic assumptions.

Some cosmopolitans argue strictly for the creation of just institutions, whereas others also view personal morality as a legitimate target for cosmopolitan reflection. The difference between those two strands of cosmopolitanism is also reflected in their respective emphasis on justice or charity. The two views are often located either in the field of theories of global justice (institutions) or of the new field of global ethics (personal morality). A third variant includes recommendations on the morality of states and other institutions. Some cosmopolitans have justified their theories in the past by reference to global interdependence. The justification of a position by reference to current circumstances has been questioned for its reliance on moving from an 'is' statement to an 'ought' statement (referred to as the Humean fallacy). However, from a practical point of view, it may be sensible to work out what we owe people under the present circumstances rather than spend time debating what we would have owed people in more abstract terms.

Another argument for less abstraction is that globalisation as a political project introducing neo-liberal policies across the globe has had an immense and negative impact on the protection of human rights. Although cosmopolitanism fits in with the traditions of thought that rely on abstract principles for the design of just institutions, an assessment of what is unjust in the present world situation, how injustice comes about and how it can be combated would assist cosmopolitanism in developing a political strategy. The human rights discourse is an obvious candidate for such a practical approach.

Human rights are often seen as an instance of cosmopolitanism and it is assumed that cosmopolitans would support human rights. The overlap between the two bodies of thought is obvious: the human rights doctrine, too, views the boundaries of nation-states as arbitrary determinants for the answer to moral questions. The development of an international system of human rights law, starting properly with the **UNIVERSAL DECLARATION** of 1948, consistently and increasingly challenged the concept of national sovereignty, as developed from the Peace of Westphalia (1648) onwards. The early criticisms of the governments of states for how they treated their citizens were initially met by arguments referring to national sovereignty and governments hid behind the position that the treatment of their citizens was an internal matter. The gradual development of specific conventions, the sending in of special rapporteurs and the setting up of the implementation system of governmental reporting duties all contributed to an erosion of this strong conception of national sovereignty. The more recent argument put forward by state governments taking a defensive position when criticised for their human rights record refers to cultural relativism. Yet even this defence, although opening up the space to review some of the post-colonial arrogance and inequality of power in the international system, has now been largely laid to rest, especially since the Vienna Conference in 1993 where it was agreed that human rights are universal and interdependent. Although disagreement still exists on human rights and the relevance of culture, the position that human rights are a matter of concern globally is undisputed.

The human rights doctrine also coincides with cosmopolitanism in respect of its individualism. The cosmopolitan emphasis on the individual as the ultimate unit of moral concern is directly replicated in most international human rights law which explicitly entitles individuals to the rights enshrined in its sources. There are a few exceptions to this general rule: the Universal Declaration contains the right to **SELF-DETERMINATION** which is a collective right as it refers to states and peoples. African human rights documents also include references to collectivities and the parts of international law that safeguard **MINORITY RIGHTS** as well as those that protect the **RIGHTS OF INDIGENOUS PEOPLES** grant group rights as well as individual rights.

The third common aspect of cosmopolitanism, generality, is also an explicit part of the human rights doctrine. The preamble to every important human rights convention states the applicability of the human rights doctrine to every human being alive, wherever they are in the world and whatever identities they hold.

No doubt the full implementation of the human rights doctrine would bring the vision of a cosmopolitan world closer. Yet it would not necessarily bring it about completely. Cosmopolitanism is a more overarching perspective than the human rights doctrine for the following five reasons:

1. A cosmopolitan vision would go beyond the legalistic framework of human rights and require a change in moral values. The motivation to behave justly towards all other human beings would need to be rooted in political culture as well as in personal morality and not rely solely on legal measures to become reality.

2. Cosmopolitans would argue for more than the minimal provision of human rights. For example, the human rights doctrine provides legal back-up of the right to an adequate standard of living; it does not represent the more egalitarian concerns of many cosmopolitans who view global taxation and redistribution as their ideal.

3. Cosmopolitans would also strive for stronger institutions of global governance and for their democratisation as well as a meaningful conception of global citizenship. This would have an impact on ideas of entitlements in specific territories and would, according to some, lead to (nearly) open borders between nation-states.

4. Cosmopolitan theory has also (just) moved in the direction of providing an explanation for the current injustice in the world. This means that cosmopolitan approaches engage with theorisation of structural factors as well as individual and collective agency whereas the human rights doctrine typically stops at providing legal mechanisms and calling for their further implementation. To be fair, academic work on human rights (mainly but not exclusively in other disciplines than law) has also provided this type of analysis.

5. Finally, cosmopolitanism, although sometimes disjointed in its work on different issues, brings together a body of theory in respect of a wide range of interlinking issues such as conflict resolution, global governance, combating poverty, respecting the environment and handling the problems caused by migration, whereas the human rights doctrine deals with different categories of rights in quite separate ways. However, the cosmopolitan debate would be strengthened by further engagement with these topics in an even more integrated perspective.

Although human rights and cosmopolitanism clearly have affinity, they are not the same and do not necessarily fit together. Cosmopolitans sometimes opt for a different moral language than rights (See: **THE CAPABILITY APPROACH, NEEDS, INTERNATIONAL CITIZENSHIP**) and human rights can be defended within one nation-state or within a liberal-nationalist framework without a cosmopolitan stance on the global scope of justice.

Still, better implementation of human rights would safeguard at least a minimalist version of a cosmopolitan approach. And even cosmopolitans using a different 'currency of justice' often include human rights in their theories at some level. For example, Gough's theory of basic needs relies on human rights for their implementation, and Sen and Nussbaum in their respective versions of the capability approach include rights as a means to human development.

Further Reading

Anderson-Gold, Sharon (2001) *Cosmopolitanism and Human Rights*, Cardiff: University of Wales Press.

Jones, C. (1999) *Global Justice: Defending Cosmopolitanism*, Oxford: Oxford University Press.

O'Neill, O. (1996) *Towards Justice and Virtue. A constructive account of practical reasoning*, Cambridge: Cambridge University Press.

Pogge, T. (2002) *World Poverty and Human Rights*, Cambridge: Polity Press.

van den Anker, C. (1999) 'Global Justice: the Moral Implications of Globalisation' in Shaw, M. (ed.) *Politics and Globalisation. Knowledge, Ethics and Agency*, London: Routledge, pp. 127–142.

Contributor: Christien van den Anker

THE COUNCIL OF EUROPE

'We must all turn our backs upon the horrors of the past and we must look to the future ... If Europe is to be saved from infinite misery and indeed from final doom, there must be this act of faith in the European family ... Can these peoples of Europe rise to the heights of the soul and of the instinct and spirit of man? ... Let there be justice, mercy, and freedom. The peoples have only to will it and all will achieve their hearts' desire.'

Winston Churchill, speech, 19th September 1946, Zurich University.

These sentiments summed up the feeling across a large part of Europe in the wake of the Second World War. The euphoria of the Allied victory soon gave way to revulsion at the horrors inflicted during the conflict and fear of further European discord. There quickly developed a determination among European leaders to create institutions that would bind the continent together in the pursuit of common aims in order to reduce the risk of future strife and to focus attention on the rights of individuals that had been so cruelly violated throughout the first half of the century.

'This agreement lays the foundations of something new and hopeful in European life. We are witnessing today the establishment of a common democratic institution on this ancient continent of Europe.'

Ernest Bevin, speech on the signing of the Statute of the Council of Europe, 5 May 1949

The Hague Congress in May 1948 canvassed the ideas that would mould the Council of Europe and the European Union, such as the establishment of an economic and political union, a consultative assembly elected by national parliaments and a human rights charter presided over by a court. Originally envisaged as a single movement, the Council of Europe developed separately from economic and political union due to disagreement over the nature of future European integration. The Council was eventually established by ten founding members, with the signing of the Statute of the Council of Europe on 5 May 1949 in London. Since then it has grown to 46 member states, with over 800 million citizens within its area of influence.

Six members went on to establish the European Coal and Steel Community, which was the beginning of the modern European

© Council of Europe

Union. The organisations remain distinct although all members of the Union are also members of the Council of Europe and membership is seen as one of the essential prerequisites to ultimate membership of the Union. Originally a western European construct, the Council now stretches right across the continent and into Asia following the fall of the Berlin Wall in 1989 and the subsequent accession of Eastern European nations. The Council now unites the former opponents in the cold war in the most comprehensive and sophisticated human rights alliance in the world.

The Statute of the Council of Europe provides as follows:

'The aim of the Council of Europe is to achieve a greater unity between its Members for the purpose of safeguarding and realising the ideals and principles which are their common heritage, and facilitating their economic and social progress ... This aim shall be pursued through the organs of the Council by discussion of questions of common concern and by agreements and common action in economic, social, cultural, scientific, legal and administrative matters and in the maintenance and further realisation of human rights and fundamental freedoms.'

These aims are diverse and reflect a concern not just with the protection of basic civil rights but also with the enhancement of the democratic ideal and the socio-economic prosperity of citizens (See: **DEMOCRACY**

AND HUMAN RIGHTS; SOCIAL RIGHTS; ECONOMIC RIGHTS). The Council of Europe now sees its role as encompassing the following:

- the protection of rights, pluralist democracy and the rule of law;
- promoting awareness and development of Europe's cultural identity and diversity;
- seeking solutions to problems facing European society such as discrimination, intolerance, environmental protection, terrorism, crime etc.;
- consolidating democratic stability in Europe by backing political, legislative and constitutional reform. (Council of Europe, 2003).

With such a broad remit, there can be some difficulty in maintaining a coherence of purpose and it is clear that the role of the Council of Europe has changed over the years as it has responded to the changing political landscape within Europe. The core concern of the Council, though, is the well-being of individual citizens within the member states and the strategy for entrenching the value of individual rights via international conventions and awareness. This is neatly summed up by Mary Robinson as follows: 'At the centre of those values is the human being. From this everything else radiates. It is the leitmotif of the Council of Europe. In a true sense, therefore, the Council is the ethical and humanist dynamo of the developing Europe' (speech to the Council of Europe, 26 April 1994) (See: **FOREWORD**).

The Office of the Commissioner for Human Rights was created in 1999 to focus on human rights education, national human rights institutions and promoting respect for human rights in all member states. Alvaro Gil-Rables is the commissioner, at the time of writing.

The chief vehicle for the development of common standards throughout Europe is the international treaty. The first and still the most important of these in terms of its international impact and influence is the **EUROPEAN CONVENTION ON HUMAN RIGHTS AND FUNDAMENTAL FREEDOMS** which came into force in 1953 and was the world's first international human rights enforcement framework adjudicated by a Commission and a Court (replaced by a unified Court in 1998).

This is just one of over 180 treaties, conventions and protocols that have been the responsibility of the Council of Europe.

Other significant agreements include:

- **THE EUROPEAN SOCIAL CHARTER** (1961, revised in 1996) is a bill of economic, social and cultural rights including education, health employment, housing, anti-discrimination etc. The enforcement mechanisms are not as robust as the Convention on Human Rights but the recent revision has attempted to significantly tighten up enforcement. There is a European Committee of Social Rights comprising 15 independent members which is responsible for monitoring whether states have complied with the obligations in the Charter. Member states report annually to the Committee and various interested bodies such as trade unions, employers' federations and NGOs can make complaints to the Committee which may lead to a resolution from the Council of Europe, possibly with specific recommendations for a state to change its law or procedure. The Committee publishes an annual survey of compliance with the Social Charter.

- The European Convention for the Prevention of Torture and Inhuman or Degrading Treatment or Punishment supplements the European Convention on Human Rights by providing a more proactive monitoring and protection regime for those who are detained. The Convention thus establishes an independent Committee for the Prevention of Torture (CPT) with unlimited access to institutions where people are detained in order to monitor how such people are treated. Following visits, the CPT prepares a report of its findings and recommendations. The system is confidential but states have routinely permitted publication of reports and government responses (See: **FREEDOM FROM TORTURE**).

- The Framework Convention for the Protection of National Minorities came into force in 1998 and is the first legally binding multilateral instrument for the protection of the interests of national minorities. The principles include ensuring equality of treatment in law, preserving and developing minority cultures and identities including language, protecting religions and enabling cross-border exchanges. There is an Advisory Committee of 18 independent experts which advises the Committee of Ministers on compliance with the Framework in light of reports received from member states. The Committee of Ministers can also receive 'shadow' reports from NGOs and minority interest groups. Recommendations are made to state parties following the monitoring procedure (See: **MINORITY RIGHTS**).

This provides a flavour of the activity of the Council of Europe in the field of human rights. It is clear that the organisation works by seeking to bind diverse governments to international norms, thereby recognising a common heritage and forging a common future.

The main decision-making body is the Committee of Ministers, which comprises the foreign ministers of each of the member states or their representatives. There is also a Parliamentary Assembly of 313 members drawn from the national legislatures plus delegations from non-member states. Unlike the EU Parliament, the Assembly is not directly elected and does not have a pivotal role in making laws or treaties. This also helps to confirm the position of the Council of Europe not as a legal system itself but as the catalyst for the development of international norms and agreements. The Assembly elects judges from the member states to the European Court of Human Rights, which since 1998 has been a full-time court with judges elected for a six-year period. A standing Congress of Local and Regional Authorities of Europe is split into two chambers representing the interests of local and regional government respectively. The Secretary General presides over a Secretariat of approximately 1800 staff split into the following directorates:

- political affairs
- legal affairs
- human rights
- social cohesion
- education, culture and heritage, youth and sport
- administration and logistics.

The Secretary General prepares an annual intergovernmental programme of activities, which must be approved by the Committee of Ministers. There is ongoing debate and dialogue between the Committee of Ministers and the parliamentary, regional and local representative bodies. The latter bodies put forward recommendations to the Committee of Ministers which determines the action, if any, to be taken thereon and on other proposals emerging from the various intergovernmental committees and conferences.

The main 'output' of the Council of Europe includes:

- conventions and other international agreements – as mentioned above, the Council has been responsible for over 180 conventions since its inception. These do not become binding on member states until they have been signed by governments and ratified through the appropriate national process;
- recommendations to member states in respect of problems that have been identified and possible solutions;
- declarations and resolutions regarding compliance with and progress towards agreements;
- monitoring compliance with convention standards – this has become increasingly important as the membership of the Council has grown to embrace a hugely diverse range of legal and political systems with different historical and cultural approaches to human rights;
- organisation and sponsorship of conferences and other meetings between politicians, experts, NGOs and interest groups;
- initiatives for training and the sharing of expertise, such as the Confidence-Building Measures Programme aimed at assisting new member states to develop and entrench the institutions of democratic civil society;
- research projects – to provide a factual or statistical basis for recommendations and other initiatives;
- awareness campaigns;
- cultural events, for example the European Capital of Culture initiative.

If success is measured by an organisation's growth and its output then the Council of Europe has been a phenomenal achievement. It now encompasses the vast majority of European states and has formal links with other powerful nations (the United States, Japan and Canada have observer status). It has introduced a vast number of international agreements across a diverse range of political, legal and other issues. Nevertheless, it has not been able to prevent the implosion of various parts of the continent and ultimately can only encourage the willing rather than force the recalcitrant.

WEBSITES

www.coe.int
www.conventions.coe.int

Further Reading

Council of Europe (2003) *Council of Europe: 800 Million Europeans*, Strasbourg: Council of Europe.

Schieder, Peter (2004) *Building one Europe*, Strasbourg: Council of Europe.

Van Dijk, P. and Van Hoof, G. (1998) *Theory and Practice of the European Convention on Human Rights*, Leiden: Kluwer, 3rd edn.

Contributor: Kevin Kerrigan

CREATIVE PROBLEM SOLVING

Creative problem solving is an approach to law and lawyering that views legal problems beyond the litigation paradigm. The traditional legal model defines the client as the individual or the entity which is being represented. A creative problem solving approach, however, views the identity of the client more broadly, in terms of relations. Thus, in any given situation the true client may not be merely the individual or entity who presents a problem but a family, a group or a community. Because the focus is on the web of interconnections, a lawyer who is also a creative problem solver understands the nuances of group process, cross-cultural communications and interdisciplinary collaboration in solving a problem. This specific training provides the creative problem solver with a unique set of skills to address problems of a global society, such as those involving human rights.

In using creative problem solving, lawyers attempt to broaden the inquiry concerning legal problems and bring to bear a broader range of skills for the effective resolution of those problems. This has distinct relevance to the field of human rights law.

In the decades which followed the founding of the **UNITED NATIONS**, a plethora of international human rights conventions and United Nations General Assembly declarations was promulgated. While the original focus of this body of law was the articulation of human rights, eventually mechanisms for the prosecution for those responsible for human rights atrocities were developed: the Optional Protocol for the International Covenant on Civil and Political Rights (creating a right of individual petition); the Inter-American Convention on Human Rights (with its automatic right of individual petition); and the rise of Security Council-mandated human rights tribunals. Further, lawsuits based on the Alien Tort Claims Act in the United States became more prevalent, together with similar national laws in Europe which provided for standing and a cause of action for human rights atrocities committed extraterritorially.

In these new fora, the litigation model of lawyering became predominant. And rightly so. The litigation model of lawyering is ideal for the advocacy context like the tribunals. But does the litigation model of lawyering fully satisfy the needs of the defendants, witnesses and participants? While several human rights institutions like the UN **HUMAN RIGHTS COMMITTEE**, the **INTER-AMERICAN COMMISSION ON HUMAN RIGHTS** and the tribunals to be established under the Rome Statute are powerful mechanisms for exposing human rights atrocities, they might not be the best venues to allow for healing. Do they allow for empathy and victim empowerment through storytelling? What about the role of the perpetrators?

Although the role of lawyer as advocate is sometimes appropriate, particularly in the defence of people arbitrarily detained, treated inhumanly or even tortured, these are not the only skills that society needs from lawyers in the human rights context. Increasingly, lawyers are being asked to approach problems more creatively. The rise of truth and reconciliation commissions has forced lawyers to expand their tools beyond litigation (See: **TRUTH COMMISSIONS**). These alternative fora for dispute resolution allow for empathy and a sense of empowerment by encouraging the victims of human rights abuses (and arguably those who perpetrated the crimes) to participate in the process. The simple gunslinger, shark-like model is not necessarily the best way to assist the client or other participants in the healing process.

Because the creative problem solver views his or her primary role as the building, fostering, repairing and strengthening of the client's relationships with others, the lawyer must do more for the client than mere advocacy. Since litigation is essentially divisive, the vindication of individual rights through the adversary process is viewed as a creative solution only in extreme cases such as torture or other aggression against the client. Litigation should never be undertaken without full assessment of its risks and its impact on the many present and future relationships in which the client's interests are embedded.

The model of the lawyer as creative problem solver poses numerous challenges to traditional legal norms. For example, the adversary model places a premium on questioning. The creative problem solving model, meanwhile, places a premium on listening and restating what has been said in order to fully understand the views of the client and others. This may be a better approach in a truth and reconciliation commission than the standard cross-examination or direct examination methods traditionally used in more adversarial processes. The adversary model emphasises confidentiality and imposes numerous restrictions on communications with others. Often, human rights fora are constituted to bring to light the events of dictatorships, civil wars or other cases of government oppression.

Creative problem solving understands moral judgements as situation-attuned perceptions, sensitive to the dynamics of particular relationships. Traditional lawyers are trained to be dispassionate. Creative problem solving defines moral reasoning to include caring, empathy and concern. Traditional law emphasises individual rights and norms of formal equality and reciprocity. The model of the lawyer as a creative problem solver emphasises norms of responsiveness and responsibility in our relationship with others.

With its ability to assist clients to achieve a more holistic solution, creative problem solving can be a most potent tool for lawyers. Yet because it is situational, creative problem solving will always elude precise definition, much like the right of self-determination. Precise definition is an attribute of traditional legal thinking, which seeks universal, binary solutions to complex problems. Much of the power of the concept of creative problem solving lies in its ambiguity – its ability to evoke a variety of responses. Since the fashioning of creative solutions depends on the ability to recognize, respect and synthesise apparently contradictory and conflicting needs, tolerance for ambiguity and the skill to acknowledge and accept differing subjective realities are hallmarks of the discipline of creative problem solving.

Further Reading

Barton, Thomas D. (1998) 'Creative Problem-Solving: Purpose, Meaning and Values', 34 *California Western Law Review.* 273.

Brown, Stephen I. & Walter, Marion I. (1990) *The Art of Problem Posing*, 2nd edn. Hillsdale, NJ: Lawrence Erlbaum Assoc.

Cooper, James M. (1998) 'Toward a New Architecture: Creative Problem Solving and the Evolution of Law', 34 *William and Mary Law Review.* 297.

Menkel-Meadow, Carrie (1996) 'The Trouble with the Adversary System in a Postmodern, Multicultural World', 38 *William and Mary Law Review.* 5.

Nathanson, Stephen (1997) *What Lawyers Do: A Problem-Solving Approach to Legal Practice.* London: Sweet and Maxwell.

Contributors:

James Cooper and Janeen Kerper

CRITICAL RACE FEMINISM AND HUMAN RIGHTS

Critical race feminism puts an emphasis on the legal concerns of those who are both women and people of colour. Emerging at the end of the 20th century in US jurisprudence initially, critical race feminism focuses on the plight of women of colour, as they constitute a group who are disproportionately mired at the bottom of global society according to all indicators. Yet these women constitute a significant portion of the worldwide workforce for the 21st century.

Existing national and international legal paradigms have permitted women of colour to fall between the cracks – becoming literally and figuratively voiceless and invisible under so-called neutral laws or solely race-based or gender-based analyses. Critical race feminism attempts not only to identify and theorise about those cracks in the legal regime but to formulate relevant solutions as well.

The choice of the term 'critical race feminism' to describe an emphasis on women of colour was a conscious one, indicating its links to critical legal studies, critical race theory and feminist jurisprudence. The Conference on Critical Legal Studies was organized in the late 1970s by politically progressive white male academics. Like these men, critical race feminists endorse a progressive perspective on the role of law, critiquing both conservative orthodoxies and legal liberalism. Challenging the notion of law as neutral, objective and determinate, critical legal studies may also use the deconstruction methodology of European postmodernists like Jacques Derrida and Michel Foucault to expose how law has served to perpetuate unjust class, race and gender hierarchies. Some people of colour, white women and others were attracted to critical legal studies because it challenged orthodox ideas about the inviolability and objectivity of laws that oppressed dark peoples and white women for centuries. But some of these scholars also felt that some of the critical legal studies adherents often marginalised the perspectives of people of colour and white women and were not able to expand their analyses beyond the world view of progressive white male elites.

Emphasizing race and ethnicity, critical race theory emerged as a self-conscious entity in 1989, although its intellectual underpinnings can be found in the work of Harvard University law professor Derrick Bell and other scholars from the mid-1970s onwards. Critical race theory articles cover a wide array of topics including affirmative action in education and employment, hate speech, criminal law, federal Indian law – all challenging the ability of conventional legal strategies to deliver social and economic justice. While the intellectual fire in critical legal studies has died down, the still relatively young critical race theory movement of which critical race feminism is a part, has produced hundreds of articles and a growing number of books. Additionally, there are several energetic off-shoots of critical race theory, including LAT-CRIT, an emphasis on Latinos and Latinas, AsianCrit, QueerRaceCrit and critical white studies, a focus on the way whiteness functions as a social organizing principle.

Its adherents are particularly interested in legal manifestations of white supremacy and the perpetuation of the subordination of people of colour. It sometimes uses the narra-tive or storytelling technique as methodology. Additionally, it endorses a multidisciplinary approach to scholarship in which the law may be a necessary but not sufficient basis to for-mulate solutions to racial dilemmas. There are now critical race theory scholars in other disciplines besides law and in other countries besides the United States.

The third jurisprudential trend that criti-cal race feminism draws from is feminism. Some women of colour realized that certain perspectives presented in critical race theory literature may have assumed that women of colour's experiences were the same as those of men of colour. As the experiences of males may differ significantly from females, critical race feminism is thus a feminist intervention within critical race theory. Additionally, criti-cal race feminism constitutes a race interven-tion in feminist discourse, in that it necessarily embraces feminism's emphasis on gender oppression within a system of patriarchy. But most critical race feminism proponents have not joined the mainstream US/western European feminist movements. While reasons vary, in some cases the refusal to become asso-ciated is due to those movements' essentialisa-tion of all women, which subsumes the variable experiences of women of colour with-in the experience of white middle-class women. Mainstream feminism has paid insuf-ficient attention to the central role of white supremacy's subordination of women of colour, effectuated by both white men and women. Critical race feminism also draws from the black feminism or womanist femi-nism in the liberal arts as typified by the work of bell hooks, Audre Lorde, Patricia Hill Collins, Toni Morrison and Alice Walker.

While critical race feminism has strands that derive from critical legal studies, critical race theory and feminism, it has also made some analytical contributions distinct from these movements. The first notion is that of anti-essentialism. Critical race feminism pro-vides a critique of the feminist notion that there is an essential female voice, that all women feel one way on a subject. Instead, crit-ical race feminism notes that the essential voice actually describes the reality of many white middle or upper-class women, while mas-querading as representative of all women. So it highlights the situation of women of colour, whose lives may not conform to an essentialist norm. A concept linked to anti-essentialism is what has come to be called intersectionality theory as popularised by critical race feminism foremother Kimberlé Crenshaw, a UCLA/Columbia law professor. To understand the anti-essentialist plight of women of colour, you must look at the intersection of their race and gender identities. US-oriented critical race feminism topics have included a wide variety of 'civil rights' themes (to use US legal terminol-ogy), intersecting with such areas as criminal justice, constitutional law, employment dis-crimination, torts, domestic violence, sexual harassment, reproductive rights, family law, the Internet and even tax law. Scholars who have written in the American legal context include Professors Lani Guinier, Angela Harris, Anita Hill, Mari Matsuda, Dorothy Roberts and Patricia Williams.

Critical race feminism has moved beyond a purely US-based focus and is also enhancing the development of international and com-parative law, which includes the subfields of public international law, international busi-ness transactions and especially human rights. These are areas that developed primarily based upon principles first enunciated by American and European white male scholars. Men of colour from the developing world did not become involved until their respective nations gained independence or sufficient clout in entities like the United Nations. Their voices are still muted, but often rise in discus-sions of cultural relativism and human rights. Western women have only recently become engaged in attempting to reconceptualise international law from feminist perspectives. Global feminists have noted that international law has failed to address what takes place in the private sphere of the family, where most women spend a significant part of their time (See: **WOMEN'S RIGHTS** and **VIOLENCE AGAINST WOMEN**).

Critical race feminism contributes to the development of international law, global feminism and postcolonial theory by demarginalising women of colour in a theoretical and practical sense. Women of colour may be simultaneously dominated within the context of imperialism, neocolonialism or occupation as well as local patriarchy, culture and customs. They have often had to choose between the nationalist struggle for independence or self-determination and the women's struggle against patriarchy. The nationalist struggle usually has prevailed and the women who have just helped throw off the yoke of outsider oppression have then been forced back into the 'women's work' of taking care of the house and the children. Open acceptance of feminism can be seen as an unpatriotic embrace of western values that may be regarded as inimical to local culture. One of the dilemmas for those who do choose to be known as feminists is whether and how to embrace the universality of women's international human rights within their own cultural context.

Global human rights topics have included all of the domestic US themes, as well as the full array of international political and civil rights and economic, social and cultural rights issues. Topics include multiculturalism, the conflict between religion and custom, conflicts between customs and western constitutional norms, communitarianism versus individualism, immigration law, sexual slavery, female genital surgeries, female infanticide, economic development, HIV/AIDS and so on. Critical race feminism authors have noted that the problems of this century will continue to be race and ethnicity, but also compounded with a heightened awareness of gender, class, disability and sexual orientation. The events of September 11 2001 have brought the salience of identities such as nationality, religion, language, culture and political ideology to the forefront as well. Global critical race feminism authors have included Professors Azizah al-Hibri, Penelope Andrews, Elvia Arriola, Taimie Bryant, Devon Carbado, Lisa Crooms, Isabelle Gunning, Berta Hernandez, Sharon Hom, Kevin Johnson, Hope Lewis, Martha Morgan, Vasuki Nesiah, Leslye Obiora, Catherine Powell, Jenny Rivera, Celina Romany, Judy Scales-Trent, Antoinette Sedillo Lopez, Leti Volpp and Adrien Wing.

*Parts of this article were drawn from the Introductions to *Critical Race Feminism* and *Global Critical Race Feminism*, both edited by the author Adrien Katherine Wing.

Further Reading

Crenshaw, Kimberlé Williams (1989) 'Demarginalizing the Intersection of Race and Sex: A Black Feminist Critique of Antidiscrimination Doctrine, Feminist Theory and Antiracist Politics', University of Chicago Legal Forum 139.

Delgado, Richard and Stefancic, Jean (eds) (1999) *Critical Race Theory: The Cutting Edge*, 2nd edn, Philadelphia: Temple University Press.

Matsuda, Mari (1992) 'When the First Quail Calls: Multiple Consciousness as Jurisprudential Method', 14, *Women's Rights Law Reporter*, 297.

Wing, Adrien Katherine (ed.) (2003) *Critical Race Feminism: A Reader*, 2nd edn, New York: New York University Press.

Wing, Adrien Katherine (ed.) (2000) *Global Critical Race Feminism: An International Reader*, New York: New York University Press.

Contributor: Adrien Katherine Wing

CULTURAL RIGHTS

The notion of culture is not very ancient – we can trace its origins to 19th-century anthropology, when it was first used to describe the differences between colonisers and native populations. The word 'culture' is a word that carries different meanings:

1. A style of social and artistic expression.
2. The social behaviour patterns, beliefs, characteristics of a community or population that are transmitted to the members of the said community.
3. The customary beliefs, social forms and material trait of a racial, religious or social group.

Each of these meanings is reflected in different provisions of international human rights law. There are some debates on the notion, but generally from a legal perspective culture is simply a way of talking about collective identities. A culture, even though expressed through different patterns of speech and action, is largely unconscious unless exposed to other cultures. In this sense cultural identity is usually defined in opposition to or in confrontation with other cultures. In this mostly unconscious confrontation, human rights come into play in situations where a culture is under threat or competes for freedom and resources with other cultures; in other words, when the equality is lacking in a context of cultural diversity and multiculturalism.

Historically, there has been some resistance towards the development of cultural rights. International law has long been the tool to impose western values and colonise other cultures. The ideal of the modern state is based on the notion of a people as culturally homogenous; 18th-century politicians and philosophers viewed a people and a nation as a community bound together by an implicit common good and common institutions and traditions that form a dominant culture. The general view was that the people who are not sharing such common culture should gradually be assimilated within the dominant society. From such a perspective international law was used as a 'tool' to assimilate and thus destroy the cultures of minorities (See: **MINORITY RIGHTS**) and **INDIGENOUS PEOPLES**.

International law has used words such as 'savages' and 'civilisation' and in doing so been a vehicle of the idea that 'culture' was the part of the 'civilised peoples' as opposed to the so-called 'savages'. Even though such a slant is still visible in the content of international law (the UN Charter refers to the law of 'civilised nations'), contemporary international law is based on the principle of equality between all different cultures. More specifically, the human rights law discourse has taken the view that all cultures are equal and should be treated equally. During the drafting of the first human rights instruments, the inclusion of cultural rights was contested along the lines of the East–West divide on collective rights. Nonetheless, when the **UNIVERSAL DECLARATION OF HUMAN RIGHTS** was drafted, cultural rights were added to the list of recognised universal human rights. There is a dual nature to the right to culture within the International Bill of Rights: on the one hand, cultural rights mean the protection of the arts and sciences, and on the other hand, cultural rights mean the protection of specific cultures and minority groups.

The 1948 Universal Declaration contains a number of articles relating to socio-economic and cultural rights. The definition of cultural rights focuses on education and the right to participate in 'cultural life'. Article 27 UDHR says:

1. Everyone has the right freely to participate in the cultural life of the community, to enjoy the arts and to share in scientific advancement and its benefits.
2. Everyone has the right to the protection of the moral and material interests resulting from any scientific, literary or artistic production of which he is the author.

The **INTERNATIONAL COVENANT ON ECONOMIC, SOCIAL AND CULTURAL RIGHTS** expressly refers to 'cultural rights' and its Article 15 recognises 'the right of everyone ... to take part in cultural life'. In this context 'cultural rights' are taken in the sense of arts and sciences rather than focusing on the respect of cultural differences and redress for colonised peoples. Whereas the accent in the Universal Declaration and ICESCR is put on a right to culture in the sense of arts and sciences, the emphasis in the **INTERNATIONAL COVENANT ON CIVIL AND POLITICAL RIGHTS** is on the right to enjoy one's own culture. The right to enjoy one's own culture has been much more enforced through the protection offered by the ICCPR. This protection has come under the banner of non-discrimination, through rights such as freedom of expression and religion and also under the banner of minority rights. Article 27 on minority rights has been interpreted to include the recognition of some cultural practices as well as the symbolic recognition and the material support for the expression and the preservation of cultural distinctiveness. One central angle of human rights law is the protection of those living in 'minorities' within a society and thus the protection of their specific culture.

Cultural rights are also part of several other international instruments. For example, even though the Convention on the

Prevention and Punishment of the Crime of Genocide rejects the notion of ethnocide, its Article 2 prohibits the deliberate destruction of a people's culture. The United Nations Educational, Scientific and Cultural Organization principles on International Cultural Co-operation (1966) recognise that 'each culture has a dignity and value which must be respected and preserved'. The Vienna Declaration and Programme of Action also insists on the duty of states to protect and promote cultural diversity. At the regional level, Article 17 of the African Charter on Human and People's Rights guarantees the right to take part in the cultural life and Article 22 provides for the right to cultural development. Similarly, Article 13 of the American Declaration of the Rights and Duties of Man states that every person has the right to take part in the cultural life of the community.

Many international human rights instruments require the state not to interfere with the pursuit of individual cultural desire, for example: choose and practise a religion, associate with whomever one pleases, raise a family; but none of these rights addresses a collective right to cultural protection. However, such a hierarchy between individual civil and political right and collective economic, social and cultural rights is blurred when one looks at cultural rights. For example, even though, apart from the right to SELF-DETERMINATION, all the rights within the ICCPR are individual rights, the Human Rights Committee (HRC) has departed from its purely individualistic approach through its progressive jurisprudence regarding indigenous peoples' right to enjoy their own way of life. In several cases involving individual complaints from members of indigenous communities the HRC has established a link between culture and traditional forms of livelihood. One of the difficulties for the HRC was to appreciate what constitutes 'an activity forming an essential element of indigenous peoples' culture'. The HRC has clearly stated that the notion of culture in Article 27 is not 'frozen'. The view is that this provision can be invoked to support indigenous traditional cultural ways of life even when they have evolved and incorporated modern technology over the centuries. For example, in a case between a Sami community and Finland, the HRC took the view that 'the fact that the Sami have adapted their methods of reindeer herding over the years and practise it with the help of modern technology does not prevent them from invoking Article 27 of the Covenant'. Human rights law is not advocating keeping indigenous cultures frozen in time, but allows indigenous peoples to develop in their own way and offers protection for their right to enjoy their own traditional culture.

The notion of one's culture is subjective. Addressing cultural rights might be contentious in part because cultural rights are related to values of what we believe is important, what is good and what is bad. Each culture should be understood in its own context and none is superior or inferior. It has been argued that there is a clash between human rights and cultural rights. The critics address the universality of the human rights system as such universality will clash with the cultural values that should be viewed only in a specific context. In this regard human rights law is viewed as a way to impose dominant Western values in all other parts of the world. The reality is more that so-called 'cultural relativism' usually allows governments to maintain inegalitarian and repressive political systems, thus 'cultural difference' or 'cultural tradition' are often used as a means of disregarding universal norms (See: UNIVERSALISM and PLURALIST UNIVERSALISM). Communities have the right to maintain their specific cultural differences, but are also required to respect the constraints imposed by human rights norms onto governments, including the equal respect due to all members of society. The recognition of the right to enjoy one's culture plays an increasing role in this debate that should be seen not only at the level of the 'cultural relativism' versus 'universal rights' debate. Human rights law is in favour of cultural diversity and culture is a notion that is flexible, evolves and is not frozen in time. Cultural relativism arguments oversimplify the complexity of culture by treating it as a monolithic moral norm. Culture should not be viewed in isolation. Human rights law has a role to play in this debate, as often the diversity of cultures is viewed as something abnormal.

The current development of international norms regarding cultural rights invites states to give some space within their national political, judicial and legislative systems to diversity by offering minority groups the right to enjoy their own culture within the national system. By advocating the protection of cultural diversity, human rights law is based on the idea that cultural diversity is a natural and normal phenomenon that should be encouraged and protected.

Further Reading

Eide, Asbjørn, Krause, Catarina and Rosas, Allan (eds) (2001) *Economic, Social and Cultural Rights: A Textbook*, 2nd edn, Dordrecht: Martinus Nijhoff Publishers.

Asbjørn, Eide (2002) 'Cultural Rights and Minorities: Essay in Honour of Erica-Irene Daes' in Alfredsson, G. and Stavropolou, M. (eds), *Justice Pending: Indigenous Peoples and Other Good Causes. Essays in Honour of Erica-Irene Daes*, The Hague: Kluwer Law International, pp. 83–97.

Kuper, Adam (1999) *Culture: The Anthropologists' Account*, Cambridge, MA. and London: Harvard University Press.

Scheinin, Martin (2000) 'The Right to Enjoy a Distinct Culture: Indigenous and Competing Uses of Land' in Theodore S. Orlin et al. (eds.), *The Jurisprudence of Human Rights: A Comparative Interpretive Approach*, Turku: Åbo Akademi University Institute for Human Rights, pp. 159-222.

Wilson, Richard (1997) *Human Rights, Culture and Context: Anthropological Perspectives*, London: Pluto.

Contributor: Jérémie Gilbert

CUSTOMARY INTERNATIONAL LAW

Customary international law is binding on states and may have the force of law. In accordance with the Statute of the International Court of Justice, the laws which the Court applies to resolve disputes include international custom, as evidence of a general practice accepted as law and the general principles of law recognised by civilised nations (Article 38). Customary international law differs from **TREATIES** in that customary international law may not be written down. States do not 'sign up' to customary international law or ratify it in the conventional way. Rather, customary international law refers to a practice which states follow because they feel legally obligated to do so. Customary international law was a very early form of international law. To a large extent, particularly in human rights, it has been superseded by treaties – prescribed formal legal obligations in written form.

There are two criteria which must be met for customary international law:

1. *Actual behaviour/practice of states.* The International Court of Justice demands that for behaviour to constitute customary international law, it must be 'constant and uniform'. Consistency is a key requirement – states must act in conformity with the rule. Not all states have to act in the specified manner; particular emphasis is given to those states which are particularly affected by the law in question. For international human rights, it would be necessary that almost all states act in conformity with the measure. There is no prescribed length of time during which states should engage in the behaviour. As with so many norms of law, much depends on the circumstances of the law in question. With international human rights, the practice will usually have evolved over a long period of time. State practice can be evidenced in a number of ways. Recourse can be had to actual practice, diplomatic statements, national law, treaties agreed to etc. With international human rights, treaties and national law are probably the easiest elements of state practice/behaviour to identify though national constitutions and legal systems can be surveyed to gather evidence of consistency. The number of states acquiescing to international and regional human rights instruments is another obvious indicator.

2. *Legal reason for such behaviour.* There is a need for *opinio juris* to be demonstrated when establishing customary international law. In other words, it is necessary to demonstrate that states are acting in a consistent manner because they feel they are under a legal obligation to do so. The International Court of Justice has noted how essential it is that states feel they are

acting in conformity with what amounts to a legal obligation. Mere social usage does not suffice; the obligatory quality of the practice must be demonstrated before the practice can be enforced as customary international law. Of course, it is difficult to prove the reasons for the actions of any given state – politics, economics and diplomacy may all influence state practice. With international human rights, the problem is compounded as human rights by nature involve the actions of a state towards its nationals and other residents, an area traditionally outside the competency of international law. It is necessary to indicate that the state feels subservient to international law in its actions. In other words, the state does not have the option to treat its nationals in a different manner. This has broad repercussions for the notion of national/parliamentary supremacy as it requires a state to acknowledge that it does not exist in a vacuum but rather that its actions, even within its own territory, are shaped by international obligations.

Both actual state practice and a legal obligation to comply with the 'law' must be demonstrated before a rule of customary international law can be found. In the event of an international dispute, it is the state arguing the existence of a rule of customary international law which must demonstrate that the criteria are met and thus the other state should have acted in conformity with it.

Customary international law may alter over time, reflecting maturing state practice and in response to international and national events. Again the new rule gains stature as customary law if it is actively complied with by a number of states acting under a perceived legal obligation. Just as with treaties, states can opt out of customary international law. However, any state refuting a customary rule must do so from the inception of the practice in question. If a state becomes part of the international community only after the rule of customary international law has been established, then that state is bound by the rule whether it likes it or not. Given the international community has increased almost fourfold in the last 50 years, the importance of pre-existing binding customary international law cannot be overlooked.

With a plethora of international and regional treaties, contemporary international human rights law is very much grounded in treaties. However customary international law does play a role as some human rights are arguably now custom. The **UNIVERSAL DECLARATION OF HUMAN RIGHTS** (a declaration of the General Assembly) is not in itself legally binding, though it is indicative of international opinion. The Universal Declaration was adopted without a dissenting vote although eight states abstained. Since then the Declaration has become recognised as the definitive statement on international human rights being frequently referred to in international, regional and national instruments and courts. Many of the rights enunciated in the Declaration are so well accepted that they have crystallised into international law and thus bind all states in the international system. There are two reasons for this: some aspects of the Declaration have acquired the force of law through acceptance and practice over time; some elements of the Declaration enshrined pre-existing elements of custom, i.e. the right or freedom in the Declaration was already binding on states as customary international law. This opinion has even been expressed in the International Court of Justice, though not in a legally binding part of a judgment. Not all the rights in the Universal Declaration, however, can be regarded as customary international law. As discussed above, it is necessary to determine the extent to which states respect the right or freedom in question and the reason for their action.

The prohibitions on torture and slavery are excellent examples of international human rights law which have transcended all instruments and are now accepted as part of customary international law. States are thus bound not to engage in slavery or forms of severe torture irrespective of whether they have signed up to any international human rights treaties.

> Freedom from torture has become part of customary international law, as evidenced and defined by the Universal Declaration of Human Rights.
> (Circuit Judge Kaufman, *Filartiga v Pena-Irala* (1980) F 2d 876 (2d Cir. 1980))

Further Reading

Byers, M. (1999) *Custom, Power and the Power of Rules*, Cambridge: Cambridge University Press.

Malanczuk, P. (2004) *Akehurst's Modern Introduction to International Law*, 8th revised edn, London: Routlege.

Contributor: Rhona K.M. Smith

CUSTOMARY LAW IN THE SOUTH PACIFIC

The South Pacific region includes Micronesia, Polynesia and Melanesia and covers the area from the Marshall Islands in the north-west to Tonga in the south-east. The region is diverse in almost every imaginable respect – culturally, linguistically, historically and politically. There are also significant differences in the stages of development around the region, as well as within the countries themselves; however, the majority of the population are subsistence farmers and fishermen.

With the exception of Tonga, which was a British Protected State, all the countries in the region were colonised by Western powers during the 19th century. The focus of this chapter is on those countries that were colonised by English-speaking countries rather than by France. Between 1962 and 1980, the majority of these countries became independent sovereign states. The general pattern adopted upon independence was to replace pre-existing constituent laws with a new constitution and to establish a representative parliament, whilst retaining generally the English common law model of legal system.

Prior to colonisation, customary law was the only form of law to exist in all the countries in the region. Although the customary legal systems varied across the region, they shared some fundamental characteristics. Each society was small and communal and consequently each member of the group was bound to other members by an intricate web of familial links and mutual obligation. One of the fundamental differences between customary legal systems and Western legal systems is the absence of a central state to enforce commands. Although some societies had broad-based hierarchies of hereditary chiefs whose word was law and other societies

had so-called 'Big M[...] wielded power and maa[...] for every society that the [...] resolution was largely based on [...] compromise. Such practices were [...] itated by the gradual elimination [...] during the second half of the 19th c[...] The norms that regulated the societies a[...] on the interpersonal and group relationship[...] and authority structures and also on ties to land and the environment. These norms were not often explicitly articulated as legal rules are in Western societies and were also in oral rather than written form. They were usually claimed to be merely restatements of the established practices and customs of the community. In many ways the focus of customary law is more on its dispute resolution processes and techniques for the maintenance of order, together with the community-based principles or values applied in decision making, rather than on substantive rules (Powles, 1997).

During colonisation customary law was largely ignored by the colonisers, who introduced their own systems of law based on the common law model, establishing courts which were not authorised to apply customary law. Although to varying degrees customary law continued to operate in practice at a local level, in some places as the informal law of local government and generally as a dispute resolution system, at the official level it was not recognised as a source of law.

One reason for taking this approach to customary law was that for many years legal philosophers denied that indigenous customs and dispute-settlement processes should be accorded the status of law. Nineteenth-century thinkers such as Austin depicted law as the command of a sovereign directed towards members of the society, with failure to comply being met with 'sanctions'. Clearly customary law, as the legal system of stateless societies, fails to fit these criteria (see Roberts, 1979). This positivist view of customary law was successfully challenged by the emerging school of legal pluralism in the 1970s and 1980s, which argued that there is often more than one legal order in any given society existing independently or at least semi-autonomously of each other, and that law does not need to be made, sanctioned or enforced by a central or unitary state. Support for this view also came from the work of anthropologists. For example,

© R. K. M. Smith

Malinowski demonstrated that in the Trobriand Islands there was a variety of forces that operated to maintain peace in the society, including factors such as the cohesive force of relationships of reciprocal obligation. Although the debate concerning the nature of customary law is ongoing, today its legal nature is generally recognised. However, as is discussed below, there are a number of difficulties surrounding its continued practice in the region today.

After the attainment of independence or self-government, regional governments and legislatures became increasingly interested in ensuring that customary laws formed part of the legal fabric of the country. However, the role given to customary law in the legal systems of the countries in the region varies significantly. In Tonga, for example, although the constitutional and legislative provisions for government reflect the traditional authority of chiefs, there is no provision for customary law as such to be applied by any court.

Consider land: due to the centrality of land in the lives of Pacific Islanders, in all other countries there is provision for customary law to be applied to determine rights and interests in customary land. In some countries, for example Kiribati, the Marshall Islands and Tuvalu, this is to be applied by ordinary courts, whereas in others, such as Fiji and Niue, it is to be applied by special courts or tribunals.

Consider general recognition: in some countries, for example Kiribati, Nauru, the Solomon Islands, Tuvalu, Vanuatu and Samoa, provision is made for customary law to be applied as part of the law of the country by all courts, subject to certain restrictions. These restrictions vary, but generally provide that customary law will not be applied if it is inconsistent with the Constitution, legislation, subsidiary legislation, and in some countries, principles of common law and equity (for further details see Corrin Care, *et al.*, 1999).

The restriction upon the application of custom in cases of inconsistency with the Constitution may be quite significant as in all countries the written Constitutions contain provisions recognising and protecting rights of individuals to **LIFE**, **LIBERTY**, enjoyment of **PROPERTY**, protection of the law and freedom from **DISCRIMINATION** and to the further freedoms of assembly, **ASSOCIATION**, conscience and movement. These rights are often contrary to customary law, which may restrict individuals' rights and freedoms. One reason for this potential conflict is that while human rights are based on individualistic notions of justice, customary law, as we have seen above, is often based on communal values and tends to be directed towards the re-establishment of peace and harmony in a community.

Two examples can demonstrate the way in which customary law may be restricted by the fundamental rights provisions in constitutions. In R v Loumia (1984) SILR 51, the High Court of Solomon Islands held that a custom of a tribe in the Solomon Islands that made it a duty for a member of that tribe to avenge the injuring or killing of other members of the tribe by killing the persons responsible was contrary to the right to life provided by the Constitution of the Solomon Islands and could not be accepted by the Court as a defence to a charge of murder. Another example is the case of Public Prosecutor v Kota and Others (1989–1994) 2 VLR 661, where the defendants were charged with inciting to commit kidnapping after the first defendant's wife was compelled to attend a reconciliation meeting conducted by chiefs from her home island and upon the order of the chiefs, forcibly placed on a boat to return to that island against her will. Considering the conflict between customary law and the Constitution and statutory law of Vanuatu, Justice Downing of the Supreme Court of Vanuatu stated at 664:

I think that the Chiefs must realise that any powers they wish to exercise in Custom is subject to the Constitution of the Republic of Vanuatu, and also subject to the Statutory Law of Vanuatu. Article 5 of the Constitution makes it quite clear that men are to be treated the same as women, and women are to be treated the same as men. *All people in Vanuatu are equal and whilst the Custom may have been that women were to be treated or could be treated as property, and could be directed to do things by men, whether those men be their husbands or chiefs, they cannot be discriminated against under the Constitution.* [emphasis added]

For an interesting commentary on this case, see Zorn, 2003.

There is another philosophical debate that underpins many of the issues about the role of customary law today: whether the Pacific is in a stage of 'development' to become like the West (an evolutionist view) or whether it has got its own path to follow. Powles (1990) notes that this first view argues that the inevitable sweep of Western liberal philosophy and the market orientation of economies require the adoption of systems of representative responsible government and judge-administered law which will develop the notion of the individual citizen as the possessor of equal rights under a common law. The other view attaches higher priority to the preservation of traditional cultures and inherited value systems which utilise familiar customary law and the traditional authority of chiefs and leaders.

A final point to be made here about the role of customary law in the region today is about the difficulties experienced in actually applying it in the state legal systems. The role accorded to customary law in the state system is actually significantly smaller in practice than a reading of the Constitutional provisions might suggest. Difficulties include the following: the state system utilises procedures which are very different to those of customary law; often the state system is administered by officials trained in common law legal systems rather than customary law, who therefore tend to overlook customary law and, importantly, where there is no constitutional or statutory provision to state otherwise, courts have treated customs as matters of fact that have to be proved to the court by evidence given by witnesses, documents or public records in the same way as any other matter of fact. Clearly, when dealing with customary law, the problems of proof arising from restrictions on hearsay evidence and the rules requiring that little weight be given to the evidence of witnesses who have a special interest in the proceedings mean that much relevant customary law may be excluded.

The above discussion suggests that the role of customary law in the region is limited. In terms of the state legal system this is certainly true. However, it should not be overlooked that very often in many of these countries, in part due to the weakness and/or inadequacy of central government, the customary legal systems continue to operate much as they have since time immemorial, unrecognised by the state legal system but playing a vital role in the maintenance of peace and justice in the society.

Further Reading

Corrin Care, J. *et al.* (1999) *Introduction to South Pacific Law*, 24–47. London: Cavendish Publishing.

Farran, S. (1997) 'Custom and constitutionally protected fundamental rights in the South Pacific Region – the approach of the courts to potential conflicts', 21, *The Journal of Pacific Studies*, 103-122.

Powles, G. (1997) 'The common law at Bay? – The scope and status of customary law regimes in the Pacific' 21, *Journal of Pacific Studies*, 61.

Powles, C.G. (1990) 'Traditional Authority in the Contemporary Pacific: Conflict and Compromise in Legal and Political Systems' in Conference Papers of the 9th Commonwealth Law Conference, CCH (NZ) Ltd, Auckland New Zealand.

Roberts, S. (1979) *Order and Dispute: an Introduction to Legal Anthropology*, 23.

Zorn, J. (2003) 'Issues in Contemporary Customary Law: Women and the Law' in Jowitt, A. and Newton Cain, T. (eds) *Passage of Change: Law, Society and Governance in the Pacific.* Canberra: Pandanus Books.

Contributor: Miranda Forsyth

DEMOCRACY AND HUMAN RIGHTS

In Western countries, the concepts of democracy and human rights are often referred to in one breath, with the implication that they inevitably go together. This harmony is captured in the idea of 'liberal democracies', which are held to be constituted democratically within a framework of civil and political human rights, to which appeal can be made if decisions by majorities come to threaten the rights of minorities. However, the situation is not as simple as this account suggests and the philosophical relation between democracy and human rights is in fact a complex and contested one.

While many see an intrinsic relationship between human rights (especially understood as civil and political rights) and the institutions of democratic government that may seek to realise them and that are legitimately constrained by them, others point to violations of human rights that occur even in established Western democracies, such as the case of capital punishment in the United States (See: **THE RIGHT TO LIFE: THE DEATH PENALTY**). Further, democracy and human rights have often been treated separately within different disciplines – law in the case of human rights, political science in the case of democracy (Beetham, 1999). Within philosophy as well, although many theorists see human rights as the fundamental conception, which in turn gives rise to the norm of democracy, others place priority on the idea of democracy itself by justifying human rights as necessary preconditions for democratic government.

In the human rights documents themselves, the status of democracy as a right is not as clear as one might wish. Perhaps surprisingly, the **UNIVERSAL DECLARATION OF HUMAN RIGHTS** does not refer explicitly to 'democracy,' although Article 21 does enunciate a right of everyone 'to take part in the government of his country, directly or through freely chosen representatives' where 'the will of the people shall be the basis of the authority of government', conceived as expressed 'in periodic and genuine elections ... by universal and equal suffrage ...'. This is further clarified in Article 25 of the **INTERNATIONAL COVENANT ON CIVIL AND POLITICAL RIGHTS**, which makes reference to a right 'to vote and to be elected at genuine periodic elections'. Certainly, the normative requirement for democracy has come to be widely recognised among contemporary nation-states and is most often regarded as itself one of the civil and political human rights. This latter subset of rights ('first stage rights') tends in turn to be taken as the core meaning of human rights and is sometimes held to exhaust this meaning. Nonetheless, **ECONOMIC** and **SOCIAL RIGHTS** – 'second stage rights,' if not also the group or **DEVELOPMENT** rights of the third stage – are increasingly acknowledged to be also essential to a full account of human rights. We may then ask how this multiplicity of human rights can in fact be related to democracy, as itself a right and as a form of institutional organisation, and also ask how the fundamental philosophical principles of democracy and human rights connect to one another.

One view is that civil and political rights are a necessary condition for democratic participation and thus are justified relative to it. Such rights as freedom of speech, press and **ASSOCIATION** are clearly required if people are to take part effectively in their government and communicate their will to their representatives (Beetham, 1999). Another view is that these rights have a more independent ground in a conception of the equal freedom or agency of persons and therefore can legitimately constrain political decisions that violate them (Gould, 2004). Still other theorists regard popular sovereignty and human rights as mutually presupposing each other and as coming into being together within a sphere defined by law (Habermas, 1996).

The economic and social rights – that is, to means of subsistence, health care or education – are not always seen as closely implicated in democracy, though without an adequate level of well-being, people cannot be expected to have the time, energy or resources to participate in democratic politics (Shue, 1980). Again, insofar as democracy is not only a set of procedures but also a form of political organisation designed to further people's well-being, it may aim at fulfilling these economic and social rights in order to produce a level of welfare for the populace as a whole. It is clear, then, that democracy and human rights are conceptually and practically interdependent in various ways, especially inasmuch as the fulfilment of at least a set of basic rights – both to liberty and to means of subsistence – is a precondition for effective democratic participation, while conversely people need the right to democratic participation so that they can defend and further realize their own human rights (Shue, 1980).

Nonetheless, there are significant tensions between the two conceptions of democracy and human rights. For example, the scope of democratic decision making may be unnecessarily narrowed by too robust a list of rights, understood as protected by the courts. This has often been recognized as a problem in the case of national constitutions and judicial review that set powerful limits on the democratic decisions of legislatures; yet the conflict may become even sharper if human rights are taken to extend universally, across borders, in current contexts of regionalisation or **GLOBALISATION**. Thus some theorists have proposed the adoption of a system of cosmopolitan law with a common framework of human rights, accompanied by the introduction of more global forms of democratic decision making (Held, 1995) (See: **COSMOPOLITANISM AND HUMAN RIGHTS**). In the shorter term, such developments as the **EUROPEAN COURT OF HUMAN RIGHTS**, the **INTER-AMERICAN COURT OF HUMAN RIGHTS** or (in a different way) the **INTERNATIONAL CRIMINAL COURT** present important avenues for appeal and redress for rights violations, but also raise the issue of how much limitation is acceptable both on national sovereignty and on democratic decisions within nation-states, decisions that may be subjected to review by regional or international human rights courts. Further, a prospective extension of human rights of this

sort raises questions concerning the cross-cultural interpretation of these rights. Whereas human rights previously were regarded as appropriately embodied within national constitutions, the introduction of transnational jurisdictions requires making room for a certain level of diversity in the cultural and historical interpretations of such rights, and of the forms of democracy that they may come to frame.

Finally, it can be argued that the fulfilment of human rights, including the richer list of economic, social and **CULTURAL** rights beyond the civil and political ones, should be one of the main goals of democratic decision making, as practised both within nation-states and in newer transnational multilateral organizations (Gould, 2004). Since economic, technological and political globalisation means decisions taken in one locality often significantly affect those at a distance and can make it more difficult for them to realise their human rights, it is apparent that potentially global consequences need to be taken into account in such decision making. These people at a distance may then have commensurate rights of input into the decisions that affect them, if not always rights of full democratic participation in making them. Within nation-states, democratic institutions are formed and utilised in part for the sake of realising the human rights of their citizens. The question now arises whether emerging contexts of transnational democracy likewise require that political institutions contribute to the fulfilment of the human rights of individuals both near and at a distance.

Further Reading

Beetham, David (1999) *Democracy and Human Rights*, Cambridge: Polity Press, Chapter 5.

Gould, Carol (2004) *Globalizing Democracy and Human Rights*, Cambridge: Cambridge University Press.

Habermas, Jürgen (1996) *Between Facts and Norms*, trans. William Rehg, Cambridge, MA: The MIT Press.

Held, David (1995) *Democracy and the Global Order*, Stanford: Stanford University Press.

Shue, Henry (1980) *Basic Rights*, Princeton: Princeton University Press.

Contributor: Carol C. Gould

DEROGATIONS AND RESERVATIONS

In order to balance the legitimate rights of sovereign states on the one hand and human rights and fundamental freedoms of individuals on the other, international human rights law allows states to take various measures to limit human rights under certain circumstances and on specific conditions. Derogation from human rights is one of the lawful restrictions, albeit exceptional and temporary, permitted by some human rights conventions. A number of the most important human rights instruments contain provisions that permit state parties, in times of public emergency which threatens the life of the nation such as international or internal armed conflict, to take measures derogating from their obligations. Article 4 of the **INTERNATIONAL COVENANT ON CIVIL AND POLITICAL RIGHTS**, Article 15 of the **EUROPEAN CONVENTION ON HUMAN RIGHTS**, Article 30 of the **EUROPEAN SOCIAL CHARTER** and Article 27 of the American Convention on Human Rights (ACHR) (See: **THE REGIONAL SYSTEM OF THE AMERICAS**) are the most remarkable examples of the derogation clauses. Some other human rights conventions, such as the **INTERNATIONAL COVENANT ON ECONOMIC, SOCIAL AND CULTURAL RIGHTS**, however, contain no comparable provisions regarding the rights of state parties to derogate from their obligations. However, the text of the Covenant is more programmatic and requires only gradual steps from states towards its provisions.

The right of state parties to derogate from their human rights obligations is subject to a number of restrictions spelled out in the relevant instruments. Firstly and most importantly, not all rights guaranteed in the instruments may be derogated from. All human rights conventions containing a derogation provision clearly stipulate that the derogation from certain rights shall not be permitted. The rights to **LIFE**, freedom from **TORTURE**, freedom from **SLAVERY** and servitude, and the prohibition of retroactive criminal law are not subject to derogation even in times of emergency and therefore are usually referred to as 'non-derogable rights'. In addition to this catalogue, the prohibition of imprisonment merely on the grounds of inability to fulfil contractual obligations (the so-called 'imprisonment for debt'), the right to recognition as a person before the law, as well as freedom of thought, conscience and religion in the **INTERNATIONAL COVENANT ON CIVIL AND POLITICAL RIGHTS**, the right not to be tried or punished twice (the so-called principle of 'ne bis in idem') in Protocol No. 7 to the **EUROPEAN CONVENTION ON HUMAN RIGHTS**, and the right to juridical personality, the rights of the **FAMILY**, the right to a name, the rights of the **CHILD**, the right to a nationality and the right to participate in government in ACHR are also recognised as non-derogable rights under respective instruments. The Human Rights Committee, in its General Comment 29 regarding the derogation from provisions of the Covenant during a state of emergency (paragraph 13), is of the opinion that there are some other rights not listed in Article 4 that also cannot be made subject to lawful derogation. Article 30 of the European Social Charter, however, does not list any non-derogable rights therein.

Secondly, rights may be derogated from only to the extent strictly required by the exigencies of the situation, which means the extent and scope of the derogation measures must stand in a proportionate relation to the necessity of combating the public emergency. This proportionality test constitutes, in addition to the catalogue of non-derogable rights, a significant limitation on the permissible derogation measures. Thirdly, derogation measures must not be inconsistent with other obligations under international law assumed by state parties. Most notable international obligations in this regard are those under other human rights instrument than the one containing the derogation provisions, and both **CUSTOMARY** and conventional rules under international **HUMANITARIAN LAW** and international **LABOUR** law. Fourthly, with the exception of the European Convention on Human Rights and European Social Charter, derogation measures must not involve **DISCRIMINATION** solely on the ground of race, colour, sex, **LANGUAGE**, **RELIGION** or social origin. The prohibition of discrimination in the context of derogation entails that derogation measures shall not be intentionally taken to aim at certain racial, ethnic, linguistic or religious groups. In contrast to regional human rights instruments, the International Covenant on Civil and Political Rights also requires that only when the existence of a public emergency is officially proclaimed can a state party lawfully derogate from its obligation under the Covenant.

Under the respective instruments, state parties taking derogation measures are also obliged to inform other state parties through the intermediary of the Secretary General of United Nations (International Covenant on Civil and Political Rights) or the Secretary General of the Organisation of American States (American Convention on Human Rights), or inform the Secretary General of the **COUNCIL OF EUROPE** (European Convention on Human Rights and European Social Charter), respectively, of the provisions having been derogated from, the derogation measures and reasons for the derogation, as well as the date on which the derogation will terminate.

As of February 2002, 25 state parties to the International Covenant on Civil and Political Rights had made one or more derogations pursuant to Article 4 of the Covenant. The Human Rights Committee issued General Comments No. 5 in 1981 and General Comment No. 29 – replacing the former one – in 2001 to assist state parties to meet the requirements of Article 4 as regards derogation during a state of emergency.

Entering reservations to human rights instruments is another means by which state parties may lawfully be exempted from their conventional human rights obligations. As defined in Article 2(1)(d) of the Vienna Convention on the Law of Treaties, '"reservation" means a unilateral statement, however phrased or named, made by a state when signing, ratifying, accepting, approving or acceding to a treaty, whereby it purports to exclude or to modify the legal effect of certain provisions of the treaty in their application to that state'. The question of reservations to human rights treaties involves a number of issues and thus has been one of the most controversial subjects in contemporary international law.

All major human rights covenants and conventions have received a great number of reservations and interpretative declarations and understandings that amount to reservations, far more than other multilateral treaties. Many state parties to human rights treaties have made reservations, inter alia, to ensure the prevailing effects of their domestic laws and/or have made general or 'sweeping' reservations that do not specify the exact provisions subjected to reservations. Reservations to human rights treaties, especially those made to substantive provisions, thus have greatly weakened the obligations of state parties or made their obligations extremely obscure and consequently have undermined the effective implementation of human rights treaties.

The right of state parties to make reservations to international treaties is not unlimited however. In accordance with Article 19(c) of the Vienna Convention on the Law of Treaties, which is generally regarded as a codification of relevant rules of customary international law in this area, a state may not formulate a reservation if the reservation is incompatible with the object and purpose of the treaty. Most human rights treaties on a universal level either contain no explicit provisions regarding reservation or merely reiterate Article 19(c). Reservations to human rights treaties therefore have to be measured against the compatibility test. Reservations incompatible with the object and purpose of the treaty concerned shall then not be permissible. Nevertheless, due to the non-reciprocal nature of human rights treaties, only very few state parties have objected to those reservations they deem incompatible with the object and purpose of the human rights treaty concerned. Furthermore, the legal effect as to whether the objection may preclude the entry into force of the treaty in question between the objecting and reserving states varies in state practice.

In view of all the problems, the Vienna Declaration and Programme of Action, adopted in 1993, encourages states to avoid resorting to reservations as far as possible and 'to consider limiting the extent of any reservations they lodge to international human rights instruments, formulate any reservations as precisely and narrowly as possible, ensure that none is incompatible with the object and purpose of the relevant treaty and regularly review any reservations with a view to withdrawing them' (A/CONF.157/24, Part I, paragraph 26 and Part II, paragraph 5).

Treaty bodies charged with monitoring the compliance of human rights covenants and conventions are not officially empowered to judge upon the compatibility and admissibility of reservations, even though some commentators have strongly suggested they should be. Nevertheless they have expressed serious concerns regarding the issue. The Committee on the Elimination of Discrimination Against Women has issued two general recommendations regarding the compatibility, validity and legal effect of reservations to the Convention. The Human Rights Committee issued General Comment No. 24 (52) in 1994 on issues relating to reservations to the International Covenant on Civil and Political Rights, representing the most comprehensive and aggressive views of treaty bodies regarding the subject of reservations to human rights treaties. The reservations to human rights treaties have also been a major issue dealt with by the International Law Commission (see, for example, the Second Report of Special Rapporteur of the International Law Commission, Alain Pellet, on reservations to treaties, A/CN.4/477/Add.1,1996) and the Sub-Commission on the Promotion and Protection of Human Rights (see, for example, 'Reservations to human rights treaties', working paper submitted by Ms Françoise Hampson pursuant to Sub-Commission decision 1998/113, E/CN.4/Sub.2/1999/28, 1999).

Further Reading

Fitzpatrick, Joan (1994) *Human Rights in Crisis: The International System for Protecting Human Rights during States of Emergency*, Philadelphia: University of Pennsylvania Press.

Lijnzaad, Liesbeth (1995) *Reservations to UN-Human Rights Treaties: Ratify and Ruin?*, Dordrecht: Martinus Nijhoff Publishers.

International Commission of Jurists, *States of Emergency: Their impact on human rights*. Geneva, 1983.

Gardner, J.P. (ed.) (1997) *Human Rights as General Norms and A State's Right to Opt out: Reservations and Objections to Human Rights Conventions*, London: The British Institute of International and Comparative Law.

Contributor: Shiyan Sun

DEVELOPMENT COOPERATION AND HUMAN RIGHTS: ACP–EU RELATIONS

Increasingly, multiple connections are being made between human rights and development, both in relevant theory and in policy practice. Even nowadays it is fairly common to regard the fulfilment of basic human rights as part and parcel of the development process. This conception straightforwardly brings up complex questions about the exact relationship between human rights and development cooperation. The European Union is a major donor of development assistance and has long-standing and extensive cooperation relations with developing countries across the globe. For a relatively long period, from the mid-1970s until the 1990s, the EU was a forerunner in conceptualising links between development and human rights and in creating formal institutional and policy frameworks for addressing matters in this area. While the EU itself did not label its activities in this way, one could qualify the EU record in development cooperation as one of shaping a rights-based approach to development because of its emphasis on legally binding bases for both development cooperation in general and for connecting human rights and development in particular.

Since the 1990s EU policies in this field are perhaps no longer as distinctive as they were before, as human rights have gradually found a more or less firm place in the missions of other organisations that seek to promote development (such as the United Nations Development Programme, the International Financial Institutions or the United Nations Children's Fund). Nevertheless, the relations between the EU and a group of now 77 states in Africa, the Caribbean and the Pacific (the so-called ACP countries) still stand out as a key example of a development cooperation relationship in which more than average attention is paid to the human rights dimensions of development processes and in which concrete consequences are attached to either positive or negative human rights situations or performance records (See also: **THE RIGHT TO DEVELOPMENT**).

The ACP countries comprise all of sub-Saharan Africa and significant parts of the Caribbean and the Pacific. Many ACP countries are former colonies of EU member states and more than half of them are least-developed countries. The terms of ACP–EU development cooperation and trade have been laid down in a string of successive legal instruments, starting with the association paragraph in the treaty creating the European Economic Community in 1957. Since the 1960s the terms of ACP–EU cooperation are set out in negotiated treaties, respectively in the Yaoundé Conventions (1963–1975), the Lomé Conventions (1975–2000) and, until 2020, in the Cotonou Agreement.

At first human rights and development cooperation were linked primarily in a negative way in ACP–EU relations, that is by suspending development aid (partially or fully) in response to flagrant human rights violations in a recipient country. Such a suspension occurred for the first time after explicit and formal decision making by the European Community Council of Ministers on the human rights situation in Uganda under Idi Amin in 1977 (See also: **AFRICA: THE REALITY OF HUMAN RIGHTS**). According to long-standing EC/EU policy, such drastic negative measures are taken only as a last resort. And when suspension of aid materialises, it is mainly the structural EU development assistance to the government in place that is affected. However, if circumstances allow, in situations where suspension of aid is deemed necessary the EU will normally try to avoid double punishment of the population involved by keeping up its direct assistance to that population, for example by channelling development aid through non-governmental organisations or by extending humanitarian or emergency aid. More recently, efforts have been made to devise 'smart' sanctions that directly affect individuals in leadership positions in the government concerned or, for example, in the army of the country involved. Visa restrictions for such people and their close relatives are a common example (See also: **SANCTIONS**).

Over time very rough criteria have been developed for identifying situations that justify and/or require punitive measures. These criteria can primarily be distilled from policy documents issued by the European Commission, from relevant resolutions or other statements adopted by the Council of Ministers and from the ever more detailed provisions on human rights, democratic principles and the rule of law in the successive Lomé Conventions and the Cotonou Agreement (see Arts, 2000). Among other things, under pressure from the ACP countries, a procedure has been developed gradually which, except in cases of 'special urgency', shall precede the taking of any negative measures. This procedure includes a formal consultation with the ACP country involved. The consultation practice that has unfolded since mid-1998 is fairly constructive and reasonably well recorded in documents issued and/or decisions made by the European Commission and Council of Ministers, and in press releases of the ACP Group (Arts, 2003). This procedural evolution certainly has enhanced the transparency of the human rights sanctions practice of the European Union.

The limited effectiveness of human rights sanctions, the (anti-)humanitarian effects of (some) sanctions and the general desire to develop more constructive policy instruments that may help to address the root causes of the problems involved gradually shaped insight that it is necessary to combine negative policy responses with positive ones. However, it is only since the 1990s that serious work has been put into positively linking human rights and ACP–EU development cooperation. In the latest version, according to Article 9(4) of the Cotonou Agreement (2000), the ACP–EU 'Partnership shall actively support the promotion of human rights, processes of democratisation, consolidation of the rule of law, and good governance'. This active support will be extended through a range of different positive instruments. Human rights, democratisation and governance matters will be focused on in the development strategies that are drawn up for each ACP state and that determines how the resources made available to the ACP state involved will be spent. A structural political dialogue process will take stock of progress achieved in the domain of human rights, democratisation and governance. In addition, concrete support for human rights or democratisation projects or for 'political,

institutional and legal reforms and for building the capacity of public and private actors
and civil society' (Cotonou Article 9) will be
made available by the EU. In actual practice
such projects for example seek to combat
racism or gender discrimination, to prevent
torture or to rehabilitate victims of torture, to
promote press freedom and more broadly free
media, to strengthen parliamentary
institutions, to monitor and support electoral
processes or to support reconciliation
initiatives such as the Truth and Reconciliation
Commission in Sierra Leone or the special
Gaçaça trials in Rwanda (See also: **FREEDOM
FROM TORTURE; FREEDOM OF EXPRES-
SION; THE RIGHT TO VOTE AND DEMOC-
RACY; DEMOCRACY AND HUMAN
RIGHTS** and **TRUTH COMMISSIONS**).

The insights gained from operationalising
human rights concerns in ACP–EU development cooperation subsequently tend to be
applied in EU development cooperation with
non–ACP countries and even in EU external
relations at large. Virtually all other external
cooperation treaties now contain explicit
human rights clauses or at least hold clear references to such rights. Human rights, democratisation and governance have become regular
items of political dialogue although it should be
noted that countries that are especially important partners for the European Union, in trade
or otherwise, may still opt out of the standard
arrangements. For example, the human rights
dialogue with China is a clear case in which
the standard arrangements have often not
been applied. The generally available budget
lines for funding human rights-related activities outside the European Union have been
grouped under the title 'European Initiative
for Democracy and the Protection of Human
Rights' since 1994. The EIDHR supports projects in the fields of human rights, democratisation and conflict prevention. In 2002 €104
million was available for this purpose, which
was largely spent in developing countries and
countries in transition. In the same year the
thematic priorities within the EIDHR were
support for abolition of the death penalty;
combating racism, xenophobia and discrimination against minorities and indigenous peoples; support for efforts to combat torture and
impunity; and support for democratisation,
good governance and the rule of law
(European Commission, 2003: 65–66).

ACP–EU practice on human rights and
development shows obvious problems and
challenges, for example in the spheres of adequately balancing positive and negative
approaches, in achieving consistent application of the formal policies and procedures,
and in providing the practical facilities and
expertise required for full implementation
(Arts, 2003). Nevertheless, the ACP–EU
record of attempts to integrate human rights
and development co-operation presents an
interesting and worthwhile experience
through which many insights into the complex
relationship between human rights, democracy, development and international cooperation have been gained. ACP–EU relations have
always been in the forefront of this domain
and have set trends subsequently followed by
others. These trends include the incorporation of human rights clauses in development
cooperation treaties and emphasis on the
importance of taking a supportive approach to
the matters involved until such moment that
negative measures have become unavoidable.
This ACP–EU record is all the more relevant as
it has been built over time in a negotiation
process between a very important donor of
development assistance and a rather large
group of diverse developing countries in
Africa, the Caribbean and the Pacific.

Further Reading

Alston, Philip (ed.) (1999) *The EU and Human
Rights*, Oxford: Oxford University Press.

Arts, Karin (2000) *Integrating Human Rights
into Development Cooperation: The Case of the
Lomé Convention*, The Hague/Boston/
London: Kluwer Law International.

Arts, Karin (2003) 'Meeting the human rights
commitment of the Cotonou Agreement:
political dialogue requires investment', in *The
ACP–EU Courier*, no. 200 (September–
October), pp. 21–23, http://www.
europa.eu.int/comm/development/body/
publications/courier/courier200/pdf/en_
021.pdf.

European Commission (2003) *Annual report
on the European Community's Development Policy
and the Implementation of External Assistance in
2002*, Luxembourg: Office for Official
Publications of the European Communities.

Williams, Andrew (2004) *EU Human Rights Policies: A Study in Irony*, Oxford: Oxford University Press.

Contributor: Karin Arts

DEVELOPMENT, THE RIGHT TO

The origins of the right to development (RTD) can be found within the **UNIVERSAL DECLARATION OF HUMAN RIGHTS** through its determination to 'promote social progress and better standards of life in larger freedom'. The connection between human rights and development was made explicit in the 1968 International Conference on Human Rights, following which several studies were commissioned to consider the possible dimensions, scope and content of a distinct RTD. These culminated in the United Nations Declaration of the Right to Development (DRD) in 1986. The DRD defines development as a 'comprehensive economic, social, cultural and political process, which aims at the constant improvement of the well-being of the entire population and of all individuals on the basis of their active, free and meaningful participation in development and in the fair distribution of benefits resulting therefrom'.

Despite some vagueness about the substantive content of the RTD beyond fulfilling rights outlined in previous documents, the DRD makes five crucial contributions. First, in the context of apartheid and in the wake of colonialism it reaffirms the right to **SELF-DETERMINATION** and sovereignty over natural resources. Second, in divergence from the strict individual focus of the Bill of Human Rights, it affords the RTD to all persons and peoples. Third, in departure from relatively narrow economic conceptions of development that had been prominent in international development programmes, it emphasises the human person as both the active participant and beneficiary of the RTD. Fourth, it stresses the importance of both first (civil and political) and second (**ECONOMIC, SOCIAL** and **CULTURAL**) generation rights to development and prohibits the denial of either type of rights in the pursuit of development. Fifth, despite assigning primary responsibility to states for the creation of conditions favourable to development, it also highlights the role of the international community in the realisation of the RTD.

The DRD did not receive unanimous international support and is not a legally binding document, however the RTD has been strengthened by a consensus reached at the Vienna World Conference on Human Rights in 1993. A dual mechanism to explore ways of implementing the RTD has been established. This involves an open-ended working group on the RTD (which meets annually) and an independent expert who conducts research and makes recommendations for action.

The RTD remains a highly controversial and contested concept, particularly between northern and southern states and academics. A common tension during the cold war was the traditional elevation of the status of 'first generation' civil and political rights in Western rights discourses and the favouring of 'second generation' economic, social and cultural rights by communist countries. The RTD, however, in articulating rights relating to peoples is sometimes referred to as a 'third generation' right and brings its own discord. Southern states have tended to endorse the RTD to a much greater extent than northern states, for example the Organisation of African Unity proclaimed the RTD five years before the United Nations in the 1981 African Charter on Human and Peoples Rights, which is legally binding on ratifying countries (See: **AFRICAN COURT AND COMMISSION** and **NEPAD**). The main source of the north–south conflict is over the role of rights-holders (those who can claim rights) and duty-bearers (those responsible for respecting, protecting and fulfilling rights) in the RTD. Broadly speaking, southern states tend to champion the RTD as a new and distinct legal right, with states or communities as the primary rights-holders and the international community as primary duty-bearers. Northern states have tended to downplay the RTD as merely a synthesis of previously documented rights, outlining international morality but not necessarily law, with individuals as rights-holders and their states as duty-bearers.

This conflict is significant. It reflects traditional cultural differences in interpretations of the **AUTONOMY** of individuals, but it also goes much further. Southern states protest that the primary obstacles to development exist in the international arena, especially in the context of **GLOBALISATION**, and fear neo-colonial control over their governing activities in the form of excessive aid conditionality. Northern states claim obstacles to development that reside within corrupt and inefficient states and have alleged that developing states may use the RTD simply to claim international assistance rather than actually committing to realising the right at a national level. More bluntly, northern states are keen to resist legal obligations for them to assist with international development. Some believe that development can be meaningful only as a collective right, while others fear collective rights may undermine the fundamental **UNIVERSALITY** of human rights and their role in protecting and empowering the individual with respect to his/her state.

The confusion over rights-holders and duty-bearers has provoked criticism relating to the operability of the RTD. The DRD offers little guidance on how to implement the RTD, for example how to prioritise development programmes within limited national budgets. Some sceptics propose that trade-offs between rights in development programmes are unavoidable and that civil and political rights can impede development, thus revealing a fundamental conflict between rights and development. One of the strengths of the DRD, however, is that it does not permit any rights to be denied in the realisation of the RTD. This ensures a balance between first and second generation rights. The independent expert illustrates the operability of this approach using a novel conception of the RTD as a right to a particular process of development, thereby including human rights as both the means and outcomes of development. He has a vision of the RTD as a vector, which allows for development to be qualified as at least the improvement of some rights, while no rights deteriorate.

The DRD can be criticised for lacking accountability mechanisms. It does not have the machinery for people to hold their states or the international community accountable for violating their RTD. More problematically, development is greatly influenced by international institutions (such as the World Bank), non-governmental organisations (see: **SOCIAL MOVEMENTS AND HUMAN RIGHTS** and **GLOBAL CIVIL SOCIETY AND HUMAN RIGHTS**) and multinational corporations (See: **BUSINESS AND HUMAN RIGHTS**) which are further distanced from accountability as they are not parties to the human rights system. As such it has been argued that the RTD adds nothing to existing human rights instruments that cover similar ground with clearer enforcement mechanisms.

It may seem surprising that accountability is considered by others to be one of the strengths of the RTD. Simply by integrating development into the human rights discourse with its framework of clear entitlements, claimants and responsibilities, development becomes a more accountable process. The transparent international legal framework of human rights provides a firm basis for national and global advocacy and campaigning on development issues. The language of rights transforms development from a matter of charity to a matter of entitlements, thus empowering the beneficiaries of aid. The DRD focus on participation means that development programmes will be locally meaningful and avoid inappropriate imported solutions.

Until recently, development and human rights have followed quite separate paths, so what contribution has the RTD made to development practice? To date few development actors have made direct use of the RTD in their work; however the assertion of the RTD has encouraged an increasing number to utilise rights-based approaches. Rights-based approaches to development see rights and development as sharing common motivations and goals and allow development programmes to incorporate the principles of human rights, while avoiding the conceptual chaos of what the RTD means. An example is the Millennium Development Goals (www.developmentgoals.org). Rights-based approaches may be in accordance with human rights, but they are not derived from the RTD. The danger is that by not acknowledging development as a right it remains a matter of conscience and charity rather than entitlement and duty.

At worst, rights-based approaches may allow actors to adopt the morally impenetrable rhetoric of human rights to justify practice that is not in the best interests of the underdeveloped or to justify existing practice without challenging the status quo.

At best, however, they offer hope for the

future of the RTD. As development and human rights organisations increasingly work together they will gain advocacy and programming strength and will increase the utilisation of shared concepts. The RTD emphasises the interdependence of rights which means development actors are increasingly realising the value of first generation rights in their work and human rights actors are increasingly acknowledging the importance of second generation rights. This use of rights-based approaches may yet serve to break down some of the regional disagreements about categories of rights and further the realisation of development not as an aspiration but as an entitlement.

There is a need for greater clarity concerning the content of the RTD if it is to be universally realised, but the independent expert continues to present innovative and challenging ideas that appear satisfactory to both north and south. The problems facing the RTD are not dissimilar from the problems initially faced by the rights discourse in general. Over time soft law has been made fast and human rights are proving effective in improving the lives of millions. The RTD will yet prevail.

Further Reading

Barry, B. (2000) 'Is There a Right to Development?' in Coates, T. (ed.) *International Justice*, Aldershot: Ashgate.

Buitenweg, R. (1997) 'The Right to Development as a Human Right?' in *Peace and Change*, 22 (4), 414–431.

United Nations (1986) Declaration on the Right to Development. Geneva: Office of the United Nations High Commissioner for Human Rights.

United Nations Development Programme (2000) *Human Development report 2000: Human Rights and Human Development*, New York: Oxford University Press.

Uvin, P. (2002) 'On High Moral Ground: The Incorporation of Human Rights by the Development Enterprise' in *The Fletcher Journal of Development Studies*, vol. XVII, 1–11.

Contributor: Rebecca Shah

DISABILITY AND HUMAN RIGHTS LAW

Disability has been described as '... part of the human condition ...' (United Nations Department of Public Information). It is a situation that directly or indirectly affects millions of people. However, the fact that people with disabilities face discrimination, harassment and negative attitudes that lead to their marginalisation raises the question of equality before the law since 'All human beings are born free and equal in dignity and rights ...' (**UNIVERSAL DECLARATION OF HUMAN RIGHTS** 1948): thus such discrimination against human beings runs counter to legal human rights principles. The question of the discriminatory treatment of people with disabilities therefore is ripe for human rights law intervention. To what extent does human rights law take account of the discrimination and unequal treatment faced by people with disabilities?

> Over 600 million people, or approximately 10 per cent of the world's population, have a disability of one form or another. While their living conditions vary, they are united in one common experience – being exposed to various forms of discrimination and social exclusion.
>
> (http://www.unhchr.ch/disability/index.htm)

Generally speaking, where Western legal regimes have evolved in relation to people with disabilities they have been premised on a policy steeped in 'paternalistic' concerns to protect people with disabilities. This concern was fashioned on the notion that people with disabilities were outside the socially constructed norm of personhood, in particular that they did not have sufficient capacity to make their own decisions (Quinn, 1999, p. 285). The idea of disability was thus seen as a problem of the person labelled disabled and not one imposed by society through reductionism and isolationism (Liachowitz, 1988). Predictably, then, the law was predisposed to respond within a paradigm that stressed rehabilitation into the societal norm. Furthermore, governmental response to the way in which public institutions should consider people with disabilities was generally inclined towards the 'caring' professions and 'special needs'. This 'welfare' or 'medical model' of disability was seen as an end in itself rather than as one strategy whose aim might be to provide part of the armoury with which to combat such discrimination (Quinn, p. 286). This climate of opinion has been severely criticised for reinforcing the ideological and practical boundaries that have kept people with disabilities outside the mainstream. However, since the 1970s the 'rights-based' approach to discrimination of people with disabilities, as well as the model that urges equality of opportunity, has gained ground in influencing both policy and the law. The 'rights-based' approach to disability moves away from the person as a problem to the issue of societal barriers. This paradigm emphasises the right to participation on an equal footing with other members of society. A human rights focus is crucial in this regard since it shows that violations can cause disability, for example torture, hunger and so on, and it is an avenue through which dominant norms can be challenged. Human rights law can act as a catalyst for change where its focus is on empowerment of the person with a disability. Let us consider these matters in the context of the international regime, regional law and national law concerning disability.

The idea that people with disabilities should have the right to equality before the law had little grounding at international level until relatively recently following the work of the United Nations that aimed to change the general mindset concerning people, disability and discrimination. Events that helped to mark this turning point in attitude and policy included the 1981 International Year of Disabled Persons and the 1983–1992 United Nations Decade of Disabled Persons. These were consciousness-raising events that stressed the other side to disability, namely ability, rights, choice and equal opportunities. This new philosophy fed the paradigm that resulted in a new international instrument entitled the UN Standard Rules on the Equalisation of Opportunities for Persons with Disabilities. Agreement was reached on these non-binding rules in 1993. This provision covers matters such as equal rights as citizens to receive education, medical care and take an active part in the social and economic strata of society. Equality of opportunity is promoted by requiring that governments develop mandatory rules to prohibit discrimination and increase equal participation in areas such as employment, family life, recreation and culture (See: EQUALITY). Under part III (implementation measures) these include policy, planning and legislation. Furthermore there is an expectation that effective implementation requires the setting up of appropriate monitoring mechanisms that seek to incorporate the advice of people with disabilities. The Standard Rules have no binding legal force but are authoritative worldwide and were adopted by the European Commission in 1996 (Equality of Opportunity for People with Disabilities: A New Community Disability Strategy).

There are a number of international instruments which, although they do not explicitly refer to disability, are interpreted to support the notion that the issue of people with disability should be dealt with from a rights-based paradigm. These include the INTERNATIONAL COVENANT ON CIVIL AND POLITICAL RIGHTS and the INTERNATIONAL COVENANT ON ECONOMIC, SOCIAL AND CULTURAL RIGHTS. The International Labour Organisation has produced a document which promotes equality of opportunity and equality of treatment for people with disability in vocational rehabilitation, training and employment, as reflected in Convention No. 159 concerning Vocational Rehabilitation of Employment of Disabled Persons, 1983 and the ILO Code of Practice on Managing Disability in the Workplace adopted in 2001.

Principle 15 of the COUNCIL OF EUROPE's SOCIAL CHARTER 1961 relates to disabled people and the right to vocational training, rehabilitation and resettlement whatever the nature of their disability. This Charter was revised in the light of the 'rights-based' approach with Revised Social Charter 1996, new principle 15, which, while not yet in operation, states that 'Disabled persons have the right to independence, social integration and participation into the life of the community' (Quinn, p. 298).

There is a plethora of cases before the EUROPEAN COURT OF HUMAN RIGHTS regarding breach of Convention rights and people with disabilities; however, Article 14 of the **EUROPEAN CONVENTION ON HUMAN RIGHTS** does not include the term 'disability'. Applicants seeking to rely on this provision have found that it is restrictively drawn. This is no longer in line with rights-based policy. The wording used in Article 14 refers to enjoyment of rights within the convention without discrimination on any ground such as 'other status'. This ground was relied on before the European Commission of Human Rights (which now exists only to deal with outstanding applications – Wadham and Mountfield, 1999) in *Maurizio Botta v Italy* (App. No. 21439/93) relying on Article 8 ECHR right to private life. The Commission did not interpret the term 'any other status' to include people with disabilities. In *SP v United Kingdom* (App. No. 28915/95, decision of Commission, 17 January 1997), the Commission considered claims under Article 2 of the First Protocol in relation to the educational provision for a child with dyslexia. The Commission decided that the question whether lack of an assessment for educational provision had a bearing on weak educational progress and behavioural problems should not be answered in the affirmative. In *Cohen v United Kingdom* (App. No. 25959/94, decision of Commission, 28 February 1990) Protocol 2 and Articles 13 and 14 were read restrictively in relation to children with special needs and access to school transport. Article 14 is not being read to include disability which Quinn argues appears to contradict the stance that has evolved within the Council of Europe.

European Union law has evolved in a more positive way since the UN Standard Rules were endorsed by the Council of Ministers in Resolution 20, December 1996 on Equality of Opportunity for People with Disabilities (OJC 186, 2.7. 1999, p. 3) adopting a human rights-based approach to disability. A Commission proposal for a Council Decision on the European Year of People with Disabilities 2003 (Brussels, 29. 05. 2001. COM (2001) 271 Final, 2001/0116(CNS)) was adopted on 3 December 2001. The purpose of the proposal was to provide an impulse and framework to address attitudes towards people with disabilities by raising awareness, encouraging reflection and exchange of experiences as well as cooperation among relevant stakeholders. The EU has been keen to address the issues

such as the fact that one in ten Europeans of all ages has a disability. Many face barriers, especially in terms of employment, accessible transport and buildings and facilities and access to education and training and to technologies that would empower full involvement. In particular these barriers negate the guarantee of free movement of workers to European citizens by Article 39 (formerly Article 48) of EEC Treaty. The problem with Article 39 is that the discriminatory barrier is expressed in terms of nationality which would prove an anathema to a person with a disability. There has been limited jurisprudence on the issue of disability which had tended to arise in relation to equal treatment and social security (Directive 79/7 [1979] OJ L6/24 on statutory social security and Directive 86/378 as amended by Directive 96/97 [1986] OJL225/40 and [1997] OJ L 46/20 on occupational social security – these relate to employment-related social security and cover the working population whose employment has been affected by illness, 'invalidity' and old age). In Case 150/85 *Drake v Chief Adjudication Officer* [1986] ECR 1995 the question of who was a member of the working population for the purposes of Article 3(1) Directive 79/7 was read broadly to cover a woman who had given up work to care for her disabled mother. In Case C-31/90 *Johnson v Chief Adjudication Officer* [1991] ECR I-3723, the ECJ held that a woman who had become an 'invalid' after she gave up work was not entitled to an invalidity pension or severe disablement allowance because the issue according to the court was to do with social protection of women who remained at home. It has been argued that this is a narrow interpretation of the provision and does not open the door for those who want to work but are prevented from doing so because of a disability (Craig and De Burca, 1998).

A more promising measure is Article 13 which amended the EC Treaty and provides that the Council may take appropriate action to combat discrimination based on, inter alia, disability. Article 13 has provided the legal basis for a Directive establishing a General Framework for Equal Opportunity in Employment and Occupation (2000/78/EC, OJ L303, 2.12.2000, p.16) and the Community Action Programme to Combat Discrimination, 2001–2006, (OJ L303,

2.12.2000, p. 23). In relation to people with disabilities the Directive provides a legislative framework for member states. They are under a legal duty to implement provisions in relation to employment. This includes the prohibition of unlawful discrimination, including harassment, scope of positive action, appropriate remedies and enforcement measures. Whittle (2002) states that while the material scope of the Directive is limited to employment and occupation, it covers private and public sectors, vocational training and guidance and is based on the principle not of special but of equal treatment on the basis of meritocracy. A very important provision is the duty to accommodate provided in Article 5. The focus here is on the job rather than on the individual person's disability. The employer is required to provide reasonable accommodation. This provision can be seen as 'special treatment rather than equal treatment' and the danger is that the provision might be interpreted restrictively, as has happened with the equivalent provision in the USA. An important case shows how the EU has still not sorted out its priorities despite the Commission having adopted on 12 May 2000 a Communication with the purpose of 'mainstreaming' people with disabilities in 'Towards a Barrier Free Europe for People with Disabilities' (COM (2000) 284 FINAL), committed to developing a comprehensive and integrated strategy to tackle social, architectural and design barriers related to unnecessary restrictions regarding access for people with disabilities to social and economic opportunities. Thus in the recent Helsinki Concordia Bus Case (C-513/99) the ECJ held that when considering a tender the overall economic benefit for the local community can be taken into account in the final choice of the contract to be tendered, contrary to the Commission's view that the award criteria must be of a purely economic nature. This decision opens the door for the consideration of the wider public such as people with disabilities in relation to award criteria for public procurement contracts (see European Disability Forum Press Release, Brussels, 17 September 2002).

The United Kingdom Disability Discrimination Act (DDA) 1995 primarily prohibits unlawful discrimination against people with disabilities in employment in the provi-

sion of goods, facilities and services. The Special Educational Needs and Disability Act (SENDA) 2001 applies to education in mainstream schools. Section 1 (1) of the DDA defines disability as 'a physical or mental impairment which has a substantial and long-term adverse effect on his ability to carry out normal day-to-day activities' and includes a person who has had a disability (Section 2(1)). Jurisprudence has evolved in relation to this Act. In *Glover v Lawford* (MA 202633, 10 March 2003), Harrogate County Court, a person with visual impairment alleged unlawful discrimination under the DDA when his guide dog was refused access to a restaurant on account of its 'no dogs in the eating area' policy. The court held that the '... refusing to allow a guide dog on to the premises means refusing to provide a service to the owner for a reason relating to their disability ...' (paragraph 21), furthermore, that the refusal was not objectively justified on the grounds of health and safety (paragraphs 22–30). The court also decided that the respondent had not discharged the '... duty under section 21 [DDA] to make [reasonable] adjustments to his policy of 'no dogs in the eating area' as the policy made ... it impossible or unreasonably difficult for a disabled person such as Mr Glover to use the service provided' (paragraphs 31–36).

In terms of provision of education in mainstream, see *Anthony Ford-Shubrook v Governing Body of St Dominic's Sixth Form College*, in the Manchester County Court, 27 August 2003, where a mandatory injunction was granted in order that the applicant, who suffered from cerebral palsy, would be admitted to commence his advanced level education. Under the Americans with Disability Act of 1990 (which came into effect 26 July 1992) a number of issues have arisen in relation to the duty to provide reasonable accommodation in employment (Section 102 5(A) and (B)). The cases *Downey v Crowley Marine Services* US C A, 9th Circuit (2001), *Prilliman v United Airlines*, 53 Cal. App. 4th 935 (1997) and *Braun v American* Int'l Health & Rehabilitation Services, Inc., 846 P.2d 1151 (Or. 1993), show that the courts expect employers to comply with their statutory obligations. However Geariety and Lonborg (2001) are critical of the ambiguity that appears to have arisen regarding when the duty to accommodate arises.

The British Disability Rights Commission (DRC) (April 2000), set up under the Disability Rights Commission Act 1999, has statutory responsibility for work in relation to the elimination of discrimination, equal opportunities and the promotion of good practice (Section 2(1)). The DRC is empowered to make proposals to ministers and other state actors and to undertake research. There is a similar body that oversees the ADA–US Equal Employment Opportunity Commission.

Further Reading

Craig, P. and De Burca, G. (1998) *EU Law: Text, Cases and Materials*, Oxford: OUP, p. 871.

Geariety, K. and Lonborg, K. (2001) 'Reasonable Accommodation of an Employee's Disability – When is the Employer Supposed to Act?', *Special Employment Law Advisory Bulletin*, Winter.

Liachowitz, Claire H. (1988) *Disability as a Social Construct: Legislative Roots*, Philadelphia: University of Pensylvania Press.

Quinn, G. (1999) 'The Human Rights of People with Disabilities under EU Law', in Alston, P. (ed.), *The EU and Human Rights*, Oxford: OUP.

United Nations Standard Rules for Equalization of Opportunities for Persons with Disabilities, A/RES/48/96 of 20 December 1993.

Wadham, J. and Mountfield, H. (1999) *Blackstone's Guide to the Human Rights Act 1998*, Blackstone Press.

Whittle, R. (2002) 'The Framework Directive for equal treatment in employment and occupation: an analysis from a disability rights perspective', paper presented to the EDF Seminar on Current and Future Disability Rights at EU level, Brussels, 8–9 February.

Contributor: Fernne Brennan

DISCRIMINATION, FREEDOM FROM

The right of everyone, 'without distinction', to enjoy all human rights and fundamental freedoms lies at the heart of international human rights law. This right was first articulated in the Charter of the United Nations in 1945 which prohibited distinctions based on 'race, sex, language or religion'. It was reaffirmed and extended by the **UNIVERSAL DECLARATION OF HUMAN RIGHTS** in 1948 and has been repeated in every human rights instrument adopted since then. Indeed, it would not be an exaggeration to say that the principle of non-discrimination and its concomitant principle of equality have fuelled most of the human rights developments that have flowed from the UDHR. Put another way, discrimination, often on multiple and intersecting grounds, is at the foundation of virtually all human rights abuses.

The **INTERNATIONAL COVENANT ON ECONOMIC, SOCIAL AND CULTURAL RIGHTS** and the **INTERNATIONAL COVENANT ON CIVIL AND POLITICAL RIGHTS**, which were adopted in 1966 to give legal effect to the UDHR, describe the grounds covered by the norm of non-discrimination using the same terms. They require state parties to ensure that all the rights enumerated in each Covenant will be enjoyed without 'discrimination [distinction] of any kind, such as race, colour, sex, language, religion, political or other opinion, national or social origin, birth or other status' (Article 2(2) ICESCR and Article 2(1) ICCPR). In both Covenants Article 3 also requires that women and men equally enjoy the rights enumerated. This listing of prohibited grounds is not exhaustive, which opens the way for further grounds of prohibited discrimination to be recognised. Further grounds that are expressly recognised by other human rights treaties include descent, ethnic origin, marital status, property and disability. The CONVENTION ON THE RIGHTS OF THE CHILD (CRC) also prohibits discrimination against children on the basis of the attributes, status, activities and expressed opinions or beliefs of their parents, legal guardians or family members.

The human rights treaty committees, that have been established to monitor and facilitate states' compliance with their treaty obligations, have interpreted the treaties to cover additional grounds of prohibited discrimination, including physical or mental disability, age (older persons), sexual orientation and health status (including HIV-AIDS), as well as on the basis of indigenous or Roma heritage. These developments illustrate the flexibility that is provided by the open-ended listing of grounds of discrimination, which enables human rights law to respond to previously unrecognized forms of discrimination. While there may be some limits to groups that fall into the category of 'other status,' these limits have yet to be settled.

Neither of the Covenants defines non-discrimination. However, the two treaties that focus on specific forms of discrimination, the INTERNATIONAL CONVENTION ON THE ELIMINATION OF ALL FORMS OF RACIAL DISCRIMINATION (ICERD) and the CONVENTION ON THE ELIMINATION OF ALL FORMS OF DISCRIMINATION AGAINST WOMEN (CEDAW), do provide definitions which are similar. The treaty committees that monitor the Covenants have adopted the same definition, which promotes consistency across the field. There are several features of this definition that are important to note. Firstly, the acts of discrimination are widely defined as 'any distinction, exclusion, restriction or preference'. These terms should be inclusive of all types of discriminatory conduct. Secondly, the definition includes both direct and indirect forms of discrimination by prohibiting acts that have a discriminatory 'purpose or effect'. This means that, in addition to prohibiting purposeful discrimination, apparently neutral conduct that has discriminatory effects is also prohibited, even where there is no discriminatory intent or motivation. Thirdly, the discrimination must bring about the specific result of 'nullifying or impairing the [equal] recognition, enjoyment or exercise of human rights and fundamental freedoms'. This means that the right to non-discrimination does not stand alone; the alleged discrimination must prevent the equal enjoyment of specific rights or freedoms such as the right to education or the freedom to express an opinion.

Finally, the definition requires that the discrimination must be experienced in a specified 'political, economic, social, cultural, or any other field of ... life'. It is in this respect that the ICERD and CEDAW definitions differ significantly, as the former is limited to the field of 'public life', while CEDAW is not. Article 2(e) of CEDAW, for example, makes it clear that states' obligations include taking measures to eliminate discrimination against women by private actors – 'any person, organization or enterprise'. This extension is important as discrimination against women often occurs in the 'privacy' of the domestic sphere. The other treaty committees have followed the CEDAW approach by not confining the scope of the prohibition against discrimination to the public sphere. Even the Committee on the Elimination of Racial Discrimination (CERD) has required state parties to ensure that private institutions do not violate the obligations they have assumed by ratifying ICERD.

Human rights law does recognise that there may be a need to take discriminatory measures in order to address the historical and structurally embedded disadvantages suffered by some groups in order to accelerate the realization of *de facto* equality (substantive or factual equality), as distinct from *de jure* equality (formal equality) which may result from treating everyone in the same way. Therefore, positive discrimination or affirmative action is allowable and may even be necessary in some circumstances. However, such special measures must not lead to separate rights or to the maintenance of unequal or separate standards for different groups and must be discontinued when the object of equality has been achieved. The acceptance that special measures may be necessary indicates that substantive equality is the goal of the right of non-discrimination.

The implementation of the right to non-discrimination does not only require state parties to refrain from discriminatory conduct; that is, it does not involve only a negative obligation to respect human rights without discrimination. As the Committee on Economic, Social and Cultural Rights (CESCR) has emphasised, the realisation of all human rights includes positive as well as negative obligations and the right to non-discrimination is no different. These positive obligations include measures to protect against discrimination by private actors and to fulfil or ensure the actual enjoyment of human rights without discrimination. Further, the right to enjoy human rights and fundamental freedoms without discrimination is an immediate obligation. Even where the realisation of the full right, such as the right to social security, is able to be progressively realised because of resource constraints, the available resources must be distributed in a non-discriminatory way. Finally, state parties are expected to adopt legislation that protects the right to non-discrimination and to provide effective remedies in the event that discrimination occurs.

It is only recently that the treaty committees have been attentive to the ways in which discrimination may not always be based on a discrete ground, but may be due to multiple and intersecting grounds. The CERD's General Recommendation on gender-related forms of racial discrimination is leading the way by recognising that unique forms of discrimination may be produced by the intersection of race and gender. (CERD General Recommendation XXV (2000)). The other treaty committees are also gradually developing practices that are more alert to the complex origins of many forms of discrimination and the more nuanced measures that may be necessary in order to fully address it.

Although enormously important, the right to non-discrimination does have some limitations. In order to prove that discrimination exists, there is the need to rely on a comparison with an appropriate standard; for example, women are compared with men, people of one race with those of another, homosexuals with heterosexuals, people with disabilities with able-bodied people, and so on. These comparisons are effective in highlighting discrimination when the experience of the two groups is comparable, as for example in exercising the right to vote. But where experience differs, as in the experience of indigenous relationships with the land or of women's reproductive potential, non-discrimination is an inadequate principle on which to base the realisation of equality. This highlights a second limitation of the non-discrimination approach which is that it cannot create 'new' rights; it is only able to ensure equality in the enjoyment of existing rights. Despite these limitations, the right to non-discrimination resonates with the experience of many people who remain disadvantaged and marginalised and continues to provide a powerful language for the mobilisation of local movements seeking dignity and equality through claiming their human rights.

Further Reading

Banton, Michael (1996) *International Action against Racial Discrimination*, Oxford: Oxford University Press.

Bayefsky, Anne F. (1990) 'The Principle of Equality or Non-Discrimination in International Law', 11 *Human Rights Law Journal*, 1.

Committee on the Elimination of Racial Discrimination (2000) General Recommendation 25, 'Gender Related Dimensions of Racial Discrimination': 20 March, contained in UN Doc. A/55/18, annex V.

International Covenant on Civil and Political Rights (2000) General Comment 28, 'Equality of Rights between Women and Men (Article 3)': 29 March, UN Doc. CCPR/C/21/Rev.1/Add.10.

Otto, Dianne (2002) '"Gender Comment": Why Does the UN Committee on Economic,

Social and Cultural Rights Need a General Comment on Women?' 14 *Canadian Journal of Women and the Law*, 1.

Contributor: Dianne Otto

ECONOMIC RIGHTS

The **UNIVERSAL DECLARATION OF HUMAN RIGHTS** 1948, founded on respect for human dignity and the equality of rights, listed rights which the global community recognised and agreed to respect. For reasons of pedagogy, these rights were commonly classed as civil and political rights and economic, **SOCIAL** and **CULTURAL RIGHTS**. But in adopting the Universal Declaration, it was clear that human rights were indivisible, not 'pick and mix', they must be applied to every country and citizen in their entirety: they are indivisible, complementary and universal.

Although the logic of the Universal Declaration would have rendered it desirable that the same rights applied in all states, it was not to be. The Commission on Human Rights finally agreed not one text, but two: the **INTERNATIONAL CONVENANT ON CIVIL AND POLITICAL RIGHTS** (ICCPR) and the **INTERNATIONAL COVENANT ON ECONOMIC, SOCIAL AND CULTURAL RIGHTS** (ICESCR). Both were adopted in 1966 and entered into force in 1976.

Although some writers considered it imperative to adopt one instrument incorporating all the rights, the geographical context of the time was not conducive to this: the cold war divided the world. The USA and the UK were suspicious of economic, social and cultural rights which they considered essentially an objective additional to true 'instant' human rights which were immediately applicable. On the other hand, while the socialist states considered economic, social and cultural rights the true test, they were reluctant to permit examination of their internal policies and human rights enforcement mechanisms by an independent committee of experts.

The status of the two Covenants is very different, reflecting the importance which was accorded to civil and political rights. Accordingly, it is advisable at all times to bear in mind one important point: the effect, immediate or progressive, of each Covenant.

The International Covenant on Civil and Political Rights has immediate application in terms of Article 2: 'Each State Party to the present Covenant undertakes to respect and to ensure to all individuals within its territory and subject to its jurisdiction the rights recognised ... Where not already provided for by existing legislative or other measures, each State Party to the present Covenant undertakes to take the necessary steps, in accordance with the constitutional processes and with the provisions of the present Covenant, to adopt such legislative or other measures as may be necessary to give effect to the rights recognised in the present Covenant.' On the contrary, Article 2(1) of the International Covenant on Economic, Social and Cultural Rights states: 'Each State Party to the present Covenant undertakes to take steps, individually and through international assistance and cooperation, especially economic and technical, to the maximum of its available resources, with a view to achieving progressively the full realisation of the rights recognised in the present Covenant by all appropriate means, including the adoption of legislative measures.'

This difference in approach, between rights immediately realisable and those progressively realisable, does not mean that the states which ratify the ICESCR have no immediate obligations. States agree to guarantee 'that the rights enunciated in the present Covenant will be exercised without discrimination of any kind as to race, colour, sex, language, religion, political or other opinion, national or social origin, property, birth or other status'. They must act to the maximum of their resources to ensure equality in the exercise of rights. The Committee on Economic, Social and Cultural Rights in General Comment 3 defined the nature and extent of the obligations incumbent on the State immediately in terms of the Covenant.

The protected rights are essentially the right to work (Articles 6–8), family rights, especially for mothers and infants (Article 10), the rights to an adequate standard of living (Article 11), to health (Article 12), to education (Articles 13–14) and to culture (Article

15). The rights which are strictly economic are found in Article 11(1): 'The States Parties to the present Covenant recognise the right of everyone to an adequate standard of living for himself and his family, including adequate food, clothing and housing, and to the continuous improvement of living conditions. The States Parties will take all appropriate steps to ensure the realisation of this right, recognising to this effect the essential importance of international cooperation based on free consent.'

One can say that this article is fundamental to all the other rights in the Covenant, as an adequate standard of living is essential to respect for human dignity, a life free from hunger and inclemency. Respecting these rights requires appropriate policies, legislative guarantees of non-discrimination in access to rights and action plans aimed at attaining the objectives.

To illustrate the foregoing, two economic rights will be briefly analysed: the rights to food and to adequate housing.

Recognised initially in the Universal Declaration (Article 25), Article 11(2) of the Covenant provides 'The States Parties to the present Covenant, recognising the fundamental right of everyone to be free from hunger, shall take, individually and through international cooperation, the measures, including specific programmes, which are needed: (a) to improve methods of production, conservation and distribution of food by making full use of technical and scientific knowledge, by disseminating knowledge of the principles of nutrition and by developing or reforming agrarian systems in such a way as to achieve the most efficient development and utilisation of natural resources; (b) taking into account the problems of both food-importing and food-exporting countries, to ensure an equitable distribution of world food supplies in relation to need.' In General Comment 12 (at paragraph 6), the Committee defined the normal meaning of this right and the obligations incumbent upon states. 'The right to adequate food is realised when every man, woman and child, alone or in community with others, has physical and economic access at all times to adequate food or means for its procurement … states have a core obligation to take the necessary action to mitigate and alleviate hunger as provided for in paragraph 2 of Article 11, even in times of natural or other disasters.'

The right requires that food provides sufficient quality of nutrition without dangerous contamination and is available as and when required. Accessibility to food is both economic and physical. The principal obligation undertaken by states is to act to progressively ensure the full realisation of the right to adequate food, progressing as quickly as possible towards the objective. The Committee (at paragraph 15, General Comment 12) distinguishes three levels of obligation: to respect, to protect and to fulfil. That is to say the state must abstain from impeding the realisation of the right, take measures to ensure others cannot impede the right and proactively ensure access to food resources, where necessary by distributing provisions.

Should any question of a violation of the Covenant arise, the state must show that every effort has been made, using all the resources at its disposal in order to comply, as a priority, with the minimum obligations in accordance with Article 2(1) of the Covenant (General Comment at paragraph 17). Note that any discrimination in access to food constitutes a violation of the Covenant (Article 2); the prohibition on discrimination is instantaneous, not progressive.

States have a margin of discretion in realising the right though all national strategies should comply with principles of accountability, transparency, peoples' participation, decentralisation, legislative capacity and independence of the judiciary (General Comment paragraphs 21–23). The Committee supports the adoption of appropriate national and international strategies, the FAO and UNICEF providing appropriate expert advice where required.

The right to housing, briefly mentioned in Article 11 of the Covenant, is addressed in more detail in two General Comments: No. 4 on adequate housing and No. 7 on forced evictions. The right to housing is broad, i.e. the right to a place where you can live safely, in peace and dignity. The adequacy of needs is essentially part of the definition (needs-based approach). Some criteria have been highlighted by the Committee (General Comment 4, paragraph 8).

1. Legal security of tenure: there should be legal protection against forced eviction, harassment and other threats. State parties

must take immediate measures aimed at conferring legal security of tenure on those currently lacking such protection, in consultation with those concerned.

2. Availability of services, materials and infrastructure: such facilities are essential for health, security, comfort and nutrition. Adequate housing requires access to safe drinking water, energy for cooking, heating, lighting, sanitation and washing facilities, refuse facilities and emergency services.

3. Affordability: the cost of adequate housing must be at a level which does not threaten or compromise the realisation of other basic needs. Thus the state parties should ensure that housing costs reflect income levels, financial support is available for the most needy and that tenants are protected against unreasonable rent levels and increases.

4. Habitability: to be adequate, housing must be habitable, that is to say, it must provide sufficient space and afford protection against cold, heat, humidity, rain, wind and other threats to health. The World Health Organisation has adopted guiding principles (Health Principles of Housing 1990) which States should apply. Therein, it is recognised that inadequate and deficient housing is invariably associated with increased mortality and morbidity rates.

5. Accessibility: adequate housing must be available to those entitled to it, with priority accorded to the most vulnerable. Ideally a state's housing policy should increase access to land for the impoverished and those without.

6. Location: adequate housing must be located in a place with employment opportunities, health care services, schools, childcare and other social facilities. At the same time, housing should not be built on polluted sites nor close to sources of pollution which threaten the right to health of the occupants.

7. Respect for cultural heritage: architecture, building materials and supporting policies must respect cultural identity and diversity of housing.

Some measures should be undertaken immediately by state parties irrespective of the state of development. Many of the measures necessary for the right to housing merely require the government to abstain from certain practices while facilitating 'self-help' for affected groups. International cooperation should be sought for any shortfall in state resources in accordance with Article 11(1), 22 and 23 of the Covenant.

The means required to guarantee the full realisation of the right to adequate housing vary considerably from state to state, but the Covenant clarifies the obligation states must take to comply. The Global Strategy for Shelter 'defines the objectives for the development of shelter condition, identifies the resources available to meet these goals and the most cost-effective way of using them and sets out the responsibilities and time-frame for the implementation of the necessary measures' (paragraph 32, adopted by General Assembly Resolution 43/181, 1988). These strategies must be inclusive, notably to those people who are badly housed or homeless. An appropriate balance between public and private sector measures should be utilised and effective, but in any number of countries the strategies of self-help will be most adaptable to the needs of the affected groups.

Provision of national legal remedies is an important aspect of the right to housing. The Committee is particularly interested in information on legal appeals against eviction and demolition orders, judicial procedures for indemnity against illegal evictions or other illegal measures carried out by or with the support of landlords (discrimination in access to housing, insalubrious accommodation, etc). In this respect, the Committee considers that forced evictions are, *prima facie*, contrary to the Covenant, and they are not able to be justified except in the most exceptional circumstances and in accordance with the applicable principles of international law (General Comment 4 at paragraphs 17 and 18). Once again, elements of economic rights are not 'progressive' rights.

Economic rights should not be disassociated from the human rights: civil, political, social and cultural. The indivisibility of human rights must become a universal reality, in accordance with the Universal Declaration. These rights should influence the actions not only of states but also of individuals and the plethora of international institutions, notably financial institutions such as the World Bank and

International Monetary Fund and commercial organisations such as the World Trade Organisation. The right to development (associated with the struggle against poverty) is a primary objective of the United Nations for the decade to come. It requires 'recognition of the inherent dignity and of the equal and inalienable rights of all members of the human family' which form, according to the Premable of the Universal Declaration, 'the foundation of freedom, justice and peace in the world'.

Further Reading

Chapman, A. (1996) 'A "Violations Approach" for Monitoring the International Covenant on Economic, Social and Cultural Rights' in 18.1 *Human Rights Quarterly*, pp. 23–66.

Committee on Economic, Social and Cultural Rights, General Comment No. 4 on the right to adequate housing, UN Doc E/1992/23.

Committee on Economic, Social and Cultural Rights, General Comment No. 7 on the right to adequate housing: forced evictions, UN Doc E/1998/22, annex IV.

Committee on Economic, Social and Cultural Rights, General Comment No. 12 on the right to adequate food, UN Doc E/C.12/1999/5.

Craven, M. (1998) *The International Covenant on Economic, Social and Cultural Rights: A perspective on its development*, Oxford: Clarendon.

Eide, A., Krause, C. and Rosas, A. (eds) (2001) *Economic, Social and Cultural Rights*, The Hague: Martinus Nijhof.

Contributor: Philippe Texier
Translated and edited from French original by Rhona Smith and Audrey Guichon

ECONOMIC, SOCIAL AND CULTURAL RIGHTS, THE FUTURE OF

Economic, social and cultural rights are not mere constitutional aspirations, nor is their materialisation guaranteed solely by the formulation of policies, plans and programmes. Their implementation does, in the very first place, require an approach based on the respect, protection and fulfilment of human rights, like the materialisation of civil and political rights.

Secondly, full enjoyment of economic, social and cultural rights is essential to the empowerment and participation of individuals and groups in the economic, social and cultural spheres. All the powers entrusted with competencies to mitigate and solve problems derived from non-enjoyment of these rights share responsibilities in combating and eradicating phenomena such as poverty, hunger, illiteracy, disease and, in general, all inequalities in so far as they hamper or impede the full and equal enjoyment of economic, social and cultural rights. Thirdly, economic, social and cultural rights are greatly underpinned by the interdependence of economic and social policies in ensuring sustainable people-centred development. Fourthly, the issue of overlap and inconsistencies with other rights is assessed by examining how the denial of another right has affected the enjoyment of specific economic, social and cultural rights. As an example, as regards the denial of the right to self-determination, an indigenous population could be deprived of the enjoyment of economic, social and cultural rights if eviction from their ancestral lands had left them without the resources to enjoy an adequate standard of living, contained in Article 11 of the International Covenant of Economic, Social and Cultural Rights (See: INDIGENOUS PEOPLES' RIGHTS; INTERNATIONAL COVENANT ON CIVIL AND POLITICAL RIGHTS AND THE INTERNATIONAL COVENANT OF ECONOMIC, SOCIAL AND CULTURAL RIGHTS).

In spite of the general consensus on the universality, indivisibility, interdependence and interrelatedness of all human rights, as reaffirmed in the 1993 World Conference of Human Rights in Vienna, economic, social and cultural rights are still not given the same priority as civil and political rights, one of the reasons being the argument that the principle of indivisibility and interdependence of all human rights does not imply equal implementation. Particularly as concerns the rights enshrined in the ICESCR, there are many who share the view that these rights are not clearly focused and that some of them are not expressed with the clarity needed to enable state parties to establish clear and binding obligations which would, in turn, lead to their justiciability.

It is true that human rights provisions are formulated in general terms, but it is equally true that interpretation and clarification follow from experience and analysis of concrete situations and cases. The issue of the justiciability of the dispositions of the Covenant has been widely discussed between the UN Committee for Economic, Social and Cultural Rights and state parties to the Covenant in the context of the national reporting procedure. National implementation reports, as well as the reports of the Special UN Rapporteurs on the rights to **FOOD**, adequate **HOUSING**, **HEALTH** and **EDUCATION**, refer to examples of national case law and of case law of the regional human rights systems in Europe, in the Americas and in Africa, that demonstrate that the general demand for the justiciability of economic, social and cultural rights is no longer subject to doubt and that the courts have taken decisions to clarify any disposition that may have not been clear at the outset.

The principle of progressive realisation is fundamental for the implementation of economic, social and cultural rights. But this has at times been understood by state parties as the possibility to decide how and when to implement the obligations derived from the ratification of the ICESCR. It is easy to understand state parties' concerns that the lack of resources can constitute a real obstacle to the full enjoyment of economic, social and cultural rights and that only the more affluent state parties would be in a position to guarantee Covenant obligations, given the nature and the amplitude of economic, social and cultural rights. However, the principle of progressive realisation, expressed in Article 2 of the Covenant, establishes that the socio-economic context of each state party needs to be taken into consideration when referring to the allocation and use of the 'maximum of its available resources'. The experience of the Committee has shown that the insufficient implementation of economic, social and cultural rights is not only due to the lack of resources but also and above all to the development of domestic priorities that do not attribute sufficient relevance to economic, social and cultural rights and, very often, to the fact that material and financial resources, in themselves scarce, are not targeted and used to the fullest extent possible for their implementation.

There can be no doubt, on the part of state parties that have ratified the Covenant, that ratification implies taking immediate measures for the materialisation of the core obligations by bringing national legislation in to conformity with the Covenant, by allocating the necessary resources for their implementation and by providing the legal remedies adequate to the nature and extension of the violation of a Covenant right.

There can also be no doubt that the Covenant rights 'will be exercised without discrimination of any kind as to race, colour, sex, language, religion, political or other opinion, national or social origin, property, birth or other status' (See: **FREEDOM FROM DISCRIMINATION**).

The international dimension of economic social and cultural rights has been the subject of heated debates, not only as part of official development assistance commitments but also in the context of the opportunities and challenges posed by globalisation (See: **THE RIGHT TO DEVELOPMENT; POVERTY AND HUMAN RIGHTS; AFTERWORD**). Article 2 of the Covenant calls on state parties to 'undertake to take steps, individually and through international assistance and cooperation, especially economic and technical, to the maximum of its available resources'. Given the fact that national capacity is one of the key factors in implementing economic, social and cultural rights and in fulfilling domestic responsibilities, the obligation contained in Article 2 is threefold. It requires developing countries in need of such assistance to ask for it. It is also a reminder to developed countries that have not yet achieved the 0.7 per cent target of their gross national product as official development assistance to developing countries of the importance of their cooperation and assistance in enabling all countries to achieve the internationally agreed development goals, including those contained in the United Nations Millennium Declaration. It also requires state parties and international financial institutions to take into full account the need for the enjoyment of economic, social and cultural rights by all sectors of the population, particularly the most vulnerable, when drawing up structural adjustment programmes.

Presently under discussion by an open-ended working group, the Draft Optional

Protocol to the Covenant contains various issues of significant relevance to the future of economic, social and cultural rights. This Optional Protocol will not constitute a new obligation but rather a complaints supervisory mechanism, to be used when all the domestic avenues to redress violations have been exhausted.

The issue of justiciability, that is fundamental to the future of these rights and to their acceptance as being as relevant as civil and political rights, will be greatly strengthened by a Protocol with a comprehensive approach to allow for individual and collective complaints against violations of the substantive rights contained in Articles 6–15 of the Covenant. The Protocol will also strengthen the mutually reinforcing nature of national, regional and international case law. When finally adopted, hopefully sooner than later, the Protocol will be another tool for the interpretation and implementation of Covenant rights, in conjunction with the General Comments of the UN Committee on Economic, Social and Cultural Rights and the reports and joint statements of the UN Special Rapporteurs on various rights.

Non-governmental organizations are key players in the present and future status of economic, social and cultural rights through their concerted efforts to raise awareness and to systematically assist state parties in developing a better understanding of the difficulties and shortcomings encountered in the progressive realisation of the full range of rights that underpins individual and collective well-being (See: **GLOBAL CIVIL SOCIETY; SOCIAL MOVEMENTS AND HUMAN RIGHTS**).

Further Reading

Resolution 2004/29, adopted at the 60th session of the Commission of Human Rights, in April 2004, on the question of the realisation in all countries of the economic, social and cultural rights contained in the Universal Declaration of Human Rights and in the International Covenant on Economic, Social and Cultural Rights, and study of special problems which the developing countries face in their efforts to achieve these rights.

United Nations International Human Rights Instruments. Compilation of general comments and general recommendations adopted by human rights treaty bodies (HRI/GEN/1/Rev.6. 12 May 2003).

United Nations Millennium Declaration Resolution adopted by the General Assembly at its 55th session (A/55/L.2. 18 September 2000).

Contributor: Virginia Bras Gomes

EDUCATION, THE RIGHT TO

A Constitutional Court determines that pregnant girls should not be punished and diverted from regular education; a movement of millions forces a constitutional amendment to guarantee the right to education; two decades of debt-induced charging for primary education are reversed (www.right-to-education.org). The realisation of the right to education requires action, oversight and commitment.

As the gateway from poverty to prosperity, from exclusion to inclusion and from exploitation to emancipation, the right to education includes civil and political as well as **ECONOMIC, SOCIAL** and **CULTURAL RIGHTS** aspects. In translating the **UNIVERSAL DECLARATION ON HUMAN RIGHTS** into binding human rights treaties, the right to education was included in both International Covenants of 1966 (See: **THE INTERNATIONAL COVENANT ON CIVIL AND POLITICAL RIGHTS AND THE INTERNATIONAL COVENANT ON ECONOMIC SOCIAL AND CULTURAL RIGHTS**). Civil and political rights aspects include the freedom of parents to ensure the education of their children according to their religious or philosophical convictions; economic, social and cultural rights aspects include the role of education in the preservation of minority languages and culture, and the right to an education from which one may draw benefit (See: **MINORITY RIGHTS; LANGUAGE RIGHTS**).

The realisation of the right to education thus depends on an interdependent approach to implementing human rights obligations. It will be compromised where **FREEDOM OF ASSOCIATION** and rights to collective bargaining of teachers are ignored – how can teachers be expected to uphold the rights of children in the classroom where their own right to a decent standard of living and labour

Education © LWA-Dann Tardif/CORBIS

rights' guarantees are violated? Where **FREEDOM OF EXPRESSION** of both teachers and students is not safeguarded to ensure that rights abuses in education are exposed by those most affected and that education remains free of indoctrination?

Education is also an enabling right, in that higher levels of education permit greater political participation, **HEALTH**, employment and **EQUALITY**. The full realisation of the right to health, for example, will be greatly facilitated by the inclusion of basic education for the avoidance of preventable diseases. The **CONVENTION ON THE RIGHTS OF THE CHILD** includes in Article 24 the right to education for health and the Committee requires states to report on measures taken to realise this obligation, not least in the inclusion of sex and sexuality education in the curriculum.

The International Labour Organisation recognises the essential link between the right to education and the elimination of child labour. According to the 138th ILO Convention of 1973 the age of completion of compulsory education should be the same as the minimum age for employment and should not be below 15 (Melchiorre, 2004). Where

this is not the case, the effectiveness of guarantees of compulsory education will be questionable where children may be involved contemporaneously in full time employment. Equally, where children may not legally be employed for some years after the completion of compulsory education, economic exigencies will make them vulnerable to economic exploitation.

A broad understanding of the role of the right to education, at the crossroads of the International Covenant on Civil and Political Rights and the International Covenant on Economic Social and Cultural Rights, led to the development of a 4-A scheme of governmental obligations under the right to education: to ensure that education is available, accessible, acceptable and adaptable (Committee on Economic, Social and Cultural Rights, General Comment No. 13). According to this framework the government, as the 'provider of last resort' should ensure that education is acceptable according to human rights principles, that it adapts to help realise them (and adapts to the individual) and that no barriers (real or metaphorical) block access and completion.

The right to education has been recognised in international jurisprudence since at least the Universal Declaration of Human Rights in 1948 (Article 26). The development of the two Covenants in the following 20 years saw the inclusion of the right to education in both the International Covenant on Civil and Political Rights (Article 18) and the International Covenant on Economic, Social and Cultural Rights (Articles 13 and 14). It has since been included in a range of international and regional human rights treaties, including the Convention on the Rights of the Child, to which the entire world except the USA and Somalia is party. In addition, at least 142 countries have included a guarantee of the right to education in their constitutions (www.right-to-education.org).

Freedom of education guarantees focus on parents' rights to ensure their children's education according to their philosophical and/or religious convictions (The International Covenant on Civil and Political Rights Article 18 and Article 2 of the First Protocol to the EUROPEAN CONVENTION ON HUMAN RIGHTS) and to ensure pluralism in education, essential for the realisation of minority rights. More recent instruments have focused on children's rights in education (CRC) which include the civil rights' guarantees of education which is in keeping with the child's identity (as a member of a minority; as an indigenous girl with a language other than the official language as her first language) and human dignity (including freedom from inhuman and degrading treatment in disciplinary measures used in the school), as well as the right to education of children in specific circumstances (children of migrant workers, refugee or asylum-seeking children). International criminal law has equally prohibited attacks on educational establishments in times of armed conflict, thus furthering the right to education at such times (See: HUMANITARIAN LAW AND HUMAN RIGHTS IN CONFLICT and HUMAN RIGHTS BETWEEN WAR AND PEACE). Indeed, three individuals have been successfully prosecuted in the International Criminal Tribunal for the Former Yugoslavia for, inter alia, the war crime of attacks against educational institutions (See: *The Prosecutor v Tihomir Blaskic* IT-95-14).

Key formulations vary little and all place priority on the realisation of the right to free and compulsory primary education. This obligation is of immediate effect and states which have not yet achieved free and compulsory education must develop plans and a time frame to do so. Secondary and higher education should be made available and accessible progressively, including in particular the introdution of free education. This standard is currently under threat, with an increasing tendency to discuss higher and even secondary education as services and therefore chargeable. The recent university reforms in the United Kingdom and the reaction of the Committee on Economic, Social and Cultural Rights to them (United Kingdom of Great Britain and Northern Ireland, ICESCR, E/2003/22 (2002) 40 at paragraphs 225 and 244), are a case in point. More generally, the General Agreement on Trade in Services has led some to question whether the world is moving towards the progressive liberalisation of trade in education services or the progressive realisation of the right to education (Annual Report of the Special Rapporteur on the right to education, UN Doc. E/CN.4/2002/60, paragraphs 19-21).

Widespread codification of the right to education has not uniformly led to its realisation. Even its most fundamental element, free and compulsory primary education for all children, is not yet realised in at least 91 countries (Tomaševski, 2003b). In Europe there are still a disproportionate number of Roma children being diverted into special schools for the physically and mentally handicapped and inclusive education remains a distant dream, even 50-odd years after the most famous civil liberties decision in education, where the US Supreme court found that 'Separate educational facilities are inherently unequal' (*Brown v Board of Education of Topeka* 347 US 483 (1954)).

WEBSITE

www.right-to-education.org, Right to Education Project

Further Reading

Committee on Economic, Social and Cultural Rights, General Comment No. 13, 'The right to education', UN Doc. E/C.12/1999/10.

Hammarberg, T. (1997) 'A School for Children with Rights', UNICEF Innocenti Lectures Series, Florence.

Melchiorre, A. (2004) 'At What Age … are school children employed, married and taken to court?', Right to Education Project, UNESCO-IBE.

Tomaševski, K. (2003a) *Education Denied*, London: Zed.

Tomaševski, K. (2003b) School fees as hindrance to universalising primary education: background study for the Education for All Global Monitoring Report 2003/4, UNESCO, 2003, www.efareport.unesco.org

Contributor: Duncan Wilson

EQUALITY AND HUMAN RIGHTS

The idea of equality is widely endorsed in contemporary societies and is often mentioned in legislation and constitutions as well as in such international documents as the **UNIVERSAL DECLARATION OF HUMAN RIGHTS**. However, this apparent consensus obscures the fact that there are several different interpretations or conceptions of equality. One way of classifying these conceptions is under the headings of basic equality, liberal egalitarianism and equality of condition.

Basic equality is the cornerstone of all egalitarian thinking: the idea that at some very basic level all human beings have equal worth and importance and are therefore equally worthy of concern and respect. It is not easy to explain quite what these ideas amount to, since many of the people who claim to hold them defend a wide range of other inequalities, including the view that some people deserve more concern and respect than others. Perhaps what is really involved in basic equality is the idea that every human being deserves some basic minimum of concern and respect, placing at least some limits on what it is to treat someone as a human being. The minimum standards involved in the idea of basic equality include prohibitions against inhuman and degrading treatment, protection against blatant violence and at least some commitment to satisfying people's most basic **NEEDS**.

A key assumption of liberal egalitarianism is that there will always be major inequalities between people in their status, resources, work and power. The role of the idea of equality is to provide a fair basis for managing these inequalities, by strengthening the minimum to which everyone is entitled and by using equality of opportunity to regulate the competition for advantage. Liberal egalitarians vary in both these respects. For some, the minimum to which all should be entitled barely differs from basic equality. Others have a more generous idea of the minimum, for example by using an expanded idea of what counts as a basic need or by defining **POVERTY** in relation to the normal activities of a particular society. The most ambitious liberal principle is Rawls's 'difference principle', which states that 'social and economic inequalities' should work 'to the greatest benefit of the least advantaged' members of society.

Liberal equality of opportunity means that people should in some sense have an equal chance to compete for social advantages. This principle has two major interpretations. The first, non-**DISCRIMINATION** or 'formal' equal opportunity, is classically expressed in the French Declaration of the Rights of Man

© R.K.M. Smith

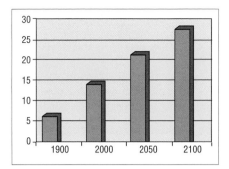

This illustrates and projects the percentage of the population of the world aged over 60. (Statistics from the UN Department of Economic and Social Affairs, Population Division)

(1789) as the principle that all citizens 'are equally eligible for all positions, posts and public employments in accordance with their abilities' (Article 6). A stronger form of equal opportunity insists that people should not be advantaged or hampered by their social background and that their prospects in life should depend entirely on their own effort and abilities. Rawls calls this principle 'fair equal opportunity'.

Liberal egalitarianism is based on the assumption that many major inequalities are inevitable and that our task is to make them fair. The idea of what can be called 'equality of condition' sets out a much more ambitious aim: to eliminate major inequalities or at least massively to reduce the current scale of inequality. The key to this much more ambitious agenda is to recognise that inequality is rooted in changing and changeable social structures and particularly in structures of domination and oppression. These structures create, and continually reproduce, the inequalities that liberal egalitarians see as inevitable. But since social structures have changed in the past, it is at least conceivable that they could be deliberately changed in the future.

Discussions of equality sometimes contrast the liberal idea of equality of opportunity with the idea of 'equality of outcome'. Although the distinction is a good shorthand account of the difference between liberal egalitarianism and equality of condition, it can be misleading, since equality of condition is also concerned with people having a wide range of choices, not with their all ending up the same. The difference is in how equal opportunity is understood. Liberal equal opportunity is about fairness in the competition for advantage. It implies that there will be winners and losers, people who do well and people who do badly. An 'opportunity' in this context is the right to compete, not the right to choose among alternatives of similar worth.

Equality of condition is about opportunities in this stronger sense, about enabling and empowering people to exercise what might be called real choices among real options. Inevitably equality in these fields of choice would lead to different outcomes, which could have profound effects on people's lives: wasting money on useless things, falling in love with the wrong person, choosing an occupation that doesn't suit. But these outcomes, precisely because they would take place in a context of continuing equality in the overall conditions of people's lives, would not undermine people's roughly similar prospects for making further choices.

Equality of condition would require much more equality in the distribution of material resources, but would allow for inequalities that reflect people's different needs. It is also concerned with promoting relations of equal respect and recognition, with enabling people to enter into relations of love, care and solidarity, with democratising power relations, and with providing working and learning opportunities that people find satisfying and fulfilling.

The idea of human rights is a fundamentally egalitarian one, resting as it does on the Universal Declaration's assertion that 'all human beings are born free and equal in dignity and rights' (Article 1). In terms of the three conceptions of equality outlined above, the human rights agenda clearly encompasses basic equality. It is also closely connected to liberal egalitarianism because it is primarily concerned with the setting of minimum standards and promoting key principles of non-discrimination. Some of the principles proclaimed by liberal egalitarians are more demanding than those included in the major human rights documents. For example, Rawls's principle of fair equal opportunity and his difference principle are both stronger than anything found in the Universal Declaration or the **EUROPEAN**

CONVENTION. But liberal egalitarians and human rights activists have broadly similar aims. The protection of human rights also forms part of the idea of equality of condition. However, equality of condition sets out a much more ambitious agenda than is found in human rights documents.

It is plausible to think of the protection of human rights as a step on the way to the more demanding principles found in some forms of liberal egalitarianism and in equality of condition, since human rights are concerned with the most basic and urgent of egalitarian aims. However, it can be argued that it is precisely the existence of substantial inequalities of condition that has enabled the privileged to violate the human rights of others. Even in liberal democracies, severe inequalities of status, resources and power mean that the human rights of marginalised groups can be violated with impunity by dominant majorities. For this reason, the struggle for human rights seems to entail a broader struggle for greater equality of condition.

Further Reading

Baker, John, Lynch, Kathleen, Cantillon, Sara and Walsh, Judy (2004) *Equality: From Theory to Action*, Basingstoke: Palgrave Macmillan.

Clayton, Matthew and Williams, Andrew (eds) (2002) *The Ideal of Equality*, Basingstoke: Palgrave Macmillan.

Rawls, John (1971) *A Theory of Justice*, Oxford: Oxford University Press.

Contributor: John Baker

ETHICAL FOREIGN POLICY AND HUMAN RIGHTS

All states have an 'ethical' foreign policy. In many parts of the world, particularly in liberal democratic societies, the ethical dimension of foreign policy is openly defended. Elsewhere, while the rhetorical appeal to ethical principles may be less in evidence, foreign policy is still regarded as a tool to promote certain kinds of values, such as security or prosperity or influence. To put the point boldly, ethics cannot simply be cut out of the foreign policy portfolio of modern states.

Why, then, is the idea of an ethical foreign policy so contested both in theory and in practice? The discussion below focuses on these two dimensions: the conceptual part draws on arguments from the field of international relations and the practical part links to the attempt by the UK Labour Governments (1997–2001 and 2001 onwards) to promote an ethical dimension in their foreign policy.

According to realism, the dominant theory of international relations, conventional moral values should not exert an influence over the high decisions of statecraft. The task for responsible leadership is to promote the interests of the state, whether this is expressed through various practices, such as defence, diplomacy, alliance politics, the balance of power, and the preparedness to use force in the last resort. Let us characterise this realist approach to ethics and foreign policy in terms of the primacy of the national interest.

There is an important assumption underlying this realist argument: interests are fixed and remain constant over time. Values, however, are determined by political parties and the process of argumentation in domestic society. The implication here is that whichever ideology triumphs within domestic society, the course of foreign policy ought to remain unaltered. Realists would argue that US foreign policy during the cold war illustrated exactly this tendency. Republican and Democratic presidents all pursued core US national interests of containing the Soviet threat, promoting European integration, maintaining hemispherical dominance in the Americas and ensuring favourable access to key energy sources in the Middle East. These priorities ensured that ethical values to do with human rights were seen either as being peripheral or indeed as a barrier to achieving the kind of position in the international system that maximised US security and economic interests.

What is the source of this division between politics inside the state and policy formulation for outside state boundaries? According to realists, this distinction results from the nature of the international system which they characterise as being 'anarchic'. This term is not equated with chaos, as it often is in everyday usage; instead, it is used to denote the absence of rule. What is meant here is that in domestic orders we have a government to legislate and implement rules, whereas in the international order there is no equivalent enforcer.

Before moving to consider the limitations of the realist viewpoint, it is perhaps worth thinking through ways in which this perspective resonates with people's everyday political experience. It is instructive to recall at this point one of the most famous campaign quotations in recent political history. In the run-up to the 1994 US presidential election campaign, the on-message slogan of William Jefferson Clinton's team was 'it's the economy, stupid'. In other words, the perceived weakness of President George Bush's administration was that it was too preoccupied with foreign policy questions. Broadening the point still further, political debates in the UK media about the European Union suggest that realists are right to emphasise the strength of feeling aroused by perceived threats to the national interest.

The one persistent theoretical alternative to the realist idea of the primacy of the national interest is the Liberal and Social Democratic notion of internationalism. While there are different versions of this doctrine, at its core internationalism maintains that states are more likely to be secure if they agree to cooperate with others and act in ways that strengthen global justice (See: COSMOPOLITANISM AND HUMAN RIGHTS). At a minimum, an internationalist foreign policy requires states to comply with international rules on a variety of issues, from arms control to environmental protection. More maximally, internationalism means states have a responsibility to promote and protect human rights everywhere. In practice, this means pursuing greater justice through redistributive mechanisms such as development aid and fairer terms of trade. Ethical states also have a duty to militarily defend the rights of non-citizens by providing a secure environment in which aid agencies can operate, or in cases of genocide or ethnic cleansing, internationalism may require the waging of war (so-called humanitarian intervention, see HUMANITARIAN INTERVENTIONS).

In the post-cold war period, there have been a number of cases where Western states have used armed force for humanitarian purposes. Such a measure has generally been welcomed if the action has received the consent of the UN Security Council and if it has been with the permission of the host government. Such was the case in September 1999 when an Australian-led military force intervened in East Timor to impose order following the ballot in which the overwhelming majority of East Timorese voted for independence from Indonesia. There have been other cases, notably Kosovo, where intervention has taken place without explicit UN authorisation, leading to questions about whether in fact such actions ought to be permitted in cases where there is a humanitarian emergency but no collective agreement among the permanent members of the UN Security Council (See also: AFTERWORD: GLOBALISATION WITH A HUMAN FACE).

Internationalists argue that we have a duty to protect human rights and we ought to be morally ashamed when we fail to 'do something'. The tragic example here is the international community's failure to intervene to halt the genocide in Rwanda. According to military experts on the ground, a rapid deployment of a few thousand well-armed troops might have saved the lives of hundreds of thousands civilians. Realists do not believe it is meaningful to talk of duties in this way: first and foremost, the responsibility of governments is to provide for the security and the prosperity of their citizens. Well-intended interventions overseas can have adverse consequences in terms both of risking soldiers' lives and compromising the national security of the state in question by weakening its defence capability.

While the vexed issue of humanitarian war often dominates debates about ethics and foreign policy, it is important to recognise that this is an issue for only a minority of states which have the capacity to project military power around the world. Many small states, such as Norway and the Netherlands, conceive of promoting humanitarian values in non-militaristic ways. Here it is important to note the role that culture plays in shaping political outcomes. In the words of the founding constitution of the United Nations Educational, Scientific and Cultural Organization, 'since war begins in the minds of men (sic), it is in the minds of men that the defences of peace must be constructed.'

An explicit link between ethics, foreign policy and human rights was made by UK Foreign Secretary Robin Cook in his 'mission statement' of 12 May 1997. In an evocative phrase, Cook claimed that 'the Labour government does not accept that political values can be left behind when we check in our passports to travel on diplomatic business'. He went on to add that the government 'would put human rights at the heart of our foreign policy'. This claim was greeted with disdain in parts of the media, as though having an 'ethical dimension' was particularly new. As noted above, all foreign policies are driven by moral purposes: what set the Labour government apart from its predecessors was the centrality accorded to human rights.

From 1997 to the beginning of 1999 the government's claim to have an ethical foreign policy was favourably received. The architects of the policy were regularly praised for their courage and many of their substantive policy commitments were thought to have enhanced a human rights agenda, including the formation of a Department for International Development (DFID), significant increases to the aid budget and the successful humanitarian intervention in Sierra Leone where the usual menu of interests were negligible. As the then Amnesty International Director put it, the government had a good record on human rights 'in many respects'. To this he bracketed one qualification: the record had been marred by arms sales to regimes with bad human rights records.

This last point illustrates a perennial dilemma for states which seek to pursue an internationalist foreign policy. The sale of British-made jets to Indonesia did significant harm to the policy's credentials. On 11 September 1999, Cook announced that the government had suspended the planned sale of nine Hawk trainer/ground-attack jets. Unfortunately this came far too late – what the Labour government should have done on arrival in office was to cancel the order for the Hawks. Governments which are 'gross violators' of human rights should be denied arms irrespective of their declared usage. The inescapable conclusion is that Britain failed to act as an ethical state in its relations with Indonesia because it placed selfish economic advantage above human rights concerns.

The other major dilemma associated with both Blair governments has been the use of force for humanitarian ends. At the declaratory level, it is clear that the government has believed itself to be fighting a humanitarian war. During the campaign in Kosovo, in April 1999, the Prime Minister boldly argued: 'We need to enter a new millennium where dictators know that they cannot get away with ethnic cleansing or repress their people with impunity. We are fighting not for territory but for values. For a new internationalism where the brutal repression of ethnic groups will not be tolerated.' In practice, the brutal repression of ethnic groups has been tolerated, particularly when it has occurred inside the borders of great powers such as China and Russia.

The experience of the UK governments under Tony Blair nicely illustrates a number of practical problems associated with trying to pursue an internationalist foreign policy. One is the problem of double standards. While it may be pragmatic to treat China's abuse of Tibetans differently to Serbia's abuse of Kosovars, the reasoning behind it runs counter to most people's understanding of what constitutes principled action. The second is the observation that moral values in world politics often conflict. To intervene is a moral value, so is non-intervention; self-defence is a moral value, so is a prohibition on the sale of certain categories of weapons. Such ambiguities reflect in part the tension between the world of states where power and authority reside and the parallel development of a global human rights culture which is an expression of our sentiments and aspirations.

Further Reading

Erskine, Toni (ed.) (2003) *Can Institutions Have Responsibilities? Collective Moral Agency and International Relations*, Basingstoke: Palgrave Macmillan.

Hill, Christopher (2003) *The Changing Politics of Foreign Policy*, Basingstoke: Palgrave Macmillan.

Smith, Karen E. and Light, Margot (eds) (2001) *Ethics and Foreign Policy*, Cambridge: CUP.

Wheeler, Nicholas J. and Dunne, Tim (2004) 'Moral Britannia? Evaluating the Ethical Dimension in Labour's Foreign Policy', *Foreign Policy Centre: Global Thinking Essay Series*, April.

Wheeler, Nicholas J. and Dunne, Tim (1998) 'Good International Citizenship: A Third Way for British Foreign Policy' in *International Affairs* 74.4 pp. 847–870.

Contributor: Tim Dunne

THE EUROPEAN CONVENTION ON HUMAN RIGHTS

The European Convention on Human Rights is often heralded as the greatest achievement of the **COUNCIL OF EUROPE**. It was signed in 1950, two years after the proclamation of the **UNIVERSAL DECLARATION OF HUMAN RIGHTS** by the United Nations. The Convention possessed over the Declaration the advantage of creating an international mechanism of enforcement. Not surprisingly it did not seek to protect as many rights as its UN counterpart. It came into force in 1953, following ratification by ten states. Forty-five states were party to it in 2004. It has inspired the **REGIONAL SYSTEMS** of human rights protection set up on the American and African continents.

The Convention originally provided for 13 civil and political rights: the rights to life (Article 2), not to be submitted to torture, cruel or inhuman treatment or punishment (Article 3), not to be enslaved (Article 4), to remain free (Article 5), to fair trial (Article 6), not to be punished without law (Article 7), to privacy and family life (Article 8), to freedom of religion and thought (Article 9), to freedom of expression (Article 10), to freedom of association (Article 11), to marry (Article 12), to a national remedy (Article 13) and to non-discrimination in the enjoyment of the above rights (Article 14).

Protocols to the Convention have added further rights. Protocol no. 1 (signed in 1952, in force since 1954) provides for the rights to peaceful enjoyment of possessions, education and free elections; Protocol no. 4 (1963, 1968) for the rights not to be imprisoned for failure to fulfil a contractual obligation, to freedom of movement and residence, not to be deported from one's own state and not to be collectively expelled; Protocol no. 6 (1983, 1985) concerns the abolition of the death penalty, especially in peacetime; Protocol no. 7 (1984, 1988) deals further with the expulsion of aliens, with review of criminal conviction and sentence, compensation for miscarriages of justice, the right not to be tried twice for the same offence and equality of rights between spouses; Protocol no. 12 (2000, not in force at time time of writing) aims to create a freestanding right to non-discrimination; Protocol no. 13 (2002, 2003) provides for the elimination of the death penalty in all circumstances. These protocols are binding on the states that have ratified them. (Those protocols omitted from the list concern purely procedural issues.)

Article 15 of the Convention makes it possible for a state to derogate from its obligations under the Convention in time of 'public emergency threatening the life of the nation'. Some rights, however, are not derogable, namely those conferred by Article 2 in peacetime and by Articles 3, 4 (1) and 7 of the Convention. Most rights are explicitly subjected to exceptions. For example, Article 2 provides that the right to life is not contravened when the authorities resort to a use of force that is 'no more than absolutely necessary', including in order to effect a lawful arrest or for the purpose of quelling a riot. Articles 8 to 11 contain escape clauses, but for state interference with the right guaranteed by the Convention to be legal, it must 1) be provided by law, 2) pursue an aim that is specifically listed in the relevant provision and 3) be 'necessary in a democratic society'.

The concrete application of the substantive provisions of the Convention has led the **EUROPEAN COURT OF HUMAN RIGHTS** to identify general principles of interpretation, including:

- effectiveness, which rests on the idea that the Convention guarantees rights which are 'practical and effective' rather than 'theoretical and illusory';
- evolutive interpretation, which regards the Convention as a 'living instrument', adaptable to new realities;
- the controversial doctrine of the margin of appreciation, which posits that states are in principle better placed than the Court to assess what local circumstances require when the Convention provides for rights that can be curtailed;
- proportionality, which demands that state interference with a right guaranteed by the Convention, even when allowed, must pursue a legitimate aim, be suitable for its purpose, be strictly necessary and justified overall.

The enforcement mechanism provided by the Convention in 1950 was revolutionary in that an international court could be called upon to examine petitions emanating from states but also from individuals. The Strasbourg institutions had registered 20 inter-state applications in 13 cases and 133,158 individual petitions by 31 December 2003.

The Convention originally provided for the establishment of a European Commission of Human Rights and a European Court of Human Rights. This happened in 1959. The Committee of Ministers, created by the Statute of the Council of Europe, also played a role under the Convention. These institutions sat, part-time, at Strasbourg. In the 1980s, it became clear that the exponential increase of individual petitions necessitated a thorough procedural reform. Protocol no. 11 (signed in 1994 and in force since 1998) led to the demise of the Commission and the establishment of a permanent Court. The jurisdiction of the Court and the right of individual petition are automatic under Protocol no. 11. Beforehand, each had depended on a specific declaration by the defendant state.

The defunct Commission was a body of independent legal experts. Its first function, fulfilled by the new Court since November 1998, was to act as a filtering body. Most decisions of inadmissibility were and are taken by unanimous 'Committees of Threes', who are satisfied that the case does not require further examination. If not stopped initially, a case is declared admissible or inadmissible by a Chamber, which can act by majority. The great majority of applications (around 80 per cent today, more in the past) fail to pass the admissibility stage, mostly on the ground that they are 'manifestly ill-founded' or that national remedies have not been exhausted, contrary to the principle of 'subsidiarity'. Only cases that are declared admissible can be examined on their merits. In the past, failing a 'friendly settlement' between the parties, the Commission, having established the facts, expressed a reasoned opinion on whether there had been a breach of the Convention. Either the Court or the Committee of Ministers took the final decision. The Court is now the sole body which decides upon a case. It deals with admissibility and merits separately (except in repetitive cases about excessive length of judicial procedure).

The Court is competent to rule as to whether the defendant state has violated the Convention. By the end of 2003 it had reached verdicts of violation in 2853 cases, about half of which involved Article 6 (fair trial) issues. The Court can also award a 'just [financial] satisfaction' to the applicant. Judgments are normally adopted by a Chamber (now of seven judges); by a Grand Chamber (the Plenary Court until 1993) in relinquished or, since Protocol 11, referred cases. The 'national judge' sits ex officio – every state party to the Convention has one judge. Judgments are commonly adopted by majority and can include 'separate opinions'. The state must do whatever is necessary to bring its practice and/or legislation into line with the Convention's requirements. The supervision of the execution of the judgments of the Court is the responsibility of the Committee of Ministers.

Even before Protocol no. 11 came into force, it was widely felt that the accession to the Convention of Eastern and Central European countries following the collapse of communism would necessitate a 'reform of the reform'. Protocol no. 14 was signed in May 2004. Once in force, it will be possible for applications to be declared inadmissible by one-judge formations, including on the new criterion that 'the applicant has not suffered a significant disadvantage'.

The Convention system is often presented as a model for the rest of the world to follow. This is understandable given its overall efficiency and its contribution to entrenching individual rights. However, there is no place for complacency. Firstly, many petitions are dismissed. Secondly, the success of the system may be due less to its intrinsic qualities than to the privileged conditions prevailing in Europe. Thirdly, the system faces new challenges, including having to deal with situations where the rule of law is not established and being confronted with the development of a human rights agenda in the European Union context. Fourthly, the Convention system is not immune from the major critiques of human rights – including by **MARXISTS**, **UTILITARIANS**, **FEMINISTS** and cultural relativists (See: **PLURALIST UNIVERSALISM**). If one can accept that human rights are a good idea, especially in a world which is largely state-based, they cannot be expected to achieve in practice the utopia they seem to promise. Their practical translation, including in the European Convention system, is therefore by nature problematic.

Further reading

Janis, Mark, Kay, Richard and Bradley, Anthony (2000) *European Human Rights Law: Text and Materials*, Oxford: Oxford University Press.

Leach, Philip (2001) *Taking a Case to the European Court of Human Rights*, London: Blackstone.

Dijk, P. van and Hoof, G.J.H van (1998) *Theory and Practice of the European Convention on Human Rights*, The Hague: Kluwer.

Contributor: Marie-Bénédicte Dembour

THE EUROPEAN COURT OF HUMAN RIGHTS

The Court (present seat in Strasbourg, France) was established in virtue of Article 19 of the European Convention on Human Rights, 1958. It came into existence on 21 January 1959 when eight signatories subscribed a declaration acknowledging the compulsory jurisdiction of the Court. All the democratic states in Europe (45 at the time of writing) have submitted to its jurisdiction. Protocol no. 11 of the Convention, effective from 1 November 1998, transformed the Court radically, from part-time to full-time. It also abolished the European Commission of Human Rights. The function of the Court is 'to ensure the observance of the engagements undertaken' by the contracting parties relating to the Convention and its protocols.

Broadly, the jurisdiction of the Court subdivides into three: inter-state cases, applications by individuals against contracting states, and advisory opinions in accordance with Protocol No. 2. Numerically, individual applications outnumber by far inter-state cases (12 so far) and advisory opinions (only one). The Court consists of a number of judges equal to that of the contracting parties to the Convention. The judges, elected for a six-year term, perform their duties in an individual capacity and have no institutional or other ties

with the state in respect of which they have been elected. The Convention requires judges to be of high moral character and to possess qualifications for high judicial office or be jurisconsults of recognised competence. Election of judges to the Court is by a majority vote in the Parliamentary Assembly of the Council of Europe, after each contracting state has submitted a list of three candidates. This procedure is followed to fill casual vacancies, to elect new judges after the expiry of their term of office and on accession of new states to the Convention. Judges retire at the age of 70, but continue to hold office until replaced and to deal with cases they already have under consideration.

To assure the independence of the Court, judges are barred from participating in any activity incompatible with independence and impartiality; a judge enjoys temporal security of tenure and may be dismissed from office only if the other judges decide, by a two-thirds majority, that he or she has ceased to fulfil the required conditions. Membership of the Court entitles judges to the privileges and immunities provided for by Article 4 of the Statute of the **COUNCIL OF EUROPE** and in agreements made thereunder. The Plenary Court consists of an assembly of all the judges. It has no jurisdictional functions but deals with the election of the president, vice-presidents, registrar and deputy registrar, and with administrative matters, discipline, working methods, reforms, the establishment of Chambers and the adoption of the Rules of Court.

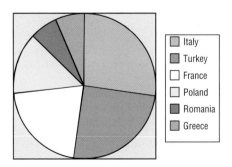

Percentage of total cases brought against those states with the highest number of judgements in 2003.
(Information from the 2003 Council of Europe Survey of Activities)

To perform its jurisdictional functions, the Court sits in Committees of three judges, Chambers of seven judges and a Grand Chamber of 17 judges. On registration, individual applications are assigned to a judge rapporteur. If he or she believes that the claim cannot be proceeded with, they refer it to a Committee of three judges, which may, by unanimous vote, declare it inadmissible or strike it out of the list of cases. The decision is final. Referral to a Committee happens in cases incompatible *ratione materiae, ratione temporis* or *ratione personae*, or that cannot be proceeded with on formal grounds, such as non-exhaustion of domestic remedies, lapse of six months from the last internal decision complained of, anonymity, substantial identity with a matter already submitted to the Court or with another procedure of international investigation. If, on the other hand, the judge rapporteur is of the opinion that the application is not such as to fall under the competence of a Committee, he or she refers it to a Chamber of the Court which, unless it deems the application inadmissible, communicates it to the respondent government for its observations. The Chamber may opt to relinquish jurisdiction in favour of the Grand Chamber in cases which raise serious questions of interpretation or when it feels it ought to depart from previous case law. Relinquishment is possible only with the consent of all parties. In all other cases the Chamber deliberates and delivers judgment on admissibility and merits. The judge elected in respect of the respondent state sits *ex officio* in the Chamber and the Grand Chamber.

The Grand Chamber was charged with determining cases still pending from the former Court before the 1998 reforms; moreover it hears cases in which the Chambers have relinquished jurisdiction and cases exceptionally referred to it by either of the parties within three months from the judgement of a Chamber. A panel of five judges decides whether to accept the referral on grounds that the case raises serious questions of interpretation and application of the Convention or a serious issue of general importance. The Committee of Ministers may, by majority vote, request the Court to give advisory opinions on legal questions concerning the interpretation of the Convention, provided that the opinion would not refer to the content and scope of fundamental rights which the Court might have to consider in consequence of proceedings that could be instituted in accordance with the Convention. Rules applicable to judgments about majority, reasons and separate opinions apply to advisory opinions which are communicated to the Committee of Ministers.

The adjudicatory mechanism of the Court may be set in motion in one of three ways: by any person, non-governmental organisation or group of individuals alleging to be victims of a breach of a substantive right or rights enunciated by the Convention, attributable to a contracting party. The latter, on their part, undertake not to hinder the effective exercise of this right. Again, any contracting party may sue another contracting party before the Court for any alleged breach of the Convention (inter-state cases); thirdly, the Committee of Ministers of the Council of Europe may request advisory opinions from the Court.

The powers of the Court include ordering interim measures, striking out an application from the list when it is of the opinion that an applicant does not intend to pursue the claim, or that the matter has been resolved, or that it is no longer justified to continue with the examination. The Court may later return to the examination of the application if 'respect for human rights' so requires and may restore a case to the lists if in its view circumstances justify such a course. After a preliminary finding of admissibility, the Court pursues the examination of the case together with representatives of the parties and undertakes any investigation it deems necessary. The contracting states are bound to furnish the Court with all necessary facilities for this purpose. In confidential proceedings the Court places itself at the disposal of the parties with a view to securing a friendly settlement and in the process monitoring that any agreement respects human rights.

The Convention requires that hearings, save in exceptional circumstances, be public. In practice, however, by far the largest number of cases is dealt with *in camera* following written pleadings. All documents in the registry are public unless the president decides otherwise.

The judgments of the Grand Chamber are final. Those of a Chamber become final within three months of delivery if no reference to

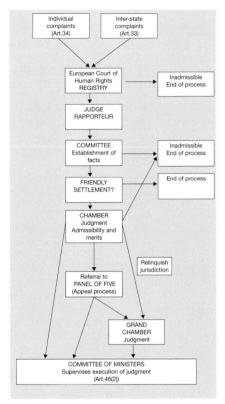

Procedure for complaints before the European Court of Human Rights. © R. K. M. Smith

the respondent state to pay material and/or moral damages and those legal costs incurred in the domestic fora to prevent or redress the violation and those related to the Strasbourg proceedings. The Court has, so far, held it has no competence to order specific measures of *restitutio in integrum*, the reopening of proceedings or the repeal of offending laws or administrative practices. It is the Committee of Ministers which oversees that states align their laws and practices with the findings of the Court or put in place individual measures to redress the violation found.

The Court's budget is funded by the Council of Europe. A registry assists judges in their functions. Central to this are the services rendered by the Court's jurists. The Court's activities have gathered irreversible momentum. In its early years few cases reached the Court and it seemed as if the Convention's protection system would fail. In the 1980s the trend was reversed and, since the 1990s, with the accession to the Convention of the former Soviet states, the Court is foundering under an intractable load. Today over 800 million people enjoy its protection in Europe, from the Atlantic to the Urals. It is now a victim of its own success, with inadequate structures and resources to cope with the daily flood of applications – 39,000 new ones in 2003 alone. While in the first 45 years, up to the reforms of 1998, the Court and the Commission had given a total of 38,389 judgments and decisions in all, the new single court has disposed of 61,633 cases in five years.

The situation is nearing breaking point and only radical rethinking can avoid a total collapse. Protocol no. 14, which aims to reform the European human rights protection mechanisms, is being debated with a sense of urgency and doom. Whether the proposed reforms go too far or not far enough remains to be seen.

The Court is now, for most intents and purposes, Europe's constitutional court, exercising a profound legal and moral authority on the democratic profile of the continent. Its landmark judgments have contributed forcefully in making human rights a tangible reality and in improving the face of democracy in Europe.

WEBSITE

www.echr.coe.int

the Grand Chamber has been made or when the panel of the Grand Chamber rejects the request for referral. Decisions on admissibility and merits record the reasons of the Court. Differently from some other international tribunals, judges who disagree with the conclusion or with the reasoning deliver separate opinions, dissenting or concurring. The Court may at a later stage, correct or clarify its decision. The contracting parties undertake to abide by the Court's final decision. The Committee of Ministers of the Council of Europe supervises its execution. In practice judgments enjoy an extremely high level of compliance.

When the Court rules on a violation of the Convention it affords, if necessary, just satisfaction to the injured party. Since its earliest days the Court has taken the view that just satisfaction shall consist only in a declaration that a violation has occurred and in orders on

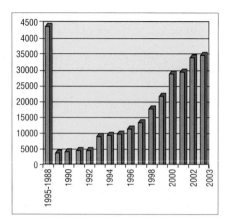

Number of applications lodged over the years. (Statistics from the 2003 Council of Europe Survey of Activities)

Further Reading

Gomien, Donna, Harris, David and Zwaak, Leo (1996) *Law and Practice of the European Convention on Human Rights and the European Social Charter*, Strasbourg: Council of Europe.

Harris, D.J., O'Boyle, M. and Warbrick, C. (1995) *Law of the European Convention of Human Rights*, London: Butterworths.

Kempees, Peter (1998) *A Systematic Guide to the Case-Law of the European Court of Human Rights* (three volumes), Leiden: Martinus Nijhoff.

van Dijk, P. and van Hoof, G.J.H. (1998) *Theory and Practice of the European Convention of Human Rights*, The Hague: Kluwer.

Contributor: Giovanni Bonello

THE EUROPEAN SOCIAL CHARTER

While the **EUROPEAN CONVENTION ON HUMAN RIGHTS** is concerned broadly with political rights (although there is no watertight division), the protection of **SOCIAL** and **ECONOMIC** rights has largely been the province of the European Social Charter (ESC), 1961, as revised. The ESC came into force on 26 February 1965 and the protection of social and economic rights within the purview of the **COUNCIL OF EUROPE** has undergone expansion, both in terms of the rights protected and the mechanisms for

enforcement, since that time. As is common in the case of social and economic rights, the ESC does not grant a right of individual petition to a person who claims to be the victim of a violation. Enforcement takes place via a system of supervision of state reports and while there is no equivalent of the individual right of petition to the **EUROPEAN COURT OF HUMAN RIGHTS** under the European Convention on Human Rights, a 1995 Additional Protocol aimed at improving the enforcement of the Charter provides for a system of collective complaints. The situation under the ESC is thus the reverse of Article 34 ECHR which does not admit of an *actio popularis*, requiring instead that an applicant should be a victim of a Convention violation.

The language of the ESC is very different from the language of the ECHR. In contrast with Article 1 ECHR which requires states to 'secure rights to everyone', the Charter provides in Part I that states accept 'as the aim of their policy, to be pursued by all appropriate means ... the attainment of conditions' in which the enumerated rights 'may be effectively realised'. There then follows a list of recognised rights. Part II ESC elaborates upon the nature of the contracting parties' obligations in relation to each of the rights set out. The focus of the instrument is on the nature of the state's obligations rather than the 'right'. To take one example, in relation to the right to just conditions of work (Article 2), the contracting parties undertake, *inter alia*, to provide for reasonable working hours, to provide a minimum of two weeks' paid holiday, to provide for additional holidays or reduced working hours where an employee is engaged in a dangerous or unhealthy occupation and to provide a weekly rest period to coincide with the day traditionally recognised as a rest day. Unlike the UN **INTERNATIONAL COVENANT ON ECONOMIC, SOCIAL AND CULTURAL RIGHTS** there is no reference to the extent of the state's obligation being tied to 'available resources' or steps being taken towards the 'progressive realisation' of the rights protected.

The ESC as originally formulated contains 19 rights, of which the following are the 'core' rights: the right to work (Article 1); the right to organise (Article 5) and bargain collectively (Article 6); the right to protection of health (Article 11); the right to social security

(Article 12); the right to social and medical assistance (Article 13); and the right of the family to social, legal and economic protection (Article 19). These rights are 'core' in the sense that Article 20 ESC requires states to consider themselves bound by at least five of them. In addition to the core articles a contracting party must undertake to consider itself bound by such number of articles or numbered paragraphs of Part II to ensure that it is bound by not less than 10 articles or 45 numbered paragraphs (Article 20 ESC).

In 1988 an Additional Protocol to reflect evolving perceptions of social and economic rights was opened for signature. It contains the following: the right to equal opportunities and equal treatment in employment without discrimination on the grounds of sex (Article 1); the right for workers to be informed and consulted within their undertaking (Article 2); the right for workers to take part in the determination of their working conditions (Article 3); and the right of elderly persons to social protection.

The Revised ESC was opened for signature in 1996 and came into force on 1 July 1999. It contains the rights set out in the original ESC plus those in the 1988 Protocol, together with a number of new rights, including the right to protection against poverty and social exclusion (Article 30) and the right to housing (Article 31). The Revised ESC exists in parallel with the original Charter and its protocols.

Following the formulation of the ECHR, the obligations undertaken within it and the ESC may be subject to such limitations as are prescribed by law and are necessary for the protection of the rights and freedoms of others or for the protection of public interest, national security, public health or morals. There is also the possibility of derogation in time of war or other public emergency (See: DEROGATIONS AND RESERVATIONS).

There is a significant difference between the ESC and the ECHR in terms of the scope of protection. The basic principle of the ESC is reciprocity between the contracting parties so that the guarantees in both the ESC and Revised ESC 'include foreigners only in so far as they are nationals of other Parties lawfully resident or working within the territory of the Party concerned'. There is thus a sharp cleavage between the reach of the ECHR ('everyone within the jurisdiction of the state') and the

ESC. The European Court of Human Rights has held that in relation to entitlement to emergency unemployment benefit, 'very weighty reasons would have to be put forward before the Court could regard a difference of treatment based exclusively on the ground of nationality as compatible with the Convention' (*Gaygusuz v Austria* (1997) 23 EHRR 364).

The contracting parties are required to submit a report every two years regarding the 'core' article obligations that they have undertaken. They report on other provisions every four years. These reports are examined by a Committee of Independent Experts 'who assess from a legal standpoint the compliance of national law and practice' with the ESC obligations (Article 2 of Protocol of 1991, substituting a new Article 24 ESC). The views of the Committee of Experts are then scrutinised by the Governmental Committee which selects on the basis of social, economic and other policy considerations the situations which should be the subject of recommendations to the relevant contracting parties (Article 4 of Protocol of 1991, substituting a new Article 27 ESC).

A significant step towards the greater protection of social and economic rights was taken in 1995 with the adoption of an Additional Protocol to the ESC providing for a system of collective complaints. This Protocol, which entered into force on 1 July 1998, is the subject of a burgeoning jurisprudence, which has breathed life into, and enhanced the 'legalisation' of, ESC rights. Complaints by individuals cannot be made, nor can a collective complaint relate to individual cases. Under this Protocol, the Committee of Experts has a new role of determining whether a complaint is admissible and, if so, determining the merits of such a complaint. This is a system of collective complaints, according to which four groups have *locus standi* under the Additional Protocol: international organisations of employers and trade unions that take part in meetings of the Governmental Committee; international non-governmental organisations that have consultative status with the Council of Europe and have been put on a list established for this purpose by the Governmental Committee; representative national organisations of employers and trade unions within the jurisdiction of the contracting parties; and representative national non-governmental organisations with particular competence in Charter matters, where their competence has been recognised by a contracting party making an optional declaration under the Protocol to this effect.

Where a complaint is made that a contracting party has not 'ensured the satisfactory application' of a Charter provision, the Committee of Experts will determine whether the complaint is admissible and then draw up a report describing the steps taken to examine the complaint and present its conclusions. The Committee of Ministers then adopts a resolution and where satisfied that the Charter has not been applied in a satisfactory manner will adopt a recommendation addressed to the relevant contracting party. The contracting party is then required to give information on the steps it has taken to redress the situation in its next biannual report.

It will be appreciated that unlike petitions to the European Court of Human Rights, determination of a complaint does not give rise to a legally binding decision, but that is not to underestimate the important 'soft law' contribution of the collective complaints mechanism to the progressive enhancement of ESC rights within the contracting parties.

The European Social Charter has undergone a process of 'revitalisation' since the late 1980s, with the introduction of revisions to the monitoring process and the introduction of new rights as well as the collective complaints procedure. Reports may be submitted several months late, but compliance is generally good. A glance at the Council of Europe website reveals that a significant number of collective complaints are being made so that the workload of the Committee of Experts is growing, as is the body of jurisprudence in relation to social and economic rights.

Further Reading

Gomien, D., Harris, D. and Zwaak, L. (1996) *Law and practice of the European Convention on Human Rights and the European Social Charter,* Strasbourg: Council of Europe Publishing.

Harris, D. 'The Council of Europe (II): (1999) The European Social Charter' in Hanski, R. and Suksi, M. (eds), *An Introduction to the Protection of Human Rights,* Turkn: Abo Akademi Institute for Human Rights.

'The Social Charter of the 21st Century' (1997) Colloquy organised by the Secretariat of the Council of Europe, Strasbourg: Council of Europe Publishing.

Contributor: Jane Wright

THE EUROPEAN UNION CHARTER OF FUNDAMENTAL RIGHTS

The text of the Charter of Fundamental Rights of the European Union was jointly proclaimed in December 2000 by three of its key institutions – the European Parliament, the Council of the European Union and the European Union. It represents a further step in a long process whereby efforts have been made to respond to concerns, particularly within member states, about the need for a human rights dimension to the law governing the Union. Recognition of the importance of such a dimension has grown as the scope for the capacity for the Union's activities to affect human rights has either increased or been appreciated. The Charter differs from other regional and global instruments in that it is not primarily directed to the member states of the organisation that generated it but to the institutions of the organisation itself, although those states are also meant to be addressees of it when they are implementing Union law.

The treaties that established the original European Communities did not contain a catalogue of human rights similar to the bills of rights often found in national constitutions, although certain provisions – such as those dealing with equal treatment and free movement of persons – embodied human rights elements. However, from the late 1960s the European Court of Justice began the development of what is now a substantial body of case law, in which it drew on the constitutions and international commitments of member states – most notably the **EUROPEAN CONVENTION ON HUMAN RIGHTS** – in elaborating human rights as part of the general principles of law that are supposed to govern the validity of measures adopted by the European institutions. This case law covers a wide range of human rights issues but, unlike a catalogue of rights, there is inevitably an ad hoc character to those which it identifies and thus this development has not assuaged the call for a more comprehensive approach.

In parallel to the development of this case law, acceptance of human rights norms – notably the European Convention and its right of individual petition – became a prerequisite for membership of the Communities. Furthermore, proposals were made for the Communities themselves to accede to the European Convention, a Community Charter on Fundamental Social Rights of Workers was adopted, human rights became an element of the Union's relations with non-member states and the obligation to respect fundamental rights, as guaranteed in the latter instrument and as derived from the constitutional traditions common to the member states, was imposed by the Maastricht Treaty on what had then become the Union. This last development endorsed and formalised the approach that had already been pursued by the European Court of Justice but the latter subsequently found, in a controversial ruling, that accession to the European Convention was not possible because the institutions had no power to enact rules on human rights or to conclude international conventions in this field.

With accession to the Convention apparently foreclosed unless there was an amendment to treaties on which the Union was based, the elaboration of a discrete instrument came to be seen as a way of making the overriding importance and relevance of human (or rather fundamental) rights more visible to the Union citizens. The Charter was drafted by a Convention of representatives of the member states, national parliaments, the European Parliament and the European Commission in a process that also sought to engage the participation of citizens and non-governmental organisations. Work on it was undertaken without any agreement as to its eventual status in the legal architecture of the Union but on the understanding that it might ultimately be incorporated into the treaties. Ultimately the Charter was adopted only in the form of a political declaration.

The Charter is the most comprehensive human rights instrument yet to be adopted at the regional or international level. It embodies both civil and political and economic and social rights for the first time since the **UNIVERSAL DECLARATION OF HUMAN RIGHTS**, but its coverage of them is more extensive. Moreover, it includes provisions directed at particular groups – such as children, the disabled and the elderly – that are more commonly found in instruments devoted solely to them than in general instruments. Furthermore it is unusual in having not only provisions dealing with both environmental and consumer protection but also requirements of good administration and access to official information. Only a few rights – dealing with accountability, diplomatic and consular protection, movement and voting – are restricted to citizens of the European Union. The language of some provisions has been shaped by the European Convention but in several instances there has also been an element of reformulation and updating, as well as a degree of elaboration. The link with the European Convention is further underlined by a requirement that rights in the Charter corresponding to the former instrument's provisions should have the same meaning and scope as them (Article 52(3)). However, there is no explicit requirement to consider the case law of the European Court of Human Rights and no comparable link is made to the other international human rights instruments from which Charter provisions have been derived, although a general reference is made to both the case law and the instruments in the preamble and there is an affirmation that the provisions will not restrict or adversely affect internationally or constitutionally guaranteed human rights (Article 53).

The Charter also differs from other instruments by its organisation of them into six thematic groupings – dignity, freedoms, equality, solidarity, citizens' rights and justice – which may help promote an understanding of their different character but could also point to different priorities influencing their interpretation. Unlike many civil and political rights instruments, there is no provision for **DEROGATION** in an emergency but there is undoubtedly scope for taking the measures required under the general limitations provision (Article 52(1)). However, its requirement that all limitations must have a legal basis, respect the essence of the right or freedom concerned, be proportionate and be necessary and genuinely meet objectives of general interest or protect the rights and freedoms of others is also an important guarantee against arbitrary action.

Although not given any formal legal status, the Charter has still been invoked in proceedings before the European Court of Justice and the Court of First Instance. It is also used as a point of reference by both the European Commission and the European Parliament, which have established an EU Network of Independent Experts in Fundamental Rights which since 2002 has analysed the situation of fundamental rights in the Union and member states by reference to the Charter's provisions (http://www.europa.eu.int/comm/justice_h ome/cfr_cdf/index_en.htm). It is likely that compliance with the Charter's provisions will become one of the bases for the Council judging whether it is appropriate to take action because of a serious and persistent breach by a member state of the principles on which the Union is founded – namely, **LIBERTY**, **DEMOCRACY**, respect for human rights and fundamental freedoms and the rule of law – or a clear risk thereof (Article 7 of the Treaty of European Union), which could entail the application of so far unspecified penalties against the state concerned.

Resistance to the Charter having legal force is based partly on a concern about duplication of existing instruments but, notwithstanding the use made of them by the European Court of Justice, none of these involves international obligations for the Union. A more fundamental objection is that such force might lead to an enhancement of the Union's competence in the field of human rights at the expense of member states. This objection led to unsuccessful efforts to have it excluded from the draft Treaty establishing a Constitution for Europe but also to the inclusion in the Charter of an explicit statement that it does not establish any new power or task for the Union or modify powers and tasks defined by the Treaties (Article 51(2)), which has been made even more explicit in the version now in the draft treaty. Further efforts to limit the Charter's potential impact include the addition to the draft treaty version of a requirement to interpret provisions resulting from common constitutional traditions of member states in harmony with those traditions (Article 51(4)) and the stipulation that principles shall be judicially cognisable only in the interpretation of legislative and executive acts taken in the implementation of Union law and in rulings

on their legality (Article 51(5)). Nonetheless, if the Treaty is adopted, the Charter's provisions on social and economic rights will be among the first to be truly justiciable. However, continuing concern about ensuring that the European Court of Justice's interpretation of provisions corresponding to those in the European Convention is consistent with that of the **EUROPEAN COURT OF HUMAN RIGHTS** should be allayed both by the requirement in Article 52(3) already cited and by the increasing prospect of technical obstacles to ratification of this instrument by the Union being removed and greater political enthusiasm for such a step.

Further Reading

Alston, P. (ed.) (1999) *The EU and Human Rights*, Oxford: Oxford University Press.

Feus, K. (2000) *The EU Charter of Fundamental Rights: Text and Commentaries*, London: Feral Trust.

Hervey, T.K. & Kenner, J. (eds) (2003) *Economic and Social Rights Under the EU Charter of Fundamental Rights: A Legal Perspective*, Hart.

House of Lords Select Committee on the European Union (2003) 'The Future Status of the EU Charter of Fundamental Rights', HL Paper 48.

Contributor: Jeremy McBride

ENVIRONMENTAL RIGHTS AND JUSTICE

Environmental justice is inherently a socio-political concept that engages environmental issues with social justice. As Bullard (1994) has argued, environmental justice is a politically charged term, one that demands remedial action to correct an injustice imposed on a specific group of people anywhere in the world. In the pursuit of environmental justice, public policy decisions should be governed by the idea of fairness to **FUTURE GENERATIONS** which is central to their human rights. The practice of sustainability would ensure that our children and grandchildren would have at least a similar if not improved quality of life to our own. However, in terms of the big 'three Es' – environment, economy and equity – central to a sustainable society, equity has been the poor relation and least represented in policy debates. In this context, the evidence to date points more towards acts of environmental injustices rather than environmental justice, especially in developing countries where individual human rights are often dishonoured.

Environmental justice as a key issue of concern is recent – the first use of the term can be traced back to the late 1970s when increasing evidence indicated that racial minorities and low income-groups in the US bore a disproportionate burden of environmental risks. The link between social justice and environmental issues was clearly made by communities objecting to the siting of toxic chemical plants, land-fills and rubbish incinerators close to their homes. The movement for environmental justice grew as a reaction to the limitations of mainstream environmentalism, which was viewed by many as being dominated by elitist 'white upper-class environmental' individuals and reflected their narrow range of views. Further, many argued that the traditional environmental movement was not adequately addressing issues such as race, power and inequality. Environmental justice can be regarded as a heterogeneous movement as it seeks to incorporate anti-racist, feminist and anti-corporate and post-colonial politics. In sum, the movement has sought to include the most marginalised and excluded groups in society, those least able to defend themselves or articulate their thoughts against more powerful private sector companies or state institutions. Academics and activists have sought to highlight how indigenous peoples, women and children and the poorest in society are not only the most vulnerable to environmental hazards but are also largely excluded from key decisions that impact on their quality of life. In this sense their human rights have often been violated.

Somewhat ironically, while the world appeared to show increasing concern for environmental matters – for example the plight of the rainforests, global warming, acid rain, ozone layer depletion, the misuse of pesticides and so on – it became clear that there was a neglect of concerns related to (human) justice. This included equity considerations based on class, gender, race and nation. The development of environmental justice has sought to correct this neglect.

As mentioned above, at its inception the concept of environmental injustice referred to the disproportionate burden of environmental cost borne by minorities and the poor resulting from industrial activities at specific locations. More recently, however, such injustice is recognised to have the capacity to occur over much wider spatial and temporal scales. A high-profile example is the negative consequences of climate change that will be felt greatest by those in the future and by nations currently emitting relatively small volumes per capita of greenhouse gasses. Such multiple scale environmental injustice has been increasingly identified by nations and their populations and is viewed with growing concern. In the case of Scotland it has been observed as occurring on three levels (Agyeman, Bullard and Evans, 2003):

- 'As in the rest of the UK, poorer and less powerful social groups have an increased risk of living in a degraded environment.'
- 'Scotland, being on the periphery of the European economic bloc, tends towards economic activities which are environmentally detrimental, in order to maintain a comparative advantage.'
- 'Scotland shares responsibility for international environmental injustice. The elevated consumption of natural resources contributes to circumstances whereby globally, less powerful groups suffer disproportionate environmental damage and enjoy fewer benefits.'

Encouragingly, the existence of some of this injustice was recognised by Scotland's First Minister Jack McConnell in early 2002 when he declared: '... damage to our environment hits the poorest hardest. Traffic fumes, pollution and poor quality housing all affect the most vulnerable in our society: the old, the very young and those who have least.' (www.scotland.gov.uk). Although activists and green politicians welcomed such official recognition of environmental injustice, they also emphasise that much needs to be done to rectify the situation and that addressing the unjust environmental impact that developed countries such as Scotland place on peoples in other parts of the world and on future generations is a critical challenge to the delivery of sustainable development (Dunion, 2003).

Central to these challenges is a need to tackle an observed root factor present behind environmental injustice at all scales – a lack of accountability. Commonly, this is in terms of both the state and business to local people. Furthermore, although the level of environmental and social accountability that business and industry afford to surrounding communities often meets the standards required by government and regulatory bodies, it may not always ensure a healthy environment for local people. Indeed, professional declarations by such bodies and industry, delivered in the language of technical expertise and finding an area is safe, are often not trusted by the communities concerned. This lack of trust is frequently exacerbated by both the reduced rights of communities and by the limited resources to uphold them when compared with those of private enterprise.

In such contexts other mechanisms for increasing business accountability to local people have been explored. One such mechanism is Good Neighbour Agreements (GNAs). These originated in the US and are voluntary or legally enforceable negotiated agreements between a company and the surrounding community regarding aspects of company behaviour identified by the community as being of concern. Although GNAs are individual to the local situation, common elements agreed include: community access to information concerning the facility in question; community rights to inspect the facility; public input into an available accident plan; measures to increase pollution prevention; commitment to local employment; and funding by the company of a community benefit fund. The potential for the widespread adoption of the GNA mechanism in the case of Scotland has been investigated by Friends of the Earth Scotland (www.foe-scotland.org.uk). This research found that although US style GNAs would not have to change significantly for adoption, critically required precursors were lacking. These included sufficient community capacity (community resources and skills) and the ability of communities to exert leverage on business (for example through the existence of a 'credible threat' of litigation). The resulting report commented that it was hard to conceive of communities obtaining such leverage in the absence of enforceable rights.

So how could such rights come about? Of promise is the United Nation's Aarhus Convention which is centred on themes of access to information, participation and justice, while the **EUROPEAN CONVENTION ON HUMAN RIGHTS** is considerate to the concept of a right to a clean environment for all. Additionally, through the requirement for greater consideration of sustainability at policy and planning levels, the EU Strategic Environmental Assessment (SEA) Directive provides the opportunity to consider the accumulative impact on environmental quality. A further avenue for increased environmental justice in Scotland comes through the Freedom of Information Act coming into force in January 2005. This will create for people the general right to information (including environmental information) held by local authorities and a system of appeal against a decision to withhold it. Additionally, an independent Scottish Information Commissioner, with the power to disclose information deemed in the public interest, was appointed in early 2003. The Commissioner also has powers to resolve disputes over access to information and is responsible for ensuring the public know of their right to this access (www.itspublicknowledge.info).

The extent to which the mechanisms highlighted above will deliver greater environmental justice within Scotland has yet to be seen. However, environmental injustice in relation to nations such as Scotland operates over much larger scales than the purely intra-national. The fight for environmental justice is not just local but increasingly global. Environmental injustices, wherever they take place in the world, need to be challenged and corrected, and both private corporations and public institutions need to take more seriously any potential impacts of their plans and actions as well as taking greater responsibility for their actions. With respect to this, government legislation to secure universally recognised rights is crucial in helping to set a context which addresses environmental justice issues. In the absence of such rights it is no surprise that environmental justice has become an important site for activism.

* The authors would like to thank Friends of the Earth (Scotland) for helpful discussions and access to relevant research findings.

Further Reading

Agyeman, J., Bullard, R.D. and Evans, B. (eds) (2003) *Just Sustainabilities: Development in an Unequal World*, 1st edn, UK and USA: Earthscan Publications Ltd.

Bullard, R.D. (ed.) (1994) *Unequal Protection: Environmental Justice and Communities of Color*, San Francisco, CA: Sierra Club Books.

Dobson, A. (1999) *Justice and the Environment: Conceptions of Environmental Sustainability and Dimensions of Social Justice*, 1st edn, Oxford: Oxford University Press.

Dunion, K. (2003) *Troublemakers: The Struggle for Environmental Justice in Scotland*, 1st edn. UK: Edinburgh: Edinburgh University Press.

Martinez-Alier, J. (2003) *The Environmentalism of the Poor: A Study of Ecological Conflicts and Valuation*, 1st edn, UK and USA: Edward Elgar.

Contributors:

Chris McWilliams and Jonathan Walton

EVIDENCE OF HUMAN RIGHTS VIOLATIONS

As human rights researchers, we analyse data and present the results of those analyses to give undeniable, credible evidence about human rights violations. A rigorous analysis will show what happened, counter perpetrators' claims, provide an undeniable record to bring closure to victims and survivors and provide evidence about the status of economic, social and cultural rights. Such evidence can be used for indictment and prosecution of perpetrators in tribunals and national courts, for truth and reconciliation commissions, and to convince legislators, arouse human rights workers to action and get media cooperation in spreading the word.

When we analyse data, we can assess the magnitude and scope of human rights violations, find patterns of violation that help identify perpetrators, determine the patterns of violations against different ethnic groups, sexes, age groups, etc. and relate violations to the actions of perpetrating regimes or organisations, show how acts of repression are coordinated throughout a country or region, show the changes over time of human rights performance indicators, provide analytical meas-ures of the extent to which rights are granted or denied and show the dependence of human rights performance indicators on region, ethnicity, etc.

The key principles of data analysis are clarity, numeracy and credibility. We need to be clear about our findings, goals and work. Our work must have clarity so that we, and others, can see things as they are, not as we would like them to be, and so that we cannot fail to see what the data are telling us. Clarity has its greatest value when it helps us to see the unexpected. When the data are available, such imprecise statements often result from a lack of numeracy, which we define as the capacity or willingness to use quantitative thought and expression. Without numeracy, there is no clarity. When a human rights report contains such imprecise statements as the following, the reader cannot have a clear picture of what has happened.

> Most of the victims showed torture stigmata.
> The majority of the disappeared were young males.
> The proportion of children showing wasting rose dramatically.
> Several massacres took place.

Sometimes you will have no choice but to use imprecise statements because you have no data. But when you have data, to use imprecise and vague words instead of numbers will damage your credibility and diminish the magnitude of violations you are reporting and not do justice to the victims' suffering.

'Most' and 'majority' are often used interchangeably, and either word is close to meaningless in describing a number, since to be a majority, the count needs only to exceed 50 per cent and colloquial usage usually is taken to mean that the count falls short of the total. If there were 1000 victims, to say that most showed torture stigmata means some number between 501 (more than half) and 999 (not all). This makes your statement unclear to your audience. 'Rose dramatically' again reduces a measurement to a subjective interpretation. Within a different context or to a different person, your 'dramatic' rise may be 15 per cent or 300 per cent – or any other value! 'Several' means only 'more than one' and leaves the audience lacking an understanding of the magnitude of the number of events. 'Massacres' is a term that must be defined in context. The dictionary meaning, 'the act or an instance of killing a number of usually helpless or unresisting human beings under circumstances of atrocity or cruelty' is adequate for rhetoric, but not for making a case in a tribunal or truth commission or to an aware public. Almost all killings of more than one victim in human rights situations could fit this definition.

You will not always have or be able to get the numbers. However, when you know the numbers, use them! When they are unknown, say so. When the numbers are available, you gain clarity by using tables or graphs, which make the data clear to everyone. If you discuss complex interrelationships among data using words buried in dense paragraphs, you will risk discrepancies or errors in the data or logic.

Credibility, the power to inspire belief, has two faces for a human rights worker. Firstly, you want your own reports of violations to be credible, to be believed by others. Secondly, you must be able to judge the credibility of reports you receive from others. For example, when creating a report, you try to eliminate errors because other people will conclude that you cannot be trusted if they find numerical errors in your work. Conversely, when you are evaluating a report, you must check whether it has numerical errors. Below, we discuss some of the issues in establishing and evaluating credibility. We discuss them from the standpoint of the creation of reports, but they are the same principles you use to evaluate the credibility of someone else's reports.

Most people when judging a report transfer good or bad performance to everything that person has done. We call this tendency the Halo effect. Thus, if you have written an otherwise sound report in which there are a few numerical errors, the reader will assume that the rest of the report is filled with errors. Lawyers are skilled at using this effect to destroy the credibility of witnesses, and in the adversarial environment of truth commissions, tribunals and legislative bodies, human rights workers can expect that simple errors will be used to attack their credibility.

Another issue is the need for confirmation. Nothing earns credibility like agreement among different sources. Data analysis is one

way to establish credibility by determining the level of agreement among observations from different sources, different regions or different samples taken from the same situation. You can gain credibility from showing that the process by which you got your data and results is sound and set up to make checks at different times and places. For instance, when asking for a victim's age, it is essential to also ask for birth date, to check the two statements and if necessary reconcile them. If you do not reveal how you collected the data, readers will suspect that you have either deliberately hidden your methodology because you do not think it was good or that you do not know what you did with the data.

Confirmation of your source data is essential for credibility. Someone who makes claims in the press that 4000 victims were buried in a mass grave and then has to retract those claims when new data emerges afterwards will not be credibile in the future. Serious charges should be checked in several sources before being released to the public. Some organisations have high standards; they insist on confirmation of violations from at least two independent sources and are known for handling data and information with great care. They have high credibility and you and others can trust them. As a human rights researcher you must track all of your data sources.

It is important to show that you have considered alternative explanations so that you cannot be accused of bias in your data collection. Your work should not show that you started out to prove a point and then did everything you could to do so, ignoring all possible alternative explanations for what might have taken place.

Your work must make sense and flow in a logical way. If you start out saying that you intend to investigate trafficking of women and then report on violations of the right to education, you will appear to be confused and hence not credible. Therefore, you need to create a logic chain.

An important issue is the choice of the unit of analysis. Do you want to analyse violations? Do you want to know how many murders, disappearances, tortures, etc. have occurred and when, to people of what age, etc.? Then you would find it hard indeed to analyse your data if you organised your list by victim identification. A victim could have been tortured twice, held in illegal detention three times and ultimately disappeared. If you had the victim identification as the unit of analysis, you would have to list all these different violations against this individual in the same row of your database list. How would you find out how many people were tortured one, two, three or even more times? What do you do about people who are victims in one incident and perpetrators in another? The unit of analysis is defined by your purpose. If you want to analyse the amount and types of confiscated property, you would use Item of Property as the unit of analysis. If you were studying vigilante raids on encampments of street children, you would use Raid as the unit of analysis.

Respected research statisticians in many fields observe these rules for their data analyses; the same rules must apply to human rights data. Using sophisticated statistical tools, however, does not excuse the user from the basic rules of numeracy, credibility and clarity.

Further Reading

Ball, P. (1996) *Who Did What to Whom? Planning and Implementing a Large Scale Human Rights Data Project*, Washington, D.C.: American Association for the Advancement of Science.

Ball, P., Spirer, H. and Spirer, L. (2000) *Making the Case: Investigating Large Scale Human Rights Violations Using Information Systems and Data Analysis*, Washington, D.C.: American Association for the Advancement of Science.

Ball, P. (1999) *Policy or Panic? The Flight of Ethnic Albanians from Kosovo, March–May 1999*, Washington, D.C.: American Association for the Advancement of Science.

Contributors: Louise and Herbert Spirer

EXPRESSION, FREEDOM OF

Freedom of expression has a long history, predating modern human rights instruments. One of the earliest and most striking defences of freedom of expression came in 1644, when John Milton published *Aeropagitica* in reaction to an attempt by the English Parliament to prevent 'seditious, unreliable, unreasonable and unlicensed pamphlets'. He made a number of powerful assertions that hold true today: that a nation's unity is created through blending individual differences rather than imposing homogeneity from above; that the ability to explore the fullest range of ideas on a given issue was essential to any learning process and truth cannot be arrived upon unless all points of view are first considered; and that by constricting free thought, censorship acts to the detriment of material progress. On the other hand, Milton argued, if the facts are laid bare, truth will defeat falsehood in open competition but this cannot be left for a single individual to determine. It is up to each individual to uncover their own truth; no one is wise enough to act as a censor for all individuals.

The protection of freedom of expression is a key element of all modern human rights instruments. Article 19 of the UNIVERSAL DECLARATION OF HUMAN RIGHTS, guarantees the right to freedom of expression in the following terms:

Everyone has the right to freedom of opinion and expression; this right includes the right to hold opinions without interference and to seek, receive and impart information and ideas through any media and regardless of frontiers.

The UDHR, though not intended to be binding on states, is widely regarded as having acquired legal force since its adoption in 1948 as customary international law (See: CUSTOMARY LAW; UNIVERSALISM).

The 1966 INTERNATIONAL COVENANT ON CIVIL AND POLITICAL RIGHTS, ratified by over 145 states, imposes formal legal obligations on state parties to respect a number of the human rights set out in the UDHR. Article 19 of the ICCPR guarantees the right to freedom of opinion and expression in terms very similar to those found in Article 19 of the UDHR. Guarantees of freedom of expression are also found in all three major regional human rights systems – in Article 10 of the EUROPEAN CONVENTION FOR THE PROTECTION OF HUMAN RIGHTS AND FUNDAMENTAL

FREEDOMS, Article 13 of the American Convention on Human Rights (See: **THE INTER-AMERICAN HUMAN RIGHTS SYSTEM**) and Article 9 of the African Charter on Human and Peoples' Rights (See: **THE AFRICAN COMMISSION AND THE COURT ON HUMAN AND PEOPLE'S RIGHTS**).

Milton's defence of freedom of expression is couched in rich prose that has never been bettered. In the more prosaic language of international law, freedom of expression is recognised by almost all international instruments as a multi-faceted right that includes much more than merely the right to express, or disseminate, information and ideas. It is defined as including at least three distinct aspects:

■ the right to seek information and ideas;
■ the right to receive information and ideas;
■ the right to impart information and ideas.

There are differences in how international standards treat this mix. Most standards recognise the right to hold an opinion as a right directly associated with freedom of expression. Article 19 of the UDHR recognises them as one composite right, as does the ECHR (Article 10). The American Convention (Article 13) recognises freedom of thought as an integral part of the right to free expression. However, the ICCPR (Article 19) recognises a distinction between free opinion and expression. The former is recognised as an absolute right that cannot be constrained. Freedom of expression, on the other hand, can be subjected to a regime of limitations under the ICCPR formula (see below).

The right to freedom of expression articulated by the above instruments also recognises that the right could be exercised through any medium of one's choice (e.g. orally, in writing, in print, through the Internet or through art forms) and without regard to frontiers. This means that the protection of international law extends to the means of expression as well as the content. This is particularly important for the media, which plays a special role as the bearer of the general right to freedom of expression for all of us (it is through the media that the expression of views takes a public form) (See: **THE MEDIA AND HUMAN RIGHTS**).

The media has a specific role in supporting freedom of expression as

■ a vessel for transmitting ideas and opinions;
■ a crucible that shapes a democratic culture (by allowing debate; by asking awkward questions and by reporting the views of opposition politicians and groups);
■ a watchdog which guards the people from the state by subjecting the state to constant scrutiny.

However, it shouldn't be forgotten that free expression is not only the concern of journalists. It is a right for everyone and particularly for vulnerable groups such as women in some societies, children and refugees to name but three. It is the responsibility of all citizens to support those who wish to receive and impart information and ideas. More specifically, protecting the means of expression means that equipment used by the electronic media or the print medium will also attract the protection of human rights law (such as Article 10 of the ECHR). Similarly, airwaves over which the electronic media broadcast information and ideas are protected. The right to free expression regardless of boundaries has also been interpreted to mean the right to exercise the right regardless of geographic/international boundaries.

Another important point is that the right is guaranteed to 'everyone' and not only to 'citizens'. The right can be invoked, therefore, not only by natural persons but also by juridical persons such as media organisations.

Current international standards have, for the most part, redefined the historic view that freedom of expression should be seen solely as something which guarantees individual integrity. They assert that freedom of expression should be seen as a pillar of democracy,

Less than 20 countries have statutory right of access of official documents through a freedom of information statute. Countries (with date of statute in parenthesis) include Sweden (1766), USA (1966), Australia, Canada and New Zealand (1982), Thailand (1997), South Korea (1998), Japan (1999) and the United Kingdom (2000).

(Taken from O'Byrne, D., Human Rights, an introduction, Pearson, Harlow 2003)

human rights and social development. In this context it is now argued that restrictions on freedom of expression can be imposed in support of human rights and democracy so long as they are narrowly drawn and independently policed. In this sense, freedom of expression is perhaps less of a fundamental right but nevertheless remains of central importance as a foundation right in the ongoing battle to inform and secure all other rights. Needless to say this view is highly controversial and there are tensions between free speech 'fundamentalists', often US based, and those who come from a more international human rights background.

All instruments recognize that freedom of expression has to be subjected to limitations in the interests of the rights of others and of larger society. However, the need to ensure that state authorities do not abuse the limitations regime is addressed by most of the instruments. Freedom of expression guarantees, therefore, have put in place 'limitations on limitations'. All the instruments examined permit the imposition of limitations on freedom of expression only by law. With the exception of the African Charter, all other instruments permit limitations only in the interests of prescribed grounds such as protecting the rights and reputations of others, national security, public order, public health or morals. The ECHR has a much more extensive list of grounds of limitation.

In addition to fulfilling those two requirements, however, authorities have to establish that the limitations imposed are necessary in a democratic society. This means that the authorities cannot impose a limitation in an arbitrary manner even though it is imposed by law and is based on any one of the prescribed grounds. While the ECHR expressly spells out this last requirement, the other instruments have been interpreted by their respective interpretive authority as requiring the fulfilment of this aspect.

The American Convention (AmC) goes on to prohibit prior censorship except in the interests of protecting childhood and adolescence. It also stipulates that freedom of expression may not be limited by indirect methods adopted either by government or private sources. This is an important issue in an era when powerful owners can censor the views they don't like as much as governments can.

While limitations may be imposed according to the conditions as described above, the ICCPR (Article 20) and the AmC (Article 13 (5)), on the other hand, mandate state parties to prohibit any propaganda for war and expression that advocates national, racial or religious hatred that constitutes incitement to violence, hostility or discrimination.

Finally, the most controversial area is the question of whether it is necessary to maintain harmonious relations among various groups in a pluralistic society by prohibiting what is known as 'hate speech'. The Special Rapporteurs on Freedom of Expression of the UN and the OAS and the OSCE Representative on Freedom of the Media met on the occasion of the World Conference Against Racism in 2001 and issued a statement on 'racism and media'. The statement pointed to the need to curb hate speech while keeping in mind the fundamental tenets of freedom of expression. It argued that the best defence against hate speech was more speech and suggested that no penalties should be imposed for hate speech unless there was proof of an intention to incite discrimination, hostility or violence.

The prohibition of propaganda for war, on the other hand, is problematic. Even though such speech may be undesirable and even deplorable, prohibition of mere propaganda would certainly be contrary to the spirit of the free marketplace of ideas essential to sustain democracy. This area remains one of the most difficult for human rights activists and free speech supporters to reconcile.

WEBSITE

www.article19.org

Further Reading

Article 19 (2002) *Virtual Freedom of Expression Handbook: Case Briefs*. www.article19.org

Council of Europe (2002) Strasbourg: Freedom of Expression in Europe.

Gordon QC, Richard (2004) *Freedom of Expression*, London: Sweet and Maxwell.

Jones, Thomas David (1998) *Human Rights: group defamation, freedom of expression and the law of nations*, The Hague: Nijhoff.

Pare, Michele and Desbarats, Peter (eds) (1998) *Freedom of Expression and New Information Technologies*, Montreal: IQ Collectif.

Contributor: Andrew Puddephatt

FAIR TRIAL, THE RIGHT TO A

The right to a fair trial is one of the most important rights enshrined in the UNIVERSAL DECLARATION OF HUMAN RIGHTS and codified in the INTERNATIONAL COVENANT ON CIVIL AND POLITICAL RIGHTS. Article 10 of the Universal Declaration states: 'Everyone is entitled in full equality to a fair and public hearing by an independent tribunal, in the determination of his rights and obligations and of any criminal charge against him.' Article 11 provides for the presumption of innocence, public trial, 'all guarantees necessary for [one's] defence' and the right to be free from retroactive punishment or penalties. Other provisions of the Universal Declaration – for example, as to arbitrary arrest, the right to an effective remedy or legal redress, the right to be free from torture, and the right to security of person, and privacy – relate to the fairness of the trial process in particular cases.

The ICCPR further elaborates – particularly in its Articles 14 and 15, but also in Articles 9, 2, 6, 7 and 10 – upon the fair trial rights identified in the Universal Declaration. Article 14 of the ICCPR recognises the right to 'a fair trial and public hearing by a competent, independent and impartial tribunal established by law'. Every person is 'equal before the courts and tribunals' under Article 14(1). Article 14 also distinguishes between the sort of fair hearing required for civil cases, on the one hand, and criminal cases, on the other.

Article 14(3) deals with the 'minimum guarantees' required in the determination of any criminal charge, the observance of which are not always sufficient to ensure the fairness of a hearing. Among the minimum guarantees in criminal proceedings prescribed by Article 14(3) are the right of everyone to be

'The Justices of the High Court and of the other courts created by the Parliament:

(i) Shall be appointed by the Governor-General in Council;

(ii) Shall not be removed except by the Governor-General in Council, on an address from both Houses of the Parliament in the same session, praying for such removal on the ground of proved misbehaviour or incapacity;

(iii) Shall receive such remuneration as the Parliament may fix; but the remunerations shall not be diminished during their continuance in office.'

(s72 of the Australian Constitution which seeks to ensure the independence of the judiciary)

informed of the charge against him/her in a language which the accused understands; to have adequate time and facilities for the preparation of a defence and to communicate with counsel of one's own choosing; to be tried without undue delay; to examine or have examined the witnesses against the accused and to obtain the attendance and examination of witnesses on one's behalf under the same conditions as witnesses against the accused; to the assistance of an interpreter free of any charge if the accused cannot understand or speak the language used in court; and not to be compelled to testify against oneself or to confess guilt. Article 14 also gives the accused the right to have one's conviction and sentence reviewed by a higher tribunal according to law; to compensation if there was a miscarriage of justice; and not to be subjected to trial or punishment for a second time (*non bis in idem*). Under Article 14(4) juveniles have the same right to a fair trial as adults but are also entitled to certain additional safeguards. Article 15 codifies the principle of *nullum crimen sine lege* (no crime without law) and also gives the accused the benefit of any decrease in penalty which is promulgated after the person has committed an offence.

The Human Rights Committee was established by the ICCPR to interpret and apply the Covenant's provisions. The Committee has evolved a considerable jurisprudence on issues relating to the administration of justice – particularly as to the right to a fair trial. For example, many prisoners have complained to the Human Rights Committee that they have not received a prompt trial and the Committee has sought to interpret that requirement. In 1984 the Human Rights Committee issued General Comment 13 authoritatively interpreting Article 14 of the Covenant and stating that the right to trial without undue delay relates not only to the time by which a trial should commence but also to the time by which it should end and judgment be rendered; all stages must take place 'without undue delay'. It must be ensured, by means of an established procedure, that the trial will proceed 'without undue delay', both in the first instance and on appeal.

The ICCPR identifies in Article 4 certain rights as non-derogable, that is, those rights which cannot be the subject of suspension during periods of emergency that threatens the life of the nation. While Article 4 does not specify Article 14 (right to a fair trial) as expressly non-derogable, it does mention Articles 7 (prohibition of torture), 15 (*nullum crimen sine lege* (no crime without law)) and 16 (recognition of every person before the law) as non-derogable. Furthermore, the Human Rights Committee has interpreted other non-derogable rights (e.g. the right not to be subjected to arbitrary deprivation of life) as implying that the basic fair trial provisions of Article 14 cannot be suspended during periods of national emergency. The Human Rights Committee has, accordingly, strengthened the non-derogable nature of the right to a fair trial by issuing a further General Comment 29 stating 'any trial leading to the imposition of the death penalty during a state of emergency must conform to the provisions of the Covenant, including all the requirements of Articles 14 and 15'. In that General Comment the Human Rights Committee further stated that:

Safeguards related to derogation, as embodied in Article 4 of the Covenant, are based on the principles of legality and the rule of law inherent in the Covenant as a whole. As certain elements of the right to a fair trial are explicitly guaranteed under international humanitarian law during armed conflict, the Committee finds no justification for derogation from these guarantees during other emergency situations. The Committee is of the opinion that the principles of legality and the rule of law require that fundamental requirements of fair trial must be respected during a state of emergency.

The **CONVENTION ON THE RIGHTS OF THE CHILD** elaborates on the rights of juvenile offenders in the ICCPR and other treaties. Article 12 safeguards each child's right to be heard in legal proceedings. Article 37(b) provides that '[n]o child shall be deprived of his or her liberty unlawfully or arbitrarily'. Furthermore, Article 37(d) provides that '[e]very child deprived of his or her liberty shall have the right to prompt access to legal and other appropriate assistance, as well as the right to challenge the legality of the deprivation of his or her liberty before a court or other competent, independent and impartial authority, and to a prompt decision on any such action'. Article 40 of the Child Convention addresses the same fair trial issues as Article 14 of the ICCPR.

Common Article 3 of the four Geneva Conventions for the protection of victims of armed conflict and Article 6 of Additional Protocol II contain fair trial guarantees for times of non-international armed conflict. Articles 96 and 99–108 of the Third Geneva Convention prescribe the rights of prisoners of war in judicial proceedings, essentially creating a fair trial standard. Articles 54, 64–74 and 117–26 of the Fourth Geneva Convention contain provisions relating to the right to fair trial in occupied territories. Article 75 of Additional Protocol I extends fair trial guarantees in an international armed conflict to all persons, including those arrested for actions relating to the conflict.

The **UN** has also issued a number of global non-treaty standards which relate to the right to a fair trial, including: Basic Principles on the Independence of the Judiciary; Basic Principles on the Role of Lawyers; Code of Conduct for Law Enforcement Officials;

General Augusto Pinochet Ugarte was arrested in London in 1998, on the basis of a Spanish warrant, for a series of human rights violations which allegedly occurred during his 17-year rule in Chile. In London, elements of a fair trial were examined when it transpired one of the English judges had links to Amnesty International and thus his independence could be considered compromised. Pinochet was subsequently returned to Chile on medical grounds. In a landmark decision, he was indicted for various offences committed by others during his term of office. However, the Chilean authorities decided in 2002 to terminate legal action against him on health grounds.

Human Rights Watch comments on these proceedings: 'Until recently, it seemed that if you killed one person, you went to jail, but if you slaughtered thousands, you usually got away with it. Times change.'

(Human Rights Watch, www.hrw.org)

Guidelines on the Role of Prosecutors; Principles on the Effective Prevention and Investigation of Extra-legal, Arbitrary and Summary Executions; and Safeguards guaranteeing protection of the rights of those facing the death penalty. In addition, regional human rights treaties in Africa, Europe and the Inter-American system protect the right to a fair trial. Furthermore, the statutes of the **INTERNATIONAL CRIMINAL COURT**, the ad hoc criminal tribunal for the former Yugoslavia and the ad hoc criminal tribunal for Rwanda contain provisions seeking to guarantee the right to a fair trial for the accused.

The United Nations, regional organisations and other international structures have codified a substantial framework of fair trial standards, which have been accepted, albeit not always followed, by most nations and which have begun to be used in the context of international criminal tribunals. In addition to the codified standards, several human rights institutions, including particularly the Human Rights Committee and the **EUROPEAN COURT OF HUMAN RIGHTS**, have interpreted and applied fair trial norms

to particular cases and have thus generated an impressive corpus of jurisprudence which lawyers and judges worldwide should consult.

Further Reading

Amnesty International (1998) *Fair Trials Manual.* London.

Chernichenko, S. & Treat, W. (1994) 'The right to a fair trial: Current recognition and measures necessary for its strengthening', final report, UN Doc. E/CN.4/Sub.2/1994/24.

Manual on Human Rights for Judges, Prosecutors and Lawyers (2004) Office of the UN High Commissioner for Human Rights, Professional Training Series, No. 9.

Weissbrodt, David (2001) *The Right to a Fair Trial under the Universal Declaration of Human Rights and the International Covenant on Civil and Political Rights.* Brill: Leiden.

Weissbrodt, David & Wolfrum, Rüdiger (eds), (1998) *The Right to a Fair Trial.* Berlin and Heidelberg: Springer-Verlay.

Contributor: David Weissbrodt

FEMINIST CRITIQUES OF HUMAN RIGHTS

The women's human rights movement has achieved two significant successes in the area of human rights: the recognition that violence against women in the home is subject to human rights scrutiny, adopted at the World Conference on Human Rights in Vienna in 1993, and the recognition of women's rights to equality, enshrined in the **CONVENTION FOR THE ELIMINATION OF ALL FORMS OF DISCRIMINATION AGAINST WOMEN**. Despite these achievements and the proliferation of advocacy in the area of women's human rights, there are some concerns as to the ways women's human rights have been addressed subsequently. One is the focus on issues of violence against women, which tends to reproduce women, especially from the global south, as victims and invites protectionist (and at times highly moralistic) responses from states. Another is the tension between women's rights to equality and the right to freedom of religion.

The 1993 Vienna World Conference on Human Rights marked the culmination of a long struggle to secure international recognition of women's rights as human rights. The final document that emerged from Vienna acknowledged that, partly as a result of the artificial line drawn between the public and private sphere, certain gender-specific issues had been left out of the human rights arena (Article 38, Vienna Declaration). The document provides that a broad spectrum of harms experienced by women in the family be subjected to human rights scrutiny. The demand to include violence against women as a human rights issue was reiterated at the Women's Conference in Beijing in 1995 and in the UN General Assembly Declaration on Violence Against Women, 1993. Since that time, women's human rights movements along with states have continued to focus primarily on the issue of violence against women (VAW). Pursuant to the Declaration, the UN appointed a Special Rapporteur on Violence Against Women to investigate issues of violence. Even recommendation 19 of the CEDAW document which deals with violence against women and is a non-binding recommendation made by the committee to state parties has received an extraordinary amount of visibility: indeed at times even more so than the actual CEDAW convention, whose articles remain largely unimplemented.

The focus on violence against women (VAW) has had some extremely important and beneficial consequences. It has drawn attention to the lack of domestic governmental responses to women's demands for more effective rape laws, laws against child sexual abuse and domestic violence laws. The VAW campaign has succeeded partly because of its appeal to the victim subject, which has enabled women to speak out about abuses that have remained hidden or invisible in human rights discourse. A powerful form of this presentation has been through personal testimonials in public tribunals, as at Vienna, or through international video links. These accounts are usually graphic and horrifying and are told through the location of the victim subject.

The problem with the focus on violence and the victimisation of women is two-fold. The first is that it treats women, especially from the global south, as weak and vulnerable and in need of rescue and protection. The second is that women's human rights are today primarily equated with a focus on issues of violence against women. This focus has triggered a spate of domestic and international reforms of the criminal law, which are used to justify state restrictions on women's rights – in the name of protecting women. Although the issue of violence has provided a common foundation on which to build a shared movement and vision, the focus on the victim produces a subject which is ahistorical, invoked to analyse issues concerning women from the lens of a universal, unemancipated subject. At times, it has facilitated and justified neo-imperialist interventions in the developing world, where women are represented as being brutalised by their cultures, in need of rescue and rehabilitation by a civilising 'West'. The anti-trafficking campaign, with its focus on violence and victimisation, is but one example. It has spawned initiatives that treat women's consent as irrelevant, invariably link trafficking to sex work and justify restrictions on women's movement. These initiatives have specifically affected the rights of women who move from the global south, who choose to move for a variety of reasons. Advocates must address the ways in which states are enthusiastically taking up issues of violence against women in a manner that is not necessarily facilitating women's human rights.

The almost exclusive focus on the issue of violence against women also narrows the scope of the women's human rights project. It deflects attention from the ways in which states are not implementing their obligations under a range of human rights documents, including CEDAW, which, if implemented, could remove both structural and formal impediments that may contribute to women's experience of violence. The focus on violence against women has thus encouraged a focus on wrongs, in particular sexual wrongs, rather than on rights and the facilitation and promotion of these rights.

Parts of CEDAW may be seen to be in conflict with some religions. Article 5(a) of CEDAW stipulates: 'States Parties shall take all appropriate measures: (a) To modify the social and cultural patterns of conduct of men and women, with a view to achieving the elimination of prejudices and customary and all other practices which are based on the idea of the inferiority or the superiority of either of the sexes or on stereotyped roles for men and women.' Article 2 of CEDAW stipulates that the state parties should take all appropriate measures including legislation to abolish practices and customs that discriminate against women and to eliminate discrimination against women by any person, organisation and enterprise. These articles instruct state parties to actively intervene in people's social and cultural practices in order to eliminate practices that discriminate against women.

Unfortunately, the Convention has been largely unsuccessful in combating religious and cultural practices that discriminate against women, partly due to its weak enforcement mechanisms and the extensive use of reservations by state parties. The problem has been aggravated by the fact that the role and influence of religion has intensified in the global north and the global south. These forces are influencing the way in which women's rights issues are being addressed, especially issues of equality. Although at times the issue of women's equality has been taken up in opposition to religion, more recently we are seeing evidence of women's equality issues being defined by the conservative and religious right. In other words, these forces are advancing their own agendas in and through the discourse of women rights. For example, the Vatican has become a major player in the international arena, developing sophisticated tactics on women's rights which speak to the way in which rights are sites of contest and that their meanings cannot be automatically equated with a progressive, justice-seeking agenda. It has sought to reconcile women's rights to equality with its own religious agenda. Although it continues to oppose abortion and contraceptive practices, its strategy has not been one of opposition. It has highlighted the equal dignity of women, how women's differences complement those of men, and has condemned violence against women. Although the shift is a subtle one, the Vatican's model of equality challenges the formal model, while not at the same time endorsing a substantive model of equality that is one based on redressing the historical disadvantage women have experienced on grounds of gender. Finally, the Vatican calls attention to issues of poverty and some of the economical-

ly exploitative policies of industrial countries in the developing world. It thus claims to represent a broader cross section of women than feminists who are cast as elite and anti-family because of their continuous focus on violence in the home.

Religious groups and conservative voices are beginning to appropriate women's human rights discourse in ways that advance women's rights, but within a framework that reinforces dominant familial and sexual norms. In failing to engage with the complex terrain of religion, the position of women's human rights advocates is invariably perceived as being in opposition to religion. As a result they are forcing women to choose between their gender and religious identities. Furthermore their failure to engage with this terrain has left it open for more conservative and orthodox voices to define the terrain and aggravate the tension between women's human rights and religion.

Women's human rights is a deeply contested arena. Although these rights have been recognised as important human rights, advocates and practitioners need to monitor the ways in which these rights are being taken up and by whom. There is a need to appreciate that advocacy must focus on more than just rights claims but must also begin to focus on the discursive contest over the meaning of rights that are taking place, something that the Vatican, and in fact right-wing ideologues and conservatives in many different countries, are already doing.

WEBSITE

Violence Against Women
http://www.un.org/rights/dpi1772e.htm

Further Reading

Askin, K.D. and Dorean, M.K. (1999) *Women and International Human Rights Law*, New York: Transnational Publishers Inc.

Human Rights Watch World Report 2000: *Women's Human Rights*. Palgrave.

Patman, R.G. (ed) (2000) *A Review of Universal Human Rights*, London and Basingstoke: Palegrave Macmillan.

Peters, Julie and Wolper, Andrea (eds) (1995)

Women's Rights, Human Rights, New York: Routledge.

Thornton, M. (1995) *Fragile Frontiers: Feminist Debates from Public and Private*, Oxford: Oxford University Press.

Contributor: Ratna Kapur

FOOD AND CLEAN WATER, THE RIGHT TO

We live in a world overflowing with riches, yet 842 million people still suffer hunger and malnutrition (FAO, 2003). Every seven seconds a child under the age of ten dies directly or indirectly of hunger somewhere in the world (WFP, 2001). More than 2 billion people worldwide suffer from 'hidden hunger' or micronutrient malnutrition. Born malnourished, children are left mentally and physically stunted, deformed or blind, condemning them to a marginal existence. Régis Debray calls them 'crucified at birth'. This is a scandal of outrageous proportions and the situation is getting worse.

The UN Food and Agricultural Organisation (FAO) has shown that progress in reducing world hunger has virtually come to a halt (FAO, 2002). Promises made by governments at the World Food Summit to halve the number of victims of undernourishment are not being met. Few countries have made progress (FAO, 2001) and the FAO reports that in recent years the situation is seriously deteriorating rather than improving, particularly in Africa. Over recent years, hunger has also increased in Afghanistan, Bangladesh, Congo, India, Iraq, Kenya, Democratic People's Republic of Korea, Tanzania, Uganda and the Occupied Palestinian Territories. Hunger is not unique to developing countries: many developed countries also admit food insecurity among their poorest populations. All this in a world which, according to the FAO, already produces more than enough food to feed the global population.

In the face of growing hunger, malnutrition, poverty and inequality, social movements and civil society organisations are beginning to take up the language of human rights to challenge the power relations that allow such hunger to persist. Relegated for many years to

an inferior position behind **CIVIL AND POLITICAL RIGHTS, ECONOMIC, SOCIAL AND CULTURAL RIGHTS** are now being proclaimed, declared and defended by an emerging civil society in the south and in the north and occupy an ever more important place within the **UNITED NATIONS**. Economic, social and cultural rights, which include the right to food, provide a powerful language to challenge the persistence of hunger and **POVERTY**. From the perspective of the right to food, persistent hunger is neither inevitable nor acceptable and usually amounts to a violation of the human right to food.

> The right to food is also protected under Articles 24 and 27 in the Convention of Rights of the Child, and Article 12 in the Convention on the Elimination of Discrimination Against Women, which also ensure provision for adequate nutrition. Article 1 (2) of the ICCPR and of the International Covenant Economic, Social and Cultural Rights states that 'in no case may a people be deprived of its own means of subsistence'. Numerous national constitutions also protect the right to food.

The right to food, including its most basic expression as the right to be free from hunger, is protected under Article 11 of the **INTERNATIONAL COVENANT ON ECONOMIC, SOCIAL AND CULTURAL RIGHTS**, as well as numerous other instruments. For the 148 governments that have ratified this International Covenant, guaranteeing the right to food is a binding legal obligation. Guaranteeing food security for everyone is a legal obligation, not simply a policy choice or preference. The Committee on Economic, Social and Cultural Rights is the key UN human rights body charged with monitoring the implementation of the **INTERNATIONAL COVENANT ON ECONOMIC, SOCIAL AND CULTURAL RIGHTS**. The Committee has defined the right to food as:

> 'the right of every man, woman and child alone and in community with others to have physical and economic access at all

times to adequate food or means for its procurement in ways consistent with human dignity.' (General Comment 12).

The right to food includes availability of food but also access to food. Adequate food must be physically and economically accessible to everyone and it must meet standards of nutritional adequacy and cultural acceptability.

The right to food does not mean handing out free food to everyone. Rather, it means that governments must respect, protect and fulfil the right to food. The obligation to respect means that governments must not violate the right to food (e.g. evict people from their land, destroy crops). The obligation to protect means that governments must protect their citizens against violations by other actors (e.g. by instituting regulations on food safety, protecting against potential abuses by transnational corporations (See: **BUSINESS AND HUMAN RIGHTS**). The third obligation to fulfil the right to food means that the government must first facilitate the right to food by providing an enabling environment for people to feed themselves and proactively engage in activities intended to strengthen people's access to and utilisation of resources and means to ensure their livelihood and food security (e.g. engage in land reform, stimulate employment). Secondly, the government must be the provider of last resort in cases where people cannot feed themselves for reasons beyond their control (e.g. social safety net programmes, food stamps, food provision in prison).

The right to water is also closely linked to the right to food. Safe, clean drinking water is essential to our daily diet and also to agriculture. Yet over 1.1 billion people in the world are not connected to a modern water supply system. Over 2.4 billion people do not have adequate sanitation and 2 billion cases of diarrhoea are recorded every year. Over 5 million people, mostly children and babies die from water related diseases every year – largely because the food is mixed with unsafe, unclean drinking water (WHO, 2002).

In 2001, my mandate as Special Rapporteur on the Right to Food was extended to include access to safe drinking water. There have been recent advances in strengthening the protection of the right to water. The UN Committee on Economic, Social and Cultural Rights has stated that water is

© R.K.M. Smith

essential to human life and defines the right to water as follows:

'The human right to water entitles everyone to sufficient, safe, acceptable, physically accessible and affordable water for personal and domestic uses.' (General Comment 15).

The Committee also recognises that the right to water is inextricably related to the right to food and requires that: 'Priority in the allocation of water must be given (...) to the water resources required to prevent starvation and disease' (General Comment 15). This includes ensuring basic access to water resources for livelihoods based on subsistence farming, primarily to protect the equal access to water for poor, marginal farmers, especially women and other marginalised groups including indigenous peoples.

Again, the right to water does not mean that free water should be given to everyone but that ways must be found to ensure that even the very poorest have access to a basic minimum quantity and quality of water. As does the right to food, the right to water entails obligations to respect, protect and fulfil for governments which have ratified the International Covenant on Economic, Social and Cultural Rights.

That food and water are both essential to life itself is self-evident, yet to conceive of access to adequate food and water as basic human rights continues to be disputed at the international level. Despite the creation of my mandate as Special Rapporteur on the Right to Food by the UN Commission on Human Rights, some governments vote regularly against my mandate because of ideological convictions that economic, social and cultural rights are not real rights at all but merely aspirations (See: **INDIVISIBILITY**). However, although it is true that economic, social and cultural rights are subject to the availability of resources and should be progressively realised, this should not be used as an excuse for failing to address the terrible suffering created by hunger and poverty in rich countries that have the resources to ensure an enabling environment where every person has basic access to food and water. The right to food and the right to water are basic, fundamental human rights for every human being.

At the same time, we need to push forward the boundaries of traditional human rights to focus on other powerful actors that affect the implementation of these rights. Creating an enabling environment for the realisation of the right to food is primarily the responsibility of national governments, but in an age of globalisation and liberalisation, governments must start to think of the impact of their policies not only on their own citizens but on citizens in other countries. The injustice and imbalances in the implementation of liberalisation required by the WTO Agreement on Agriculture, and the ways in which subsidies accorded to farmers in the north impact on the right to food of farmers in the south, is just one way in which the right to food in one country can be affected by the policies implemented in another. In this sense, international organisations (World Bank, IMF, WTO) also have responsibilities towards human rights, as well as governments. Furthermore, in a world in which transnational corporations have unprecedented control over food and water systems, it is time to develop a coherent system of accountability to ensure that they do not abuse this power (See the report of the Special Rapporteur on the Right to Food presented before the Commission on Human Rights in 2004 E/CN.4/2004/10). Just as human rights were originally developed to put limits on governments' abuse of power they must now be developed to circumscribe future abuses of power by large corporations.

As Jean-Jacques Rousseau wrote many years ago: 'Between the powerful and the weak, it is liberty that oppresses and it is the law that liberates.' To stop the daily massacre of hunger, the right to food and the right to water must be respected.

WEBSITES

www.righttofood.org

www.unhchr.ch/html/menu2/7/b/
mfood.htm

www.fao.org/Legal/rtf/rtf-e.htm

www.nutrition.uio.no/iprfd/
introduction.html

www.fian.org/

www1.umn.edu/humanrts/edumat/IHRIP/
circle/modules/module12.htm

Further Reading

Committee on Economic Social and Cultural Rights (1999) 'General Comment 12: The right to adequate food', UN Doc E/C.12/1999/5.

Committee on Economic Social and Cultural Rights (2002) 'General Comment 15: The right to water', UN Doc E/C.12/2002/11.

Eide, A. (1984) *Food as a Human Right*, Tokyo: The United Nations University (UNU), p. 289.

FAO (1998) 'The right to food in theory and practice' Rome: FAO, http://www.fao.org/Legal/rtf/booklet.pdf

FAO (2003) 'The state of food and security in the world', Rome: FAO.

FAO Committee on World Food Security (2001) Twenty-seventh session: Fostering the Political Will to Fight Hunger, Rome.

World Food Programme (WFP) (2001) 'World Hunger Map', Geneva: WFP.

WHO (2002) 'The Right to Water'.

Ziegler, J. (2002) 'The right to food', report by Jean Ziegler, UN Special Rapporteur on the Right to Food to the UN Commission on Human Rights, UN.Doc.E/CN.4/2002/58 www.righttofood.org

Contributors: Jean Ziegler with
            Sally-Anne Way and Christophe Golay

FUTURE GENERATIONS, THE RIGHTS OF

Our actions have potentially enormous impact on those who will live in the future. Perhaps the most significant impact is that our decisions affect who those future people will be and even whether there will be any future people at all. If we measure the moral significance of an action by the number of people it affects and the impact it has on them, our obligations to future generations deserve to be the central topic of moral philosophy. Potential environmental crises give a new urgency to this discussion as we now have some inkling of the magnitude of our impact on future generations.

One obvious way to account for our obligations to future generations is by reference to their rights. For instance, one might argue that it is wrong to pollute the environment, as this would violate the right of future generations to live in a clean world. Unfortunately, the language of rights is problematic with regard to future generations. The principal philosophical puzzle is not so much what rights future people might have but how they could have any rights at all. This is because, for various reasons, traditional accounts of the basis and strength of rights break down when applied to people who do not yet exist.

In his classic discussion of our obligations to future generations, Derek Parfit (1986) distinguishes two kinds of moral choice. A Same People Choice occurs whenever our actions affect what will happen to people in the future but not which people will come to exist. If our actions do affect who will get to exist in the future, then we are making a Different People Choice. Parfit makes two central claims. The first is that Different People Choices occur very frequently and in situations where we might not expect them. The second is that many traditional moral theories cope much better with Same People Choices than with Different People Choices.

Taken together, these two claims constitute the Non-Identity Problem, so called because, in a Different People Choice, those who will exist in one possible outcome are not identical to those who will exist in an alternative possible outcome. To illustrate the Non-Identity Problem, consider the following simple thought experiment.

The Risky Policy: As a community, we must choose between two energy policies. The more expensive policy is completely safe. The risky policy involves the burial of nuclear waste in areas where, in the next few centuries, there is no risk of an earthquake. But since this waste will remain radioactive for thousands of years, there will be risks in the distant future. We choose the Risky Policy. Many centuries later, an earthquake releases radiation, killing thousands of people. However, these people still have lives that are worth living.

Intuitively, adopting the Risky Policy seems very wrong. Yet it is hard to account for this in terms of rights. The language of rights, like most other moral language, evolved to discuss Same People Choices, where we can ask

© R.K.M. Smith

whether our action leaves the person worse off than they would otherwise have been. We can then say that a right is violated if and only if the person is worse off in a morally significant way.

In a Different People Choice, such as the Risky Policy case, the relevant comparisons cannot be made as the person we are concerned with would not have existed at all if we had acted otherwise. If we create a person whose life is worse than not living at all, then perhaps we can say that their rights have been violated. (A possibility that becomes relevant for wrongful life suits regarding the births of severely disabled children.) Suppose, however, that future people have lives which are worth living, even though they suffer from minor disabilities due to our pollution policy. If we had chosen another policy, then those people would not have existed. It thus looks as if they cannot claim that we have violated their rights, we have made them worse off than they would otherwise have been.

Utilitarians (See: **UTILITARIANISM AND HUMAN RIGHTS**) respond by rejecting rights-based approaches to inter-generational justice. They argue that, instead, we should base justice on the promotion of value, seeking to maximise the well-being of future people irrespective of their identity. Accordingly, utilitarians ask what makes different possible futures valuable and how we can compare them. This in turn leads to a host of paradoxes involving the comparative values of outcomes containing different numbers of people. For instance, should we aim for a future where a comparatively small number of people have very rich lives or one where a much larger population each have a smaller share of resources? (See: **POVERTY AND HUMAN RIGHTS**).

Others respond by attempting to explain how a person's rights can be violated even by actions which do not leave them worse off than they would otherwise have been. One common approach links rights with interests: x violates some right of A's if it results in a vital interest of A's not being met, even if A is better off overall. A classic example concerns a person denied an airline ticket on racial grounds. If the aircraft subsequently crashes, the person is better off as a result of this action, yet their rights have still been violated. We might still violate the rights of future people even if our actions leave them better-off overall. Attention then focuses on which interests of future people might give rise to rights and whether these interests can legitimately be traded off against one another. For instance, is it acceptable to deprive future people of the use of some non-renewable natural resource if we compensate them with additional technology?

Even if we accept that future people have rights, we must still ask how these are to be balanced against the rights of present people. This balancing is philosophically problematic, as many traditional attempts to balance political rights fall apart when applied to future people.

Our relations with future generations provide a striking case of the absence of reciprocal power relations. The quality of life of future generations depends to a very large extent on the decisions of the present generation. By contrast, the quality of life of the present generation does not seem to be affected at all by the decisions of future generations. We are in a position to do a great deal to (or for) posterity but posterity cannot do anything to (or for) us. The significance of this is that many accounts of the foundations of rights are based on an (actual or hypothetical) social contract. Many, though not all, contractarians argue that morality, human society and political institutions all are (or should be seen as) systems of mutual advantage. People come together to

make agreements which are mutually advantageous to all of them and these agreements constitute just political arrangements.

In inter-generational justice, where reciprocal power relations are entirely absent, this
contract-based approach cannot get off the
ground. This would mean that the rights of
future generations cannot outweigh those of
present people and there would be nothing to
stop the present generation pursuing a policy
with the result that, three centuries in the
future, there would be millions of people with
lives which were much worse than nothing.

Similar problems face more moderate contract-based theories. For instance, John Rawls,
whose *A Theory of Justice* was probably the most
influential work in political philosophy in the
20th century, generates his principles of justice using an Original Position, where people
choose the principles to govern their society
from behind a Veil of Ignorance. The
choosers know what their society will look like
if any given principle is adopted, but they do
not know who they will be in that society. To
take a simplified example, suppose that, in a
very simple society, there are two groups: the
Rich and the Poor. To discover what justice
requires in such a society, we ask the following
question: Which principles of justice would a
rational person choose if they did not know
whether they themselves would be one of the
Rich or one of the Poor?

Assume that we have placed the present
generation in the Original Position. If these
people choose as rational egoists, they will
choose the general principle that people in the
present generation can do whatever they like to
future generations. After all, they know they
will not be on the receiving end of that principle themselves. By contrast, they would not
choose a principle which permitted the Rich to
do whatever they like to the Poor, as they would
not know whether or not they would end up on
the receiving end of such a principle.

One solution is to stipulate that those in
the Original Position do not know what generation they belong to. Unfortunately, the
existence and identity of future people
depend upon the behaviour of the present
generation. So this would amount to the
assumption that those in the Original Position
do not know even whether they will exist at all.
They would then choose to maximise the size
of the future population, at almost any cost, in

order to maximise their own chances of existing. Unsurprisingly, this tends to produce very
strange principles of justice.

Both actual and hypothetical contracts
have their defenders, who seek to imagine fair
inter-generational bargains. Other philosophers argue that its inability to accommodate
future people disqualifies the contract
approach altogether and that we should seek
an alternative account of the foundations of
inter-generational justice.

Further Reading

Arhennius, G. (1999) 'Mutual Advantage
Contractarianism and Future Generations',
Theoria, pp. 25–35.

Barry, B. (1978) 'Circumstances of Justice and
Future Generations', in Sikora, R. and Barry,
B. (eds) *Obligations to Future Generations*,
Philadelphia: Temple University Press, pp.
204–48.

Gosseries, A. (2001) 'What do we owe the next
generation(s)?', *Loyola of Los Angeles Law
Review*, vol. 35, pp. 293–354.

Parfit, D. (1986) 'Overpopulation and the
Quality of Life' in Singer, P. (ed.) *Applied
Ethics*, Oxford: Oxford University Press, pp.
145-64.

Rawls, J. (1971) *A Theory of Justice*, Cambridge:
Harvard University Press.

Contributor: Tim Mulgan

GENOCIDE, FREEDOM FROM

Although the Convention for the Prevention
and Punishment of the Crime of Genocide
says 'that at all periods of history genocide has
inflicted great losses on humanity', the term
'genocide' itself was devised only in 1944, by
the Polish–Jewish jurist Raphael Lemkin. He
created the term 'genocide' from two words:
genos, which means race, nation or tribe in
ancient Greek, and *caedere*, meaning to kill in
Latin. He then introduced it in his book *Axis
Rule in Occupied Europe*. The impetus for its

recognition as a distinct category of international crime was driven by states that were unhappy with the restriction that the law of the Nuremberg tribunal had put on the cognate concept of crimes against humanity, namely that they be committed in association with international armed conflict. Accordingly, Article 1 of the Genocide Convention recognises that it may be committed 'in time of peace or in time of war'.

Actually, genocide is an aggravated form of crime against humanity, that is, a widespread and systematic attack aimed at the destruction of an ethnic group. In its first judgment, in 1998, the International Criminal Tribunal for Rwanda described genocide as 'the crime of crimes'. Genocide is defined in the 1948 Convention as one of five specific acts 'committed with intent to destroy, in whole or in part, a national, ethnical, racial or religious group, as such'. Despite frequent criticism that the definition excludes important vulnerable groups, defined for example by political opinion, economic and social status or gender, the text adopted by the General Assembly in the 1948 Convention has stood the test of time. It is repeated essentially without change in the Rome Statute of the International Criminal Court (1998), the statutes of the ad hoc tribunals for the former Yugoslavia and Rwanda, and in most attempts by national legislators to implement the Convention.

Although narrow, the definition's focus on national, ethnic, racial and religious groups is certainly not irrational; it corresponds with a determined orientation in international human rights law to the protection of what are sometimes called 'national minorities'. It also reflects the antipathy towards racial discrimination and xenophobia that is manifested in such instruments as the International Convention for the Elimination of All Forms of Racial Discrimination. As a trial chamber of the International Criminal Tribunal for the former Yugoslavia wrote, '[t]he preparatory work of the Convention shows that setting out such a list was designed more to describe a single phenomenon, roughly corresponding to what was recognised, before the second word war, as 'national minorities', rather than to refer to several distinct prototypes of human groups. To attempt to differentiate each of the named groups on the basis of scientifically objective criteria would thus be inconsistent with the object and purpose of the Convention.' (*Prosecutor v Krstic* (Case no. IT-98-33-T), Judgment, 2 August 2001, para. 556).

The terminology of the protected groups – national, racial, ethnic and religious – has not always been easy to apply because modern social science rejects the legitimacy of concepts such as racial groups. In this respect, it is helpful to consider what was meant by these terms when they were initially adopted in 1948. On a practical level, to borrow an expression from a justice of the United States Supreme Court (who was speaking of pornography), it may be difficult to define but 'I know it when I see it'.

The Genocide Convention lists five punishable acts of genocide: killing members of the group; causing serious bodily or mental harm to members of the group; deliberately inflicting on the group conditions of life calculated to bring about its physical destruction in whole or in part; imposing measures

Case Study

The Prosecutor v Radislav Krstic

The definition and scope of genocide is continually evolving. Systematic rape is included as is the targetting of only men. In Srebrenica in 1995, the VRS (Bosnian Serb Army) massacred men in the community irrespective of whether they did or could actually serve in the military (many were civilians and some were incapacitated, others were young boys or elderly). As several thousand men were killed, genocidal intentions could be deduced. Evidence was produced to suggest that Krstic in his command position knew that the murders were occurring. The Appeals Chamber of the International Criminal Tribunal for the Former Yugoslavia unanimously found Krstic guilty of aiding and abetting genocide in its judgment delivered on 19 April 2004. It sentenced him to 35 years imprisonment. The tribunal thus pronounced that genocide had been carried out against Bosnian Muslims in Srebrenica in 1995.

intended to prevent births within the group; forcibly transferring children of the group to another group. The enumeration is an exhaustive one, a consequence of efforts by the drafters to prevent expansion of the concept into what is sometimes called 'cultural genocide'. In effect, the intent was to confine the crime of genocide to acts aimed at the physical and biological destruction of a group, leaving attacks on culture, such as prohibition of use of a national language or religion, to other areas of international human rights law. All that remains in the Convention of an initially extensive proposal covering cultural genocide is the prohibition on transferring children from one group to the other.

The exclusion of cultural genocide from the scope of genocide raises difficulties with respect to the contemporary notion of 'ethnic cleansing'. Although not officially defined, 'ethnic cleansing' is generally considered to encompass acts of terror, including killing and rape, intended to drive a national minority from its homeland. The goal of the perpetrator of ethnic cleansing, then, is not the physical destruction of the group but rather its displacement. It is easy to understand why when the Genocide Convention was being drafted, in the aftermath of the Second World War, many of the great powers were nervous about extending the concept of genocide to encompass forced population transfers. The Potsdam Agreement had authorised the expulsion of millions of Germans from Poland and elsewhere in Eastern and Central Europe, often with great violence and resulting loss of life. In recent years, some national and international courts have indicated a willingness to expand the definition of genocide to cover such behaviour. While this adds to the stigmatisation of 'ethnic cleansing', which is in any event a crime against humanity, it has the undesirable consequence of diluting the stigma of full-blown genocide, such as occurred in Rwanda in 1994.

Initially, some states also hoped the Genocide Convention would recognise genocide as a crime of universal jurisdiction, subject to prosecution by courts wherever the suspected perpetrator could be found. But in the 1940s, many found this to be too provocative and the Genocide Convention only admits prosecution by the courts of the territory where the crime took place or by an international criminal court. Cold war tensions prevented establishment of international criminal tribunals until the 1990s, however. In the meantime, the Israeli courts ruled that genocide was subject to universal jurisdiction under customary law, convicting Nazi bureaucrat Adolph Eichmann for crimes committed in Europe.

The Genocide Convention requires that states provide 'effective penalties' for the crime. In the first national conviction, Israel made an exception to its unconditional opposition to capital punishment: Eichmann was executed and his ashes sprinkled over the Mediterranean Sea, so as to deprive his perverse admirers of a shrine. After 15 years without an execution, Rwanda too returned to the practice of capital punishment in 1998, when 22 convicts were shot before large crowds. The international criminal tribunals, however, in keeping with contemporary human rights standards, have set life imprisonment as the maximum penalty for genocide. Most of those persons convicted of genocide by the International Criminal Tribunal for Rwanda have been given life terms.

Because the focus of the Genocide Convention is on prevention of the crime, it was deemed important to make incomplete or preparatory acts punishable. As a result, in addition to participation in the crime of genocide itself, the Convention mandates prosecution of conspiracy to commit genocide, attempted genocide, and direct and public incitement to commit genocide. It has proven important here to draw a clear line between punishable manifestations of hate speech and what should be treated as legitimate if distasteful exercise of freedom of expression.

The emphasis on prevention of genocide also imposes a duty on states to intervene to prevent the crime being committed. The scope of this obligation remains uncertain, however. In 1994, powerful members of the United Nations Security Council hesitated at using the term genocide to describe mass killing of the Tutsi minority in Rwanda, out of concern that this legal qualification would entail a duty to act, something they were not prepared to do because the problems of a small country in central Africa were of no great strategic interest. Arguably, then, their behaviour confirmed the fact that when an accurate determination can be made that genocide is under way, there is a legal obligation to prevent. This is often referred to as the doctrine of humanitarian intervention. But here the Genocide Convention must be reconciled with the Charter of the United Nations: states cannot use force unilaterally on the grounds that genocide is being committed, they must act pursuant to a Security Council authorisation, in accordance with Chapter VII of the Charter of the United Nations.

Further Reading

Chalk, Frank and Jonassohn, Kurt (eds) (1990) *The History and Sociology of Genocide*, New Haven and London: Yale University Press.

Lemkin, Raphael (1944) *Axis Rule in Occupied Europe: Laws of Occupation, Analysis of Government, Proposals for Redress*, Washington: Carnegie Endowment for World Peace.

Schabas, William A. (2000) *Genocide in International Law*, Cambridge: Cambridge University Press.

Contributor: William A. Schabas

GLOBAL CIVIL SOCIETY AND HUMAN RIGHTS

Globalisation and the international human rights regime have contributed to create operational and legal openings for non-state actors to enter international arenas which were once the exclusive domain of national states. Various, often as yet very minor, developments signal that the state is no longer the exclusive subject for international law or the only actor in international relations.

Subnationally, these trends, along with neo-liberal deregulation and privatisation, are contributing to an incipient unbundling of the exclusive authority over territory and people we have long associated with the national state. The most strategic instantiation of this unbundling is probably the global city, which operates as a partly denationalised platform for global capital and at the same time is emerging as a key site for the most astounding mix of people from all over the world. Further, the growing intensity of transactions among these cities worldwide is creating strategic cross-border geographies – for capital, for professionals, for immigrants, for traders – which partly bypass the national state. This holds even for a state as powerful as that of the US. The new network technologies further strengthen these transactions, whether they are electronic transfers of specialised services among firms or Internet-based communications among the members of globally dispersed diasporas and interest groups. A good illustration of this is the coordinated demonstrations against the war on Iraq that enabled demonstrations on 15 February 2003 in at least 600 cities around the world.

These cities and the new strategic geographies that connect them can be seen as constituting part of the infrastructure for global civil society. They do so from the ground up, through multiple microsites. Among these microsites and microtransactions are a variety of organisations concerned with transboundary issues covering immigration, asylum, international women's agendas, anti-globalisation struggles and many others. While these are not necessarily urban in their orientation or genesis, their geography of operations is partly inserted in a large number of cities. Ironically the new network technologies, especially the Internet, have strengthened the urban map of these transboundary networks. It does not have to be that way, but at this time cities and the networks that bind them function as an anchor and an enabler of cross-border struggles. These same developments and conditions also facilitate the internationalising of terrorist and trafficking networks.

There is a growing tension between the legal equality contained in the institution of citizenship and the normative project of substantive equality. Enhanced inclusion has been an aim of various minorities and disadvantaged sectors. The struggles of the 1960s were one such effort. Today the US is seeing an even broader array of minoritised citizens who are not satisfied with formal equality and are seeking visibility and recognition for their claim making. A critical matter here is the failure in the US (and, indeed, in most countries) to achieve what citizenship is supposed to give: substantive equality, not merely formal equality.

Insofar as citizenship is at least partly shaped by the conditions within which it is embedded, today's novel landscape may well lead to a set of changes – one more in the long history of the institution. These may not yet be formalised and some may never become fully formalised. But the US has certainly been one country in the modern era that has evinced considerable determination on the part of minorities to gain rights. There is a specific American condition in all of this, given partly how the country was created: disadvantaged populations colonising the lands of others and making them into disadvantaged peoples; **SLAVERY**; robber barons. That is perhaps why few modern national states have experienced the American trauma of the sharp tension between citizenship as a formal legal status and the reality of life as a citizen if one was not among the privileged. For the large masses of disadvantaged in the US, citizenship emerges as a normative project or an aspiration. It is the substantive exclusions suffered by lawful citizens which have in turn produced the strong politics of claim making and of minority group rights that has characterised US history. The formal equality of citizens in the US after the Civil Rights legislation of the 1960s has rarely embodied the need for substantive equality in social terms.

Today, with over 50 million Americans living below the poverty line and a massive attack on the civil rights of particular groups of citizens, we see a growing emphasis on rights and aspirations that go beyond the formal legal definition of rights and obligations. The growing prominence of an international human rights regime has produced areas of convergence even as it has underlined the differences between citizenship rights and human rights. The actual content and shape of the legal rights and obligations may also change.

There is in all of this a very American response. Because the principle of equal citizenship remains unfulfilled, even after the successful struggles and legal advances of the last five decades (Karst, 1997), there is a proliferation of political and academic initiatives. Groups which still face various exclusions from full participation in public life have multiplied their self-definitions – by race, ethnicity, religion, sex, sexual orientation and other 'identities'. This is especially so at the level of practices and high-visibility claim making. Secondly, because full participation as a citizen rests on a material base (cf. T.H. Marshall, Joel Handler), poverty excludes large sectors of the population and the gap is widening. Feminist and race-critical scholarship have highlighted the failure of gender and race-neutral conceptions of citizenship and of rights. At the same time, the disadvantaged position of these different groups also engendered the practices and struggles that forced changes in the formal institution of citizenship itself.

In brief, citizenship is partly produced by the practices of the excluded. This very American history of interactions between differential positionings and expanded inclusions signals the possibility that the new conditions of inequality and difference evident today and the new types of claim making they produce may well bring about new forms of inclusion.

Individuals, even when undocumented immigrants, can move between the multiple meanings of citizenship. The routines of undocumented immigrants in their daily life in the community where they reside (raising a family, schooling children, holding a job) earn them a particular type of recognition. It is often referred to as an informal social contract between such undocumented immigrants and their communities of residence (Schuck and Smith, 1985). Indeed, unauthorised immigrants who demonstrate civic involvement, social deservedness and national loyalty can apply for legal residency in the US. Less formally, some interpret this as giving these undocumented immigrants informal citizenship claims even as the formal status and, more narrowly, legalisation may continue to evade them. In many countries around the world, including the US, long-term undocumented residents often can gain legal residence if they can document the fact of this long-term residence and 'good conduct'. US immigration law recognises such informal participation as grounds for granting legal residency. Different from the undocumented immigrant whose practices allow her to become accepted as a member of the political community is the case of those who are authorised residents yet not recognised as political subjects. Beyond the case of discriminated minorities, this may also hold for regular natives who are not discriminated against.

Research on immigrant women in the US not surprisingly shows that their regular wage work and improved access to other public realms has an impact on their culturally specified subordinate role to men in the household and in their role as housewives. Immigrant women gain greater personal autonomy and independence while immigrant men lose ground compared with their condition in cultures of origin. Women gain more control over budgeting and other domestic decisions. More to the point of the argument here is the fact that it is precisely in their role as housewives that they are responsible for taking care of the children which includes dealing with public state agencies: schools, the health system, police, civic obligations. There are two arenas where immigrant women are active: institutions for public and private assistance and the immigrant/ethnic community. These immigrant women are more active in community building and community activism and they are positioned differently from men regarding the broader economy and the state. They are the ones who are likely to have to handle the legal vulnerability in the process of seeking public and social services for their families. All of this amounts to participation in the public sphere and their possible emergence as public actors. They are often the ones in the household who mediate in this process. It is likely that some women benefit more than others from these circumstances. Yet the important dynamic to recover is that precisely in their role as housewives, a non-political subject, they emerge as a type of informal political/civic subject. These are dimensions of citizenship and citizenship practices which do not fit the indicators and categories of mainstream frameworks for understanding citizenship and political life. Women in the condition of housewives and mothers do not fit the categories and indicators used to capture participation in public life.

It is in this sense that those who lack power, those who are disadvantaged, outsiders, discriminated minorities, can gain presence in public domains, presence vis à vis power and presence vis à vis each other. This gaining of presence is enabled in the complex space of cities and assumes international dimensions in the case of global cities. This signals, for me, the possibility of a new type of politics centred in new types of political actors. It is not simply a matter of having or not having power. These are new hybrid bases from which to act.

We are seeing in the US a whole new wave of claim making. Many of these tranformations become legible in cities. In the city, these dynamics easily take concrete forms: the enactment of a large array of particular interests, from protests against police brutality, protests for the rights of immigrants, to sexual preference politics and house squatting by anarchists. I interpret this as a move towards citizenship practices that revolve around claiming rights to the city. These are not exclusively or necessarily urban practices. But it is especially in large cities that we see simultaneously some of the most extreme inequalities as well as conditions enabling these citizenship practices. In global cities, these practices also contain the possibility of directly engaging strategic forms of power, a fact that is significant in a context where power is increasingly privatised, globalised and elusive.

WEBSITES

APCWNSP (Association for Progressive Communications Women's Networking Support Programme). 2000. 'Women in Sync: Toolkit for Electronic Networking.' Acting Locally, Connecting Globally: Stories from the Regions (Vol. 3). Available at www.apcwomen.org/netsupport/sync/sync3.html.

Coalition to Abolish Slavery and Trafficking (CAST) www.trafficked-women.org

Continental Direct Action Network http://cdan.org/

Corporate Watch www.corpwatch.org/

50 Years is enough www.50years.org/

Fundacion ESPERANZA www.fundacionesperanza.org.co

Global Alliance Against Traffic in Women www.inet.co.th/org/gaatw

Global Exchange www.globalexchange.org/

Immigrant Workers Resource Center www.communityworks.com/html/mgd/iwrc.html

International Association of refugee law judges www.iarlj.nl/

International Forum on Globalization www.ifg.org/

Jubilee South www.jubileesouth.net/

SPARC www.sparcindia.org

Student Environmental Action Coalition www.seac.org/

Further Reading

'Symposium: The State of Citizenship' (2000) Indiana Journal of Global Legal Studies, vol. 7.

Handler, Joel (1995) *The Poverty of Welfare Reform*, New Haven, CT: Yale University Press.

Isin, Engin F. (ed.) (2000) *Democracy, Citizenship and the Global City*, London: Routledge.

Jessop, Robert (1999) 'Reflections on Globalization and its Illogics' in *Globalization and the Asia-Pacific: Contested Territories*, Olds, Kris *et al.* (eds), pp. 19–38, London: Routledge.

Glasius, Marlies, Kaldor, Mary and Anheier, Helmut (eds) (2002) *Global Civil Society Yearbook*, London: Oxford University Press.

Karst, Kenneth (1997) 'The Coming Crisis of Work in Constitutional Perspective' in 82.3, *Cornell Law Review*, 523–71.

Marshall, T. H. (1977) [1950] 'Citizenship and Social Class' in *Class, Citizenship and Social Development*, Chicago, IL: University of Chicago Press.

Sassen, Saskia (2005) *Denationalization: Territory, Authority and Rights in a Global Digital Age*, Princeton, NJ: Princeton University Press.

Schuck, Peter and Smith, Roger (1985) *Citizenship without Consent: Illegal Aliens in the American Polity*, New Haven, CT: Yale University Press.

Contributor: Saskia Sassen

GROUP RIGHTS

A 'group right', in its primary sense, is a right held by a group as a group rather than by its members severally. The qualification 'group' describes the nature of the right-holder. For example, if there is a right of national SELF-DETERMINATION, that must be a group right – a right possessed by a nation as a group. It is simply implausible to suppose that an individual, merely as an individual, could have a right that a nation should be self-determining. The rights of a people to its territory or its natural resources or its culture are other examples of rights that are group rights in this sense.

Rather confusingly, the term 'group right' has recently come to be used in a second, different sense in which it connotes a right that is unique to the members of a group. Here 'group' indicates not the nature of the right-holder but the range of people who hold the right: 'insiders' have the right; 'outsiders' don't. Group rights, in this sense, are sometimes ascribed to INDIGENOUS PEOPLES who, because of their special circumstances and vulnerability, are held to need special protective rights that they alone should possess. But many other rights also qualify as 'group rights' in this sense; for example, the rights people hold as members of trade unions or sports clubs or universities. A better term for these rights, coined by Will Kymlicka, is 'group-differentiated rights'. That is a better term because rights that are unique to a group need not be group rights in the primary sense: group-differentiated rights may be held by a group qua group, but they may also be held and exercised by the members of a group severally and so be 'individual' rights. For example, the rights possessed by the members of a trade union or sports clubs or university are most commonly rights held and exercised by members individually rather than by the group as a collectivity.

Group-differentiated rights cannot be straightforwardly human rights simply because they are group-differentiated rather than universal to mankind. However, they may be justified by way of human rights. For example, an indigenous minority may be situated such that it needs special protective rights if its members are to enjoy human rights on terms equal with the majority population. Hereinafter, I use the term group right only in its primary sense, in which it describes a right held by a group rather than a group-differentiated right.

The relationship between group rights, in their primary sense, and human rights is both complex and controversial. Group rights sometimes figure in catalogues of human rights. The most prominent example is the right of peoples to self-determination that is announced in the first articles of the INTERNATIONAL COVENANT ON ECONOMIC, SOCIAL, AND CULTURAL RIGHTS (1966) and the INTERNATIONAL COVENANT ON CIVIL AND POLITICAL RIGHTS (1966). The use of the term 'peoples' signals that the right is ascribed to each people as a group rather than to individuals.

Another example of a group right embedded in a human rights document is the right of the members of a religious faith that their sacred sites shall not be desecrated (Vienna Declaration, 1993). Sometimes, rather than being subsumed within human rights, group rights are presented as a separate category of right, though one that still complements human rights, as, for example, in the **AFRICAN CHARTER ON HUMAN AND PEOPLES' RIGHTS** (1981).

Yet the inclusion of group rights in official human rights documents is often regarded as a grave error. One simple objection is that human rights are rights held by human individuals, so that the mere fact that group rights are group rights disqualifies them as human rights. Some critics go further and challenge the very idea of group rights: groups are not real entities, they are mere aggregations of individuals and to conceive groups as right-holding entities is, they say, to dabble in metaphysical nonsense. In addition, group rights are often thought to be dangerous. If we ascribe rights to groups, we risk creating moral or legal juggernauts that will crush all who stand in their way. Human rights aim to safeguard human individuals but the rights of mere individuals may be easily overridden when set against the mighty rights of large groups. Proponents of human rights may therefore have reason to view group rights with fear and suspicion.

In assessing the relationship between group rights and human rights, much depends upon how we conceive the right-holding group. Those who are hostile to the idea of group rights typically suppose that these require us to conceive groups as unitary entities. We might describe this as the 'corporate' conception of group rights. On this conception, a group is viewed as a corporate entity that mimics a human person; indeed, it might be conceived as a group-person or group-individual. Analysts of groups do sometimes ascribe to groups thoughts, intentions, agency and other features that we normally ascribe to human persons. It is this way of conceiving groups that most frequently incurs scepticism: can we plausibly think of a group as a sort of macro-individual possessed of characteristics that befit it to wield rights? In fact, in law there is nothing unusual in ascribing rights (and duties) to corporate entities, but,

in the absence of legal incorporation, it is much harder to sustain a corporate conception of groups. In addition, since this conception of group rights entails ascribing to a group a moral standing that is ultimately rather reducible to the standing of its individual members, it seems at some distance from human rights thinking.

There is, however, another way of conceiving groups as right-holders that is much more consonant with human rights. We might describe this as the 'collective' conception. Here there is no attempt to turn groups into super-individuals. Rather, group rights are conceived simply as rights that individuals hold jointly rather than severally. Individuals may have some interests as discrete individuals and, in virtue of those discrete interests, may possess certain rights as separate individuals. But they may also have interests that they share with others. Those shared interests may be sufficiently significant to give rise to a shared or 'collective' right, in circumstances where the interest of any individual, taken singly, would not suffice to ground a right. In that case, we have a genuine group right, though one very different in character from a corporate right. It is a genuine group right because it is a right that the relevant individuals hold jointly or collectively, as a group, and that none of them possesses as an independent individual. This collective conception of group rights is much more in sympathy with human rights thinking in that it grounds these rights in the moral standing of the several individuals who make up the relevant group rather than in any supposed group entity. We might, for example, interpret the right of peoples to self-determination as a collective human right: it is a human right because it ranges over all human persons but it is a collective right because it is possessed and exercised by individuals not singly but only collectively or jointly as members of political communities.

Three significant questions confront proponents of group rights. Firstly, which groups possess rights? If we take the case of self-determination, for instance, is that right possessed only by 'nations' or 'peoples' or can it also be claimed, perhaps in a modified form, by indigenous minorities or subnational groups? Secondly, how should we individuate groups for right-holding purposes? For example, among those who embrace the idea of national self-determination there is often deep disagreement about which segments of humanity constitute nations possessed of rights of self-determination. Thirdly, which rights do (or should) groups have and, more particularly, how should we strike the balance between the rights of groups and the rights of individuals?

So-called 'solidarity' or 'third generation' human rights, which focus on goods such as **PEACE, DEVELOPMENT**, a healthy **ENVIRONMENT**, communication and ownership of the common heritage of mankind, are frequently characterised as group rights because of the collective nature of the goods to which they lay claim. The status of these putative rights is controversial but, conceptually, some do make sense as group rights. For example, development is a good that is public to the society whose development is at stake and a right to a public good will normally be a group right possessed by the relevant public. Whether we should conceive all 'solidarity rights' as group rights is more questionable, but that turns more on their status as rights than on their group character. In so far as they present aspirations for mankind as a whole, rather than claims that we can make against one another, they are better conceived as common objectives or ideals for humanity than as rights. The language of rights is not appropriate to every form of human endeavour, whether individual or collective.

Further Reading

Baker, Judith (ed.) (1994) *Group Rights*, Toronto: University of Toronto Press.

Cassesse, Antonio (1995) *Self-Determination of Peoples*, Cambridge: Cambridge University Press.

Galenkamp, Marlies (1993) *Individualism versus Collectivism: the Concept of Collective Rights*, Rotterdam: Rotterdamse Filosofische Studies.

Jones, Peter (1999) 'Human Rights, Group Rights and Peoples' Rights', in *Human Rights Quarterly*, 21, 80–107.

Shapiro, Ian and Kymlicka, Will (eds) (1997) *Ethnicity and Group Rights*, New York: New York University Press.

Contributor: Peter Jones

HEALTH, THE RIGHT TO

The **UNIVERSAL DECLARATION OF HUMAN RIGHTS** in Article 25(1) states that 'Everyone has the right to a standard of living adequate for the health and well-being of himself and his family, including food, clothing, housing and medical care and necessary social services'. The inclusion of 'health' and 'medical care' to the UDHR has led to an Article each in the **ESCR COVENANT** (Article 12), the **EUROPEAN SOCIAL CHARTER** (Article 11) and the **AFRICAN CHARTER OF HUMAN AND PEOPLES' RIGHTS AND DUTIES** (Article 16). All these covenants recognise the right of everyone to the enjoyment of the 'highest' or 'best' attainable standard of physical and mental health. Among the aspects singled out for special mention are also infant mortality (which also could be an aspect of the right to life); environmental and industrial hygiene; epidemic and occupational diseases; the development of medical services; and the encouragement of individual responsibility in matters of health. The relevant provisions in the European Social Charter have been considered by the Strasbourg Committee of Experts, which has laid down the minimum standards which the state parties to that treaty must observe in the health field if they are to be regarded as fulfilling their obligations.

Related human rights are the **RIGHT TO LIFE,** and the right that 'No one shall be subject to cruel, inhuman or degrading treatment or punishment'. In addition, rights to equality and non-discrimination are central in this context, particularly when we discuss the treatment of terminally ill patients (due to either incurable diseases such as fatal cancer, HIV/AIDS or various genetic conditions). These rights are also relevant when we consider individuals' wishes in relation to their end-of-life decisions such as refusing treatment or to be resuscitated, or when asking for euthanasia (See: **RIGHT TO LIFE: EUTHANASIA**) or physician-assisted suicide. In addition, rights to equality and non-discrimination are essential in relation to the rights of anyone who is physically or mentally disabled and thus easily disadvantaged or marginalised in a society.

The World Health Organization uses a holistic definition of 'health' according to which health does not merely consist of the absence of disease or handicaps but refers to the highest attainable standard of physical, mental and social well-being. While this definition is more inclusive and allows various aspects of life to be taken into account in health issues, this wide understanding of 'health' can be a double-edged sword. On the one hand, it appears to avoid restricted, paternalist or imperialist interpretations of the concept, but on the other hand, it leaves plenty of room for relativist interpretations of what is to be included in 'health' and what it means to be 'healthy'. After all, even when we think about 'health' merely in terms of lack of disease or handicap, there might be differences in interpretations of its meaning across cultural, national and generational borders. What is considered a disease or abnormality in one place or at one time may not be seen as such somewhere else or any longer. As French philosopher Michel Foucault has noted, social power relations also have an impact on what we consider to be 'normal' or 'healthy'. This is important from the point of view of human rights because when we set a variety of normative standards for 'health' against which we judge some people as 'abnormal' or 'sick', there is a danger that we may insist that for their own good they should get treatment to be cured – whether we talk about mental, physical or genetic conditions or even sexual orientation. This can lead into inequality in the form of discrimination and stigmatisation.

Much of the contents of our actual legal rights to health and medical care depend, first, on the conditions of the individual patient and second, on health services available, as the claims for 'highest or best attainable standard of health' implies. If I have an incurable disease, I no longer can claim my right to be 'fully healthy', but at least I have a chance to claim certain medical services and health care, which may not be able to cure me but may provide me nevertheless with the 'highest attainable quality of life'. These services, for their part, often depend not only on the resources available but also on the chosen policies based on various concepts of distributive justice.

It is therefore central to consider what distributive considerations are relevant in establishing some universal minimum health standards. We tend to refer to different types of rights within different politico-economic systems. If we defend negative rights, that is our civil and political rights of non-interference and participation, our rights to life and health would mean that others have a responsibility not to harm us. However, negative rights leave us vulnerable if we have lost our health (or were born disabled one way or another) without any particular person's fault, since they also promote state non-interference in economic and social matters. Positive rights, for their part, assume that either the state (or the society as a whole) has a responsibility to help us to create the social conditions that support our health and well-being. Positive rights are substantive rights that give us social entitlements and set a state or a society a duty to assist us to realise our health by also supporting the availability of justly distributed health care and medical services.

The promotion of positive rights in relation to health and well-being often raises the question of social and individual responsibility. How much responsibility do we have for our own health? In order to enforce responsibility a state might set legal requirements (such as a law to use seat belts or helmets in traffic, a smoking ban or restrictions on selling alcohol and drugs). The state can also enforce policies for routine vaccinations or screening for various genetic conditions (with the latest diagnostic technology) in order to promote 'public health'. The requests for social and individual responsibility turn into a human rights question when an individual's concept of well-being conflicts with the national public health goals that might lead to paternalistic interference that limits one's **AUTONOMY** and freedom, and in the worst

> In the next 24 hours, almost 30,000 children under five will die, most from preventable or treatable diseases. That is more than 10 million children per year. Sub-Saharan Africa with only 10 per cent of the world's population accounts for 43 per cent of all deaths among children under five.
>
> (From Save the Children USA)

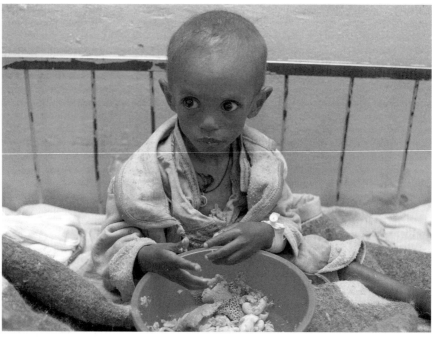

© Reuters/CORBIS

case might lead to discrimination. Similarly, conflicts may occur when we have to prioritise between the needs and rights of people who are not infected with HIV/AIDS (measures of prevention) and people living with HIV/AIDS (access to treatment).

While the issues of distribution of resources are central in protecting human rights to life, health and well-being, there is also a need to discuss how we can best combine different cultural interpretations of the concepts of 'health' and 'well-being', particularly when we consider health care practitioners working across geographical and cultural borders. The rather vague demand to promote 'the highest attainable standards of health' as such does not help medical practitioners to decide when to treat and how to treat in difficult situations and in different cultural contexts. Sometimes even if we want to help and have the best intentions in sharing our skills and resources, what Western doctors and experts think is best for Africa or Asia might not gain agreement among individual patients or their communities. The discussion on universality of the codes of professional medical ethics and plausibility of their global

application is therefore important for human rights promotion.

In addition, the question whether it is morally justifiable to try to force people to live healthier lives in order to provide the best attainable health is further complicated when set in an international context. People from affluent societies – whether medical practitioners or not – may reprimand those living in poor conditions about such health-threatening traditions as female genital mutilation (FGM), but at the same time they themselves may engage in lifestyles that danger their own health (by smoking, eating unhealthy food, and so on).

The issues of paternalism, privacy and self-determination arise also when we ponder national and international health goals. Different countries and regions may have different health concerns, but how can we fit them within the international human rights context? This is not only about particular diseases or resources needed to deal with them – whether in the form of prevention, care or cure – it is also about the sharing of information across borders. What kind of information and knowledge about health is relevant for assessing international and national policies and institutions that are designed to decrease child mortality and increase life expectancy, provide opportunities for good health and access to health care resources?

Many of the violations against rights to health and to standards of living that would be adequate to promote our health and well-being are due to uneven distribution of resources. Most of us feel that it is morally unacceptable that millions of people in poor countries not only lack access to basic health services but die from hunger and preventable diseases, while the abundance of resources has led many in rich countries to suffer from obesity, eating disorders and heart diseases. Attempts to guarantee everyone 'the highest possible health and well-being' are then related to the available resources. In the poor, developing countries the focus might be on combating such curable diseases as malaria, tuberculosis, cholera and diarrhoea, while the affluent, technologically and scientifically advanced societies can offer such complicated and expensive treatments as organ transplantation, gene therapy and various forms of expansive fertility treatments. However, while unequal distribution of resources is a global problem, it is also a local problem and a sign of general lack of respect for equal human rights.

In many poor countries, for instance, women's health issues and well-being receive the least attention. Women are socially the most disadvantaged and vulnerable (due to lack of access to education, lack of nutrition and satisfaction of basic NEEDS, mistreatment of girl children and domestic violence, including rape (See: VIOLENCE AGAINST WOMEN: DOMESTIC VIOLENCE), which, for its part, leads to the spread of HIV/AIDS and other sexually transmitted diseases). Thus, in order to improve women's position and to promote women's health the human rights agenda places a special emphasis on WOMEN'S RIGHTS as human rights and particularly on women's reproductive needs.

The relationship between human rights and health is complex and often appears to involve questions on conflicting rights. The right to EQUALITY, for instance, is related to the rights to privacy and confidentiality which, however, may conflict with the requirement for social responsibility. Individual rights con-

flicts occur when we discuss whether an individual has the 'right not to reveal' or even 'not to know' his or her health status' (for instance in relation to various genetic diseases or HIV/AIDS) if and when other individuals might directly be affected by their condition.

Nevertheless, the main problem is still the unequal global and local distribution of resources: a) the lack of access to basic standards of living as well as the lack of EDUCATION create suffering and promote the spread of various diseases; b) lack of access to the most basic health care generates difficulties in prevention and cure of not only serious illnesses but also other more minor health problems.

Further Reading

Cook, Rebecca *et al.* (2003) *Reproductive Health and Human Rights: Integrating Medicine, Ethics and Law (Issues in Biomedical Ethics)*, Oxford: Oxford University Press.

Farmer, Paul (2003) *Pathologies of Power: Health, Human Rights, and the New War on the Poor*, Los Angeles: University of California Press.

Foucault, Michel (1973) *The Birth of the Clinic, Archaeology of Medical Perception*, Random House, New York.

Gostin, Lawrence and Hodge, James (eds) (2004) *Health and Human Rights*, London: Ashgate Publishing.

Mann, Jonathan (ed.) (1999) *Health and Human Rights*, London: Routledge.

WHO (2002) *25 Questions and Answers on Health and Human Rights*, WHO, Geneva. http://whqlibdoc.who.int/hq/2002/9241545 690.pdf

Contributor: Sirkku Hellsten

THE HISTORICAL ROOTS OF HUMAN RIGHTS BEFORE THE SECOND WORLD WAR

The term 'human rights' was rarely used before the Second World War. However, when the UNITED NATIONS declared, in the preamble to its Charter of 1945, that it was determined 'to reaffirm faith in fundamental human rights', it was 'reaffirming', not inventing, the principles of human rights. The idea of human rights is a transformation of older ideas.

There are two main approaches to the history of human rights. The first assumes that the concept is derived from broader and deeper moral ideas, such as those of justice and human dignity, that are found in many cultures, including the world's ancient religions. This approach has the advantage of making the concept inclusive and of providing a basis for the claim that human rights are universal (See: UNIVERSALISM). The second approach emphasises the distinctiveness of the concept of 'rights' and claims that it is Western and modern. On this view, the Western origin of the idea is consistent with the view that it ought to be universalised under contemporary conditions.

Many ancient social codes and religions emphasised duties to others and especially to those suffering from abuse or misfortune. These duties were often derived from a belief that there was a universal source of truth for all human beings. In the Jewish (See: JEWISH TRADITION AND HUMAN RIGHTS), Christian and Islamic (See: ISLAM AND HUMAN RIGHTS) traditions, this derives from a belief in a single, universal God and the worth of all his creation. This implies moral limits on the powers of rulers and obligations to the needy. The universalism of moral duty has sometimes been explicitly extended to strangers. Concepts such as benevolence, compassion and love are found in Confucianism (See: CONFUCIANISM AND HUMAN RIGHTS), Buddhism (See: BUDDHISM AND HUMAN RIGHTS) and Christianity. The emphasis of these ancient codes was, however, on duties rather than on rights. They also commonly excluded from their protection various groups, such as foreigners, non-believers, women, slaves and homosexuals. Some rulers did, however, recognise the principle of religious toleration. The ancient world had no conception of human rights, but it had the concept of the rule of law and various conceptions of justice that implied rights for various categories of persons.

Ancient religions, such as Judaism and Buddhism, and secular philosophies, such as those of Confucius and Plato, had a conception of the 'human' without a clear conception of rights. The political philosophy of Aristotle

had a clear conception of citizens' rights but no conception of human rights since citizens' rights did not extend to women, slaves and foreigners. The Stoic philosophers developed the idea of a universal moral law. Classical philosophy, therefore, recognised the idea of citizens' rights and that of universal moral law, but did not combine them in the concept of universal human rights.

The idea of rights passed from the classical to the modern world through medieval Christian philosophy. This process was complex and remains rather obscure. Christian philosophers incorporated the classical idea of natural law into the Christian conception of divine law in their attempts to justify the right to private property. At the same time various medieval power-holders, such as landowners and urban corporations, asserted claims to customary and legal rights against monarchs seeking to increase their own power and wealth. The Magna Carta (1215) is a famous example of such demands. The Protestant Reformation made freedom of conscience a fundamental political issue of early modern Europe. In 17th-century England the principles of property rights and religious toleration came together in resistance to the absolutist pretensions of the Stuart monarchy. John Locke gave these ideas philosophical expression in his *Second Treatise of Government*, in which he claimed that everyone had natural rights to life, liberty and property, and that government was a trust established to protect these rights through the rule of law. His theory was based on Christian natural-law philosophy but provided the outlines of the modern conception of human rights.

The idea of natural rights was particularly influential in America, where the demand for freedom of conscience and resistance to excessive taxation were exceptionally strong, and in France, where absolute monarchy was reluctant to grant civil liberties, such as freedom of expression and conscience, that had been won in England. The American Declaration of Independence (1776) justified the revolt against British rule in terms of 'unalienable rights' to life, liberty and the pursuit of happiness. In 1791 the Americans added the Bill of Rights as a set of amendments to the US Constitution and included rights to freedom of religion, the press, expression and assembly, protection against

> It is in truth not for glory, nor riches, nor honours that we are fighting, but for freedom – for that alone, which no honest man gives up but with life itself.
>
> Declaration of Arbroath, Scotland, 1320

unreasonable search and seizure, the right not to incriminate oneself and the right to due process of law. Although the Americans appealed to the philosophy of natural rights, the specific rights that they claimed had long been established in colonial and English law.

In 1789 King Louis XVI of France convened the Estates-General – an antiquated medieval parliament – in an attempt to raise more taxes to finance France's rivalry with Britain. Negotiations among the monarchy, aristocracy, clergy and the 'third estate' (commoners) broke down and the third estate established a national assembly and proclaimed a Declaration of the Rights of Man and the Citizen as a set of principles for a new constitution of France. The Declaration affirmed the rights to liberty, property, security and resistance to oppression; equality before the law; freedom from arbitrary arrest; the presumption of innocence; freedom of expression and religion; and the right to property. Whereas the American Revolution had ignored the rights of women and the question of slavery, the French Revolution raised both issues, only to suppress them quickly. The rights proclaimed by both these revolutions were universal in theory, but restricted in practice to propertied, white males. Despite these limitations, the French Declaration was the most important historical inspiration for the **UNIVERSAL DECLARATION OF HUMAN RIGHTS** adopted in 1948.

The upheavals of the French Revolution discredited the idea of the Rights of Man. Political philosophers, such as Edmund Burke and Jeremy Bentham (See: **UTILITARIANISM AND HUMAN RIGHTS**), criticised it for subverting social order and/or as unscientific. The rise of industrial capitalism changed the emphasis of social philosophy from forms of government to the dynamics of the economy and society. Karl Marx criticised the Rights of Man as the ideology of the bourgeois class

(See: **THE MARXIST CRITIQUE OF HUMAN RIGHTS**). Nevertheless, several developments that were important for the future of human rights took place in the 19th century: the anti-slavery movement (See: **FREEDOM FROM SLAVERY**); the campaign for the social and political rights of women; workers' and socialist movements, trade unions and political parties; the development of the humanitarian laws of war; concern for religious and ethnic minorities; and protests against racial discrimination and colonialism.

These campaigns were important in two particular respects. The first was their emphasis on what are now called economic and social rights, such as fair working conditions, health and education. These are sometimes called 'second generation' rights, in contrast to 'first generation' civil and political rights, but this is misleading, both because earlier generations of rights advocates had been concerned with economic rights, such as the rights to subsistence and property, and because, from the 17th to the 20th centuries, campaigners (for example, workers and women) demanded political rights partly in order to defend their economic and social rights.

The second important aspect of these movements was their internationalism (See: **COSMOPOLITANISM AND HUMAN RIGHTS**). Struggles for the rights of minorities, workers and women all had an international dimension and the international solidarity of non-governmental organizations, which is a prominent feature of contemporary human rights struggles, was pioneered as the industrial revolution made international travel and communication faster and easier.

The First World War was a humanitarian catastrophe, but it also advanced the causes of economic and social rights, the rights of women and minorities, and the right of national self-determination (See: **THE RIGHT TO SELF-DETERMINATION**) against imperial domination. At the end of the war the League of Nations was established and although both its Covenant and its practice proved to be disappointing to those concerned with human rights, it addressed questions of minorities, workers' rights, slavery, the rights of women and children and the plight of refugees. Thus, even if the League was a political failure, it contributed to the very idea of the United Nations and its commitment to human rights.

The historical struggles of property owners, intellectuals, colonists, workers, women, national minorities and anti-colonial campaigners all contributed to the development of the contemporary conception of human rights. The discourse of rights derives from classical Western philosophy, Roman law, medieval Christianity and modern liberal and socialist ideologies. The idea of human rights is, however, rooted in a set of fundamental moral and religious beliefs that are far from exclusively Western. These beliefs were developed into conceptions of rights in response to tyrannical government and oppressive social and economic conditions that are not particularly Western. The human rights movement has been global since the conditions for global social movements came into being. The idea and the specification of human rights have always been controversial in theory and practice. They have evolved as men and women have struggled for a life of dignity under changing conditions. This struggle will continue, globally.

Further Reading

Burgers, J.H. (1992) 'The Road to San Francisco: The Revival of the Human Rights Idea in the Twentieth Century', in *Human Rights Quarterly*, 14 (4), 447–77.

Freeman, M.A. (2002) *Human Rights: An Interdisciplinary Approach*, Cambridge: Polity Press.

Lauren, P.G. (1998) *The Evolution of International Human Rights: Visions Seen*, Philadelphia, PA: University of Pennsylvania Press.

Tierney, B. (1997) *The Idea of Natural Rights*, Atlanta, GA: Scholars Press.

Waldron, J. (ed.) (1987) *'Nonsense Upon Stilts': Bentham, Burke and Marx on the Rights of Man*, London: Methuen.

Contributor: Michael Freeman

HOUSING, THE RIGHT TO ADEQUATE

Over the past two decades, the human right to adequate housing has been consistently reaffirmed as a distinct human right by various bodies in the UNITED NATIONS system, numerous national constitutions and legislations, and civil society organisations across the world. It also found repeated recognition as a fundamental human right in the Istanbul Declaration and the Habitat Agenda, resulting from the World Conference on Human Settlements (1996), with states reaffirming 'our commitment to the full and progressive realisation of the right to adequate housing, as provided for in the international instruments'. In spite of this welcome acknowledgement, the right to adequate housing remains unrealised for the vast majority of poor and vulnerable people and communities across the world.

Indeed, it is estimated that 600 million urban dwellers and over 1 billion rural people live in overcrowded and poor quality housing without adequate water, sanitation and drainage or garbage collection. An additional 100 million people are essentially homeless, being forced to live with no shelter. Statistics, however, do not fully capture the global dimensions of inadequate and insecure housing. Consider, for example, just some of the types of distressed housing in which people and communities are forced to live across the world: slums and squatter settlements, makeshift housing, old buses, shipping containers, pavements, railway platforms and alongside railway tracks, streets and roadside embankments, cellars, staircases, rooftops, lift enclosures, cages, cardboard boxes, plastic sheets and aluminium and tin shelters.

The emergence and persistence of economic GLOBALISATION has limited the capacity of states to provide adequate resources for fulfilling ECONOMIC, SOCIAL and CULTURAL RIGHTS, including the right to housing. The attendant reliance on privatisation of land and civic services, growing speculation of housing and land and the widening gap between income groups have all contributed towards increasing the number of people living in inadequate and insecure housing and living conditions, including the millions who are homeless and landless.

If we acknowledge this global reality and the affront to the dignity of people and entire communities that such distressed housing and living conditions represent, it is clear that only a human rights paradigm, which includes a housing and land rights approach, can offer the radical and systemic changes that are necessary to solve this global crisis. Such a focus on human rights is all the more critical as we are faced with growing inequality, poverty and social exclusion. The human rights approach enables a sharper critique of government responsibility and provides benchmarks for interventions by all sectors of society, including those marginalised and suffering from discrimination.

Since the proclamation of the **UNIVERSAL DECLARATION OF HUMAN RIGHTS** in 1948, the right to adequate housing has found explicit recognition in a wide range of international instruments. On the basis of the provisions established in the UDHR, the right to adequate housing was further elaborated and reaffirmed in the **INTERNATIONAL COVENANT ON ECONOMIC, SOCIAL AND CULTURAL RIGHTS** in 1966. Article 11.1 of the Covenant states that: 'The States Parties to the present Covenant recognize the right of everyone to an adequate standard of living for himself and his family, including adequate food, clothing and housing, and to the continuous improvement of living conditions. The States Parties will take appropriate steps to ensure the realization of this right, recognizing to this effect the essential importance of international cooperation based on free consent.'

The right to adequate housing is also recognised in several other international instruments that have focused on the need to protect the rights of particular groups such as in the **CONVENTION ON THE ELIMINATION OF ALL FORMS OF DISCRIMINATION AGAINST WOMEN** (1979), the **CONVENTION ON THE RIGHTS OF THE CHILD** (1989) and the **INTERNATIONAL CONVENTION ON THE ELIMINATION OF ALL FORMS OF RACIAL DISCRIMINATION**.

Issues related to the right to adequate housing were also highlighted in declarations and programmes of action adopted by several of the United Nations global conferences and summits held during the 1990s, including Agenda 21 adopted at the United Nations Conference on Environment and Development (1992), the Copenhagen Declaration and the Programme of Action of the World Summit for Social Development

(1995), the Beijing Declaration and Platform for Action of the Fourth World Conference on Women (1995) and the Habitat Agenda of the second United Nations Conference on Human Settlements (Habitat II) (1996).

During the past two decades, numerous UN bodies and civil society groups have made significant efforts to clarify and provide a broad interpretation to the content of the right to adequate housing. The most comprehensive interpretation has been made by the Committee on Economic, Social and Cultural Rights, in its General Comment no. 4 on the right to adequate housing. The General Comment reflects both the holistic conception of the right and the value it gains from the aspect of dignity and adequacy. Based on this broad interpretation, the General Comment identified seven aspects of the right to housing that determine 'adequacy': (a) legal security of tenure including legal protection against forced evictions; (b) availability of services, materials, facilities and infrastructure; (c) affordability; (d) habitability; (e) accessibility for disadvantaged groups; (f) location; and (g) cultural adequacy.

Based on, and inspired by, this interpretation and the strident work of civil society groups worldwide to capture the grassroots-level experiences and aspirations of the right to housing, I have made an attempt to define the human right to adequate housing as 'the right of every woman, man, child and youth to gain and sustain a secure home and community in which to live in peace and dignity'. Notwithstanding the wide legal recognition of the right to adequate housing, it is, however, a fact that the norms and principles contained in international instruments have not yet been sufficiently reflected in national policy frameworks in the housing sector or transformed into operational measures. Some have even argued that the right to adequate housing – and other economic, social and cultural rights – is not enforceable but aspirational, since it is claimed these rights are not justiciable and their fulfilment depends on the availability of public resources that many countries do not have.

Proper understanding of the nature of state obligation is, therefore, critical in dispelling such misconceptions. The principles that permeate the international human rights instruments offer an invaluable guide to understanding the scope of the right to housing. Indivisibility of human rights requires that the right to housing has to be seen as a congruent right along with the right to security of the person and home, the right to participation, the right to freedom of movement, the right to information, the right to water and the right to be free from inhuman and degrading treatment. Gender equality indicates that women and men have equal rights to an adequate standard of living, which includes the right to housing. Non-discrimination calls for affirmative action and the retention of subsidies for vulnerable people and communities to stem the growing phenomenon of segregation and ghettoisation in terms of housing and living conditions and the attendent denial of civic services. Non-retrogression requires that there is no stepping back from progress made in societies towards improving housing and living conditions, including to ensure that judicious legislation and policies are not bargained away. The right to a remedy requires that the right to housing is justiciable and that those who are responsible for guaranteeing this right demonstrate political and economic accountability.

The misconceptions that surround the right to housing can also be removed by understanding what the right to housing is not. Work carried out by UN human rights bodies has clarified that the obligations of states do not imply: that the state is required to build housing for the entire population; that housing is to be provided free of charge by the state to all who request it; that the state must necessarily fulfil all aspects of this right immediately upon assuming duties to do so; that the state should exclusively entrust either itself or the unregulated market to ensuring this right to all and that this right will manifest itself in precisely the same manner in all circumstances or locations.

The human rights approach to housing also needs to be understood from the perspective of the rights of specific groups. Inadequate and insecure housing and living conditions such as overcrowding, indoor pollution, precarious housing, lack of water and electricity and inadequate building materials affect women to a larger extent than men. Women living in extreme poverty face a much greater risk of becoming homeless or finding themselves in inadequate housing and health conditions. The horrific lack of adequate housing, particularly for women, is a strong indicator of the extent to which governments across the world are failing their people.

Given these dire conditions, it is heartening to see that more and more civil society initiatives across the world, including large scale local and national campaigns and movements, are taking up the human right to adequate housing as a rallying demand. Recent national constitutions, such as those of South Africa and Kenya, are also recognizing this right as fundamental. Given, however, the manifold threats to this essential right as outlined above, it is clear that even more strident civil society action is required. Such action needs to demonstrate alternative solutions and ensure human rights education at all levels of society such that people and communities can know and claim their human rights. The moral, ethical and legal basis of all human rights, in particular economic, social and cultural rights, as contained in the international human rights instruments, must form the organising principles for all policy and advocacy interventions by governments and civil society alike. Such a clear direction in policy formulation and action would necessarily require, as a priority, land and wealth redistribution, including urban and rural land reform. Only then will we see an improvement in the housing and living conditions of millions across the world.

WEBSITES

www.unhchr.ch/housing

www.hlrn.org

www.choike.org

www.cohre.org

www.unhabitat.org

http://home.mweb.co.za/hi/hic/

www.achr.net

Further Reading

Centre on Housing Rights and Evictions (2000) *Sources 4: Legal Resources for Housing Rights: International and National Standards*, Geneva: COHRE.

Centre on Housing Rights and Evictions (1994) *Legal Provisions on Housing Rights: International and National Approaches*, Utrecht.

Farha, Leilani (2002) 'Is There a Woman in the House?: Re-Conceiving the Human Right to Housing', 14 *Canadian Journal of Women and the Law*, pp.118–141.

Leckie, (1995) 'The Justiciability of Housing Rights' in Coomans and van Hoof (eds), *The Right to Complain about Economic, Social and Cultural Rights*, SIM, Utrecht: COHRE.

Office of the High Commisioner for Human Rights, Fact Sheet No. 21: 'The Human Right to Adequate Housing', available at: http://www.unhchr.ch/housing/fs21.htm

The Right to Adequate Housing. Report of the Special Rapporteur, 52 pages, sales no. E.96.XIV.3. ISBN: 92-1-154120-4. United Nations.

Contributor: Miloon Kothari

HUMAN RIGHTS BETWEEN WAR AND PEACE

In times of strife, when a situation is no longer peaceful but before it can be qualified as an armed conflict, human rights law may become nebulous. Indeed, during this period between peace and war – sometimes called the 'grey zone' – states may derogate from some of their human rights obligations.

It is important to emphasise that one of the strengths – as well as one of the weaknesses – of the entire human rights regime is based on the possibility for states to diminish human rights protection in times of emergency, through the 'derogation clause' (see: **DEROGATIONS AND RESERVATIONS**). On the one hand, this clause allows increased protection in non-emergency times: states will be all the more willing to grant strong human rights guarantees in ordinary times because they may reduce some standards when the life of the nation is at stake. In addition, the identification of the legal framework that applies in states of emergency allows for the recognition of a hardcore of inalienable rights, namely the rights defined in clauses that may never be derogated from, even in the most extreme emergency. In the **INTERNATIONAL COVENANT ON CIVIL AND POLITICAL RIGHTS** (1966) the list of inalienable rights and the conditions under which states may derogate from their human rights obligations are spelled out in Article 4.

While the derogation clause may play a positive role, an improper use of the clause could lead to an excessive decrease in human rights protection, such as permanent states of emergency. Indeed, it happens that governments prolong states of emergency and the legal framework that should apply only in exceptional situations becomes *de facto* the regular law. This is even more worrying given that states willing to diminish human rights guarantees will also often be those where the most vulnerable people will need greater protection, due to civil strife.

Consequently, one of the key aspects for effective human rights protection in situations of emergency will be the existence of an actual and efficient control, by an independent and impartial body, over the use of the derogations clause by states. Under a democratic regime where the legislative, executive and judiciary powers are separated, the national tribunals will be responsible for controlling the use of the derogation clause by the government. Judges will verify that the conditions spelled out in Article 4 of the Covenant are respected, as well as other specific conditions according to domestic law. In particular, they will make sure that no inalienable right will be affected by the exceptional measures and that these measures are not inconsistent with the state's other obligations under international law. Judges will also verify the existence of a public emergency that threatened the life of the nation, without which no derogation is possible. Further, the derogating state will have to demonstrate that every exceptional measure was strictly required by the exigencies of the situation and respected the principle of proportionality. Finally, the derogation measures must not involve discrimination solely on the ground of race, colour, sex, language, religion or social origin.

When the public emergency is such that the life of the nation is threatened, it seems only natural that the authorities are allowed to take exceptional measures to restore peace and security. Amongst the possible exceptional measures is the possibility for a state to derogate from some of its international human rights obligations. In fact, all but the inalienable human rights may somehow be restricted under special circumstances. Yet a strange phenomenon appears under international law. In the most extreme emergencies, namely when the situation is so tense that it becomes an armed conflict – that is when the International Law of Armed Conflict or **INTERNATIONAL HUMANITARIAN LAW** (IHL) applies – human rights protection starts to increase again. In other words, human rights may appear relatively well protected under normal circumstances and in times of armed conflict, while being much weaker in situations 'in between', during an emergency.

The **RIGHT TO A FAIR TRIAL** is an interesting illustration of this phenomenon. Under the Covenant, the right to a fair trial (Article 14) is not categorised as an inalienable right. In theory the clause may be derogated from, so long as the state respects the conditions spelled out in Article 4 of the Covenant. However, when the situation qualifies as an armed conflict and both the Geneva Conventions and their Additional Protocol apply, the due process rights guaranteed (with respect to protected persons) are almost the same as those covered by Article 14 of the Covenant. It appears that the right to a fair trial could enjoy equivalent protection in times of peace and war, while it may be limited under mere emergency situations. Why is this the case?

Despite some similarities in the content of the norms, the philosophies behind the two sets of law are totally different. During an armed conflict there is no longer a balance of power between individuals (even grouped together) and states. Humanitarian law is, originally, a law that applies to relationships between states (namely armies composed of combatants) or between an 'official' power and 'dissenting' powers (rebels, freedom fighters and so on). The code of conduct of hostilities defined by humanitarian law is common to all belligerents and the parties have a direct interest in respecting the rules of war in order to ensure that they are respected, in return, by the enemy combatant. Thus, in humanitarian law reciprocity is regarded both as the rationale behind the norm and as an important factor in its efficacy. In contrast, the concept of human rights stands in an individual/state relationship which excludes any reciprocity: what a state grants to an individual cannot be given back to the state by the individual. Consequently, states were always more disposed to develop guarantees under human-

itarian law than human rights law. This also explains why the codification of humanitarian law started long ago, while the drafting of international human rights law treaties is more recent.

Furthermore, humanitarian law does not apply instead of the human rights that were in force during the state of emergency but in addition to them. The hardcore of human rights that might have been reduced to its minimum – where only rights expressly listed as inalienable may never be diminished – starts growing again once the situation is qualified as an armed conflict, by contrast to internal tensions or states of emergency.

The fact that human rights law imposes more constraints upon governments may explain why states are sometimes so reluctant to name situations of strife as armed conflicts but rather call them 'terrorism' (such as in Chechnya nowadays), 'events' (Algeria during the war of independence) or 'troubles' (Northern Ireland). What first appears as a paradox – namely the fact that some human rights might enjoy better protection during armed conflicts than during other, less serious crises – has its justifications. Yet this does not mean that such a situation is satisfactory.

Scholars and monitoring human rights bodies have made various efforts to increase human rights protection under states of emergency. For example, the **INTER-AMERICAN COURT** and **COMMISSION OF HUMAN RIGHTS** developed the argument that the rights necessary to allow inalienable rights to be effective are themselves non-derogable. In particular, in its Advisory Opinion on 'Habeas Corpus in Emergency Situations' (1987), the Inter-American Court emphasised that, although the right to *habeas corpus* was not listed as an inalienable right in the Convention, it may never be suspended or rendered ineffective. The Inter-American Court explained that the immediate aim of *habeas corpus* is to bring the detainee before a judge, thus enabling the latter to verify whether the detainee is still alive and whether or not he has been subject to **TORTURE**. And indeed, the clauses guaranteeing the **RIGHT TO LIFE** and the right not to be tortured may never be derogated from. In other words, the purpose of *habeas corpus* is to guarantee the effectiveness of inalienable rights; by extent it necessarily becomes inalienable.

Similarly, the EUROPEAN COURT OF HUMAN RIGHTS, responsible for monitoring the respect by member states of their human rights obligations under the EUROPEAN CONVENTION OF HUMAN RIGHTS, emphasises that the Convention is intended to guarantee not rights that are theoretical or illusory but rights that are practical and effective (see, for example, the decision *Wemhoff v Germany*, 1968). For a right or a remedy to be effective, it must be capable of producing the result for which it was designed.

The ultimate basis of this reasoning relies on the argument that states party to a human rights treaty have an obligation to respect the rights and freedoms recognised in the treaty in an effective manner and to ensure to all persons subject to their jurisdiction the free and full exercise of those rights and freedoms. Through the theory of effectiveness it may be possible to both respect the letter and the spirit of human rights treaties while increasing the scope of inalienable human rights that must be respected even in times of public emergency that threaten the life of the nation.

Further Reading

Eide, A., Rosas, A. and Meron, T. (1995) 'Current Development: Combating Lawlessness in Grey Zone Conflicts Through Minimum Humanitarian Standard', 89 *American Journal of International Law*, 215.

Fitzpatrick, J. (1994) *Human Rights in Crisis. The International System for Protecting Rights during States of Emergency*, Philadelphia, University of Pennsylvania Press.

Meron, T. (1983) 'Note and Comment: on the Inadequate Reach of Humanitarian and Human Rights Law and the Need for a New Instrument', 77 *American Journal of International Law*, 589.

Olivier, C. (2004) 'Revisiting General Comment No. 29 of the Human Rights Committee. About Fair Trial Rights and Derogations in Times of Public Emergency' in *The Leiden Journal of International Law*, 17, 2.

Oraa, J. (1992) *Human Rights in States of Emergency in International Law*, Oxford: Clarendon Press, Oxford.

Contributor: Clémentine Olivier

HUMAN RIGHTS EDUCATION

The UNIVERSAL DECLARATION OF HUMAN RIGHTS germinated the idea of human rights education. Several decades later, this fructified in the United Nations Human Rights Education Decade ending in 2005. The Universal Declaration insists that 'every individual and organ of society' shall 'try by teaching and education to promote respect for these rights and freedoms ...'. In this figuration, the embryonic human right to human rights education emerges simultaneously as an aspect of human rights and fundamental freedoms and as a co-equal measure of human rights obligations of all individual human beings. Only such a reading renders sensible the affirmation of everyone's right to education (Articles 26, 29), including human rights education, as a crucial aspect of the attainment of 'freedom, justice and peace in the world.'

The shift in the human rights education terrain is marked by human rights education's remarkable articulations: the 1974 UNESCO Recommendation, the 1993 Montreal Declaration and the 1993 Vienna Declaration on Human Rights. These simultaneously enlarge as well as limit the plenitude of human rights education. The enlargement occurs through the proclamations of human rights education hypergoals that now link it with the promotion of 'international understanding', 'cooperation' and 'peace', 'friendly relations between peoples and states' and 'respect for human rights and fundamental freedoms'. The limits stand posed variously by the practices of structural adjustment of human rights in a heavily globalising world, now exacerbated by the 'war on terror' that, all over again, constitutes a global recession of human rights futures.

Even so, we need to pursue some human rights education itineraries. The UNESCO Declaration in particular emphasises the 'international education', as entailing 'Intellectual and emotional development;' 'a sense of responsibility and of solidarity with less privileged groups' such that results in 'observance of principles of equality in everyday conduct' (Article 5); a culture of 'inadmissibility of recourse to war' and understanding of responsibility to strengthen world peace (Article 6); the incompatibility of 'the true interests of people' and with interests of 'monopolistic groups holding economic and political power, which practice exploitation and ferment wars' (Article 15); 'inter-cultural understanding' (Article 17); meaningful opportunities for 'active civic training,' enabling cooperative endeavor in 'the work of public institutions' imparting competence to political participation [Article 13]; and capabilities to eradicate 'conditions which perpetuate major problems affecting human survival and well-being' and which enhance 'international cooperation' to this end [Article 18].

The 1993 UNESCO Montreal Declaration links human rights education to the spread of democracy. It declares that all education, especially human rights education, should 'promote societal transformation based upon human rights and democracy in ways that enhance the universality of human rights by rooting these rights in different cultural traditions' and evolve 'special and anticipatory strategies aimed at preventing the outbreak of violent conflicts' and related human rights violations. Human rights education should itself be 'participatory and operational, creative, innovative and empowering at all levels of civil society.' The Vienna Declaration on Human Rights marks yet another milestone in the development of human rights education. Its most excitingly innovative dimension is, of course, the reference to 'human rights needs of women.' The Plan of Action for the United Nations Human Rights Education Decade further defines as its principal objective a community of concern between 'democracy, development and human rights'. Human rights education aims at the 'building of a universal culture of human rights' through the 'imparting of knowledges, skills and moulding of attitudes.' Human rights education should provide literacy in human rights values, norms and standards in ways that remain 'relevant to the daily lives of the learners, respecting equal participation of women and men of all age groups and all sectors of society both in formal learning ... and non-formal learning through institutions of civil society, the family and the mass media'.

The lofty human rights education hypergoals pose problems of overload to a point where it signifies at the same moment everything and nothing. The pursuit of incredibly diverse and often contradictory goals understandably does not occur at any historically meaningful pace. Where national budgetary allocation for education remains pathetically low, human rights education itself may attract minuscule resources, if any. Existing patterns of 'social capital' manifest in curricular and pedagogic traditions do not yield easily to human rights education's multifarious agenda. The hypergoals further tenaciously address huge constituencies, entailing tasks of re-education of the already much 'educated' ruling classes, including state and security personnel, key business/industrial elites and learned professions especially in the spheres of law, science and technology. Paradigmatic global sites such as the White House and Whitehall continue to relentlessly cancel even the small gains of human rights learning across the board. And human rights education now needs to address urgently the emergence of trade-related and market-friendly paradigms pitted against the paradigm of universal human rights.

In a world dizzy with unprecedented acceleration of history, the human rights education tasks ahead resist simple-minded prescriptions. The emergent initiatives at the 'world system' level require not just complex and contradictory forms of inter-agency collaboration within the United Nations system but also exemplary dedication by human rights education NGOs and movements, beset by constant perils of co-optation. Even so, the unfolding work of two Special Rapporteurs of the United Nations Commission on Human Rights (Katarina Tomaševski on the Right to Education and Arjun Sengupta on the Right to Development) remains crucial to the worldwide system of human rights education.

Noteworthy also in this regard remains the remarkable innovation of grassroots human rights education under the auspices of The People's Decade for Human Rights Education. This initiative has provided leadership in constructing human rights cities and communities and by a radical summation of the tasks involved (in the words of its founder, Shulamith Koenig) in overcoming 'the vicious cycle of humiliation'. Kindred ventures, across local, regional, national, supranational and international arenas, now define the human rights education movement, in diverse contexts, in terms of empowerment of subaltern or rightless peoples. What is needed is a critical and engaged overview towards which the Peoples' Report on Human Rights Education (to be published in 2005) makes a significant contribution.

This leaves the specific tasks ahead as follows:

- relating literacy and primary and elementary education to the human rights education mandate and mission;
- inventing human rights education strategies that aspire meaningfully to combat mass impoverishment;
- constricting zones of violent social exclu-

sion, emanating from recalcitrant combinatory state and civil society formations, stemming from entrenched patterns of hostile race, gender and 'disability' discrimination;

- revisiting theory and practice of academic freedom, in terms of both the freedom to teach and to learn;
- innovating practices of multiculturalism that empower disadvantaged, dispossessed and deprived groups with pertinent political voice via some distinct reversals of state control over education;
- ensuring 'fiscal allocations for public education';
- relating, at the ground level, the right to development to human rights education as a human right of everyone;
- specifying non-negotiable human rights content in the delivery of educational services under state and civil society auspices;
- targeting specific human rights education constituencies, especially through programmes and measures of continuing non-formal human rights education;
- education for political classes, security personnel, judges and law enforcement officials, including state and private lawpersons, and the reformation of management, science/technology educational systems and programs;
- reconstructing transnational advocacy networks and developmental discourse in ways that takes seriously nascent approaches to theories of global justice.

In thus silhouetting this formidable agendum, I invite attention to the tasks of differentiation (in some recent languages of business ethics) between the enunciation of hypergoals and their conversion into intelligible hypernorms. This translation illustrates at the one and the same moment both the possibility and impossibility of human rights education. However, the process of conversion of benign visions into a specific code of tasks at the very least directs attention to the Montreal Plan's human rights education criteria by which 'success' of any mission may be evaluated. It would be successful when it changes 'conduct leading to a denial of rights', creates a climate of 'respect' for 'all rights' and transforms the civil society in a peaceful manner and participatory model.

The setting of human rights education hypergoals represents (according to Reinhardt Koselleck) a horizon of expectation, which always overruns the horizon of experience. Vast impoverished and subjugated rightless masses of human beings necessarily tend to view the manifold human rights education endeavours as yet another ruse of governance. At the same moment, some empirical studies indicate the utility, and even the value, of human rights education. Across the world, it is shown to nurture a measure of lived and embodied triumph of hope over experience.

Overall, human rights education makes historic sense only as 'pedagogy of the oppressed.' The various human rights education declarations explain what it may mean; the task, however, is to change its transformative praxes. In this historic sense, we may well say with Schiller, concerning human rights education tasks ahead: What is left undone one minute is restored by no eternity.

Further Reading

Andreopoulos, George J. and Pierre Claude, Richard (eds) (1997) *Human Rights Education for the Twenty-first Century*, Philadelphia: University of Pennsylvania Press.

Office of the United Nations High Commissioner for Human Rights (1999) *The United Nations Decade for Human Rights Education, 1995–2004*, no. 2: human rights education and human rights treaties, New York: United Nations.

Office of the United Nations High Commissioner for Human Rights (1999) *The United Nations Decade for Human Rights Education, 1995-2004*, no. 3: the right to human rights education: a compilation of provisions of inernational and regional instruments dealing with human rights education New York: United Nations.

Ray, Douglas et al. (eds) (1994) *Education for Human Rights: an International Perspective*, Paris: UNESCO: International Bureau of Education.

Starkey, Hugh (1991) *The Challenge of Human Rights Education*, London: Cassell.

Contributor: Upendra Baxi

HUMAN RIGHTS AND GLOBALISING MEMORY CULTURE

The contemporary international human rights movement has to be seen together with the explosion of a transnational memory culture in recent decades. Both are concerned with protecting basic human rights today and righting wrongs committed in the past. Both grew to a large degree out of legal, moral and philosophical discourses about genocide. The Holocaust and related atrocities committed by the Nazi regime continue to play an important role for both memory and human rights discourses. If the human rights movement functions as the legal and judicial arm of this global phenomenon, transnational memory culture provides the cultural backdrop without which the public awareness of human rights issues would not be what it is today. Public commemorations, monuments and museums as well as representations of **GENOCIDE** and human rights violations in the media, in literature, film and the visual arts are the necessary supplement for the success of human rights activism (Huyssen, 2003; Young, 1993).

Strangely enough, this obvious link between transnational memory culture and the human rights movement is largely ignored in the pertinent literature. Human rights discourse and memory discourse, closely intertwined in practice all over the world, usually remain separated by the disciplinary gap between the humanities and legal studies. But it is precisely the humanities' focus on language and image, translation and cultural difference, memory and its representation that has much to offer to one of the main debates endangering the acceptance of human rights as universal rights, namely the debate about (Western) **UNIVERSALISM** versus cultural relativism (See: **PLURALIST UNIVERSALISM AND HUMAN RIGHTS**). Given their historical and interpretive depth, the humanities are well equipped to argue for the truth of cultural diversity without giving up the claim of universal human rights.

The rise of memory as a keyword of contemporary culture and politics and its surprising spread across the world begs itself to be historically explained. Memory discourses of a new kind first emerged in the 1960s in the wake of decolonisation and the new **SOCIAL MOVEMENTS** with their search for alternative and revisionist histories. The search for other traditions in the post-colonial world and for the traditions of 'others', of minorities and ethnic groups in the West, radically challenged the *idée reçue* of a homogeneous modernity, exemplified for instance in the American notion of the 'melting pot' or in the understanding of national cultures as unitary, based on language and ethnic identity. Memory discourses accelerated in the early 1980s in the US and in Europe, energised then by the ever broadening debate about the Holocaust (triggered by the television series *Holocaust* and the somewhat later testimony movement) as well as by a whole series of politically loaded 40th and 50th anniversaries relating to the history of the Third Reich, its demise and the victory of the allies. These historical commemorations were widely covered in the international media and they helped stir up post-Second World War recodifications of national history in Germany, France, Austria, Italy, Switzerland and even the US. But soon enough, resonances of Holocaust and Third Reich memories spread beyond the Northern Transatlantic, attaching themselves to politically and historically very different events and situations in post-dictatorship Latin America or post-apartheid South Africa. Indeed, one can now observe something like a 'globalisation' of Holocaust memory (Levy and Sznaider, 2001; Huyssen, 2003).

The recurrence of genocidal politics in Rwanda, Bosnia and Kosovo in more recent times made Holocaust memory discourse pertinent for evaluating present-day events. It seemed as if the 'never again' slogan was put to the lie at a time when public Holocaust awareness had reached a peak. In the case of ethnic cleansing in the Balkans and the organised massacres of Rwanda, comparisons with the Holocaust were at first fiercely resisted by politicians, the media and much of the public, not because of the undeniable historical differences but rather because of a basic unwillingness to intervene. Public opinion changed in the late 1990s with Kosovo. Streams of refugees across borders, women and children packed into trains for deportation, stories of atrocities, systematic rape and wanton destruction all mobilised a politics of guilt in Europe and the US associated with the appeasement

politics of the 1930s. Holocaust memory helped legitimise NATO's military intervention in Kosovo, but only years after the failure to intervene in a timely fashion in the Bosnian genocide of 1992. The Kosovo intervention thus confirms the increasing power of memory culture in the late 1990s, but it also raises difficult issues regarding the use of the Holocaust as universal trope for historical trauma, organised massacres and genocide.

Extending the Holocaust beyond its original historical reference point and using it as a template to judge other cases of massive human rights violations leads to what I would call the globalisation paradox. On the one hand, the Holocaust has become a cipher for the 20th century as a whole. For some it is the logical result of the failure of the project of enlightenment and it serves as proof of Western civilisation's failure to reflect on its constitutive inability to live in peace with difference and otherness and to understand the insidious relationship among enlightened modernity, racial oppression and organised violence. On the other hand, this totalising dimension of Holocaust discourse, so prevalent in much post-modern thought, is accompanied by a legitimate desire to particularise and to localise. It is precisely the emergence of the Holocaust as a universal trope in recent memory culture that allows Holocaust memory to latch on to specific local situations, which are historically distant and politically distinct from the original event that gave shape to the genocide convention in the first place. In the transnational movement of Holocaust memory into other contexts, the Holocaust loses its quality as index of the specific historical event and begins to function as metaphor for other traumatic histories and memories. The Holocaust as universal trope is thus a prerequisite for its decentring and its use as a powerful prism through which we may look at other instances of genocide and organized massacres.

The global and the local aspects of Holocaust memory have entered into a new constellation that begs to be analysed case by case in its implications for the strengthening of human rights regimes anywhere. At the same time, we need to recognise that while the comparison with the Holocaust may rhetorically energise some public discourses of traumatic memory and human rights claims, it may also serve as a screen memory or simply block insight into specific local histories. When any real or imagined human rights violation becomes another 'Holocaust', the trope may lose its specific exemplarity and become something like white noise. To recognise this danger, however, is not to accept the argument of those who insist on the absolute uniqueness of the Holocaust. As an integral part of the Genocide Convention the Holocaust can legitimately be used to evaluate other historical cases, lest we make the demand 'never again' into an empty shell.

Clearly, the politically most interesting uses of Holocaust memory in relation to human rights have occurred in nations struggling to create democratic policies and civil societies in the wake of histories of mass extermination, apartheid, military dictatorship or totalitarianism. Countries such as South Africa, Argentina and Chile are facing the unprecedented task of securing the legitimacy and future of their emergent polity by finding ways to commemorate and adjudicate past wrongs (Coombes, 2003; Feitlowitz, 1998). The political site of memory practices and the struggle for human rights is still national, not post-national or global. At the same time, national memory debates are always shot through with the effects of the global media and their coverage of genocide and ethnic cleanings, migration and **MINORITY RIGHTS**, victimisation and accountability.

There is no doubt that in our time memory politics and human rights are more intimately connected than ever and the continuing strength of memory culture remains essential for securing human rights in the future. But as much as its presence is essential for establishing human rights regimes where they do not yet exist, memory may also nurture human rights violations. Mythic and imagined pasts are mobilised to support aggressively nationalist, fundamentalist or religion-based politics (post-communist Yugoslavia, India, most recently the United States). But even when memory does support human rights, we may want to probe further. With the fading of the social and political utopias of the 20th century – the imagined futures of fascism, communism and global capitalist modernisation – and the mountains of corpses the dictatorships of this dark century have bequeathed to humanity, it sometimes seems as if too much of the struggle for human rights focuses on righting past wrongs (See: **REPARATIONS**). Securing the past may be as perilous an undertaking as trying to secure the future. If human rights activism were to become a prisoner of the past and of memory politics, it would mean only that it will always have come too late.

Further Reading

Coombes, Annie E., (2003) *History After Apartheid: Visual Culture and Public Memory in a Democratic South Africa*, Durham and London: Duke University Press.

Feitlowitz, Marguerite (1998) *A Lexicon of Terror: Argentina and the Legacies of Torture*, Oxford: Oxford University Press.

Hartmann, Geoffrey (ed.) (1994) *Holocaust Remembrance: The Shapes of Memory*, Oxford: Basil Blackwell.

Huyssen, Andreas, (2003) *Present Pasts: Urban Palimpsests and the Politics of Memory*, Stanford: Stanford University Press.

Levy, Daniel and Sznaider, Natan (2001) *Erinnerung im globalen Zeitalter: Der Holocaust.* Frankfurt am Main: Suhrkamp.

Young, James (1993) *The Texture of Memory: Holocaust Memorials and Meaning*, New Haven and London: Yale University Press.

Contributor: Andreas Huyssen

HUMANITARIAN INTERVENTION

Three months after NATO concluded its 78-day campaign over Kosovo in 1999, Secretary-General Kofi Annan presented his annual report to the UN General Assembly. In it, he presented in stark terms the dilemma confronting those who privileged international law over the need to respond to gross and systematic violations of human rights:

To those for whom the greatest threat to the future of international order is the use of force in the absence of a Security Council mandate, one might ask – not in the context of Kosovo – but in the context of Rwanda: If, in those dark days and hours leading up to the genocide, a coalition of States had been prepared to act in defence of the Tutsi population, but did not receive prompt Council authorization, should such a coalition have stood aside and allowed the horror to unfold?

The hypothetical neatly captured the ethical dilemma as many of the acting states sought to present it. Could international law truly prevent such 'humanitarian' intervention?

The problem, however, is that this was not the dilemma faced in the context of Rwanda. Rather than international law restraining a state from acting in defence of the Tutsi population, the problem in 1994 was that no state wanted to intervene at all. When France, hardly a disinterested actor, decided to intervene with Operation Turquoise, its decision was swiftly approved in a Council resolution – though reference to 'impartiality', a two-month time limit and five abstentions suggested wariness about France's motivation.

The capriciousness of state interest is a theme that runs throughout the troubled history of humanitarian intervention. While much ink has been spilt on the question of the legality of using military force to defend human rights, it is difficult to point to actual cases that demonstrate the significance of international law on this issue. States do not appear to have refrained from acting in situations like Rwanda (or Kosovo) simply from fear of legal sanction. Nor, however, do any of the incidents frequently touted as examples of 'genuine' humanitarian intervention correspond with the principled articulation of such a doctrine by legal scholars. Returning to the Secretary-General's analogy, the type of problem confronting human rights today is not Kosovo but Rwanda. Put differently, the problem is not the legitimacy of humanitarian intervention but the overwhelming prevalence of inhumanitarian non-intervention.

While the bombs were falling over Kosovo, many international lawyers sought cover under references to the inadequacy of 'traditional' international law; few were willing to condemn NATO for taking action against a brutal leader who clearly wished ill on the Albanian population of Kosovo. Though academic commentators tended, with hindsight, to become more polarised on the question, the more sober assessments by the acting states themselves have continued to blur the question of legality. In a report on the intervention, the United Kingdom Foreign and Commonwealth Office concluded that 'at the very least, the doctrine of humanitarian intervention has a tenuous basis in current international customary law, and that this renders NATO action legally questionable'. In proceedings before the International Court of Justice, only Belgium sought to establish that its participation in the NATO air strikes did not violate Article 2(4) of the UN Charter, which prohibits the threat or use of force. Other states emphasised the relevance of Security Council resolutions (which fell well short of authorising the use of force), or made reference to the existence of a 'humanitarian catastrophe' – apparently wary of invoking the doctrine of humanitarian intervention by name. Such reticence to reach a firm position on the legality of the intervention was not restricted to the states participating in it. Two well-respected independent commissions also returned Solomonic verdicts. The Kosovo Commission, headed by Richard Goldstone, concluded that NATO's intervention was 'illegal but legitimate'. The International Commission on Intervention and State Sovereignty, chaired by Gareth Evans and Mohamed Sahnoun, took a more political tack. Acknowledging that, as a matter of 'political reality', it would be impossible to find consensus around any set of proposals for military intervention that allowed for intervention not authorised by the Security Council or the General Assembly, the Commission sought to present this as a political rather than a legal problem:

[T]hat may still leave circumstances when the Security Council fails to discharge what this Commission would regard as its responsibility to protect, in a conscience-shocking situation crying out for action. It is a real question in these circumstances where lies the most harm: in the damage to international order if the Security Council is bypassed or in the damage to that order if human beings are slaughtered while the Security Council stands by.

Most legal analysis of humanitarian intervention – defined here as the threat or use of force for the purpose of protecting human rights – considers the provenance and future of Article 2(4) of the UN Charter. The passage agreed to by states at the San Francisco conference of 1945 was broad in its scope:

All Members shall refrain in their international relations from the threat or use of force against the territorial integrity or political independence of any state, or in any other manner inconsistent with the Purposes of the United Nations.

The prohibition was tempered by only two exceptions. First, the Charter preserved the 'inherent right of individual or collective self-defence'. Second, the newly established Security Council was granted the power to authorise enforcement actions under Chapter VII. (Although this latter species of military action is sometimes considered in the same breath as unilateral humanitarian intervention, Council authorisation changes the legal questions to which such action gives rise.) Most serious legal analysis of the alleged 'right' of humanitarian intervention seeks to justify it either within a tortured reading of the terms of Article 2(4), or within a broad interpretation of Security Council resolutions not explicitly authorising the use of force – especially where it is alleged that a properly authorising resolution is blocked only by capricious use of the veto.

The political tension underlying such recourse to legal justifications for military action is most evident in James Rubin's account of debates between the NATO capitals on the legality of proposed NATO action in the weeks prior to the air campaign. A series of strained telephone calls between US Secretary of State Madeleine Albright and UK Foreign Secretary Robin Cook had led him to cite problems 'with our lawyers' over using force in the absence of UN endorsement. Albright's reply, reportedly, was: 'Get new lawyers.'

Equivocation about the role of international law in decision-making processes is hardly new; the history of international law is to some extent a struggle to raise law above the status of being merely one foreign policy justification among others. In the course of the US operation to oust Manuel Noriega from Panama in 1989, for example, Attorney General Richard Thornburgh was first called in to advise President George Bush that the United States had clear legal authority to act on 19 December 1989 – two days after President Bush had authorised the operation and a matter of hours before 24,000 marines actually landed in Panama. Legal advisers today appear to have greater involvement in some decisions, especially on questions of targeting high-precision weapons, but on fundamental questions of whether and when to use force they are commonly marginalised. Nevertheless, the rhetoric of international legality continues to be invoked frequently. At the beginning of the 1990s the United States, while proclaiming itself the victor in the cold war, magnanimously asserted that this provided an opportunity for the United Nations to fulfil its long-promised role as the guardian of international peace and security. The Security Council saw new possibilities for action without the paralysing veto; Secretary-General Boutros Boutros-Ghali laid out grand plans with An Agenda for Peace. In President Bush's words, 'the rule of law would supplant the rule of the jungle'.

The rhetoric was euphoric, utopian and brief. As quickly became clear, international security issues continued to be resolved by reference to Great Power interests; notably, the role of the UN Security Council was reduced to something akin to the League of Nations Council, with power merely to give advice on matters of collective security. There is, now, a real danger that the United Nations will be used only when it is geopolitically convenient or useful to do so.

Any such development should be treated with great caution. The 1990s were remarkable for the fact that recourse was had to international institutions at all: the United States sought authorisation to intervene in the hemisphere previously demarcated as its own under the Monroe Doctrine; France sought leave to intervene in its former African colonies; Nigeria (belatedly) sought legitimacy for operations in its sphere of influence. The politics might well have been the same as those that beset the old world order, but they had assumed a very different form – it was the abandonment of even this form that made Kosovo all the more dangerous a precedent.

Further Reading

Annan, Kofi (1999) *The Question of Intervention: Statements by the Secretary-General*, New York: United Nations Department of Public Information.

Chesterman, Simon (2001) *Just War or Just Peace? Humanitarian Intervention and International Law*, Oxford: Oxford University Press.

International Commission on Intervention and State Sovereignty (2001) *The Responsibility to Protect*, Ottawa: International Development Research Centre, December, available at www.iciss.gc.ca

Tesón, Fernando R. (1997) *Humanitarian Intervention: An Inquiry into Law and Morality*, 2nd edn, Dobbs Ferry, NY: Transnational Publishers.

Wheeler, Nicholas (2000) *Saving Strangers: Humanitarian Intervention in International Society*, Oxford: Oxford University Press.

Contributor: Simon Chesterman

HUMANITARIAN LAW AND HUMAN RIGHTS IN ARMED CONFLICT

International humanitarian law (IHL) is a body of rules specifically intended to solve humanitarian problems caused by armed conflicts. Its principal aim is to protect people and property that are, or may be, affected by an armed conflict and to limit the rights of the parties to use methods and means of warfare of their choice. While rules regulating warfare have existed in various forms for centuries, modern IHL is associated with the adoption, in 1864, of the Geneva Convention for the Amelioration of the Condition of the Wounded in Armies in the Field. International humanitarian law is today made up of dozens of treaties, the most commonly referred to being the Four Geneva Conventions of 1949 and their two Additional Protocols of 1977. There is also a large body of customary international humanitarian law rules.

In contrast to human rights law, which is in principle applicable at all times, IHL is applicable only in situations of armed conflict, whether international or non-international. International armed conflicts (wars) are those involving two or more states, regardless of whether a declaration of war has been made or whether the parties involved recognise that there is a state of war. Non-international armed conflicts are those involving government forces and organised armed groups, or organised armed groups among themselves.

International humanitarian law governs the protection of people and property, as well as the conduct of hostilities, once an armed conflict has occurred. It does not regulate the right to resort to force, an area of international relations governed by the UN Charter. There are no 'just' or 'unjust' wars in terms of IHL. Its application is triggered whenever an armed conflict happens in practice, regardless of any justification that may be given.

International humanitarian law aims primarily to protect people who do not or are no longer taking part in hostilities. As their very titles indicate, the four Geneva Conventions of 1949 deal with the treatment, in international armed conflict, of wounded and sick members of the armed forces on land (Geneva Convention (GC) I), wounded, sick and shipwrecked members of the armed forces at sea (GC II), prisoners of war (GC III) and civilians (GC IV). Similarly, the rules applicable in non-international armed conflict (article 3 common to the Geneva Conventions and Additional Protocol II) deal with the treatment of people not taking, or no longer taking part in the hostilities, taking account of the fact that the people involved are nationals of the same state. In all circumstances IHL prohibits acts of violence against people in enemy hands, including murder, torture, rape, inhuman treatment, collective punishments, the taking of hostages, denial of the right to a fair trial and a range of other assaults on human life, health and dignity.

International humanitarian law protects civilians not only by specifying the treatment they must be accorded once they are in the power of the enemy but by means of norms on the conduct of hostilities (Additional Protocol I). It is a fundamental rule of IHL that parties to an armed conflict must at all times distinguish between civilians and combatants and between military objectives and civilian objects. Neither the civilian population as a whole nor individual civilians may be the object of attack. Attacks against military objectives are also prohibited if they would cause disproportionate harm to civilians or civilian objects. In short, the beneficiaries of international humanitarian law are civilians and others – including combatants – who are or may be subject to the effects of an armed conflict.

The common underlying purpose of international humanitarian and international human rights law is the protection of the life, health and dignity of human beings, albeit in different circumstances. It is therefore not surprising that the content of some of the rules is similar. Both bodies of law aim, for example, to protect human life, prohibit torture or cruel treatment, prohibit discrimination, prescribe basic rights for persons subject to criminal process, include provisions for the protection of women and children and regulate aspects of the right to food and health.

On the other hand, IHL deals with many issues that are outside the purview of human rights law, such as the already mentioned principles on the conduct of hostilities, combatant and prisoner of war status, the use of weapons in armed conflict and the protection of the Red Cross and Red Crescent emblems. Likewise, human rights law deals with aspects of life in peacetime that are not governed by international humanitarian law, such as freedom of the press, the right to assembly, the **RIGHT TO VOTE**, the right to strike, etc. What is important to know is that the comprehensive protection of persons in armed conflict requires the complementary application of IHL and human rights, as well as of other bodies of law.

The similarity of purpose and, to an extent, of content between international humanitarian and human rights law is evidenced by several treaties containing a mix of international humanitarian law and human rights provisions. The **CONVENTION ON THE RIGHTS OF THE CHILD** and, in particular, its Protocol on the Involvement of Children in Armed Conflict are cases in point. The Rome treaty establishing a permanent **INTERNATIONAL CRIMINAL COURT** also pools together violations of separate bodies of law – war crimes, genocide and crimes against humanity.

Even though international humanitarian and human rights law share certain features, there are important distinguishing characteristics stemming from their distinct scope of application. Humanitarian law is the special law ('*lex specialis*') specifically designed for situations of armed conflict. An exceptional circumstance such as war by its very nature demands that no derogations from any of the obligations of the parties be allowed if humanitarian law is to serve its protective purpose. Thus, in contrast to certain human rights treaties, the totality of humanitarian law norms is non-derogable. Just as importantly, international humanitarian law binds all parties to an armed conflict, which may include both state and non-state armed actors. As is well known, international human rights law governs relations between a state and individuals; whether non-state actors can be responsible for violations of human rights that do not reach the level of international crimes remains controversial.

Another distinguishing feature of international humanitarian law is the extraterritorial applicability of its norms. There is no question that the parties to an armed conflict remain bound by their humanitarian law obligations regardless of where hostilities may take place. The extraterritorial application of international and regional human rights treaty law, by contrast, is still being clarified by means of human rights jurisprudence.

The duty to implement international humanitarian law lies first and foremost with states. States have a duty to take a number of legal and practical measures – both in peacetime and in armed conflict situations – aimed at ensuring full compliance with international humanitarian law. States must, for example, adopt national legislation implementing their treaty obligations, disseminate the rules of international humanitarian law, train military and other personnel to apply them, translate the relevant texts and have legal advisers guiding them in the application of norms. They also have a duty to search for persons suspected of having committed or having ordered the commission of 'grave breaches' and to bring such persons either before their own courts or to hand them over to another state for trial. They should also enable their courts to exercise universal jurisdiction over other

The US authorities have recognised former Iraqi President Saddam Hussein as a prisoner of war, according him the full protection of the Geneva Conventions. In contrast, those terrorist suspects held in Guantanamo Bay, Cuba have been deemed 'illegal combatants'.

serious violations of the laws and customs of war, i.e. war crimes, whether committed in international or non-international armed conflict.

As regards international implementation, states have a collective responsibility under Article 1 common to the Geneva Conventions 'to respect and to ensure respect for' the Conventions 'in all circumstances'. The supervisory system also comprises the Protecting Power mechanism, the enquiry procedure and the International Fact-Finding Commission envisaged in Article 90 of Additional Protocol I. Pursuant to that Protocol state parties also undertake to act in cooperation with the **UNITED NATIONS** in

situations of serious violations of the Protocol or of the Conventions.

The ICRC is a key component of the international supervisory system by virtue of the mandate entrusted to it under the Geneva Conventions and their Additional Protocols, as well as under the Statutes of the International Red Cross and Red Crescent Movement. These texts contain numerous provisions specifically mandating or allowing ICRC to perform a variety of tasks aimed at protecting and assisting victims of war, at encouraging states to implement their humanitarian law obligations and at promoting and developing the law. As a neutral, independent and impartial humanitarian organisation, the ICRC also has a right of initiative which permits it to offer its services or to undertake any action which it deems necessary to ensure the faithful application of international humanitarian law.

WEBSITE

ww.icrc.org

Henry Dunant

Henry Dunant was Swiss. On 24 June, 1859 he travelled to northern Italy for a meeting with Napoleon III. He was horrified when he encountered thousands of casualties of the War of Italian Unification sheltering in villages and, in 1862, published a book on his experience, concluding 'Would it not be possible, in time of peace and quiet, to form relief societies for the purpose of having care given to the wounded in wartime by zealous, devoted and thoroughly qualified volunteers?'. The book was widely translated and circulated. It prompted the meeting of a group comprising Dunant, Gustave Moynier, General Guillaume-Henri Dufour, Dr Louis Appia and Dr Théodore Maunoir, initially called the International Committee for Relief to the Wounded which met for the first time on 17 February 1863. This quickly evolved into the International Committee of the Red Cross (ICRC).

(From www.icrc.org)

Further Reading

Dinstein, Y. (1984) 'Human Rights in Armed Conflict: International Humanitarian Law', in *Human Rights in International Law: Legal and Policy Issues*, Meron, Theodor (ed.), Oxford: Clarendon, vol. II, pp. 345.

Doswald-Beck, Louise and Vité, Sylvain (1993) 'International Humanitarian Law and Human Rights Law', in *International Review of the Red Cross*, no. 293, p. 94–119.

Eide, Asbjørn (1984) 'The Laws of War and Human Rights – Differences and Convergences', in *Studies and Essays on International Humanitarian Law and Red Cross Principles in Honour of Jean Pictet*, Swinarski, Christophe (ed.), ICRC and Martinus Nijhoff Publishers, p. 675.

Meron, Theodor (1989) *Human Rights and Humanitarian Norms as Customary Law*, Oxford: Clarendon.

Moir, Lindsay (2002) *The Law of Internal Armed Conflict*, Cambridge: Cambridge University Press.

Contributor: Jelena Pejic

THE HUMAN RIGHTS COMMITTEE

Article 28 of the INTERNATIONAL COVENANT ON CIVIL AND POLITICAL RIGHTS establishes the Human Rights Committee to monitor the implementation of the Covenant. The Committee is composed of 18 independent experts serving in their individual capacity, elected by a meeting of state parties to the Covenant. The Committee performs a number of functions related to the monitoring of the effective implementation of the Covenant. In practice, the most important of these functions are the consideration of periodic reports submitted by states (Article 40), the adoption of General Comments that systematise the Committee's interpretation of specific provisions or aspects of the Covenant (Article 40.4) and the consideration of individual communications on alleged violations of the Covenant (Optional Protocol). Being a treaty body, the Committee's mandate is determined by the substantive human rights provisions in Articles 1 to 27 of the Covenant and exists only in respect of states that are bound by the Covenant, either through formal ratification or accession or in certain cases on the basis of continuity of human rights obligations.

The reporting obligation prescribed in Article 40 of the Covenant is the main procedural obligation of state parties to the Covenant. An initial report is to be submitted within one year of the entry into force of the Covenant in respect of the state in question. Thereafter, periodic reports are due 'whenever the Committee so requires'. Previously the Committee applied a uniform periodicity of five years between two consecutive reports. In July 2001, however, it adopted an approach of specifying separately for each state the due date of its next periodic report. In addition, the Committee may request a so-called special report irrespective of the decided due date, for instance if the human rights situation appears to deteriorate rapidly. A periodic report shall consist of information on the measures adopted by a state party to give effect to the rights recognised in the Covenant and the progress made in the enjoyment of those rights. Reports shall also indicate the factors and difficulties affecting the implementation of the Covenant.

The system of periodic reporting operates as a continuous cycle in which the consideration of a report in a public hearing before the Committee forms a high point, followed by the Committee's concluding observations. Usually the Committee allocates two meetings (i.e. six hours) to each report, during which time a delegation sent by the reporting state answers to written and oral questions posed by the Committee and its individual members. The Committee prepares the consideration by hearing non-governmental and intergovernmental organisations, by studying written information from these and other sources and by drawing up a written list of issues which is sent to the state party well before the oral hearing. Since 2002, the Committee appoints from among its members a so-called task force of four to six members to handle the consideration of any particular report.

The Committee's concluding observations give recognition to positive aspects in the implementation of the Covenant but the main part of them is devoted to expressions of concern and recommendations for further action. The state party is expected to publicise the concluding observations and to use them as a starting-point for the next reporting cycle. The Committee's reporting guidelines recommend so-called focused reports which are based on the Committee's concluding observations from the previous round and any new developments that emanate from the national human rights discussion. The due date of the next periodic report is set at the end of the Committee's concluding observations.

In 2002, the Committee introduced two further reforms. Firstly, it has started to tackle the problem of long overdue reports by scheduling a country for consideration even in the absence of a report. The first experiences of this new approach are promising, as it appears to facilitate the production of reports that were seriously overdue. Secondly, the Committee instituted a follow-up procedure to its concluding observations. At the end of the concluding observations, a follow-up submission is requested within 12 months on some of the concerns. Also, one member of the Committee was appointed Special Rapporteur on follow-up under Article 40.

According to Article 40, paragraph 4, the Committee may adopt, on the basis of its consideration of state reports, 'such general comments as it may consider appropriate'. By

April 2004, the Committee had adopted 31 general comments, most of them outlining its understanding of one substantive right covered by the Covenant. Some of the general comments, however, deal with cross-cutting issues such as reservations (General Comment no. 24), continuity of obligations (no. 26) or the right of states to derogate from some of their Covenant obligations during a state of emergency (no. 29). The most recent general comment (no. 31) deals with Article 2 of the Covenant and addresses many general issues of state obligations under the Covenant, such as state responsibility for action by private parties or for extraterritorial conduct.

Article 41 of the Covenant allows for inter-state complaints by those states that have made a separate declaration recognising the Committee's competence in this respect. So far, 47 states have given such a declaration but not even a single inter-state complaint has been submitted. Potentially, the procedure is an important mechanism for the collective responsibility of the state parties over the effective implementation of the Covenant.

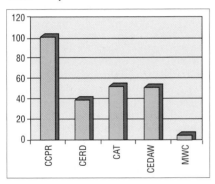

Enforcement – number of states consenting to individual communications under the principal international human rights treaties (Statistics from www.unhchr.ch)

Out of the 152 states that in early 2004 were parties to the Covenant, 104 had also ratified the Optional Protocol that allows for submission of individual complaints of violations of Covenant rights. Complaints, or individual communications as they are referred to in the Optional Protocol, are first handled by the Office of the UN High Commissioner for Human Rights in Geneva, where a Petitions Team specialises in dealing with individual communications to the various treaty bodies.

A case summary is presented to one member of the Committee who acts as the Committee's Special Rapporteur on new communications and decides on the registration of communications and their transmittal to the state party for observations. Particularly in cases involving the death penalty the Special Rapporteur also decides, on behalf of the Committee, whether to request interim measures of protection from the state party. According to Rule 86 of the Committee's Rules of Procedure such measures may be requested 'to avoid irreparable damage to the victim of the alleged violation'. In addition to death penalty cases this rule is applied in some deportation cases, usually because of a risk of torture or other inhuman treatment. After the registration of a communication and its transmittal to the state party concerned, the state can either separately contest the admissibility of the communication within two months or present within six months its observations on both the admissibility and the merits of the case. The main rule nowadays is that the plenary Committee deals only once with a communication, addressing both its admissibility and, if appropriate, the merits.

Any submission received from either the individual or from the state is always transmitted to the other party which then has an opportunity to comment. The Optional Protocol procedure is, hence, based on the principles of equality of arms and *audiatur et altera pars*. However, contrary to what is customary in full judicial proceedings the Committee has no oral hearings but restricts itself to 'written information made available to it by the individual and the state party concerned'. The admissibility conditions include the victim requirement, i.e. that the communication is submitted by or on behalf of a natural person whose Covenant rights have been violated, the requirement of exhausting domestic remedies, an obstacle to simultaneous consideration of the same matter by more than one international court or treaty body and the requirement of the Committee's competence *ratione materiae*, i.e. that the claims presented fall within the scope of the Covenant. In the practice of the Committee, the requirement of substantiating any claim by facts and arguments is also applied as an admissibility condition.

In cases declared admissible the Committee

proceeds to its decision on the merits, called 'Final Views'. This expression reflects the absence of a treaty provision on the legally binding nature of the Committee's decision. However, it would be wrong to categorise the Committee's Views as mere 'recommendations'. They are the end result of a quasi-judicial adversarial procedure before an international body established and elected by the state parties for the purpose of interpreting the provisions of the Covenant. It would be incompatible with these preconditions of the procedure if a state that voluntarily subjected itself to such a procedure would, after first being one of the two parties in a case, simply replace the Committee's Views with its own interpretation of the Covenant. Hence, the Committee's views in Optional Protocol cases are usually treated as the authoritative interpretation of the Covenant under international law. In cases where the Committee finds one or more violations of the Covenant, it also addresses the question of an effective remedy to be afforded. Basing itself on Article 2, paragraph 3 of the Covenant, the Committee declares that the victim of a violation has a right to an effective remedy and the state party a corresponding legal obligation under international law to provide the remedy. Thereafter, the Committee proceeds to express its own view on what, in the circumstances of the case, would constitute an effective remedy. The Committee's pronouncements of an effective remedy range from, for instance, the commutation of a death sentence or release, to compensation or a new trial. One member of the Committee acts as Special Rapporteur on follow-up under the Optional Protocol.

WEBSITES

Office of the United Nations High Commissioner for Human Rights (Geneva) www.ohchr.org
Treaty Body Database www.unhchr.ch/tbs/doc.nsf
University of Minnesota www.umn.edu/humanrts/ (see the section on the Human Rights Committee under UN materials)
Netherlands Institute of Human Rights http://sim.law.uu.nl/ (see the databases for case law and concluding observations)

Further Reading

Boerefijn, Ineke, (1999) *The Reporting Procedure Under the Covenant on Civil and Political Rights*, Antwerpen: Intersentia – Hart.

Hanski, Raija and Scheinin, Martin (2003) *Leading Cases of the Human Rights Committee*, Turku/Åbo: Åbo Akademi University Institute for Human Rights.

Joseph, Sarah, Schultz, Jenny and Castan, Melissa (2000) *The International Covenant on Civil and Political Rights: Cases, Materials and Commentary*, Oxford: Oxford University Press.

McGoldrick, Dominic (1991) *The Human Rights Committee: Its Role in the Development of the International Covenant on Civil and Political Rights*, Oxford: Clarendon Press.

Nowak, Manfred (1993) *UN Covenant on Civil and Political Rights: CCPR-Commentary*, Kehl: N.P. Engel.

Contributor: Martin Scheinin

HUMAN SECURITY AND HUMAN RIGHTS

In recent years concerns for human security have emanated from a number of societal conditions rooted in the tension between a post-Second World War system of international relations based on the Westphalian model and forces that have been undermining its functioning. These concerns have been articulated with an increasing degree of explicitness and urgency. Unequal structures of power in governance at national and international levels during the 50 years of the existence of the United Nations have resulted in neither a just world nor global stability. The current multilateral system is vulnerable to action being taken unilaterally by individual states or groups of states seeking to ensure their own immediate security – action which detracts from global security in the longer term (See: **HUMANITARIAN INTERVENTION**).

Dissatisfaction has grown with the Westphalian concept of security – one which reifies the state, sanctioning use of military power in defence against threats to territorial autonomy and domestic political order. This tradition is blind to the polymorphous nature of social power – gender, class, ethnicity, religion and age – and its deployment within and across territorial boundaries. The intersections between the various power bases have created complex matrices of human rights abuse within the domestic jurisdiction of many nation-states. These abuses have either remained invisible or been purposely concealed in the name of national security and social and/or cultural order. In addition, new non-military security issues with human rights implications have emerged and acquired transnational characteristics since the end of the cold war and in conjunction with the intensification of global economic integration. These have included for example environmental threats, the HIV/AIDS pandemic, the instability of the global financial system, illicit and unsafe population movements across borders and the spread of organised crime networks engaged in drugs, arms and human trafficking (See: **SLAVERY**; **THE MIGRANT WORKERS' CONVENTION**). More threatening are acts of terror led by states, as well as non-state actors aspiring for the capture of formal power or the assertion of causes that are not adequately addressed by national and international systems of arbitration (See: **TERRORISM AND HUMAN RIGHTS**). The sources of such threats are multiple, progressive and cumulative and their manifestations diffused through everyday life. Clearly, the state-centric approach to security has severe limitations in redressing a situation in which the configurations of security have become transnational. The vulnerability of individuals, groups and their social institutions has been exacerbated, particularly those who found themselves at the intersection of various frameworks of jurisdiction. Such are the cases of displaced people fleeing from conflict situations, those on the move across borders through illicit means in search of work and those who live under the surrogate governance of an alien state or an organised criminal group commanding territorial authority in regions of a given nation through the use of arms.

The emergence of human security as a concept expresses a collective search among communities of policymakers, academic institutions and civic organisations for a renewed ethical and theoretical framework that will bring security issues into better focus. Significant in this new endeavour is the ability

to comprehend and respond to threats to human life and dignity as outcomes of interplay between global forces and those forces embedded in national and local structures.

Initially formed through collective action in the campaign against landmines, the Human Security Network was formally launched in 1999 in Norway. Based on a pluralistic approach to human security and guided by a commitment to human rights and **HUMANITARIAN LAW**, the Network consists of a group of like-minded countries from all regions in the world – Austria, Canada, Chile, Greece, Ireland, Jordan, Mali, the Netherlands, Norway, Switzerland, Slovenia, Japan and Thailand, and South Africa as an observer. It seeks to maintain dialogue at the level of Foreign Ministers, to build an interregional perspective with co-existing agendas, and to foster strong links with civil society and academia in order to address vital and quotidian security issues. The Network's basic aim is to energise all political processes and to gear them towards conflict prevention and resolution, thereby promoting peace and development as inexorably related phenomena (See: **THE RIGHT TO PEACE; THE RIGHT TO DEVELOPMENT**).

The United Nations Commission on Human Security, co-chaired by Amartya Sen (See: **THE CAPABILITIES APPROACH AND HUMAN RIGHTS**) and Sadako Ogata, was mandated in 2001 to provide ways of achieving the Millennium Declaration's goals – endorsed in 2000 by 180 states – of attaining freedom from fear and freedom from want for all people. The Commission had worked on six areas related to conflict and poverty: protection of people from violent conflict, protection of people on the move, protection of people in post-conflict situations, overcoming economic insecurity (See: **POVERTY AND HUMAN RIGHTS**), improvement of health and health services (see: **THE RIGHT TO HEALTH**) and imparting knowledge and skills. The Commission's 2003 report Human Security Now endorses the definition of human security as 'the protection of the vital core of all human lives in ways that enhance human freedoms and human fulfilment'. Its approach integrates human rights, human development and human security as three facets of a common ethical base for the protection of human life and dignity as enshrined in the **UNIVERSAL DECLARATION OF HUMAN RIGHTS** and the subsequent Human Rights treaties. The main premise of this integration is the idea that human life and dignity are basic values which all societies must seek to protect. A society that can guarantee human security for all its members is one which secures harmony not just by preventing strife but by enhancing factors such as freedom from want, freedom from fear and the freedom for future generations to inherit a healthy natural and social environment (See: **ENVIRONMENTAL RIGHTS**). These forms of freedoms are interrelated and are essential foundations for ensuring security and enabling society to flourish. The moral requirement to warrant for the existence and functioning of these freedoms is a social contract between government and its citizens and between different governments of interacting states within the global community. The attempt to unleash the moral power of the Universal Declaration of Human Rights seeks to find means to create viable, co-existing pluralistic security regimes by which to address the needs of different referents: the individual, the group and the nation-state.

Challenges to the Commission's key point on its agenda – to mainstream human security in the work of global, regional, and national security-related organisations – are many. Most glaring is the fact that the referents of security are not equal, therefore a formula must be found for weighting competing needs. The lack – so far – of a universally accepted definition of human security makes this task difficult. To date, two dimensions of human security have benefited from quantification efforts, notably poverty and violence. Caution is necessary when drawing the correlations between poverty and violence; simplistic approaches may overshadow deeper cultural causes. Quantifying positive dimensions are challenging tasks still ahead. These may include, among others, the capacity of a society or group to reach peaceful conflict resolution or the capacity to reduce the degree of susceptibility to environmental destruction, disease and other threats. Last but not least, an appropriate approach to the quotidian issues of human security affecting vulnerable groups requires comprehending their social world by other means than normative assessment of entitlements and assets. Ways must be

found to integrate the concept of 'intersectionality' as a tool to assess human insecurity as interplay between various axes of social power (gender, age, ethnicity, religion) and its effects on coping mechanisms of individuals and groups.

A vision of human security is coalescing, based on some form of transnational democracy, the salient features of which are as follows. As provider of security, the nation-state remains a key player in the global field, but the significance of 'security' needs to be extended in many directions: inwardly to vulnerable individuals and groups, outwardly to international systems and the biosphere, and from military to political, economic, social and environmental security. Political responsibility is best diffused through many layers of governance: local, national, local/global civic associations and networks, regional governments and markets. Threats to human security can no longer be conceptualised as residues or side effects of reforms within particular national boundaries. Rather, sources of tension in political processes of reform at national and global level must be resolved through dialogic and peaceful means – a proactive obligation by all governments to protect the vital core of all human lives. The courses of reform require monitoring and scrutinising by civic associations with transnational links in order to prevent any derogation by the state from the duties laid down by the Universal Declaration of Human Rights and the subsequent Human Rights treaties.

Despite the consensus about the core values human life and dignity, controversy does arise when it comes to which humans, where and when, and what forms of protection are feasible and which authority can be held accountable. The task of specifying the particular and general threats to human security remains a critical test ahead. Defining the contexts of human security and its referents and the charting of appropriate courses of action may well get left open to interrogation and scrutiny from a variety of perspectives and authorities. This leaves policy choices for human security vulnerable to competing claims unless a global will can be fostered, basing itself on the urgency of the survival of humankind – an entity blessed with feelings and a conscience – beyond and above the concerns of specific individuals, communities and nation-states. A qualitative shift of conscious-ness that can inscribe interdependence as a normative value shared by rulers and ruled within and across nations in their everyday dealings is imperative, yet remains to be realised.

Further reading

Agosin, Marjorie (ed.) (2001) *Women, Gender and Human Rights: A Global Perspective*, New Brunswick, New Jersey and London: Rutgers University Press.

Commission on Human Security (2003) *Human Security Now*, New York: United Nations

Hettne, Bjorn and Bertil, Oden (eds) (2002) *Global Governance in the 21st Century: Alternative Perspectives on World Order*, Stockholm, Sweden: Almkvist and Wiksell International.

Nef, Jorge (1999) *Human Security and Mutual Vulnerability: The Global Political Economy of Development and Underdevelopment*, Ottawa, Canada: International Research Development Centre.

Sen, Amartya (1999) *Development as Freedom*, New York: Alfred A. Knoff.

Truong, Thanh-Dam (2004) 'Reflections on Human Security: A Buddhist Contribution' in *Religion and Visions of Peace*, ter Haar, Gerrie and Busuttil, James, Leiden: Brill.

Contributor: Thanh-Dam Truong

INDIGENOUS PEOPLES' RIGHTS

It is estimated that 300–500 million indige-nous peoples populate the Earth. There is no general agreement on the definition of the term 'indigenous peoples', although it is usu-ally agreed that there are three relevant crite-ria to the definition. Indigenous peoples are descendants of the first known inhabitants of territories on which they live, they have dis-tinct cultures which set them apart from the dominant society and they have a strong sense of self-identity. The proposed definition refers to a mix between objective criteria, such as his-torical continuity, and subjective factors including self-definition. The crucial factors are the occupation of ancestral lands, or at least part of them, a common ancestry with the original occupants of these lands and a non-dominant position within the society. Based on such particularities, indigenous peo-ples' claims under human rights law do not fit the classical regime of human rights law as such claims are closely related to their partic-ular history as well as to their collective rights over their traditional territories.

Indigenous peoples' relations with inter-national law have been long and painful. Until recently international law had been a tool to legally organise and justify the territorial dis-possession of indigenous peoples. These were the first victims of the rules governing title to territory, fashioned in a way which declared that indigenous peoples were not deemed civilised enough to legally own their territo-ries. After this first experience of dispossession, indigenous peoples experienced another discriminative approach of interna-tional law which played an important role as a tool for their assimilation. Indeed the League of Nations had a paternalistic and patronising approach to indigenous peoples that it quali-fied as 'peoples not yet able to stand by them-selves under the strenuous conditions of the modern world'. The view was that indigenous peoples should be forcibly assimilated within the main society and their culture should dis-appear to give way to so-called progress and civilisation.

One of the first human rights initiatives concerning indigenous peoples came from the International Labour Organisation. Since its creation in 1919, the ILO has defended the rights of native workers (See: **LABOUR RIGHTS**). As a result in 1957 the ILO adopted the first international convention on the rights of indigenous populations, ILO Convention 107. Despite being advanced in recognising the need to especially address indigenous peoples' rights, ILO Convention 107 was criticised for its assimilationist approach. As a result, the ILO adopted Convention 169 which recognises the rights of indigenous peoples. The general spir-it of the Convention is to invite governments to respect indigenous peoples' way of life, and in a number of articles the Convention insists on consultation with indigenous peoples before

© Jack Fields/CORBIS

states take decisions affecting them.

Parallel to this development, in 1970 the **UNITED NATIONS** Sub-Commission on Prevention of Discrimination and Protection of Minorities (See: **MINORITY RIGHTS**) recommended that a comprehensive study be made of the problem of discrimination against indigenous populations. The Special Rapporteur appointed for the study submitted his final report to the Sub-Commission during 1981–1984. This notably resulted in the establishment in 1982 of the United Nations Working Group on Indigenous Populations, which was the first forum in which indigenous peoples could participate. In 1993, the Working Group agreed on a final text of the draft declaration on the rights of indigenous peoples. After its adoption by the Sub-Commission the draft, which promised to be the first universal instrument on indigenous peoples' rights, was then submitted to the Commission on Human Rights, which established a working group for consideration of the draft. It was hoped the draft would be adopted by the General Assembly within the International Decade of the World's Indigenous People (1995–2004). The goal of the Decade was to strengthen international

cooperation for the solution of problems faced by indigenous people in such areas as human rights, the environment, development, education and health. However, at the time of writing the Decade had been disappointing, as one of its main goals was the adoption of the Declaration yet only two of its 45 articles had been approved. The positive developments of the Decade were the establishment of the Permanent Forum in 2000 and the appointment of a Special Rapporteur in 2001. The Permanent Forum is an advisory body to the Economic and Social Council which consists of both indigenous peoples and state representatives; it meets once a year. The Special Rapporteur on the situation of the human rights and fundamental freedoms of indigenous people was appointed in order to gather and receive information and communications on violations of indigenous peoples' human rights and fundamental freedoms from all relevant sources, including governments, indigenous people themselves, their communities and organisations.

Human rights treaty bodies have paid special attention to the situation of indigenous peoples. The **HUMAN RIGHTS COMMITTEE** (HRC) has affirmed that

The International Day of the World's Indigenous Peoples is celebrated annually on 9 August which was the date of the first meeting of the UN Working Group on Indigenous Populations in 1982.

indigenous peoples need special protection and that their **CULTURAL RIGHTS** are closely associated with territory and use of natural resources. When states undertake operations within indigenous peoples' territories, the HRC applies the tests of **SUSTAINABILITY** for the indigenous way of life and their participation in the process. Similarly, the Committee on the Elimination of Racial Discrimination has adopted a General Recommendation on the rights of indigenous peoples which 'calls upon states parties to recognise and protect the rights of indigenous peoples to own, develop, control and use their communal lands, territories and resources and, where they have been deprived of their lands and territories traditionally owned or otherwise inhabited or used without their free and informed consent, to take steps to return those lands and territories'. The Committee on Economic, Social and Cultural Rights has also carefully monitored the treatment of indigenous peoples and the **CONVENTION ON THE RIGHTS OF THE CHILD** specifically mentions the rights of indigenous children.

At the regional level the **INTER-AMERICAN COMMISSION ON HUMAN RIGHTS** has developed a large jurisprudence on indigenous peoples' rights. The Court has recognised indigenous peoples' right to collective ownership of their lands and the obligation of states to put in place special measures of protection. The Organisation of the American States is working on the adoption of a regional declaration on the rights of indigenous peoples. The **EUROPEAN COURT OF HUMAN RIGHTS** has received some communications from members of Sami communities in Scandinavia. The African Commission on Human and Peoples' Rights has established a working group of experts on the rights of indigenous or ethnic communities in Africa to examine the concept of indigenous people and communities in Africa and to study the implications of the **AFRICAN**

CHARTER ON HUMAN RIGHTS for the well-being of indigenous communities. These steps show that indigenous peoples' human rights are rapidly evolving at the regional level.

Despite the increased access of indigenous peoples to the UN system, states remain reluctant to develop indigenous peoples' human rights. During the debates for the adoption of the draft declaration, states have expressed their opposition to indigenous peoples' right to **SELF-DETERMINATION**, and more generally to the recognition of their collective rights (See: **GROUP RIGHTS**). At the heart of indigenous peoples' struggle is the issue of control over their territories. Indigenous peoples from all over the world share the same attachment to their traditional lands because preserving land means protecting their way of life and language and promoting their culture.

This issue of land ownership is one of the most contentious. Traditionally international law favours states' territorial integrity, which results in states' reluctance to recognise indigenous peoples' territorial claims. The issue of land restitution and compensation for past abuses is at the centre of the human rights discourse on non-discrimination. At the World Conference Against Racism, indigenous peoples united their concerns with victims of past human rights violations. Human rights law can operate as a platform for reconciling the rights of indigenous peoples and the interests of the state through apologies, **REPARATIONS**, the establishment of special measures and the restitution of lands. For example, human rights have been a cornerstone of the negotiations in the establishment of the recent peace agreements on the rights of indigenous peoples in Guatemala and Mexico (See: **LATIN AMERICA: THE REALITY OF HUMAN RIGHTS**).

Overall, the instruments concerning indigenous peoples intend to allow for a high degree of autonomous development as the provisions regarding indigenous peoples seek to give them authority to make their own decision. Human rights law also invites the recognition of customary indigenous laws and systems of governance (See: **CUSTOMARY LAW IN THE SOUTH PACIFIC**). Thus, despite states' reticence, the rights of indigenous peoples are gaining momentum under the human rights regime. Indigenous peoples from all over the world have been successful in organising their common plight and in bringing it to the top level of the human rights agenda. Slowly but surely the human rights discourse is breaking the history of injustices and indigenous peoples may finally have a right to remain different and enjoy their different way of life.

Further Reading

Aikio, Pekka and Scheinin, Martin (eds) (2000) *Operationalizing the Right of Indigenous Peoples to Self-Determination*, Institute for Human Rights, Turku/Åbo: Åbo Akademi University.

Alfredsson, G., and Stavropoulou, M. (eds) (2002) *Justice Pending: Indigenous Peoples and other Good Causes*, The Hague: Martinus Nijhoff Publishers.

Anaya, S. James (1996) *Indigenous Peoples in International Law*, New York: Oxford University Press.

Kingsbury, Benedict (2001) 'Reconciling Five Competing Conceptual Structures of Indigenous Peoples' Claims in International and Comparative Law', in Alston, Philip, *Peoples' Rights*, Oxford: Oxford University Press.

Thornberry, Patrick (2002) *Indigenous Peoples and Human Rights*, New York: Juris Publishing.

Contributor: Jérémie Gilbert

INDIVISIBILITY OF HUMAN RIGHTS

During the cold war, international human rights were divided, primarily for ideological reasons, into three 'generations' or dimensions. Western countries, above all the US, alleged and in part still maintain today that only the 'first generation' of civil and political rights, which were in principle perceived as negative rights to ward off state interference, constituted 'real' individual rights with corresponding legal entitlements that could be enforced against governments by means of judicial remedies. A typical example of such an understanding is the right not to be subjected to TORTURE which, according to the official definition in Article 1 of the UN Convention against Torture of 1984, can only

be committed by or at the instigation or with the consent of a public official.

Socialist states, which considered any meaningful effort of international human rights protection as undue interference with their national sovereignty, argued that the practical enjoyment of civil and political rights was dependent on a sufficient level of development in the enjoyment of the 'second generation' of ECONOMIC, SOCIAL and CULTURAL RIGHTS by all people which, in principle, could be guaranteed by socialist countries only through a comprehensive set of positive measures. Freedom of information and EXPRESSION was meaningless for illiterate people and the protection of the home was considered a luxury which homeless people could not enjoy. Consequently, the right to free and equal access to EDUCATION for all was a precondition for the exercise of political rights and freedoms, the right to HOUSING was a precondition for the enjoyment of the right to PRIVACY, and the right to work, which could only be guaranteed in a society without unemployment, was considered as the main precondition for any meaningful enjoyment of other human rights. Finally, southern states put the human rights discourse in the context of colonialism and imperialism by arguing that the full enjoyment of individual human rights was possible only in a society in which the collective rights of the so-called 'third generation', in particular the right of peoples to SELF-DETERMINATION and DEVELOPMENT, were fully secured through individual and collective efforts by all states.

With the end of the cold war, these ideological concepts of 'three generations' slowly gave way to an understanding which stresses the EQUALITY, similarity and interdependence of all human rights rather than their inherent differences. The second World Conference on Human Rights, held in 1993 in Vienna, achieved recognition as having acted as a catalyst for achieving a new and common understanding of human rights, which is based on their universality and indivisibility (See: UNIVERSALISM). With the disappearance of the Socialist states from international politics, the industrialised countries of the north had developed a certain human rights activism towards the south which was based on the notion of the universality of human rights, although in practice was confined to civil and political rights (democratisation, 'good governance', rule of law, and so on). The developing countries of the south reacted to this new form of 'human rights colonialism' by stressing the importance of the right to development and the concept of the indivisibility and interdependence of all human rights. In other words, the notion of the universality of human rights was accepted only if it related to all human rights ('all human rights for all'). In order to save the principal recognition of the universality of human rights and the legitimacy of their international protection, the north, including the US government, finally agreed to accept the right to development and the indivisibility of all human rights. This important compromise is laid down in paragraph 5 of the Vienna Declaration and Programme of Action as follows: 'All human rights are universal, indivisible and interdependent and interrelated. The international community must treat human rights globally in a fair and equal manner, on the same footing, and with the same emphasis.'

What does this political compromise mean in practice? Can any legal consequences be derived from it? First of all, the doctrine of the indivisibility of all human rights has put an end to the 'three generations' theory. It is widely accepted that no set of human rights can claim priority over other human rights. While the fulfilment of economic, social and cultural rights can be regarded as one of the major preconditions for an effective enjoyment of civil and political rights, the same argument can be applied vice versa. As Amartya Sen (2001) has argued convincingly, hunger and starvation usually do not occur in well-functioning democracies with a high level of enjoyment of civil and political rights. International development agencies and financial institutions, such as the United Nations Development Programme and the World Bank, recognise today that effective POVERTY reduction strategies should not aim only at developing sustainable institutions in economic, social and cultural fields, such as small scale enterprises, primary education and health care, but also at institution building in the fields of pluralist DEMOCRACY, the rule of law and other civil and political rights.

Secondly, governments increasingly realised that the division of human rights into various 'generations' was not based on real differences but on an ideological construction. This means that more states, also in Europe, are willing to treat economic, social and cultural rights in their constitutions and, with respect to domestic judicial remedies, on an equal footing with civil and political rights. A major step in this direction was the adoption of the in 2000, which will soon be incorporated into a legally binding constitution of the European Union. Such an understanding presupposes, however, that economic, social and cultural rights are interpreted in a more realistic manner than by the former Socialist states. Not every unemployed person constitutes a violation of the right to work by the respective state, but governments have a legal obligation to take appropriate measures aimed at achieving full and productive employment and must provide adequate social security for those in need, including the unemployed. On the other hand, civil and political rights are today interpreted in a much broader manner than originally perceived in the Western human rights theory and jurisprudence. In addition to respecting the enjoyment of civil and political rights by abstaining from government interference, states have an obligation to secure these rights by a comprehensive set of positive measures, including legislation in all fields of law, institution building, development of proper procedures, investigating past human rights violations and bringing the perpetrators to justice, as well as affirmative action and practice. In other words, no government can claim that it has taken sufficient measures for the full realisation of human rights. There is ample room for further improvements in the 'progressive realisation' of all human rights in all states and in our global society.

In contemporary human rights theory and practice, the following three state obligations have evolved which equally apply to all human rights. Firstly, the obligation to respect human rights means that states should refrain from intervening unless such measures are considered admissible or even necessary under the relevant limitation and restriction clauses. Secondly, the obligation to ensure human rights by positive measures can be divided into two sub-categories. The obligation to fulfil means that states shall take legislative, administrative, judicial and practical measures necessary to ensure that the rights in question are implemented to the greatest extent possible. Thirdly, the obligation to protect refers to state protection of the individual against human rights violations by private parties.

These three state obligations shall be explained by the example of one civil and one social right. The obligation to respect the civil right to a fair trial means that government officials (judges, prosecutors and so on) shall respect the presumption of innocence and other minimum rights of the accused in a criminal trial, such as the right to a defence counsel and to examine witnesses. The obligation to fulfil requires states to build courts, to train and employ a sufficient number of judges and prosecutors and to ensure that justice is provided without unnecessary delay. The obligation to protect means that the state has to take sufficient measures to protect individuals against powerful groups (for example workers against transnational corporations) by providing equal access to justice for all (for example through legal aid in labour disputes) and by ensuring equality of arms and fairness. The obligation to respect the social right to health means, for example, that states shall not interfere with traditional health practices and shall respect the right of women to reproductive health. The obligation to fulfil requires states to build hospitals and primary health care facilities, to train and employ a sufficient number of doctors and nurses, to ensure the progressive reduction of infant mortality and to provide to all people the 'highest attainable standard of physical and mental health'. Finally, the obligation to protect means, for example, that states should protect vulnerable groups, such as children, against practices by their parents and families that are detrimental to their health, such as female genital mutilation in many African societies or the prohibition of life-saving blood transfusions by Jehovah's Witnesses.

Further reading

Nowak, Manfred (2003) *Introduction to the International Human Rights Regime*, Leiden, Boston.

Nowak, Manfred (ed.) (1994) *World Conference on Human Rights*, Vienna.

Sen, Amartya (2001) *Development as Freedom*, Oxford: Oxford University Press.

Steiner, Henry and Alston, Philip (2000) *International Human Rights in Context: Law, Politics, Morals, Texts and Materials*, 2nd ed., Oxford: Oxford University Press.

Symonides, Janusz (ed.) (2000) *Human Rights: Concept and Standards*, Aldershot: UNESCO.

Contributor: Manfred Nowak

THE INTER-AMERICAN COMMISSION ON HUMAN RIGHTS

The Commission is a principal organ of the Organisation of American States (OAS). The OAS is the world's oldest regional organisation, dating back to 1890 when it was known as the International Union of American Republics. Following the creation of the United Nations, the OAS was created in Bogotá, Colombia in 1948. The essential purposes of the OAS are to strengthen peace and security in the hemisphere; to promote and consolidate representative democracy, with due respect for the principle of non-intervention; to prevent possible causes of difficulties and to ensure peaceful settlement of disputes that may arise among the member states; to provide for common action on the part of those states in the event of aggression; to seek the solution of political, juridical and economic problems that may arise among them; to promote, by cooperative action, their economic, social and cultural development; and to achieve an effective limitation of conventional weapons that will make it possible to devote the largest amount of resources to the economic and social development of the member states.

The OAS has 35 member states (see: www.oas.org). In addition, it has granted permanent observer status to over 55 States as well as to the European Union. The Commission is comprised of seven members who represent the 35 member states. At the time of writing, the seven members are Dr José Zalaquett, the President, from Chile, Dr Clare Roberts, the first Vice-President, from Antigua, Dr Susana Villarán, the second Vice-President, from Peru, Dr Evelio Fernández, from Paraguay, Dr Freddy Gutiérrez from

Venezuela, Dr Florentín Meléndez, from El Salvador and Dr Paulo Sergio Pinheiro from Brazil. The seven members are elected to four-year terms and may only be re-elected once.

The Commission was created in 1959, pursuant to a political resolution, to study the human rights situation in the Americas and to make general recommendations to the member states. The Commission had been receiving individual petitions alleging human rights violations from the date of its creation, but was not authorised to deal with them. In 1965, the political bodies granted the Commission the competence to examine and decide on violations of human rights set forth in the American Declaration on the Rights and Duties of Man. The Commission exercised jurisdiction over all the member states of the OAS and applied the rights set forth in the American Declaration.

In 1969, the American Convention on Human Rights was adopted by the member states of the OAS. This treaty recreated the Inter-American Commission on Human Rights (IACHR) and created an Inter-American Court of Human Rights, following the model of the European system which had existed since the early 1950s. The treaty entered into force on 18 July 1978 when the 11th ratification, of Grenada, was received. The treaty created legally binding obligations on the part of the states that ratified or acceded to the Convention. In March 2004, there were 25 state parties to the American Convention: Argentina, Barbados, Bolivia, Brazil, Chile, Colombia, Costa Rica, Dominica, Dominican Republic, Ecuador, El Salvador, Grenada, Guatemala, Haiti, Honduras, Jamaica, Mexico, Nicaragua, Panama, Paraguay, Peru, Suriname, Trinidad and Tobago, Uruguay and Venezuela.

The other ten states that have not yet ratified the American Convention continue to be subject to the American Declaration on the Rights and Duties of Man. This group includes Antigua and Barbuda, the Bahamas (Commonwealth of), Belize, Canada, Cuba, Guyana, Saint Kitts and Nevis, Saint Lucia, Saint Vincent and the Grenadines and the United States.

The inter-American system has adopted a number of human rights treaties and protocols following the adoption of the American Declaration and the American Convention. These treaties cover specialised areas. All of these instruments have entered into force for the states that have ratified or acceded to them. The texts of these instruments are available on the Commission's website: www.cidh.oas.org

The main function of the Commission is to promote respect for and the defence of human rights. The two most important tasks of the Commission are the processing of individual petitions and carrying out on-site visits and the preparation of country reports. In the exercise of its mandate it has the following functions and powers: 1) to develop an awareness of human rights among the peoples of America; 2) to make recommendations to the governments of the member states when it considers such action advisable, for the adoption of progressive measures in favour of human rights within the framework of their domestic law and constitutional provisions as well as appropriate measures to further the observance of those rights; 3) to prepare such studies or reports as it considers advisable in the performance of its duties; 4) to request the governments of the member states to supply it with information on the measures adopted by them in matters of human rights; 5) to respond, through the General Secretariat of the Organisation of American States, to inquiries made by the member states on matters related to human rights and, within the limits of its possibilities, to provide those states with the advisory services they request; 6) to take action on petitions and other communications pursuant to its' authority under the provisions of Articles 44 through 51 of this Convention; and 7) to submit an annual report to the General Assembly of the Organisation of American States.

In recent years the Commission has designated its members to serve as Rapporteurs for the different countries in the hemisphere and for specific subjects such as indigenous peoples, children, prisoners, women, migrants and the internally displaced. Furthermore, the Commission has appointed Eduardo Bertoni to serve as Rapporteur for Freedom of Expression.

The first session of the IACHR took place from 3–28 October 1960. As of March 2004 the Commission had held 119 sessions. The first country report of the Commission was a

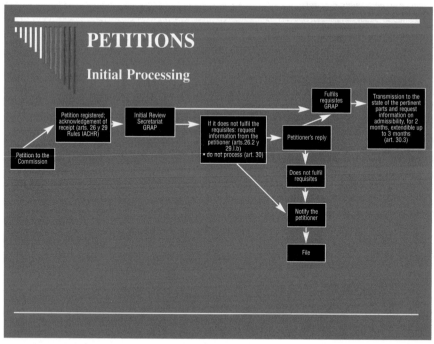

Processing petitions to the Inter-American Commission. © C. Cerna.

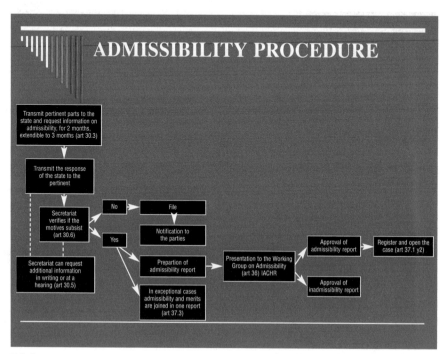

© C. Cerna.

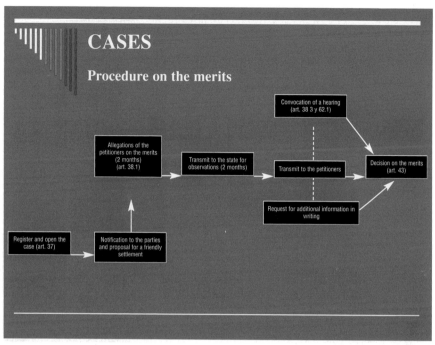

© C. Cerna.

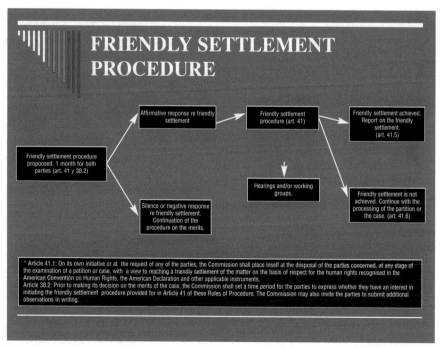

The Friendly Settlement Procedure. © C. Cerna.

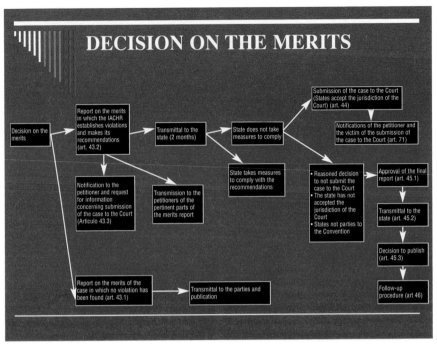

© C. Cerna.

Report on the Situation of Human Rights in Cuba, which was issued in 1962. The Commission has prepared approximately 55 country reports over the years. Parts of the session reports and all of the country reports are available on an American University Law School database website: www.wclamerican.edu/pub/humright/digest/inter-american/index.html.

The Commission has issued decisions on individual cases since 1965 under the American Declaration and since 1979 under the American Convention. The decisions on these cases are included in the Commission's Annual Report to the OAS General Assembly. The Annual Reports are published on the Commission's website, as decisions on new cases as they are adopted throughout the year but primarily during the two ordinary sessions that the Commission celebrates for three weeks in February–March and then again in October.

The American University Law School with the assistance of the Netherlands Institute of Human Rights (SIM) has compiled a 'Repertorio' of the Commission's jurisprudence which is tracked to every article of the American Convention. Unfortunately this Repertorio exists in Spanish only, but is accessible to all on the website: www.wcl.american.edu/humright/repertorio.

Any person, group or non-governmental organisation may lodge a petition with the Commission alleging violation of the American Declaration or the American Convention by a member state of the OAS. In order for the Commission to admit a petition, the petitioner must demonstrate that domestic remedies have been exhausted at the national level up to the highest court possible. The petitioner then has six months from the date of notification of the final judgment to present the petition. A petitioner can find guidance for filling out the petition form on the Commission's website: www.cidh.oas.org/denuncia.eng.htm

In serious and urgent cases and to avoid irreparable harm to persons the Commission has the power to grant precautionary measures. The petitioner may seek one of two kinds of measures: measures in the form of an injunction, to prevent the state from carrying out an action that would violate the petitioner's rights, or measures in the form of protection, to protect the petitioner from a possible irreparable harm. The following flowcharts demonstrate how the petition is processed in the system.

All international human rights instruments presume a democratic state as a condition for the enjoyment of human rights. The Inter-American Commission has been a key player in the democratisation of the Americas. The OAS, beginning in 1959, was the first international body to attempt to define the 'attributes' of democracy in the first 'Declaration of Santiago' named after the city in which it was adopted, despite the fact that many states were not democratic. The Commission's reports on the situation of human rights in Nicaragua (1978), Argentina (1980), Chile (1985), Guatemala (1985), Paraguay (1987), Haiti (1988), to cite just a few notable examples, served to focus hemispheric doubt on the legitimacy of governments that violated human rights internally on a massive scale. These country studies, prepared by the Commission following on-site visits to these countries, contributed to the eventual democratisation of the hemisphere.

In 1991, the OAS held its General Assembly in Santiago, Chile and reaffirmed its commitment to democracy and the rule of law. At that time, every member state, except for Cuba, had a democratically elected head of state. On 11 September 2001, the OAS member states adopted the Inter-American Democratic Charter by which they attempt to guarantee representative democracy as the only acceptable form of government in the region.

Further Reading:

Harris, David and Livingstone, Stephen (1998) *The Inter-American System of Human Rights*, Oxford: Oxford University Press.

Introductory Note to the new Rules of Procedure of the Inter-American Commission on Human Rights (2002) 40 ILM 748.

Medina, Cecilia (1988) *The Battle of Human Rights*, The Hague: Martinus-Nijhoff.

Contributor: Christina M. Cerna

THE INTER-AMERICAN COURT OF HUMAN RIGHTS

The Inter-American Court of Human Rights is the sole judicial organ of the **INTER-AMERICAN HUMAN RIGHTS SYSTEM**. It was established by the Organisation of American States in 1979 upon the entry into force of the American Convention on Human Rights, also known as the 'Pact of San Jose'. The seat of the Court is in San Jose, Costa Rica where it usually convenes. Alternately, the Court may meet in any state of the OAS, with the prior consent of that state, so long as a majority of the judges on the Court deem the alternative meeting place desirable.

The Court consists of seven judges who must be nationals of the member states of the OAS. The judges are elected in their individual capacity. As such, they are independent and do not represent states. They must be jurists of the highest moral authority, be recognised for their competence in human rights and possess the qualifications to fulfil the highest state judicial functions. The official languages of the Court are Spanish, English, Portuguese and French – the languages of the Americas. The Court agrees on its working languages each year. It may authorise any person appearing before it to use his or her own language if the witness does not have sufficient knowledge of the working languages. The Inter-American Court has contentious jurisdiction, advisory jurisdiction and the authority to order a state to take provisional measures.

Under its contentious jurisdiction, the

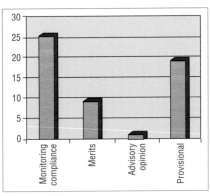

Inter-American Court of Human Rights – status report
from 2002 Annual Report

Inter-American Court rules on whether a state has violated the human rights of any person that is subject to the state's jurisdiction. The human rights allegedly violated must be those that are set forth in the American Convention on Human Rights. All individual complaints of human rights abuse must first be filed with the **INTER-AMERICAN COMMISSION ON HUMAN RIGHTS**. Only after the Commission has completed its procedures may the State or the Commission submit the case to the Inter-American Court. A case can be submitted to the Court only if the state concerned has accepted the Court's compulsory jurisdiction or its jurisdiction for that case. As of 1 March 2004, 21 state parties to the American Convention had accepted the compulsory jurisdiction of the Inter-American Court. The states subject to the Court's jurisdiction are Argentina, Barbados, Bolivia, Brazil, Chile, Colombia, Costa Rica, Dominican Republic, Ecuador, El Salvador, Guatemala, Haiti, Honduras, Mexico, Nicaragua, Panama, Paraguay, Peru, Suriname, Uruguay and Venezuela. Trinidad and Tobago denounced the American Convention and the jurisdiction of the Inter-American Court in 1998, its denunciation coming into effect one year from the date of notification. The states in the Western hemisphere that have not ratified the American Convention or accepted the jurisdiction of the Inter-American Court are Canada, the United States of America, Chile and some Caribbean nations.

Individuals do not have standing to bring a case to the Inter-American Court. Once an application, which must be submitted by the Commission or the state, has been admitted by the Court, the alleged victims, their next of kin or their duly accredited representatives may submit their pleadings, motions and evidence autonomously throughout the proceeding. The Court must assess the truth of the applicant's allegations and determine whether the facts as proved constitute a violation of the Convention imputable to the state. The Court generally considers written pleadings and holds a public hearing to hear oral testimony. The contentious proceedings of the Court are generally divided into preliminary objections, merits and reparations.

If the Court determines that the state is responsible for the violation of a right or freedom protected by the American Convention, the Court may award reparations to the victim. Court-ordered reparations vary depending on the violation. The Court generally orders the state to make financial compensation to the victim or the victim's next of kin. Such pecuniary reparations compensate the victim for material damages such as loss of earnings, medical expenses and the costs and expenses incurred in bringing the case before the domestic authorities and the Inter-American Commission and Court. A financial award may also compensate the victim for moral damages, which are non-economic in nature, such as the pain and suffering of the victim and the emotional distress of family members. In addition, the Inter-American Court may order a state to take or refrain from taking specific actions. For example, in the Loayza Tamayo case (Loayza Tamayo: Series C, No.33, 17 September 1997) the Inter-American Court ordered Peru to release a college professor from prison. The Court has also ordered states to pass domestic legislation to bring its laws into compliance with the American Convention or to amend or repeal any law that violates the American Convention. In the Hilaire, Constantine and Benjamin *et al.* cases (Hilaire *et al.*: Series C, No.44, 21 June 2002), the Court ordered Trinidad and Tobago to modify the domestic law that mandatorily imposed the death sentence on any person convicted of murder. In the Barrios Altos case (Barrios Altos: Series C, No.75, 14 March 2001), the Court held that Peru's amnesty laws, which granted immunity to the perpetrators of human rights violations, are contrary to the American Convention and, therefore, had no legal effect. The Court also consistently orders the state to thoroughly investigate the violation and to identify, prosecute and punish the violators. The Inter-American Court has not ordered the state to pay punitive damages. An Inter-American Court judgment is final, not subject to appeal and binding on the parties to a case.

The American Convention allows state parties to file complaints against other states provided that both states have recognised the competence of the Inter-American Commission to consider the inter-state complaints. These cases could subsequently be referred to the Inter-American Court if the states concerned had accepted the Court's jurisdiction. As of 1 March 2004, there had been no inter-state complaints filed in the Inter-American system.

The Inter-American Court also has jurisdiction to issue advisory opinions. An advisory opinion is an authoritative but non-binding explanation of a legal question or issue. Under the advisory jurisdiction of the Inter-American Court, the member states and organs of the OAS may request the Court's interpretation of provisions of the American Convention or of other treaties concerning the protection of human rights in the American states. Also, any OAS member state may request an advisory opinion as to whether its domestic laws comply with the American Convention or the human rights provisions of other treaties to which the state is a party. Although an advisory opinion is not binding, it does have undeniable legal and moral effects on both national and international law.

The Inter-American Court has the authority to order a state to take provisional measures in cases of extreme gravity and urgency and when measures are necessary to avoid irreparable damage to persons. An order of provisional measures may require that the state take positive action such as providing protection for human rights activists or for witnesses in a case. Alternatively, provisional measures may call for the state to refrain from taking action such as by not extraditing people or delaying the execution of prisoners until their cases have been resolved. The Inter-American Court is not limited to ordering provisional measures when the case is before the Court. At the request of the Commission, the Court may order a state to take provisional measures in a case that is before the Commission but that has not yet been submitted to the Court.

WEBSITE

Inter-American Court http://corteidh.or.cr

Further Reading

Basic Documents Pertaining to Human Rights in the Inter-American System (2001) OEA/Ser.L/V/I.4 rev. 8, 22 May.

Harris, David J. and Livingstone, Stephen (eds) (1998) *The Inter-American System of Human Rights*, Oxford; Clarenden Press.

García Ramírez, Sergio (2002) *Los derechos humanos y la jurisdicción interamericana*, Universidad Nacional Autónoma México.

Pasqualucci, Jo M,(2003) *The Practice and Procedure of the Inter-American Court of Human Rights*, Cambridge: Cambridge University Press.

Contributor: Jo M. Pasqualucci

THE INTER-AMERICAN HUMAN RIGHTS SYSTEM

The inter-American system for the promotion and protection of human rights is today a major component of the Organisation of American States, which has developed comprehensive legal norms, supervisory institutions and petition procedures to address the topic. Concern for human rights in the Americas pre-dates the creation of the OAS, however, and can be traced to the 1826 Congress of Panama, urged by Simon Bolivar to consider a confederation of Latin American States. The Treaty of Perpetual Union, League and Confederation adopted at the 1826 meeting would have joined Colombia (which included Ecuador, Panama and Venezuela), Mexico, Central America and Peru, but the treaty never entered into force.

Despite the failure of Confederation, the Congress of Panama set the precedent for a series of regional meetings to discuss matters of concern and regional cooperation. Prior to 1890, the meetings were convoked in response to specific problems or needs. They were institutionalised with the First International American Conference, held in Washington DC in 1889–90. The conferences continued to be held periodically until the Ninth Inter-American Conference, convened in Bogotá in 1948, adopted the Charter of the Organisation of American States and created the present regional organisation. The American States manifested their concern with the promotion and protection of human rights from the very first regional meeting. The 1826 Treaty of Perpetual Union, League and Confederation recognised the principle of judicial equality of nationals of a state and foreigners; in addition, the contracting parties pledged themselves to cooperate in the abolition of the slave trade. Later meetings adopted agreements on the rights of aliens, on nationality and asylum and on the **RIGHTS**

OF WOMEN. Conference resolutions related to human rights became common prior to Second World War. Between 1938 and 1945, special conferences on issues of war and peace adopted resolutions on the defence of human rights, persecution for racial or religious motives, racial DISCRIMINATION and international protection of the rights of man.

The OAS Charter has been amended by four protocols: Buenos Aires (1967), Cartagena de Indias (1985), Washington (1992) and Managua (1993). The Charter still contains few references to human rights, although there are provisions specifically devoted to representative democracy, human rights and equality, economic rights and the right to education. The most important reference to human rights appears among the principles proclaimed by the Organisation which reaffirms 'the fundamental rights of the individual without distinction as to race, nationality, creed or sex'.

The Ninth International Conference of American States not only concluded the Charter of the Organisation of American States, but it adopted Resolution XXX, better known as the American Declaration of the Rights and Duties of Man. The Declaration became the early cornerstone of the inter-American system for the promotion and protection of human rights. The American Declaration was adopted as a conference resolution and not as a treaty. The Declaration affirms, however, that 'the international protection of the rights of man should be the principal guide of an evolving American law'. More recently, the INTER-AMERICAN COURT OF HUMAN RIGHTS declared in its tenth advisory opinion that the term human rights as it appears in the OAS Charter has been given 'authoritative interpretation' and defined by the American Declaration, which is thereby a source of international obligation related to the Charter for OAS member states.

In 1959, the OAS by resolution created an INTER-AMERICAN COMMISSION ON HUMAN RIGHTS, composed of seven members elected as individuals and charged with furthering respect for human rights. The Commission began functioning in 1960 and became a principal organ of the OAS when the Charter was amended by the Protocol of Buenos Aires (which entered into force in 1970).

The American Convention on Human Rights was adopted in 1969 at an inter-governmental conference convened by the OAS in San Jose, Costa Rica. The Convention draws heavily on the American Declaration, the EUROPEAN CONVENTION ON HUMAN RIGHTS AND FUNDAMENTAL FREEDOMS and the INTERNATIONAL COVENANT ON CIVIL AND POLITICAL RIGHTS. It contains 82 articles and codifies more than two dozen rights, including the right to juridical personality, to LIFE, to humane treatment, to personal LIBERTY, to a FAIR TRIAL, to PRIVACY, to a name, to nationality, to participate in government, to equal protection of the law, and freedom of conscience, RELIGION, thought and EXPRESSION, as well as FREEDOM OF ASSOCIATION, movement and residence, besides prohibiting the application of ex post facto laws and penalties. In contrast to the Convention, the Declaration also addresses numerous ECONOMIC, SOCIAL, AND CULTURAL RIGHTS, such as the right to PROPERTY, culture, work, health, EDUCATION, leisure time and social security. Only the first of these rights is guaranteed by the Convention, although Article 26 of the Convention calls for progressive measures by state parties to achieve 'full realisation of the rights implicit in the economic, social, education, scientific, and cultural standards set forth in the Charter'.

The Convention's Protocol on Economic, Social and Cultural Rights obliges parties to it to take progressive action, according to their degree of development, to achieve observance of the right to work and to just, equitable and satisfactory conditions of work; the right to organise trade unions and to strike; the right to social security; the right to HEALTH; the right to a healthy ENVIRONMENT; the right to FOOD; the right to education; the right to the benefits of culture; and the right to the formation and protection of families. In addition, special protections are afforded to certain vulnerable groups, such as CHILDREN, the elderly and the DISABLED. The Convention's petition procedures extend to two rights in the Protocol: the right to form trade unions (Article 8a) and the right to education (Article 13). Implementation of the remaining rights is supervised through a system of state reports.

Some recognised rights may be limited or suspended under certain circumstances. The Declaration and the Convention each contain a clause that provides that the rights of each person are limited by the rights of others, by the security of all and by the just demands of the general welfare in a democratic society. In addition, some rights in the Convention are accompanied by specific provisions that permit limitations in the interest of national security, public safety or public order, or to protect public health or morals or the rights or freedoms of others.

Article 27 of the Convention permits a state party to suspend one or more rights during a period of national emergency. Any such measure must be non-discriminatory and 'strictly required by the exigencies of the situation'. In addition, it is never permitted to suspend the rights to juridical personality, life, humane treatment, freedom from slavery, freedom from ex post facto laws, freedom of conscience and religion, rights of the family, right to a name, rights of the child, right to nationality and the right to participate in government. In all cases, the judicial guarantees essential for the protection of human rights, including procedures of *amparo* and *habeas corpus*, must be maintained.

In recent years, the OAS General Assembly has approved new instruments to strengthen the inter-American system. At the time of writing current normative instruments of the regional system are:

- American Declaration of the Rights and Duties of Man (1948)
- American Convention on Human Rights (1969)
- Inter-American Convention to Prevent and Punish Torture (1985)
- Additional Protocol to the American Convention on Human Rights in the Area of Economic, Social and Cultural Rights (1988)
- Protocol to the American Convention on Human Rights to Abolish the Death Penalty (1990)
- Inter-American Convention on Forced Disappearance of Persons (1994)
- Inter-American Convention on the Prevention, Punishment and Eradication of Violence Against Women (1994)
- Inter-American Convention On The Elimination Of All Forms Of Discrimination Against Persons With Disabilities (1999)
- Statute and Regulations of the Inter-American Commission on Human Rights
- Statute and Rules of the Inter-American Court of Human Rights.

The various treaties in force are binding only on those OAS member states that have accepted them, while the OAS Charter and the American Declaration establish human rights standards for all OAS members. The American Declaration is invoked primarily against states that have not ratified the American Convention, but states that are parties to the Convention must keep in mind that its Article 29 precludes any interpretation of Convention rights and obligations that would limit the effect of the American Declaration.

States are obliged not only to respect the observance of rights and freedoms but also to guarantee their existence and the exercise of all of them. The Torture Convention and the Convention against Disappearances create a further duty on state parties to establish criminal liability for the commission of or attempt to commit torture or forced disappearance. Other provisions require compensation of victims, training of police and custodial officials, and extradition of those accused of having committed torture or forced disappearance.

The Inter-American Commission on Human Rights promotes the observance and protection of human rights and serves as a consultant to the OAS on human rights matters. The Commission also has specific competence over matters relating to the fulfilment of obligations undertaken by state parties to all human rights conventions adopted in the regional framework, with the exception of the Convention on Persons with Disabilities which creates a separate supervisory committee. The Court also has some functions extending to all OAS member states (primarily in respect to advisory opinions), but mainly concerning parties to the American Convention, the Convention on **VIOLENCE AGAINST WOMEN** and the Disappearances Convention.

The inter-American system is undoubtedly stronger than it was a decade ago, as its institutions have achieved legitimacy, have become widely known and are able to challenge almost any government action that violates human rights. But there are threats to its continued progress, especially due to the lack of staff and resources to process cases quickly and efficiently. With growing attention being paid to enhancing the effectiveness of international human rights procedures, advocates and scholars should become more aware of the strengths and weaknesses of the inter-American system and participate in efforts to enhance the former and reduce the latter.

Further Reading

Buergenthal, Thomas and Shelton, Dinah (1995) *Protecting Human Rights in the Americas*, 4th ed. Kehl, Germany and Arlington, VA: N.P. Engel.

Davidson, Scott (1996) *The Inter-American Human Rights System*, Dartmouth: Aldershot.

Harris, David and Livingstone, Stephen (1998) *The Inter-American System of Human Rights*, Oxford: Clarendon Press.

OAS (2003) Basic Documents Pertaining to Human Rights in the Inter-American System, OAS also available at http://www.oas.org

Stoetzer, O.C. (1993) *The Organisation of American States*, 2nd edn, New York: Praeger.

Contributor: Dinah L. Shelton

INTERNATIONAL CITIZENSHIP AND HUMAN RIGHTS

Recent literature that seeks to reconcile the imperatives of human rights with processes of economic, social and political **GLOBALISA-TION** has focused on international citizenship. Linklater (1992), for example, proposes a system of overlapping citizenship, where the state citizen, the international citizen and the cosmopolitan citizen exist in harmony and mutual tolerance. According to Linklater, this can be achieved through developing what he takes to be the three dimensions of international citizenship.

■ The first dimension concerns the collective responsibility of states to maintain order, an order that provides the basis for experimenting with new forms of citizenship within a changing world order. This is important because while it acknowledges

historic conflicts between states, the amelioration of these conflicts is seen as prior to the task of developing the notion of international citizenship and human freedoms on the global stage.

■ The second dimension concerns respect for other states, including processes that seek out and support international consensus through, for example, international law and diplomacy. Following Hedley Bull, this is a call to further develop the institutions of international society, where the rights of the citizen are identified with those of the state.

■ The third dimension concerns the right to self-determination. For Linklater, this is the universal moral principle upon which the tensions between particular and universal claims of citizen's rights rest. The right to self-determination suggests that legitimacy in both domestic and international relations should be decided by measures that seek the consent of all groups, including those excluded from full social, economic and political engagement. Accordingly, any national policy decision should fulfil the obligation not to take action that frustrates the right of others to achieve self-determination.

By proposing the project of international citizenship Linklater tries to take full account of the previous period, where the state was the main actor on the international stage, and the new era of globalisation, where the individual's identity and loyalty to the state are said to be in decline. Although the account of international citizenship proposed by Linklater and others is intended to offer a possible solution to the pressing problems found in a rapidly changing world, any solution that relies upon some notion of citizenship may also offer support for existing practices that are the cause of many human rights violations and much human misery.

Three reasons may be offered for this conclusion. First, although the central aim in proposing international citizenship is to find a solution to the tensions in the relationship between state and citizen, juxtaposed to the broad needs of humanity, Linklater's project remains largely state-centric. As Hutchings (1996) has observed, so long as state citizenship remains integral to developing international citizenship it appears that international

© The Purcell Team/CORBIS

citizenship will emerge only with the states' permission. This suggests that the rights attached to international citizenship are bestowed from above rather than demanded and developed from below. If this is so, then the **COSMOPOLITAN** claims of human rights appear to take second place to the rights of the state.

This criticism also raises questions about the links made between human rights and **DEMOCRACY**. Proponents of international citizenship observe the growing number of transnational actors, including NGOs, TNCs, international financial institutions and international organisations, and see this as an exciting and revolutionary phenomenon that demands a new democratic project for global governance. However, this fails to acknowledge any possibility that these trends may lead to new loyalties that are not necessarily conducive to the protection of human rights.

Furthermore, the state-centric approach to citizenship places the responsibility for promoting human rights onto states through the medium of international law. In this way human rights become a technical issue concerned with agreements and disagreements over the internal logic and elegance of law, its coherence, extent and meaning. More complex questions to do with the prevailing social, economic and political context in which human rights are supposed to be protected by international law are excluded. Given the arguments about the changing nature of sovereignty under conditions of globalisation, it remains unclear how international law – as a system of law that reflects traditional, state-centric thinking on world politics – is expected to ameliorate the human rights consequences characteristic of globalisation.

The second broad criticism of the project of international citizenship is that it does not avoid the problems that arise in the relationship between the citizen and civil society. International citizenship draws on a

'Where, after all, do universal human rights begin? In small places, close to home – so close and so small that they cannot be seen on any maps of the world. Yet they are the world of the individual person; the neighborhood he lives in; the school or college he attends; the factory, farm, or office where he works. Such are the places where every man, woman, and child seeks equal justice, equal opportunity, equal dignity without discrimination. Unless these rights have meaning there, they have little meaning anywhere. Without concerted citizen action to uphold them close to home, we shall look in vain for progress in the larger world.'

(Eleanor Roosevelt www.udhr.org)

neo-liberal framework to understand the relationship between state and citizen. In this, the task of protecting the freedom of the individual from interference in the pursuit of economic interests is assigned to the public sphere of the state. Citizenship is therefore concerned with protecting civil and political rights, rights which the state guarantees in the name of the private sphere of civil society. Although in formal terms ECONOMIC and SOCIAL RIGHTS are often afforded parity with civil and political rights, according to the neo-liberal conception of citizenship, civil and political rights must be prioritised in order to provide the conditions for wealth creation. Only when these conditions are achieved can citizens turn their attention to what Linklater sees as honouring a duty to promote the widest possible good. While the citizen has the right to seek legal protection if personal and political freedoms are threatened, those suffering economic deprivation have no such rights but must instead rely upon the good faith and charity of others. The duty placed upon the citizen is not even one to protect the poor and vulnerable from further violations, a duty that implies positive action, but rather the lesser requirement to promote their cause in some indeterminate fashion (See: POVERTY AND HUMAN RIGHTS).

This reinforces the centrality of the individual in the human rights debate at the expense of structural causes of violations. It confuses the rights of the individual with the rights of the citizen and does not take full account of the relationship between civil society, the state and the citizen. While a citizen can claim rights by appealing to the state, the individual claiming universal human rights has no such privilege. Following MARX, civil society represents the private sphere; a sphere intended to guarantee the liberty necessary to pursue private satisfactions. Human rights that can be claimed through civil society are concerned with the egoistic, atomised, isolated individual, separated from community. Furthermore, to maintain social order there remains a need to create an imaginary space, the state, in which to fabricate the institutions of unity, including those associated with EQUALITY, democracy and citizenship.

As Ellen Meiksins Wood (1996) has argued, this interpretation of civil society constitutes relations between public and private spheres that offer a unique opportunity for new forms of social power. Social power is located in the legitimation of rights, which are claimed by individuals as members of civil society. Importantly, social power is now relocated in the separate private sphere of civil society. The role of the state is to oversee the existing order rather than to initiate change, which is the role of civil society (See: SOCIAL MOVEMENTS AND HUMAN RIGHTS). In this reading of civil society the state is more concerned with property, appropriation, exploitation and securing the domination of particular economic interests, and acts accordingly to protect the violation of these values. If some groups emerge within civil society with agendas that seek to challenge inequalities, the dominant forces within civil society can appeal to the state to defend the existing order. In short it is civil society that constitutes the limits, form and extent of rights, not the state. The inevitable conclusions from this analysis suggest that the protection of human rights, particularly economic and social rights, cannot be achieved through mechanisms associated with the state, international law and the idea of the international citizen.

The third broad criticism of the project of international citizenship is concerned with its call for a new form of tolerance and recognition. This is a fundamental principle of pluralism. However, proponents of neo-liberal ideas of civil society do not intend that tolerances should be extended to all groups, ideas and values. Instead tolerance is extended to those who accept the general purposes of civil society by adopting its values and following the 'correct' procedures for realising a particular vision of the 'good life'. Marcuse (1969), for example, has referred to this as 'repressive tolerance'. He contends that tolerance in the neo-liberal order is little more than a 'market place of ideas' in which notions of the 'good life' compete for attention within the confines of a particular version of civil society. Those who are seen as a threat to the principles manifest in civil society are marginalised, either by labelling them 'mad' and therefore not worthy of 'rational' consideration (See: **MENTAL DISABILITY AND INTERNATIONAL HUMAN RIGHTS**) or, if that fails, by mobilising 'legitimate' violence. Tolerance may therefore perform the task of 'closure' by excluding alternatives that threaten the existing order, for example by defining peace in terms of the preparation for war or human rights as a legal problem rather than one best understood within the context of the political economy (See: **CAPITALISM AND HUMAN RIGHTS**).

Thus, the idea of international citizenship is not unproblematic and, in its current conceptualisation, may not deliver the outcomes that proponents seek. The argument is not that some form of citizenship cannot lend support to protecting human rights but, rather, that it cannot be done unless we contextualise human rights within the current configuration of social forces, forms of state and world order.

Further Reading

Evans, T. (2000) 'Citizenship and Human Rights in the Age of Globalization', in *Alternatives* 25, no. 4, 415-38.

Hutchings, K. (1996) *The Idea of International Citizenship*, Holder, B. (ed.) Basingstoke: Macmillan.

Linklater, A. (1992) *What is a Good International Citizen?*, Keal, P. (ed.) Canberra: Allen and Unwin.

Marcuse, H. (1969) *Repressive Tolerance*, Wolff, R.P. Moore, B. and Marcuse, H. (eds) Boseon: Beacon Press.

Wood, E.M. (1996) *Democracy Against Capitalism*, Cambridge: Cambridge University Press.

Contributor: Tony Evans

THE INTERNATIONAL COVENANTS ON CIVIL AND POLITICAL RIGHTS AND ON ECONOMIC, SOCIAL AND CULTURAL RIGHTS

Together with the **UNIVERSAL DECLARATION OF HUMAN RIGHTS**, the two **UNITED NATIONS** Human Rights Covenants constitute the International Bill of Rights, that is the core of the present universal human rights standards. As the only general human rights treaties of the United Nations, the Covenants cover a wide spectrum of civil rights (for example **THE RIGHTS TO LIFE**, personal **LIBERTY**, security and integrity, **PRIVACY**, **FAIR TRIAL**, **RIGHT TO MARRY**), political rights and freedoms (for example **THE RIGHT TO VOTE** and participate in the conduct of public affairs, **FREEDOM OF EXPRESSION**, assembly and **ASSOCIATION**), **ECONOMIC RIGHTS** (for example the right to work, right to just, safe and healthy working conditions (See: **LABOUR RIGHTS**), right to form and join trade unions, right to strike), **SOCIAL RIGHTS** (for example **THE RIGHTS TO HEALTH**, social security and to an adequate standard of living, including adequate **FOOD**, clothing and **HOUSING**), **CULTURAL RIGHTS** (for example the rights to **EDUCATION** and participation in cultural life) as well as the right of all peoples to **SELF-DETERMINATION** as the most important example of the so-called 'third generation' of collective rights. In addition, the Covenants include a comprehensive right to **EQUALITY** and non-discrimination (See: **FREEDOM FROM DISCRIMINATION**) as well as a number of human rights for special groups, such as members of minorities (See: **MINORITY RIGHTS**), aliens, women (See: **WOMEN'S RIGHTS**) and children (See: **CHILDREN'S RIGHTS**).

As core human rights treaties of the United Nations, the Covenants are supplemented by a wide range of special human rights treaties for specific groups (for example the Geneva Refugee Convention, the Convention on Political Rights of Women, the CONVENTION ON THE RIGHTS OF THE CHILD or the MIGRANT WORKERS CONVENTION), for combating discrimination (for example the CONVENTION ON THE ELIMINATION OF ALL FORMS OF RACIAL DISCRIMINATION and the CONVENTION ON THE ELIMINATION OF ALL FORMS OF DISCRIMINATION AGAINST WOMEN) or for enhancing the protection of specific human rights (the Genocide Convention (See: FREEDOM FROM GENOCIDE), the Convention against Torture (See: FREEDOM FROM TORTURE) and ILO Conventions on Forced Labour and Freedom of Assembly).

The international community, in reaction to the Nazi Holocaust, recognised the need for international human rights protection for the first time by adopting the UN Charter in 1945. The promotion and encouragement of respect for human rights constitutes one of the three main purposes of the United Nations, but the Charter neither defines human rights nor does it provide for specific mechanisms to protect human rights. The states, therefore, established the Commission on Human Rights and entrusted it to develop a universal human rights system in three steps: by drafting a non-binding declaration in order to define a universal consensus on the contents of human rights, by drafting a convention in order to create binding legal obligations of states, and by developing a system of international supervision for monitoring states' compliance with their international legal obligations (See: THE HISTORICAL ROOTS OF HUMAN RIGHTS BEFORE WWII and UNITED NATIONS SINCE THE UNIVERSAL DECLARATION OF HUMAN RIGHTS OF 1948).

The first step was reached within a surprisingly short period of time. With the adoption of the UNIVERSAL DECLARATION OF HUMAN RIGHTS on 10 December 1948, the international community achieved a universal consensus on those civil, political, economic, social and cultural rights which constitute the core of the international human rights regime. But the drafting of a binding human rights convention encountered serious difficulties at the beginning of the cold war in the early 1950s. By insisting on an essential differ-

ence between civil and political rights on the one hand, and economic, social and cultural rights on the other, the Western states in the General Assembly forced the Commission to draft two separate treaties with two different monitoring mechanisms. The socialist and most southern states never accepted this division and reacted by filibustering and by watering down the contents and monitoring mechanisms of the Covenant on Civil and Political Rights. It took until 1966 to draft and adopt both Covenants and another ten years until their international entry into force in 1976 and the establishment of two separate monitoring mechanisms. At the time of writing, both Covenants have been ratified by some 150 States all over the world. The 2nd Optional Protocol to the Covenant on Civil and Political Rights, aiming at the abolition of the death penalty, was adopted in 1989 and entered into force in 1991. It has been ratified by only some 50 states, primarily from Europe and Latin America.

The ideological differences between west and east regarding the so-called first and second generations of human rights are reflected in the formulation of state obligations in Article 2 of both Covenants as well as in the adoption of different monitoring mechanisms. Under the Covenant on Civil and Political Rights (CCPR), every state party undertakes 'to respect and to ensure to all individuals within its territory and subject to its jurisdiction the rights recognised' in this Covenant without any discrimination and with direct and immediate effect as from the day of entry into force. A state party to the Covenant on Economic, Social and Cultural Rights (CESCR), on the other hand, undertakes only 'to take steps, individually and through international assistance and co-operation, especially economical and technical, to the maximum of its available resources, with a view to achieving progressively the full realisation of the rights recognised' therein. The Western states, which had pushed for this distinction, maintained until recently that only civil and political rights can be considered as human rights in the real sense of legal and judicially enforceable individual entitlements, whereas economic, social and cultural rights were merely regarded as programmatic rights without any immediately applicable and judicially enforceable corresponding state obligations.

This ideological doctrine of an essential difference between these two sets of human rights was, however, abandoned after the cold war and replaced by the doctrine of the indivisibility, equality and interdependence of all human rights, as universally agreed upon during the Vienna World Conference on Human Rights in 1993 (see: INDIVISIBILITY).

With respect to the monitoring mechanisms, the only common denominator which could be accepted by all states during the cold war was the state reporting procedure, that is the obligation of governments to submit periodic reports to the United Nations on the measures which they have adopted for the domestic implementation of the respective rights and on the progress made in the enjoyment of these rights. Whereas the examination of state reports under the CCPR was entrusted to an independent body of experts, the Human Rights Committee, states originally could not agree to establish a similar body in respect of the CESCR. Instead, the consideration of such reports was entrusted to the Economic and Social Council (ECOSOC), that is one of the main political bodies of the United Nations composed of state representatives. Already in 1985, governments realised, however, that a reporting procedure before a governmental body does not function and established the Committee on Economic, Social and Cultural Rights which, like most other treaty monitoring bodies, consists of 18 independent experts from all geopolitical regions. Although both committees are not judicial bodies and cannot adopt any legally binding decisions, they have developed the reporting procedure into a fairly effective monitoring mechanism. Non-governmental organisations play an important role in assisting the committees in carrying out their supervisory function in this procedure (See: THE ROLE OF NGOS IN HUMAN RIGHTS PROTECTION and SOCIAL MOVEMENTS AND HUMAN RIGHTS). Reports are examined in public and in direct confrontation with high-level government representatives, and both committees issue Concluding Observations, in which they recognise achievements but at the same time also strongly criticise governments for non-compliance with their international legal obligations. In addition, both Committees adopted a considerable number of General Comments based on consensus, in which they provide authoritative interpretations of the relevant Covenant provisions, including most individual rights, state obligations and procedural questions.

The CCPR also provides for a fairly weak optional inter-state communication procedure which has, however, been accepted by only comparably few states and never been applied in practice. According to the first Optional Protocol (OP) to the CCPR, which was adopted in 1966 and entered into force together with the CCPR, the Committee also has the power to decide on so-called 'communications' from individuals who allege to be victims of human rights violations. This procedure has been accepted by more than 100 state parties from all regions. Although it is formulated in fairly weak terms, the Human Rights Committee has turned it into a surprisingly effective quasi-judicial individual complaints procedure, which is even comparable to those before the European and Inter-American Court of Human Rights.

Since its establishment in 1977, the Committee has adopted almost 500 decisions on merits which, although not legally binding, are argued like judgments and delivered to the state parties with specific recommendations. These decisions cover a broad range of issues, including difficult legal problems related to the death penalty, torture and ill-treatment, enforced disappearances, arbitrary detention, fair trial, privacy, freedom of religion and expression, political rights, minority rights, equality and non-discrimination. These decisions, most of which are adopted by consensus, represent the most important source of inspiration for the universal interpretation of civil and political rights. At the time of writing, the UN Commission on Human Rights was in the process of drafting an Optional Protocol to the CESCR which will soon provide victims of violations of economic, social and cultural rights with the right to submit individual communications to the Committee on Economic, Social and Cultural Rights, too (See: THE FUTURE OF ECONOMIC, SOCIAL AND CULTURAL RIGHTS).

Further Reading

Arambulo, Kitty (1999) *Strengthening the Supervision of the International Covenant on Economic, Social and Cultural Rights: Theoretical and Procedural Aspects*, Antwerp: Hart Publications.

Eide, Asbjörn, Krause, Catarina and Rosas, Allan (eds) (2001) *Economic, Social and Cultural Rights – A Textbook*, 2nd edn, Dordrecht/Boston/London:

Joseph, Sarah, Schultz, Jennifer and Castan, Melissa (2000) *The International Covenant on Civil and Political Rights – Cases, Materials and Commentary*, Oxford: Oxford University Press.

Nowak, Manfred (2004) *UN Covenant on Civil and Political Rights – CCPR Commentary*, 2nd edn, Kehl/Strasbourg/Arlington:

Contributor: Manfred Nowak

THE INTERNATIONAL CRIMINAL COURT

Since 1 July 2002, the international community has been endowed with a permanent International Criminal Court (ICC) that will bring to justice individuals, including leading state officials, allegedly responsible for the most serious international crimes such as **GENOCIDE**, ethnic cleansing and sexual slavery and put an end finally to the impunity so often enjoyed by those in positions of power (UN Doc. A/CONF.183/9). These crimes are considered to be of such a heinous nature that they are of 'concern' to the international community and dictate prosecution because humanity as a whole is the victim.

The process of establishing the ICC has been very slow. The idea of prosecuting war criminals is ancient: during an armed conflict, human beings are expected to behave appropriately. However, until recently the prosecution of war crimes remained ineffective because it was conducted by national courts and mainly limited to the vanquished (See: **INTERNATIONAL CRIMINAL LAW AND THE REGIONAL TRIBUNALS**). The idea of establishing a permanent International Criminal Court goes back to the aftermath of the First World War with numerous aborted attempts. The end of the Second World War saw the creation of the Nuremberg and Tokyo Tribunals, which brought about the adoption of the 1948 Convention on the Prevention and Punishment of the Crime of Genocide (See: **FREEDOM FROM GENOCIDE**) and the four 1949 Geneva Conventions. These Conventions constitute the basis of **INTERNATIONAL HUMANITARIAN LAW** with regard to international crimes. As early as 1948 the United Nations mandated the International Law Commission (ICL) to draft a statute of such a court, but because the issue was discussed periodically it came to fruition only in 1994. Rather ironically, the atrocities committed recently in many parts of the world gave the new impetus to creating this permanent mechanism to bring to justice the perpetrators of these serious crimes. Events in Rwanda and the former Yugoslavia led the UN Security Council to create specific tribunals, but this turned out to be expensive and lengthy. A permanent tribunal will be more effective and efficient and hopefully provide a strong deterrent to committing serious crimes. Potential war criminals might reconsider carrying out their plans when they know that they may be held accountable as an individual, even if they are a head of state.

In 1994, the ICL produced a draft text to establish a permanent criminal court which was finally adopted in July 1998 by 120 UN member states and entered into force on 1 July 2002. The United Kingdom signed the ICC Statute on 30 November 1998 and ratified it on 4 October 2001. The USA has not.

With the creation of the ICC, a legal void is filled. Whereas the International Court of Justice examines cases between states, the ICC will deal with cases of individual responsibility and make sure that acts of genocide and violations of human rights no longer go unpunished. The ICC Statute sets out the laws, rules and procedure of the Court which must be applied in accordance with international law. Eighteen elected judges, including a president and two vice-presidents, make up the composition of the court (Article 36 ICC Statute). The Court consists of a Pre-Trial Chamber, a Trial Chamber and an Appeals Chamber. The mandate of the Office of the Prosecutor is to conduct investigations and prosecutions of crimes that fall within the jurisdiction of the Court. The first Chief Prosecutor is Luis Moreno-Ocampo. It is interesting to note that the Prosecutor has the power, if there is enough cause and evidence, to initiate investigations of his or her own accord and does not need to rely on a state party to be asked to do so.

The Court's jurisdiction is based on the

principle of complementarity, which means that the Court can exercise its jurisdiction only when a national court is unable or unwilling to genuinely do so itself. For the United Kingdom, the International Criminal Court Act 2001 incorporated the offences of the ICC statute into domestic law. According to this, proceedings shall not be instituted except with the consent of the Attorney General (section 53 (3)). In other words, the Attorney General has a duty to apply the law. It is therefore necessary first to submit any request to investigate to the Attorney General.

The ICC Statute carefully sets out the Court's jurisdiction which is to try highly placed individuals in either a military or governmental capacity who are responsible for the most serious crimes of concern to the international community committed after July 2002, the date the ICC Statute entered into force. These crimes are genocide, crimes against humanity, war crimes and eventually crimes of aggression. The crimes are not limited to those committed during an armed conflict but include international humanitarian crimes, as long as the appropriate conditions are met.

1. Genocide (Preamble and Article 5 ICC Statute) – the crime of crimes. Genocide is defined as a list of prohibited acts committed by an individual with the specific 'intent' to destroy, in whole or in part, a national, ethnical, racial or religious group. Such acts are the killing or causing serious bodily or mental harm to members of the group (torture, rape, sexual violence or inhuman and degrading treatment), imposing conditions on the group calculated to destroy it (forced marches), preventing births within the group and forcibly transferring children from the group to another group.

   The required element of intent means that only the individuals at the top may be prosecuted. Most of the participants in a genocide will fall outside this definition, simply because they may lack the knowledge of the context of the crime. This is in line with the statute's objective to prosecute only the serious criminals such as leaders, organisers and instigators. In cases where the intent is lacking, prosecution may still be possible for crimes against humanity or war crimes.

2. Crimes against humanity (Article 7 ICC Statute). Crimes against humanity include the extermination of civilians, enslavement, torture, rape, forced pregnancy, persecution on political, racial, national, ethnic, cultural, religious or gender grounds and enforced disappearances, but only when they are part of a 'widespread or systematic attack' directed against a civilian population. The requirement that the attack must be either 'widespread' or 'systematic' sets a high threshold to differentiate between a crime of a particular magnitude and random acts of violence, such as rape, murder or even torture, that could be carried out, perhaps even by soldiers in uniform, but which may not actually qualify as crimes against humanity.

   The crime of genocide and crimes against humanity can never be random and will be prosecuted only when planned or committed on a large scale. This is not the case of the third category of crimes: war crimes.

3. War crimes (Article 8 ICC Statute). War crimes include grave breaches of the Geneva Conventions and other serious violations of the laws and customs applicable in international armed conflict or in large-scale armed conflict committed against members of the armed forces *hors de combat* or nationals. Examples of war crimes include the use of weapons of a nature to cause superfluous injury or unnecessary suffering, or which is indiscriminate, the murder of a prisoner of war or a civilian.

   As indicated above, a single instance of any of these acts committed by an individual soldier acting without direction or guidance from higher up can constitute a war crime. However, the ICC has jurisdiction over war crimes only when committed as part of a plan or policy or as part of a large-scale commission of such crimes.

The Court, when applying the definitions of crimes found in Articles 6, 7 and 8 of the ICC Statute, can refer to the Elements of Crime. In accordance with Article 9 of the ICC Statute, the Elements of Crime were adopted in September 2002 (ICC.ASP/1/3, pp. 108-

155). These are an interpretational aid to assist the Court.

Aggression is defined as the use of force by one state against another, not justified by self-defence or other legally recognised exceptions (Article 1 of the UNGA Resolution 3314 of 14 December 1974). International law condemns wars of aggression as a crime against international peace. The prohibition on international aggression is a fundamental principle of international criminal humanitarian law of armed conflict and aggression gives rise to international responsibility. Regrettably, the crime of aggression was excluded by Article 5(2) ICC Statute pending the adoption by the state parties of an agreement on the definition of crimes of aggression and the conditions under which the court could exercise its jurisdiction. So far, this has proven difficult, but as a consequence crimes of aggression are not yet punishable, in accordance with Article 5(2) ICC Statute.

Since the ICC is up and running, the international community possesses a mechanism to bring to justice perpetrators of these heinous crimes. With the invasion and subsequent occupation of Iraq by, among others, the UK (the USA has not acceded), all eyes are cast towards the ICC Prosecutor to see whether he believes there to be sufficient cause and evidence to investigate the actions of the salient officials. For such a youthful and immature institution as the ICC, this may be a daunting prospect. However one should not forget that prosecution is a medium by which international criminal law will progress and strengthen itself and there will always remain scope for ICC decisions to be refined over time.

WEBSITES

International Criminal Court: www.icc-cpi.int/

Rome Statute of the International Criminal Court: www.un.org/law/icc/

International Law Commission: www.un.org/law/ilc/

Further Reading

Cassese, A. (1991) 'The Statute of the International Criminal Court: Some Preliminary Reflections', 10 *European Journal of International Law*, pp. 144–71.

Cassese, A. (2003) *International Criminal Law*, Oxford: OUP.

De Than, C. and Shorts, E. (2003) *International Criminal Law and Human Rights*, London: Sweet & Maxwell.

Dörmann, Knut (2003) *Elements of War Crimes under the Rome Statute of the International Criminal Court: Sources and Commentary*, Cambridge: Cambridge University Press.

Schabas, W. (2004) *An Introduction to the International Criminal Court*, 2nd edn, Cambridge: Cambridge University Press.

Contributor: Solange Mouthaan

THE INTERNATIONAL CRIMINAL COURT, THE FUTURE OF

There can be little argument that the creation of the **INTERNATIONAL CRIMINAL COURT** (ICC) has taken the field of international criminal law, a somewhat disputed legal category, one step closer to becoming a 'discipline'. Much literature has already described the importance of that step. With the prospect of a functioning international court having the resources and the resolve to investigate and prosecute individuals both from the frontline and from political command centres, comes a sense that international law is finally responding to the need for consistent action in the name of humanity.

It would be wrong, however, to restrict the ICC's operations to the confines of such a 'new' discipline. No matter how true Kittichaisaree's suggestion that '[i]nternational criminal law is distinguishable from international human rights law in general' (Kittichaisaree 2001: 3-4), the fact is that the Court is fundamentally infused by human rights matters concerned with the most blatant forms of crimes against humanity and violence. Although focused on 'the most serious crimes of concern to the international community' (Article 5(1) ICC Statute), fundamental human rights lie at the core of the new court's domain. Crucially, Article 21(3) ICC Statute insists that the application and interpretation of law by the Court 'must be consistent with internationally recognised human rights, and be without any adverse distinction founded on grounds such as gender, age, race, colour, language, religion or belief, political or other opinion, national, ethnic or social origin, wealth, birth or other status'. The adherence to principles of non-discrimination reinforces the human rights basis for the ICC's operations.

Consequences of real practical importance for human rights enforcement and development flow from these observations. As a result of the explicit and implicit philosophical and legal underpinning of its Statute, and the scope of its jurisdiction, the Court has in effect created itself as a new, dynamic forum for human rights victims and activists to be heard and to seek justice.

This potential of the ICC for human rights strategies can perhaps best be measured by the example of the 2003 war in Iraq and that country's subsequent occupation by Coalition forces. Here we can see that in possessing the capacity to scrutinise and address issues of political responsibility, the use of weapon systems and strategic and tactical decisions made by the 'victors' of a conflict, as well as dictatorial regimes overthrown, the ICC now represents a formidable presence in the human rights world in the search for accountability. This proposition requires a little more discussion.

The prospect of military intervention in Iraq by Coalition forces during 2003 provoked intense debate on questions of international law. At the forefront of discussion was the legality of any military action without specific authorisation by a UN Security Council Resolution (see for example Lowe, 2003). However, an ancillary legal concern soon became apparent in relation to the UK's specific involvement in the conflict.

As the UK signed the ICC Statute on 30 November 1998 and ratified it on 4 October 2001, and with the entry into force of the Statute in July 2002, the UK government was, for the first time, embarking upon military action in the full knowledge that its operations could be subject to scrutiny and even prosecution. The UK had explicitly agreed for its citizens to be held accountable to an international tribunal in relation to its operations. Although the crime of aggression was outside the jurisdiction of the ICC (Article 5(2) ICC

Statute), crimes against humanity and war crimes fell firmly within the Court's ambit. Even the armed forces were aware of this new legal regime and acted accordingly: Air Marshall Burridge confirmed whilst giving oral evidence to the House of Commons Defence Committee in June 2003 that the armed forces operated a policy of 'heavy lawyering' in order to ensure that operations were conducted within international law.

UK government spokespeople were clearly unabashed by this new circumstance. They were happy to acknowledge the presence of the ICC at the same time as asserting that all military activity would be carried out in accordance with international humanitarian law. Despite such assurances, as the conflict in Iraq developed, serious concerns began to be expressed regarding aspects of the Coalition's operations. Specifically, the number of civilian casualties, the deployment of certain weapon systems such as cluster munitions and the striking of particular civilian targets were all highlighted by human rights agencies. Even when the war ceased on 1 May 2003, agencies expressed grave disquiet over the methods and consequences of military occupation. In 2004 the treatment of prisoners held by both the USA and the UK was subject to severe criticism by the International Committee of the Red Cross.

All of these issues are firmly within the ICC's domain. They potentially fall within the definition of war crimes under Article 8(2)(b) ICC Statute, which brings within the jurisdiction of the Court 'serious violations of the laws and customs applicable in international armed conflict, within the established framework of international law'. Thus, with the appointment of the Chief Prosecutor, Luis Moreno-Ocampo, in June 2003, a direct avenue became open to investigate these grave concerns. Although the Prosecutor may have rejected complaints made to him regarding the conduct of the USA in relation to Iraq (on the basis that neither country is a state party to the Statute), this does not preclude an investigation into the actions of the UK during the war and the subsequent occupation. Nor does it preclude consideration of UK citizens' potential complicity in war crimes committed by US forces under Article 25 ICC Statute.

For human rights activists concerned with

addressing the 'crime of silence', as well as seeking justice for victims of both war and occupation, the ICC therefore presents notable possibilities. Three specifically come to mind in the context of the Iraq War and occupation.

First, activists supplying information detailing possible war crimes can encourage an investigation into a particular situation by the Prosecutor. Even though the main methods of commencing an investigation are through complaint by a state party or referral by the UN Security Council (Article 13 ICC Statute), the Prosecutor is entitled to act on his own initiative under Article 15 ICC Statute. He is also expressly empowered to seek additional information from NGOs to determine the seriousness of the alleged crimes (Article 15(2) ICC Statute). Consequently, human rights groups are able to bring violations to the Prosecutor's attention without necessarily having to compile a dossier of evidence that would of itself sustain a prosecution. Thus, pressure can be applied to ensure that the potential commission of war crimes is taken seriously.

Second, the ICC Statute provides a recognised means of holding accountable not only perpetrators of crimes but also those individuals who exercise effective command responsibility over the actions of military forces. Article 27 ICC Statute makes clear that anyone operating in 'an official capacity' such as head of state or government minister will not be exempt from 'criminal responsibility'. Equally, anyone exercising 'effective authority and control' over subordinates can be held responsible under Article 28(b) ICC Statute for crimes within the Court's jurisdiction where they knew or 'consciously disregarded information which clearly indicated' crimes were being or about to be committed and failed to 'take all necessary and reasonable measures' to prevent or repress the commission of those crimes or to investigate and prosecute them. Such provision underlines the scope of the ICC to hold accountable those 'in command' howsoever that term may be defined. In terms of military conflict, any strategic decisions, which might for instance include the deployment of weapons known by governments to be indiscriminate and likely to cause 'incidental loss of life or injury to civilians' (Article 8(2)(b)(iv) ICC Statute), may thus come under scrutiny by the Prosecutor. Indeed, Guy Goodwin-Gill has suggested to the authors that it is not beyond the bounds of reason that the ICC Statute's possible application might be used to encourage state parties to undertake full investigations whenever military force is used. The impetus to conduct such an enquiry becomes even more urgent when loss of life has resulted, thus *prima facie* breaching the right to life.

Third, given the nature of the crimes against humanity and the war crimes defined by the ICC Statute and the Elements of Crimes that accompany it, military personnel of state parties can no longer assume that they can operate in a bubble of immunity. All actions and decisions may be scrutinised by the ICC. Thus, allegations of murder, torture or imprisonment 'in violation of fundamental rules of international law' that are committed 'as part of a widespread or systematic attack against any civilian population' (Article 7(1) ICC Statute) are specifically within the Court's jurisdiction. This is particularly pertinent in the context of the occupation of Iraq after the war in 2003, where accountability has suffered from the lack of transparent and independent inquiries into alleged human rights violations.

Given the clear and immediate responsibility of government members under the ICC outlined above, there is now a permanent arena for holding individuals criminally accountable for some of the most serious human rights abuses. Whether or not this leads to stricter systematic surveillance and control of the armed forces of an ICC state party (such as the UK), or empowers human rights victims to attain some kind of justice in a court setting, will depend on the willingness of states to embrace the jurisdiction of the ICC. Equally, it will depend on the ICC's willingness to pursue difficult questions of accountability. The case of Iraq may well determine which direction states and the Court take.

WEBSITES

www.amnesty.org Amnesty International

www.hrw.org Human Rights Watch

www.icc-cpi.int The International Criminal Court

www.iraqbodycount.net Iraq Body Count

www.medact.org MEDACT

www.peacerights.org Peacerights

Further Reading

Cassese, Antonio (2003) *International Criminal Law*, Oxford: Oxford University Press

Dörmann, Knut (2003) *Elements of War Crimes under the Rome Statute of the International Criminal Court: Sources and Commentary*, Cambridge: Cambridge University Press

Kittichaisaree, Kriangsak (2001) *International Criminal Law*, Oxford: Oxford University Press

Lowe, Vaughan (2003) 'The Iraq Crisis: What Now?', 52 *International and Comparative Law Quarterly* 859-71

McGoldrick, Dominick (2004) *From 9-11 to the Iraq War 2003: International Law in an Age of Complexity*, Portland, OR: Hart

Contributors: Andrew Williams, Solange Mouthaan and Phil Shiner

INTERNATIONAL CRIMINAL LAW AND THE REGIONAL TRIBUNALS

Although war crimes and other international crimes have long been violations of both international law and of basic human rights, the recognition and acceptance by international courts of individual criminal responsibility for humanitarian crimes is a relatively new phenomenon (See: **HUMANITARIAN LAW; THE INTERNATIONAL CRIMINAL COURT**). Before 1945 individuals were of course prosecuted for violations of international law during war, but such cases were either dealt with under the limited jurisdiction of military tribunals or, rarely, in national courts. The change came after the dramatic circumstances of the Second World War when the Nuremberg and Tokyo tribunals set up by Allied states applied criminal sanctions, including the death penalty, to those found guilty of war crimes and of the new category of offences, crimes against humanity. Thus for the first time individuals were held accountable not only for specific infringements of the conventions and customary rules of international humanitarian law but also for conduct felt to shock the very essence of humanity.

Thus the seeds of international criminal jurisdiction of tribunals were sown, albeit without a truly international genesis. However, it was not until the early 1990s that the international community again called for a judicial solution to the horrific crimes against humanity being perpetrated in the Federal Republic of Yugoslavia. In the intervening years many international violations of humanitarian law were being committed which would have justifiably warranted the prosecution of heads of government and high-ranking military officials for their offences. Prime examples include the atrocities of the regimes led by Pol Pot in Cambodia, Idi Amin in Uganda and Saddam Hussein in Iraq. However, dictatorships, as a rule, are not stopped by concerns over the criminality of their actions or the possible judicial consequences, at least, within their own borders. Psychologically, they see themselves as somehow being immune from any outside interference. This attitude is no doubt aided by Article 2(7) of the United Nations Charter preventing the **UNITED NATIONS** from intervening in matters which are essentially within the domestic jurisdiction of the offending state. Indeed between the Nuremberg trial in 1946 and the establishment of the tribunal for breaches of humanitarian law in the former Yugoslavia in 1993, the apathy towards punishing individuals for their violations of international criminal law was such that respect for international humanitarian laws was being seriously undermined.

However, after the break-up of the Soviet Union in 1989 the role of Security Council became more effective and poignant. Under Article 29 of the UN Charter the Security Council is given wide powers whereby it 'may establish such subsidiary organs as it deems necessary for the performance of its functions'. Since the Security Council is charged with the maintenance of international **PEACE** and security, this seemingly includes the power to create a judicial tribunal, the purpose of which would be to prosecute individuals who pose a threat to peace and security in violation of international law under Chapter VII and in particular Articles 39, 41 and 42 of the Charter. It should be noted that establishing such a tribunal has the disadvantage that it exists only whilst the threat to peace itself lasts, as an ad hoc tribunal, and therefore once the threat has subsided the legitimacy of the continuity of such a tribunal would also cease to exist.

With the creation of independent Balkan states in the territory of former Yugoslavia the realisation grew that this transformation was not going to be a smooth and peaceful process. When Bosnia-Herzegovina, Croatia, Slovenia and Macedonia declared independence from the Former Republic of Yugoslavia armed conflict and widespread humanitarian atrocities reminiscent of the Second World War erupted. Reports and media film emanating from those territories depicted scenes of horrific human rights violations. Such atrocities included civilians being indiscriminately murdered and thrown into mass graves, the starvation of the civilian population, the establishment of concentration camps, deportation, ethnic cleansing and widespread and systematic rape of women and girls. In 1991 and again in 1992 negotiations took place between the various interested parties to reach a peaceful settlement, but without success. Eventually in 1993, under the authority of Chapter VII, the Security Council adopted resolution 808 (reaffirming the previous resolution 764[1992]) which declared

'that all parties are bound to comply with the obligations under international humanitarian law and in particular the Geneva Conventions of 12 August 1949, and that persons who commit or order the commission of grave breaches of the Convention are individually responsible in respect of such breaches ... and to take effective measures to bring to justice the persons who are responsible for them.

(And) that an international tribunal shall be established for the prosecution of persons responsible for serious violations of international humanitarian law committed in the territory of the former Yugoslavia since 1991.'

It should be noted that failure by the UN at this time to take some form of constructive action would no doubt have resulted in the credibility of the UN itself being seriously undermined.

After the Secretary General submitted a report on the situation to the Security Council,

Resolution 827 reaffirmed the establishment of an international tribunal. Thereafter, in 1993, the International Criminal Tribunal for the Former Yugoslavia (ICTY) came into being as well as the Statute of the International Tribunal (SITY) governing the offences, rules and procedures of the Tribunal. Article 1 of the Statute states that the Tribunal has the power to prosecute individuals for serious violations of international humanitarian law. Jurisdiction is limited to crimes within the territory of the former Yugoslavia and then only for those crimes that took place after 1 January 1991. Under Article 9(1), although the Tribunal and national courts shall have concurrent jurisdiction to prosecute people, the Tribunal will have primacy over the national courts; thereby permitting the Tribunal to request a national court to defer the case to its jurisdiction at any stage of the proceedings (Article 9(2)). Once tried by the Tribunal for crimes under the Statute, the accused may not be tried again by a national court. Conversely, if tried by a national court the accused may still be indicted by the Tribunal if '(a) the act for which he or she was tried was characterised as an ordinary crime; or (b) the national court proceedings were not impartial or independent, were designed to shield the accused from international criminal responsibility, or the case was not diligently prosecuted' (Article 10).

Within Articles 2–5 there is an exhaustive list of the categories of crimes for which individuals may be prosecuted, namely, grave breaches of the Geneva Conventions of 1949 against protected persons and property (Article 2), violations of the laws or customs of war (Article 3), genocide (Article 4) and crimes against humanity (Article 5). The Tribunal sits in The Hague.

The second major regional criminal tribunal applying international law also had its roots in violence on a massive scale. The International Criminal Tribunal for Rwanda was created in response to the genocidal policies, mass murders and other inhumane and grave violations of international humanitarian and human rights law of the then Hutu government in that state in 1994. The conflict had deep historical roots, with prejudices strengthened by the former colonial power. Even prior to independence in 1962 armed insurrection between the two main ethnic groups, the Tutsis (Rwandan Patriotic Front) and the Hutu Rwandan government forces (Forces Armées Rwandandaises), for political domination in Rwanda continued unabated. After independence the policies of the first Hutu government only exacerbated the situation and many Tutsis were forced to take refuge in neighbouring states or else suffer severe reprisals if they remained. The next ten years saw fierce cross-border fighting between the groups and despite a military coup in 1973, little was achieved in alleviating an already volatile situation. Civil war broke out in 1990 between the Hutu extremists and the Tutsis. On 6 April 1994 President Habyarimana was killed in a plane crash after returning from Tanzania where a tentative peace agreement had been reached. Immediately after this the genocide began and in the short period from April to July 1994 it is estimated that between 500,000 and 1 million people were slaughtered, the vast majority of whom were Tutsis. The scale of other forms of violence, principally sexual violence, was beyond belief (see: **VIOLENCE AGAINST WOMEN IN WAR TIME**).

The United Nations was very slow to acknowledge or take any positive action to prevent what was to become one of the worst genocidal tragedies of the 20th century. The peacekeeping forces already there were wholly inadequate for preventing further bloodshed. As a judicial response, on 8 November 1994 the Security Council (Resolution 955) established the International Criminal Tribunal for Rwanda (ICTR) for the prosecution of those responsible for serious violations of international humanitarian law in Rwanda and its neighbouring states. The Tribunal sits in Arusha, Tanzania, but the Appeals Chamber and Office of the Prosecutor are in The Hague. The Statute of the International Tribunal for Rwanda (the Rwandan Statute) sets out three separate categories of crime which come within the Tribunal's jurisdiction: genocide (Article 2), crimes against humanity (Article 3) and serious violations of Article 3, common to the Geneva Conventions 1949 (murder, outrages upon personal dignity etc.) and Additional Protocol II of 1977 (Article 4). Overall, the Rwandan Statute is set out in comparable terms to that of the Yugoslav Tribunal, with differences related to the different nature of the conflicts (Yugoslavia as principally international armed conflict,

Rwanda as internal armed conflict).

A few differences between the two tribunals' statutes are important to note. Article 1 of the Rwandan Statute grants the Tribunal the power to prosecute people for serious violations of international humanitarian law. However, unlike the territorial restriction of Article 1 of the Yugoslav Statute which relates only to crimes within the territory of the former Yugoslavia, the Rwandan Tribunal's powers extend to 'violations committed in the territory of neighbouring states'. Moreover, under the Rwandan Statute prosecutions are limited to those crimes which took place between the period 1 January and 31 December 1994, while under the Yugoslav Statute the period commences on 1 January 1991 and continues thereafter.

With hindsight, the two regional tribunals have had great positive effects upon international criminal law. In spite of their remarkably small number of completed cases, each has created a large and unprecedented body of international criminal law, evidence and procedure; the impact of such developments cannot be overestimated. Without the tribunals' concern for the rights of both victims and defendants, international human rights would have had a smaller role in international criminal law and the Statute of the International Criminal Court. The tribunals were to a large extent an unintended 'pilot project' for the ICC. Judges have developed the definitions of existing international crimes and invented new ones; their effect on international law has broken through their limitations to a great extent via the citing of cases from regional tribunals in national and regional courts. There has been a process of cross-pollination between international humanitarian law, international criminal law and international human rights, since the tribunals for the former Yugoslavia and for Rwanda intrinsically blend all three within their jurisdiction and in the presentation of their judgments, applying human rights conventions and cases to criminal conduct. Thus they have reduced the grey areas and conflicts within **CUSTOMARY LAW** and aided the interpretation of treaties.

The criminalisation of wartime sexual violence in international law has been greatly aided by tribunal decisions. Liability for genocide has finally been imposed in an international criminal tribunal; the principles and availability of universal jurisdiction have been expanded; and head of state immunity has been denied effect. But, most significantly of all, international criminal law has been rendered enforceable for the first time since the Nuremberg trials, with criminal sanctions against individuals for violations of some of the most fundamental human rights. Although limited by geography and time, this is still a major achievement in the fight against impunity for the most heinous human rights violators and a step towards a new international climate seeking justice for their victims.

However, there are still some problems due to the lack of efficiency of the tribunals. Each has a huge backlog; it is estimated that the tribunal for the former Yugoslavia will not finish its limited task for at least another decade. Moreover, the limits of time and geography have an obvious effect. The consequent reliance upon co-operation between states and police forces makes the process of bringing fugitives to justice frustrating and slow and the trials themselves are long and lead to high numbers of appeals. The application of substantive law is contested as the expansion of legal principles can be viewed as inaccuracy of interpretation of existing law. Confusion has sometimes been caused in the case law due to the conflicts between decisions and the lack of clear rules as to which court's judgments bind others. Of the 46 changes suggested in a UN report on the effectiveness of the regional tribunals, fewer than half have been put into practice. Finally, individual criminal responsibility may not be the most effective method of vindicating human rights when in so many cases through practical problems the tribunals are unable to gain physical custody of fugitive suspects, or when those convicted are a long way down the chain of command.

The creation of the ICC does not prevent future use of 'temporary' international criminal tribunals, but makes them less likely.

WEBSITES

www.ictr.org Tribunal for Rwanda
www.un.org/icty Tribunal for the former Yugoslavia

Further Reading

Ackerman, J. and O'Sullivan, E. (2000) *Practice and Procedure of the International Criminal Tribunal for the Former Yugoslavia, with Selected Materials from the International Criminal Tribunal for Rwanda*, Leiden: Brill.

Cassese, A. (1997) 'The International Criminal Tribunal for the Former Yugoslavia and Human Rights', in *EHRLR* (4), 329–352.

de Than, C. and Shorts, E. (2003) *International Criminal Law and Human Rights*, London: Sweet and Maxwell.

McGoldrick, D. (1999) 'The Permanent International Criminal Court: an End to The Culture of Impunity?' in *Criminal Law Review*, August, 627–655.

Contributor: Claire De Than

THE INTERNATIONAL LABOUR ORGANISATION

The International Labour Organisation, established in 1919, survived the demise of the League of Nations to become the first specialised agency of the UN system. Its primary mandate is the world of work and it is only fairly recently that its pioneering work on international human rights has begun to become better known in the human rights community.

The ILO's deliberative bodies are tripartite, composed of representatives of governments, employers and workers. This structure has been a great source of strength for the ILO, which is the only intergovernmental organisation in which governments do not have the exclusive right to debate and decide. The ILO is comprised of three main bodies. The International Labour Conference consists of tripartite delegations from all member States. The Governing Body consists of 56 members, 28 representing governments (including permanent seats for the ten countries of 'chief industrial importance') and 14 each representing employers and workers. The International Labour Office is the permanent secretariat of the organisation.

The principal human rights instruments of the ILO are its standards and the ILO is the most active standard-setting body in the UN system. Conventions and Recommendations are adopted by the Conference. Most of these standards concern some aspect of human rights, as understood in the **INTER-NATIONAL COVENANT ON ECONOMIC,**

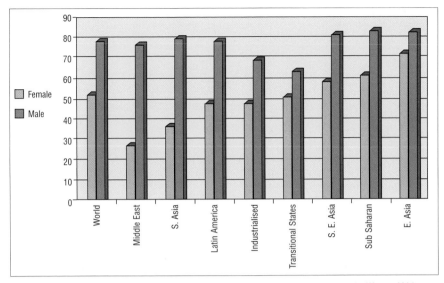

Labour force participation rates by region 2003. (Statistics from ILO Global Employment trends for Women 2004, Geneva, March 2004)

SOCIAL AND CULTURAL RIGHTs. Some relate directly to the ILO's principal human rights concerns as laid down in the 1998 Declaration (see below). Others cover aspects of the right to a decent working environment – wages, conditions of work, occupational safety and health, etc. The ILO is also responsible for the only international conventions specifically relating to the protection of indigenous and tribal peoples. These Conventions are widely ratified – over 7,000 ratifications in all, with most of the fundamental human rights conventions in the ILO system having well over 150 ratifications – they thus provide significant international human rights coverage around the world.

In 1998, the ILO adopted a new kind of instrument. The Declaration of Fundamental Rights and Principles at Work codifies the ILO's long understanding of the fundamental human rights contained in its Constitution and standards as comprising freedom of association and the right to bargain collectively, freedom from forced labour, freedom from child labour and freedom from discrimination. It provides that all states, even if they have not been able to ratify the Conventions which embody these principles, have 'an obligation, arising from the very fact of membership in the Organisation, to respect, to

promote and to realise, in good faith and in accordance with the Constitution, the fundamental rights which are the subjects (of the eight ILO Conventions recognised as fundamental)'. Global reports are prepared under the Declaration, each focusing on one of the four subjects covered, examining its application around the world and giving rise to a plan of action for technical assistance. All of this work is done in a promotional framework.

In other cases, standards are laid down in texts less formal than Conventions and Recommendations. These include, for example, the Tripartite Declaration of Principles concerning Multinational Enterprises and Social Policy, adopted by the Governing Body in 1976 and updated in 2000, and Conference resolutions on such questions as the independence of the trade union movement and the relation of trade union rights and civil liberties. The ILO has also adopted a number of codes of conduct and guidelines illustrating best practice in various respects, such as the Code of Practice on HIV/AIDS adopted by the ILO Governing Body in June 2001.

The most remarkable thing about the ILO and human rights is the supervision of standards' application. Most supervision takes place on the basis of regular reporting and dialogue between states and the ILO's supervisory bodies. The reports supplied by governments on the application of Conventions and of Recommendations are examined in the first instance by the Committee of Experts on the Application of Conventions and Recommendations, which is composed of 20 independent people. Some 2000 reports are received and examined each year. The Committee's comments take the form either of 'observations' contained in its printed report or of 'direct requests' addressed directly to the governments concerned. The reports of the Committee of Experts are submitted to a tripartite Committee on the Application of Conventions and Recommendations at each session of the International Labour Conference. This body discusses with the representatives of the governments concerned selected important cases on the basis of the Committee of Experts' annual report.

In addition to supervision based on regular reporting, the ILO Constitution provides for two kinds of complaints procedures. The procedure of complaint under Article 26 of the ILO Constitution allows complaints to be filed by any member state against another member state on the application of a Convention that both have ratified. This procedure may also be initiated by the Governing Body on receipt of a complaint from a delegate to the Conference or on its own motion. As an example, a complaint filed in 1996, following the examination of earlier representations, alleged massive forced labour in Myanmar and the Commission of Inquiry found that these allegations were amply justified. Commissions of Inquiry receive written submissions, hear witnesses and, when necessary, make on-the-spot visits. A number of other complaints have been referred to the Committee on Freedom of Association or were the subject of an agreed settlement reached with the assistance of the ILO. The Myanmar case led in June 2000 to the first instance of the ILO's use of Article 33 of the Constitution, which provides that the Governing Body may propose to the Conference 'such measures as it may deem wise and expedient' to secure observance of the findings of a Commission of Inquiry. The ILO continues to follow up

this case.

Representations may be made under Article 24 of the Constitution by employers' or workers' organisations on the ground that a state does not secure the application of a ratified Convention. They are considered by a three-member committee of the Governing Body and then by the Governing Body itself. Fewer than 100 representations have been submitted during the existence of the ILO, since 1919, but the increase in recourse to this procedure in recent times appears to reflect growing difficulties in numerous countries in securing observance of ratified Conventions. In the field of freedom of association, the ILO set up special machinery in 1950, in agreement with the Economic and Social Council of the United Nations, for examination of complaints by governments or by employers' or workers' organisations. Since the procedure draws its authority from the ILO Constitution, it may be invoked against states which have not ratified the freedom of association Conventions. The machinery comprises two bodies: the Committee on Freedom of Association is a tripartite body, appointed by the Governing Body from among its members. It has dealt with over 2000 cases on a wide range of issues. The Fact-Finding and Conciliation Commission, composed of independent people, may undertake more extensive investigations, similar to a commission of inquiry. A case may not be referred to the Commission without the consent of the government concerned and, in the early years, several governments refused to give their consent. Subsequently, a number have done so, but if the governments concerned have ratified the Conventions the tendency is to resort to the Article 26 procedure which does not require consent.

The first important thing to retain about the ILO's supervisory procedures is that they function regularly and in detail and that they feed into the ILO's active technical advice and assistance programmes. For many years, the ILO has operated a rights-based development approach, ensuring above all that none of the assistance it provides is in conflict with ILO standards. The second thing is that the ILO's standards system has produced tangible results through the years, improving the lives and working conditions of people all over the world.

WEBSITES

The interactive data base ILOLEX, available online at www.ilo.org or on CD-ROM.

Further reading

Ahmed, Iftikhar and Doeleman, Jacobus A. (eds) (1995) *Beyond Rio: The Environmental Crisis and Sustainable Livelihoods in the Third World*, New York: St Martin's Press.

Figueiredo, J. and Gore, C. (eds) (1998) *Social Exclusion: An ILO Perspective*, Geneva: ILO.

Forastieri, Valentina (1997) *Children at Work: Health and Safety Risks*, Geneva: ILO.

Reinhart, Arian (2000) *Sexual Harassment: An ILO Survey of Company Practice*, Geneva: ILO.

Swepston, Lee (1998) 'The Universal Declaration of Human Rights and ILO Standards: A comparative analysis on the occasion of the 50th Anniversary of the Declaration's adoption', Geneva: ILO.

Contributor: Lee Swepston

© R.K.M. Smith

ISLAM AND HUMAN RIGHTS

Like all religions, Islam has been lived and understood in different ways through time and space. The interpretations of Islam have been as many and as variable as the societies across the world which have adopted it through its 14-century history. If we stopped there (and we could), discussing 'Islam and human rights' would be an enormous, even impossible task. There is, however, a common body of religious precepts and beliefs which forms the basis of the Islamic religion and from which our discussion of Islam and human rights can commence. The content of this common body of precepts remains disputed; outlining its salient points requires a considerable degree of abstraction and simplification. But despite the problems associated with this process, it is a helpful first step in tackling the question at hand.

The first thing to note with regard to the fundamentals of the Islamic religion is that many of them are in contradiction with international human rights principles. For example, Islam stresses the submission of the individual to Allah and human freedom is understood as surrendering to the divine will. Only God has rights, people do not. There are major inequalities between Muslims and non-Muslims: the Koran asserts that idolaters must be slain and Jews and Christians in Muslim societies are second-class citizens. There are many inequalities between men and women, too. Men can have up to four wives; women's rights to divorce, inheritance and custody of the children are limited, and so on. Apostasy is punishable by death. The *hadd* penalties (harsh corporal punishments such as flogging or cutting off limbs for theft) are enjoined and slavery is condoned.

But none of these precepts and ideas were unusual for the seventh century AD, which is when Islam appeared. It would be unreasonable to expect that a traditional body of thought would contain the notion of human rights, which is a modern idea. Human rights are inalienable and unconditional. They belong to all human beings irrespective of race, sex, religion and nationality. By contrast, traditional, pre-modern belief systems emphasised duty rather than right and rights, or privileges, were accorded because of who people were or what they did. It would therefore be futile trying to locate the concept of human rights in traditional Islamic doctrine, as some Muslim apologists do. It would also lead to a forced and false conciliation between Islam and human rights, similar to the one contained in the ISLAMIC DECLARATION OF HUMAN RIGHTS.

However, what we can locate in the fundamental precepts of Islam are ideas that can serve as the foundation for developing a conciliation between Islam and international human rights principles – resulting in a genuine Islamic liberalism. For example, Islam elevated the status of the individual and stressed his/her dignity by introducing the idea that he/she is the vicegerent of God/Allah on earth. His/her relationship with Allah would be direct, without intermediaries. Because of the belief that all believers are equal, the Islamic belief system is strongly egalitarian (within the community of the faithful only, but the idea could be extended). The ruler in Islam must uphold the Islamic law (*sharia*) and can be removed from his position by the believers should he fail in this important duty. The institution of *shura* (consultation among the faithful) contains the idea that authority must rest on consensus. Islam was a progressive religion. Compared with pre-Islamic Arabia, it elevated the status of women and gave them certain, albeit limited, rights. Non-Muslim minorities living in Muslim societies, especially Jewish and Christian, were guaranteed protection and a measure of autonomy.

Is it, therefore, the case that Islamic doctrine – in so far as we can abstract it from historical reality – has the potential to be interpreted in either an authoritarian or a liberal fashion in equal measure? Some would not be convinced. They would claim that the 'dice' are loaded in favour of authoritarianism in Islam and that it would be very difficult to reconcile Islamic doctrine, even in modern times, with human rights principles. They would use two arguments to support their position. Firstly, they would point to the cardinal Muslim belief that the Koran is the word of God and that, as a consequence, no good Muslim should contravene what is in the holy book. This implies that, for example, injunctions about the position of women and non-Muslims or the *hadd* punishments can never be abandoned, thereby creating a serious ten-sion with international human rights principles. Secondly, they would argue that, because the door of *ijtihad*, the use of independent reasoning to construct a workable law, was 'closed' in the ninth century, Islamic law stopped adapting to changing historical circumstances, again leading to serious tensions between Islam and human rights principles as they developed in modern times.

How can we think about these two arguments? There is no doubting the centrality of the Koran in the Islamic religion. However, there is considerable dispute between Muslims about the true meaning of the Koran. There are those who argue, for example, that the Koran says that the hand of the thief should be stopped, not cut. There is also disagreement between Muslims on whether the spirit, as opposed to the letter, of the Koran must be respected. This has important implications for the relationship between Islam and human rights. For instance, some Islamic feminists argue that because Islam elevated the status of women compared with pre-Islamic Arabia, it is the duty of Muslims to carry on the progressive impulse contained within the Koran by constantly revising the position of women. Finally, we have cases where ideas or institutions which are contained in the Koran are so fundamentally at odds with modern times and values that they are hardly ever defended, at least openly, by any Muslim religious or Islamist thinkers. The major example here is slavery.

What about the argument that because the door of *ijtihad* closed in the ninth century Islamic law cannot adapt to changing historical circumstances and needs? Here we are confronted with an interesting, albeit not unusual, set of tensions between myth and reality. It is self-evident that no society can function without a workable law that meets its needs. In reality, while the myth that *ijtihad* was no longer practised remained powerful – at least in the mainstream Sunni Islamic world – Islamic law pragmatically adapted to changing circumstances. At the same time, a body of secular law of administrative rules and regulations developed in parallel with Islamic law to serve the needs of Muslim societies.

Let us, then, concede that it is possible to find ways of conciliating Islam with human rights principles. This means that a society can be Islamic and also liberal. But now we are confronted with another serious objection. It is often held that liberalism can flourish only in secular societies and that allowing religion – any religion – into the public (let alone political) sphere introduces a level of intolerance, which is detrimental to human rights. The problem with Islam, the argument continues, is that it can never separate itself from politics – Muhammad, after all, was both a political and a religious leader – and be, simply, a private matter. Therefore, if secularism is an impossibility in the Muslim world, so is respect for human rights.

Once again, this view carries considerable conviction, not least because so many Muslims believe it to be true. But even a cursory look at Islamic history is sufficient to demonstrate that for long periods government was 'Islamic' only in name. In the 20th-century Middle East, for instance, secular ideologies – namely nationalism in all its hues – captured and held the imagination of the great majority of the people for decades on end. Political Islam, far from being the 'natural' choice of the Muslim Middle East, arose in response to the many failures of secular ideologies and the inability of the Middle Eastern state to deliver on its promises of welfare and independence.

Further Reading

An Naim, Abdullahi (1990) *Towards an Islamic Reformation: Civil Liberties, Human Rights and International Law*, Syracuse, NY: Syracuse University Press.

Binder, Leonard (1988) *Islamic Liberalism: A Critique of Development Ideologies*, Chicago, IL: University of Chicago Press.

Dalacoura, Katerina (2003) *Islam, Liberalism and Human Rights: Implications for International Relations*, London: I.B. Tauris.

Contributor: Katerina Dalacoura

THE ISLAMIC DECLARATION ON HUMAN RIGHTS

Does adherence to Islam require a distinctive approach to human rights? There are many indications to the contrary. Representatives of Muslim countries made important contributions to the formulation of the UN human rights instruments, governments of Muslim countries have generally acknowledged their authority and Muslim human rights activists rely on them. However, a substantial segment of Muslim opinion has rejected aspects of the International Bill of Human Rights, often classifying their precepts as being 'secular' or 'too Western'. With the increasing influence of political Islam since the 1970s, numerous efforts have been made to formulate Islamic counterparts to the international bill at the same time that some governments have been asserting that they have cultural and religious reasons for deviating from international standards.

The most prominent of the models purporting to offer an Islamic version of human rights was the 5 August 1990 Cairo Declaration on Human Rights in Islam, embodying an approach that was endorsed in a meeting of the foreign ministers of the Organisation of the Islamic Conference (OIC), to which all Muslim countries belong. This international organisation indicates in the preamble to its charter that its members are 'reaffirming their commitment to the UN Charter and fundamental Human Rights [sic], the purposes and principles of which will remain one of the important factors of achieving progress for mankind'. Despite this commitment, the OIC's 1990 declaration was sharply at variance with UN human rights principles.

The declaration reveals an ongoing ambivalence about whether in matters of human rights Muslims should be bound by Islamic precepts as these were formulated by jurists centuries ago. Reflecting divisions among the OIC members, the Cairo Declaration, like many other attempts at formulating Islamic versions of human rights, is a hybrid of international and Islamic elements. It contains many terms and concepts borrowed from the International Bill of Human Rights and combines these with elements selectively appropriated from the Islamic legacy without offering any coherent theory to account for this hybridity.

The central concept of the Cairo Declaration is that rights and freedoms afforded in international human rights law are excessive – with the concomitant need for reducing their number and restricting the scope of those preserved. After asserting that 'fundamental rights and universal freedoms in Islam are an integral part of the Islamic religion', the declaration proceeds to enumerate rights and freedoms, all of which are subject to vague 'Islamic' qualifications. For example, Article 24 provides that 'all the rights and freedoms stipulated in this Declaration are subject to the Islamic Shari'ah' without offering any indications for how the shari`a-based constraints should be defined – or by whom. No added clarity is provided by Article 25, which states: 'The Islamic Shari'ah is the only source of reference for the explanation or clarification of any of the articles of this Declaration.' Interpretations of shari'a requirements have differed vastly among different sects and schools, and various contemporary trends have proposed new ways of understanding the Islamic sources, so the Islamic qualifications envisaged by the Cairo Declaration remain open-ended, opening the door to nullifying rights protections.

Not only does the Cairo Declaration dilute rights via vague qualifications, it also eliminates many rights, including some very basic ones. For example, no guarantee of **FREEDOM OF RELIGION** is afforded. Naturally, the absence of provision for freedom of religion will tend to be detrimental for non-Muslims, but it could also have a harmful impact on Muslims, given the amount of discrimination and persecution to which Muslim dissenters and members of minority sects are exposed in Muslim countries. There is no unequivocal affirmation of the **EQUALITY** of all persons, Article 1 stating that human beings 'are equal in terms of basic human dignity and basic obligations and responsibilities', but offering no guarantee of equality in rights and freedoms. Article 6 provides that 'woman is equal to man in human dignity' – again not providing for any equality in 'rights'. Moreover, the declaration makes no provision for equal protection of the law. Article 6 imposes on the husband support obligations and the responsibility to care for the family, duties that directly correlate with the husband's traditional legal prerogatives under Islamic law, including his right to demand obedience from his wife, who is presumed to be dependent. Thus, this provision effectively calls for perpetuating gender stereotypes and patterns of inequality in the husband-wife relationship. In this declaration, where guarantees for equal rights for women and non-Muslims have been deliberately eliminated, when Article 19a provides that 'all individuals are equal before the law, without distinction between the ruler and the ruled', this means only that there may be no favouritism in the law for rulers – not that all individuals are being accorded equality regardless of gender or religious affiliation.

No guarantees of freedom of assembly or **FREEDOM OF ASSOCIATION** are afforded and no provisions for free and democratic elections are included. Article 5 provides that on **THE RIGHT TO MARRY** there should be 'no restrictions stemming from race, colour or nationality', but does not prohibit restrictions based on religion. The extensive provisions in the international instruments that are designed to guarantee fairness in criminal procedure are largely ignored.

Some provisions are opaque and their potential impact will be apparent only to those familiar with how Islamic law is interpreted in countries like Iran and Saudi Arabia. For example, the principle set forth in Article 19d allows the Shari'a to determine crimes and punishments, which could result in imposing the death penalty for apostasy from Islam and for certain categories of extramarital sexual intercourse and utilising penalties such as floggings, amputations, and stonings.

The Cairo Declaration makes no pretence of religious neutrality, being forthright in favouring Islam at the expense of other religions. Article 10 states 'Islam is the religion of unspoiled nature' and prohibits 'any form of compulsion on man or to exploit his poverty or ignorance in order to convert him to another religion or to atheism'. The impression is conveyed that pressures to effectuate religious conversions would not be prohibited where they were employed to convert people to Islam.

Reflecting the Third World setting in which Muslim nations elaborate their positions on human rights, Article 11b states that colonialism is 'totally prohibited', implying that there could be no qualifications, not even Islamic ones, placed on this particular principle. It also states that 'peoples suffering from colonialism have the full right to freedom and

SELF-DETERMINATION', a principle lacking in express antecedents in traditional Islamic doctrine that has been borrowed from UN instruments. According to Article 2b of the Declaration, it is prohibited 'to resort to such means as may result in the genocidal annihilation of mankind'. This provision seems to be loosely modelled on the prohibition of GENOCIDE in international law, constituting another instance where in fashioning principles the OIC went beyond the Islamic sources, the modern concept of genocide not being a concept expressly prefigured therein. Article 11a provides that no one has the right to enslave human beings. Of course, for many centuries SLAVERY was a salient feature of Muslim societies, as evinced in the work of the classical jurists, where slavery was treated as a given and was extensively regulated. This is an instance where the Cairo Declaration implicitly repudiates traditional readings of Shari'a law, adopting norms in accordance with the international instruments.

Subsequent developments proved that the Declaration did not signal the emergence of a unified Islamic stance on human rights. Individual Muslims, Islamic institutions and governments of various Muslim countries have continued to differ widely in their degree of readiness to embrace international human rights law. In addition, the Declaration did not prompt Muslim countries that were not previously disposed to exploit Islam as the rationale for denying human rights to do so, nor did it influence such countries to remodel their laws along the lines of the rights in the declaration, which in many cases fell below the standards embodied in domestic laws and constitutions.

The Cairo Declaration does not reflect a coherent Islamic philosophy of human rights and has not been endorsed by general Muslim opinion, which remains deeply divided on human rights. Rather than setting forth the definitive restatement of how the Islamic heritage bears on human rights, it offers a rough and inchoate vision of the project of integrating human rights within an Islamic framework.

WEBSITE

Qantara.de www.qantara.de/webcom/ show_link.php/_c-449/i.html

Further Reading

Khan, Saad S. (2001) *Reasserting International Islam: A Focus on the Organisation of the Islamic Conference and Other Islamic Institutions*, Oxford: Oxford University Press.

Mayer, Ann Elizabeth (1999) *Islam and Human Rights: Tradition and Politics*, Boulder: Westview.

Contributor: Ann Elisabeth Mayer

JEWISH TRADITION AND HUMAN RIGHTS

Human rights as understood in Jewish tradition are responsibilities incumbent on the Jewish individual by Divine Decree. These are specified in 248 positive commandments (to do) and 365 negative commandments (not to do). The 613 commandments (*mitsvot*) are placed in two wide-ranging categories: the ones pertaining to the realm between the human and God (*ben adam la makom*), the others to the realm between human and human (*ben adam lechawero*).

Central principles in Jewish tradition are the sacredness of human life, the preservation and the protection of human dignity, for human beings were created in the image of God, 'Male and female he created them' (Genesis 1,27), and as co-creator with the task to mend the world (*letaken olam*). The use of the plural in the expression of the deed of creation 'Let us create the human' (*naase adam*) is to be understood as an indication that God could create the human only with his cooperation. 'You and I let us together create a mensch with free will' (Hassidic commentary). Man is thus not only in search of God but God is also in search of man.

Ethics as *Imitation Dei*, the imitation of God, the walking in his ways is the highest norm determining the actions of the Jew (Deuteronomy 28,9). The clothing of the naked, the visiting of the sick, the comforting of the bereaved, the burial of the deceased are a holy obligation, following the example given by the holy blessed be he (Talmud Sota 14A).

The Torah. © Image Source/CORBIS

It is clearly paralleled by the *Imitation Hominis*, the way God as it were is asked to obey the rules of the highest form of human behaviour. Thus Abraham challenges God when confronted with his plan to destroy the evil cities of Sodom and Gomorrah and the consequence that righteous ones will be punished with the wicked. 'Shall the judge of the whole Earth not do Justice' (Genesis 18,25) is an extraordinary commentary on the text '... that you will know that God is trustworthy' (Deuteronomy 7,4).

God is asked to act according to the righteous water carrier who saves life by providing water and rescue his daughter who is drowning. 'When I went out towards you I found you on the way towards me,' writes the medieval poet Yehuda Halevi.

Although the human should always remember that he or she has been created later than the lowest animal and should care for all living, he or she is according to the psalmodist little lower than the angels crowned with glory and might, ruling over the work of the creation of God (Psalm 8). Thus one who destroys one human being is considered as if they have destroyed the whole universe and one who saves one human being is considered as one who has saved the whole universe (Talmud Sanhedrin 37A). The overriding principle is *Pikuach nefesh*, the obligation to preserve life, also one's own, even when by doing so one is breaking the commandments. There are only three specified instances in which martyrdom is required: when one is ordered to murder, to rape or to worship idols publicly (Talmud Sanhedrin 74A). 'Once a man came to his teacher and informed him: "The ruler of my city told me to kill this one and if not that I would be killed." The teacher replied: "You should be

killed and not kill. How do you know that his blood is redder than yours, maybe his blood is redder?"' (Talmud Psachim 28B).

This injunction was taken to the extreme during the Holocaust. Parents had the opportunity to save their sons' lives by arranging for others to be put in their place on the list kept by the commander of the Nazi concentration camp, but they refused to do so. The pre-eminence given to the concept of *Pikuach nefesh* to save life is of utmost importance in the decision making of political leadership in Israel today. As the leading shepherd rabbi of our generation has stated: '... and therefore if it is possible for us to give back territories and to avoid the dangerous war with our enemies we must do so on account of the commandment to save life' (oz ver shalom 3, 1982).

The commandment, the golden rule 'Thou shalt love thou neighbour as thyself, I am the ever being God' (Lev. 19,18) gives direction to all legislation. Although the plain meaning of 'neighbour' or 'brother' in the Bible is Israelite, it is clear from the verse later in the chapter (19,34), 'you should love the stranger, for strangers you have been in the land of Egypt', that the term is all inclusive. The Talmud (Gittin 61) states: 'The poor of the gentiles are to be supported together with the poor of Israel, the sick of the gentiles are to be visited together with the sick of Israel and the dead of gentiles are to be interred even as we inter the dead of Israel in order to achieve the "ways of peace" and "one whole Torah exists only for the sake of the ways of peace"' (Gittin 59B).

The down-to-earth restatement is this principle by Hillel: 'Do not do unto others what you don't want others to do to you.' This has become the cornerstone of the teaching of good human behaviour. And it all flows from the simple injunction in chapter 19 of Leviticus: 'You shall not curse the deaf and you shall not put a stumbling block in the way of the blind' (14,14).

Moral behaviour is based on the principle that one should act justly and protect the human rights of the other not out of fear of punishment. God has given the ten commandments to humans, who have free choice to obey, or not to obey and not to angels, who are not capable of doing wrong. These commandments constitute the basis of a just society.

There are two reasons given in the commentaries for the fact that these commandments were given to the Jewish people: one, that the people themselves were the only ones who chose to accept them (*naase vemishma*: we shall study them and carry them out), the other, that God gave the people of Israel no choice: 'You shall keep them or you shall die.' In that respect, to be chosen is not to have a choice. In any case, the people are the messengers of the universal charge. You shall not serve idols, profane God, murder, commit adultery, steal, be a false witness, be obsessive by wanting to have what is your neighbour's. The specific additional commandment to the Jewish people is to live with the knowledge of God who has taken you out of the land of Egypt and freed you, the God of historical, existential experience, and to observe the Sabbath day. Jews are obligated to let non-Jewish members of the household, slaves and strangers, enjoy the day of rest.

Later the seven commandments of the sons of Noah were enumerated as minimum requirements to enter decent society, forbidding idolatry, bloodshed, profaning God's name, robbery, cutting the flesh or a limb from a living animal and the positive injunction to install courts of justice (Genesis Rabba 34,8).

The rules to protect the rights of the weak in society, including slaves and strangers, are very strict to ensure their physical integrity, sustenance and dignity. One should not reap the full harvest but leave the corners of the field for the poor and the stranger. The loving treatment of the stranger is commanded all through the Torah, the five books of Moses. Moreover, all inhabitants and strangers, the free and the slaves, are protected by laws and regulations. Thus one can be convicted only on the basis of the testimony of at least two witnesses, after a due course of justice. The death penalty can be given only, reluctantly, after intensive deliberations of the full Sanhedrin of 71 members. A Sanhedrin that metes out several death penalties is called 'a murderous one'. In cases where someone has caused death but it is not certain whether they acted wilfully or by accident, they should be allowed to reach one of the six cities of refuge, to escape the blood revenge. The life of the slave should be protected. Thus when a master has hit his slave so that he loses his tooth or his female servant so that she loses her eye, he should let them go free (Exodus, 21,21). The passage which states this follows the one which deals with a life for a life, an eye for an eye, a tooth for a tooth. It is clear from the context that one is commanded to apply moderation – not taking more than a tooth.

During warfare, even in the most precarious circumstance, the dignity of the individual should be protected. Thus even the sensitivity of the captured woman should be considered. She should have time to mourn the loss of her family, in peace. One should always attempt to conclude a peace treaty before assaulting a city, even when war is commanded in order to protect life and property. During the siege one should leave open an escape route. One should never resort to starving the inhabitants of a besieged city and should not deprive them of the necessary medicines (Sifre). These are the bases of the rules of conduct during warfare that are applied in the Israeli defence forces. They are known as *taharat haneshek*, the keeping clean of the weapons. One is obligated to always probe the justice of an order and to disobey when it is inhuman.

To obey these rules of ethics is a formidable task and an ongoing challenge. I am writing these lines of summary of the protection of human dignity, keenly aware, in my bones, that I am alive thanks only to the courage of my foster parents, devoted Catholics, who understood the necessity to protect a then anonymous Jewish baby, even if by doing so they risked their lives. Van der Kemp, their memory be a blessing.

While it is true that the emphasis of ancient religiously motivated codes was more on duties and responsibilities than on rights, there are in the Jewish legacy similarities with international standards of human rights, such as the treatment of prisoners of war, property rights, the right of return, citizens' rights, freedom of speech, assembly and learning. It should be noted that international documents now also include reference to religious traditions, unlike the **UNIVERSAL DECLARATION OF HUMAN RIGHTS**. The Earth Charter, for example, draws upon non-Western religious and spiritual traditions in its broad perspectives of rights and responsibilities in respect to ecological integrity, social and economic justice and peace and democracy.

WEBSITE

www.earthcharter.org

Further Reading

Agus, Jacob B. (1966) *The Vision and the Way, An Interpretation of Jewish Ethics*, Frederic Unger Publishing.

Cohen, Arthur A. and Mendes-Flohr, Paul (eds) (1988) *Contemporary Jewish Religious Thought*, New York, NY: The Free Press and London: Collier Macmillan.

Collier (1987) *Contemporary Jewish Religious Thought*, Macmillan Publishers.

Herzberg, Arthur (1961) *Judaism*, London: Prentice Hall International.

Lamm, Norman (1974) *The Good Society: Jewish Ethics in Action*, Viking Press.

Spero, Shubert (1983) *Morality, Halakka and the Jewish Tradition*, Yehhiva University Press.

Contributor: Awraham Soetendorp

LABOUR RIGHTS

'Labour rights are human rights' is an often repeated phrase among scholars, trade unionists and other human rights activists. Why is this simple phrase even necessary? This phrase implies that labour rights were somehow different from human rights at some point in time. Labour rights or workers' rights must be understood as a subset of human rights rather than as some newly discovered phenomenon.

The articulation of workers' rights began during the industrial revolution as agrarian workers moved to cities and factories. In 1787 the first society to abolish slavery was formed. As the industrial revolution gained steam, trade unions began to evolve, become stronger and more highly organised as they sought to address issues such as working conditions and wages in various industries. The development of workers' rights owes much to the struggle and sacrifice of these early activists.

In 1919 moral and geo-political factors, such as the Bolshevik Revolution, the end of the First World War and a century of struggle for workers' rights led to the creation of an international organisation that would define and protect these rights – the International Labour Organisation. The ILO was established the same year as the League of Nations (1919) by the Treaty of Versailles. Its origins in the First World War and a century of worker struggles are expressed in a statement of principle in the first sentence of the constitution's preamble. 'Universal and lasting peace can be established only if it is based upon social justice.' The constitution argues that where labour is exploited, threats to peace exist. As such, the constitution calls for improvements in hours of work, prevention of unemployment, a living wage, health and safety, the protection of children, young persons and women. These have been further developed in international human rights law and international labour law since 1919.

After the Second World War the community of nations declared that both workers' rights and human rights were founded on the same premises. In 1944 the ILO adopted the Declaration of Philadelphia and incorporated it into the ILO constitution in 1946. This Declaration reaffirmed the central belief of the constitution that 'lasting peace can be established only if it is based on social justice'. Only a few years later the newly created United Nations General Assembly adopted the **UNIVERSAL DECLARATION OF HUMAN RIGHTS** which declared that 'Whereas recognition of the inherent dignity and the equal and inalienable rights of all members of the human family is the oundation of freedom, justice and peace in the world.' Workers' rights and human rights are thus based on notions of justice and peace and grew out of events that represented immense threats to these two values.

An important demonstration of the relationship between human rights and workers' rights is found in the references to workers' rights in human rights instruments. The Universal Declaration of Human Rights addresses workers' rights in Articles 20, 22, 23, 24 and 25. These include freedom of **ASSOCIATION, DISCRIMINATION**, equal pay for equal work, the right to just and favourable remuneration, right to rest and leisure, including reasonable limitation of working hours and periodic holidays with pay. The same year the UDHR was adopted the International Labour Conference (ILC) adopted Convention 87 concerning freedom of association and the right to organise and in 1949 Convention 98 on the right to organise. Workers' rights are also dealt with in both international human rights covenants which are often believed to separate human rights into civil and political rights and economic, social and cultural rights.

The International Covenant on Economic, Social and Cultural Rights (ICESCR) and the International Covenant on Civil and Political Rights (ICCPR) both deal with workers' rights. Articles 6–10 of the ICESCR deal with workers' rights including many of the same rights dealt with in the UDHR. Articles 8 and 22 of the ICCPR deal with freedom of association and the right to organise. Furthermore, the text of the ICCPR addresses the linkage between human rights and workers' rights clearly in Article 22(3) which states that nothing in Article 22 of the ICCPR authorises states which have ratified Convention 87 to take measures that prejudice the guarantees of the convention. The fact that such fundamental human rights instruments as the ICESCR and ICCPR deal with workers' rights, and that they even seek to address potential conflicts between themselves and ILO standards, demonstrates that workers' rights are not something separate from human rights but integral to them. It is also interesting to note that ILO Conventions have been adopted relating to all the labour rights contained within the UDHR, the ICESCR and the ICCPR.

One right which deserves particular attention is freedom of association. This right is contained in the UDHR, ICCPR, ICESCR as well as the ILO constitution, ILO Conventions 87 and 98, in addition to numerous regional instruments. Its importance rests on several key concepts. First it is integrally linked with civil liberties such as freedom of expression, the right not to be subjected to arbitrary arrest, detention and exile and the right to a fair and public hearing to name just a few (See: LIBERTY). Second, freedom of association is an enabling right which allows people to exert power in protection of their rights. Finally, freedom of association includes the

right of individuals to associate b
rights to organisations. There is o...
much more to this right but these three characteristics are important in understanding the centrality of freedom of association to other labour rights. The right of workers to establish and join organisations gives them power that helps them advance their interests but that has also put trade unions at the centre of many struggles for freedom and DEMOCRACY in the world.

Much time is spent today on the fundamental conventions of the ILO. Various standards have been considered 'core' by different groups, including conventions on forced labour, freedom of association, the right to organise and discrimination. Later child labour and the minimum age for admission to employment were also included. Whether the rights of workers' representatives and health and safety should be included in a list of core conventions has also been discussed. By the beginning of the 1990s the world had changed. GLOBALISATION, the Internet revolution, the end of the cold war and the emergence of a consensus on the principle of open markets created concern about the social and labour impacts of the market economy and liberalisation. This concern manifested itself in the debate about trade and labour standards. In response, the World Trade Organisation's Ministerial Conference in 1996 called on governments to respect core labour standards and noted that these were the responsibility of the ILO. In addition the ILO Governing Body identified eight conventions referred to as the Fundamental ILO Conventions in the areas of child labour (C. 138 and 182), equal opportunity and non-discrimination (C. 100 and 111), freedom of association and collective bargaining (C. 87 and 98) and forced labour (C. 29 and 105). Some commentators have expressed concern that the focus on fundamental ILO Conventions as human rights detracts from the fact that other ILO Conventions also cover internationally proclaimed human rights.

These developments helped pave the way for the ILO Declaration on Fundamental Principles and Rights at Work in 1998. In adopting it, the members recognise that they have an obligation to work towards the realisation of certain fundamental principles and rights that are inherent in the ILO Constitution, namely freedom of association and the right to collective bargaining, the elimination of forced or compulsory labour, the abolition of child labour, and the elimination of discrimination in respect of employment and occupation. This obligation exists even if they have not yet been able to undertake to accept the more detailed provisions of the Conventions the ILO has adopted on these questions. Member states are required to submit annual reports on the fundamental rights for which they have not ratified the corresponding ILO Convention. A promotional follow-up was also adopted to determine the needs of States and the way in which they can be met.

Workers' rights are an integral part of the human rights discourse today. They have developed in national and international law and political thinking over 300 years and are among the most well-defined human rights. As scholars and activists we have much to learn from their foundations and much more to contribute to their observance.

Further Reading

Alcock, Antony (1971) *History of the International Labour Organisation*, Basingstoke: Macmillan Press.

International Labour Review Special Issue: *Labour Rights, Human Rights*, Vol. 137, No. 2, pp. 197–290.

Leary, Virginia (1996) 'The Paradox of Workers' Rights as Human Rights' in Compa, Lance and Diamond, Stephen *Human Rights, Labor Rights and International Trade*, Pennsylvannia: University of Pennsylvania Press.

Swepston, Lee (1998) 'The Universal Declaration of Human Rights and ILO Standards: A comparative analysis on the occasion of the 50th Anniversary of the Declaration's adoption', Geneva: ILO.

Contributor: Michael Urminsky

LANGUAGE RIGHTS

The question of language is fundamental in human society because *homo sapiens* are, by definition, 'language animals'. Language also plays a central role in terms of economic opportunity and success, since the dominance of one language in a state will be advantageous in terms of access to and distribution of public resources to individuals who have greater fluency of the official or majority tongue. Those who have a different primary language will often be seriously disadvantaged. This is perhaps why language rights are so important and indeed why language figures prominently in a number of violent conflicts worldwide.

It should be made clear from the outset that language rights are human rights. A large number of documents such as the Framework Convention for the Protection of National Minorities, the UN Declaration on the Rights of Persons Belonging to National or Ethnic, Religious or Linguistic Minorities and the European Charter for Regional or Minority Languages, in addition to the human rights provisions of treaties, acknowledge that the speakers of the world's thousands of languages have rights – human rights – that must legally be respected. Not all of these instruments are legally binding treaties, nor do most of them aim to protect languages as objects of law. They nevertheless recognise that language rights are not simply a 'good idea' and are concretely enforceable standards that must be complied with.

All individuals thus have numerous rights in relation to language, some in treaties and others repeated in documents from the **ORGANISATION FOR SECURITY AND CO-OPERATION IN EUROPE** and other intergovernmental organisations. While these latter examples do not for the most part constitute legally binding documents, they do represent political and moral obligations and reflect a generalised consensus as to what are the human rights and standards that are applicable in the area of language. Although not having the same force as a legally binding

In Europe, more people speak Catalan (the language of north-eastern Spain) than Greek and more people speak Welsh than Icelandic. Both Catalan and Welsh are deemed minority languages, their survival under threat.

right, political commitments do signal acceptance of an individual's entitlement to use his or her language in various situations, including persons who belong to a linguistic minority (See: **MINORITY RIGHTS**).

A problem which often arises when trying to understand what language rights exist in international law is that many human rights standards tend to be rather vague or general. This means that it is not always clear what is the exact content of a particular right in relation to language in concrete situations, or what exactly governments may have to do in order to fulfil their legal obligations. One of the most prevalent misunderstandings is to confuse language rights with some kind of nebulous 'right to language'. There is no 'right to language' in international law, in the sense that there is no such thing as a wide-ranging panoply of 'language rights' as soon as one invokes the presence of a distinct language. This has been unequivocally shown by the **EUROPEAN COURT OF HUMAN RIGHTS** in the Belgian Linguistic Case ([1968] 1 Yearbook of the European Convention on Human Rights 832). What exists instead is a series of human rights with a linguistic content which states must comply with as part of their international obligations under instruments such as the **INTERNATIONAL COVENANT ON CIVIL AND POLITICAL RIGHT**s. Language rights therefore exist in those situations which fall under specific human rights provisions and only to the extent provided for in these specific human rights and treaty obligations.

Broadly speaking, language rights can be divided into two categories: first, rights or freedoms that are related to private linguistic activities and expression and which can be linked to specific traditional liberties such as **FREEDOM OF EXPRESSION**, right to private life and the right of a member of a minority to use his/her language with other members of the group; second, rights to have public authorities use to some extent the language preferred by individuals, whether it is an official language or not.

The first category of rights in the area of private usage is relatively straightforward. If public authorities prevented the use of a minority language in private activities, this would breach a number of rights that are well established in international law and increasingly recognised in bilateral and multilateral treaties and other documents. Attempts by public authorities to regulate the language used in the private sphere could in all likelihood violate the right to private life, freedom of expression, non-discrimination or the right of people belonging to a linguistic minority to use their language with other members of their group if it prevents them from using their language of choice. To give one example, freedom of expression includes the right to linguistic expression. There is therefore a human right which is at the same time a linguistic right to use one's language of choice in private 'expression' activities under this freedom. This includes outdoor commercial signs and other private displays of a commercial, cultural or even political nature.

> There are currently some 300 million indigenous peoples, 4 per cent of the world's population. They speak over 5000 languages and live in some 70 countries.

The second category of language rights where public authorities must use another language – in addition to the state's official or national language – in contact with individuals is still much debated, but there is increasing consensus on where it may be exercised and under what conditions.

It would seem that public authorities have an obligation to use an individual's language – even if not official – in appropriate circumstances, such as where numbers and geographic concentration of the speakers of a minority language make it a reasonable or justified arrangement. These rights are clearly spelt out in two treaties of the **COUNCIL OF EUROPE** in particular, the Framework Convention on the Protection of National Minorities and the European Charter for Regional or Minority Languages. For example, in local administrative districts where speakers of a particular language are concentrated, local authorities must generally provide for an increasing level of services in the language used locally as the number of speakers of a particular language increases. Beginning at the lower end of this 'sliding scale' and moving to a progressively higher end, this could imply, as described in the European Charter for Regional or Minority Languages:

1. making available widely used official documents and forms for the population in the non-official or minority language or in bilingual versions;
2. the acceptance by authorities of oral or written applications in the non-official or minority language;
3. the acceptance by authorities of oral or written applications in the non-official or minority language and response thereto in that language;
4. having in place sufficient officers who are in contact with the public to respond to the use of the non-official or minority language;
5. being able to use the non-official or minority language as an internal and daily language of work within public authorities.

Treaties, international and European documents often embody this concept of a sliding-scale formula in order to determine the situations in which individuals are entitled to have 'language rights', in other words to have their language used by public authorities to an appropriate degree. The Framework Convention for the Protection of National Minorities refers in Article 10 to the situation involving 'areas inhabited by persons belonging to national minorities traditionally or in substantial numbers, if those persons so request and where such a request corresponds to a real need, the Parties shall endeavour to ensure, as far as possible ...'. The European Charter for Minority or Regional Languages essentially does the same in slightly different wording in Article 10 when it indicates that this is to occur 'within the administrative districts ... in which the number of residents ... justifies the measures specified below and according to the situation of each language', while the Oslo Recommendations regarding the Linguistic Rights of National Minorities uses in Recommendation 13 the words 'where persons belonging to a national minority are present in significant numbers and where the desire for it has been expressed'.

This is not a 'right to a language', since it does not appear for every language that individuals may prefer or use. It is only a right which an individual can assert when factors such as the number of speakers of a language, the level of demand for the use of a language, territorial concentration, a state's available resources, the type of service being requested and the relative ease or level of difficulty in responding to the demand are satisfied.

The right to have public authorities use a language where reasonable or justified is also referred to in an increasingly large number of resolutions, declarations and other documents in the Council of Europe, the European Union (where respect for minority rights is now part of the political criteria for admission of new States to the EU), the Organisation for Security and Co-operation in Europe and the United Nations.

Finally, some experts also believe this right is guaranteed in international law from the application of non-discrimination as to language, although this has not yet been firmly established. In some cases, individuals have the right to have another language used by public authorities regardless of this requirement. For example, every person facing criminal proceedings who does not understand the language used in these proceedings has the right to be informed promptly, in his or her minority language, of the reasons for their arrest and of the nature and cause of any accusation against them, and to defend themselves in this language.

Further Reading

de Varennes, Fernand (1996) *Language, Minorities and Human Rights*, The Hague: Martinus Nijhoff.

de Varennes, Fernand (2000), *A Guide to the Rights of Minorities and Language*, Hungary, Budapest: Constitutional and Legal Policy Initiative (COLPI).

Dieergardt et al. v. Namibia, Views of the UN Human Rights Committee, UN Doc. CCPR/C/69/D/760/1997 6 September 2000.

Trifunovska, Snezana (ed.) (2001) *Minority Rights in Europe: European Minorities and Language*, The Hague: T.M.C. Asser Press.

Contributor: Fernand de Varennes

LATIN AMERICA: THE REALITY OF HUMAN RIGHTS

Since the signing of the UNIVERSAL DECLARATION OF HUMAN RIGHTS in 1948, the history of human rights in Latin America is often divided into two broad but overlapping phases: the 'era of dictatorships' and the 'era of democratic transition'. The first, beginning with the US-backed military coup that deposed the Arbenz government in Guatemala in 1954, proceeded to spread across the Americas. It brought in its wake a legacy of brutal violations of human rights across the continent. State-sanctioned 'murder and disappearances', 'TORTURE', 'arbitrary detention', 'removal of the right to freedom of opinions and EXPRESSION', 'peaceful assembly and ASSOCIATION', 'the right to take part in the government of their country' all became casualties of the struggle for 'order and state control' as those left out of the highly unequal development model sought to challenge contemporary social relations through electoral politics and, when that path was blocked, through guerrilla insurgency.

In exploring this period we can talk of the three Ds: dirty wars, death squads and disappearances.

■ The phrase 'dirty wars' emerged to describe a counter-insurgency war where the state used TERROR and widespread human rights violations to attempt to eliminate opposition. Unlike in a conventional war where combatants can be identified, in the 'dirty war' the notion of the 'subversive enemy' provides a loose definition of any potential opponents of the state. In Argentina, during the 1970s over 30,000 people were killed. The victims included peasants, teachers, intellectuals, human rights workers, liberal professionals, politi-

cians and artists. Similar patterns of targets can be found in Guatemala from 1954, Chile after the 1973 military coup, El Salvador in the 1980s, Peru under Fujimori in the 1990s and in Colombia today where it is estimated that 6,000 people are assassinated every year for political reasons.

■ The second D, 'death squads', was a phrase which emerged in Brazil in the 1960s when unofficial units within the police began murdering and torturing beggars and alleged criminals. By 1969 this had extended to 'subversives' and the practice spread during the 1970s to many other parts of Latin America: Chile, Uruguay, Argentina, Colombia, El Salvador, Nicaragua and many other countries. Despite protestations by states that these actions were the work of far-right extremists, human rights research has revealed widespread involvement by state military and law enforcement apparatus in all of the countries that have suffered from this phenomenon.

■ The third D, 'Disappearances', is a phrase used to describe practices that emerged from the 1950s where state and 'para-state' forces kidnapped political opponents who were never seen again. In Guatemala after the military coup it is estimated that over 30,000 people were 'disappeared' over three decades. These practices were repeated in Nicaragua under the Somoza dictatorship, in Brazil after the 1964 military coup, in Chile after the 1973 military coup and in Argentina particularly after the 1976 military coup. In Argentina it is estimated that over 9000 people were 'disappeared'; many dropped from helicopters into the ocean. In the 1980s these practices extended to El Salvador, Peru and they continue today in Colombia (Corradi et al., 1992).

Similarities in the patterns of human rights abuses across Latin America during this period led to a well-documented finger of suspicion being pointed at the United States and its 'counter-insurgency' policies that intensified in the wake of the Cuban revolution in 1959, and the challenge that alternative development models posed to US hegemony. The role of the US Army's 'School of the Americas' (SOA) that has trained over 64,000 Latin American military personnel since its creation

Ms Enriqueta Estela Barnes de Carlotto
Ms Enriqueta Estela Barnes de Carlotto is the President of the Asociación Abuelas de Plaza de Mayo [Association of Plaza de Mayo Grandmothers] which was established in 1977 in response to the forced or involuntary disappearance of hundreds of children following the military coup in Argentina in 1976 when hundreds of children were abducted with their parents. She initially joined the Association in search of her own daughter and grandson.

The Association has located many missing and kidnapped children and restored them to their rightful families. It is also helping to ensure, by demanding the punishment of the culprits and advocating the rights of the child at both the national and international levels, that these abhorrent violations of children's rights will not be repeated.

Ms Barnes de Carlotto also chairs the Argentine Committee on Follow-up and Implementation of the International Convention on the Rights of the Child and has written widely on the subject of the 'disappeared' children of Argentina. She was one of the people awarded the 2003 United Nations Prize in the Field of Human Rights.

(from www.un.org/events/humanrights/awards.html)

in 1946 was highlighted as a major player in diffusing counter-insurgency practices. Due to the activities of its graduates, it gained the nickname the 'school of assassins' and the 'school of coups'. In 1984, the Panamian president, Jorge Illueca, demanded that the School leave Panama, calling it 'the biggest base for destabilisation in Latin America'. Now located in Fort Benning, Georgia and renamed the Western Hemisphere Institute for Security Cooperation (WHINSEC), graduates continue to be trained in 'counter-insurgency techniques' and implicated in widespread human rights abuses. WHINSEC's 'Hall of Fame' includes many of the most notorious human rights violators in the region (see SOAW, 2004).

The second phase that defines human rights history in Latin America, 'the era of democratic transition', marked the end of the military dictatorships in the 1980s in Argentina, Chile, Uruguay and Brazil and signalled a glimmer of hope to those human rights activists who had fought against state-sanctioned terrorism. 'Nunca mas' (never again) became the collective rallying cry of many of the human rights organisations which sought to utilise the new possibilities of **DEMOCRACY** to document and investigate the systematic human rights violations that had occurred during the period of dictatorships. The reconstruction of historical memory continues to provide a key field of contestation in the attempt to punish the guilty, compensate the victims and ensure that the horrors of the period are neither forgotten nor repeated (Jelin, 2003). However, political compromises have meant that few human rights violators of the era have been punished.

Despite real gains in the realms of civil and political rights in many parts of the region, the widespread application of neo-liberal economics during the 1980s rapidly undermined initial optimism for a new human rights environment. The region-wide debt crisis in the early 1980s provided the mechanism through which the International Monetary Fund and the global financial institutions spread stringent economic policies throughout the

Case study

Velasquez Rodriguez v Honduras

The systematic and repeated nature of disappearances, either permanently or briefly, to create a general state of anguish, insecurity and fear was held to infringe the American Convention on Human Rights. Disappearance and lack of information over a period of years could allow a presumption that the person had been killed. Presumption can be inferred that state authorities decided the fate of individuals and executed them without recourse to the rule of law.

continent. These included reduced state budgets and privatised natural resources and facilitated the large-scale entry of multinational corporations into all spheres of the economy. **ECONOMIC** and **SOCIAL RIGHTS** were undermined during these 'lost decades of the 1980s and 1990s' and **POVERTY** and social inequality increased.

While useful for exploring the historical development of human rights and its violations in Latin America, the two 'eras' of 'democracy' and 'dictatorship' often obscure the more dynamic relationship between political and civil rights and economic, social and **CULTURAL RIGHTS**. The brutal US-backed military coup in Chile was triggered by the onset of a limited programme of social reform and redistribution implemented by the elected government of Salvador Allende. Struggles for social, economic and cultural rights in Latin America continue to bring in their wake the repression of political and civil rights. Inequality provides the link between the two 'eras' and remains the major obstacle to the integrated implementation of human rights in their political, civil, social, economic and cultural domains. While the vast majority of Latin America's population remain excluded from the benefits of economic growth they are likely to continue to struggle for their rights and if the state is unwilling to address these demands, either due to external pressure from the international markets or internal pressure from national elites and privileged sectors, then the cycles of repression and resistance are likely to continue bringing new waves of human rights violations.

The dangers of this are clearly demonstrated in Colombia where popular resistance to neo-liberal economic reforms since the late 1980s has met with fierce state repression. Since 1988, more than 4000 trade unionists have been assassinated by paramilitary death squads closely linked to the Colombian state. Further, an average of 6000 people are assassinated for 'political reasons' every year. The election of the authoritarian Uribe government in 2002 on a mandate to end the long-running civil war and implement deeper neo-liberal reforms has led to the setting up of 'special security zones' where many basic human rights have been suspended and where the military has wide-ranging powers (Livingstone, 2003, Stokes, 2004).

In the wake of September 11th 2001 and the subsequent War on Terror a green light has been given for an array of repressive measures aimed at 'subversives' across the continent. The example being set by the global hegemon, the USA, in Guantanamo Bay, Afghanistan and Iraq does not bode well for the future of human rights in Latin America.

WEBSITES

Equipo Nizcor provides an excellent contemporary database on human rights violations: www.derechos.org/nizkor/la/eng.html

Latin American Network Information Centre (LANIC), based at the University of Texas provides a range of links to key documents on the human rights situation in Latin America: http://lanic.utexas.edu/la/region/hrights/

Colombia Journal Online provides an excellent source of information in English on the human rights situation in Colombia: www.colombiajournal.org/index.htm

Colombia Solidarity Campaign, UK is a campaigning organisation working for the promotion and protection of human rights in Colombia, and runs an Urgent Action Network: www.colombiasolidarity.org.uk/index.shtml

SOAW (2004) School of the Americas Watch, available at www.soaw.org/new/

Further reading

Corradi, J. *et al.* (1992) *Fear at the Edge: State Terror and Resistance in Latin America*, Berkeley: University of California Press.

Jelin, E. (2003) *State Repression and the Struggles for Memory*, London: Latin American Bureau

Livingstone, G. (2003) *Inside Colombia: Drugs, Democracy and War*, London: Latin American Bureau.

Stokes, D. (2004) *Repackaging Repression: US Intervention in Colombia After the Cold War*, London: Zed Books.

Contributors: Mario Novelli and Berenice Celeyta

RETURN, THE

me of unprecedented interna-
ent: goods and capital now cir-
culate with greater ease than ever before and
people increasingly move across borders. In
contrast, the role of the sovereign state in the
control over migration has greatly intensified
in recent decades. The challenges posed by
migratory movements to the international
community call for a comprehensive understanding of the normative framework, the
legal content and the practical terms of two
interdependent rights of unequal importance:
the right to leave and the right to return.

This subject is vast, with great opportunities for ambiguity and confusion, as the relevant literature demonstrates. Some
preliminary definition of scope and terms is
necessary, therefore although it does not aim
to state a consensus on principles which are
subject to very different interpretations. Who
are we talking about? The right to return is
related to a state's own nationals, while the
right to leave does not distinguish between citizens and non-citizens. In opposition to the
right to leave, which has never been considered an absolute right (there are some permissible restrictions), the right to return – as a
right based on nationality – is, in principle,
beyond dispute.

The right to leave and the right to return
are not equivalent to the freedom of movement. These rights clearly share in the more
general value attributed to the freedom of
movement that has six aspects: freedom to
choose a residence within the territory of a
state; freedom to enter/return to a state; freedom to move about within the borders of a
state; freedom from expulsion of a state; and
freedom from exile (Sieghart 1984: pp178–9).
The freedom of movement includes 'the right
to remain'. The 'right to remain' is nowhere
in universal or regional human rights instruments, but it can be understood as a 'concept
deduced from a variety of others [...] necessary to realise the full potential of the link
between people and territory' (Goodwin-Gill,
1995). In this regard, the right to leave and
return does not guarantee a complete freedom from persecution or a solution to the
flight from a country, but they are essential
elements in the right to remain.

The right to leave any country, including

one's own, is embodied in numerous multilateral instruments relating to human rights at
international level, beginning with the
UNIVERSAL DECLARATION OF HUMAN
RIGHTS of 10 December 1948 (Article 13
(2)), which acknowledges that right immediately after the right to freedom of movement
and residence within the borders of each
state. The general provision of the Universal
Declaration has been detailed in the 1966
INTERNATIONAL COVENANT OF CIVIL
AND POLITICAL RIGHTS which uses the
same contextual approach and gives the right
to leave a firm and broad conventional basis.
Formulations of this right can be found in var-
ious specialised universal instruments that
specify the provisions of the Covenant within
their own fields of application: Article 5 of the
1965 INTERNATIONAL CONVENTION ON
THE ELIMINATION OF ALL FORMS OF
RACIAL DISCRIMINATION, Article 2 of the
1973 Convention on the Suppression and
Punishment of the Crime of Apartheid,
Article 5 (2) of the 1985 Declaration on the
Human Rights of Individuals Who are not
Nationals of the Country in Which They Live,
Article 10(2) of the 1989 CONVENTION ON
THE RIGHTS OF THE CHILD and Article 8
of the 1990 International Convention on the
Protection of the Rights of All Migrant
Workers and Members of their Families (See:
MIGRANT WORKERS' CONVENTION:
PROTECTING MIGRANT WORKERS'
RIGHTS).

Regional instruments also recognise the
right: 1963 Protocol no. 4 to the 1950
EUROPEAN CONVENTION FOR THE
PROTECTION OF HUMAN RIGHTS AND
FUNDAMENTAL FREEDOMS (Article 2 (2)
and (3)); the 1969 AMERICAN CON-
VENTION OF HUMAN RIGHTS (Article
22); and the 1981 African Charter on Human
and Peoples' Rights (Article 12) (See:
AFRICAN COURT AND COMMISSION).

To sum up, there is ample evidence to support the existence of a right to leave under
international law. The controversy is on permissible restrictions, as described below.

The right to leave, available to nationals
and aliens alike, covers both temporary stays
abroad (right to travel) and long-term departure from a country (right to emigrate).
Furthermore, this right implies a two-fold obligation for the state: a negative obligation to not

impede departure from its territory, on the one hand, and a positive obligation to issue travel documents, on the other (Chetail, 2003).

The right to leave is not, however, an absolute right. Numerous conventions provide for restrictions under certain circumstances (for example, when they are provided by law, purported to protect the legitimate state interests and the other rights and freedoms recognised in human rights treaties, and necessary for achieving this purpose). Some restrictions are clear: for example, the right to leave the country could not be claimed in order to escape legal proceedings or to avoid such obligations as national service and the payment of fines, taxes or maintenance allowances.

However, the huge bureaucratic and legal barriers imposed by state practice to the right to leave remain a source of concern, particularly in a context where public order and national security clearly prevail: 'lack of access for applicants to the competent authorities and lack of information regarding requirements; the requirement to apply for special forms through which the proper application documents for the issuance of a passport can be obtained; the need for supportive statements from employers or family members; exact description of the travel route; issuance of passports only on payment of high fees substantially exceeding the cost of the service rendered by the administration; unreasonable delays in the issuance of travel documents; restrictions on family members travelling together; requirement of a repatriation deposit or a return ticket; requirement of an invitation from the state of destination or from people living there; harassment of applicants, for example by physical intimidation, arrest, loss of employment or expulsion of their children from school or university; refusal to issue a passport because the applicant is said to harm the good name of the country' (**HUMAN RIGHTS COMMITTEE**).

In brief, except for the limited notion of the right to leave to seek and enjoy asylum, which is the only aspect in international law that is recognised as imposing any duty on states, the right to leave is recognised by states as long as it does not impose either obligations or expectations on them. The exceptions of the right to leave should consequently be defined more precisely and applied in a more restrictive sense, by taking more into account individual freedoms (Boutkevitch, 1997).

By contrast to the right to leave as understood in the practices of states, the right to return has an absolute character. Indeed, the various regional and universal instruments do not envisage restrictions to its application, except the term 'arbitrarily' contained in the 1966 International Covenant on Civil and Political Rights that may imply some possible limits to its benefit (Chetail, 2003).

A second difference between the right to leave and the right to return lies in their personal scope. Both the European Convention and the American Convention expressly limit the right of return to the State of which the person is a national. On the contrary, the Universal Declaration, the International Covenant and the African Charter speak of 'his country' or 'his own country' without specifying that there must be a link of nationality. Although it is commonly admitted that this ambiguous expression covers both nationals and permanent residents on the territory of state parties (Human Rights Committee), one may ask why public international law does not support a clear right of return for long-term residents in the country.

The right to return is connected to the duty to admit. In other words, at the traditional level of state-to-state relations, the state's obligation to admit its nationals (or long-term residents) is the correlative to other states' right of expulsion. As such, there is a clear international dimension of this right (Goodwin-Gill, 1995). There are, however, some unsolved questions and problems in relation to the right of return. Some intractable political situations centre around this right to return. One of the key elements of the conflict between Israel and Palestine is that of the right to return to their original homes in what is now Israel of the descendants of those who fled the 1947 war and have since been refugees in neighbouring countries or in the Occupied Territories. Israel denies that this right exists, as its implementation would dilute the Jewish character of Israel, while the Palestinians insist that an acceptable solution must be negotiated.

Other situations make the right of return impossible to implement. Some countries refuse to recognise some individuals as their nationals: for example, all the Russians who fled their country after the 1917 Revolution were stripped of their nationality in 1925, thus becoming officially stateless people, and could not go back. Other countries have at time refused to issue travel documents.

This right to return is also often invoked by state authorities forcibly expelling foreigners, be they illegal migrants or failed asylum seekers, often provoking huge public debates in the host country.

Further Reading

Boutkevitch, V. (1997) Working paper on the right to freedom of movement and related issues, E/CN.4/Sub.2/1997/22.

Chetail, V. (2003) 'Freedom of Movement and Transnational Migrations: A Human Rights Perspective' in Aleinikoff, T. Alexander and Chetail, Vincent (eds), *Migration and International Legal Norms*, Migration Policy Institute, Washington D.C., the Graduate Institute of International Studies, Geneva, and the International Organization for Migration, Geneva.

Goodwin-Gill, G.S (1995) 'The Right to Leave, the Right to Return and the Question of a Right to Remain' in Gowlland-Debbas, V. (ed.) *The Problem of Refugees in the Light of Contemporary International Law Issues*, The Hague/Boston/London: Martinus Nijhoff Publishers, pp. 93-108.

Human Rights Committee (1999) 'General Comment 27 on Freedom of Movement', CCPR/C/21/Rev.1/Add.9, 2 November.

Sieghart, P. (1984) *The International Law of Human Rights*, Oxford: Oxford University Press.

Contributors: François Crépeau and
Delphine Nakache

THE ROLE OF LAWYERS IN PROMOTING HUMAN RIGHTS

The legal profession seeks excellence and ethics from each of its members in the application of their skills yet the global results of their collective efforts seem as if there is a collusion in cruel indifference to the fate of millions year on year. 'The legal profession' here represents all those involved in the administration of justice. As a law service industry it has members in all countries and the numbers are vast. Human rights form part of the complete code of legislation known as 'the Rule of Law'. There is an inextricable link between the Rule of Law and the legal profession. If justice is not being delivered there is a collective professional responsibility to remedy the defects. 'Access to justice' is a phrase of aspiration and some achievement but is an unattainable aspect of survival for many millions in most countries. Without access to justice an individual victim is without remedy for suffered wrongs and so to that victim the Rule of Law is a concept without any active connection or impact.

The duty of the legal profession as a whole is to provide access to justice in those places where the state cannot or will not provide for administration of justice and will not provide or allow lawyers of that community to deliver the service required by the victims. The reality of the extent of the distance between the victims of human rights abuses and enforcement of human rights and access to justice and the administration of justice through legal workers is that there is no mechanism for intervention and assistance by lawyers of one state to represent victims of another state. Whilst there is global responsibility, there is no global system to discharge that responsibility.

'No international procedure exists today for bringing an international civil action against an individual human rights violator.' (Dinah Shelton, 1999). Therein lies the extent of the gap between actuality and aspiration. There are attempts to bridge the gap but the gap still exists.

Law societies and bar associations and law colleges offer assistance and involvement with disadvantaged colleagues. The International Bar Association is developing the International Legal Assistance Consortium. Governments and inter-governmental groups and private foundations provide educational programmes. Law lecturers transmit knowledge in countless courses and classes. Law firms are operating in many jurisdictions and some purport a global network. Law publishers print pages of legal texts in books and magazines and journals that require miles of shelving each year for new library space. The

Internet allows the transmission of accessible material to individual computer terminals. Law conferences contribute to the culture of discourse and debates among all participants and at all levels within the legal profession and throughout the world. There is a plethora of non-governmental organisations involved in human rights, indicating that this voluntary effort is much needed still.

Such an overview would suggest a global asset of dedicated administrators of justice. Yet each day brings tales of human rights abuses throughout the world, often on a massive scale. The differential between legal resources and justice is a gap that blights the profile of a profession dedicated to the delivery of justice to all.

The quest is to find a mechanism so that the Rule of Law can prevail as a global culture (See: **CREATIVE PROBLEM SOLVING**). One mechanism could be the establishment and the implementation of a new global civil court, which crosses boundaries and operates without national government interference and is accessible to all relevant litigants to hear complaints of abuse of human rights and with powers and personnel to enforce judgments. Such a court might be called the International Civil Court of Human Rights. That court would symbolise the determination of the legal profession to provide access to justice for the citizens of the globe and thereby promote the role of lawyers and the Rule of Law as key contributors to providing a satisfactory quality of life for all in accordance with the **UNIVERSAL DECLARATION OF HUMAN RIGHTS**.

There are several international courts. The International Court of Justice at The Hague deals primarily with inter-state litigation. The **INTERNATIONAL CRIMINAL COURT** to which the USA will not subscribe is an attempt to promote a global criminal court. The ad hoc International War Crimes Tribunals of the former Yugoslavia and Rwanda and Sierra Leone are focusing on the leaders responsible for atrocities. There are regional civil courts including the **EUROPEAN COURT OF HUMAN RIGHTS** and **INTER-AMERICAN COURT OF HUMAN RIGHTS** and the **AFRICAN COURT ON HUMAN AND PEOPLES RIGHTS**. There have been **TRUTH AND RECONCILIATION COMMISSIONS** in

Chile and South Africa. The American Alien Tort Claim Act has allowed claims in respect of offences outside America to be litigated inside America if the defendant is resident in America. The UK courts have accepted claims to be litigated in its courts where the damages occurred in a foreign jurisdiction. Conventions between nations have been created to provide reciprocal enforcements of judgments. Commissions for compensation for victims of the Holocaust and of the Kuwait invasion, of Chinese slaves and of Korean comfort girls, of rape victims of soldiers on foreign training trips and colonial abuse of native peoples all illustrate other types of programmes for providing some remedies for human rights violations. Enquiries into the performance of governments, such as during military rule in Argentina when many disappeared or the shootings of civilians in Northern Ireland or East Timor, show how retrospective analysis and evaluation is an important part of community interest in human rights disasters.

Yet many countries and regimes will not tolerate either courts or commissions to enquire into abuses of human rights. There is a continuum of conflict year after year and the present day reality is of human rights abuse on a pandemic scale. The genocidal slaughters across Africa between races and tribes and nations, for instance, create contemporary holocausts.

Unless all states allow and encourage the creation and operation of courts as the essence of the administration of justice and provide places and people to manage dispute resolution programmes, there is no alternative available to the abused victims but to seek revenge or even solace through inflicting violence on others who then become victims themselves. Thereafter the pendulum of perpetual violence ensures that more misery begets more misery and revenge becomes a generational opportunity or obligation.

The only proven method of bringing social stability to communities is a system of delivery of justice. The legal profession is the deemed deliverer of justice. Therefore it follows that the legal profession must be proactive in producing the methods and management of universal justice without gaps and no-go zones. Sovereignty and respect for national jurisdictions is a concept of legalised non-intervention which has been eroded by a resolve at supra-governmental level in the United Nations to interfere in the interests of human rights abuses. The UN should be the sponsor of this case for an International Civil Court of Human Rights.

With such a court and its associated systems including personnel and places and procedures and powers, the legal profession would have an operational base and supervisory regulations from which to develop and demonstrate the potential to provide social structures to ensure the compliance with the entitlement of each individual to protection under the rule of law and promotion of their own human rights. Without such a court there will be an excuse for lawyers and others to avoid intervention and responsibility for the abuses of the Rule of Law.

The UN covenant and commitment to the Rule of Law should be emphasised by the engineering of programmes to deliver the desired results. The corps of members of the legal profession have the resources and know-how to operate such programmes. They merely need legal authority. This would be an additional special status court and justice programme in an existing portfolio of judicial programmes in each country. The cost would be colossal but insignificant, even incidental, within the context of the cost of existing damage control or limitation exercises. The social cost and the causative consequences of rampant injustices predict the prospects for continuing humanitarian disasters. The experiences of the victims of those disasters will influence the performance of activists on their behalf who will seek to effect change. Thereby the risks of direct action on indirectly involved individuals become inevitable.

The dilemma for governments is whether or not to delegate such an influential impact on community management to an independent internationally mandated professional organisation over which they have no ultimate control. The International Civil Court for Human Rights would provide a forum for individuals to take their case against those responsible for violations, whether individual or government. Further, by being internationalised the advocates and administrators would be immunised from the influences and abuses of national governments, which have so

imperilled indigenous practitioners.

The challenge for the legal profession is whether it can assume a collegiate responsibility for the global consequences of lawlessness. The United Nations and the legal profession together can bring implementation of the ideals of universal justice. Otherwise they are conspirators to the lack of mechanisms for the enforcement of human rights and consequential disrespect for the Rule of Law.

Further Reading

Mathisen, Ralph W. (2001) *Law Society and Authority in Late Antiquity*, Oxford: OUP.

Menski, Werner F. (2000) *Comparative Law in a global context. The Legal Systems of Asia and Africa*, London: Platinum.

Philippe Sands (1999) *Manual on International Courts and Tribunals*, London: Butterworths.

Shelton, Dinah (1999) *Remedies in International Human Rights Law*, Oxford: OUP.

Steiner, Henry J. and Alston, Philip (2000) *International Human Rights in Context*, Oxford: OUP.

Contributor: David Hallmark

LESBIAN AND GAY RIGHTS

The phrase 'lesbian and gay rights' became widely used as a slogan in the 1980s and 1990s in campaigns by sexual minority groups who were felt to be the victims of unjust treatment by the law and in society more broadly. It first crept into political discourse – in the gender-specific form gay rights – as an indirect consequence of the 1969 Stonewall Riot in New York. One of the riot's direct consequences was the emergence on both sides of the Atlantic of the gay liberation movement, which had a socially and politically revolutionary focus. The liberation movement quickly collapsed as an active political force, but by giving prominence to the notion of sexual identity politics – and in particular, to the idea that a lesbian or gay identity was a positive attribute rather than something to be hidden or despised – it laid the groundwork for a more moderate reformist, civil or human rights-focused politics in subsequent decades. This form of politics gained further momentum with the onset of the AIDS crisis in the mid-1980s. Given its linkage with the concept of sexual identity, the idea of lesbian and gay rights has more recently been reformulated as LGBT rights, 'LGBT' standing for lesbian, gay, bisexual, transgender and transsexual.

A wide variety of rights claims can fall within this heading, although the claims which are made in any given society will depend upon pre-existing levels of legal protection and social tolerance. The most basic legal rights claims are for the decriminalisation of consenting sexual activity between people of the same sex and for the removal of rules such as unequal ages of consent which unduly restrict LGBT individuals by contrast with heterosexuals. Another relatively basic claim is for the prohibition of discrimination in the workplace and the public sphere. In more morally pluralistic societies, claims for the legal recognition of same-sex partnerships and for the removal of discriminatory restrictions relating to the upbringing of children have also become widespread. For people who feel impelled to change sex, the availability of appropriate surgery, the prohibition of discrimination in the workplace and the ability to alter one's birth certificate – something which has important consequences for partnership rights – are crucial.

The idea of LGBT rights is effectively an umbrella phrase used to encompass a broad variety of rights-related claims which are united by their close connection with the rightholder's minority sexual orientation – a point which underlines the idea's place in the politics of sexual identity. Depending on the legal system concerned, LGBT rights claims have tended to rest on concepts such as privacy, equal treatment/non-discrimination and respect for human dignity. In turn, the range of claims which we associate with LGBT rights may vary depending upon the underlying legal concept in play.

Supporters of LGBT rights are keen to promote the social understanding and fair treatment of members of sexual minority groups. This in turn has an important connection with gender equality, given that it involves a challenge to – and hopefully the elimination of – unjust gender stereotypes concerning what counts as 'proper' behaviour of a 'masculine' or 'feminine' variety. For this reason, some theorists have argued that dis-

crimination against members of sexual minority groups is effectively a form of sex discrimination; this view is not universally shared, however. Nonetheless, its existence again demonstrates the role of LGBT rights claims in the politics of sexual identity.

Despite the inclusion of sexual orientation as a prohibited ground of discrimination in many contemporary human rights codes, claims to freedom from discrimination sometimes meet with opposition from those religious groups whose doctrines condemn non-heterosexual behaviour. Some scholars have disputed whether such opposition rests on an accurate understanding of the doctrines concerned. In any event, the existence of conflicts between claims to non-discrimination and assertions of religious freedom pose serious questions for the meaning and reach of human rights norms (see: **FREEDOM OF RELIGION AND BELIEF; UNIVERSALISM; PLURALIST UNIVERSALISM**).

For different reasons, the idea of LGBT rights is not universally popular with those campaigning for the elimination of discrimination. One criticism is that it is artificial to explain rights claims in terms of a person's lesbian or gay sexual orientation when people in reality have any number of social identities and often possess several simultaneously. This is often connected to a second criticism, namely that campaigners who use the language of LGBT rights often conflate myriad different sexual, ethnic and class-based identities when talking of the needs of lesbians and gay men. On this view, it is both artificial and unjust to equate the needs of a poorly educated and economically deprived person with those of a wealthy professional solely because they both happen to be lesbian or gay: a risk that we run if we view their respective positions solely though the lens of sexual orientation. Indeed, some activists and writers have adopted the language of queer rights, suggesting that real freedom will be achieved only if all sexual identity categories are subverted.

A third criticism is that a sexual identity-based politics may not be useful to people who live in societies which do not share contemporary Western notions of sexual identity. While people in such societies may have strong claims to be freed from social and legal oppression, the language of LGBT rights might not be of great assistance to them in framing those claims. This provides a good example of the difficulties faced by arguments that human rights are capable of being understood in a single, universally applicable way.

A very different question is whether, given the emergence in North America and Europe of demands for the legal recognition of same-sex partnerships, it remains appropriate to talk specifically of LGBT rights rather than talking of the making available to everyone – regardless of gender and sexual orientation – of the general human rights to marry and not to suffer discrimination on the basis of their sexual identity or of the consensual sexual acts and sexual and emotional relationships in which they engage. In short, do sexual minority groups need to root their arguments in the language of sexual identity politics any longer?

Defenders of the idea of LGBT rights

February 2004 brought major debate on same-sex marriages in the USA. The Supreme Court of Massachusetts decreed that same-sex marriages should be permitted in accordance with non-discrimination laws the day after the State of Ohio legislature passed measures banning same-sex unions. Meanwhile, in California, the mayor and county clerk of San Francisco agreed to issue marriage licences to gay couples.

Court challenges to this are ongoing. Both the Governor of California, Arnold Schwarzenegger, and the President of the USA, George W. Bush, have condemned moves towards same-sex marriages in California. The issue is set to dominate the American political agenda. Gay marriages are legal at present in Canada, Belgium and the Netherlands.

Plans are in place in the UK to allow civil partnerships for same-sex couples. This brings the UK into line with many other countries – same-sex partnerships are recognised in Croatia, Denmark, Finland, France, Germany, Hungary, Iceland, Norway, Portugal and Sweden. Other countries extend legal benefits to same-sex couples.

might respond by saying that, as an approach, it nonetheless steers a useful middle course. Large numbers of people nowadays self-identify as lesbian, gay, bisexual, transgendered or transsexual, something which is reflected in contemporary literature and in the provision of commercial services relating to leisure, travel and accommodation. By dropping the 'LGBT' from the picture, we would unrealistically ignore this aspect of their identity, both as a general matter and when framing legal rights claims in response to specific acts of discrimination (which, many would argue, are both motivated by and hurt the claimant because of the assault on minority notions of sexual identity. This is an important point given the levels of social hostility which LGBT individuals still face even in the Western world). In a similar vein, the language of LGBT rights can be used to highlight particular social and legal injustices without going so far as to launch the type of general assault on all sexual identity categories which is involved in the queer rights approach.

However we describe the human rights claims made by sexual minority groups, it remains important to understand why such claims are morally justifiable. The clearest argument relates to the moral dignity of the individual. A person's sexual and emotional feelings are among the deepest and most centrally personal aspects of what makes them human. The forced denial of sexual feeling which follows on the heels of the prohibition or severe restriction of consenting sexual activity between adults can cause profound misery, as well as infantilising the adults involved. More broadly, since most adults find union with a compatible partner to be crucial to their well-being, it can be profoundly damaging to a person to force them not to engage in or to look for a consenting relationship, or to have to conceal its existence on a day-to-day basis. It is also highly demeaning – and damaging to the moral dignity of all concerned – to deny relationships between people of the same sex the same level of respect as is offered to heterosexual relationships and to deny fair treatment to LGBT individuals. Subject to the requirement of consent, which also stems from respect for moral dignity, the ability to express oneself sexually and to form loving relationships is an important aspect of anyone's human rights.

Further Reading

Bamforth, Nicholas (ed.) (2005) *Sex Rights: the Oxford Amnesty Lectures 2002*, Oxford: Oxford University Press.

D'Emilio, John (1992) *Making Trouble: Essays on Gay History, Politics, and the University*, New York: Routledge.

Richards, David A.J. (1999) *Identity and the Case for Gay Rights: Race, Gender, Religion as Analogies*, Chicago: University of Chicago Press.

Santford, Theo, Schuyf, Judith, Duyvendak, Jan Willem and Weeks, Jeffrey (eds) (2000) *Lesbian and Gay Studies: An Introductory, Interdisciplinary Approach*, London: Sage.

Wintemute, Robert and Andenaes, Mads (eds) (2001) *Legal Recognition of Same-Sex Partnerships*, Oxford: Hart Publishing.

Contributor: Nicholas Bamforth

LIBERTARIANISM AND HUMAN RIGHTS

In my view, we get a lot more mileage out of staring at the word 'rights' than out of staring at the word 'human' when discussing human rights. If we focus on the way that rights claims characteristically figure in our moral reasoning, we can narrow the range of possibilities quite a lot. It is useful to make three background assumptions which seem reasonably uncontroversial.

1. We don't want a set of human rights that occupies the whole space of moral reasoning. Rights are unquestionably good things – values – but they're not the only good things. That is, not all our moral duties are ones correlative to rights claims. Many of our moral duties – and, among them, some very significant ones – are duties that go well beyond what we can strictly be said to owe to others. Indeed, many of them have nothing to do with other people at all. These can include such duties as those of courage and cultivating one's talents, and duties of caring for the environment and animals of other species.
2. We don't want a set of human rights that demands the impossible. So, among other things, we want all duties correlative to those rights claims to be, at least in principle, jointly performable.
3. We don't want a set of human rights that requires a lot of discretionary judgement. What I have in mind here are judgements that, in determining whether some act violates a human right, can reach a conclusion only either by deploying some prejudice or interest of those doing the judging or, for reasons which I will indicate presently, by appealing to some other moral value.

The characteristic way in which rights claims figure in our moral thinking is as items which are invoked in what I'll call adversarial circumstances. What are adversarial circumstances? Well, one feature of them is certainly disagreement. If all of us always and everywhere agreed on what would be the best thing to do in any particular situation, rights would quickly disappear from our language. But disagreement is only a necessary, not a sufficient, condition of adversarial circumstances. The sufficient condition is what I call deadlock. Broadly speaking, deadlock occurs when two people's chosen courses of action intersect: that is, when what each proposes to do or have done would preclude the occurrence of what the other proposes to do. Their two courses of action are jointly unperformable.

It is in these circumstances that people begin to think about ringing up their solicitors and making rights claims. Of course, before they start reaching for their rights, each will presumably try to convince the other that their own proposed action is the better of the two. And sometimes, hopefully often, one of these attempts at persuasion will succeed. If it does succeed, it eliminates the deadlock by eliminating the disagreement.

But what if two adversaries cannot eliminate their disagreement? What if they do not share that same aim or, even if they do, they do not prioritise it in the same way in relation to their other aims? It's here, I think, that rights-claims really come into their own. For the function of such claims is to eliminate deadlocks without eliminating the disagreements that generate them. Rights give people reasons to back off from interference when they have no other reason to allow the performance of the action they are interfering with.

If this suggestion is correct, then – abstract and general as it admittedly is – one important inference that we can draw from it is this: the general content of rights cannot be derived from any of the values/priorities motivating the disagreement between the adversarial parties, for, *ex hypothesi*, they have already been down the road of searching for a consensus on these values or priorities and have returned empty-handed. These values don't supply either of them with sufficient reasons to do the requisite backing off. So if appeals to rights are going to do any work in resolving their deadlock, without falsely presupposing the absence of their disagreement, those rights have to be (in some sense) neutral with respect to the relative merits of the adversaries' competing values, interests or, more generally, cultures.

The job of rights, then, is to demarcate individuals' private domains – their spheres of activity within which their practical choices must not be subjected to interference – and to demarcate them without reference to the value of the choices they make within those spheres. By means of a not very extended argument, it's possible to show that rights are thus allocations of liberty and that the only allocation of liberty that possesses the kind of neutrality I have been gesturing at is an equal one, and this chiefly because any unequal one logically requires the stipulation of an ex hypothesi unacceptable criterion for apportioning those inequalities. Rights thus embody, or are grounded in, the principle of equal liberty.

By means of another not very extended argument, it is also possible to show that, for this set of rights to be a possible set – for all the correlative duties it entails to be jointly performable ones – these rights must be understood as something like property rights: mutually differentiated titles to physical things. For unless people's action domains can be mutually differentiated in this way, there is no reason why two persons, whose respective obligatory actions are deadlocked, might not both be acting within their rights. In which case, no appeal to rights can eliminate that deadlock, which is precisely what rights are meant to do.

If people's rights are basically property rights, then to find out whether on any particular occasion they are acting within their just rights, we need to have an account of just property rights. And here I think there are strong conceptual reasons for taking a Lockean approach and saying that what people have property rights to are, in the first instance, their own bodies – their bodies are, so to speak, owner-occupied (see: **THE RIGHT TO PROPERTY: PROPERTY IN THE BODY**) – and, beyond that, the products of their labour. That is, they can justly do whatever they like with these things, provided that they don't encroach on the similar rights of others.

But there's a problem here which both Locke and, more recently, Nozick acknowledge. And this is that the world is inhabited not only by self-owned persons and the products of their labour but also by natural resources. Indeed, there can be no labour products – no activity at all – without the use of some natural resources. And cutting a long story very short, it's possible to show that the same principle of equal freedom that gives people rights to their own bodies and labour also gives them rights to an equal share of the value of natural resources.

Here I must confess that I have simply no idea of what the aggregate value of natural resources is in today's world. Whatever it is, this view of rights would entitle each person to an equal share of it. One author has estimated that, in 1985, the aggregate value of American natural resources would have yielded a guaranteed income of $20,000 under that entitlement to each average size American family (Andersen, 1985: 153).

It should immediately be said, however, that the kind of right I'm sketching here is one with an inherently global reach: entitlements to the value of American natural resources are not confined to Americans. And the same is true of all other societies' natural resources. So what I'm suggesting is that such a right implies something like a global fund: one that pools all natural resource values and in which each person, whatever society he or she is a member of, is an equal shareholder. I think such a regime would foster a considerable global reduction in social and economic inequalities. For here we must remember that natural resources encompass not only what can be found, as it were, under the ground but also surface space and, for that matter, the air space and electromagnetic spectrum above it. No one would want to suggest that the value of an acre in downtown Manhattan or the City of London or central Tokyo is negligible. And each person is entitled to an equal portion of it.

So, returning to the question posed for us, the upshot of this very telescoped argument is that there are essentially only two basic human rights. One is the right to self-ownership and that right, along with the various familiar types of right and civil liberty that can be shown to derive from it, more or less implicates a laisser faire social order devoid of anything resembling the multifarious targeted provisions and taxes of the regulated economy and the welfare state. But the second human right, being one to an equal share of global natural resource values, amounts to an entitlement to what has recently come to be called an unconditional basic income or an initial capital stake which, I conjecture, would not be paltry.

Further Reading

Andersen, A. (1985) *Liberating the American Dream*, New Brunswick, N.J.: Transaction Books.

Steiner, H. (1994) *An Essay on Rights*, Oxford: Blackwell.

Contributor: Hillel Steiner

LIBERTY, THE RIGHT TO

Liberty is a fundamental value which underlies most notions of human rights and the relationship between the individual and the state in a democracy. Under international law, it tends to enjoy the much narrower meaning of freedom from arbitrary arrest or detention. However, even this more focused definition of liberty constitutes a significant hallmark of modern democracies where individuals should fear neither the night-time knock on the door nor the 'disappearances' of loved ones.

It is in these terms that the right to liberty appears in UK law as early as the 13th century in the Magna Carta. This stated:

'no freeman shall be taken or imprisoned ... but ... by the law of the land.'

US 5th Amendment:

'no person shall be ... deprived of life, liberty, or property, without due process of law'.

Declaration of the Rights of Man 1789 – Article 7:

'no one shall be accused, arrested or imprisoned, save in the cases determined by law, and according to the forms which it has prescribed.'

Universal Declaration of Human Rights 1948 – Article 9:

'Everyone has the right to liberty and security of person. No one shall be subjected to arbitrary arrest or detention. No one shall be deprived of his liberty except on grounds and in accordance with such procedure as are established by law.'

It appears in similar terms in the fifth amendment to the United States Constitution, in Article 7 of the French Declaration of the Rights of Man of 1789 and in Article 9 of the Universal Declaration of Human Rights 1948. It is also the basis for Article 5 of the European Convention for the Protection of Human Rights and Fundamental Freedoms 1950 ('the Convention') and Article 9(1) of the International Covenant on Civil and Political Rights (1966).

The right to liberty was formally enshrined

Liberty is a UK-based civil rights campaign group. Since its formation in 1934, it has worked to protect and promote human rights and fundamental freedoms. From supporting the Hunger Marches in the 1930s, promoting rights issues in the course of two world wars and the cold war through to fighting to end internment in 2004, Liberty has been at the forefront of civil liberty campaigning for 70 years.

with the incorporation into UK law of all of the rights and freedoms guaranteed by the Convention through the introduction of the Human Rights Act 1998. The Act was the culmination of hopes and aspirations for a new age when human rights would become the fundamental values of Parliament, the judiciary and wider society.

The right to liberty under Article 5 of the Convention is essentially made up of two key elements. Paragraph 5(1) sets out an exhaustive list of circumstances under which a person may lawfully be deprived of their liberty. The list broadly consists of four categories – those suspected or convicted of criminal activity, minors, those who are of unsound mind and illegal immigrants. The second section (paragraphs 5(2–5) sets out the due process requirements for detention to be lawful for example the right to be informed of the reasons for detention (5)(2) and so on.

There have been some positive developments in 'due process' in recent times. One example is the European Court of Human Rights case of *Stafford v United Kingdom*, (Application no. 46295/99). The court held that the Home Secretary had violated Article 5 when he overturned a decision of the Parole Board to release on licence a convicted murderer who had exhausted his tariff (of punishment) on the grounds that he might commit a non-violent offence. The Home Secretary has said that he was 'disappointed' with the judgment and is now taking steps to fix tariffs for those serving life sentences.

However, it is difficult not to conclude that important achievements are undermined, if not negated, by a more general trend towards compromising the traditional principles of Article 5. This can be seen most clearly in the treatment of foreign nationals. In the case of *R v Secretary of State for the Home Department ex parte Saadi and others* (2002) UKHL 41, the House of Lords took an extraordinarily broad-brush approach to the meaning of Article 5(1)(f) and the circumstances under which immigrants/asylum seekers could lawfully be detained. Four asylum seekers had been detained at Oakington Reception Centre for between seven and ten days while their applications for asylum were considered and decided. Each had promptly sought asylum on arrival in the UK and none was feared to be at risk of absconding.

Their Lordships held that 'detention to achieve a quick process of decision making for asylum seekers is not of itself necessarily and in all cases unlawful' (paragraph 32). They concluded that administrative convenience can lawfully be considered an objective within Article 5(1)(f). This extraordinary decision begs the question as to whether such a loose interpretation of the right to liberty could apply to UK citizens. Could one, for example, envisage a situation where a UK national is detained while his tax return is considered and a decision made as to whether his declaration of income is accurate or fraudulent?

The decision effectively bypasses the exhaustive grounds for lawful detention set out under Article 5(1)(f) in favour of the populist concern of reducing 'asylum overload'. The case marks a significant departure from the human rights values of the Convention and from the 'culture of human rights' so enthusiastically promoted by the government with the introduction of the Act in 1998.

The 1996 case of *Chahal v UK* (1996) 1 BHRC 405 ECtHR established that deportation of foreign nationals, even suspected terrorists, to face torture in their country of nationality breached Article 3 of the Convention (absolute prohibition of inhuman and degrading treatment and torture). The case also found that Mr Chahal's extensive detention (over six years) without recourse to an appropriate court breached Article 5. Detainees who could not be deported without breaching Article 3 would have to be released. Faced with this human rights inconvenience and in the context of the post 9/11 War on Terror the Home Secretary approached the competing interests of national security and natural justice with a creative zeal. The Special Immigration Appeals Commission (SIAC) was created (post Chahal) to provide an immigration deportation appeal for cases of national security where none previously existed. However, none of the usual rules of evidence of trial apply. The test is of 'reasonable suspicion' based on intelligence rather than proof. Suspicion of involvement with terrorism can amount to no more than loosely defined 'links'. Both the appellant and his lawyers are excluded from closed hearings when intelligence information is discussed and a special advocate probes the intelligence but cannot disclose such information to the appellant or discuss it with him or her.

Greater creativity still was used to exploit a legal loophole in the Convention which prevented derogation from Article 3 but allowed derogation from Article 5 pursuant to Article 15. Article 15 allows derogation 'in time of war or other public emergency threatening the life of the nation' provided the measures adopted derogated 'only to the extent strictly required by the exigencies of the situation'.

In derogating from Article 5 the Home Secretary said that he was declaring a 'technical state of emergency' rather than responding to intelligence on any specific threat. The result has been the creation of the UK's very own Guantanamo Bay and the convenience of indefinite detention without trial. Sixteen men have since been detained, some for over two-and-a-half years. In a further chilling connection between arbitrary detention and torture, the Home Secretary refuses to rule out reliance on intelligence gained by torture around the world in his decisions to detain without trial.

For the time being UK nationals retain their rights under Article 5. SIAC's finding that differences in the treatment of foreign nationals amounted to unlawful discrimination was rejected with the aid of 'judicial deference' by the Court of Appeal. The court concluded that there could be no discrimination since foreign detainees, unlike UK nationals, have no right to remain in the UK. It is hard to avoid the conclusion that different human rights standards are believed to apply for different human beings.

There are many other examples of the trend against 'liberty'. Under s44 of the Terrorism Act 2000 the police now have the power to stop and search without the normal requirement for reasonable suspicion. The power was intended as an 'emergency power' to be used in extreme circumstances and in relation to specific risks. In practice, however, the power has been used in rural and urban areas of the UK to deter peaceful political protest at events such as arms fairs and anti-war demonstrations. In the case of *R (Laporte) v Chief Constable of the Gloucestershire Constabulary* (2004) EWHC 254 (Admin) the court held that the police had breached Article 5 when they detained a coach of peace protestors heading towards a protest at an RAF/US Air Force base at Fairford and escorted them back to London.

In a post 9/11 era of competing and conflated concerns about migration and crime it has perhaps never been clearer that human rights cannot exist in a legal bubble. The black letter of the law provides limited protection in the absence of societal will to promote and protect precious democratic values. As the UK government rightly stated on the passing of the Human Rights Act, a 'culture of human rights' is essential for ensuring the protection of human rights. It is disappointing that the state has been less than enthusiastic in leading this cultural transformation.

Further Reading

Human Rights Act 1998, c42 (UK).

Stafford v United Kingdom (Application no. 46295/99) ECtHR.

Chahal v UK (1996) 1 BHRC 405 ECtHR.

R v Secretary of State for the Home Department ex parte Saadi and others (2002) UKHL 41.

R (Laporte) v Chief Constable of the Gloucestershire Constabulary (2004) EWHC 254 (Admin).

Contributors: Shami Chakrabarti and
                                  Kathryn Kenny

LIFE, THE RIGHT TO: ABORTION

The debate over the application of the 'right to life' to abortion raises different issues to the application of this right in other contexts. Crucially the question is not just what entitlements the right to life imparts to the right-bearer, as for example in the discussion of the death penalty, but more fundamentally to whom the right to life applies. At the heart of the abortion debate (polarised as 'pro life' vs. 'pro choice') is the question of the status of the embryo. Is the embryo a person? And if so, is the embryo a 'full person' entitled to the same human rights as any other person? If the embryo is a 'full person' and consequently entitled to the same protection, then it is on this presumption of equality that the claims of the potential mother's rights (for example, to privacy, integrity and reproductive freedom) are based. Yet despite the fact that the debate over abortion often assumes this equality (presenting the embryo's rights as deserving equal consideration to those of the carrying woman's) in law the embryo is usually not considered to be a person and therefore cannot be considered to be a bearer of human rights. However, although the embryo becomes a 'person' only at birth and only then is entitled to claim the protection of human rights, implicit in the laws concerning abortion (even in countries where it is permitted) is the assumption that the embryo merits some protection. Moreover, the protection the embryo is entitled to generally increases as it develops and the nearer to birth and to the possibility of 'viability', the more 'rights', or at least protections, are accorded to the embryo.

There has been much discussion about attempting to define a 'point' at which the embryo becomes a person. Historically in the West the soul was thought to enter the body at 'quickening' (the first movement of the embryo) and this has been updated in the scientific era with discussion about personhood beginning when the 'primitive streak' is formed (14–15 days after conception) and commonly, in abortion legislation, when 'viability' is reached. However, none of these methods is agreed upon, with the pro-life lobby maintaining that 'life' and 'personhood' begin at conception and the extreme end of the 'pro-choice' lobby maintaining that the embryo is never a person and that the woman has a right to abortion at any point of the pregnancy. Even the criterion of 'viability' which has been intuitively if not overtly used in much abortion legislation has now been rendered pragmatically less useful as technical

advances lower the 'viability' level. 'Viability' is now approaching 20 weeks, a time when pregnant women are still waiting for the results of anti-natal tests (such as amniocentesis) which, if the result is positive, often lead to termination.

For the pro-life lobby, such considerations are of course immaterial, as the 'right to life' applies from conception and no other considerations can nullify this absolute right. However, to all other actors in the debate the issues of the potential quality of life of the embryo (the potential person) and the woman's rights to privacy and reproductive autonomy are relevant to the rights and wrongs of abortion – although termination of pregnancy as a result of a positive amniocentesis raises additional ethical issues about how 'quality of life' is defined, in particular whether such actions are discriminatory to non-able-bodied persons. The general tendency has been to assume that there is no 'fixed point' at which an embryo becomes a person but as the pregnancy progresses the embryo is entitled to more protection. This assumption is evident in English Law both in the Abortion Acts (1967, 1990, 2002) and in the provision for protection of embryos found in the Human Fertilisation and Embryology Act (1990) (Lee and Morgan, 2001). Moreover, while the debate over the status of the embryo continues, there is increasingly international acceptance at least of the principle that the woman's 'right to life' outweighs that of the foetus and UN committees have found that high maternal mortality rates resulting from the prohibition of abortion are unacceptable (CCPR/C79/Add. 82, 1997; UN Doc.E/C.12/1998/26, 1998). According to 1997 WHO statistics, around 55,000 unsafe abortions continue to take place every day, leading to the death of approximately 200 women (Cook, Dickens and Fathalla, 2003). Hence, as abortion continues in jurisdictions where it is prohibited, the permitting of abortions may actually save lives.

It is the conflict of the embryo's 'rights' (or more accurately 'interests', as attributing 'rights' to the embryo is problematic) with the woman's rights that has formed the crux of the abortion debate. Despite the fact that an embryo is not a 'person' and has no 'legal existence' (Lee and Morgan, 2001) separate from the mother, the fact that abortions can be ille-

Most international treaties avoid the issue of abortion by not defining when the right to life begins. There is one noticeable exception: 'Every person has the right to have his life respected. This right shall be protected by law, and, in general, *from the moment of conception*. No one shall be arbitrarily deprived of his life.'

(emphasis added, Article 4 of the American Convention on Human Rights 1969)

gal makes the claim that the embryo has no 'rights' or 'interests' which merit protection academic. Even in liberal countries which permit abortion the 'right' of women to choose abortions is balanced with the embryo's interests (and concerns about its potential right to life and right to a good quality of life). Most obviously, there is a time limit for legal abortions (in Europe the average is 12 weeks) and also abortions have to be justified according to specific criteria. For example, in the UK (where the law is applied liberally) an abortion is permitted up to 24 weeks when certified by two doctors and performed in a hospital or licensed clinic, when there is a risk to the physical and mental health of the woman or her existing children. The wide variety of abortion legislation in Europe points to the unease about the status of abortion and concern for the rights and interests of the embryo; for example, both Spain and Portugal prohibit abortion except in rare exceptions (in cases where there is risk to life of the mother or embryo or when the pregnancy is a result of rape). Moreover, the tendency is for abortion laws to become less liberal, particularly in Eastern Europe which previously under Soviet leadership had exceptionally liberal attitudes to abortion, not only permitting but assisting women to have abortions for legal, social and moral reasons. Since the break-up of the communist bloc, restrictive abortion laws have been swiftly introduced, for example, in Poland the 1993 Abortion Act (referred to as the 'Anti-abortion Law') limits abortion only to circumstances that threaten the life of the mother or foetus or when the pregnancy is the result of an offence. These differences raise additional issues as only those women who can afford to travel are able to obtain abortions and so exercise their reproductive rights: most commonly women travel to the UK, the Netherlands and France (France attempted to curtail 'abortion-tourism' by demanding three months residency to qualify for an abortion; however, this was overturned in 2000 as being contrary to the European Convention for the Protection of Human Rights).

Therefore, while embryos do not have any absolute right to life, and while in a case of conflict the woman's right to life outweighs that of the foetus, a certain respect for the potential right of the embryo is enshrined if not in law, in the limits to the rights of women

and the implicit assumption that the foetus has interests which could perhaps be regarded as potential rights. These rights are taken into account implicitly and the 'potential right to life' (and to a certain quality of life) is increasingly evident in the regulation of pregnancy and indeed can often be considered to outweigh the rights of the women. This is evident not only in the laws preventing abortion but in increasing pressure upon women to provide the 'best start in life' by having a 'good' pregnancy – not smoking, not drinking, eating well and taking supplements. All of which involves a curtailing of the women's usual freedom and is enforced in a general way by social pressure, but also in certain cases by legal measures. For example, pregnant drug-takers (particularly of 'hard drugs') are increasingly facing legal penalties and being forced and coerced to live their lives in a different manner in order to protect the foetus (Bewley in Dickenson, 2002). Even where liberal laws to abortion prevail, as in the USA – as a result of the *Roe v Wade* judgment in which a constitutional right to abortion was granted under the right of privacy (Baird and Rosenbaum, 2001) – this does not necessitate access to abortion. Indeed, under the Republican government of George W. Bush funding has been withdrawn not only to abortion clinics but to any activities connected with abortion, including funding to aid organisations which provide information, counselling and advice about abortion.

Taken together, then, despite the recognition of women's rights to privacy and reproductive autonomy evidenced in some access (however limited) to abortion, the embryo's moral if not always legal 'right to life' remains a consideration throughout the debate. However, in the age of technological advances and ever-increasing options of new reproductive technologies (NRT), the abortion debate may enter a new era in which 'quality of life' rather than life itself becomes paramount. The increasing dominance of quality of life considerations is the impetus behind the growing pressure on women to make the necessary life changes to ensure a 'good' pregnancy and also in the debates about whether there is a duty not to reproduce and the so-called 'wrongful life' cases. ('Wrongful life' suits claim that 'an infant has been harmed and/or wronged by being brought to birth in a less than satisfactory condition or in adverse circumstances'

(Harris, 1992).) As genetic and pre-natal testing provides information about the health of the embryo and future health of child and adult, questions are raised about whether it is one's duty in certain circumstances not to reproduce. This is exactly the claim in 'wrongful life' cases: that the person should never have been born and thus should be compensated accordingly (Harris, 1992). Thus, the suggestion is that there is a 'right not to be born' or at least a 'right to a certain standard of life' rather than an absolute 'right to life'.

Further Reading

Baird, Robert M. and Rosenbaum, Stuart E. (2001) *The Ethics of Abortion: Pro-Life vs. Pro-Choice*, New York: Prometheus Books.

Cook, Rebecca J., Dickens, Bernard M. and Fathalla, Mahmoud F. (2003), *Reproductive Health and Human Rights*, Oxford: Clarendon Press.

Dickenson, Donna (2002) *Ethical Issues in Maternal-Fetal Medicine*, Cambridge: Cambridge University Press.

Harris, John (1992) *Clones, Genes and Immortality: Ethics and the Genetic Revolution*, Oxford: Oxford University Press.

Lee, Robert G. and Morgan, Derek (2001) *Human Fertilisation and Embryology: Regulating the Reproductive Revolution*, London: Blackstone Press Limited.

Contributor: Heather Widdows

LIFE, THE RIGHT TO: ASSISTED SUICIDE

Although sometimes equated with voluntary **EUTHANASIA**, assisted suicide (usually referred to as physician-assisted suicide) raises some distinct issues for consideration. Euthanasia is a crime at common law and is covered by the law in respect of murder. In England and Wales, however, assisting suicide is a statutory offence, to be found in the Suicide Act 1961. The Act makes it a crime to counsel, procure aid or abet suicide (S. 2(1)). The position in Scotland is less clear. As Mason, McCall Smith and Laurie (2002) note, 'it is difficult to imagine a common law offence of aiding and abetting an act which is

not, itself, a crime' (see also Ferguson, 1998). The main distinction, however, between voluntary euthanasia and physician-assisted suicide lies in the fact that in the former, a third party directly causes the death whereas in the latter the person themselves takes the final step. In physician assisted suicide, then, the third party provides the means to bring about death; the person wishing to die administers it him or herself.

Perhaps because of this distinction, opposition to assisted suicide is sometimes less strong than that which confronts proponents of voluntary euthanasia, although it is by no means uncontroversial. The fact that assisted suicide is more easily conceptualised as just another form of suicide, which is not a crime, has arguably contributed to the fact that it is not outlawed in some jurisdictions, such as the Netherlands, Belgium and the US state of Oregon.

Whatever the philosophical arguments, the law in England and Wales is clear: it is a criminal offence to assist someone to die, even with their consent. The Scottish position, while different, seems likely to equate in principle to that which exists in England and Wales, even although, as we have seen, there is some lack of clarity about precisely what the crime would be. As the most recent attempt to obtain assistance in dying specifically concerned the Suicide Act 1961, no further consideration of Scots law will be undertaken here.

It is not always clear what amounts to a criminal act in terms of the relevant legislation. For example, what amounts to 'counselling' is not self-evident. Is a crime committed by someone who discusses an intended suicide with a distressed friend and agrees with their decision for death? What is clear, however, is that the mere distribution of factual information is unlikely to amount to a crime in terms of the Act. (A-G v Able [1984] 1 All ER 277). However, the majority of cases are likely to arise where people, suffering from a degenerative disorder and physically unable to kill themselves, seek the help of a doctor or other third party in assisting in their death.

In the Canadian case of *Rodriguez v A-G of British Columbia* ((1993) 107 DLR (4th) 342), for example, a woman suffering from amyotropic lateral sclerosis (a progressive neurological condition) sought the authority of the Supreme Court to permit her medical assistance in dying at a time of her choosing. Her condition was such that she would eventually be entirely unable to do anything for herself; to evacuate waste or even to breathe unaided. However, she would remain aware of her condition. Ms Rodriguez did have the option of committing suicide, but wished to live for as long as she was not in terrible discomfort so as to spend more time with her children. At that point, she would have been unable to kill herself. She argued that the Canadian Charter of Rights and Freedoms should be interpreted as providing her with a right to assistance in her dying. Human rights discourse, therefore, was central to her case. Although the case hinged on the particular terms of the Charter of Rights and Freedoms, one rationale for denying Ms Rodriguez the interpretation she sought is common to those jurisdictions where assisted suicide remains a crime. Sopinka, J. said that the prohibition on assisted suicide was there to protect those who were particularly vulnerable as a result of their medical condition, concluding that:

> In order to effectively protect life and those who are vulnerable in society, a prohibition without exception on the giving of assistance to commit suicide is the best approach ... The formulation of safeguards to prevent excesses has been unsatisfactory and has failed to allay fears that a relaxation of the clear standard set by the law will undermine the protection of life and will lead to abuses of the exception. (p. 410)

Following the incorporation into United Kingdom law of the European Convention on Human Rights by the terms of the Human Rights Act 1998, the language of human rights has direct relevance in the United Kingdom. However, the extent to which this kind of discourse would have any impact was not clear until the European Court of Human Rights considered the case of *Pretty v United Kingdom* (66 BMLR 147 (2002)). In this case, Mrs Pretty, who suffered from motor neurone disease (a progressive neurological condition), challenged the terms of s 2(1) of the Suicide

Brian Pretty, right, and his paralyzed wife Diane leave the House of Lords, London, following a Law Lords judgement Thursday 29 November 2001. The terminally ill woman lost her appeal to Britain's highest court for the right to die with her husband's help. © AP Photo/Alastair Grant

Act, and the failure of the Director of Public Prosecutions to offer a guarantee that, should her husband assist in her death, he would not be prosecuted. Mrs Pretty based her case on a number of Convention rights: Articles 2, 3, 8, 9 and 14. Article 2 protects the right to life. Mrs Pretty argued that this right, while designed to protect people from killing, should be interpreted as encapsulating a right to choose. She argued that:

> While most people want to live, some want to die, and the article protects both rights. The right to die is not the antithesis of the right to life but the corollary of it, and the state has a positive obligation to protect both. (p. 155)

However, the court was disinclined to accept this argument, saying:

It is not enough for Mrs Pretty to show that the United Kingdom would not be acting inconsistently with the Convention if it were to permit assisted suicide; she must go further and establish that the United Kingdom is in breach of the Convention by failing to permit it or would be in breach of the Convention if it did not permit it. Such a contention is in my opinion untenable ... (p. 159)

Article 3 prohibits inhuman and degrading treatment. Mrs Pretty argued that this Article imposed a positive obligation on states not to inflict the proscribed treatment, which – she said – could include the suffering caused by her condition. Even if the court had accepted that a medical condition amounted to treatment for the purposes of the Convention, it concluded that:

... it could not ... be said that the United Kingdom is under a positive obligation to ensure that a competent, terminally ill, person who wishes but is unable to take his or her own life, should be entitled to seek the assistance of another without that other being exposed to the risk of prosecution. (p. 162)

Articles 8 and 9, which protect respectively the integrity of the individual and freedom of thought, religion and conscience, were also, in the Court's view, not engaged by Mrs Pretty's argument, rendering consideration of Article 14 (the right not to be discriminated against) unnecessary, as this last right is based on a breach of other Convention rights.

Mrs Pretty lost her case and died shortly thereafter without the assistance she had wanted.

Although assisted suicide and euthanasia raise some distinct questions, for one purpose they are inherently the same. That is, proponents of each argue that people should have a right to choose the timing and the manner of their own death. Moreover, some would argue that the law's prohibition on

killing is in fact a prohibition only on 'unlawful' killing. Thus, it is pointed out, killing in some circumstances, such as in self-defence, is not a crime (see, for example, Battin, 1994). Just as forcefully, opponents argue that deliberate killing is always wrong, irrespective of motive. As with euthanasia, opinion poll evidence suggests that the majority of the public (and some health care professionals) would support the legalisation of assisted suicide. At the time of writing in the United Kingdom, parliament has the opportunity of reconsidering the current law during debates on the Assisted Dying for the Terminally Ill Bill (HL Bill 17, 2004). Although it is not expected that this bill will become law, it provides a real opportunity for this complex and sensitive debate to be aired in public.

Further Reading

Battin, M.P., Rhodes, R. and Silvers, A. (1998) *Physician Assisted Suicide: Expanding the Debate*, London: Routledge.

Battin, M. (1994) *The Least Worst Death: Essays in Bioethics on the End of Life*, New York, Oxford: OUP.

Ferguson, P.A. (1998) 'Killing 'Without Getting Into Trouble?' Assisted Suicide and Scots Criminal Law' 2, *Edinburgh Law Review* 288.

Mason, J.K., McCall Smith, R.A. and Laurie, G.T. (2002) *Law and Medical Ethics*, (6th edn.), London: Butterworths.

McLean, S.A.M. (ed.) (1996) *Death, Dying and the Law*, Aldershot: Dartmouth.

McLean, S.A.M. and Britton, A. (1997) *The Case for Physician Assisted Suicide*, London: Pandora.

Contributor: Sheila A.M. McLean

LIFE, THE RIGHT TO: THE DEATH PENALTY

Like the prohibition of slavery and the slave trade in the 18th and 19th centuries (See: **FREEDOM FROM SLAVERY**), the abolition of capital punishment is one of the clearest examples of progress in the protection and promotion of human rights in the 20th century. At the end of the Second World War, as the modern international human rights legal regime was beginning, the death penalty was still practised in most countries. Many European countries that had allowed it to lapse for many years revived the supreme punishment in order to deal with war criminals and enemy collaborators. Ironically, the prosecutions included trials of Nazi jurists who were eventually convicted of crimes against humanity for their excessive and barbaric use of capital punishment (*United States of America v. Alstötter et al.* ('Justice trial'), (1948) 3 TWC 1, 6 LRTWC 1, 14 Ann. Dig. 278 (United States Military Commission), p. 1201 (TWC)).

The **UNIVERSAL DECLARATION OF HUMAN RIGHTS**, adopted on 10 December 1948, did not speak directly to the subject, although there was much discussion about capital punishment in the General Assembly when the Declaration was being debated. A proposal to explicitly recognise the death penalty as an exception to the right to life was defeated, but then so was another amendment prohibiting the death penalty in peacetime. The consensus lay somewhere in the middle: states were beginning to see that the

abolition of capital punishment the 'common standard of ach. expressed in the Universal Declarat. were still wary of outright prohibition of th. practice, given its persistence in their own legal systems.

As the years went by, the trend towards abolition became unarguable and increasingly remarkable. By the mid-1990s, somewhat more than half the states in the world had abolished capital punishment either in law or in fact. Whereas in the 1940s the international war crimes tribunals at Nuremberg and Tokyo had executed offenders, the 1990s versions – the ad hoc tribunals for the former Yugoslavia and Rwanda and the **INTERNATIONAL CRIMINAL COURT** – set life imprisonment as the maximum penalty.

Historically, criminal punishment has been associated with barbaric sanctions, including various forms of torture and mutilation. In the Middle Ages, convicted criminals were often drawn and quartered as part of carrying out a sentence of death. They might be hung up in a public place and left to die a slow and agonising death from starvation and exposure. Limbs of the executed might be displayed for weeks or months. As societies

© Tim Wright/CORBIS

became more advanced, they eliminated many of these practices. One of the reforms of the French Revolution was universal application of a rapid and apparently painless form of execution, named after its inventor, Dr Guillotin. But corporal punishment remained widely practised, even in Europe, until the late 20th century (*Tyrer v United Kingdom*, April 25, 1978, Series A, No. 26, 2 E.H.R.R. 1).

The modern abolitionist movement begins with an Italian penal reformer of the Enlightenment, Cesare Beccaria. His book *Dei delitti et delle pene* (*Cesare BECCARIA, On Crimes and Punishments*, trans. Henry Paolucci, Indianapolis: Bobbs-Merrill, 1963) convinced such revolutionary thinkers and statesmen as Voltaire, Jefferson, Paine, Lafayette and Robespierre of the uselessness and inhumanity of capital punishment. Beccaria's writings prompted a few ephemeral efforts at abolition, in Austria and Tuscany. As the debate evolved, the practice of capital punishment became increasingly restricted. It was applied to fewer and fewer crimes, certain categories of individuals, such as pregnant women and juvenile offenders were automatically excluded, and there were several efforts to improve the actual method of execution so as to make it more humane.

There are now several international human rights conventions that abolish capital punishment altogether. The first was adopted by the **COUNCIL OF EUROPE**, in 1983. Approximately 70 states have ratified these treaties. Another 80 states have ratified one of the more general international human rights treaties, such as the **INTERNATIONAL COVENANT ON CIVIL AND POLITICAL RIGHTS**. Although these instruments do not totally prohibit the death penalty, they impose strict limitations. Moreover, Article 6(6) of the Covenant says '[n]othing in this article shall be invoked to delay or to prevent the abolition of capital punishment by any State Party to the present Covenant'. The **HUMAN RIGHTS COMMITTEE**, which monitors compliance with the Covenant and provides for its authoritative interpretation, considers that the general prohibition in article 6(1) on arbitrary deprivation of the right to life means that countries where capital punishment has already been abolished cannot participate in it, even indirectly, by for example extraditing someone to another country where it might

be imposed (*Judge v Canada* (Case No. 829/1998), 13 August 2003, UN Doc. CCPR/C/78/D/829/1998).

Fewer and fewer professionals in the field of criminology attempt to justify capital punishment on scientific grounds. In the 1960s, studies commissioned by the Council of Europe and the **UNITED NATIONS** rejected the idea that the death penalty had a valid deterrent effect (Marc Ancel, The Death Penalty in European Countries, Strasbourg: Council of Europe, 1962; Capital Punishment, UN Doc. ST/SOA/SD/9, Sales no. 62.IV.2). Deterrence is a difficult thing to analyse because of the difficulty in identifying people who have in fact been deterred by the threat of punishment. What seems clear is that little or no additive deterrent effect can be demonstrated when the death penalty is compared with other forms of severe punishment, such as life imprisonment.

The other argument often invoked to defend the practice of capital punishment is its retributive value, sometimes described as the theory of 'just desserts'. It is said that society requires an offender to pay the price for violent crime. Some suggest that where it fails to do so, ordinary citizens will take the law into their own hands and that this will lead to social chaos.

Perhaps the best argument against the death penalty is that, like torture, mutilation and other barbaric forms of punishment that have long been abandoned, it is a violation of human dignity. Societies that impose what amounts to state-sanctioned planned and premeditated murder degrade themselves and violate the right to dignity of their citizens.

International law now universally condemns the practice of execution for crimes committed while under the age of 18. The prohibition is contained in the **CONVENTION ON THE RIGHTS OF THE CHILD**, adopted in 1989. At the time, several states still conducted occasional executions of juvenile offenders. Since 1989, they have systematically abandoned the practice, often explaining their decisions with reference to their international obligations under the Convention. Now, only the United States and Iran continue to execute juvenile offenders.

Several international tribunals and constitutional courts have also condemned the practice of the mandatory death penalty. Legislation that makes capital punishment the inevitable consequence of a conviction for a specific offence eliminates the relevance of various individual mitigating factors. In this way, it falls foul of the international prohibition of 'arbitrary' deprivation of life.

Most countries where the death penalty has been abolished now refuse to extradite offenders to states where it may be imposed, failing an assurance from the state seeking extradition that capital punishment will not be imposed. The **CHARTER OF FUND-AMENTAL RIGHTS OF THE EUROPEAN UNION**, adopted December 2000, declares it a violation of fundamental rights to extradite an individual to a country where capital punishment is threatened.

Often, the practice of capital punishment will cease as a result of executive clemency long before it is actually abolished by legislation. For this reason, statistics on abolition take into account de facto abolitionist states. In fact, political leaders are ready to abandon the practice even though public opinion may still support the death penalty. Public opinion on the subject is volatile and will fluctuate particularly following the commission of an atrocious crime. Because of the tendency to de facto abolition, there has been a strong call within international organisations for a moratorium on capital punishment in states where it has not been abolished. Critics of the moratorium strategy fear that it will only allow for the more egregious flaws in the death penalty system to be repaired. In most countries, however, de facto abolition or imposition of a moratorium is the first step in an inevitable and irreversible process towards total abolition.

Many countries argue that the death penalty corresponds to a level of economic and social development, and that poor or developing countries cannot eliminate it immediately. They point to the success of abolition in the most developed countries, specifically Europe, as support for this socio-economic argument. But it is incorrect for several reasons. Many poor and developing countries, especially in sub-Saharan Africa and in South America, do not conduct executions. Moreover, abolition in Europe became widespread only very recently. It corresponds not so much to levels of economic develop-

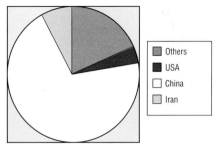

31 countries executed at least 1,526 people in 2002. In the USA, 65 were executed in 2003 and over 3,500 people remain under sentence of death. (Statistics from Amnesty International http://web.amnesty.org/pages/death-penalty-facts-eng)

ment as to commitments to fundamental principles of human rights that became widespread within Europe only in the second half of the 20th century. And, of course, there is the fact that the most developed country in the world, the United States of America, remains a keen practitioner of capital punishment.

The persistence of capital punishment in the United States is a puzzling anomaly. In recent decades, the Supreme Court of the United States has come extremely close to judicial abolition of capital punishment (*McCleskey v Kemp*, 481 US 279, 107 S.Ct. 1756, 95 L.Ed.2d 262 (1987)). Public support for the death penalty within the United States has dropped considerably from a high point in the early 1980s. With occasional exceptions, the practice is confined to only a few jurisdictions within the country, with Texas in the lead. They had been slave states prior to the Civil War and, as Franklin Zimring (2003) has recently demonstrated, were also the main practitioners of lynchings of African-Americans until the middle of the 20th century. In other words, the contemporary enthusiasm for the death penalty in certain parts of the United States follows in a direct line from a violent history of racial discrimination. While other factors may also be involved, this is probably the best explanation for the persistence of capital punishment in the United States at a time when it has virtually disappeared from the rest of the developed world.

Further Reading

Hodgkinson, Peter & Schabas, William A. (2004) *Capital Punishment: Strategies for Abolition*, Cambridge: Cambridge University Press.

Hood, Roger (2002) *The Death Penalty, A Worldwide Perspective*, 3rd edn, Oxford: Oxford University Press.

Schabas, William A. (2003) *The Abolition of the Death Penalty in International Law*, 3rd ed., Cambridge: Cambridge University Press.

Zimring, Franklin A. (2003) *The Contradictions of American Capital Punishment*, Oxford: Oxford University Press.

Contributor: William A. Schabas

LIFE, THE RIGHT TO: EUTHANASIA

Much was expected of the incorporation of the **EUROPEAN CONVENTION ON HUMAN RIGHTS** into United Kingdom law by the Human Rights Act 1998. For the first time Convention rights became directly enforceable in the UK and many expected that the theoretical underpinnings of rights discourse would provide them with a means of vindicating their interests. Particular expectation surrounded Article 2, the **RIGHT TO LIFE**, interestingly not just from those who wanted to debate issues about life, but also from those who sought to argue that a necessary corollary of the right to life was the 'right' to die.

It must be said at the outset that rights language cannot easily embrace any such thing as a 'right' to die. Death is inevitable and the closest we can come to a 'right' to die is, arguably, the recognition of the lawfulness of suicide. However, to use the language of human rights in terms of assisted dying it is necessary to reconceptualise what is being argued for. That is, the argument is not about the 'right' to die but rather the right to choose death; a fine, but important, distinction. Its main significance lies in the fact that the debate must then be couched in the specific terms of self-determination rather than being focused on death itself. In other words, the primary issue becomes people's right to

choose how they should live their lives, including controlling the end of that life (See also: **THE RIGHT TO LIFE: ASSISTED SUICIDE** and **AUTONOMY AND HUMAN RIGHTS**).

Medical advances mean that many people who would previously have died a natural death can now be artificially maintained. Perhaps inevitably, this has led some of them to question the reason for continued existence, perhaps in pain or emotional distress, and sometimes subject to conditions which, for them, may be seen as degrading. It has even been proposed that an increasing number of elderly people in the United States have been choosing suicide rather than waiting for the ravages of illness and the consequential intrusion of medical treatment (Angell, 1990). Conceptualised as an issue of choice, then, the question becomes the extent to which states can or should intervene in essentially private decisions about quality of life, and the picture is further confused by the fact that the law does permit some choices for death. Thus, for example, a competent adult person can refuse life-sustaining treatment (*Ms B v An NHS Hospital Trust* 65 BMLR 149 (2002)) for any reason (Re T (adult: refusal of treatment) 9 BMLR 46 (1992)).

Equally, patients in a permanent vegetative state (pvs), (*Airedale NHS Trust v Bland* 12 BMLR 64 (1993); *Law Hospital NHS Trust v Lord Advocate* 1996 SLT 869) and even some in 'near-pvs', (Re G (adult incompetent: withdrawal of treatment) 65 BMLR 6 (2001)) have had life sustaining treatment withdrawn by authority of the courts, even although their wishes were not known. Finally, patients may be provided with ever increasing analgesia (to kill pain) when it is foreseen, but not intended, that this may hasten their death; the so-called principle of double effect (accepted by law in the case of *R v Adams* [1957] Crim LR 365).

The reason for this apparent difference rests on a number of distinctions drawn by the law, each of which is open to critique. First, the right to refuse life-sustaining treatment depends on the fact that the third party involvement in the death is passive rather than active. That is, the doctor who respects the patient's autonomous choice for death does not directly cause it. Rather he or she permits the death to occur. There are, however, a number of reasons to question this acts/omissions distinction. It has been described as 'most problematic and unsatisfactory ... the distinction is of debatable moral and philosophical significance' (Otlowski, 1997, p. 12). This opposition to the acts/omissions principle stems from two main sources. First, although we are generally not liable for our omissions in criminal law, we become liable when we have a duty of care, as doctors clearly do in respect of their patients. Second, the purpose, intention and outcome are precisely the same, irrespective of the means of bringing about the death. As for the principle of double effect, it is often questioned on what basis a distinction can be drawn between what is foreseen and what is intended; the difference, it might be said, is at best nugatory.

In the United Kingdom, euthanasia in any form is governed by the criminal law of murder. Although it is now lawful in some European countries (such as Belgium and the Netherlands), euthanasia remains a serious crime in the UK. Few prosecutions are, however, brought, and the perpetrator is generally dealt with sympathetically by courts. One example of this is the case of Dr Nigel Cox, who was prosecuted for responding to his patient's repeated requests for him to stop her pain (*R v Cox* 12 BMLR 38 (1992)). Dr Cox injected his patient with potassium chloride, which had no therapeutic purpose, and his patient died. Lack of clarity about the actual cause of death meant that he was charged with, and convicted of, attempted murder, was given a suspended sentence, admonished by the General Medical Council and continued in his employment subject to some restrictions.

In 1994, the House of Lords Select Committee on Medical Ethics restated society's commitment to, and rationale for, the prohibition of euthanasia. The Committee's report said:

That prohibition [of intentional killing] is the cornerstone of law and of social relationships. It protects each of us impartially, embodying the belief that all are equal ... We acknowledge that there are individual cases in which euthanasia may be seen by some to be appropriate. But individual cases cannot reasonably establish the foundation of a policy which would have such serious and widespread

repercussions. Moreover, dying is not only a personal or individual affair. The death of a person affects the lives of others, often in ways and to an extent which cannot be foreseen. We believe that the issue of euthanasia is one in which the interest of the individual cannot be separated from the interest of society as a whole. (HL Paper 21–1, paragraph 237)

Moreover, the Council of Europe has recommended:

... that the Committee of Ministers encourage the member states of the Council of Europe to respect and protect the dignity of terminally ill or dying persons in all respects ... (c) by upholding the prohibition against intentionally taking the life of terminally ill or dying persons ... (Council of Europe Recommendation 1418, adopted 25/6/1999, of the Parliamentary Assembly of the Council of Europe, paragraph 9).

In 2002, Diane Pretty's case was heard by the European Court of Human Rights. Her case is considered in depth in the entry on **THE RIGHT TO LIFE: ASSISTED SUICIDE**, but it merits some consideration in this context because of its implications for euthanasia as well as assisted suicide. As part of her argument, Mrs Pretty sought to distinguish between voluntary euthanasia and assisted suicide, claiming that she was concerned that the latter should be legalised in her case, whereas seeking to avoid comment on the former. However, the Court was unimpressed by this argument, saying:

... there is in logic no justification for drawing a line at this point. If Article 2 does confer a right to self-determination in relation to life and death, and if a person were so gravely disabled as to be unable to perform any act whatever to cause his or her own death, it would necessarily follow in logic that such a person would have a right to be killed at the hands of a third party without giving any help to the third party and the state would be in breach of the Convention if it were to interfere with the exercise of that right. (*Pretty v United Kingdom* 66 BMLR 147 (2002), at p. 156)

Arguments about the rights and wrongs of euthanasia are fierce and, despite the fact that opinion poll (and therefore anecdotal) evidence suggests that a majority of people would wish to see voluntary euthanasia legalised, past attempts to achieve legalisation have failed. At the time of writing, the Assisted Dying for the Terminally Ill Bill (HL Bill 17, 2004) is progressing through the UK parliament, although it is thought unlikely to become law. The bill would legalise assisted dying, which, the bill explains, means:

> The attending physician, at the patient's request, either providing the patient with a means to end the patient's life or if the patient is physically unable to do so ending the patient's life. (s 1 (2))

Qualifying patients must have been informed of their diagnosis and prognosis, what will happen if they are assisted to die, and the alternatives available to them, including palliative care (id). Patients would need to be certified as terminally ill and as 'suffering unbearably' as a result of that illness (s.2). The patient must then make a written declaration witnessed by two individuals, one of whom must be a solicitor (s.4).

The impact of human rights discourse on the euthanasia question has to date been essentially to reinforce the law's previous position. No right to choose death has been recognised where the death can be brought about only with active assistance from a third party. The state's claimed interest in safeguarding all human life without distinction is a powerful – although not unarguable – force in maintaining this prohibition. Despite this, social attitudes are changing and the arguments about voluntary euthanasia seem likely to continue for the foreseeable future.

Further Reading

Angell, M. (1990) 'Prisoners of Technology: The Case of Nancy Cruzan', 322, *New England Journal of Medicine*, 1226.

Ethical Eye, Euthanasia (2004) Council of Europe Publishing.

Glover, J. (1977) *Causing Death and Saving Lives*, London: Penguin.

Griffiths, J., Bood, A. and Weyers, H. (1998) *Euthanasia and Law in the Netherlands*, Amsterdam: Amsterdam University Press.

Otlowski, M.F.A. (1997) *Voluntary Euthanasia and the Common Law*, Oxford: Clarendon Press.

Keow, J. (ed.) (1995) *Euthanasia Examined: ethical, clinical and legal perspectives*, Cambridge: Cambridge University Press.

Contributor: Sheila A.M. McLean

MARRIAGE AND A FAMILY, THE RIGHT TO

The right to marry and found a family is enshrined in the **UNIVERSAL DECLARATION OF HUMAN RIGHTS** (Article 16), the **INTERNATIONAL COVENANT ON CIVIL AND POLITICAL RIGHTS** (Article 23) and the **EUROPEAN CONVENTION ON HUMAN RIGHTS** (Article 12), as well as in the constitutions of numerous countries. Gender equality in the exercise of the right to marry is emphasised by Article 16 of the **CONVENTION ON THE ELIMINATION OF ALL FORMS OF DISCRIMINATION AGAINST WOMEN**, while the **CONVENTION ON THE ELIMINATION OF RACIAL DISCRIMINATION** prohibits race, ethnicity and national origin discrimination in the right to marry and choice of spouse (Article 5).

The debate as to the universality of human rights standards is particularly acute in the context of marriage because of the extent to which the institution is embedded in religious traditions and culturally specific customs. Some ethnically and culturally diverse states such as South Africa have omitted specific mention of the right to marry in their constitutions to obviate arguments about the nature of the right.

Problems are posed by legal pluralism: even if statute law is compatible with human rights, **CUSTOMARY** or religious law may not be. In addition, there may be a wide gulf between law and practice. Cultural practices such as child marriage, forced marriage and widow inheritance, or restrictions on marriages between those of different faiths or races violate the freedom to marry enshrined in human rights instruments.

The right to marry does not prevent a state from enacting laws that place restrictions on the form that a valid marriage must take or on the ability of certain couples to marry, for example because they are closely related to one another or because they are too young. Most formulations of the right to marry state that the couple must be of 'full' or 'marriageable' age and attempts have been made to outlaw the practice of child marriage (see for example the African Charter on the Rights and Welfare of the Child).

The minimum age for marriage is linked to the ability to give a valid consent to marriage. The Convention on Consent to Marriage, Minimum Age for Marriage and Registration of Marriages requires the presence, as well as the 'full and free' consent, of both parties to the marriage. Whether this means that only the consent of the parties is required is open to question: the validity of marriages contracted without parental consent is under debate in Pakistan.

Related to this is the question: what are the parties consenting to? Polygamy is permitted by tradition or religion in many countries in the developing world, although the extent to which Islam allows polygamy is contested – is it an absolute right or one conditional on the man's ability to act justly between his wives? A number of signatories to the Convention on the Elimination of All Forms of Discrimination Against Women – such as Algeria, Egypt, Morocco and the Maldives – have entered reservations to Article 16 insofar as it contradicts Shariah law. However, human rights advocates are clear that polygamy should be abolished as inconsistent with equal treatment of men and women, since women are not allowed multiple spouses. Countries such as Turkey, Cyprus, Tunisia and Côte d'Ivoire have abolished polygamy, while others have limited men's rights in this regard. In Pakistan, for example, a husband wishing to

take another wife must obtain the permission of his existing wife or wives and submit an application to the Arbitration Council. The recent Protocol to the **AFRICAN CHARTER ON HUMAN AND PEOPLE'S RIGHTS** on the Rights of Women in Africa declared that State parties should ensure that monogamy was encouraged as the preferred form of marriage, while protecting the rights of women in polygamous marriages.

Turning to the Western world, at present there are two key issues in debates over the right to marry: first, should a transsexual be allowed to marry as a member of his or her reassigned gender, and second, should marriage be opened up to same-sex couples? The traditional concept of marriage is a union of one man and one woman. But how is the sex of a transsexual to be determined for the purpose of marriage? The decision of the English High Court in *Corbett v Corbett* (1971) p. 83, which held that sex was determined at birth by genital, gonadal and chromosomal factors and could not be changed, has been remarkably influential. However, this view was never universal – Sweden has regulated and recognised gender reassignment since 1972, Germany since 1980 and Italy since 1982 – and has now lost its sway. **THE EUROPEAN COURT OF HUMAN RIGHTS** has finally held – reversing a line of previous decisions on this point – that the refusal to recognise a transsexual's reassigned sex for the purposes of marriage is in breach of Article 12. It acknowledged that while the right to marry was subject to the national laws of the contracting states, 'the limitations thereby introduced must not restrict or reduce the right in such a way or to such an extent that the very essence of the right is impaired' (*Goodwin v UK* [2002] 2 F.C.R. 576 at 604).

Similarly, Australia decided in Re Kevin (2003) FamCA 94 that the marriage between a post-operative female-to-male transsexual and a woman was valid, emphasising the evolutionary nature of marriage. In England and Wales, Parliament has introduced a Gender Recognition Bill that will allow even transsexuals who have not undergone surgery to be recognised and to marry in their reassigned sex.

At the same time, the definition of marriage as a union between a man and a woman is under challenge. A number of countries,

© R.K.M. Smith

beginning with Denmark in 1989, have introduced registered partnerships open to same sex couples, which are functionally equivalent to marriage. In recent years there have been a number of initiatives to open up marriage to same-sex couples. As with the introduction of transsexual marriages, some developments have been instigated by the courts, while others are the result of legislative action. The Netherlands was the first jurisdiction to pass legislation allowing marriage between same-sex couples in 2001 and Belgium followed suit in 2003. In the USA, the Hawaii Supreme Court ruled as far back as 1993 that the denial of marriage to same-sex couples was unconstitutional. However, the state legislature responded with legislation banning same-sex marriages, while in 1996 Congress passed the Defense of Marriage Act defining marriage as the union of one man and one woman for federal purpose and allowing states not to recognise same-sex marriages celebrated in other states. The same pattern has recently been repeated in Massachusetts, although the legislature proposed civil unions at the same time as banning same-sex marriage. In February 2004 thousands of same-sex couples flocked to be married in San Francisco after the Mayor

decided to issue marriage licences to same-sex couples in defiance of Californian state law, but California's Supreme Court subsequently ordered officials to desist. The majority of US states have now passed legislation banning same-sex marriage – Ohio became the 38th to do so in February 2004 – and an amendment to the constitution defining marriage as exclusively heterosexual is under consideration.

By contrast, over the border in Canada, a number of provinces have held that the denial of marriage to same-sex couples is a violation of the Canadian Charter of Rights and Freedoms, since it discriminates against them on the basis of their sexual orientation. At the time of writing, legislation was under consideration by the federal government, pending a referral to the Supreme Court, which is expected to report in 2005. In the meantime, Ontario and British Columbia have begun to allow same-sex couples to marry and Nunavut has declared that it will recognise such marriages.

Article 9 of the recent **EU CHARTER OF FUNDAMENTAL RIGHTS** reflects these changing social norms: the implicitly heterosexual formulation of 'men and women' in earlier versions is gone and 'the right to marry' is stated as distinct from 'the right to found a family'. Similarly, while in *Rees v UK* (1993) 2 FCR 49 the European Court of Human Rights stated that Article 12 of the Convention was 'mainly concerned to protect marriage as the basis of the family' (at paragraph 49), in the more recent *Goodwin v UK* it noted that the inability of a couple to conceive did not remove their right to marry.

Many of the key human rights instruments were formulated with the view of protecting the individual from the state and conceived of 'the right to found a family' as the right to be free from state interference in procreation. In recent years, the development of techniques for assisted reproduction has raised the question whether the state has a positive duty to assist the founding of a family and if so, whether that duty extends beyond the traditional married couple to same-sex couples and single fertile women. The right to marry and found a family thus raises issues that range from the place of customary practices to the use of cutting-edge technology.

Further Reading

Ali, S.S. (2002) 'Testing the Limits of Family Law Reform in Pakistan: A Critical Analysis of the Muslim Family Laws Ordinance 1961' in *International Survey of Family Law*, 317.

Bala, N. (2003) 'Controversy over couples in Canada: The Evolution of Marriage and Other Adult Interdependent Relationships', 29, *Queen's Law Journal* 41.

Benedek, W. Kisaakye, E.M. and Oberleitner, G. (eds) (2002) *The Human Rights of Women: International Instruments and African Experiences*, London: Zed Books.

Brems, E. (2001) *Human Rights: Universality and Diversity*, The Hague: Kluwer Law International.

McConvil, J. and Mills, E. (2003) 'Re Kevin and the Right of Transsexual Person to Marry in Australia', 17, *International Journal of Law, Policy and the Family* 251.

Contributor: Rebecca Probert

THE MARXIST CRITIQUE OF HUMAN RIGHTS

Based mostly on what Karl Marx wrote about rights in *On the Jewish Question and Critique of the Gotha Program*, most detractors (and even supporters) of Marx have interpreted him to be highly critical of rights in general, including human rights. Marx writes that rights promote egoism and alienation of persons from one another. The need for rights is based on the belief that there are those who are out to violate the rights of others, especially in terms of property and well-being. Furthermore, Marx refers to rights as 'absolute rubbish' and 'ideological nonsense'. At times he seems to challenge the legitimacy of certain 'equal rights'. But Marx also seems to heap scorn on rights in general. Indeed, this is precisely how Marx is interpreted, namely, as one who criticises rights per se because all rights are pernicious as they in reality protect the interests and freedoms of the bourgeoisie rather than those of the proletariat. Rights are, Marx argues, alleged to create and protect equality among citizens. Yet in fact they promote inequality. They protect the rights of the bourgeoisie over those of the working class, providing unequal protection under the law. Thus on this traditional interpretation, Marx is construed as an enemy of rights and so it would seem to follow that a Marxist regime would be one that disavows rights in light of Marx's own critique of them.

It turns out that this is a most unfortunate misconception of Marx on such an important matter as rights. As Joel Feinberg (1980) has argued, a society without rights is 'Nowheresville,' a society lacking sufficient resources to provide humanity with what is of paramount importance to its members: dignity, self-empowerment, liberty and self-determination, self-respect and respect for others. A right is either institutional, non-institutional or both. Institutional rights, such as legal rights, are those stipulated by a valid system of

Prima facie rights
Prima facie rights are rights that are held in the main but are not absolute in that there may be considerations that override those rights under certain circumstances.

rules. Non-institutional rights, including moral rights, are grounded in valid moral claims or interests quite apart from what legal rules might stipulate concerning what rights persons (or non-persons) might possess. Human rights include a broad set of interests and/or claims that are said to be valid by virtue of human personhood. All persons have them, though some such rights might be construed as being absolute, while others are merely *prima facie* rights (see box). Indeed, a morally acceptable society must be rights-based, though this need not imply that rights are the only things important in a good society. Duties and obligations are also important, for instance. In fact, there is a strong correlation between rights and duties, though not an absolute one. Thus a society without rights is lacking in a fundamental respect. And to attribute to anyone, especially a philosopher as distinguished as Marx, the view that rights per se are to be rejected because of their problematic nature, perhaps is either accurate (as the traditional interpretations of Marx have it) or is a pernicious form of misunderstanding in the form of the straw man fallacy.

© R.K.M. Smith

The straw man fallacy
The straw man fallacy is the mistake of using a very strong version of an argument against one's own position in order to knock it down easily.

Is the traditional interpretation of Marx on rights accurate? Or is it based on an embarrassing misreading of Marx? In attempting to answer these and related queries, it is crucial to distinguish certain claims about what Marx may have thought concerning rights. First, one might say that Marx failed to acknowledge that persons have rights. Second, one might hold that Marx held a position, one of the unacknowledged propositions of which implied that persons have no rights. Third, one might aver that Marx acknowledged that none of the rights of persons should be enforced by institutional structures of law. And fourth, one might argue that Marx held a view, one of the unacknowledged claims of which implied that none of the rights of persons should be enforced by institutional structures of law. In each case, one must ask whether or not Marx has in mind rights per se, rights in capitalism or rights under socialism and/or communism.

One must also distinguish between the having a right from the exercise of it. One might have a right yet choose not to exercise it for whatever reasons. Or one might have a right yet not exercise it out of ignorance that one has it. And this is true of legal and moral rights. Human rights would fall under both of these categories insofar as certain elements of international law provide for human rights that are, of course, supported by the balance of human reason. This distinction between having a right and exercising it is important to Marx's critique of rights in that Marx might well be engaged in a scathing critique of the ways in which rights are exercised rather than the ways in which they ought to be exercised and/or protected. Furthermore, Marx's critique of rights might well target the ways in which rights are exercised and/or protected in capitalist societies, but not necessarily in socialist or communist ones.

So the fact that Marx scorns various rights (even 'equal rights') is not sufficient to show that Marx criticises rights as such other than the ones that protect bourgeois interests. Marx singles out certain rights for criticism: 'the rights of man' and perhaps even 'the rights of the citizen' (the rights to liberty, **PROPERTY**, **EQUALITY**, security and certain other political rights). For these, Marx argues, promote egoism in capitalist societies. But Marx importantly does not criticise the right to resist oppression in Article 2 of the 1789 Declaration of the Rights of Man and of the Citizen. Perhaps, though not necessarily, this implies that Marx accepts this right and does not reject all rights. Furthermore, when Marx refers to capitalist exploitation as 'robbery' and an 'injustice' he seems to affirm an implied (moral) right to be free from these forms of exploitation. Also implied in Marx's critique of **CAPITALISM** is the moral right to not be alienated from other persons, the product of one's own labour, from labour itself and even from oneself by the capitalist means of forcing workers to sell their labour power. Indeed, Marx's theory of surplus value implies that insofar as workers are forced to sell their labour power they have a right to not be so coerced by capitalist means of production. And the capitalist extraction or theft of the surplus value of workers' labour is condemned by Marx, perhaps because Marx implicitly holds that workers have a right to the full value of their labour power, uncoerced as it ought to be in capitalism, and uncoerced as it would be in socialism and/or communism. More generally, what little Marx writes of socialist and/or communist societies leads one to think that both individuals and groups therein would freely choose to produce the bounty of their societies and how they want to engage in productive activity. And if this is true, then there is an implied individual and collective right to self-determination in Marxian societies, one hardly acknowledged by the traditional interpretation of Marx on rights.

Thus Marx's critique of rights is hardly universal in scope. Rather, it targets certain rights that seem to protect bourgeois interests in capitalist societies. For Marx's critique of capitalism itself implicitly acknowledges certain moral rights (rights that humans ought to have respected) that when respected protect the interests and legitimate claims of all persons.

Further Reading

Buchanan, A.E. (1982) *Marx and Justice*, Totowa: Rowman & Littlefield.

Cohen, G.A. (1985) *History, Labour, and Freedom*, Oxford: Oxford University Press.

Corlett, J. Angelo (2005) *Ethical Dimensions of Law*, Dordrecht: Kluwer Academic Publishers.

Feinberg, Joel (1980) *Rights, Justice, and the Bounds of Liberty*, Princeton: Princeton University Press.

Journalists for Human Rights, 'Human Rights, 2003' www.jhr.ca/usefullinks.html

Marx, Karl and Engels (1995) F. *Collected Works*, New York: International Publishers.

Contributor: J. Angelo Corlett

MEDIA AND HUMAN RIGHTS

Media freedom itself is an essential human right. If freedom of expression is absent, few other rights can be fully realised. An 'active open media' can promote human rights, **DEVELOPMENT** and **DEMOCRACY** by informing people of their rights, encouraging participatory governance, increasing transparency and demanding accountability of the broadest range of societal actors. But by commission or omission, media can also subvert basic liberties by encouraging acquiescence to or active support for human rights violations.

The media's moral and professional responsibilities in reporting or promoting human rights are robustly debated. Media outlets owned by governments, political parties, religious institutions and secular groups have varied agendas and many others' primary motive is profit. The pluralist view of media describes a 'fourth estate' watchdog that as a counterweight to powerful interests exercises 'eternal vigilance' over societal actors. The tradition of crusading and investigative journalists challenging entrenched interests and championing rights is indeed alive and thriving in many countries.

Complementing this watchdog function is the media's 'public interest' role. 'Public' or 'civic' journalism proponents argue that both state and private media should work to identify societal problems and encourage debate about their solution. Media's watchdog and public interest roles, pursued vigorously, produce the ideal described here as an 'active open media'.

Human rights and social justice advocates work in a crowded marketplace of ideas and products. They sometimes compete with each other and almost always against governments and other interests whose resources usually far outstrip those of even the most prominent human rights groups. Powerful institutions often deploy disinformation or lies to discredit criticism and may resort to economic pressure, legalised suppression, intimidation or physical attacks against both rights advocates and media if their perceived vital or vested interests are threatened. Among the most prominent groups that promote freedom of expression and media rights are Article 19 (www.article19.org), Index on Censorship (www.indexonline.org), the Committee to Protect Journalists (www.cpj.org) and Reporters Sans Frontiers (www.rsf.org).

Reporting on human rights and humanitarian issues also faces structural obstacles inherent in the journalistic style that prevails in most television, radio and daily newspaper reports. These usually emphasise events over process, description over explanation and post-facto analysis over prediction and early warning. Sources used to comment on events and the language of discourse and description most often reflect dominant paradigms supporting the status quo that condition audience perceptions and reactions.

Beginning in the mid-1800s, changes in technology and governance converged to increase media's power. The telegraph enabled the first electronic transmission of news and other information. In Britain and the United States, competitive, mass-produced newspapers vied for market share among a growing literate public as steam power allowed the first mass printing and circulation of newspapers. Growing press freedom permitted media to challenge those in power. Most important, elected governments, despite a legitimacy tempered by limited franchise, had to answer to the voters. The strength of these three markers – media freedom and independence, wide dissemination of and access to media content, and official accountability – today remain the most accurate measures of media's potential to influence public opinion and policy.

In both the UK and the USA, abolitionists organised extensive media campaigns in their 19th century fight against SLAVERY. A globalised news industry operating on a 24-hour news cycle and the spread of electoral democracy have since greatly magnified media's role in public life. 'Sovereignty' over any communications or cultural production is steadily dissipating. National and cultural control or organisation of information is increasingly challenged by the organic growth of virtually linked affinity groups that identify by affiliations other than geography, kith or kin.

The growing permeability of information frontiers fostered by evolving information and communications technologies offer local, national and regional human rights advocates increasingly greater and cheaper access to worldwide networks of resources and influence, particularly to marginalised groups – those typically most subject to the most persistent and egregious human rights violations.

Case study

Observer and Guardian v United Kingdom

Peter Wright, a former member of the British Security forces, wrote his memoirs, entitled 'Spycatcher', following his retirement. The British government banned the book in England for national security reasons. A ban followed in Scotland hours later although the first edition of Scottish newspapers were published with excerpts from the book. Further bans were sought in Australia. Despite this, the book was published and became a bestseller in the USA, especially at airports with direct flights to the UK.

When the European Court of Human Rights was asked by the Observer and Guardian newpapers to consider the continuation of the ban, it declared that the material was already in the public domain and widely known, thus the ban could not be upheld as a justifiable limitation on freedom of expression. The book was subsequently published.

Rights activists are growing adept at using tools of modern mass media to move their message, from community radio stations that raise local awareness to sophisticated websites that mainstream information from traditionally excluded communities, to global advocacy networks (See: **SOCIAL MOVEMENTS**).

Only a few of the world's most reclusive and repressive lands still seek to exclude information. Inevitably, open access to information that is the prerequisite, and not a perquisite, of modern economies spurs political debate as well as economic development.

The global standard for media freedom is utterly unambiguous. Article 19 of the **UNIVERSAL DECLARATION OF HUMAN RIGHTS** states succinctly that 'freedom of expression' includes the right 'to seek, receive and impart information and ideas of all kinds, regardless of frontiers, either orally, in writing, or in print, in the form of art, or through any other media …'.

Mass media can be the most powerful vehicle for free expression. Even in mature and prosperous democratic states that enjoy the rule of law, media's watchdog role remains crucial to balancing the tremendous power that inheres in government, is amassed by businesses, and is sometimes exercised by other societal actors.

Active open media can also provide early warning of conflicts or other threats. Nobel laureate Amartya Sen credits India's free press for helping that country avoid major famines since independence because their reporting stirred elected governments to action when hunger reached life-threatening levels. Sen compares this to massive but almost unreported famines in China, during which Beijing's unaccountable authoritarian leaders faced neither domestic nor international pressures to save their citizens. The role of media is especially crucial in reporting on war and other conflicts, when the people of democratic societies must share responsibility for lives and treasure spent in state-sanctioned violence. The Crimes of War Project, (www.crimesofwar.org) offers detailed explanations and examples of reporting on humanitarian issues, particularly in conflict situations.

The importance of media ownership is encapsulated in A.J. Liebling's (1960) aphorism, 'Freedom of the press is guaranteed only to those who own one'. State-controlled media is often blatantly biased, with human rights abuses unreported or denied. And self-censorship and even free editorial choices may produce information no less skewed than official propaganda. Private media is often much less than balanced and fair and utilised to pursue the grand prize of power.

Even moderate critiques of existing media structures in the most democratic societies urge much greater popular participation in generating media content and decentralisation of dissemination. In many developing countries, domestic media are often even more beholden to the state or elite interests through official control or the narrow economic base of most private media enterprises. In many cases, mass media consent is merely mandated rather than even manufactured.

Human rights advocates also face mounting obstacles from concentrated commercial mass media whose pursuit of profit often precludes serious coverage of social justice issues. The marketplace's demands may be no less insidious than a government's dictates and can reduce pluralism by making content no more than a servant to ratings, even if media is free enough to be more than a 'stenographer to power'.

The informational role for media in developing democracies is more complex than in mature democracies. The structures and processes of new or newly empowered institutions that protect rights require explanation. Awareness of rights must be widespread if they are to be asserted and respected. Very basic **HEALTH**, literacy and other social services information that serve **ECONOMIC, CULTURAL** or **SOCIAL RIGHTS** may also be an important part of effective and useful media in developing democracies (See: **THE RIGHT TO DEVELOPMENT**). In countries that have not yet begun democratic transitions, or those with limited, restricted or mistrusted local media, surrogate external media such as the British Broadcasting Corporation can be important sources of more balanced or accurate information.

But accepting that media can and should play important human rights and pro-democracy roles does not demand that such roles be imposed by fiat. Political parties, advocacy groups, religious organizations and purely commercial interests may operate media for their own parochial purposes. Private media, beyond reasonable regulation of incitement and libel in the context of guarantees of free expression, should bear no such official responsibility. When media clearly incite conflict and local authorities cannot or will not intervene (or might be party to incitement), however, difficult decisions on whether and how external actors should restrict media dissemination of messages inciting violence must be considered.

'Eternal vigilance is the price of liberty' is an adage adorning the masthead of several newspapers worldwide. Media theorist Marshall McLuhan neatly turned this conventional wisdom to the age of mass media consumption by warning 'the price of eternal vigilance is indifference'. 'Compassion fatigue' that desensitises media consumers to others' suffering has been identified as a negative outcome of reporting on humanitarian crises and human rights abuses.

But McLuhan's 'indifference' must be recognised as the result not of eternal vigilance but of feelings of powerless and resignation in the face of enormous and complex problems. The media's position in the human rights firmament is complex and at times highly problematical. All sectors of society need to gain better skills to suggest solutions and to demand action for problems the media exposes. And the media must unrelentingly defend its own right to serve as a watchdog and promoter of rights for all, and to give voice to those struggling for theirs.

WEBSITE

Journalists for Human Rights (2003)

www.jhr.ca/usefullinks.html

Further Reading

Kaplan, Roger (ed.) (2002) *Journalism, Media and the Challenge of Human Rights Reporting*, Geneva: The International Council on Human Rights Policy.

Liebling, A.J. (1960) 'Do You Belong in Journalism?' in *New Yorker*, 4 May.

McDow, Dodie (2001) *Making the Most of the Media: Tools for Human Rights Groups Worldwide*, New York: The Center for Sustainable Human Rights Action.

McLuhan, Marshall (1965) *Understanding Media, The Extensions of Man*, New York: McGraw Hill.

Sen, Amartya (1999) *Development as Freedom*, New York: Knopf.

Contributor: Thomas R. Lansner

MENTAL DISABILITY AND INTERNATIONAL HUMAN RIGHTS

It is still often the case that the rights of people with mental disorders are viewed, expressly or implicitly, as somehow peripheral to 'real' human rights issues. Such should not be the case. Mental disability law frequently involves the confinement of individuals. It also often involves the non-consensual introduction of chemicals or electricity into their bodies, with the objective of inducing a change in personality or experience of the empirical world. Certainly, some (but not all) recipients of such treatment are grateful afterwards and treatment providers will usually act with the best of motives. In appropriate circumstances the interventions may be socially desirable and legally justifiable. They nonetheless raise fundamental issues in human rights law.

Two prejudices must be dismissed immediately. First, mental disorder is not the same as mental incapacity. People with serious mental illness may nonetheless be capable of making choices about their well-being and of exercising their rights. The principle of **AUTONOMY** at the heart of human rights law means that they ought to be permitted to do so. They are often acutely aware of the situations they are in and the difficulties they face. Second, mental illness cannot be equated with dangerousness. While current human rights law does appear to allow controls to be placed when people pose significant risks to themselves or others, the vast bulk of people with mental disorders are not dangerous, and blanket restrictions on their rights cannot be justified on this ground.

It is only relatively recently that the rights of people with mental health difficulties have become a matter of concern in international human rights law. The first case involving mental disorder under the **EUROPEAN CONVENTION OF HUMAN RIGHTS**, for example, was decided only in 1979, more than a quarter of a century after the Convention came into effect. The **UNITED NATIONS** issued a brief declaration in 1971, but its first substantial declaration was not issued until 1991. There can be little doubt that the framers of the classic human rights charters following the Second World War did not have people with mental disorders in mind. Where litigation has occurred therefore, it has involved the application of human rights provisions in a context for which they were not designed.

The European Convention of Human Rights has so far proven the most fruitful field of litigation, although the similarity of its provisions with other human rights charters discussed elsewhere in this volume suggests that similar advances may be made more broadly. Movement has so far been most significant in procedural matters. The court has, for example, held that the **RIGHT TO LIBERTY** required that detention could occur only according to clear legal process, following a reliable medical diagnosis. The patient must further have a right to challenge the detention periodically before an independent tribunal, where due process requirements apply. Application of jurisprudence under the right to life has further imposed requirements to investigate deaths in psychiatric facilities. Procedural standards seem to have met with some success.

The courts have been considerably more reticent about requiring substantive standards. The leading case of *Winterwerp v Netherlands* (1979) 2 EHRR 387 indicates that to justify detention the mental disorder must be of 'a kind or degree warranting compulsory confinement' [paragraph 39] but the court has offered little indication of what that means. Similarly, little has been said about the standards of care a facility must meet, although it is now clear that a prison may not be used for civil psychiatric confinement: *Aerts v Belgium* (1998) 29 EHRR 50. Substantive standards are contained in the 1991 United Nations Principles, however, which are considerably more prescriptive both on standards of admission and standards of facilities. Similarly, while the **EUROPEAN COURT OF HUMAN RIGHTS** has been hesitant to make findings that conditions violate the European Convention of Human Rights protections

from inhuman or degrading treatment, the European Committee for the Prevention of **TORTURE** now routinely visits psychiatric facilities with a view to ensuring appropriate institutional standards.

Even at the rudimentary level of first generation rights, the paucity of litigation particularly outside Europe must be noted. Fundamental rights such as liberty, privacy, family life and access to courts are contained in all the major human rights charters, but these provisions are not yet being litigated in the context of mental disorder. While reliable empirical studies are few, there appears to be cogent reason for concern that fundamental standards are not being met.

While fundamental rights may be essential to people with mental disorders, equally significant is access to appropriate care, treatment and services. Again, there is minimal litigation on this question and such as there is tends to be articulated in procedural rather than substantive contexts. Thus in *Johnson v UK*, (1998) 27 EHRR 296, the complainant was held by successive tribunals no longer to require detention in a psychiatry facility, but community facilities appeared not to be available. The court addressed this as a problem of the tribunal being unable to enforce its orders rather than the provision to the individual of a right to appropriate services. It is not always the case that countries have a tradition of offering appropriate services to people with mental disorders and fiscal restraints imposed on countries, in part through international financial obligations, frequently result in mental health services failing to develop, if indeed they do not deteriorate.

Human rights documents do contain a variety of potentially important provisions. Many provide rights to **HEALTH CARE, EDUCATION, WORK**, social security and community living. The difficulty here is that few of these provisions are directly enforceable by aggrieved individuals. However honourable the sentiments expressed, they count for little when not implemented. Again, the reports of non-governmental organisations suggest that in few places can there be said to be an appropriate choice and standard of service available.

A question of power arises here: who determines the appropriateness of service? In the mental health arena, is it the patient, the doctor or social worker, or the government that determines appropriateness of service? In the political reality, it tends to be government, with medical practitioners sometimes having involvement. As a matter of human rights law, however, it is at least arguable that service users ought to have a significant role in defining the services they need. Therapeutic jurisprudence would argue that such involvement may result in better medical results – a reminder that human rights law and medicine are not necessarily in conflict (see, for example, Winick, 1991).

Certainly, the availability of appropriate services cannot remove first generation human rights. It is a non-sequitur to say that when services are available, the individual is required to accept the services.

Mental disorders fall within the remit of human rights instruments governing disabilities and, consistent with those instruments, much of the recent academic discussion of human rights and mental disorder has focused on the right to be free from **DIS-CRIMINATION**. As a general principle, this is clearly an appropriate realm of analysis. People with mental health problems, like all others in society, have rights to social benefits, and there is much to be gained by applying anti-discrimination law to these fields. Consideration of some of mental health law, including consent to treatment, in this framework is similarly fruitful (see Bartlett, 2003).

This approach contains challenges to previous conceptions of human rights in mental health law, however, which are often inherently discriminatory. The 1991 United Nations principles, for example, allow the civil confinement of individuals when 'there is a serious likelihood of immediate or imminent harm to that person or to other persons' (Article 16). Such prospective confinement is discriminatory, in that confinement in other contexts cannot occur in anticipation of dangerous behaviour, but only after its occurrence. Similarly, while the non-discrimination approach may beneficially buttress the rights of individuals with mental disorders, it is not clear how these rights integrate with the rights of families. The individual has a right to privacy, for example; how does that affect the right to family life of family members, who may have coherent needs for information about the individual? The integration of non-discrimination with other human rights principles poses one of the challenges of the near future.

As noted at the beginning of this article, mental incapacity is not co-extensive with mental disorder. Consistent with the non-discrimination approach, incapacity is increasingly viewed as the borderline where decisions may be taken away from the individual, raising profound questions as to what incapacity means (Bartlett and Sandland, 2003a). There has been less articulation within a human rights framework as to how the human rights of the individual lacking capacity are to be understood. Certainly, they must retain certain first generation rights, such as the right to be free from inhuman treatment; but that sets a remarkably low threshold. For an individual unable to make decisions, should additional substantive provisions be required to ensure appropriate care? The individual lacking capacity is unlikely to be in a position to enforce these rights. Both the United Nations instruments and the Cairo Declaration on Human Rights in Islam (See: **ISLAM AND HUMAN RIGHTS**) include rights to guardianship for people lacking capacity. This in turn raises a set of administrative questions as to whether or how the guardian should be supervised and how decisions of the guardian can be challenged. It further begs the question of the degree to which the views of the individual lacking capacity should nonetheless be taken into account. These again are issues for consideration by international human rights advocates in the near future.

WEBSITES

Mental Disability Advocacy Centre, Budapest. www.mdac.info

Mental Disability Rights International, Washington DC. www.mdri.org

Further Reading

Bartlett, P. (2003) 'The Test of Compulsion in Mental Health Law: Capacity, Therapeutic Benefit and Dangerousness as Possible Criteria', 11 *Medical Law Review*, 326-52.

Bartlett, P. and Sandland, R. (2003a) *Mental Health Law: Policy and Practice*, 2nd edn, Oxford: Oxford University Press.

Lewis, O. (2002) 'Protecting the rights of people with a mental disability – the European Convention on Human Rights', 9:4 *European Journal of Health Law*, 293–320.

Rosenthal, E. and Sundram, C. (2002) 'International Human Rights in Mental Health Legislation', 12, *New York Law School Journal of International and Comparative Law*, 469–524.

Winick, B. (1991) 'Competency to Consent to Treatment: The Distinction Between Assent and Objection', 28 *Houston Law Review*, 15.

Contributor: Peter Bartlett

MIDDLE EAST: THE REALITY OF HUMAN RIGHTS

Although some attention was paid to the issues of human rights in the Middle East in the past, the current high levels of concern are relatively recent. During the second half of the 20th century the concept of 'rights' was closely related in the Arab conscience to the rights of the Palestinian people. However, since the mid–1980s, the region has witnessed significant developments related to human rights issues. This overview of the present human rights situation in the Middle East is based on four main pillars: 1) the political and cultural context of human rights in the region; 2) the emergence and development of the 'human rights movement' as represented by the NGOs working in the field and their relation with the international human rights community; 3) the stance of Arab governments towards human rights issues and the development of regional and national mechanisms to enhance and safeguard human rights; and 4) violations of human rights in the Arab countries.

The human rights record in the Middle East is less promising than that of other regions. To give a balanced assessment, an understanding of the overall political and cultural context prevalent in the region is required. The political environment in the majority of the Arab countries is relatively unsuitable for the prosperity of the values and principles of human rights. Democratic norms and the rule of law are almost totally absent, particularly when a state of emergency is imposed, as is the case in many Arab countries. Culturally, the Arab region is characterised by excessive manipulation by the authorities and the conservative Islamic and Nationalist political groups of the alleged Islamic cultural specificity of the Arab communities. Such cultural norms are invoked in rejecting the international human rights standards and breaching the international human rights obligations of the Arab states. Hence, most Arab states made reservations to the international instruments invoking Islamic Shari'a. Likewise, many patriotic and pro-governmental voices have seen human rights activities as a consequence of **GLOBALISATION** that threaten state sovereignty and the Arab national identity.

At the regional level, the region has long suffered from the repercussions of the Arab-Israeli conflict which greatly inflicted the rights of the Palestinian people in particular, and **DEMOCRACY AND HUMAN RIGHTS** in the region in general. For public opinion in the region, the failure of the international community to reach a just and durable settlement of this persistent conflict has led to a lack of credibility of the international justice system. In this context the human rights discourse, too, is being criticised for applying double standards. Politically this conflict has been manipulated by many Arab regimes in order to distract Arab public opinion from the lack of democracy and human rights in their own countries.

Human rights NGOs started to emerge in the early 1970s. They were primarily based in the countries of the Maghrib, namely, Mauritania, Morocco, Tunisia and Algeria. In Egypt, pro-governmental human rights institutions emerged as of 1975. As for the Mashriq (Eastern Arab and Gulf countries), there were no real human rights NGOs, only committees for defending freedoms that were related to political parties and powers present in the arena. There were only three human rights organisations: one with a governmental nature was established in Iraq, namely, the Iraqi Organization for Human Rights; the other was the Lebanese Association for Human Rights, which was established amidst deteriorating political conditions; the third is Al-Haq which was established in Palestine in 1979.

Nevertheless, the few writings that tackle the emergence and development of the human rights movement in the Arab region agree that it did not actually emerge until 1983 with the establishment of the Arab Organization for Human Rights (AOHR) – the first regional human rights NGO. It was established by a number of Arab professionals from various intellectual and political tendencies whether Nationalist, Islamic or Marxist (See: **ISLAM AND HUMAN RIGHTS; MARX'S CRITIQUE OF HUMAN RIGHTS**). As the Arab governments refused to host the initial meeting, the founders of AOHR had to hold their meeting outside the Arab region, in Cyprus. This rejection was emblematic for the lack of political will of the Arab governments to legally recognise such organisations and, on the contrary, the tendency to assume a hostile stance against these NGOs in most cases.

By the mid-1980s, numerous national and regional human rights NGOs existed. The emergence of global pro-civil society policies and foreign funding played a key role in enhancing the establishment of more specialised human rights NGOs in various fields such as legal aid and human rights education, and so on.

However, these developments were restricted to a few Arab states, for example the Maghrib, Egypt, Lebanon, Yemen and Palestine. With the development of human rights NGOs and related activities in these states, the authorities began taking severe stances against such institutions and charged them with being agents for foreign countries. Consequently, the issue of foreign funding became one of the most important tools to deny the political and moral legitimacy of the human rights groups. Several NGOs faced legal and political impediments, inter alia, dissolving a number of such organisations and criminalising activities related to human rights issues.

In such a hostile atmosphere, several local human rights NGOs started seeking assistance and solidarity from the international human rights community to gain strength and legitimacy. Furthermore, there were initiatives apt at bringing the different actors of the Arab human rights movement together.

The Arab region is often seen as one of the least democratic all over the world as far as civil and political rights and women's rights are concerned. Yet some Arab governments have established national institutions for enhancing and protecting human rights. However, their affiliation with the states affects their credibility among many of those concerned with human rights locally and internationally. At the regional level, the Arab Permanent Committee for Human Rights was established within the framework of the League of Arab States in 1968. In practice, the mission of this committee was restricted to criticism of Israeli practices against the Palestinian people. It never tackled the rights of citizens of Arab countries. In 1979, the Arab Permanent Committee for Human Rights began drafting an Arab Charter on Human Rights. It was adopted and proclaimed by the League of Arab States in 1997. Although weak, the Charter did not gain enough support to be ratified. Recently, with the assistance of the OHCHR, the Charter was updated in order to conform to international human rights standards; however, at the time of writing it had yet to be adopted by the Arab states.

At the international level, some Arab countries did not ratify a number of international human rights instruments. Of the Arab countries which did ratify these instruments, most did so with reservations, with reference to Islamic Shari'a law. Furthermore, none of the Arab states ratified the Statute of the **INTERNATIONAL CRIMINAL COURT** except for Jordan.

Like other areas all over the world, the Arab region witnessed blatant violations of human rights which varied from one state to another. Due to the lack of monitoring mechanisms in several Arab states, numerous violations remained invisible. National and international NGOs played a key role in exposing such violations. In addition to violations of civil and political rights as well as **ECONOMIC** and **SOCIAL** rights, the Arab region witnessed a number of more flagrant violations such as **GENOCIDE** as in the case of the Kurds under the regime of the ousted

Iraqi president, Saddam Hussein. Other countries such as Algeria and Egypt witnessed violations of the **RIGHT TO LIFE** due to the bloody confrontations between militant Islamic groups and security forces as well as other violations such as forced disappearance and military trials.

Meanwhile, other countries, particularly the Gulf countries, witnessed flagrant violations of the rights of **WOMEN** and migrant labourers (See: **THE MIGRANT WORKERS' CONVENTION**). Mauritania and Sudan were accused of not being decisive to end the traditional forms of slavery. The rights of the Palestinian people are now being paid due attention by the United Nations and the national and international human rights NGOs, in a context, however, that often fails to achieve any tangible progress in obtaining respect for the fundamental rights of the Palestinian people.

It is noteworthy that while the Arab human rights NGOs have strongly challenged the violations of civil and political rights by governments in the region, they have paid less attention to the numerous violations of economic and social rights. Moreover, the NGOs have been uncourageous in challenging violations of other rights such as the **FREEDOM OF RELIGION** or the right to freedom of sexual-orientation (See: **THE RIGHTS OF GAY, LESBIAN, BISEXUAL AND TRANSSEXUAL PEOPLE**)

Finally, the region witnessed a high degree of turbulence in the aftermath of September 11 2001 and the subsequent military strategies manifested in the the War on Terror. The invasion of Iraq the latest and probably most perilous of the factors instigating instability in the region.

WEBSITES

Arab Organization for Human Rights
www.aohr.org
Arab Institute for Human Rights
www.aihr.org.tn/
Cairo Institute for Human Rights
www.cihrs.org/
Arab Center for Independence of Judiciary and Legal Profession www.acijlp.org
Arab Committee for Human Rights
www.com.to/achr

The Middle East NGOs Gateway: www.mengos.net/default.htm
Arab Gateway: www.al-bab.com
Derechos: www.derechos.org/humanrights/mena/iot.html
Human Rights Library of The Minnesota University:
www1.umn.edu/humanrts/links/islam.html
Critical review of the updated Arab Charter for Human Rights done by Amnesty International:
http://web.amnesty.org/library/index/engmde010022004
Interdisciplinary discussion held in Cairo in March 1998 about the International Aspects of The Arab Human Rights Movement:
www.law.harvard.edu/programs/hrp/publications/cairo1.html

Further Reading

An-Na'im, Abdullah Ahmed (1990) *Toward an Islamic Reformation: Civil Liberties, Human Rights, and International Law.* New York: Syracuse.

Dalacoura, Katerina (2003) *Islam, Liberalism and Human Rights: Implications for International Relations,* London: I.B. Tauris.

Mayer, Ann Elizabeth (1991) *Islam and Human Rights. Tradition and Politics,* Boulder, Col.: Westview Press.

Contributor: Yousry Moustafa

THE MIGRANT WORKERS' CONVENTION

The growing inequality of wealth within and between countries is leading more people to make the decision to migrate. The number of people living outside their country of origin rose significantly between 1985 and 2000 from 105 million to 175 million. This figure includes migrant workers, permanent immigrants, refugees and displaced persons, but does not include irregular migrants (International Organization for Migration, World Migration, 2003). This represents a 67 per cent increase at a time when the total world population increased only by 26 per cent.

Political breakdown or economic dislocation (caused by conflict, environmental disaster, structural adjustment policies, mismanagement of the economy, etc.) undermines existing standards of living and threatens some people's ability to sustain themselves and their families. These are important factors which contribute to the number of people who seek to migrate. The demand for migrant workers is also increasing, particularly in developed countries where low fertility rates and longer life expectancy are resulting in an ageing population and leading to significant labour and skills shortages. The proportion of adults over 60 in high-income countries is expected to increase to 19 per cent by 2050, while the number of children will drop by one third (United Nations Populations Division 2002, quoted in McKinley, 2003).

Migrant workers are therefore likely to play an increasingly important role for sending (origin) countries, particularly through their remittances (that is earnings that they send back to their country of origin) and also for receiving countries where they make a vital contribution through their labour and tax contributions. Despite this, migrant workers are routinely denied both their human and labour rights. This may include torture, forced labour, restrictions on their freedom of movement, removal of documents, debt bondage, inadequate or non-payment of wages and work which does not comply with national health and safety requirements. While irregular migrants (those without the required documents to allow them to work in another country legally) are obviously most at risk of being subjected to human rights violations, regular migrants are also subjected to the types of ill-treatment outlined above. These abuses can take place in the country of origin (particularly when unscrupulous recruitment agencies are involved) or in transit, as well as in the country of destination.

There are three important international standards that specifically address migrant workers, which should be considered when seeking to protect migrants from human or labour rights violations. Despite being over 50 years old, the **INTERNATIONAL LABOUR ORGANIZATION** Convention no. 97 on Migration for Employment (Revised), 1949, still addresses problems that many migrants face today. For example, Article 6 requires states to ensure that all immigrants receive equal treatment to nationals in areas like remuneration, conditions of work, accommodation and membership of unions. However, the major problem with this Convention is that it is limited to 'any person regularly admitted as a migrant for employment' and therefore will not assist irregular migrants. Given its age and its limited scope it is disappointing that this Convention has only 42 ratifications. A ratification is the formal agreement by a state that it will ensure that its laws and practice fully comply with all the provisions of the relevant international standard.

ILO Convention no. 143 on Migrant Workers (Supplementary Provisions), 1975, also has a low number of ratifications (just 18 states have ratified it at the time of writing and none of these has done so in the last ten years). However, this Convention marks a significant step forward in international human rights law because it sets out that that both regular and irregular migrants need to be protected from human and labour rights violations. Like its predecessor, Convention 143 promotes equality of opportunity and treatment for migrant workers in regular situations, but it goes further by extending some protection against exploitation to irregular migrants. For example, Article 9 states that even where a migrant has irregular status they shall 'enjoy equality of treatment for himself and his family in respect of rights arising out of past employment as regards remuneration, social security and other benefits'. It also notes that where disputes arise in relation to this then the migrant worker, or a representative, will have the right to present their case to the competent body.

The standards set out in these ILO Conventions are reinforced in the United Nations Convention on migrant workers, which was completed in 1990. The United Nations Convention on the Protection of the Rights of All Migrant Workers and their Families, 1990, builds on the principles of ILO Conventions nos 97 and 143 and the **UNIVERSAL DECLARATION OF HUMAN RIGHTS**, in order to extend human rights law to all migrant workers and their families throughout the entire migration process. It seeks also to prevent and eliminate 'the clandestine movements and trafficking in migrant workers' and the employment of migrants in irregular situations.

The 1990 Convention is the most comprehensive international standard dealing with migrant workers and is divided into nine parts. Some of the most important aspects of the Convention are highlighted below. Part III of the Convention extends basic human rights protection to all migrant workers and their families regardless of whether they have regular or irregular status in the country of destination. This includes protection from torture, slavery or forced labour; the right to liberty and security of person; due process before the law; protection against the confiscation or destruction of their identity documents; equality of treatment with nationals in respect of remuneration and conditions of work; and the right to take part in trade union activities.

Part IV of the Convention sets out additional rights for documented migrants. This includes equality of treatment with nationals in respect to access to education, vocational training and social services; reunification with partners and dependent children; and equality of treatment with nationals in respect to protection against dismissal, unemployment benefits and access to alternative employment if work is terminated. Part VI of the Convention proposes policies to promote lawful international migration and which will reduce the number of migrants who are vulnerable to exploitation from smugglers and traffickers. These proposals include: regulating recruitment agencies; improving collaboration between states to prevent the dissemination of misleading information regarding migration; and introducing measures to prohibit and punish those responsible for the illegal movement of migrant workers or for the employment of undocumented migrants.

While this Convention has only 25 ratifications at the time of writing, the Convention is in force and a treaty monitoring body has been set up to regularly review whether the states which have ratified the Convention are in full compliance with it. The states that have ratified the Convention, as of March 2004, are Azerbaijan, Belize, Bolivia, Bosnia and Herzegovina, Burkina Faso, Cape Verde, Colombia, East Timor, Ecuador, Egypt, El Salvador, Ghana, Guatemala, Guinea, Kyrgyzstan, Mali, Mexico, Morocco, Philippines, Senegal, Seychelles, Sri Lanka, Tajikistan, Uganda and Uruguay.

A total of 65 states have ratified either one or more of the three Conventions discussed above. It is therefore a real priority to try to convince all states, and in particular those which are receiving states for migrant workers, to ratify the 1990 Convention and extend human rights protection to all migrants throughout the migration process. However, as this is likely to be a long-term goal and the majority of countries in the world are not bound by the standards set out in these Conventions, it is also important to consider what other international standards contain provisions that may be of assistance in protecting migrant workers' rights.

In this context, ILO Convention no. 29 on Forced Labour is particularly noteworthy as it has 163 ratifications and is one of the ILO's fundamental human rights conventions, with which ILO member states are supposed to comply even if they have not ratified them. The Convention can assist any migrant worker who is undertaking any work or service against their will because they have been coerced or threatened with some form of punishment if they do not. The definition of forced labour has been interpreted broadly by the ILO and has been applied to bonded labourers and trafficked people in the past. Other standards, such as the **INTERNATIONAL COVENANT ON CIVIL AND POLITICAL RIGHTS**, 1966 and **THE INTERNATIONAL COVENANT ON ECONOMIC, SOCIAL AND CULTURAL RIGHTS**, 1966 (both of which have been ratified by more than 140 states), also have articles that may assist in protecting migrant workers.

WEBSITES

International Organization for Migration, World Migration 2003, Geneva, 2003.

December 18 and Migrant Rights International website: www.december18.net

International Labour Organization website: www.ilo.org/migrant

Further Reading

Anti-Slavery International (2003) *The Migration-Trafficking Nexus: Combating Trafficking Through the Protection of Migrants' Human Rights*, London.

The International Catholic Migration Committee (2004) *How to Strengthen Protection of Migrant Workers and Members of Their Families with International Human Rights Treaties*, Geneva.

McKinley, Brunson (2003) *International Migration and Development – The Potential for a Win-Win Situation.*

Contributor: Mike Kaye

MINORITY RIGHTS

Analysing the growth of the human rights regime more than 50 years after the passage of the **UNIVERSAL DECLARATION OF HUMAN RIGHTS** 1948, it is easy to detect a sense of achievement with the extent to which this regime has progressed. The principle that governments are accountable for their actions towards groups that are numerically inferior and in non-dominant positions within the state even in times of conflict is further evidence that human rights principles are now firmly embedded within the international legal system. The relative success, incremental though it might be, of the work of the **UNITED NATIONS** Treaty Bodies, in addition to the standards being developed under the auspices of the United Nations Commission on Human Rights by Rapporteurs and Working Groups, suggests that the outlook for the future progress of the human rights regime is basically sound.

However, one lacuna that remains within human rights law is the lack of a successful regime guaranteeing the rights of minorities. Despite the growth in modern human rights regimes, it could be argued that the international regime for the protection of minority rights was stronger before the UN era.

Much discussion has taken place as to the precise nature of who a minority is. Rather than seeking a detailed analysis of this discussion, it is proposed that the oft-quoted working definition framed in a UN study published in 1979 by Francesco Caportorti be accepted.

According to Caportorti, a minority can be described as:

A group, numerically inferior to the rest of the population of a State, in a non-dominant position, whose members – being nationals of the State – possess ethnic, religious or linguistic characteristics differing from those of the rest of the population and who, if only implicitly, maintain a sense of solidarity, directed towards preserving their culture, traditions, religion or language.

This definition has some limitations in terms of its universal suitability and applicability. The first such limitation that arises is with respect to the issue of nationality. The restrictive approach of law would require that minorities be citizens of a given state, to gain protection under its laws. Thus the primary focus of international minority rights law has been concern over a state's treatment of minority groups who are citizens and who live within the state. There is also acceptance in international human rights law that states are within their rights, through the principle of state sovereignty, to distinguish between its nationals and non-nationals with regard to rights that are non-fundamental, though there are more recent efforts to constrict this differentiation. Further, the use of the term 'national' in the context of the description of a group as a minority has not been particularly useful since this accords status only to groups living in one state with the nationality of another, usually neighbouring, state. While 'national' minorities are often as vulnerable as non-national minorities, human rights law has more recently developed the principle for a broader reading to include non-national groups.

It needs to be reiterated that Caportorti's view is not definitive with the existence of other definitions that vary slightly from it but nonetheless express similar sentiments. It is also worth emphasising the famous statement of Max van der Stoel, erstwhile High Commissioner for National Minorities of the **ORGANISATION FOR SECURITY & CO-OPERATION IN EUROPE**, that he knew a minority when he saw one. To this must be added the caveat that the nature of a minority varies tremendously from state to state but that a general rule in determining whether a particular group comes within the ambit of a 'minority' is that members of the group ought to possess features through which they are readily identifiable as being different from the majority and these differentiated features that identify them should be considered by them to be relatively fundamental to the cultural identity of the group.

There has been discussion about whether other groups, for example group identity based on sexual preference or disability, ought to come within this definition, with the general consensus being that they do not fall within this category. While there are several vulnerable groups that exist in society, minority rights law is only one specific mechanism seeking to address the particular vulnerability of groups that are distinguished on the specified grounds identified above. While the principles of minority rights law can and should be extended to other groups that are similarly vulnerable, these groups do not fall within the sobriquet of 'minorities' in international human rights law.

An important question that needs to be raised, in the context of the blossoming of the human rights agenda, is whether there is need for special identification and categorisation of such rights when the core content of minority rights is already covered by general human rights norms. An argument is often posited that the particular identification of a specified group is superfluous since all human beings are entitled to human rights by virtue of being human and irrespective of any differences in identity.

The best response to this argument focuses on the historical discrimination that particular groups have faced. This discrimination has usually been constructed against minorities due to their numeric inferiority, a manifestation of inherent racism or the dominance through law or force of them. More crucially, the result of this discrimination has been the construction of chronic inequality that remains extremely difficult to dismantle. In this context, there is a pressing need to move beyond the rhetoric of the 'equal value and worth of every human being' and 'her/his inherent dignity'. Thus while the human rights agenda based on the principles of equality and non-discrimination insists that all human beings are entitled to similar treatment, such similar treatment is unlikely to visit every individual and group equally.

Further, with the human rights discourse stressing the legal/legislative route as being one of the avenues towards improved protection and accountability, it becomes imperative to ensure that groups in particular need have access to these legal developments. In this sense, the real test of human rights law is to ascertain its value and merit in protecting the most vulnerable groups within society, among which minorities fall. To be able to do this effectively requires the creation of effective mechanisms to address inequality.

The founding principle of minority rights law is posited in the principle of affirmative action (also known as positive discrimination). Minority rights law asserts that in specific situations, the most efficient way to address the gap between a minority and majority lies in the construction of specific measures seeking to raise the level of opportunities available to members of minority groups. This differential treatment, it is argued, will aim to provide individuals from minority groups with a fillip to enable them access to the opportunities and choices that those from the majority have as of right or tradition. The principle of affirmative action accepts that in taking these positive measures, individuals from the majority population will be discriminated against in the short run. This is considered to be an acceptable price, however, in the overall context of fostering greater inclusion and participation in the life and affairs of the state and towards the greater inclusion of groups that have been historically discriminated against.

In addition to the rationale for the protection of diversity and multiculturalism (See: **PLURALIST UNIVERSALISM**), the development of minority rights law is also particularly important to global peace and security. Conflicts are often sparked by persistent discrimination against particular groups, usually ethnic minorities, who have subsequently armed themselves to resist the state. This has resulted in large-scale losses of lives and significant displacement of populations, resulting in crisis levels of refugee flows. Often, the root cause of these conflicts is the persistent and historical discrimination against particular groups, who feel that the only manner to improve their living conditions is to agitate against the state and seek the creation of their own state. This phenomenon draws on romanticised notions of the struggle against oppression, as groups within post-colonial states arm themselves with a view to fighting a battle against the state. Notwithstanding the break-up of the Soviet Union, the Velvet Divorce between the Czech and Slovak Republics and the dissolution of former Yugoslavia (none of which occurred in 'colonial' settings), very few of these movements have been successful in breaking away from the post-colonial state.

The emphasis on the situation of such minorities within former colonial countries is particularly relevant since the state in these settings is often the result of the imposition of colonial boundaries that may not pertain to ethnic, religious, linguistic or cultural faultlines. It could be argued that a greater emphasis on the human rights of these groups, with an opportunity for greater participation in the life of the state, would quell or subdue these feelings of separatism, or at worst relocate discussions about separatism away from the use of force to legal, social and political fora. In this sense, the increased sophistication of minority rights and a greater emphasis on this agenda can significantly enhance the purposes and principles of the United Nations, while also striking an important blow for the principle of effective equality within human rights law.

WEBSITE

United Nations Human Rights Committee General Comment No. 23 available from www.ohchr.org

Further Reading

Alfredsson, Gudmundur and Ferrer, Erika (1998) *Minority Rights: A Guide to the UN Procedures and Institutions*, London: Minority Rights Group International & Raoul Wallenberg Institute.

Banton, M. (1996) *International Action Against Racial Discrimination*, Oxford: Oxford University Press.

Brölmann, Catherine, Zieck, Marjoleine and Lefeber, Rene (eds) (1993) *Peoples and Minorities in International Law*, Dordecht: Martinus Nijhoff.

Ezorsky, G. (1991) *Racism and Justice: the Case for Affirmative Action*, Ithaca, NY: Cornell University Press.

McKean, Warwick (1985) *Equality and Non-Discrimination under International Law*, Clarendon: Oxford University Press.

Thornberry, Patrick (1991) *International Law and the Rights of Minorities*, Clarendon: Oxford University Press.

Contributor: Joshua Castellino

MONITORING AND ENFORCING HUMAN RIGHTS

International mechanisms are an important part of the global machinery for the protection and promotion of human rights. Yet they are not a substitute for effective national mechanisms. At best international mechanisms can only supplement effective domestic mechanisms.

International mechanisms are of broadly three types: Treaty Body mechanisms created under the seven major human rights treaties (See: **TREATY BASED LAW**), Charter-based mechanisms, commonly known as 'Special Procedures', created by the UN, and other mechanisms such as the International Labour Organization, the Inspection Panel of the World Bank, the Compliance Review Panel of the Asian Development Bank, the International Criminal Court and the Ad Hoc Tribunals.

The treaty monitoring process is a fluid process and has changed considerably over the years. It is dependent to a great extent on the personalities on the different committees and the nature of the interactions that these committees have with national and international human rights organisations. The chairs of the committees meet once a year to review their work and explore possibilities of cooperation. The main activity of the committees under the treaties is to examine reports submitted by governments. Most committees adopt the procedure outlined overleaf in considering reports submitted by governments.

In addition to scrutinising government reports, committees also regularly adopt General Comments or Recommendations. A General Comment or Recommendation will take a right or issue in the Covenant, elaborate on its meaning and identify in some detail the nature of the obligations under that right.

The Committee Against Torture (CAT) (See: **FREEDOM FROM TORTURE**) and the **CEDAW** Committee are explicitly authorised to make country visits. CAT has utilised this sparingly and the CEDAW Committee has not used it at all. The Economic, Social and Cultural Rights Committee has made at least one country visit. In at least one instance the ESCRC has acted so as to prevent a violation from taking place. The Committee took the view that the proposed forced eviction of a large group of people would result in an infringement of the Filipino government's obligations under the covenant. It recommended that the evictions go ahead only if a suitable resettlement scheme had been put in place.

When Hong Kong reported under the ICESCR some years ago, the NGOs arranged for the ESCRC member in charge of the Hong Kong report to visit Hong Kong and dialogue with local NGOs prior to the Committee considering the government's report. A similar process was followed when India reported under CEDAW a few years ago.

Some committees such as the CESCR set aside time for a discussion of a specific right or article of the covenant, or of a specific issue of concern, with the objective of catalysing action among other organisations. Experts may also be asked to participate.

'Shadow' or 'Alternative' Reports are now considered by most Committees when governments report and are an integral part of the monitoring process. A Shadow Report is prepared by a national or international NGO or a group of NGOs. It presents an alternative perspective to the government report and enables the committee to come to a better understanding of the human right situation in the country it is examining. The generation of a Shadow Report within a country can have other implications. Where the process is highly participatory and involves a number of NGOs and regular public consultation, it has the potential to raise public awareness on the issues and to develop a better understanding of the rights in question. When India reported to CEDAW a few years ago, Indian NGOs designed a highly participatory process of generating a Shadow Report which included consultations with grassroots communities.

Five of the seven treaty bodies can receive

Typical Committee procedure

1. The government submits its report.

2. In the case of most Committees, a few months before its formal session, a working group or one of its members will identify the issues to be raised with the government representative.

3. It is open for national and international NGOs to prepare 'alternative' or 'shadow' reports for submission to the Committee.

4. The Committee will meet with government representatives at one of its formal sessions (usually held twice a year) for a review of the government's report. Prior to this the Committee will address a list of questions to the government concerned.

5. Some Committees permit national and international NGOs to make oral submissions before the Committee, to supplement their written reports.

6. Some Committees also invite members of the specialised agencies of the UN to make their observations.

7. The Committee will then make its concluding observations on the government report. These observations contain an assessment of the progress made in implementing the Treaty, the major problem areas and recommendations on the steps it considers the government should take. The Concluding Observations provide a lobbying tool for NGOs at the national level. Occasionally the Committee may request the government to provide additional information or a further report.

complaints from individuals alleging a violation of rights in the treaty. States would need to accept the competence of the committee in this respect before individual complaints are admitted. The ICESCR and the CRC do not provide for an individual complaints procedure. Before submitting a complaint to the treaty body the individual should have tried to obtain redress domestically. This is sometimes referred to as the principle of 'exhausting local remedies'. However, where domestic remedies are ineffective or are unduly prolonged, this rule would not apply. A treaty body is unlikely to consider the complaint where it is being considered by some other international process. In the case of CEDAW others may petition on behalf of the victim. The individual complaints procedure has the potential to provide redress to the individual where the state concerned accepts the finding of the treaty body. However, like domestic human rights litigation it may also result to changes to law and policy. Further, the jurisprudence of the treaty body may begin to establish standards and benchmarks with regard to the rights that have been considered. A common criticism of the process is that it takes too long and offers little redress to the individual concerned.

The UN Commission on Human Rights is the UN's primary body for the promotion and protection of human rights. The Commission has played a significant role in the drafting and the adoption of international standards on human rights in a number of areas. However, unlike the Treaty Bodies the Commission is a political body and many of its decisions are the result of political compromises.

The Commission meets at least once year in Geneva and has set up a number of thematic and special mechanisms. These 'Special Procedures' are of two types: country-specific procedures which are set up to examine, monitor and report on the human rights situation in a specific country or territory and thematic procedures which are set up to examine, monitor and report on specific types of human rights violations. These special procedures consist of 'working groups', 'special rapporteurs', 'special representatives' or other 'experts'. Most special procedures rely on country visits and many pay particular attention to individual or systemic violations. A few of the procedures like the Special Representative on Internally Displaced Persons and the Rapporteur on Violence against Women (See: **VIOLENCE AGAINST WOMEN IN WAR TIME** and **VIOLENCE AGAINST WOMEN: DOMESTIC VIOLENCE**) have also tried to develop an international normative framework. The Commission also resorts to the confidential 1503 Procedure to address widespread violations.

mendations contained in the Platform of Action adopted at Beijing. NGOs are allowed to lobby the CSW at its annual sessions and time is set apart specifically for this. The Commission was closely involved in drafting the Optional Protocol to CEDAW.

There are several other mechanisms, for example the Inspection Panel of the World Bank and the Compliance Review Panel of the Asian Development Bank (ADB). The Inspection Panel of the World Bank and the Compliance Review Panel of the ADB provide a unique opportunity for people affected by any of the banks' projects to complain about the operations of the bank. The panelsare, however, only advisory bodies and the decisions are not binding on the bank.

The ILO has been one of the most active international organisations in the area of human rights, adopting over 150 Conventions and Recommendations on issues pertaining to the 'right to work' and the 'rights at work'. The organisation's structure and process of work is based on the tripartite involvement of trade unions, employers' organisations and member states.

The **INTERNATIONAL CRIMINAL COURT** was established to try what the global community considered were the most serious international crimes, namely crimes against humanity, war crimes and genocide. It is the first time that the global community has set up a court with power to enforce sanctions although the court will try only those individuals whom national systems are unwilling or unable to prosecute.

The UN has also been involved in setting up two ad hoc tribunals, one for Rwanda, and the other for the former Yugoslavia, and the Special Court for Sierra Leone. Although these tribunals and the court deal with country-specific situations, their jurisprudence has an impact that goes beyond those particular societies (See: **INTERNATIONAL CRIMINAL LAW AND THE REGIONAL TRIBUNALS**).

The World Trade Organisation came into existence in 1995 and was established to regulate the rules of international trade. It is not a human rights organisation per se but many of its agreements and decisions have implications for a number of human rights.

The Sub-Commission on the Promotion and Protection of Human Rights is the main subsidiary body of the Commission on Human Rights. It was previously known as the Sub-Commission on the Prevention of Discrimination and Protection of Minorities (See: **MINORITY RIGHTS**). The Sub-Commission has a number of working groups and thematic mechanisms which study and make recommendations with regard to a variety of human rights issues.

The Commission on the Status of Women (CSW) was established in 1947. After the Beijing Conference on Women, the General Assembly asked it to follow up on the recom-

Further Reading

Alston, P. and Crawford, J. (EDS) (2000) *The Future of UN Human Rights Treaty Monitoring*, Cambridge: CUP.

Alston, P. and Megret, F. (eds) (2005) *The United Nations and Human Rights: A Critical Appraisal*, 2nd edition OUP Oxford.

Bayefsky, A. (ed.) (2000) *The UN Human Rights System in the 21st Century*, The Hague: Kluwer.

Robinson, M. (2003) 'From Rhetoric to Reality: Making Human Rights Work', *European Human Rights Law Review* pp. 1–8.

Symonides, J. (ed) (2003) *Human Rights: International Protection, Monitoring and Enforcement*, Ashgate, Aldershot.

Contributor: Mario Gomez

NATIONAL INSTITUTIONS ON HUMAN RIGHTS

'We, the peoples of the united nations ...' So starts the Charter of the **UNITED NATIONS** on which so many international human rights instruments are based. 'The States Parties to the present Covenant ... considering the obligation of States under the Charter of the United Nations to promote universal respect for, and observance of, human rights and freedoms ... agree ...' in the words of the preamble to the **INTERNATIONAL COVENANT ON ECONOMIC, SOCIAL AND CULTURAL RIGHTS** and that on **CIVIL AND POLITICAL RIGHTS**.

Every subsequent international and indeed regional human rights instrument has been agreed in the name of states. The obligations in the treaties are undertaken by the states themselves, not the international community, thus responsibility for realising international human rights is a matter primarily within the competence of states. While the last 60 years have witnessed an enormous expansion of international human rights, issues relating to implementation and enforcement remain unresolved. There are those who

> **Non-dualist state**
> States can be either monist or dualist in their approach to international and regional law. Monist states believe in one system of law, comprising international, regional and national. All relevant laws are applied within that state and often there is a hierarchy of law ascending the global order. Dualist states believe in a two-tier legal system: national law and the rest. For any international measure to enter the national system, special legislative measures are required.

argue that the international community appears impotent in the face of gross and systematic human rights abuses even though (or maybe because) primary responsibility for promoting and enforcing human rights lies with the states. Undoubtedly success has been enjoyed by the treaty monitoring bodies, the regional courts and commissions and even non-governmental organisations in forcing changes to state policy. However, somehow, somewhere, the system is still faltering. Universal human rights are not yet a reality. With the passing years, attention has thus focused on additional ways to give effect to norms of human rights. Regional systems have provided some remarkable successes (notably the high compliance level in Europe for judgments of the **EUROPEAN COURT OF HUMAN RIGHTS**). It is perhaps logical that attention has thus turned to the primary obligees under international human rights instruments (the states themselves) and mechanisms by which national institutions can protect and promote human rights.

National human rights institutions are viewed favourably by the United Nations. Shortly after the establishment of the organisation, in 1946, the Economic and Social Council expressed support for local (national) human rights bodies to support the work of the Commission on Human Rights. Further developments followed a number of United Nations workshops and meetings over the next four decades. During this period, guidelines as to the functioning of human rights institutions were drafted and a number of national bodies were established. Progress culminated in a 1991 workshop held in Paris which aimed at discussing mechanisms for increasing the effectiveness of national human rights bodies. Many national institutions participated in the sessions. The result, the Paris Principles relating to the status and functioning of national institutions for protection and promotion of human rights, remain the blueprint today (approved by the General Assembly – UN Doc. A/RES/48/134, 20 December 1993). These principles (discussed in brief below) include the composition, functions and nature of national institutions whether basic advisory bodies or those with quasi-judicial functions.

In 2002, the Secretary General, Kofi Annan, emphasised the need for the United Nations to assist and support states wishing to create national human rights institutions. This was, he opined 'what in the long run will ensure that human rights are protected and advanced in a sustained manner' (UN Doc A/57/387). Few can argue with the fact that human rights are most successfully enforced at a national/local level. There the power exists to change laws and policies. International and regional bodies have rarely claimed to exercise anything more than a supervisory function. Real power to affect human rights standards remains with the states.

The **OFFICE OF THE HIGH COMMISSIONER FOR HUMAN RIGHTS** supports the sharing of good practice among states in furtherance of the development of national human rights institutions. It also promotes the development of regional networks for the same purpose. A National Institutions Unit is located within the Capacity Building and Field Operations Branch of the OHCHR in Geneva. Elsewhere at the international level, national institutions may be accredited for participation in the sessions of the Commission on Human Rights and a National Human Rights Institutions Forum was established for researchers and practitioners in the field of national human rights institutions.

At a regional level too, there is growing support for national institutions. While many of these support the existing regional systems (for example in Europe and Africa) others are in regions without such mechanisms. In Asia, the Asia Pacific Forum of National Human Rights Institutions represents significant progress towards the creation of national insti-

tutions within the region and the awareness, more generally, of human rights (See: **THE ASIAN REGIONAL HUMAN RIGHTS SYSTEM**). The **COUNCIL OF EUROPE** has hosted a number of round table meetings of national human rights institutions and ombudspersons in that region while the third General Assembly of the Network of National Institutions of the Americas met in Buenos Aires in June 2004.

There are many examples of national human rights institutions ranging from government advisory committees to quasi-judicial and fully independent bodies constantly reviewing state practice. Titles and functions vary from state to state. Some are independent while others are linked to the government in power or the primary legislative body (although the Paris Principles specify that their composition should be pluralistic, any government participation should be advisory only and funding mechanisms should ensure independence from government – principle B1). For example, within Europe, many states have created national entities empowered to ensure compliance with the European Convention standards. Similarly many emerging democracies hail the establishment of a national human rights institution as evidence of **DEMOCRACY** and respect for the rule of law. This is especially evident in countries with a chequered history of human rights and those striving to emerge from the shadow of human rights abuses. Within the **ORGANISATION FOR SECURITY AND COOPERATION IN EUROPE**, national human rights institutions are recognised as having a role to play in furthering democracy and the rule of law throughout the region. Additionally, the creation of a national human rights body may contribute to the truth and reconciliation process as the experience of South Africa demonstrates (See: **TRUTH COMMISSIONS**).

The Paris Principles specify that a national institution shall be vested with competence to protect and promote human rights and shall be given as broad a mandate as possible (embedded in law) (Principles A1 and 2). Among the responsibilities of national institutions are 'to submit to the government, parliament and any other competent body, on an advisory basis ... opinions, recommendation, proposals and reports on any matters concerning the protection and promotion of human rights' (Principle A3(a)). The areas covered by this include violations of human rights, legislative and administrative provisions and even foreign policy. National institutions also have the responsibility for promoting human rights standards and ensuring national legislation is harmonised therewith, encouraging ratification of the international human rights instruments, contributing towards state reports to treaty monitoring bodies, cooperating with UN and regional human rights agencies, formulating programmes for teaching human rights in schools and universities and publicising human rights and the need to combat all forms of **DISCRIMINATION** (Principle A3). Not all national human rights institutions have jurisdiction to receive complaints. Irrespective of that, their establishment should raise awareness of human rights, thereby promoting the protection of human rights.

A brief description of some examples of different bodies which meet some or all of the criteria for National Institutions as specified in the Paris Principles follows.

In Norway, the first Children's Commissioner was appointed in 1981. Commissioners (or ombudspersons) as a concept originated in Scandinavia in the 19th century. The Children's Commissioner is Norway's sixth such body. It provides a focus for **CHILDREN'S RIGHTS** and can exert influence directly with those involved in the law-making process. It is often cited as a model in other countries considering establishing children's commissioners in furtherance of their obligations under the UN **CONVENTION ON THE RIGHTS OF THE CHILD**.

In Brazil, regional attorneys/public prosecutors are appointed to oversee the rights of certain groups. For example, litigation on behalf of the rights of **INDIGENOUS PEOPLES** is often instigated by publicly funded prosecutors. These people are partly funded by the state but obviously must remain independent thereof when instituting actions against the state or state-affiliated organisations.

In Northern Ireland, the role of Human Rights Commissioner was created in the wake of the establishment of a Northern Irish Assembly with quasi-legislative functions. Professor Brice Dickson is the full-time Chief Commissioner at the time of writing. He is assisted by eight part-time Commissioners. The Commission's role is to promote awareness of human rights, review law and practice and advise the legislative bodies. The Commission can also conduct investigations and assist with court proceedings within its area of competence. Although the UK devolution agreements (Scotland, Wales and Northern Ireland) enabled the establishment of regional commissioners, there is no equivalent body for the United Kingdom as a whole. However, a Joint House of Lords and House of Commons Parliamentary Select Committee (comprised of members of the legislature) considers human rights issues and has sought to influence government policy and publicise relevant issues.

In the United States of America the Supreme Court is guardian of the Bill of Rights. As a corollary to its appellate functions, it acts as a barometer on conformity with the national human rights standards. Similar constitutional courts operate in many jurisdictions. The principal problem with such a model is that international human rights standards may not be considered and little is done to promote them and raise awareness thereof. The United States Commission on Civil Rights, in contrast, reports to Congress and the President on issues of Civil Rights in accordance with its statutory powers (Civil Rights Act 1957).

Australia, like many States, combines human rights with non-discrimination in the Australian Human Rights and Equal Opportunities Commission which is an independent statutory body established in 1986. Interestingly, human rights education is one of the areas of responsibility of the Commission. Under the President of the Commission, portfolios of responsibility are divided among a number of commissioners, including one for human rights. A separate commissioner deals with indigenous rights.

Canada has provincial and federal institutions with responsibility for human rights. Ontario established the first Human Rights Commission at a local level. This was followed more than 30 years later by the Canadian Commission which operates at the federal level. Initially the provincial bodies were concerned with promoting anti-discrimination laws though their remit is now significantly broader.

An ideal national human rights institution would have the power to monitor national legislation, prompting changes as necessary to comply with emerging international and regional norms. Moreover, there should be a mechanism by which individuals and groups could complain about violations of human rights. Ultimately for as long as international law remains in its current consensual form, full realisation of international human rights standards is dependent on the actions of states. It is the states themselves which created the current regime of international human rights, so as an act of good faith they should surely take all necessary steps to conform to their obligations thereunder. Establishing effective national institutions, as many have done, is clearly a positive development. Expanding the network of national institutions across the globe should ensure that the political rhetoric of international human rights becomes a tangible reality for the intended beneficiaries.

WEBSITES

www.nhri.net – United Nations Forum for National Human Rights Institutions
www.chrc-ccdp.ca – Canadian Human Rights Commission
www.ohrc.on.ca – Ontario Human Rights Commission, Canada
www.hreoc.gov.au – Australian Human Rights and Equal Opportunities Commission
www.nihrc.org – Northern Ireland Human Rights Commission
www.usccr.gov – United States Commission on Civil Rights

Further Reading

Australian Human Rights Centre (2000) 'National Human Rights Institutions: an overview of the Asia-Pacific region', 7 *International Journal on Minority and Group Rights*, pp. 207–277.

Dickson, Brice (2003) 'The contribution of human rights commissions to the protection of human rights' *Public Law*, pp. 272–285.

Marie, Jean-Bernard (2003) 'National Systems for the Protection of Human Rights' in Symonides, J. (ed.), *Human Rights: International Protection, Monitoring, Enforcement*, Aldershot: Ashgate/UNESCO, pp. 257–80.

Klevan, Olivia (ed.) (1999) 'Human Dimension Seminar: On Ombuds and National Human Rights Protection Institutions' (Warsaw, 25–28 May 1998) (Papers in the Theory & Practice of Human Rights), Essex: University of Essex Human Rights Centre.

United Nations (1995) *National Human Rights Institutions: a Handbook on the Establishment and Strengthening of National Institutions for the Promotion and Protection of Human Rights* (Professional Training Series: 4), Geneva.

Contributor: Rhona K.M. Smith

NEEDS AND HUMAN RIGHTS

The ideas of human rights and basic human needs are closely connected. Human rights – rights that apply for every person because they are a human – can be seen as rights to the fulfilment of, or ability to fulfil, basic human needs. These needs provide the grounding for human rights. 'Behind human rights are freedoms and needs so fundamental that their denial puts human dignity itself at risk' (Goldewijk and Fortman, 1999: 117). Basic human needs are whatever people require to be able to achieve a level of functioning that satisfies a given ethical conception of the acceptable minimum. Such conceptions include, for example, human dignity or the avoidance of serious harm. The needs implied by these conceptions typically include, in particular, basic levels of physical and mental health.

Galtung refines this picture in many ways. Not all needs correspond to rights and not all rights correspond to needs. But a central set of human rights rest on basic needs. He warns that the traditional human rights approach connects better to survival needs and freedom needs, 'needs that are more clearly threatened by deliberate acts of 'evil' actors', and for which we can more readily state norms in s that imply duties by specific ~~st~~, various other needs 'are ~~ed~~ed by 'wrong' structures' ~~69~~). Here a post-traditional ~~approach is required~~: 'needs rather than rights direct us to look for causal factors rather than evil actors' (ibid, 55).

The concept of human rights forms in turn an essential partner to the discourse of basic needs. It provides an insistence on the value of each person and a strong language of prioritisation. These focus our attention and energies: 'in adverse environments, the primary meaning of human rights is to make people aware of what is basically wrong' (Goldewijk and Fortman 1999: 117). And when widely acknowledged as norms or legally recognised as instruments, rights form a major set of tools, legitimate claims, in the political struggles for fulfilment of needs.

Consider the example of the international debt of low-income countries. By the late 1990s many very poor countries paid more in debt service, largely to rich countries, than they spent on education or health. Typically their **EDUCATION** and **HEALTH** budgets had been cut at the insistence of international financial organisations after the countries had failed to service their debts following rises in oil prices and interest rates and other shocks. Sacrifice of the basic needs, the health and prospects, of millions of people in order to service debts to, directly or indirectly, far richer groups became unsurprising and normal in the 1980s and 1990s. 'Jubilee 2000' campaigners for debt relief achieved significant impact by showing how such cuts contravened the **UNIVERSAL DECLARATION OF HUMAN RIGHTS** endorsed by nearly all governments, including the debt collectors. The Universal Declaration of Human Rights prioritises access to education and health care. In welfare states, when a family goes bankrupt no child is expected to lose access to basic education and health care in order for debts to first be repaid. This principle should apply for people everywhere.

A connection between conceptions of needs and human rights has long been proposed, but has not been adopted as a standard formulation. One still encounters social science dictionaries in which adjacent entries on human needs and human rights contain no reference to each other's language. The two ideas have been primarily located in different disciplines and fora: rights more in the worlds of law and social movements, needs more within social and economic policy and planning. Added to this have been confusions around needs discourse, attacks on it by many libertarians and free-market advocates, and antagonism by some socialists and economists to rights formulations. In the past 20 years these obstacles have diminished and the fundamental connection of the two bodies of thought has become more evident in work by, for example, Galtung, Gewirth and Waldron, without gainsaying the inevitable fuzziness in such concepts.

Rights are justified claims to the protection of persons' important interests, argues Gewirth. Such 'claim-rights' have this structure: person/subject A has a right to object X against duty-bearer B by virtue of ground Y. For 'human rights' the proposed ground is that the objects X are requisites for being human in a morally acceptable sense. According to Gewirth they are 'the goods that are necessary for human action or for having general chances of success in achieving one's purposes by action'. Henry Shue refers similarly to 'basic rights', those which are necessary to enjoy all other rights. In normative needs discourse, they are basic needs.

The concept of need arises in three importantly different modes. First, 'needs' in explanatory theory are powerful underlying motives or drives. Second, needs in normative theory are justified priorities based on a 'relational formula': person A needs object X (or an equivalent 'satisfier') in order (reason Y) to do or attain goal G which is a high priority in the relevant political community. Third, instrumental needs are the requisites (X) for G. Whether, in particular cases, object X brings fulfilment of a drive or motive is a matter for positive investigation. Whether object X really is required for achieving G is an instrumental issue for examination. Whether G is or should be a high priority is a matter for normative debate and political process.

Normative needs discourse thus has the same structure as claim-rights discourse. This can be obscured by failure to distinguish the three modes and also different levels in chains of instrumental and normative relations (Gasper, 2004). Amartya Sen's categories of capability and functioning help us to discuss levels more clearly (See: **THE CAPABILITY APPROACH AND HUMAN RIGHTS**). Martha Nussbaum's *Women and Human Development* (2000) proposes that many human rights are best seen as rights to basic needs seen in turn as basic capabilities to function. She argues that capabilities language has an advantage in not being felt as eurocentric, but that rights language provides force and conveys respect for persons; and that using these languages together highlights respect for persons as choosers.

Sen holds further, in *Development as Freedom* (1999), that political rights are important for not only the promotion and defence of need fulfilment but also for the processes of specifying needs. It is not true that needs discourse inherently presumes that persons are passive and materialistic and ignores them as active rights-claiming choice-making agents. **AUTONOMY** of agency stands as the central principle in the prominent normative needs theory of Len Doyal and Ian Gough (1991).

The table uses the structure of their theory to compare ethics of capabilities, basic needs and human rights. As argued by Penz, the three are closely connected and complementary, not competitive.

Galtung warns that institutionalisation of human rights as a means towards fulfilling needs can become ineffective or counterproductive, due to the internal logics of the institutions involved. From recent South African experience, Hamilton (2003) holds that rights language bears too much the imprint of property rights and ties fulfilment of priority human needs to the ability to expensively access a remote judicial system. That system takes existing property rights as the default case; claims against them must be demonstrated beyond reasonable doubt. Basic needs of the majority can in practice become downgraded by being stated in the same rights language as that of established propertyholding, he argues. But they can be downgraded by not using rights language too. And a needs-rights conception can also influence and structure patterns of public provision, access and claiming in ways other than via the judicial system.

Comparing capabilities, needs and human rights

	Basic Criterion	Requirements in order to fulfil the basic criterion (Needs level 1)	Required satisfier characteristics (Needs level 2)	Specific required satisfiers (Needs level 3)	Required preconditions (Needs level 4)
In the categories of the capability approach and UNDP's Human Development	Priority functionings	Capabilities that are required to achieve the priority functioning	'Characteristics' of goods that are required to achieve those capabilities	The goods/ 'commodities' that are required to provide those characteristics	The societal conditions that are required to sustain the supply of those goods
Doyal & Gough's main formulation of human need	Avoidance of serious harm	Health; autonomy of agency	Nourishment; housing; security in environment, work and childhood; health care, education, etc.	Vary according to geographical, socio-economic and cultural setting	Conditions concerning production reproduction cultural transmission, and political authority
From Goldewijk & Fortman's formulation of human rights	Dignity/non-humiliation, self-respect	Equality and freedom; or equality and agency	Implications of Needs level 1 in this row	Implications of Needs level 2 in this row	

Further Reading

Doyal, Len and Gough, Ian (1991) *A Theory of Human Need*, Basingstoke: Macmillan.

Galtung, J. (1994) *Human Rights in Another Key*, Cambridge: Polity.

Gasper, D. (2004) *The Ethics of Development*, Edinburgh: Edinburgh University Press.

Goldewijk, B.K. and Fortman, B. de Gaay (1999) *Where Needs Meet Rights*, Geneva: WCC Publications.

Hamilton, L. (2003) *The Political Philosophy of Needs*, Cambridge: Cambridge University Press.

Nussbaum, Martha (2000) *Women and Human Development*, Cambridge: Cambridge University Press.

Penz, P. (1991) 'The Priority of Basic Needs', pp. 35–73 in Aman, K. (ed.) *Ethical Principles for Development: Needs, Capacities or Rights*, Upper Montclair, NJ: Montclair State University.

Sen, Amartya (1999) *Development as Freedom*, Oxford: Oxford University Press.

Contributor: Des Gasper

NEPAD (NEW PARTNERSHIP FOR AFRICA'S DEVELOPMENT) AND HUMAN RIGHTS

The New Partnership for Africa's Development (NEPAD) is a policy and programme framework established by member states of the African Union (AU) to orient and implement Africa's development agenda. Not an autonomous organisation and with no inter-governmental institutions of its own, NEPAD can more appropriately be conceptualised as a blueprint or vehicle for the African Union to achieve its development objectives and increase its participation in international affairs on the basis of partnership and not through docile compliance or exploitation.

The relatively rapid evolution of NEPAD from concept to creation has created critics and supporters of the initiative. Critics argue that like revival programmes that have come before it, NEPAD was flawed in its concept and design. They condemn the fact that the programme relies heavily on a neo-liberal market economic framework which some argue is what hampers Africa's development, thereby making NEPAD a part of the problem rather than a solution. Heavy subsidisation of commodities by developed countries undermines Africa's ability to trade and create wealth. In addition, programmes that compel African governments to repay their debts instead of investing in health care and education only reinforce dependency and underdevelopment. In contrast, supporters view NEPAD as a means to begin redressing the disadvantages that Africa faces in the global arena by acting as a forum and framework where alternative strategies can be deliberated and where localised solutions can be implemented.

NEPAD offers a broad outline for the promotion of human rights. However it is not specific about how concrete initiatives will be implemented or supported, thereby giving scope to further elaborate on the provisions for human rights protection within NEPAD, particularly with reference to ECONOMIC RIGHTS, SOCIAL RIGHTS, WOMEN'S RIGHTS, CULTURAL RIGHTS and ENVIRONMENTAL RIGHTs.

However, NEPAD does recognise that poor political leadership characterised by human rights violations, economic mismanagement as well as local and foreign corruption are additional causes of Africa's current condition. To remedy this, NEPAD further acknowledges that establishing and ensuring the rule of law is a key aspect of enhancing the African Union's capacity to monitor and promote human rights. Article 30 of The Constitutive Act of the Union states that 'governments which shall come to power through unconstitutional means shall not be allowed to participate in the activities of the Union'. This places an emphasis on constitutional government and the protection of DEMOCRACY AND HUMAN RIGHTS.

At the African Union's Assembly held in Durban in 2002, the Declaration on the Implementation of NEPAD which was adopted included a more specific Declaration on Democracy, Political, Economic and Corporate Governance that established the African Peer Review Mechanism. Member states are invited to voluntarily join the African Peer Review Mechanism for the purpose of participating in a self-monitoring programme with a clear time frame to achieve certain standards for promoting inclusive governance, participatory democracy and human rights promotion through constitutional governments.

Due to entrenched patterns of behaviour, Africa continues to be afflicted by bad leadership and economic mismanagement which result in ongoing conflicts and failing development initiatives. Beyond a doubt, resources diverted from fighting these wars could be used to promote human rights. There is a case for the dissemination of the programmes that NEPAD proposes to the African people and civil society should have a role in documenting and monitoring the progress that governments are making.

NEPAD's success in the promotion of human rights will be measured by some key indicators. In addition to the promotion of the rule of law, an indicator of NEPAD's impact on the promotion of human rights will rely on its success in protecting Africa's war-affected regions from predatory global economic forces. In particular, some multinational organisations are fuelling violent conflicts leading to human rights atrocities by supporting the illicit trade in diamonds, oil and timber with governments whose legitimacy is being challenged by sub-national groups. This is witnessed in the Democratic Republic of the Congo, the Sudan and historically in Sierra Leone, Liberia and Angola. Linked to this issue of capital flight, NEPAD should mobilise international partners to ensure that the wealth generated by Africa's natural resources is not stored away in private banks for the benefit of the few, but instead used to finance the development of viable health care, education and other economic projects in Africa. Related to this is the issue of debt cancellation which would also release funds being paid as interest on debt which could instead be used for governance, human rights and developmental projects.

An indicator of NEPAD's impact will also be the extent to which it can promote and enhance the **LABOUR RIGHTS** of the African working population. Under the current political trends and economic neo-liberal doctrine, capital can flow freely across borders but labour cannot. This places African citizens at a distinct disadvantage as capital can be siphoned out of the continent by business enterprises after exploiting the local commodities and markets. However, highly restrictive immigration laws prohibit skilled Africans from travelling to other parts of the world for employment to repatriate capital back to assist in the development of their continent.

At the time of writing the programme of action for implementing NEPAD is still evolving. There are additional issues that NEPAD needs to address including how the rights of sub-national **MINORITIES** can be protected to ensure that they do not resort to violence. The NEPAD initiative should also promote the Protocol of the African Charter on Human Rights and People's Rights, ratified on 25 January 2004, marking the creation of an African Human Rights Court. The NEPAD initiative has to deepen its collaboration with the United Nations Commission on Human Rights and civil society organisations. Some of these initiatives may include the establishment of an African Union Commissioner or Special Representative on Human Rights with a mandate to highlight human rights violations within member states and generally oversee the mainstreaming of human rights promotion across the continent.

WEBSITE

www.nepad.org

Further Reading

Bond, Patrick (ed.) (2002) *Fanon's Warning: A Civil Society Reader on the New Partnership for Africa's Development*, Trenton, NJ: AIDC.

Chabal, Patrick (2002) 'The Quest for Good Governance and Development in Africa: Is NEPAD the Answer?' in *International Affairs*, vol. 78, no. 3 (July), pp. 447–62.

De Waal, Alex (2002) 'What's New in the New Partnership for Africa's Development?' in *International Affairs*, vol. 78, no. 3 (July).

Odinkalu, Chidi Anselem (2003) 'Back to the Future: The Imperative of Prioritizing for the Protection of Human Rights in Africa', in *Journal of African Law*, 47, pp. 1–37.

Organization for African Unity (OAU precursor to the African Union) (2001) 'New Economic Partnership for Africa', July.

Contributor: Timothy Murithi

NON-GOVERNMENTAL ORGANISATIONS IN HUMAN RIGHTS PROTECTION, THE ROLE OF

In 1914, there were 1083 non-governmental organisations (NGOs) and no firm conception of universal human rights affirmed by the international community, such as it was. Now the estimated number of NGOs stands at between 37,000 and 50,000 according to the UNDP Human Development Reports and the OECD Directory of NGOs. Though contested, there are now firm conceptions of human rights as well as emerging humanitarian norms. Many NGOs were formed in the 1990s as a response to the broad requirements of this synthesis of peacebuilding, humanitarianism, human rights monitoring and advocacy. Most NGOs operate on specific issues or bridge several aspects of these areas. The most familiar NGOs working on human rights include the International Crisis Group, Amnesty International and Human Rights Watch. It is in the realms of human rights that NGOs have made what is perhaps their most important contribution.

The definition of NGOs, our understanding of their roles and the contexts of **GLOBALISATION**, global governance and **GLOBAL CIVIL SOCIETY** in which NGOs exist and operate are heavily contested. The general thrust of the currently fashionable argument is that NGOs operate in, and contribute to, the construction and facilitation of global governance and globalisation in transnational networks to advocate liberal reform (Keck & Sikkind, 1998: ix). This assertion is, of course, rather problematic given the fact that all of these concepts are contested and there is little agreement even on the nature of NGOs.

Scholars have offered various NGO typologies. Perhaps the clearest is Weiss and Gordenker's typology. This includes orthodox NGOs which are private citizens' organisations, active on social issues, not profit making, and with transnational scope. Another type is the 'quango' which is a 'quasi-non-governmental organisation' such as the Nordic, Canadian and some US NGOs, as well as the International Committee of the Red Cross (ICRC), with relative autonomy which generally decreases as reliance on government funding increases. Quangos include government contractors providing expert services (for example, the International Rescue Committee). Thirdly, DONGOs are donor-created NGOs for particular purposes, such as development and humanitarian emergencies (Weiss and Gordenker, 1996). NGO functions include documentation, lobbying, dissemination and political activism in analysing effects on human rights.

Most NGOs work in global, regional and local networks of seemingly ever-increasing density and pro-activeness. Independently or as part of a networked consortium of NGOs, they channel information, advocacy and other resources to nodal points of identifiable need. This might involve lobbying political or economic institutions, advocating changes in, and reform of, or monitoring norms and practices within institutions like the World Bank or in conflict or crisis zones, or transferring humanitarian resources into conflict zones. In particular, there is an emerging consensus that NGO efforts need to be owned by the local civil society to be effective. NGOs do not just work with a narrow, legalistic conception of human rights but have the capacity to operate in the context of a broad range of **ECONOMIC, SOCIAL** and **CULTURAL RIGHTS**, as was made clear at the 1993 UN Conference on Human Rights in Vienna (Asia Cultural Forum on Development, 1993). Many NGOs have tended to be issue-oriented but increasingly connections are being made between NGOs operating on different issues and also between operation and advocacy NGOs (van Tuijl, 1999: 439).

The antecedents of NGO human rights capacity began to emerge in the 19th century as in association with the creation of the ICRC, the ending of the slave trade, voting rights for women, international law and disarmament discourses, and many other activities organised by non-state actors aimed political, social and economic reform. Such actors soon began to proliferate: the International Rescue Committee began its life rescuing Jews from Europe during the Second World War, and was later to be involved with retrieving Hungarian refugees after the failure of the 1956 rebellion and Cuban refugees after Fidel Castro came to power in Cuba in 1959; other such organisations followed, including the Catholic Relief Service, World Vision and the Oxford

NGOs
A number of NGOs are active in international human rights. Among the most famous are Amnesty International, Survival, Article 19, Anti-Slavery Organisation, Save the Children and Greenpeace.

Committee for Famine Relief (OXFAM).

NGOs played an important role in highlighting the need for human rights to be included in the UN Charter at San Francisco in 1945 and have consistently worked to develop the UN Human Rights System. NGOs provided useful input into the drafting of the UNIVERSAL DECLARATION OF HUMAN RIGHTS (Korey, 2001). They have also been key actors in the creation of different UN treaties and convention spanning issues from the elimination of discrimination against women (1979) to the rights of children (1989) (See: WOMEN'S RIGHTS; CHILDREN'S RIGHTS). They have also played important roles in many other human rights-related UN working groups, as well as in the creation of the position of the UN High Commission for Human Rights. In the UN system their roles have fallen into three main guises: setting standards, monitoring and implementation (van Tuijl, 1999: 495). NGOs have also been able to introduce human rights mechanisms into other international organisations such as the World Bank and its Inspection Panel, which was introduced in 1993 to examine the impact of the organisations policies on human rights. International NGOs are important in bringing to light abuses by states and advocating change in their practices, and local NGOs are often crucial in re-establishing human rights in conflict and crisis zones.

What is clear is that in the realm of human rights, observation, monitoring and enforcement (which in the Westphalian international system is generally left to host states), NGOs have the ability, capacity, access and resources to work with or even to bypass host states and take on board such tasks themselves. Sometimes this is in a role which directly addresses human rights abuses or provides monitoring, or it is as a 'norm entrepreneur' in which NGOs are instrumental in bringing about the social, political and economic changes necessary to enhance human rights.

Many of these organisations have also added the contemporary mantras of development to their repertoire of human rights and humanitarian assistance (Duffield, 2002, 16), incorporating what has become known as 'human security' into policy and intellectual debates. Centred around the UN project of the creation of the 'liberal peace' (Duffield, 2002: 11) human security was formalised in policy terms in the UNDP Report of 1994 (UNDP, Human Development Report: 3) in which individuals and their security needs (security from fear and want) became the referents of security rather than the state. The human rights discourse and the role of NGOs were key to this development. Furthermore, a connection has now developed between human rights, humanitarianism and associated forms of intervention, military and non-military (See: HUMANITARIAN INTERVENTION). This has partly been because of experiences in multiple contexts – from the Middle East after and since the declaration of the state of Israel in 1948, in the attempted secession of Biafra during the Nigerian Civil War 1967–70, to the first Gulf War. This has raised the question of whether NGOs operate on a 'rights' or a 'NEEDS' basis (Chandler, 2002) distinguishing between victim and aggressor or simply assisting where it is required regardless of this issue. A further strengthening of these regimes occurred during the first Gulf War when UN Security Council resolution 688 of 5th April 1991 allowed NGO intervention to take precedence over state sovereignty (in this case, of Iraq) to deal with human rights issues, among others.

In this sense advocacy movements, epistemic communities, non-states actors, NGOs and humanitarian actors are what Wallace and Josselin have described as 'norm entrepreneurs' which privilege DEMOCRACY, human rights and forms of DEVELOPMENT in their micro-level interventions as well as in their discourse in the realm of international relations (Josselin and Wallace, 2001: 253). In this context the UN Economic and Social Council (ECOSOC) has played an important role because under Article 71 of the UN Charter it is empowered to consult with NGOs on issues within its remit, as well as on issues relating to refugees, the environment and development.

NGOs have been particularly valuable

vis-à-vis human rights because they are not necessarily bound by the norm of non-intervention, are not sovereign actors and operate in a private, non-official capacity. (Of course, given their financial relationships with donor states and international organisations, one might qualify this status as pseudo-private/non-official.) In the realm of human rights they have the capacity to monitor abuses and to publicise them, to advocate action to be taken, to take action themselves to build compliance with international law and norms and to build the necessary institutions to combat further abuses. They have been instrumental in the construction of international human rights law and regimes, humanitarian law, advocating further development and overseeing compliance. Without the presence of NGOs representing these capacities, it is unlikely that human rights regimes would be as prominent or as developed as they now are, nor would they be such a key part of the reconstruction of the liberal peace in failed states and conflict zones.

Further Reading

Asia Cultural Forum on Development (1993) *Our Voice: Bangkok NGO Declaration on Human Rights*, Bangkok: Asia Cultural Forum on Development.

Carey, Henry & Richmond, Oliver P. (2003) *Mitigating Conflict: The Role of NGOs*, London: Frank Cass.

Chandler, David (2002) *From Kosovo to Kabul*, London: Zed Books.

Duffield, Mark (2002) *Global Governance and the New Wars*, London: Zed Books.

Josselin, Daphne and Wallace, William (eds) (2001) *Non-State Actors in World Politics*, London: Palgrave.

Keck, Margeret E. and Sikkind, Kathryn (1998) *Activists Beyond Borders*, Ithaca: Cornell University Press.

Korey, William (2001) *NGOs and the Universal Declaration of Human Rights*, New York: Palgrave.

van Tuijl, Peter (1999) 'NGOs and human rights: sources of justice and democracy' in *Journal of International Affairs*, 52(2), 493–512.

Weiss, T.G. and Gordenker, L. (1996) 'Pluralizing Global Governance: Analytical Approaches and Dimensions', in Weiss, T.G. and Gordenker, L. (eds), *NGOs, the UN and Global Governance*, Boulder: Lynne Rienner, 20–21.

Contributor: Oliver P. Richmond

NORTH AMERICA: THE REALITY OF HUMAN RIGHTS

As descendants of peoples who occupied North America prior to European colonisation and settlement, the human rights of indigenous peoples are intricately related to land and authority over the territory itself. International human rights bodies such as the United Nations, the International Labour Organisation and the Organisation of American States (OAS) have all recognised both the primacy of indigenous peoples' relationships to land and their special status in states such as Canada and the US.

The UN defines indigenous peoples as original inhabitants of regions colonised or invaded by what became a dominant population. Their relationships with states are qualitatively different from other social groups such as minorities who have no human rights incumbent upon prior occupation. As indigenous peoples, American Indians in the US, Aboriginal peoples in Canada, Native Hawaiians and circumpolar Inuit are recognised as having historical and cultural continuity within particular territories, which are worthy of protection as human rights. For example, ILO Convention no. 169 and the Inter-American Commission on Human Rights (IACHR) of the OAS prescribe that governments take affirmative steps to consult and include indigenous peoples, as well as protect their cultures, and even assist them to regain stolen lands. In 1997, the UN

Committee monitoring the **CONVENTION ON THE ELIMINATION OF ALL FORMS OF RACIAL DISCRIMINATION** called upon states to protect the rights of indigenous peoples to own, develop, control and use their communal lands and resources. Moreover, inter-regional courts of human rights, such as the **INTER-AMERICAN COURT FOR HUMAN RIGHTS**, have drafted (or adopted) opinions and judgments supporting indigenous peoples' rights to their land and culture in North America.

Whether they be hunter-gatherers such as the Algonquian-speaking peoples of the Subarctic and Eastern woodlands or agriculturists such as the Pueblo Indians of the American south-west, land remains crucial to the ways of life of many indigenous peoples. Their relationships with the North American environment has provided them with sustenance, a complex cosmology and the core institutions of their societies. Despite some historical fluidity, autonomy within the physical environments of North America shaped their distinctiveness as peoples. The integrity of indigenous societies was affected by European colonisation and their viability became ever more precarious with the westward expansion of settlers, which brought their territories under foreign authority. This was solidified by the creation of the United States and the Dominion of Canada in 1776 and 1867, respectively.

The historical trajectory by which this state of affairs arose is pertinent to almost all of the human rights concerns that are being raised about the position of indigenous peoples today. Over several centuries under the Doctrine of Discovery, European powers broadly agreed among themselves that newly 'discovered' lands could only be claimed for the discoverer's monarch through negotiation with the inhabitants, who were deemed to be themselves sovereign. Indigenous consent then extinguished pre-existing sovereignty and later this became codified in colonial and the state law. In practice, however, indigenous land was appropriated through a number of legal and quasi-legal contrivances such as Royal charters, patents and fraudulently undertaken commercial transactions, which contradicted the policy of achieving consent. As late as 1898, the US simply annexed Hawaii by arrangement with Euro-American settlers

and entrepreneurs without any consent from Native Hawaiians.

However, the most influential extra-legal justifications for displacing indigenous peoples originated in Enlightenment philosophical premises and these later made their way into early international and state laws. As part of a general European perception of indigenous peoples as culturally inferior, John Locke's theory that agricultural production uniquely conveyed private property ownership was taken up by Emmerich de Vattel who made it a principle of international law in the 18th century. This legitimised the removal of indigenous hunting peoples by settler agriculturists across North America and meant that much of the European claim to the territories was based on *terra nullius*, the principle that the land was empty of people who had rights to own property. *Terra nullius* persisted until the 1990s in Canada as a justification for the confiscation of indigenous peoples' lands. Between the 1970s and the 1990s, in the Calder, Baker Lake and Delgammukw cases, the Supreme Court struck down Aboriginal rights appeals on the grounds that, although there was evidence of historical continuity, they did not constitute an 'organised society' at the time of European contact.

Alongside this tradition of treating indigenous people as if they have no rights is the contradictory idea that they constitute, at least to some degree, sovereign nations, and Canada and the US have adopted policies and practices that have always swung between the two. Following from the Doctrine of Discovery, under the Royal Proclamation of 1763, any land not ceded to the British Crown was 'reserved to them'. Even though settlers wilfully ignored this, further acquisition of such territory required written consent through treaties under the auspices of the Crown. Treaties effectively recognised pre-existing Aboriginal sovereignty and they became pivotal to Indian policy in both Canada and the US. The inherent rights of indigenous peoples were further bolstered by a series of decisions by Chief Justice John Marshall in the US Supreme Court in the 1830s. Indians still had 'a legal as well as a just claim to retain possession [of the land] and to use it according to their own discretion'. They were, in effect, 'domestic dependent nations,' who 'had always been considered distinct, independent political communities, retaining their original natural rights, as the undisputed possessors of the soil, from time immemorial'.

Unfortunately, the recognition of indigenous rights implicit in Marshall's ruling was largely ignored in the 19th century. Accompanying the rapid diminution of indigenous lands were sustained campaigns of military conquest, especially in the US, and forced assimilation through removal of native children to boarding schools. In the late 19th century, in another measure to break up the integrity of native societies, the Dawes Act required American Indians to be allotted to individual holdings on reservations under the Trusteeship of the US government. 'Surplus' Indian lands were sold off to settlers. Similarly, in Canada, 'reserves' were created under the Indian Act legislation. These reduced native land bases and **AUTONOMY** still further. Outside the areas affected by the Indian Act, the Canadian government authorised a number of coerced relocations of Northern nomadic peoples to crudely built villages. The relocations, which went on until the 1970s, were premised on perceived native cultural inferiority, but they also had the effect of opening up vast tracts of indigenous lands for natural resource extraction. Significantly, this land was often outside of the treaty areas and hence 'unextinguished', meaning that the land acquisitions were based on violations of inherent Aboriginal title rights. Predictably, the human consequences of such policies have been catastrophic, with Aboriginal peoples across Canada having some of the highest rates of suicide, alcoholism and solvent abuse in the world.

As a means of achieving unquestioned sovereignty over indigenous lands, Canada's 'land claims' treaties have been based on the assumption that it is the Aboriginal party which must 'claim' from the state and not the reverse. These policies require an exchange of a written agreement of extinguishment of Aboriginal title in exchange for cash compensation and specifically defined rights, including some measures of self-government within Canada. These procedures are heavily biased towards the state and developers. While negotiations are ongoing, Canada has unilaterally reduced several 'claim' areas by simply selling land under negotiation. In 1999, after much protest from Aboriginal peoples, the UN's

Human Rights Committee specifically condemned Canada for the practice of 'extinguishing' Aboriginal people's rights and described the situation of indigenous people as 'the most pressing issue facing Canadians'. In response, Canada amended its 'land claims' treaties so that 'extinguishment' is avoided, but in return the Aboriginal party must agree that the Treaty itself defines the totality of their rights and that they could not assert their rights granted from any previous treaties or from any violations of the Aboriginal title that may have occurred in the past. This is known as the non-assertion/fallback release policy and merely amounts to extinguishment by other means.

It was not until relatively recently that human rights concerns regarding indigenous peoples in the US reached the international arena. In the Dann case of 2003, the IACHR ruled in favour of the Western Shoshone that their rights to property in their ancestral homelands had been violated by the US government's seizure of land guaranteed by treaty in 1863. The land in question has been confiscated for open pit cyanide leach gold mining, military testing and just six months before the ruling, the US Congress authorised the use of Yucca mountain, sacred to the Western Shoshone, to entomb up to 77,000 tons of radioactive waste. The report of the IACHR recommends that the US remedy the situation either through legislation or by holding a hearing on title. Importantly, it recognised the collective rights of the Western Shoshone not to be deprived of their ancestral lands without consent and fair compensation. In other contemporary developments, the peoples of the Far North are highly susceptible to having their ways of life affected by the industrial activities to the south. In addition to noticeable climate changes in the Arctic, persistent organic pollutants such as dioxins and industrial toxins such as pesticides have shown up in the animals hunted by the Inuit and these carcinogens now threaten both the hunting activities and the health of the people. The Inuit of Alaska and Canada have filed suit at the IAHCR against the US government for its repudiation of the Kyoto protocol on global warming.

It is a matter of speculation as to how far international human rights can protect indigenous peoples from violations of their land and ways of life. The UN and the OAS

The Alaskan Native Settlement Claim Act 1971, won without racial violence, was the largest Indian settlement in history, giving Alaska's indigenous people clear title to 40 million acres (2 per cent of all land in the USA) and cash of $962.5 million. Had the Natives formed a single business entity, it would have numbered among the ten largest corporations in the country. The settlement paved the way for the trans-Alaskan pipeline.

(From Lael Morgan, Art and Eskimo Power, the life and times of Alaskan Howard Rock, Epicenter, Fairbanks 1988)

are both organisations of nation-states and many indigenous peoples believe their role is to legitimate the institution of the state itself. Most conventions, accords and international court rulings have to be not only ratified but also enforced by states. At present, little more than international embarrassment can be used as a sanction against a state violating the human rights of indigenous peoples. However, the UN Working Group on the Draft Declaration of the Rights of Indigenous Peoples has been producing a new international code, which would advocate self-determination and collective rights for indigenous peoples. Although states such as the US and Canada have already acknowledged collective rights and a measure of self-determination through various treaties and policies, they see the international recognition of such rights as a threat to their own sovereignty. Few indigenous peoples aspire to statehood, but some in the growing international movement of indigenous peoples wonder whether they could do any worse than states. If adopted, the new Draft Declaration will certainly call for major changes to Canadian and US policies towards indigenous peoples. Such an overhaul will be necessary if native North Americans are to avoid facing what many are now openly fearing – cultural extinction.

Further Reading

Asch, Michael (2000) 'First Nations and the Derivation of Canada's Underlying Title:

Comparing Perspectives on Legal Ideology,' in Cook, Curtis and Lindau, Juan D. (eds) *Aboriginal Rights and Self-Government: The Canadian and Mexican Experience in North American Perspective*, Montreal: McGill-Queen's University Press, 148–67.

Niezen, Ronald (2003) *The Origins of Indigenism: Human Rights and the Politics of Identity*, Berkeley: University of California Press.

Orkin, Andrew (2003) 'When the Law Breaks Down: Aboriginal Peoples in Canada and Governmental Defiance of the Rule of Law,' in *Osgoode Hall Law Journal*, 41, 2 and 3, 445–62.

Samson, Colin, Wilson, James and Mazower, Jonathan (1999) *Canada's Tibet: The Killing of the Innu*, London: Survival International.

Wilson, James (1998) *The Earth Shall Weep: A History of Native America*, London: Picador.

Contributor: Colin Samson

THE ORGANISATION FOR SECURITY AND COOPERATION IN EUROPE (OSCE) AND HUMAN RIGHTS

In the context of a book about human rights essentials, the Organisation for Security and Cooperation in Europe is an anomaly. This is for two main reasons. First, it has no human rights protection mechanisms and is not even directly concerned with the protection of individual human rights. Second, in contrast to the **UNITED NATIONS, COUNCIL OF EUROPE** or European Union, it has no treaties at its base. The 55 'participating states' are subject to no binding obligations.

It suffers from the further disadvantage that very few people have heard of it. Not for nothing has it been called the 'Organisation for Spreading Confusion in Europe'. And its most active organ has the most unfortunate acronym, at least in English – 'Oh Dear!', or more correctly, ODIHR, the Office for Democratic Institutions and Human Rights.

OSCE

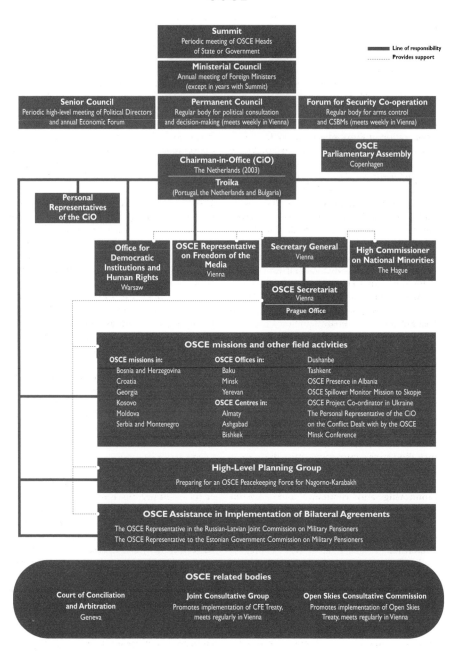

Summit
Periodic meeting of OSCE Heads of State or Government

━━━ Line of responsibility
········· Provides support

Ministerial Council
Annual meeting of Foreign Ministers (except in years with Summit)

Senior Council
Periodic high-level meeting of Political Directors and annual Economic Forum

Permanent Council
Regular body for political consultation and decision-making (meets weekly in Vienna)

Forum for Security Co-operation
Regular body for arms control and CSBMs (meets weekly in Vienna)

OSCE Parliamentary Assembly
Copenhagen

Chairman-in-Office (CiO)
The Netherlands (2003)

Troika
(Portugal, the Netherlands and Bulgaria)

Personal Representatives of the CiO

Office for Democratic Institutions and Human Rights
Warsaw

OSCE Representative on Freedom of the Media
Vienna

Secretary General
Vienna

High Commissioner on National Minorities
The Hague

OSCE Secretariat
Vienna

Prague Office

OSCE missions and other field activities

OSCE missions in:	OSCE Offices in:	Dushanbe
Bosnia and Herzegovina	Baku	Tashkent
Croatia	Minsk	OSCE Presence in Albania
Georgia	Yerevan	OSCE Spillover Monitor Mission to Skopje
Kosovo	**OSCE Centres in:**	OSCE Project Co-ordinator in Ukraine
Moldova	Almaty	The Personal Representative of the CiO
Serbia and Montenegro	Ashgabad	on the Conflict Dealt with by the OSCE
	Bishkek	Minsk Conference

High-Level Planning Group
Preparing for an OSCE Peacekeeping Force for Nagorno-Karabakh

OSCE Assistance in Implementation of Bilateral Agreements
The OSCE Representative in the Russian-Latvian Joint Commission on Military Pensioners
The OSCE Representative to the Estonian Government Commission on Military Pensioners

OSCE related bodies

Court of Conciliation and Arbitration
Geneva

Joint Consultative Group
Promotes implementation of CFE Treaty, meets regularly in Vienna

Open Skies Consultative Commission
Promotes implementation of Open Skies Treaty, meets regularly in Vienna

OSCE structures and institutions

Nevertheless, it is the largest European regional organisation, with 55 'participating states'. Its members include all the states of the Former Soviet Union and its satellites in Central Asia as well as the Caucasus and Central and Eastern Europe.

Very little has been written about the OSCE, although a detailed account would take volumes. In this short account of the essentials, I will focus on three principal achievements. First, the OSCE's predecessor, the CSCE (Conference on Security and Cooperation in Europe), can be credited with a significant role in the collapse of the USSR and its system of satellite states. Second, it has now achieved an extraordinarily important role in the reconstruction of territories of the Balkans, torn apart by armed conflict, especially Bosnia and Herzogovina, Kosovo, Serbia and Montenegro, and Macedonia. Third, and largely through the charisma and dedication of one individual, Max van der Stoel, it has helped to avert further bloodshed in the Baltic states, in Ukraine, in Central Asia and in Macedonia, which now hosts the 'Stoel University', otherwise known as the South-East European University.

As the organisation itself states on its website, www.osce.org, it is chiefly active in early warning, conflict prevention, crisis management and post-conflict rehabilitation. Thus, its guiding principle is state security and prevention of conflict. In its own words: 'The OSCE approach to security is comprehensive and cooperative: comprehensive in dealing with a wide range of security-related issues including arms control, preventive diplomacy, confidence- and security-building measures, human rights, democratisation, election monitoring and economic and environmental security; co-operative in the sense that all OSCE participating States have equal status, and decisions are based on consensus.'

It will be seen that human rights is by no means first on a list of 'security-related issues'. Nevertheless, it has accumulated a substantial 'human dimension', now published in a sizeable book, *OSCE Human Dimension Commitments, Reference Guide* (Warsaw, 2001), and at www.osce.org/documents/odihr/2001/01/1764_en.pdf.

How did the CSCE help the USSR to collapse? It must be understood that the CSCE had its own historical soil. Just as the Council of Europe was the 'ideological counterpart of NATO' at the outset of the cold war, and the European Economic Communities sought to prevent future conflict within Western Europe through economic integration, first between France, Germany and the Benelux states, the CSCE was a product of the brief period of détente in the 1970s. The Final Act of the CSCE was adopted in Helsinki on 1 August 1975 as the culmination of a process of meetings and consultations which had started on 3 July 1973. This document (not at all a treaty) was signed by 35 states including the USA and the USSR. Under Section VII, entitled Respect for Human Rights and Fundamental Freedoms, including the Freedom of Thought, Conscience, Religion and Belief, the participating states recognised 'the universal significance of human rights and fundamental freedoms'. They also confirmed 'the right of the individual to know and act upon his rights and duties in this field'.

At the time, the Helsinki Final Act was seen, on the Soviet side, as a diplomatic triumph for Leonid Brezhnev, whose chief motivation was to secure the ratification of the status quo in Europe, especially the divided Germany. The German Democratic Republic (GDR) had been admitted to the United Nations (with the Federal Republic of Germany) on 18 September 1973 and the GDR's participation and adherence to the Helsinki Final Act gave its leader Erich Honecker a great deal of satisfaction.

Ironically, the Helsinki Final Act had an unanticipated boomerang effect. It conferred vital legitimacy on human rights activists throughout the USSR and its satellites and played a crucial role in helping the system to undermine itself, in the USSR and in all its Eastern European satellites.

The CSCE's important 'follow-up' conference in Vienna in 1989, and the Copenhagen Meeting of the Conference on the Human Dimension of the CSCE in 1990 (now a fundamental source of principles and standards in the field of minority rights), provided an essential counterpoint to the revolutionary changes in the USSR. The Charter of Paris for a New Europe, adopted on 21 November 1990 by 34 states (following German reunification), contained the most solemn undertaking to abide by human rights and fundamental freedoms. The next meeting of the Conference on the Human Dimension took place in Moscow itself, only shortly before the demise of the USSR in December 1991.

It is therefore hardly surprising that the leading human rights monitoring and protection organisations in Russia and many other former Soviet and satellite countries are the Helsinki Committees, organised in the International Helsinki Federation. The President of the IHF at the time of writing is the Chair of the Moscow Helsinki Group and distinguished Russian human rights veteran, Ludmila Alekseyeva.

So to my second point. The 1990 Paris Summit mentioned above began the process of transforming what had been a series of conferences and meetings into an institution, with a Secretariat in Prague, a Conflict Prevention Centre in Vienna, an Office for Free Elections (ODIHR) in Warsaw and a CSCE parliamentary assembly, involving members of parliaments from all participating States. In July 1992, the Helsinki Summit established the Chairman–in–Office, the Troika – preceding and succeeding Chairmen – and the High Commissioner on National Minorities. This process led to the announcement, by the Budapest Summit of the CSCE: 'The CSCE is the security structure embracing States from Vancouver to Vladivostok. We are determined to give a new political impetus to the CSCE, thus enabling it to play a cardinal role in meeting the challenges of the 21st century. To reflect this determination, the CSCE will henceforth be known as the Organisation for Security and Co-operation in Europe (OSCE).'

This has been the basis for the crucial role now played by the OSCE not only in monitoring elections in all former communist states but in facilitating the transition to democracy and the rule of law in the Balkans. For example, the OSCE's Mission in Serbia and Montenegro, OMiSaM, is by far the largest international mission in Belgrade, much larger than the UN, Council of Europe and EU put together. One of the OSCE's achievements has been the establishment and training of the 'Multi-Ethnic Police' in South Serbia (the Presevo Valley), with substantial numbers of ethnic Albanian

serving alongside their Serbian – and a few Roma – counterparts. A central theme of OMiSaM's work is the 'human dimension' – human rights.

Third, the creation of the office of the High Commissioner on National Minorities in 1992, with a multi-national office in The Hague, succeeded beyond all expectations. This was largely through the 'quiet diplomacy' (Kemp, 2001) of the first High Commissioner, who served until 2001, the former Dutch Foreign Minister, Max van der Stoel. Through his confidential interventions and tireless travel, he was able to defuse a number of potentially bloody conflicts, especially in Latvia, Estonia and Macedonia. Moreover, he found a way to turn the 'soft law' of OSCE acts, documents and declarations into sets of recommendations, worked out by experts within an institution, the Foundation on Inter-Ethnic Relations, which he himself created: the Hague Recommendations of 1996 on Education Rights of National Minorities, the Oslo Recommendations of 1998 on their Linguistic Rights and the Lund Recommendations of 2000 on their Effective Participation in Public Life. His work has been continued by the present High Commissioner, Rolf Ekeus.

Further Reading

Kemp W. (2001) *Quiet Diplomacy in Action: The OSCE High Commissioner on National Minorities*, Kluwer Law International.

Packer, J. (2000) 'Making International Law Matter in Preventing Ethnic Conflict: A Practitioner's Perspective', *New York University Journal of International Law and Politics*, vol. 32, no. 3, pp. 715–724.

Ratner, S. (2000) 'Does International Law Matter in Preventing Ethnic Conflict?', in *New York University Journal of International Law and Politics*, vol. 32, no. 3, pp. 591–698.

Walker, W. (2000) 'OSCE Verification Experiences in Kosovo: November 1998–June 1999', 4, *The International Journal of Human Rights*, p. 127–44.

Wright, J. (1996) 'The OSCE and the protection of minority rights', 18, *Human Rights Quarterly*, p. 190.

Contributor: Bill Bowring

PEACE, THE RIGHT TO

The term 'peace' is generally understood to mean the absence of inter or intra-state conflict or forceful intervention. The right to peace however can be said to fall broadly within the spectrum of what are termed 'third generation rights', a category which includes, inter alia, the right to development, the right to a healthy environment, the right to communicate and the right to be different. The concept has been explicitly recognised in Article 23 of the African Charter on Human and Peoples' Rights that states, in part, 'All peoples shall have the right to national and international peace and security [...]' and by the United Nations Commission on Human Rights and the United Nations General Assembly. A 1976 UN Commission on Human Rights Resolution [5] recalls that 'everyone has the right to live in conditions of international peace and security' and in 1978 the General Assembly adopted Resolution 33/73, which states, '[...] every nation and every human being...has the inherent right to life in peace.'

The right to peace is primarily discussed as an individual right but as Sohn (1982) has argued, there is 'general agreement that any such right necessarily has both individual and collective aspects; as in the case of the right to development, these aspects reinforce one another and are not mutually exclusive'. That said, there are significant questions raised regarding the implementation of these so-called 'third generation' rights, which Alston (1984) (and others) argues, 'are much closer to general social values than to legal principles'.

Article 2(4) of the Charter of the United Nations provides that states 'shall refrain in their international relations from the threat or use of force against the territorial integrity or political independence of any state'. This principle, which according to Franck (1992) 'stands at the apex of the global normative system', is one that Epps (1998) extends to a state entitlement to peace, and quite possibly an individual right to peace. Furthermore, the 1984 General Assembly Resolution A/RES/39/11 on the Right of Peoples to Peace recognised that 'the maintenance of a peaceful life for peoples is the sacred duty of each State'. The question is therefore whether one can imply an individual right to peace from a state duty to provide it. Such an inference raises no cause for concern in the area of 'first generation' rights; for example, every individual has the right to life and, accordingly, the state has a duty to protect life and not to deprive a person of their right to life arbitrarily. The link, however, between a state's duty to provide peace and an individual justiciable right to peace is considerably more tenuous. In fact Alston's proposals for 'quality control' in the elaboration of new human rights are symptomatic of a more general trend towards the characterisation of certain human rights as hierarchically superior, arguably due to, as Meron (1986) notes, the 'proliferation of human rights instruments, sometimes of poor quality and uncertain legal value'.

Although some commentators see the recognition of the right to peace or a right to live in peace as 'a step in the right direction', it is nevertheless the case that the main beneficiaries of the adherence to the right to peace would be individuals residing in the countries that accept and abide by that right. The pertinent issue then is the protection afforded to people when the status is not one of peace.

The Fourth Geneva Convention, adopted on 12 August 1949 by the Diplomatic Conference for the Establishment of International Conventions for the Protection of Victims of War, relates to the protection of civilians during wartime. The Convention provides a set of legal principles aimed to protect civilians from the ravages of war. These include the right to be free from violence, in particular murder of all kinds, mutilation, cruel treatment and torture, the right not to be taken hostage, and freedom from outrages upon personal dignity, in particular humiliating and degrading treatment. In addition to this, Article 27 of Geneva IV provides that civilians are entitled to respect for their persons, their honour, their family rights, their religious convictions and practices, and their manners and customs. The duty to protect and respect civilians forms part of binding customary international law. According to Gasser (1995) the placing of Article 27 within the text of the Convention makes clear that it also includes all situations in which a party to a conflict comes into contact with civilians of the opposing side. Moreover, the duty to 'protect' civilians in Article 27 goes a step further, conferring a positive obligation on a state party to undertake every possible measure to shield civilians from harm.

While there are a number of legal protections afforded to civilians in time of war however, there remains a disparity between the principle and practice, suggesting that, as Jones and Cater (2001) argue, '[m]eaningful protection of civilians in and from war requires greater coherence between distinct types and level of international response than currently exists'. Although it is clear that violations of the 'laws of war' do take place, equally there is sufficient evidence to demonstrate that the protective provisions of international humanitarian law prevented or reduced great suffering in many cases.

With respect to the maintenance of international peace and security, Chapter VII of the Charter of the United Nations authorises the United Nations Security Council to employ coercive measures against a threat to or breach of the peace or against an act of aggression. Furthermore, UN Commission on Human Rights Resolution 1992/S-1/1 of 14 August 1992 states that persons who commit or order violations of the Geneva Conventions or its Additional Protocols can be held individually criminally responsible.

It is without question that even lawful actions taken during war would constitute violations of fundamental human rights if the same actions were to take place during a time of peace. Yet the proliferation of ethnic conflict and, increasingly, inter-state disputes suggest that while we may strive for peace, we must recognise the realities of war. Kant (1795) reminds us that 'the state of peace among men living side by side is not the natural state (*status naturalis*); the natural state is one of war'. To this end, the 'right' to peace may be more appropriately (and realistically) framed in terms of protections afforded by existing human rights and humanitarian law frameworks. These legally binding principles endeavour to ensure peace and security are maintained (Charter of the United Nations) and, in the event of war, that the principles of the laws of war (specifically the Geneva Conventions) are respected.

Further Reading

Alston, Philip (1984) 'Conjuring Up New Human Rights: A Proposal for Quality Control', 78, *American Journal of International Law*, 607.

Epps, Valerie (1998) 'Peace and Democracy: The Link and the Policy Implications', 4, *ISLA Journal of International and Comparative Law*, L. 347.

Franck, Thomas M. (1992) 'The Emerging Rights to Democratic Governance', 86, *American Journal of International Law*, 46.

Gasser, Hans-Peter (1995) 'Protection of the Civilian Population', in *The Handbook of Humanitarian Law in Armed Conflicts*, Fleck, Dieter (ed.), Oxford: Oxford University Press.

Jones, Bruce D. and Cater, Charles K (2001) 'From Chaos to Coherence? Toward a Regime for Protecting Civilians in War', in *Civilians in War*, Chesterman, Simon (ed.), London: Lynne Rienner.

Kant, Immanuel (1795) *Perpetual Peace: A Philosophical Sketch*, available at http://www.constitution.org/kant/perpeace.htm

Meron, Theodore (1986) 'On a Hierarchy of International Human Rights', 80, *American Journal of International Law*, 1.

Sohn, Louis B. (1982) 'The New International Law: Protection of the Rights of Individuals Rather than States', 32, *American University Law Review*, Rev. 1.

Contributors: Edel Hughes with
                             Kathleen Cavanaugh

PLURALIST UNIVERSALISM AND HUMAN RIGHTS

Two fundamental facts characterise human beings. First, they belong to a common species and share in common a set of basic capacities and needs. They are capable of entering into communicative, sexual, social, moral and other relationships with each other and sharing a common life. Their unique capacities enable them to create a rich and distinctively human world, mark them out from the rest of the natural world and give them a privileged status. They can develop their capacities and lead meaningful lives only under certain conditions, which therefore define their well-being and constitute their common fundamental interests. For convenience we shall call this the fact of common humanity.

Secondly, as being endowed with the powers of imagination, rationality and critical self-reflection, human beings seek to understand themselves and the world. They live under different natural circumstances, face different challenges, have different histories and are subject to different contingencies, and make sense of these in their own different ways. As a result they develop different cultures based on different visions of human life and different systems of meaning and significance. These cultures structure their lives, foster a distant set of human capacities, emotions and needs, and give rise to unique cultural communities. For convenience we shall call this the fact of cultural diversity.

Each of these facts has important moral consequences. The fact of common humanity implies that some basic evils and fundamental interests, and therefore some moral values, are common to all human beings. Premature death, torture, acute poverty and so on are universal evils and respect for human life and dignity, equality of moral worth, access to the conditions necessary for the development of human capacities and satisfaction of basic needs are universally desirable goods or values. The fact of cultural diversity implies that the thick moral lives that characterise all human societies and within which their members live their lives are based on different visions of the good life and moral values. Different societies structure moral relations differently, rely on different moral motivations and foster different virtues and dispositions.

Common humanity is the basis of moral universality and cultural diversity of moral plurality. To say that common humanity is the basis of moral universality does not mean that it logically entails the latter, but rather that it makes the latter possible and provides the ground on which a universal morality can be constructed. The same applies to the relation between cultural diversity and moral plurality. A coherent account of moral life must recognise both moral universality and moral plurality and explore their complex relationship.

Moral philosophers have not found it easy to do so and have emphasised one at the expense of the other. Relativism stresses moral plurality and ignores moral universality. Universalism makes the opposite mistake.

Broadly speaking, relativists argue that every society or culture is a morally self-contained whole, that its values and practices define the moral limits of its members and that they have no transcultural means of judging and evaluating these. Relativists ignore the fact that no culture is homogeneous and free of internal tensions, that it is profoundly shaped by the prevailing structure of economics and power, that its members are never so determined by it as to lack the capacity for critically reflecting on it and that cultures interact with and learn from each other. Relativists also ignore the fact that since all human beings share certain fundamental interests and are deeply damaged by certain common evils, these offer the basis for evaluating all cultures.

Although universalism takes many forms, in its dominant version it argues that moral values are universally binding, admit of no qualifications and exceptions and should form the basis of all societies. Universalists ignore the fact that moral values need to be interpreted and that this is done differently by different societies. Respect for life is a universal value, but different societies may legitimately disagree on when life begins and ends, whether and when the life of a foetus might be terminated, whether capital punishment and wars are justified and what respect for life involves. Universal values also conflict and can be prioritised and traded off differently by different societies. Universal values, again, are necessarily thin and cannot by themselves form the basis of a society's way of life. Every society integrates them differently into its thick and inevitably complex moral and cultural life.

Moral universalism and moral relativism then are incoherent extremes. Each captures a vital truth about our moral life but misinterprets, exaggerates and distorts it. We need to combine their insights and recognise the dialectical interplay of universality and diversity. A society's morality is subject to the constraints of, and can and should be evaluated in terms of, universal morality; the latter in turn needs to be adopted to the moral traditions and self-understanding of each society. If we need a name for this view, we could call it pluralist universalism.

The pluralist universalist has a distinct perspective on human rights. Human rights are rooted in common humanity and refer to those conditions and opportunities that human beings need to express and develop their uniquely human capacities and lead meaningful lives. They do not exhaust the totality of universal values, and highlight those we consider so important that we give the individual the right to demand them and require the state to set up an appropriate institutional structure. Qua universalist, the pluralist universalist champions human rights, considers them an indispensable feature of the good society and judges all societies and cultures in terms of them. Qua pluralist, he values moral and cultural diversity and appreciates that different societies interpret and prioritise human rights differently and resolve their unavoidable conflicts in their own different ways. While some might primarily rely on the state, others might turn to social pressure, collective moral ethos and other less coercive mechanisms to sustain a regime of human rights. Since different societies entertain different conceptions of the good life, they might regard some rights as human rights that others do not. While some societies might seek to foster a culture of human rights and make it the sole basis of their moral life, others might reject such a single-minded obsession with a culture of claims and demands, and foster instead a moral life in which the languages of generosity, solidarity, altruism and social responsibility balance that of human rights.

The pluralist universalist not only appreciates but welcomes these differences. This is not relativism, which absolutises the values of a particular culture, but rather relativisation or contextualisation of universal values. For the pluralist universalist, there is no single model of realising universal values including human rights, and the resulting diversity and the intercultural dialogue it stimulates offers a vitally necessary opportunity to deepen our constantly developing insights into the nature and complexity of universal values. While ensuring that universality does not become an excuse to create a morally homogeneous and suffocating world, he is equally keen to ensure that diversity does not become a licence to undermine universality and engage in unacceptable practices. This is not an easy path to travel either in theory or in practice, but there is no other.

Further Reading

Hampshire, S. (1983) *Morality in Conflict*, Oxford: Basil Blackwell.

Jones, P. (1994) *Rights*, London: Macmillan.

Nussbaum, M. and Sen, A. (eds) (1993) *The Quality of Life*, Oxford: Clarendon Press.

Parekh, B. (2000) *Rethinking Multiculturalism*, London: Palgrave.

Parekh, B. (1999) 'Non-Ethnocentric Universalism' in Dunne, T. and Wheeler, N. (eds). *Human Rights in Global Politics*, Cambridge: Cambridge University Press.

Walzer, M. (1994) *Thick and Thin: Moral Argument at Home and Abroad*, Notre Dame: University of Notre Dame Press.

Contributor: Bhikhu Parekh

POVERTY AND HUMAN RIGHTS

Human rights would be fully realised if all human beings had secure access to the objects of these rights. Our world is today very far from this ideal. Piecing together the current global record, we find that most of the current massive underfulfilment of human rights is more or less directly connected to poverty. The connection is direct in the case of basic social and economic human rights, such as the right to a standard of living adequate for the health and well-being of oneself and one's family, including food, clothing, housing and medical care. The connection is more indirect in the case of civil and political human rights associated with democratic government and the rule of law. Desperately poor people, often stunted, illiterate and heavily preoccupied with the struggle to survive, typically lack effective means for resisting or rewarding their rulers, who are therefore likely to rule them oppressively while catering to the interests of other (often foreign) agents more capable of reciprocation.

The statistics are horrifying. Out of a total of 6350 million human beings, 1000 million have no adequate shelter, 800 million are undernourished, 1000 million have no access to safe water, 2400 million lack access to basic sanitation, 2000 million are without electricity, 880 million lack access to basic health services and 876 million adults are illiterate (UNDP). Some 170 million children between the ages of 5 and 14 are involved in hazardous work (e.g. in agriculture, construction, textile or carpet production), 8.4 million of them in the 'unconditionally worst' forms of child labour, 'defined as slavery, trafficking, debt bondage and other forms of forced labour, forced recruitment of children for use in armed conflict, prostitution and pornography and illicit activities' (www.ilo.org/public/english/standards/decl/publ/reports/report3.htm). People of colour and females bear a disproportionate share of these deprivations.

Roughly one third of all human deaths, some 50,000 daily, have poverty-related causes, easily preventable through better nutrition, safe drinking water, mosquito nets, rehydration packs, vaccines and other medicines. This adds up to 270 million deaths in just the 15 years from the end of the cold war – more deaths than were caused by all the wars, civil wars and government repression of the entire 20th century.

Never has world poverty been so easily avoidable. The collective annual income of the 2800 million people living below the World Bank's '$2/day' poverty line is about $400 billion. Their collective shortfall from that poverty line is roughly $300 billion per year. This is 1.2 per cent of the gross national incomes of the high-income countries, which add up to $25,400 billion. These countries contain 15 per cent of the world's population with nearly 81 per cent of the global product. The global poor are 44 per cent of the world's population with 1.25 per cent of the global product. At market exchange rates, the per capita income of the former is nearly 200 times greater than that of the latter.

The rich countries' response to world poverty is mainly rhetorical. Official development assistance shrank steadily throughout the 1990s and the portion targeted to basic social services in 2004 stands at 7 per cent or under $4 billion per year. The citizens of the rich countries give another $7 billion annually to international NGOs.

Even the rhetoric is appalling. At the 1996

> In Asia and the Pacific, the number of people living in poverty was reduced from 34 to 25 per cent in the 1990s. Despite this 768 million people in the region subsist on less than US$1 a day.
> (UNDP, UNESCAP 'Promoting the Millennium Development Goals in Asia and the Pacific: Meeting the Challenges of Poverty Reduction' 2004)

World Food Summit in Rome, the world's governments grandly promised to halve the number of extremely poor people between 1996 and 2015, implicitly accepting 25,000 daily poverty deaths in 2015 and some 250 million such deaths in the interim. In the 2000 UN Millennium Declaration, they modified their promise – replacing 'number' by 'proportion' and extending the plan period backwards to 1990. Taking advantage of rapid population growth and a huge poverty reduction in China during the 1990s, these clever modifications greatly dilute the target: the new promise, if fulfilled, would reduce the number of extremely poor people by only 20 per cent between 2000 and 2015.

Confronted with such facts, citizens of the rich countries may concede that we affluent should do more to help the poor. But they see this as a demand of humanity or charity, not as a demand of justice and certainly not as a moral duty imposed on us by the human rights of the poor. As the US government declared after the World Food Summit: 'The attainment of any "right to adequate food" or "fundamental right to be free from hunger" is a goal or aspiration to be realised progressively that does not give rise to any international obligations.' The presumption behind this denial is that, internationally at least, human rights entail only negative duties: they require that one not deprive foreigners of secure access to the objects of their human rights, but they do not require that one help them attain such secure access by protecting them against other threats.

This presumption can be attacked by arguing that human rights do impose positive duties, even internationally. But even if the presumption is accepted, it shields the rich from human-rights-based obligations only insofar as they bear no responsibility for the existing radically unequal global economic distribution. And this claim to innocence is highly dubious at best. For one thing, the existing radical inequality is deeply tainted by how it accumulated through one historical process that was deeply pervaded by enslavement, colonialism, even genocide. The rich are quick to point out that they cannot inherit their ancestors' sins. Indeed. But how can they then be entitled to the fruits of these sins: to their huge inherited advantage in power and wealth over the rest of the world? If they are not so entitled, then they are, by actively excluding the global poor from their lands and possessions, contributing to their deprivations.

Moreover, even the causes of the current persistence of severe poverty are by no means exclusively domestic to the countries in which it occurs. The asymmetries inherent in the current global economic (WTO) regime are well documented: it allows the rich countries to collect royalties on patented seeds and drugs while continuing to favour their own companies through tariffs, quotas, anti-dumping duties and huge subsidies. UNCTAD estimates that the latter market distortions cost the developing countries $700 billion annually in lost export revenue — a huge amount relative to the needs of their poor.

To be sure, many developing countries are run by corrupt and incompetent leaders, unwilling or unable to make serious poverty-eradication efforts. But their ability to rule, often against the will and interests of the population, crucially depends on outside factors. It depends, for instance, on their being recognised by the rich countries as entitled to borrow in their country's name, to confer legal title to its resources and with the proceeds to buy the weapons they need to stay in power. By assigning these privileges to such rulers, on the basis of their effective power alone, the rich countries support their banks and secure their resource imports. But they also greatly strengthen the staying power of oppressive rulers and the incentives toward coup attempts, especially in the resource-dependent countries.

More generally, bad leadership, civil wars and widespread corruption in the developing countries are not wholly homegrown, but strongly encouraged by the existing international rules and extreme inequalities. The rulers and officials of these countries have vastly more to gain from catering to the interests of wealthy foreign governments, corporations and tourists than from meeting the basic needs of their impoverished compatriots.

Are the rich countries violating human rights when they, in collaboration with southern elites, impose a global institutional order under which, foreseeably and avoidably, hundreds of millions cannot attain 'a standard of living adequate for the health and well-being of himself and of his family, including food, clothing, housing and medical care' (**UNIVERSAL DECLARATION OF HUMAN RIGHTS** Article 25)? The Declaration itself makes quite clear that they do when it proclaims that 'everyone is entitled to a social and international order in which the rights and freedoms set forth in this Declaration can be fully realised' (Article 28).

Further reading

Beitz, Charles (1999) *Political Theory and International Relations* [1979], Princeton: Princeton University Press.

Pogge, Thomas W. (2002) *World Poverty and Human Rights*, Cambridge: Polity Press.

Rome Declaration on World Food Security, 1996 (www.fao.org/wfs).

Shue, Henry (1996) *Basic Rights* [1980], Princeton: Princeton University Press.

UNDP (United Nations Development Programme): Human Development Report, New York: Oxford University Press annually.

Contributor: Thomas Pogge

PRIVACY, THE RIGHT TO

Privacy has become one of the most important human rights issues of the modern age. At a time when computer-based technology gives government and private sector organisations the ability to conduct mass surveillance of populations, privacy has become a crucial safeguard for individual rights. According to opinion polls, concern over privacy violation is now greater than at any time in recent history. Uniformly, populations throughout the world report their distress about encroachment on privacy, prompting an unprecedented number of nations to pass laws that specifically protect the privacy of their citizens. The basis for this legal activity rests on a growing understanding that privacy is a fundamental right. Privacy is a value that underpins human dignity and other key values such as **FREEDOM OF ASSOCIA-TION** and freedom of speech (See: **FREE-DOM OF EXPRESSION**). These rights are established squarely in international covenants and protected specifically in the laws and con-stitutions of more than 60 nations.

The increasing sophistication of informa-tion technology, with its capacity to collect, analyse and disseminate information on indi-viduals, has introduced a sense of urgency to the demand for further legislation. New devel-opments in medical research and care, telecommunications, advanced transportation systems and financial transfers have dramati-cally increased the level of information gener-ated by each individual. Computers linked together by high-speed networks with advanced processing systems can create com-prehensive dossiers on any person without the need for a single central computer system.

Privacy can be defined as fundamental (though not an absolute) human right. The concept can be traced as far back as 1361, when the Justices of the Peace Act in England provided for the arrest of peeping toms and eavesdroppers. Various countries developed specific protections for privacy in the centuries that followed. In 1792, for example, the Declaration of the Rights of Man and the Citizen declared that private property is invio-lable and sacred. The history of privacy pro-tection in the United States is reflected in numerous Supreme Court decisions. In recent decades the case of *Griswald v Connecticut* found a constitutional right to privacy.

The modern privacy benchmark at an international level can be found in the 1948 **UNIVERSAL DECLARATION OF HUMAN RIGHTS**, which specifically protected territo-rial and communications privacy. Article 12 states: 'No-one should be subjected to arbi-trary interference with his privacy, family, home or correspondence, nor to attacks on his honour or reputation. Everyone has the right to the protection of the law against such interferences or attacks.'

Numerous international human rights covenants give specific reference to privacy as a right. The **INTERNATIONAL COVENANT ON CIVIL AND POLITICAL RIGHTS** rein-forced the UDHR, while the European Declaration of Human Rights expands the concept to 'private life'.

Of all the human rights in the internation-al catalogue, privacy is perhaps the most diffi-cult to define and circumscribe. Definitions of privacy vary widely according to context and environment. In many countries, the concept has been fused with data protection, which interprets privacy in terms of personal infor-mation. Outside this rather strict context, pri-vacy protection is frequently seen as a way of drawing the line at how far society can intrude into the affairs of a person. In the 1890s, US judge, Louis Brandeis, articulated a concept of privacy that urged that it was the individ-ual's 'right to be left alone'. Brandeis argued that privacy was the most cherished of free-doms in a **DEMOCRACY** and he was con-cerned that it should be reflected in the constitution.

The Preamble to the Australian Privacy Charter says: 'A free and democratic society requires respect for the **AUTONOMY** of indi-viduals, and limits on the power of both state and private organisations to intrude on that autonomy ... Privacy is a key value which underpins human dignity and other key values such as freedom of association and freedom of speech ... Privacy is a basic human right and the reasonable expectation of every person.'

The lack of a single definition should not imply that the issue lacks importance. As one writer observed: 'In one sense, all human rights are aspects of the right to privacy.' Privacy is a term widely used to refer to an accepted group of related rights. Its antithesis is surveillance. The subject area is wide, but can be divided into the following facets:

- information privacy, which involves the establishment of rules governing the col-lection and handling of personal data such as credit information and medical records;
- bodily privacy, which is concerned with protection of people's physical selves against invasive procedures such as drug testing and cavity searches;
- privacy of communications, which covers the security and privacy of mail, telephones, email and other forms of communication;

■ territorial privacy which concerns the setting of limits on intrusion into the domestic and other environments such as the workplace or public space.

Interest in the right of privacy experienced a high profile in the 1960s and 1970s with the advent of information technology (IT). The surveillance potential of powerful IT systems prompted demands for specific rules governing the collection and handling of personal information. The genesis of modern legislation in this area can be traced to national privacy and data protection laws passed by Sweden (1973), the United States (1974), Germany (1977) and France (1978). Two crucial international instruments evolved from these laws. Both the **COUNCIL OF EUROPE**'s Convention on the Protection of Individuals with regard to the Automatic Processing of Personal Data and the OECD Guidelines governing the Protection of Privacy and Transborder Data Flows of Personal Data articulate specific rules covering the handling of electronic data.

The rules within these two documents form the core of the data protection laws on the statutes of dozens of countries. These rules describe personal information as data that are afforded protection at every step from collection through to storage and dissemination. The right of people to access and amend their data is a primary component of these rules. The expression of data protection in various declarations and laws varies only by degrees. All require that personal information is obtained fairly and lawfully, used only for the original specified purpose, is adequate relevant and not excessive to purpose, is accurate and up to date and is destroyed after its purpose is completed.

In 1994, conscious both of the shortcomings of law and the many differences in the level of protection in each of its states, the European Parliament passed a Europe-wide directive that provides citizens with a wider range of protections over abuses of their data. The Directive on the Protection of Individuals with regard to the processing of personal data and on the free movement of such data sets a benchmark for national law. Each EU state has passed complementary legislation so that the flow of data throughout Europe is harmoniously protected.

The regulatory model adopted by Europe, Australia, Hong Kong, New Zealand, Central and Eastern Europe and Canada is that of a public official who enforces the data protection law. This official monitors compliance with the law and conducts investigations into alleged breaches. In some cases the official can find against an offender. The official is also responsible for public education and international liaison in data protection and data transfer. This is the preferred model for most countries adopting data protection law. It is also the model favoured by Europe to ensure compliance with its new data protection regime. Some countries such as the United States have avoided general data protection rules in favour of specific 'sectoral laws' governing, for example, video rental records and financial privacy. In such cases, enforcement is achieved through a range of mechanisms.

Data protection can also be achieved – at least in theory – through various forms of self-regulation, in which companies and industry bodies establish codes of practice. However, the record of these efforts has been disappointing, with little or no evidence that the aims of the codes are fulfilled to the satisfaction of European data protection standards.

With the recent development of commercially available encryption-based technologies, limited privacy protection has also moved into the hands of individual users. Many users of the Internet can use a range of programs and systems that will provide varying degrees of privacy and security of communications.

Further Reading

Agre, Phillip & Rotenberg, Marc (eds) (1997) *Technology and Privacy: The New Landscape*, Cambridge, Massachussetts: MIT Press.

Bennet, Colin (1992) R*egulating Privacy: Data Protection and Public Policy in Europe and the United States*, Cornell University Press.

Electronic Privacy Information Center & Privacy International, Privacy & Human Rights 2003, available free at http://www.privacy international.org/survey/phr2003/

Flaherty, David (1989) *Protecting Privacy in Surveillance Societies*, North Carolina: University of North Carolina Press.

Michael, James (1994) *Privacy and Human Rights*. Paris: UNESCO.

Contributor: Simon Davies

PROPERTY, THE RIGHT TO: PROPERTY IN THE BODY

Recent developments have renewed consideration of whether the body can be the subject of property rights. Developments in biotechnology have made the body an increasingly valuable and contested resource. Scandals involving organ stripping and retention, disputes over bodily material and debates about the organ trade have prompted concern about the control that different persons may exercise over the body, body parts and products of the body and the uses to which they may be properly put. Here we consider the extent to which it is possible to recognise property rights in the body and the interests that are served or sacrificed by the recognition of such rights.

Historically, the law recognised some property in the living body. Slavery, feudal tenures, the attachment of a debtor to act as payment for debt and the property interest of a husband in the body of his wife are some examples. However, historically the law did not recognise property in the dead body. Although rights of possession for the purpose of burial were recognised and criminal and ecclesiastical sanctions for wrongfully interfering with a corpse existed, as a general rule the common law did not recognise property in the dead body. The 'no-property' rule probably dated back to the description in Sir Edward Coke's Institutes of a cadaver as nullius in bonis ('in the goods of no one') (3 Co. Inst. 203). Coke's description was, however, probably based on error of the existing authorities and was in any case confined to caro data vermibus ('flesh given to worms'), suggesting a description only of a buried corpse. However, despite its dubious origins, the 'no-property' rule was accepted as authoritative in the 18th and 19th centuries in the common law.

While the recognition of property rights in the living body eventually diminished, the 'no-property' rule in respect of the dead body remained. At the beginning of the 20th century, however, an exception to it emerged. In the case of *Doodeward v Spence* ((1908) 6 CLR 406) a majority in the Australian High Court held a two-headed stillborn fetus preserved in fluids and displayed as a curio to be property. Affirming the 'no-property' rule, Griffith, C.J. stated an exception to it where a person lawfully in possession of a body or its parts 'by the lawful exercise of work or skill so dealt with a human body or part of a human body ... that it has acquired some attributes differentiating it from a mere corpse awaiting burial' (ibid, 413). Although Higgins, J. dissented, and Barton, J. in his concurring judgment stressed as significant the difference between the human body and the stillborn 'monster' in the case, Griffith C.J's 'work/skill' exception emerged as the central rationale of the Doodeward case. In *R v Kelly and Lindsay* ((1999) QB 621), a case involving the theft of a number of anatomical specimens, the English Court of Appeal affirmed the 'no-property' rule, but accepted an exception, following Doodeward, where 'by the application of skill' parts of a corpse 'acquired different attributes', such as, as in the instant case, dissection and preservation for the purposes of teaching and exhibition. The court also commented that another exception might be recognised where parts of a body did not acquire new attributes, but, instead, a use or significance beyond mere existence, such as parts intended for transplantation, DNA extraction and exhibition in a trial.

In envisaging an exception to the 'no-property' rule based on use or significance, the Court in *R v Kelly and Lindsay* arguably approved of property rights in parts and products of the human body, irrespective of the state they are in and irrespective of whether they derive from a living or deceased 'source'. This approach seems already to have been implicit in the treatment by the English lower courts in *R v Welsh* ((1974) RTR 478), *R v Rothery* ((1976) RTR 550) and Herbert ((1961) 25 *Journal of Criminal Law*, 163) of urine, blood and hair as property capable of being the subject of theft. It is not inconceivable that by logical extension, the law might also recognise property in a whole corpse that has acquired different attributes by the application of skill, such as plastination (the impregnation of the body with plastics) for the purpose of lifelike anatomical exhibition, as in Professor von Hagen's Body Worlds exhibition (London, March 2002–February 2003), or property in a whole corpse where it had simply acquired a use or significance such as designation for an autopsy, prior to dissection and preservation having begun.

Developments in the common law and contemporary conditions suggest, therefore, that the traditional 'no-property' rule is limited and that the possibility of property rights in the (dead) body and parts and products of the body is real. However, controversy is likely to be raised where commercial interests are at stake and where, perhaps more significantly, dispute between the 'source' and the 'user' takes place. The Californian case of *Moore v Regents of the University of California* (271 Cal.Rptr. 146 Cal.,1990) illustrates the controversy. *Moore* concerned an action raised by John Moore in respect of cells removed from his body and subsequently commercialised without his knowledge. In 1976 Moore attended the University of California at Los Angeles Medical Centre for treatment of hairy-cell leukaemia, a rare form of cancer. Dr Golde, his treating physician, recommended the removal of Moore's spleen. Unbeknown to Moore, Golde discovered that some of his cells were distinctive and commercially valuable and made arrangements to retain portions of the spleen for research. Over the course of seven years, Golde took blood, bone marrow, skin and sperm from Moore under the pretence that this was a necessary part of treatment. Golde and a researcher established a cell-line from Moore's cells, which was subsequently patented. In conjunction with the Regents, Golde negotiated agreements with several biotechnology companies for exclusive access to the cell-line and products derived from it, in exchange for substantial payments and benefits. Moore eventually became suspicious of Golde's activities and when he discovered the existence of the patented cell-line, raised a number of actions, including breach of fiduciary duty and lack of informed consent, and conversion (the tort of wrongful interference with property). The Californian Supreme Court accepted the former claim but, reversing the judgment of the Court of Appeal, rejected the latter, holding that once removed from his body, Moore did not have property rights in his cells and could not therefore succeed in a claim in conversion.

The majority in Moore considered that significant policy considerations militated against what would, as they saw it, be an extension of existing law. They were concerned primarily with the impact that the recognition of property rights of a 'source' would have on socially valuable research, feeling that research required free access to cells, the secure exchange of scientific materials and an economic incentive, which would be inhibited by recognition of property rights in the 'source'. Justice Arabian expressed particular concerns with the commercialisation inherent in Moore's conversion claim and affront to human dignity from the creation of a body marketplace. Broussard, J., dissenting, pointed to the fact that rejection of Moore's claim did not prevent an immoral trade but simply precluded the 'source' from any profits in that trade. Mosk, J., also dissenting, pointed to the inequity of permitting only the 'user' to profit and argued that there was no evidence of any detriment to research by recognition of a property right in the 'source'. Significantly, Mosk, J. suggested that recognising such a right would both respect the human body as an expression of the human persona and protect persons against exploitation by the biotechnological enterprise.

The possibility that property might respect and protect the person, as suggested by the minority in Moore, is the most perplexing possibility offered by a property regime in the body. Property implies control and recognition of the property rights of a 'source' might enhance control over their body and provide a strong protection against exploitation and unauthorised use. However, property also implies commodification and may offend a certain view of human dignity, particularly if property rights included the freedom to transact unrestrained. Irrespective of these issues, what is clear is that recognition of the rights of the 'user', as implied by the majority in Moore, but not the 'source' risks serious disadvantage to the 'source' and fails to provide protections more generally to persons from exploitation of their bodily resource.

In conclusion, it is suggested that developments in the common law indicate that, contrary to the traditional position, it may be possible to establish property rights in the body, body parts and products of the body. However, the recognition of property rights may have varying results, suggesting that it is imperative for the law to develop in this area with careful consideration to the implications of recognising property in the body, particularly for the 'source' and for society as a whole.

Further Reading

Grubb, A. (1998) '"I, Me, Mine": Bodies, Parts and Property' in 3, *Medical Law International*, 299–317.

Harris, J.W. (1996) 'Who Owns My Body?' in 16, *Oxford Journal of Legal Studies*, 55–84.

Mason, J.K. and Laurie, G.T. (2001) 'Consent or Property? Dealing with the Body and its Parts in the Shadow of Bristol and Alder Hey' in 64, *Modern Law Review*, 710–29.

Skene, L. (2002) 'Proprietary Rights in Human Bodies, Body Parts and Tissue: Regulatory Contexts and Proposals for New Laws' in 22, *Legal Studies*, 102–27.

Contributor: Shanti Williamson

PROPERTY, THE RIGHT TO: INTELLECTUAL PROPERTY RIGHTS AS HUMAN RIGHTS

The collective term intellectual property rights (IPRs) that includes patents, copyrights, trademarks and other aspects of making knowledge or information into property, can lead to confusion. The discourse of rights as regards intellectual property is a relatively recent development, entering common use only in the early part of the 20th century. Now some wish to claim that IPRs are human rights.

Intellectual property constructs scarcity of use where none necessarily exists. Knowledge and information, unlike material goods, are not usually exclusive: I can use an idea at the same time that you are thinking the same idea without any loss of utility for either of us. Without the possibility of excluding from use, securing a reward for the supply of goods or services is difficult if not impossible. Hence, IPRs construct a scarcity of use to allow a market to be constructed for knowledge and information.

Intellectual property is a market-oriented legal form, finding its origins in the grant of trade monopolies prior to the 17th century and dependent on political authority for its continued existence. The key supporters of these rights (from the very beginning) have been commercial organisations, from the stationers company and the merchant guilds in the Renaissance to the record and film industries today. One of the key arguments supporting IPRs has been that by ensuring innovators and creators can gain rewards for their intellectual products, the continued social provision of these important social goods is supported. However, political authorities have recognised for 500 years that the public benefits of wide dissemination must also be protected. This has meant that IPRs are usually temporary: currently ranging from 20 years for patents to 50 years after the author's death for copyrights. Intellectual property then enters the public domain to be used by anyone for no charge. The general historical trajectory, especially in the last half century, has been to strengthen private rights (by lengthening periods of protection and relaxing the criteria for inclusion) at the expense of the public domain. The Trade Related Aspects of Intellectual Property Rights (TRIPs) agreement during the Uruguay Round of multilateral trade negotiations that led to the establishment of the Word Trade Organisation (WTO) in 1995 was the global watershed of this expansion of private rights.

Although the TRIPs agreement does not actually mandate specific national legalisation, it does require the law covering IPRs to produce various effects and rights. To become TRIPs-compliant many WTO members have had to change their national laws, and there is considerable technical assistance available from various agencies. To support these often contentious and politically sensitive changes in law, considerable political effort has been deployed to support the (re)production of the norms underpinning the protection of property rights in knowledge and information.

Probably the most important norm is that the rendering of knowledge and information as property serves a socially useful purpose. Drawing a direct metaphorical link with material property, we are told that the use of knowledge can be made more socially efficient by awarding ownership rights. A market can be established and its operation can allocate resources to those who need them most (or can use them best) even if use is governed by wealth effects (or effective demand). However, while property rights in things are a response to their natural exclusivity as regards use, IPRs construct scarcity and thus rather than a mechanism for dealing with a specific social problem (the distribution of scarce resources) produce the scarcity that they then organise 'efficiently'.

To obscure this issue a series of narratives about IPRs have been developed to try to establish an individualised reason for recognising and protecting IPRs. Thus, it is frequently asserted that individuals have rights to reward for their (intellectual) efforts, and by so rewarding creators or innovators we stimulate their further intellectual activity. Moreover, the products of our minds to a large extent define us and therefore it is only just that we are able to control the use of such ideas and knowledge in the wider world. In recent years this desire to justify the recognition of IPRs has led to claims that the right to profit from the use of intellectual property is actually a human right.

The establishment of the global governance of IPRs has prompted a claim that IPRs are also human rights or 'natural' rights. There are two serious problems with this proposition. Article 15.1(c) of the COVENANT ON ECONOMIC, SOCIAL AND CULTURAL RIGHTS (CESCR) and Article 27 of the UNIVERSAL DECLARATION ON HUMAN RIGHTS both require the protection of authors' interest in their works, but Article 15.2 of the Covenant also requires that the diffusion of science and culture should not be compromised. However, in most cases IPRs are 'owned' not by individuals but rather by companies because many individuals can only hope to achieve significant rewards by licensing their IPRs to companies that have the resources to invest in the large-scale manufacture and reproduction. But while these companies may have significant and just rights to profit from their investment in the production of goods and services, the confusion of commercial rights with human rights leads to an over emphasis on the protection of IPRs related to others' rights. While human rights are natural rights accorded to persons with no qualification, commercial actors are legal entities subject to legal definition and limitation.

Although they find their origins in the products of individual endeavour (with natural persons), IPRs' largely commercial character and frequent effective ownership by companies suggests they are something other than human rights.

Furthermore a significant element of IPRs is not the freedom for an individual rightsholder to do something or not to have something done to them, but is rather the 'right' to halt certain behaviour by others. Although these limitations have always been circumscribed by the assertion of public benefits in most IPR-legislation, these commercial rights may still have a significant effect on the rights of others. For example there is a clear tension between the rights of AIDS patients to receive life-extending drug treatments and the rights of multinational pharmaceutical companies to receive financial rewards for the utilisation of their patents. The crucial issue is that IPRs confer rights within markets and where IPRs are in tension with other (human) rights, use becomes a wealth issue.

In national legislation such problems have been ameliorated through the use of political mechanisms such as compulsory licensing (where the government appropriates specific IPRs to allow their cheaper manufacture). In democratic societies, although imperfect, there are established mechanisms for the articulation of political interests at odds with the rights claimed by the owners of specific IPRs. However, at the global level, as the disputes and difficulties regarding AIDS medicines in poorer countries have demonstrated, the balance of claimed rights is difficult to resolve. The recognition and enforcement of IPRs may infringe and diminish the rights of others, and the claim that IPRs are human rights cannot be seen outside this context.

Although there are certainly arguments that IPRs have a human rights element especially where such rights are claimed by natural persons or where the appropriation of traditional knowledge is being resisted, because of their general commercial character alongside the demands they make on others regarding the limitation of behaviour, the presentation of IPRs as human rights is not particularly helpful. This is not to say that IPRs are not important, nor that the rights claimed are necessarily illegitimate or unjust. However, IPRs' benefits and rewards must be put into the context of their social and political deployment. This has recently been the position taken by the United Nations Development Programme, which has argued that TRIPs (and IPRs more generally) are inconsistent with many of the (human) rights established by the CESCR and its companion, the **COVENANT ON CIVIL AND POLITICAL RIGHTS**. The presentation of IPRs as natural or human rights underpins a strident (almost absolutist) claim as regards the importance of rights-holders (just) interest and fails to fully recognise that too often important human rights are compromised by the enforcement of IPRs. The rights of natural persons to the protections that human rights conventions establish must take precedence over any protection accorded commercial entities claiming equivalent (human) rights.

Further Reading

Helfer, L.R. (2003) 'Human Rights and Intellectual Property: Conflict of Coexistence?' in, 5.1 *Minnesota Intellectual Property Review*, 47–61 (available at: http://mipr.umn.edu/archive/v5n1/helfer.pdf).

May, C. (2004) 'Cosmopolitan legalism meets 'thin community': problems in the global governance of intellectual property', 39.3, *Government and Opposition*, 393–422 p836.

May, C. (2002) 'Unacceptable Costs: The Consequences of Making Knowledge Property in a Global Society' in 16.2, *Global Society*, (April) 123–44.

Monaghan, K., du Plessis, Max and Malhi, T. (2003) *Race, Religion and Ethnicity Discrimination*, a JUSTICE report, London.

Ostergard, R.L. (1999) 'Intellectual Property: A Universal Human Right?' in 21.1, *Human Rights Quarterly* (February) 156–78.

Contributor: Christopher May

PROPERTY, THE RIGHT TO: LAND RIGHTS RESTITUTION

Restitution is the act of making good the loss suffered by an individual in a way such that the claimant is placed in the same or similar position as he or she might have been before the loss occurred. In the case of land rights that

> **China**
> Proposed reforms to the Chinese Constitution in 2004 include the elaboration of the right to private property.

were lost, restitution must make good that loss by restoring the land or its equivalent.

The challenge with land restitution is that the value, and sometimes the purpose, of the lost land would have changed from the time it was taken away from or even reinstated to the claimant. That value is not always monetary because land sometimes holds many values, including the emotional, customary and sacred ties of people. The taking of the land may have occurred many years ago, often not by the current owners. The character of the land might have changed, for example a large block of apartments is currently built on it. Or the claimant might have been dispossessed of land once on the edge of the city and at the time of restitution is now in the centre of the expanded city. The question remains: who finances the changed situation and how is restitution undertaken?

The restitution of land has been an issue in many parts of the world such as Canada, the United States of America, Australia, New Zealand, Germany, Romania, Estonia, Lithuania, Zimbabwe and South Africa. In all these countries, progress has been slow and expensive where there are clear laws, if any, to deal with such claims. As an example of this process at work, some details about the progress in South Africa will be examined through a critical evaluation of successes and failures.

Since 1652 the practice of white settlers in South Africa was the 'conquest' of territory and the imposition of individual ownership over what was perceived to be communal land. Much later, in 1948, the system of separate development was created which became known as apartheid. This practice ensured that more than 80 per cent of the best land was legally designated for white South Africa, undertaken through the enactment of a number of laws that created separate areas for different race groups. In effect, the system was such that no black person had South African citizenship as he or she was assigned to an ethnic homeland.

In 1994 the Interim Constitution stressed the need to move away from the divisions and

Case study

Mabo v State of Queensland
Wik v State of Queensland

Aboriginal and Torres Strait Islanders in Australia were dispossessed of their land some two hundred years ago. The incoming colonial forces deemed the islands 'terra nullius', literally empty land. Thus Australia was not subject to recognised systems of land ownership and suitable for conquest.

Mabo v State of Queensland prompted a dramatic rethink when the High Court of Australia recognised the pre-existing native title to land in the Torres Strait islands. The Native Title Act 1993 sought to rectify the 'historic wrong', creating a system for the formal recognition of native title and compensation for the loss thereof. Further developments in *Wik v State of Queensland* extended the right by indicating that native title may continue irrespective of subsequent transfers of ownership. Native title perhaps cannot be extinguished.

strife of the past and to rebuild the society on the values of compassion, respect, human dignity and reconciliation encapsulated in the word 'ubuntu'. Key to this concept was the Restitution of Land Rights Act of 1994, which created a legal process for persons or communities who were dispossessed of their rights in land under past racially discriminatory laws to claim for the restitution of those rights from the state. Under this law a qualified claimant could apply for the land to be restored or for alternative land or for compensation where the dispossession took place after 19 June 1913. Clearly, this law did not cater for claims before that. Also, there was a fixed period in which claims could be lodged. There was a two-stage procedure: one before the Land Claims Commission and another before the Land Claims Court. First, the claim would be sent to the Land Claims Commission which had powers to investigate and verify it before informing the public. In addition, the Land Claims Commission was empowered to mediate between the competing claims. Generally, if no settlement was reached the claim would end up before the Land Claims Court. The Land Claims Court might decide to give the claimed land back to the claimant, or to provide alternative land, or even compensation under some guidelines. The Land Claims Court had to also factor in the desirability of the restitution process, the remedying of past violations of human rights and the avoiding of mass social disruption. Before the Land Claims Court determined the price to be paid to the current holder of the property, it had to also consider the requirements of fairness and

any programme of affirmative action planned for that piece of land. In addition, the Land Claims Court had to balance the public interest and the interest of those affected by considering the current use of the property, the way the property was acquired and how it was used, the market value of the property, any soft loans granted by the state to buy the property, any improvements of the property and the reason for the state taking the property. It was intended that this holistic view would determine what would be a just and equitable price for land that would be expropriated for restitution purposes.

Originally, it was envisaged that these claims would be decided in five years. It soon became clear that this was not going to be possible and the period was extended until the end of 2005. In the first four years of this process, until 1998, a mere 28 claims from a total of 42,000 submitted were resolved. A review indicated a slow rate of delivery, lack of trust and high levels of frustration with the process. There was a need to prioritise different types of land claims and eradicate management and leadership issues that hampered a smooth running of the restitution process. In response to these criticisms new administrative mechanisms for resolution were created for claims where there was no dispute, for undisputed individual urban claims for financial compensation and for the Minister to act in cases where the parties had reached a settlement among themselves. By 31 December 2002 land claims numbering 36,279 were settled from a total of 68,878 claims at a cost of 1,854,425 thousand South African rands (approximately $US 300,000).

The government has come in for sharp criticism from land reform non-governmental organisations which saw land restitution process as part of the land reform package promised by the government in 1994. The government had promised to redistribute 30 per cent of agricultural land to black farmers and to complete the land restitution programme within five years. By 31 December 2002 only 2.3 per cent of agricultural land had been transferred and half the number of land restitution claims resolved. The land restitution process has been criticised as a cautious approach that did not take into consideration the urgency of the need. The limiting of claims to the 19 June 1913 date was not satisfactory because many black people had already been dispossessed by then. The land restitution process has been seriously restricted by a limited budget. Some critics have said that under the present pattern of settlement of land restitution cases, it could take up to 150 years to complete the restitution programme.

But the main stumbling block to the state's ambitions on delivery of land restitution claims was the inability to expropriate farms at reasonable prices. In the absence of an agreement, farmers have been holding out for market value prices and the Land Claims Commission was forced to back down on just and equitable prices for these properties due to threats to take these cases to the Land Claims Court. This has now been remedied with a further amendment to the land restitution law. Now the Minister of Land Affairs can expropriate land for the purposes of restitution where the amount of the compensation paid for the land must be just and equitable.

A more objective assessment of the restitution of land rights in South Africa may be that, besides the teething problems in getting the system to work and deliver adequate results, it is a more rights-based system centred on the ideal of correcting the errors of the apartheid era. There is do doubt that it is a legalistic system which can be disempowering to those who have recently acquired rights and who are victims of the old order.

Where people were dispossessed of their lands unfairly and there is an opportunity to atone for those actions by taking corrective measures, directed at restoring the dignity of the dispossessed persons, land restitution schemes merit serious consideration. Most of them appear to have a costly and time-consuming process. Too many delays cause frustration and people may be compelled to resort to self-help. The expectation of speedier results may lead to the replication of further injustices to others. The solution may lie in finding a balance between the promise to remedy past mistakes and effective delivery mechanisms.

'1. All peoples shall freely dispose of their wealth and natural resources. This right shall be exercised in the exclusive interest of the people. In no case shall a people be deprived of it.
2. In case of spoilation the dispossessed people shall have the right to the lawful recovery of its property as well as to an adequate compensation.
...
5. State parties to the present Charter shall undertake to eliminate all forms of foreign exploitation particularly that practised by international monopolies so as to enable their peoples to fully benefit from the advantages derived from their natural resources'.

(Article 21, African Charter on Human and Peoples' Rights 1981)

WEBSITES

Monty J. Roodt, Land Restitution in South Africa.
www.badil.org/Campaign/ExpertForum/Geneva/04-M-Roodt.htm
Review of Baltic States Real Estate Market 2002. www.maamet.ee

Further Reading

Jaichand, Vinodh (1997) *Restitution of Land Rights – A Workbook*, Johannesburg: Lex Patria Publishers.

O Gutto, S.B. (1995) *Property and Land Reform. Constitutional and Jurisprudential Perspectives*, Durban: Butterworths Publishers.

Contributor: Vinodh Jaichand

RACISM, THE FUTURE OF THE STRUGGLE AGAINST

Along with protection from discrimination on grounds of sex, language and religion, the protection against race discrimination is the cornerstone of the international community's commitment to equality. The UN Charter of 1945 proclaims that the United Nation's purposes include:

'... promoting and encouraging respect for human rights and for fundamental freedoms for all without distinction as to race, sex, language, or religion' (Article 1, UN Charter).

Following the Charter's endorsement of the principle of human equality, the rooting out of racism and racial discrimination has been the main impetus for the emergence of the UN's human rights mechanisms. Half a century later, an important milestone in the history of international efforts to address racism was the World Conference against Racism, Racial Discrimination Xenophobia and Related Intolerance, which took place in August–September 2001. It was convened in Durban by the United Nations and hosted by the South African government.

The Durban Conference reaffirmed the principle of equality and non-discrimination based on race and adopted a Programme of Action for the third millennium. The Programme of Action builds on the comprehensive international framework to protect against discrimination, calls on the international community to make it more effective and identifies the thorny issues around which there must be further dialogue, understanding and action.

One of the main issues the conference tackled was the impact of historical patterns and traditions of racial or ethnic discrimination and the need to devise social measures and action plans to address victims of historical exclusion. There was recognition that equality of opportunity cannot alone be provided by general guarantees of equality and political and social participation or universal policies of access to vital services such as **EDUCATION, HEALTH CARE, HOUSING** and employment (See: **LABOUR RIGHTS**). These are the essential foundation of equality (See: **EQUALITY AND HUMAN RIGHTS**). But minorities who have experienced often generations of prejudice and exclusion require in addition targeted policies that help them to catch up. International human rights standards encourage what are termed affirmative action policies or special measures where they are designed strictly to correct inequalities of the past and are for a limited period. Some human rights treaties expressly require positive action on the part of states to eliminate discrimination on prohibited grounds. An obligation to bring about change by the imposition of a positive duty so as to tackle structural disadvantage goes further towards securing substantive equality. Such an approach is sometimes considered controversial because of the assumption that positive duties, or affirmative action, violate conventional principles of equality. Yet it does represent the high point in the protection against discrimination.

Designing effective corrective measures requires an honest assessment of the burden of history and its legacy in the present. The Durban Conference was historic in that states faced up to the past. They agreed that **SLAVERY** and the slave trade are a crime against humanity and should always have been so. While falling short of committing themselves to **REPARATIONS** for such historical injustices, these are recognised as having contributed to **POVERTY**, underdevelopment (See: **THE RIGHT TO DEVELOPMENT**), marginalisation, social exclusion, economic disparities and instability. Ultimately, states are called on to take appropriate and effective measures to halt and reverse the lasting consequences of those practices.

The Durban Conference also brought to the fore the issue of multiple discrimination. It is increasingly recognised that discrimination on multiple grounds is commonplace and creates unique experiences. It affects particularly women, whose vulnerability to discrimination is increased when they belong to a racial or ethnic minority group (See: **WOMEN'S RIGHTS; CONVENTION ON THE ELIMINATION OF ALL FORMS OF DISCRIMINATION AGAINST WOMEN**). The focus on such multiple burdens of discrimination is a further development of a new process of gender awareness in the study of human rights violations. The conference addressed the importance of applying a gender perspective in formulating policies, programmes, administrative and legal measures aimed at the eradication of racism. The UN monitoring mechanisms have acknowledged the need to focus on the circumstances in which racial discrimination only or primarily affects women, or affects them in a different way or to a different degree than men. For example, the Committee on the Elimination of Racial Discrimination – the UN treaty body that oversees compliance with the **INTERNATIONAL CONVENTION ON THE ELIMINATION OF ALL FORMS OF RACIAL DISCRIMINATION** – has shown more sensitivity to this problem and encouraged the integration of gender aspects into state reports.

Migrants and refugees constitute another vulnerable group for which more action is being called for to counter the discrimination and intolerance to which they are increasingly exposed (see: **THE MIGRANT WORKERS' CONVENTION**). Problems confronting migrants, refugees and other non-citizens are institutional and endemic in many countries. They encounter hostility and practices of racism, xenophobia and intolerance, particularly when visibly distinguishable. They often live in their host state as second class human beings. Although, as a matter of principle, basic human rights apply to everyone, citizens and non-citizens alike, legal distinctions between citizens and non-citizens continue to be enforced beyond the narrow exceptions permitted by international human rights law.

While international human rights law generally requires the equal treatment of citizens and non-citizens, the Convention on the Elimination of All Forms of Racial Discrimination itself contains a significant lacuna in that by its terms it does not apply to how governments treat non-citizens. While the CERD Committee has addressed this loophole in its General Recommendations and practice with respect to examination of state party reports, the contemporary importance of the issue requires a more direct treatment. The Durban Declaration notes 'that xenophobia against non-nationals, particularly migrants, refugees and asylum seekers, constitutes one of the main sources of contemporary racism …'. The Programme of Action urges States to address discrimination against migrants and refugees and to facilitate the full enjoyment of their human rights.

The Durban Programme of Action builds on the increasing focus by UN bodies on discrimination faced by non-nationals and on the major advances that have been made in the international elaboration of rights of non-citizens. It demonstrates the need for the establishment of an effective international legal protection regime for non-citizens and the enjoyment of those rights in practice (See: **INTERNATIONAL CITIZENSHIP AND HUMAN RIGHTS**).

The Durban Conference called also for more extensive efforts to build up a legal framework at national level to combat racism and racial discrimination. General and comprehensive anti-discrimination legislation is encouraged or prescribed by existing provisions and evolving standards at international and regional level. States have been repeatedly called upon to enact comprehensive anti-discrimination legislation, not only in the criminal sphere to suppress incitement to racial hatred and discrimination and acts of violence but also in the area of civil and administrative law. Such legislation is not only needed to direct policies and practices of public authorities and public institutions but also to prohibit racial discrimination by private institutions, enterprises and individuals with respect to such areas as employment, education, housing, health care, social security, access to supply of goods and services and to public places, as well as access to citizenship.

Positive legal developments have been most remarkable in Europe where in recent years a comprehensive body of legislation has been put in place requiring EU member states to adopt and implement far-reaching anti-discrimination provisions in the areas of everyday life, such as employment and working conditions, social security and health care, education, access to goods and services, including housing. Member states must also provide for legal protection for victims and witnesses against retaliation by employers or others, and establish bodies for the promotion of equal treatment, with a mandate to provide independent assistance to victims of discrimination, conduct surveys and studies and publish reports and recommendations.

Innovative measures, such as protection against victimisation and conferring a capacity on national institutions or non-governmental organisations to assist victims, are echoed in the Durban Programme of Action as part of provisions calling for effective remedies, recourse, redress and other measures at the national, regional and international level.

The Durban Conference has undoubtedly increased awareness of how the protection systems of international and regional mechanisms may become more effective and more relevant for victims of racism. It has improved the understanding of issues relating to discrimination through improved knowledge of this phenomenon and through evaluation of the effectiveness of policies and practices. It has strengthened organisations' means of action through exchange of information and good practice. Comprehensive implementation and follow-up to its programme would ensure that race discrimination is minimised and we move closer to the goal of its eradication.

Further Reading

Bell, Mark (2002) *Anti-Discrimination Law and the European Union*, Oxford University Press.

Fredman, Sandra (ed.) (2001) *Discrimination and Human Rights – The Case of Racism*, Oxford: Oxford University Press.

JUSTICE, Race, Religion and Ethnicity Discrimination – Using International Human Rights Law, 2003.

McDougall, Gay (2002) 'The World Conference against Racism: Through a Wider Lens' in *The Fletcher Forum of World Affairs*, vol. 26, 2, Summer/Fall.

Report of the World Conference Against Racism (2001) 'Racial Discrimination Xenophobia and Related Intolerance', Durban, 31 August–8 September, A/CONF.189/12.

Contributor: Anneliese Baldaccini

THE REFORM OF THE UNITED NATIONS

The ongoing crisis in the international political order and its institutions since 11 September 2001 dramatically demonstrates

global governance to be the pressing political issue of our times. The United States' effectiveness in combating 'global terror' through a series of costly localised wars is questionable. Yet rejecting preventative action in favour of a cold war concept of international legitimacy is also inadequate. As most questions become global, 'nation-states' are increasingly ill-suited to their solution.

This moment should be seized for a bold, imaginative reform of the United Nations to address the issues of **DEMOCRACY, PEACE,** sustainability (See: **ENVIRONMENTAL RIGHTS**) and network society defining our new century. Can these challenges be met by modest reconfiguration? Or is a drastic reconstruction necessary and desirable? The UN's status remains a valuable asset and should be preserved. While official initiatives (like the Secretary General's High Level Panel) may yield incremental progress, we now see radical reform as the only viable option.

Any plausible scheme must consider three major features: decision making in the Security Council and General Assembly; reformulation of mission statements (including the Charter) and internal organisation of the United Nations; and rationalisation of the portfolio of international policy-making entities.

Professor Philip Alston

Professor Philip Alston was appointed as an Independent Expert by the UN Secretary General, on the recommendation of the General Assembly to report on measures to ensure the long-term effectiveness of the UN human rights treaty bodies. He submitted preliminary reports in 1989 and 1993 (before the Vienna World Conference). His final report was submitted in 1997. This report lays the framework for the current system of reform being undertaken by the United Nations with respect to human rights monitoring. Professor Alston has served in a number of different positions in Australia and the UN, as well as in universities worldwide. He is a well-published academic of international repute and is currently full-time faculty in the New York University School of Law.

The United Nations faces problems both of efficacy and democracy. Although trade-offs are often sought between these two, we believe that its weakened problem-solving ability and diminished representative capacity (of people and nations) are correlated. So what can be done? Some suggest abolishing the veto of the permanent members of the Security Council or modifying the Security Council's composition and permanent membership. Others propose dismantling the Security Council, leaving all decisions to the General Assembly. But in institutional redesign, the first step should identify separate 'powers' conveying democracy and efficiency with different intensity and these should be able to counterbalance each other.

In our view the Security Council should become an executive decision-making body whose members – the biggest countries – are all permanent and which guarantees efficiency (smaller groups are better at problem solving) and stability. The General Assembly, by contrast, will ensure democracy and innovation, which normally originates with smaller players and outsiders. Its remit will be extended and its decisions taken mostly by simple majority (for example in elections to United

Rank	Country	Military expenditures – dollar figure	Date of Information
1	United States	$276,700,000,000	2002
2	China	$55,910,000,000	2002
3	France	$46,500,000,000	2000
4	Japan	$39,520,000,000	2002
5	Germany	$38,800,000,000	2002
6	United Kingdom	$31,700,000,000	2002
7	Italy	$20,200,000,000	2002
8	Brazil	$13,408,000,000	2000
9	India	$11,520,000,000	2002
10	Russian Federation	$11,400,000,000	2002
11	Mexico	$4,000,000,000	1999
12	Pakistan	$2,545,500,000	2001
13	Indonesia	$1,000,000,000	1999
14	Bangladesh	$559,000,000	2000
15	Nigeria	$374,000,000	2000

Military expenditure in 2002 in dollars (Source: www.cia.org)

Rank	Country	GDP – per capita (2002)
1	United States	$ 36,300
2	Japan	$ 28,700
3	Germany	$ 26,200
4	France	$ 26,000
5	United Kingdom	$ 25,500
6	Italy	$ 25,100
7	Russia	$ 9,700
8	Mexico	$ 8,900
9	Brazil	$ 7,600
10	China	$ 4,700
11	Indonesia	$ 3,100
12	India	$ 2,600
13	Pakistan	$ 2,000
14	Bangladesh	$ 1,800
15	Nigeria	$ 900

GDP per capita in 2002.

*Dollars 2002 International prices (Source: www.cia.gov)

Nations' bodies) but by two-thirds majority in priority areas (decisions on expulsion from membership, for instance). The Security Council could demand a higher quorum, as occasion requires.

The new United Nations must exploit a simple fact: global forces of population, economic and military power are highly concentrated. The world's six largest countries comprise 50 per cent of the global population; adding one more accounts for half of global gross domestic product. A relatively small body could still be strongly 'representative' in majoritarian terms.

Who will the new Security Council members be? The criteria should be transparent and quantitative. We propose the ten largest countries measured by population and GDP to give a list of 15 nations: the current P5 (the United States, the United Kingdom, France, the Commonwealth of Independent States and China), three more G8 states (Japan, Germany and Italy), plus India, Indonesia, Bangladesh, Brazil, Mexico, Pakistan and Nigeria. These 15 states, 7 per cent of the 191 members of the United Nations, represent 4 billion people (65 per cent of world population) and 59 per cent of worldwide Gross Domestic Product. They also account for more than 90 per cent of total military expenditure, and nearly all weapons of mass destruction, so reflecting the current balance of power. Nevertheless, a good regional balance is maintained; nor is it a 'rich club'.

One question stands out: what could convince the Security Council incumbents, especially the United States as the current sole superpower, to dilute their power? There are four additional problems: 1) countries claiming they too are big enough for the new Council (Spain and Australia on economic grounds, Egypt and Vietnam on population); 2) large states balking at having identical voting weight as the tiniest in the General Assembly; 3) today's P-5 objecting to equal status with new Security Council members; 4) inevitable rejection by today's P-5 of loss of their veto. The first problem may be easy to address: individual Security Council members may gradually be replaced by macro-regions (like the European Union) as these develop unitary capacity to contribute to global decision making. Countries too small to qualify may also increase their weight through partnerships. As to the second, General Assembly votes certainly require weighting, probably according to population (or population bands, to avoid over-representing India and China and making the smallest countries invisible). Thirdly, weighted voting may also be applied in the Security Council, at least for a period, to persuade the current P-5 to accept change: their votes might carry twice those of the other ten.

As for the veto, only the US maintains the superpower status this reflected in 1945. An institutional mechanism must be found to accommodate this reality. One option would be to concede retention of the veto to the US alone. This would prevent the United Nations from acting against the US – any such decision would anyhow be technically impossible to implement. And the US might be encouraged to take major decisions with the United Nation's consent. Not doing so, as in Iraq, is already showing itself to be politically and economically unsustainable. A 'sunset clause' must be added to all these special provisions (in other words, a provision guaranteeing a review, and potential revision, of the new arrangements after a set period of time). This would be crucial factor in maintaining the new body's dynamism and responsiveness to evolving distributions of world power and resources.

The United Nations Charter claims three main objectives in its mission statement: peace and security, **DEVELOPMENT** and aid, and freedom and human rights. The meaning of the first has changed radically: since 1945, the relationship between the two terms has been turned upside down. The guiding intention of the second objective, development and aid, may remain substantially intact, but the macroeconomic hypotheses on which it was constructed need urgently to be revisited. The third objective poses two questions that can no longer be postponed: are human rights an inextricable part of security? And is democracy integral to human rights and therefore a natural part of the United Nations mission? Answering 'yes' to the second question triggers further dilemma. What do we mean by democracy? Is there a universally acceptable definition? Should this hold any implication for the terms of United Nations membership?

The United Nations needs to revisit its foundational tenets and mechanisms for achieving its objectives. It is one thing to claim rhetorically that 'the UN promotes peace and security', but an entirely different matter to state clearly – as we would recommend – that 'no war may be prosecuted against a UN member state without explicit authorisation by a qualified majority' and that 'the UN may authorise a limitation of national sovereignty, should it decide a state threatens the security of others, or its own inhabitants'.

Many areas remain for analysis, within and beyond the United Nations galaxy. A reformed organisation could be assigned further global tasks, for example environmental protection, as we have suggested in the extended version of this article (see websites). Synergies must be leveraged and overlaps reduced – for instance, between the World Bank and the IMF which, at minimum, require vastly improved coordination, if not integration into a more rational global governance framework.

The new United Nations should avoid replicating traditional nation-state or macro-regional governance structures. Instead of instituting one huge government with a 'President of the World' at its head, different executive entities – their nature somewhere between 'agencies' and real 'government' – should be elected by the Security Council and the General Assembly. The new configuration must also be more inclusive of citizens (See: **INTERNATIONAL CITIZENSHIP** or civil society (See: **SOCIAL MOVEMENTS AND HUMAN RIGHTS**). The gulf between public opinion and international decision-making processes was starkly evident in the passionate debates preceding the Iraq war. Granting additional seats to international non-governmental organisations or political parties with sufficient cross-border representation might achieve better alignment in future. Pilots directly involving citizens on a world- or at least macro-regional footing should be undertaken. International referenda might be an organisational nightmare, yet an effective tool to market global governance. Gradually we must find ways to boost participation.

Institutional flexibility must be at the core of global governance if we are to navigate and survive the challenges and uncertainties of decades to come. This puts the idea of a 'variable geometry' for the United Nations firmly on the agenda. The United Nations, like the European Union, should assume different shapes for different tasks, programmes and projects – all under United Nations authorisation, but involving shifting subsets of members.

Achieving a grand redesign is likely to take years. It will demand, first, engaging states in sustained and structured dialogue, to persuade them of the ultimate benefit to national interests. But it will also require focused demands for change from civil society, to unblock fixed official positions. One possibility is a Convention on the Future of Global Governance, incorporating lessons about multilateral constitution building from Europe's Convention process. We plan to continue working on this agenda through TransformUN, a Vision umbrella project to explore a spectrum of ideas (reaching even beyond those presented here) and to catalyse the beginning of a process of transformation in global governance, whose time has now come.

WEBSITES

Secretary General's High Level Panel
www.un.org/News/Press/docs/2003/sga857.doc.htm.

Extended version of this entry on:
www.vision-forum.org and
www.opendemocracy.net

Further Reading

Held, D. (2004) *Global Covenant: The Social Democratic Alternative to the Washington Consensus*, Cambridge: Polity.

Held, D. and McGrew, A. (eds) (2002) *Governing Globalization: Power, Authority and Global Governance*, Cambridge: Polity.

International Development Research Centre (2002) *The Responsibility to Protect: The Report of the International Commission on Intervention and State Sovereignty*, Ottawa: IDRC.

Stiglitz, J. (2003) *Globalization and its Discontents*, London: Penguin.

Contributors: Francesco Grillo,
Simona Milio and Claire O'Brien

REFUGEE LAW

Refugee law is an integral component of the mosaic of international human rights law. The 1951 Geneva Convention Relating to the Status of Refugees and its 1967 Protocol defines for the purposes of international law a refugee. The **UNIVERSAL DECLARATION OF HUMAN RIGHTS**, Article 14, acknowledges everyone has the right to seek and enjoy in other countries asylum from persecution. This right has been omitted from subsequent international human rights instruments and

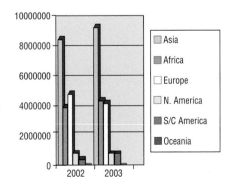

Numbers of persons of concern to UNHCR, by region
(Information from www.unhcr.ch)

© Carmen Redondo/CORBIS

has only reappeared in Article 18 of the **EUROPEAN CHARTER FOR FUNDA-MENTAL RIGHTS AND FREEDOMS**. The 1951 Convention (references to the 1951 Convention also include the 1967 Protocol) extends surrogacy of protection to individuals where normal protection is not extended by the state of nationality or place of habitual residence. As such the 1951 Convention is part of a corpus of international human rights law and such norms derived from treaty and customary international law should be employed in the application of the 1951 Convention. Essentially the granting of refugee status indicates that one or more of the claimant's basic human rights are not being respected.

The interface between other international human rights instruments and the 1951 Convention is immediately identified in the Preamble of the 1951 Convention which makes reference to the Charter of the United Nations and the Universal Declaration of Human Rights and the affirmation of the United Nations that human beings are to enjoy fundamental rights and freedoms without discrimination. The 1951 Convention is premised on all human beings enjoying fundamental rights and freedoms and a fundamental purpose of the 1951 Convention is counteracting discrimination (Lord Stein in the case of *Islam v SSHD* and *R v IAT ex parte Shah (HL)* [1999] INLR 144).

Interpretation of the 1951 Convention demands reference to international human rights instruments, in particular the terms 'persecution' and non-refoulment. Persecution is not defined in the 1951 Convention and the *United Nations High Commission for Refugees Handbook* recognises there is no universally accepted definition of the term. Article 33 of the 1951 Convention provides an individual is not to be returned to any country where his life or freedom would be threatened on account of his race, religion, nationality, membership of a particular social group or political opinion. These are the grounds set out in the 1951 Convention and for asylum to be granted a nexus has to be established between the alleged persecution and any one of the five or a combination thereof. Paragraph 51 of the *UNHCR Handbook* recognises the five grounds would constitute persecution but continues that other serious violations of human rights, for the same reasons, would also constitute persecution. Determining whether violation of human rights requires cognisance be given to the various international human rights instruments. Persecution should be interpreted on the basis of internationally recognised human rights standards:

Ruud Lubbers
Ruud Lubbers assumed the role of UN High Commissioner for Refugees in January 2001. He is the ninth UNHCR with a term of office running until December 2005. Prior to assuming his current appointment he spent twelve years as Prime Minister of the Netherlands and a period in academia. Immediately prior to entering the UN he was head of the World Wide Fund for Nature.

(From www.unhcr.ch)

'from the sustained or systematic violation of basic human rights demonstrative of a failure of state protection in relation to one of the core entitlements which has been recognised by the international community. The types of harm to be protected against include the breach of any right within the first category, a discriminatory or non-emergency abrogation of a right within the second category, or the failure to implement a right within the third category, which is either discriminatory or not grounded in the absolute lack of resources' (Hathaway, 1991, p. 114).

Professor Hathaway categorises human rights into three levels. Level one rights are the absolute rights admitting no suspension of in any circumstances, e.g. Articles 6, 7, 8 (paragraphs 1 and 2), 11, 15, 16 and 18 of the **INTERNATIONAL COVENANT ON CIVIL AND POLITICAL RIGHTS**. A failure of a state to ensure such rights will 'be tantamount to persecution'. Second-level rights are those which admit derogation during an officially declared state of emergency. Such rights include those guaranteed by Articles 9, 12, 14 and 26. Responsibility will be incurred if the state goes beyond what is strictly necessitated by the emergency (in terms of scope or duration) or where the derogation impacts on certain sub groups of the population (Hathaway, p. 110).

Level three rights are essentially those spelt out in the **INTERNATIONAL COVENANT ON ECONOMIC, SOCIAL AND CULTURAL RIGHTS**. Discrimination may amount to a violation of human rights but to constitute persecution the discrimina-

tory measures must lead to consequences of a substantially prejudicial nature for the person concerned (paragraph 54, *UNHCR Handbook*).

The corpus of international human rights norms has grown and international human rights standards are found in the Universal Declaration on Human Rights and the two 1966 UN Covenants (ICCPR and ICESCR) and also in international instruments which deal with specific rights and freedoms, seeking to extend protection to particular vulnerable groups and those seeking to prevent or eliminate specific discriminatory behaviour. Certain instruments make specific reference to refugees or apply specifically to refugees. The Convention Against **TORTURE** and other Cruel Inhuman or Degrading Treatment or Punishment (1984) defines torture in Article 1 and encapsulates the principle of non-refoulment in Article 3. Article 3 provides an individual should not be returned or extradited to another state where there are substantial grounds for believing that he/she would be in danger of being subjected to torture. An individual who has been denied Convention refugee status may invoke Article 3 of the Torture Convention (see, for example, Communication no. 13/1993 *Mutombo v Switzerland*, 15, *HRLJ*, 164 and 15/1994 *Khan v Canada*, 15, *HRLJ*, 426). Note also Article 3 of the European Convention on Human Rights and Fundamental Freedoms, which has been held by the European Court of Human Rights to be absolute in expulsion cases (see e.g. *Chahal v UK* (1996) 23 EHRR 413). The absolute nature of Article 3 is reinforced by the fact that a state returning someone to an intermediary country has got to determine whether the individual would be at risk of treatment contrary to Article 3 when returned to the country of final destination (*Ti v UK* 2000 INLR 211).

Conventions dealing with particular groups include the **CONVENTION ON THE RIGHTS OF THE CHILD**, which makes specific reference to refugee children, Article 22. International Conventions dealing with discrimination and its elimination include the international **CONVENTION ON THE ELIMINATION OF ALL FORMS OF DISCRIMINATION** and the **CONVENTION ON ELIMINATION OF ALL FORMS OF DISCRIMINATION AGAINST WOMEN** and there is a plethora of standard-setting norms to compliment these Conventions.

The provisions of the 1951 Convention are to be applied on the basis of non-discrimination, on grounds of race, religion or country of origin. Refugees within territories of contracting states are to be accorded treatment at least as favourable as that afforded to their nationals with respect to the practice of their religion and freedom as regards the religious education of their children.

20,556,781 people fell within the mandate of the United Nations High Commissioner for Refugees as of 1 January 2003.
(Figures from www.unhchr.ch, 2004)

The 1951 Convention also spells out rights which should be afforded to individuals once refugee status has been granted. Refugees should receive at least the treatment which is accorded to aliens generally. National treatment is accorded regarding the protection of artistic rights and industrial property (Article 14), access to courts (Article 16), housing (Article 21), elementary education (Article 22), labour legislation and social security (Article 24), freedom of movement (Article 26). Article 17 relates to wage earning and employment and has attracted the most reservations. Not all persons seeking refugee protection will qualify. Persons who are excluded are those not considered to be in need of protection, Article 1E, or those undeserving of protection.

The so-called 'exclusions clauses' are set out in Articles 1D, E and F of the 1951 Convention. Article 1F denies refugee protection to any individual where there are serious reasons for considering inter alia he/she has committed a crime against peace, a war crime or a crime against humanity as defined in relevant international instruments; a serious non-political crime outside the country of refuge prior to admission as a refugee and acts contrary to the purposes and principles of the UN. Given Article 1F excludes a person from international refugee protection, the crimes in question must be interpreted from an international perspective. International instruments utilised include the Convention on the Prevention and Punishment of the Crime of Genocide 1948 and the Statutes of the International Criminal Tribunal for the Former Yugoslavia (ICTY) and International Criminal Tribunal for Rwanda (ICTR). Article 1F, because of the serious consequences flowing from its application, must be strictly interpreted. Article 1F(b) seeks to balance the needs of the community of a receiving country against admission of an individual who has committed a serious common crime while still providing due justice to a refugee who has committed a common crime(s) of a less serious nature or an apolitical offence (paragraph 151, UNHCR Handbook). Application of Article IF (b) demands the striking of a balance between the offence presumed to have been committed and the degree of persecution feared (paragraph 156, ibid). An act contrary to the purposes and principles of the UN (Article 1F (c)) is generally not applicable where an individual acts in his/her capacity without a link to a state or state-like entity. The protection of the 1951 Convention will also cease when an individual is no longer regarded as being in need of international protection. Article 1C states exhaustively the occasions when refugee status shall cease.

The principle of family unity is reflected in many international human rights instruments. However, such a provision is absent from the 1951 Convention, but the Final Act of the Conference, which adopted the 1951 Convention, recommended that governments take the necessary measures to protect a refugee's family and this is further reflected in the UNHCR Handbook, paragraphs 184, 185 and 187.

The 1951 Convention is gender silent and applies to all refugees irrespective of age. However, in conformity with international human rights developments there have been efforts to make the Convention gender and child sensitive. These are reflected in the UNHCR guidelines, UNHCR EXCOM conclusions and guidelines now applicable in member states.

Refugee law for its effective application requires cognisance of international human rights law and demands that refugee decision makers come from an informed international human rights background, which is supported by a strong human rights culture. Decisions makers in determining whether Convention refugee status is warranted must have access to reliable, general, up-to-date country information reports on (non) compliance with international human rights standards. Reports from organisations such as the US Department of State, Human Rights Watch and Amnesty International provide a relevant contextual background.

WEBSITE

www.unhcr.org

Further Reading

Crawley, H. (2001) *Refugees and Gender Law, Law and Process*, Bristol: Jordans.

Goodwin-Gill, G. (1996) *The Refugee in International Law*, 2nd edn, Oxford: Clarendon.

Hathaway, J. (1991) *The Law of Refugee Status*, London: Butterworths.

Office of the United Nations High Commissioner for Refugees (re-edited 1992) *Handbook on Procedures and Criteria for Determining Refugee Status, under the 1951 Convention and the 1967 Protocol relating to the Status of Refugees*, Geneva.

Wallace, R.M.M. (2001) *International Human Rights, Texts and Materials*, London: Sweet & Maxwell.

Contributor: Rebecca M.M. Wallace

REGIONAL SYSTEMS: AN OVERVIEW

Regional systems of human rights apply to a limited number of states, usually states found in close geographical proximity. Given the problems encountered with developing universally acceptable systems of human rights, it is perhaps logical that some attempt should be made to develop human rights at a regional level. There are a number of advantages:

1. States within regions may be relatively homogenous, sharing cultural, religious and historical traditions. This means that agreement on some rights is more likely.
2. With trade and diplomatic links, neighbouring states are often more likely to comply with the agreed rights to avoid political repercussions.
3. Fewer states are involved than at the international level thus in theory achieving a consensus is more likely.

4. Regional systems are by definition more accessible to people insofar as the salient bodies are located in the same geographical area as the states concerned. The United Nations mechanisms are normally based in Geneva or New York, not necessarily the most accessible for Africans or South Americans.

Initially, the newly formed United Nations considered itself to have prime jurisdiction over establishing a universal system of human rights. Regional developments were viewed as undermining the process of developing international universal rights. However, beset by problems achieving political consensus thereon and the proven success of regional systems in Europe and the Americas, it was inevitable that this initial reticence would wane.

In 1977, the 32nd General Assembly of the United Nations recognised 'the importance of encouraging regional cooperation for the promotion and protection of human rights and fundamental freedoms', appealing to states in areas without regional systems 'to consider agreements with a view to the establishment within their respective regions of suitable regional machinery for the promotion and protection of human rights'. In furtherance thereof, the Secretary General was asked to organise seminars in appropriate regions to determine the 'usefulness and advisability of the establishment of regional commissions for the promotion and protection of human rights' (General Assembly Resolution 32/127, 16/12/1977). At the time only Europe and the Americas had functioning regional human rights systems. In subsequent sessions the following years, the General Assembly noted with approval the advance towards a regional human rights mechanism under the then Organisation of African Unity and the embryonic proposals for regional discussions in Asia.

Perhaps it was a lack of foresight as to the burgeoning of human rights instruments which shaped the early view of the United Nations. The world in 2005 is markedly different to that in 1945. The United Nations itself began with a fraction of its current membership in an atmosphere conducive to international agreement. At least it was for the first few years as states united against the 'scourge of war' and the emerging horrors of mass war crimes. In subsequent years, political ideology fractured this consensual arrangement. In the UN Charter itself, the only mention of regional arrangements is in furtherance of the maintenance of peace and security (Chapter VIII of the Charter). However, as human rights have encroached ever more on the UN agenda and the organisation has quadrupled in size, international reliance on, and development of, regional systems has grown exponentially in response. Today the regional systems are a vital part of the international protection of human rights, complementing and supplementing the UN system. Now, the United Nations actively encourages the establishment of regional systems. It was instrumental in setting up the African system. Its offices have been offered to Asian States attempting to foster a common understanding of human rights in that region.

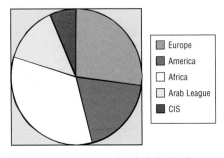

Number of member states in the principal regional systems with major human rights instruments

The principal regional systems are found in Europe (the Council of Europe), the Americas (the Organisation of American States), Africa (the African Union) and the Commonwealth of Independent States. In each instance, there is an agreed instrument enshrining the rights and a mechanism for ensuring those rights and freedoms extend to all peoples in the region. In the earlier instruments, Europe and the Americas, the rights are predominantly civil and political in nature. This reflects contemporaneous understanding of the nature of rights and the political reality of a lack of consensus on economic, social and cultural rights. Both these systems have now been augmented by elements of social, economic and cultural rights in additional instruments. However, the significant enforcement mechanisms, charac-

teristic of the principal regional treaties, do not apply to such rights.

Subsequent instruments, such as the African Charter, represent a substantive advancement in rights, including a number of economic, social, cultural and collective rights. Heralded as enshrining an African concept of human rights, the approach emphasises the universality and indivisibility of rights. The Arab League adopted a Charter on Human Rights in 1994. This instrument was drafted to reflect the Islamic Shari'a and other laws but proved merely a political tool, lacking legal ratification by states. A decade later, proposals for a revised charter are under review. Further north, the dissolution of the former USSR raised awareness of human rights in the former Soviet states. In furtherance of democratic reform, economic and social growth and strengthening law and order, the raft of new states in the **COMMONWEALTH OF INDEPENDENT STATES** adopted a regional human rights instrument in 1995.

Within the rest of **ASIA**, progress has been made although agreement on a regional mechanism still appears a long way off. In 1997, an Asian Charter of Human Rights was adopted which followed on from the 1993 Bangkok Declaration on Human Rights (adopted during preparations for the 1993 Vienna World Conference on Human Rights). In a period of dramatic and accelerated development, human rights issues are rarely far from the political agenda in Asia. Efforts will surely continue in furtherance of establishing appropriate regional systems.

Other transnational organisations increasingly respond to political concerns by adding human rights dimensions to their work. The **ORGANISATION FOR SECURITY AND COOPERATION IN EUROPE** and the **EUROPEAN UNION**, for example, have adopted instruments on human rights while the Commonwealth (of UK former colonies and dominions), the Caribbean States and even alliances of States in the South Pacific have expressed an interest in setting up a regional system.

According to the World Conference on Human Rights, regional systems should be established and strengthened in accordance with universal rights. The international system has been complemented by regional systems and now the emphasis is increasingly on states to develop national systems for ensuring respect for human rights and fundamental freedoms.

Although the later regional systems are sometimes seen as progressive for their inclusion of different categories of rights, in reality the European system is the one that functions best. This may be due to the familiarity of Europe as a continent with legal systems akin to the international system of human rights law. Human rights protection is part of a long tradition in Europe.

WEBSITES

www.coe.int – the Council of Europe

www.oas.org – Organization for American States

www.africa-union.org – African Union (formerly Organisation of African Unity)

www.arableagueonline.org – League of Arab States

www.cis.int – Commonwealth of Independent States (in Russian)

www.cis.minsk.by/english/engl_home.htm – Executive Committee of the CIS (in English)

www.forumsec.org.fj – the Pacific Islands Forum

www.thecommonwealth.org – the Commonwealth Secretariat

www.forumasia.org – Asian forum for human rights and development

---

Further Reading

Buergenthal, T., Shelton, D. and Stewart, D. (2002) *International Human Rights in a Nutshell*, 3rd edition, St. Paul, MN, West Group.

Rehman, J. (2003) *International Human Rights Law – a practical approach*, Harlow: Pearson.

Smith, R.K.M. (2005) *Textbook on International Human Rights*, 2nd edn, Oxford: OUP.

Contributor: Rhona K.M. Smith

RELIGION AND BELIEF, FREEDOM OF

The protection of freedom of religion or belief in international human rights law has had a long and difficult history. If one concentrates on its recent history, one can detect a general shift of focus along three overlapping foci: from the protection of religious minorities, to an emphasis on individual rights and non-discrimination on the basis of religion, and then to today's challenge of the full implications of 'freedom of religion or belief'.

During the negotiations on the drafting of the Covenant of the League of Nations, President Woodrow Wilson proposed the inclusion of an article on religious liberty which would condemn religious persecution and provide for the free exercise of any religious belief which did not conflict with public order and morals. This proposal remained on the agenda until just before the publication of the first draft of the Covenant in February 1919. However, when Japan sought to provide a linkage between such a clause with one on racial equality and the equality of states, both proposals were dropped due to the unpalatable nature of a racial equality clause to the drafters.

Despite this omission, numerous clauses were inserted into 15 subsequent inter-war treaties. These insisted on the protection of particular religious minorities in particular territories. This was done through special minorities treaties, treaties of peace and special declarations on the protection of minorities, which were made a prerequisite of League of Nations membership for a number of states. The guarantee of freedom of conscience and religion and the preservation of the identity of religious minorities was also guaranteed through the mandate system of the League of Nations.

The general unease of the international community with **MINORITY RIGHTS** after the bitter experiences of the Second World War, particularly because of Hitler's exploitation of the League's minority provisions to destabilise the Versailles settlement, had a negative spill-over effect for the protection of religious minorities as a group. In the early days of the formation and operation of the **UNITED NATIONS** the view was that the focus on minority groups as a whole had been erroneous. It was now believed that the new UN human rights emphasis on the protection of individual rights combined with non-discrimination would provide a better framework for the realisation of rights. The watchword now was non-discrimination on the basis of religious belief for the individual.

In this context, the **UNIVERSAL DECLARATION OF HUMAN RIGHTS** was the first official document of this new regime. Article 18 recognised that: 'Everyone has the right to freedom of thought, conscience and religion; this right includes freedom to change his religion or belief, and freedom, either alone or in community with others and in public or private, to manifest his religion or belief in teaching, practice, worship and observance'. It was primarily concern with outbreaks of racial hatred in Europe, as reflected in a UN General Assembly resolution adopted in 1960, that drove the international community to urge the UN to draft new instruments for protection against racial and religious hatred. However, insofar as drafting an instrument for protection against religious hatred was concerned, this was to mark the beginning of a tortuous 20-year effort towards a declaration. Whereas a declaration and then a convention on racial discrimination were adopted in quick succession, it was only in 1981 that the UN Declaration on the Elimination of All Forms of Intolerance and of Discrimination Based on Religion or Belief was adopted by the General Assembly by consensus. The length of time taken to adopt this instrument, and even then as a declaration rather than a legally binding covenant, is indicative of the controversy and sensitivity of the matter of religion or belief to states. In fact if this Declaration had not been adopted in 1981, it is doubtful that it could have been agreed at all in the decades that have followed.

The Declaration remains the only international instrument exclusively concerned with religion or belief. However, its purpose is not to provide a positive rendition of freedoms of religion or belief, but to eliminate discrimination and intolerance on its basis. The Declaration is largely silent on specific preventive and combative measures to be taken by states in addressing such discrimination. Unlike the **INTERNATIONAL CONVENTION ON THE ELIMINATION OF ALL FORMS OF RACIAL DISCRIMINATION**, it does not recognise the possibility of positive discrimination towards the advancement of groups disadvantaged by such discrimination, it does not spell out measures that states should take in condemning such discrimination nor a prohibition on incitement of such hatred and it does not outline the need for particular remedies, reparation or satisfaction in the case of any damage suffered from such discrimination.

In line with other international provisions on freedom of religion or belief, limitations to this freedom only concern manifestation of religion or belief (in worship, observance, practice and teaching; either individually or in community with others) where prescribed by law and necessary to protect public safety, order, health or morals or the fundamental rights and freedoms of others. This 'forum externum' may therefore be subjected to restriction in very particular instances, whereas the 'forum internum' of having a religion or belief of one's choice is absolute.

Article 6 of the Declaration is considered its key provision, as it outlines the scope and extent of the freedom of religion or belief. Article 6 seems to shift from the more material aspects required for such freedoms – such as places of worship, charitable institutions, publications and receiving contributions – to the more community dimensions of religion or belief – such as the religious leadership, days of rest, and recognising freedom of communication to religious communities. It does not go so far as the 1960 study of the UN Sub-Commission Special Rapporteur, Arcot Krishnaswami, in its specifications of which spheres of life need to be protected as central to the manifestation of religion or belief.

Secular education and religion
Various locales in Europe, notably France and Germany, were proceeding in 2004 with laws prohibiting overt religious symbols in schools. Islamic headscarves, Sikh turbans, Jewish skullcaps and Christian crosses will be unacceptable within the confines of public schools. While some may consider this a clear infringement of religious freedom, the politicians hail the proposals as essential to maintain the neutrality of the education system.

In contrast, Russia's supreme court decided in March 2003 to permit Muslim women to wear headscarves in passport photos, permitting an exception to the rule that no hats or other headwear were permissible.

Unlike some other international provisions in this area, the Declaration does not specifically express that its scope of protection extends to the protection of theistic, non-theistic and atheistic beliefs. Nor does it specify the prohibition of coercion towards the adoption and change of religion or belief. It only forbids such coercion towards the 'having' of a religion or belief of one's choice. Most surprisingly, the Declaration makes no reference to religious minorities, although the collective is clearly envisaged in some of the rights stipulated in Article 6.

Although there is no monitoring machinery associated with this Declaration, there are other means by which freedom of religion or belief is upheld and promoted through the United Nations. Through the provisions of the Convention on the Elimination of All Forms of Racial Discrimination, the **INTERNATIONAL COVENANT ON ECONOMIC, SOCIAL AND CULTURAL RIGHTS** and the **CONVENTION ON THE ELIMINATION OF ALL FORMS OF DISCRIMINATION AGAINST WOMEN** their treaty bodies grapple with particular aspects of freedom of religion or belief in relation for example to wider discrimination, education and employment and traditional or customary practices respectively. However, it is the substantial Article 18 of the International Covenant on Civil and Political Rights that enables the Human Rights Committee to have the clearest jurisdiction on matters of freedom of religion or belief.

It is essential to understand Article 18 in the light of General Comment 22 that the Human Rights Committee issued in relation to that article. The General Comment clarifies the concern of Article 18 with the theistic, atheistic and non-theistic in its oversight of religion, belief and conscience. It urges that the terms religion or beliefs need to be broadly construed. It also explains, more controversially, that Article 18(2)'s protection of the freedom to 'have' or 'adopt' a religion or belief of one's choice necessarily entails the freedom to change one's religion or belief.

Article 27 deals with minorities and states that religious minorities should not be denied the right to profess or practise their religion in community with other members of their group. Further related provisions of the International Covenant on Civil and Political Rights concern non-discrimination and the prohibition incitement of religious hatred.

Provisions relating to religious minorities are also contained in the 1992 UN Declaration on the Rights of Persons Belonging to National or Ethnic, Religious and Linguistic Minorities. This requires states to encourage the promotion of the religious identity of such minorities through appropriate legislative and other means, allow them to participate effectively in decisions concerning their group, the right to maintain their own associations and enable them to express and develop their own characteristics except where they violate national law and international standards.

In 1986 the UN Commission on Human Rights appointed a Special Rapporteur on Freedom of Religion or Belief in order to examine and monitor incidents and governmental actions inconsistent with the 1981 Declaration. What has resulted from this appointment has been twice yearly reports, transmission to governments of allegations of violations of the freedom of religion or belief of individuals, *in situ* country visits assessing the situation of freedom of religion or belief and particular initiatives such as the holding of the 2001 UN International Consultative Conference on School Education in Relation with Freedom of Religion and Belief, Tolerance and Non-Discrimination in Madrid.

At present, there is a need for the human rights doctrine and practice to grapple more effectively with the overlap that exists between individual rights and minority rights within the area of freedom of religion or belief. More particularly this concerns the individual rights encapsulated in provisions focused on freedom of religion or belief in community with others and minority rights as they concern religious minority groups. While historically these two understandings have been separate and sharply differentiated, the co-existence of these norms in existing international provisions calls for the challenge of a fuller appreciation of the balancing of the individual and group dimensions of religion or belief. As all international provisions on freedom of religion or belief acknowledge, the manifestation of religion or belief in community activities are inseparable from this right, though they may be subject to restriction in very particular circumstances.

Further Reading

de Jong, Cornelis D. (2000) *The Freedom of Thought, Conscience and Religion or Belief in the United Nations (1946-1992)*, Antwerpen: Intersentia.

Ghanea, Nazila (2003) *Human Rights, the UN and the Bahá'ís in Iran*, The Hague: Kluwer Law International.

Ghanea, Nazila, (ed.) (2004) *Religious Discrimination at the Dawn of the New Millennium*, Leiden: Martinus Nijhoff.

Lindholm, Tore, *et al* (eds) (2004) *Facilitating Freedom of Religion or Belief: A Deskbook*, Leiden: Martinus Nijhoff.

Sullivan, Donna J. (1988) 'Advancing the Freedom of Religion or Belief Through the UN Declaration on the Elimination of Religious Intolerance and Discrimination', in *American Journal of International Law*, vol. 82, issue 3.

Contributor: Nazila Ghanea

REPARATIONS FOR HUMAN RIGHTS VIOLATIONS

'All human beings are born free and equal in dignity and rights …'
UNIVERSAL DECLARATION OF HUMAN RIGHTS, Article 1

From this general statement it follows that an abuse of human beings which includes interference with the rights to freedom and to be treated with dignity and respect may constitute a violation of human rights under international law. Abuse of the rights of human beings includes murders, summary executions, forced removals, kidnapping and torture, colonialism and slavery, human trafficking, gender and racial-related discrimination as well as abuse of children. Where such violations occur the appropriate remedy may require reparations. Reparation is an expression that '… forms an active part of the lexicon of victims of gross human rights violations' (van Boven, 1997). This lexicon includes rights to restitution, compensation and rehabilitation. However, according to van Boven, it appears that victims of gross viola-tions of human rights place more on the right to demand justice by way of reparation.

Reparation has been defined in a revised set of basic principles prepared by van Boven for the United Nations Sub-Commission on the Prevention of Discrimination of Minorities. Reparation, '… shall render jus-tice by removing or redressing the conse-quences of the wrongful acts and by preventing and deterring violations. Reparations shall be proportionate to the gravity of the violations and the resulting damage and shall include restitution, com-pensation, rehabilitation, satisfaction and guarantees of non-repetition' (van Boven).

The basic principles that relate to repara-tion are known as the 'Van Boven Principles' and apply to circumstances where there may have been a gross violation of human rights. Accordingly, the basic principles require states to respect and ensure respect for human rights and humanitarian law, including the prevention and investigation of such viola-tions, the punishment of offenders and reme-dy and reparations for victims. The model that states are obliged to adhere to in respect of the protection of human rights is that of inter-national law. States have a duty to ensure effective access to remedies for the victims of human rights violations at both national and international level. Reparation claims may be made by individuals, groups, direct victims, immediate family, dependants or other per-sons connected with the direct victims. Furthermore, the procedures for making a claim should be transparent to potential claimants. Moreover, statutory limitations are to be read so as not to bar a reparations claim. Special measures may be adopted by states to ensure that there is full and effective repara-tion; this is in line with international law. The shape that reparation may take is not pre-scribed or exhaustive. This might include restitution, compensation, rehabilitation, sat-isfaction and the guarantee of non-repetition. Recent examples of such claims include the South African Truth and Reconciliation Commission set up to deal with the claim for reparations for all those who suffered under the Apartheid regime (see 'Race and Class', *Truth*, vol. 44, no. 1, July to September 2002) (See: **TRUTH COMMISSIONS**), the 1952 set-tlement between Israel and the Federal Republic of Germany in relation to the Jewish holocaust (See: **HUMAN RIGHTS AND GLOBALISING MEMORY CULTURE**). In 1990 Austria paid $25 million to Jewish Holocaust survivors. With the British Foreign Compensation Act 1950, several agreements were reached with Romania, Bulgaria, Poland and Egypt in relation to the expropriation of property that belonged to claimants. Reparation payments have been made by Japan to South Korea regarding incidents that related to invasion and occupation; furthermore Iraq has been required by the UN Security Council to pay reparations for the invasion of Kuwait in the 1990s.

The type of human rights violations that attract demand for a right to reparation include where there have been victims of '... crimes against humanity, defined in the Principles of the Nuremburg Tribunal, 1950 as: "Murder, extermination, enslavement, deportation and other inhuman acts done against any civilian population, or persecutions on political, racial or religious grounds, when such acts are done or such persecutions are carried on in execution of or in connection with any crime against peace or any war crime"' (Principles of International Law Recognised in the Charter of the Nürnberg Tribunal and in the Judgment of the Tribunal, Principle vi, c).

Launching a reparations claim can be politically controversial, particularly where the state is unwilling to fulfil obligations such as the bringing to justice of perpetrators of hate crimes. The non-governmental organisation Human Rights Watch writes that in the East Timor situation in the late 1990s thousands of East Timorese civilians were murdered and many more affected by arson and forced expulsion as a result of armed forces and Timorese militia activity, in reprisals for voting for independence. However, those among the elite responsible for the widespread human atrocities have not been brought to justice due the failure of the judicial system.

One of the outstanding issues in terms of a potential claim for reparation is that surrounding the transatlantic slave trade (See: **FREEDOM FROM SLAVERY**). Many African communities were destroyed. Parallels may be drawn with the Aboriginal peoples in Australia where 'Communities were destroyed because of the forcible removals, leading to community dissolution of cultural, linguistic and other ties as well as interference with their economic and social organisation' (Cornwall). Gifford has argued that while there is general agreement that a gross injustice was perpetrated against African people, one that continues to impact on parts of Africa and those of African descent in the Western Diaspora, there is reluctance to provide a mechanism that would enforce a reparation claim and even less '...willingness of the white world to recognise it'. While many scholars argue that a reparation claim based on the transatlantic slave trade is limited in what may be achieved (Van Bueren, 2004) or highly improbable (Thompson, 2004), other scholars argue that such an abuse of human rights must have a remedy and that a claim founded on the notion of reparation is not only internationally recognised but also possible. To this scholarly discourse must be added that which has occurred on a global scale. At the World Conference Against Racism and Xenophobia, the question of reparations was raised. The conference acknowledged that the transatlantic slave trade was a human tragedy, a crime against humanity and a major source of racism, racial discrimination, xenophobia and intolerance. Moreover, the document containing the Durban Declaration and Programme of Action suggested that Africans and people of African descent were victims and continue to be victims of the consequences of this slave trade. One of those consequences identified by the conference was the subsequent periods of colonialism and post-colonialism which, in turn, have led to contemporary forms of racism and racial discrimination affecting African people and people of African descent. Advocates of reparations such as the representative of Trinidad and Tobago contend that the World Conference '... should call upon those states that have practised, benefited or enriched themselves from slavery, the transatlantic slave trade and indenture ships to provide reparations to countries and peoples affected, and to adopt appropriate remedial and other measures in order to repair these consequences'.

Following the World Conference against Racism, Racial Discrimination, Xenophobia and Related Intolerance Conference (2001) (WCAR) the United Nations Economic and Social Council concurred with the decision of the Commission on Human Rights which resolved:

> To establish a working group of five independent experts on people of African descent, appointed on the basis of equitable geographical representation by the Chairman of the Commission at its fifty-eighth session, in consultation with regional groups, to meet for two sessions of five working days each prior to the fifty-ninth session of the Commission, in closed and public meetings (Commission on Human Rights, Resolution 2002/68 of the 25th April 2002).

The mandate granted by the Commission to the Working Group of Experts on People of African Descent was: 'To study the problems of racial discrimination faced by people of African descent living in the Diaspora ...'. Furthermore, the group was required: 'To propose measures to ensure full and effective access to the justice system by people of African descent.' This mandate related to a number of issues raised at the WCAR which the Commission considered should '... address all the issues concerning the well-being of Africans and people of African descent contained in the Durban Declaration and Programme of Action'. One of those issues was, and remains, that of reparations for the transatlantic slave trade, described by 18th century commentators as '... the mainspring of the machine which sets every wheel in motion' (J.F. Rees, 'The Phases of British Commercial Policy in the Eighteenth Century', *Economica* June 1925). This inhuman trade furnished the industrial revolution, comprised of slaves imported from Africa, exports and ships from the West and raw materials of the colonial plantations.

In terms of the van Boven Principles the hurdles that a legal claim for reparations needs to address are to identify the victims/claimants, offenders including states and African people and states that colluded in the trade, the appropriate special measures and forum. In terms of the victim/claimant issue for instance the van Boven principle requires that reparation claims may be made by individuals, groups, direct victims, immedi-ate family, dependants or other persons connected with the direct victims. Writers have argued that direct victims no longer exist and very few people can claim to be immediate family, dependants or connected with the victims (Thompson). However, it is argued that the passage of time is not necessarily a barrier to a legal claim (Gifford, 1993). There are many examples where distant descendants, relations and nation-states have successfully claimed reparations. Successors in title of owners on property in Egypt have been able to lay claim to land that was sequestrated under the Nasser government through the British Foreign Compensation Act 1950. Furthermore, Israel was able to recover reparations from the West Germany in relation to the resettlement of Jewish refugees. The fact that West Germany was not in existence and did not perpetrate gross violations of human rights against the Jewish people did not prevent the claim from materialising or being satisfied (Gifford). How successful the campaign for reparations for the transatlantic slave trade will be remains to be seen.

Further Reading

Gifford, Lord Anthony (1993) The legal basis of the claim for Reparations, By Lord Anthony Gifford, British Queens Counsel and Jamaican Attorney-at-Law, A paper Presented to the First Pan-African Congress on Reparations, Abuja, Federal Republic of Nigeria, April 27-29.

Report of the Working Group of Experts on People of African Descent on its first and second sessions (Geneva, 25–29 November 2002 and 3–7 February 2003), United Nations Economic and Social Council.

Thompson, J. (2001) 'Historical Injustice and Reparations: Justifying Claims for Descendants', *Ethics*, 112, October.

van Boven, T. (1997) 'Draft Basic Principles and Guidelines on the Right to Reparation for Victims of Gross Violations of Human Rights and Humanitarian Law', UN Doc, E/CN.4/1997/64, Annex II. (The revised document is entitled 'Basic Principles and Guidelines on the Right to Reparation for Victims of Gross Violations of Human Rights and Humanitarian Law', van Boven, 1996; see

Appendix 8). United Nations, Economic and Social Council, Distr. GENERAL E/CN.4/Sub.2/1996/17 24 May 1996).

Van Bueren, G. (2004) 'Slavery and Piracy – the Legal Case for Reparations for Slavery' in Walden, R. (ed.) *Racism and Human Rights*, Leiden/Boston: Martinus Nijhoff Publishers.

Van Bueren, G. (2004) 'Slavery and Piracy – the Legal case for reparations for the slave trade' in van den Anker, C. (ed.) *The Political Economy of New Slavery*, Palgrave, 235–47.

Cornwall, A. (2002) in relation to Aboriginal Australians, Public Interest Advocacy Centre Ltd, NSW Australia.

Contributor: Fernne Brennan

SANCTIONS AND HUMAN RIGHTS

What are the relationships between economic sanctions and human rights? The most familiar perspective is that economic sanctions are used, with varying levels of effectiveness, by liberal democratic states as a means of pressuring undemocratic states into improving their human rights record. This is indeed part of the picture, but only part of it. This article offers a broader overview in relation to three themes – the characteristics of economic sanctions; the links between economic sanctions, human rights and the neo-liberal approach to GLOBALISATION; and the negative as well as positive roles played by liberal democracies in relation to economic sanctions and human rights.

Economic sanctions can be defined as the threat or use of monetary means to impose costs for the purpose of achieving political goals – in this case, the improvement of human rights. Economic sanctions come in many different forms, such as tariffs (that is, taxes on imports from the target), boycotts (refusal to buy or accept a particular category or amount of item), embargoes (refusal to sell or provide something), price rises, fines and ending, cutting or refusing to increase aid programmes. Note that the imposition of economic costs is not necessarily a form of

economic sanctions: bombing a factory imposes economic costs but we do not usually refer to this as an economic sanction. Particular economic sanctions can blur with other means, for example reduction of subsidies for arms exports or military training in order to bring about improvements in the human rights record of a target can in some senses be seen as military in nature. Economic sanctions are coercive. They may be aimed at making human rights abuses impossible for a particular actor by crippling its ability to carry them out. More commonly, economic sanctions are aimed at persuading the target to change its behaviour with the promise of an end to the negative use of monetary means in return for that change of behaviour.

Economic sanctions do not have to have significant economic effects in order to be effective in achieving their goals. This is because they can signal willingness to use other instruments, including force. In addition, they can achieve important symbolic effects in portraying the target as being an illegitimate actor not worthy of normal economic relations and the actor imposing them as legitimate. Economic sanctions are not necessarily irrational or misconceived if they are economically costly to the actor imposing them and do not actually improve human rights. A government can point to the economic costs of such sanctions as proof that they are serious about their commitment to human rights in principle. Economic sanctions do not have to have direct economic effects on the target either to be regarded as having value. Arab states took steps to blacklist Japanese companies which traded with Israel, as part of their campaign to improve the human rights of Palestinians under Israeli rule. The use of monetary means to impose economic costs may be related to denial of future benefits, such as refusal to begin trade talks which might deliver political, military or economic gains for the target.

It should be noted that economic sanctions are not the exclusive preserve of states. For example, the consumer boycott of Nestlé products was a case of non-state actors using economic sanctions to try to improve human rights. The boycott aimed to prevent Nestlé from promoting powdered milk for babies because powdered milk is a less healthy alternative than breast milk. For the campaigners, corporate profit was being promoted at the expense of babies' **RIGHT TO LIFE** (See: **BUSINESS AND HUMAN RIGHTS**) This example points to wider issues: the relationships between economic sanctions and human rights are being reshaped by the processes of neo-liberal globalisation which are under way at present.

Theoretically, neo-liberal globalisation envisages the removal of all barriers to movements of goods and capital (though not labour). In practice, neo-liberal globalisation often involves the erosion of barriers used by weaker states to protect themselves while allowing the more powerful states to maintain most of their barriers, including subsidies to their producers which make it harder for producers in weaker states to compete. Nevertheless, increases in the degree of freedom of trade and capital contradict the use of economic sanctions for the purpose of achieving political goals in relation to human rights. For example, the United States imposes penalties on foreign companies operating in the United States if they also invest in Cuba, due to US hostility to that country's communist government. For supporters of US policy, the United States is using economic sanctions to promote the right of Cubans to elect their government. For opponents, those sanctions are violating the human rights of Cubans by undermining gains made in health and education. Neo-liberals see their project in terms of the human right to economic freedom, and the threatened or actual use of economic sanctions (such as adverse World Trade Organization rulings requiring the payment of compensation to corporations) as one of their instruments of influence. In contrast, their opponents argue that this form of globalisation uses economic coercion for corporate gain at the expense of the human rights of most people, especially those in the poorer parts of the world. Certainly, a focus only on the positive use of economic sanctions by liberal democratic states to promote human rights is insufficient.

The notion that the use of economic sanctions by liberal democratic states can harm human rights is usually framed as a dilemma in which short-term harm to human rights is traded off against possible longer-term progress on human rights. The paradigmatic case is the economic sanctions on South Africa, imposed with the aim of helping to bring about the end of its system of racial segregation, known as apartheid, or at least showing symbolic disapproval of it. Opponents of the sanctions argued that the sanctions were hurting the people they were meant to help. However, the sanctions had broad support among South Africans opposed to apartheid, perhaps partly because the costs to them were not extreme. In contrast, the comprehensive **UNITED NATIONS** economic sanctions on Iraq inflicted extremely high costs on most of the Iraqi population. The sanctions were imposed in 1990 to force Iraq out of Kuwait which it had invaded and occupied. They continued after Iraq was expelled from Kuwait in order to make it comply with UN resolutions relating to disarmament, among other things. Although it is often said that the sanctions on Iraq failed, Iraq complied with most of what was demanded of it. However, Saddam Hussein's grudging and incomplete cooperation combined with US determination to remove him ensured that the situation was resolved by a US-led invasion of Iraq in 2003. For many, these UN economic sanctions were so costly as to be regarded a severe violation of human rights in Iraq and hence unacceptable, regardless of their degree of effectiveness.

The Iraq case was the main impetus behind the development of the notion of 'smart' sanctions, that is, sanctions which target political leaders to provide maximum political effectiveness and minimum costs for the population of a state. The discourse of 'smart' sanctions also serves the ideological purpose of projecting a benign image of liberal democratic states, an image which is not deserved significantly often. For example, in 1973 the United States used its economic muscle to destabilise the Chilean economy in order to bring about a military coup. This denied the Chilean people their human right to have their own (in this case left-wing) government which they had elected democratically. Hence a liberal democratic state can use economic sanctions with the aim of violating human rights. The challenge for those concerned with promoting human rights is to work out how to prevent the use of economic sanctions in that way.

Further Reading

Baldwin, David A. (1985) *Economic Statecraft*, Princeton, NJ: Princeton University Press.

Cortright, David and Lopez, George A. *et al.* (2000) *The Sanctions Decade: Assessing UN Strategies in the 1990s*, Boulder, CO: Lynne Rienner Publishers.

Cortright, David and Lopez, George A. (2002) *Smart Sanctions: Targeting Economic Statecraft*, Lanham, MD: Rowman & Littlefield Publishers.

Doxey, Margaret (1996) *International Sanctions in Contemporary Perspective*, 2nd edn, London: Palgrave Macmillan.

Drezner, Daniel W. (1999) *The Sanctions Paradox: Economic Statecraft and International Relations*, Cambridge: Cambridge University Press.

Weiss, Thomas, Cortright, G. David, Lopez, George A. and Minear Larry (eds) (1997) *Political Gain and Civilian Pain: Humanitarian Impacts of Economic Sanctions*, Lanham, MD: Rowman & Littlefield Publishers.

Contributor: Eric Herring

SELF-DETERMINATION, THE RIGHT TO

Self-determination is one of the founding principles of human rights law. Its primary place within the human rights discourse is illustrated by its presence in Article 1 of the United Nations Charter and Article 1 of the two 1966 Covenants (See: **THE COVENANT ON CIVIL AND POLITICAL RIGHTS AND THE COVENANT ON ECONOMIC SOCIAL AND CULTURAL RIGHTS**). Throughout history self-determination has been the inspiring principle for peoples under oppression. However, from a legal perspective, the reference to the right of self-determination remains a subject of controversy. It has caused a lot of blood and ink to flow. Thus, even though self-determination is certainly the most aspirational of rights, it is also the most controversial of the International Bill of Rights.

Historically, self-determination evolved as a political principle before becoming one of the central rights of the contemporary human rights system. It was at the heart of both the American and the French Revolutions of the 18th century. The claim was for government of the people by the people; in this regard self-determination is often associated with the notion of democracy (Franck, 1992). Self-determination was also one of the cornerstones of Lenin's political ideology. At the end of the First World War, one of the most resounding consequences of President Wilson's 14-point speech remains his reference to the principle of 'national self-determination' for the ethnic groups that were carved out by the fall of the Ottoman, Austro-Hungarian, Russian and German empires. Post-Second World War, the resurgence of the principle of self-determination formed the basis of decolonisation. In addition to its inscription in Article 1 of the UN Charter, self-determination is the central principle of the General Assembly's 1960 Declaration on the Granting of Independence to Colonial Countries and Peoples, as well as the 1970 Declaration on Principles of International Law Concerning Friendly Relations. From a post-colonial perspective, self-determination refers to the right of people to exercise sovereignty over their own territory. It is with such a political background that self-determination was finally consecrated as a right by its inscription as joint Article 1 of the two 1966 Covenants. In these instruments, self-determination refers to the right of a people to express its popular will, pursue its economic, social and cultural development (See: **THE RIGHT TO DEVELOPMENT**), to be free from outside interference and to freely dispose of their natural resources. This mix of democratic entitlements and territorial rights has given rise to difficult legal controversies.

The maturing of the political principle of self-determination as a right engendered several controversies, the principal are being that self-determination clashes with the principle of state territorial integrity. Under international law, the issue of territoriality remains central to international stability. Since self-determination has fuelled the decolonisation process, it is often associated with the emergence of new states or as a right to statehood. Thus, in the shadow of self-determination there is a fear of fragmentation of existing states into a multitude of new states. Different theories have been developed to answer such a fear.

Self-determination has been qualified as a 'remedial right', i.e. a people would have a right to secede from a state that is discriminating or committing gross human rights violations. It has been interpreted as meaning a right to break away from a government that excludes people of any race, creed or colour from political representation. This inter-relation between democratic entitlements and self-determination has been further elaborated by the distinction established between so-called 'external' (meaning secession and statehood) and 'internal' self-determination (meaning self-government and autonomy) (Cassese, 1995). In the 'internal' context, self-determination is understood as the right to participate in the democratic process of governance and to exercise some form of autonomous development within the state boundaries.

Another difficulty is that self-determination is framed as a right for a people, which runs *a contrario* to the traditional individual framing of human rights law. Thus, one of the challenges is that self-determination has a dual nature; it is a right for any individual as a member of a 'people' to political representation and non-discrimination, but it is also a collective right for a people to a territory. Central to this debate is the question: who are the people entitled to self-determination? Is it people under colonial rule or under apartheid only? In the contemporary debates on self-determination, the view is that self-determination remains limited to peoples under colonial or related forms of foreign or racial domination. However, such a restricted approach is inconsistent with contemporary human rights law, as human rights law has undertaken a modern view of self-determination which is not limited to the classic post-colonial (i.e. statehood) interpretation of self-determination.

Certainly the most challenging claim to self-determination comes from INDIGENOUS PEOPLES. Their claim relies on the fact that they have traditional form of government and have specific rights over their traditional territories and thus are 'people' entitled to self-determination. In this regard, because in most countries they are living on the margins of society, facing discrimination, exploitation and dispossession, indigenous peoples seem particularly entitled to claim their right to self-determination. The HUMAN RIGHTS COMMITTEE has recognised that based on their right to self-determination, indigenous peoples have the right to

access their natural resources as a right to 'subsistence' (Scheinin, 2000).

In its concluding observations, the same Committee has also pointed out that indigenous peoples' right to self-determination entails their right to participate in decisions affecting their natural resources. From such a perspective self-determination is built on the cultural connections to natural resources as well as the right of indigenous peoples to participate in decisions affecting their territories. Self-determination implicates a right for indigenous peoples to access their means of subsistence and a relational right to participate in decisions affecting their territories. However, despite such evolution and even though the concept of statehood is a concept that remains alien to most indigenous nations, states are restraining the evolution of indigenous peoples' rights under international law based on the fear that the recognition of the right to self-determination would mean an eventual right of secession for indigenous peoples (See also: CUSTOMARY LAW IN THE SOUTH PACIFIC).

The connection between access to natural resources and a right of 'economic self-determination' will certainly become one of the future chapters of human rights law. Despite the fact that self-determination refers to the right of a people to access and benefit from its own natural resources, this right has not attracted much attention. As many peoples in the world are reclaiming the benefit of the exploitation of their own natural resources, it is important to reaffirm that the right to self-determination is also the right for all peoples to determine their own economic, social and cultural development. In the current situation of economic globalisation (See: GLOBALISATION AND HUMAN RIGHTS), such aspects of the right to self-determination could also be attractive to many peoples that are the victims of economic exploitation.

Despite being one of the oldest principles of human rights law, self-determination remains one of the most challenging rights of the human rights system. Having been at the centre of the enlightenment and decolonisation process, self-determination carries new significance in our contemporary world. It has to be borne in mind that self-determination has always acted as a banner for freedom for the oppressed. Human rights law does not evolve in a vacuum but is tied to the contemporary political agenda, while retaining its noble ideal of providing the most vulnerable with legal recourse and protection. In this regard, it is certain that self-determination remains one of the central rights of all peoples under international law. Self-determination is the right of the oppressed to influence their future, politically, socially and culturally. For example, self-determination has been raised to secure political representation for women (See: WOMEN'S RIGHTS).

Recent events have shown that methods of oppression are not fixed and can take a multitude of forms. In this sense it would be dangerous to propose a definition or precise criteria for who exactly the peoples are that are entitled to self-determination. In the development of the right to self-determination it is important to keep in mind that statehood is one of many results of self-determination; the automatic equation of self-determination with statehood is not always accurate. In this regard, indigenous peoples' claims to the recognition of their right to self-determination should be seen as an interesting new chapter in the ongoing development of the concept.

Further Reading

Aikio, Pekka and Scheinin, Martin (eds) (2000) *Operationalizing the Right of Indigenous Peoples to Self-Determination*, Turku: Abo Akademi University.

Cassese, Antonio (1995) *Self-Determination of Peoples, A Legal Reappraisal*, Cambridge: Cambridge University Press, Cambridge.

Castellino, Joshua (2000) *International Law and Self-Determination: The Interplay of the Politics of Territorial Possession with Formulations of Post-Colonial 'National' Identity*, The Hague: Martinus Nijhoff Publishers.

Franck, Thomas (1992) 'The Emerging Right to Democratic Governance', 86, *American Journal of International Law* 46.

Kirgis, Frederic L. (1994) 'The Degrees of Self-Determination in the United Nations Era', 88, *American Journal of International Law* 304.

Scheinin, Martin (2000) 'The Right to Enjoy a Distinct Culture: Indigenous and Competing Uses of Land', in Orlin, Theodore S. and

Scheinin, Martin (eds) *The Jurisprudence of Human Rights: A Comparative Interpretive Approach*, Turku: Åbo Akademi University Institute for Human Rights.

Thornberry, Patrick (1989) 'Self-determination, Minorities, Human Rights: A Review of International Instruments', 38 *International and Comparative Law Quarterly* 872.

Contributor: Jérémie Gilbert

SLAVERY, FREEDOM FROM

Slavery has existed since ancient times and the last country to outlaw it was Oman in 1970. However, despite wide belief to the contrary slavery remains prevalent in the new millennium. The first international instrument to condemn slavery was the 1815 Declaration Relative to the Universal Abolition of the Slave Trade of the Congress of Vienna. Today international law contains a large number of agreements on the outlawing and the prevention of the slave trade, both bilateral and multilateral. The first international agreements in the 19th century were bilateral and designed to abolish the trade in native Africans by European powers and empires. More than 80 separate international instruments and documents have addressed the issues of slavery, slave trade and slavery-related practices (Cherif Bassiouni, 1991). However, none of them has been totally effective. The International Court of Justice identifies the protection from slavery as one of its two examples of obligations owed by a state to the international community as a whole (Barcelona Traction, Light and Power Co. Ltd (*Belgium v Spain*), Judgment of 5 February 1971 2, *ICJ Reports*, 1970, p. 32).

The definition of slavery has always been controversial because of disagreements about which practices should be categorised as slavery and the most appropriate strategy to eliminate them. However, in order for any international body to implement their agreements on slavery it is vital to develop a consensus about these practices. Today slavery and slavery-like practices are defined in several important conventions of the UNITED NATIONS (UN) and its subsidiary bodies:

UN Slavery Convention of 25 September 1926 (http://www.hri.ca/uninfo/treaties/28.shtml)

- UN Supplementary Convention on the Abolition of Slavery, the Slave Trade and Institutions and Practices Similar to Slavery, 1956 (http://www.hri.ca/uninfo/treaties/30.shtml)
- **INTERNATIONAL LABOUR ORGANIZATION** (ILO) Forced Labour Convention, 1930 (No.29) (http://www.hri.ca/uninfo/treaties/31.shtml)
- Protocol to Prevent, Suppress and Punish Trafficking in Persons, especially Women and Children, Supplementing the UN Convention against Transnational Organized Crime, November 2000 (http://www1.umn.edu/humanrts/instree/trafficking.html)

Control and ownership are the key elements of any definition of both slavery and trafficking. These are often identified by analysis of the degree of restriction of a person's freedom of movement, control over personal possessions (e.g. passport) and the existence of full consent and understanding of the nature of any employment relationship. A review by Anti-Slavery International recognises the following forms of slavery today: chattel slavery, predial and domestic slavery, servitude, servile status, debt bondage and bonded labour, serfdom, forced or compulsory labour, servile marriage, sale of wives, forced marriage, the levirate, sexual slavery, trafficking in human beings, the entrapment and enslavement of migrant workers, particularly migrant domestic workers whose passports are taken away from them, forced and enforced prostitution, the exploitation of prostitution by others, child trafficking, child labour, the worst forms of child labour, children being sent away by their families to work for others, false adoption, the commercial sexual exploitation of children (that is to say child prostitution and pornography) and the recruitment of children as soldiers (Weissbrodt and Anti-Slavery International, 2002).

The initial responsibility for preventing all forms of slavery resides with national governments, but these are supplemented by the procedures for ensuring compliance with the international slavery conventions. The most significant of these are as follows.

- UN Working Group on Contemporary

> It is estimated that over 700,000 people are trafficked each year for sexual exploitation. According to Interpol, trafficking remains one of the more profitable activities for organised international crime.

Forms of Slavery. The Economic and Social Council of the UN set up this body in 1975, following pressure from Anti-Slavery International and others. It has a wide degree of discretion and can receive information from both member States and **NON-GOVERNMENTAL ORGANISATIONS**. Although the conventions on slavery provide for state parties to submit reports on their implementation this is rarely done and the Working Group operates by receiving reports from NGOs and then asking the relevant government(s) to comment. At the end of its annual meeting the Working Group submits a set of recommendations to its parent body the UN Sub-Commission on the Promotion and Protection of Human Rights, which normally passes them to the Commission on Human Rights for approval. Because of this long-winded procedure, the Working Group has tended to operate as an informal forum for the discussion of issues of slavery between governments and NGOs rather than an effective mechanism of calling governments to account.

- ILO Committee of Experts on the Application of Conventions and Recommendations. This is a group of experts appointed by the ILO to assess the reports submitted every five years by governments on any of the ILO Conventions they have ratified. The Committee reports to the tripartite (governments, trade unions and employers) Conference Committee on the Application of Conventions and Recommendations. In addition the ILO may set up an investigation into specific allegations that a state has failed to comply with its obligations under a convention. In 1998 the ILO agreed that its four core conventions (discrimination, child labour, forced labour, freedom of association) should be obligatory on all members, whether they had ratified the Convention or not (http://

echo.ilo.org/pls/declaris/DECLARA-TIONWEB.INDEXPAGE?var_language=EN). Each year, on a four-yearly cycle, the ILO produces a report on the implementation of one of these core areas.

Implementation of the laws against slavery and trafficking by national governments has tended to be patchy and to depend on the level of public awareness and concern for the issues. It can be argued that the current concern in the European Union and the USA for issues of trafficking in people has been generated as much by public debate about economic migration as concern for the victims of such trafficking. Generally the laws in most countries, if fully enforced, offer full protection to people from slavery. However, too little thought appears to have been given by most governments to questions of the rights of people released from slavery and how to ensure that people are enabled to build a new life in freedom. In the last few years these problems have been seen in such issues as:

- the need to find alternative possibilities for children released from sweatshops and other areas of forced labour;
- alternative employment and income-generating opportunities for men, women and children released from bonded labour in South Asia;
- difficulties of reintegrating women trafficked into prostitution into their own communities if they are returned home;
- social isolation and banishment of women and children who refuse forced marriage;
- when issues of slavery or bonded labour are linked to social structures of caste and traditional hierarchies, the difficulty of released people finding local employment or acceptance.

Unlike most international human rights instruments the slavery conventions have no specific treaty monitoring body. This means that, apart from their obligations under the **INTERNATIONAL COVENANT ON CIVIL AND POLITICAL RIGHTS** and the ILO Forced Labour Convention, governments are not called upon to report regularly on issues of slavery and this does little to encourage them to establish safeguards against all forms of slavery. Various possibilities have been sug-

gested, including extended mandate of the Working Group, appointment of a Special Rapporteur on contemporary slavery or recognition of the Working Group as a treaty monitoring body.

Further Reading

Cherif Bassiouni, M. (1991) 'Enslavement as an international crime', *New York University Journal of International Law and Politics*, vol. 23, p. 445.

A Future Without Child Labour (2002) Global report under the follow-up to the ILO Declaration on Fundamental Principles and Rights at Work, published by the International Labour Organization, March.

Anti-Slavery International/ICFTU (2001) *Forced Labour in the 21st Century.*

Miers, Professor Suzanne (2003) *Slavery in the Twentieth Century – the evolution of a global problem*, London: Altamira Press.

Stopping Forced Labour (2001) Global report under the follow-up to the ILO Declaration on Fundamental Principles and Rights at Work, published by the International Labour Organization, May.

Weissbrodt, David and Anti-Slavery International (2002) *Abolishing Slavery and its Contemporary Forms*, published by the Office of the High Commissioner for Human Rights.

Contributor: David Ould

SOCIAL MOVEMENTS AND HUMAN RIGHTS

Looked at from the point of view of recent history, the connection between social movements and human rights might seem straightforward enough. The latter half of the 20th century saw a range of social movements developing and claiming human rights. The resurgence of feminism generated claims for women's rights as human rights, indigenous peoples' movements generated claims for indigenous peoples' rights and the green movement generated debates about environmental rights as human rights and the rights of future generations. These examples suggest the link between social movements and human rights is that the former generate the latter as part of their struggles.

Yet curiously, and in stark contrast, the literature on the history of human rights makes little or no reference to social movements, nor has any such link been considered significant for theories of human rights. So does this mean that the earlier history of human rights was very different to this recent history or is it that the bulk of the human rights literature has somehow missed this link and any theoretical significance it may have? In my view it is the latter. In particular, I have argued that, for a variety of reasons, the bulk of the literature from both proponents and critics of human rights is blinded from seeing the significance of this link. Consequently, there has been a failure to properly grasp both the potentials and limits of human rights (Stammers 1999, 2004). If this is right, the shift in theoretical focus implied by taking social movements seriously could also have important implications for social movement activists and how they understand and use human rights in their struggles.

Although research in this field is sparse and in its infancy, it is nevertheless already possible to point to some potentially important implications for theories of human rights and to some more practical issues that arise from these implications. Firstly, it appears that a re-evaluation of the history of human rights is likely to show that social movements have been a major source for the construction and development of ideas and practices in respect of human rights. These initial constructions and developments arose and were used to challenge dominant relations and structures of power in particular historical epochs. Secondly, however, it also appears that when such understandings of human rights are institutionalised (for example, if and when they are codified as positive law within particular jurisdictions) then there is a very real danger that, in their institutionalised form, human rights can come to sustain rather than challenge particular forms of power. The way dominant states have cynically used human rights as a tool of their foreign policy is an example of this.

Thirdly, historical examination of the link between social movements and human rights suggests that human rights have an important expressive dimension in addition to their more obvious instrumental side. This expressive dimension is about the validation or legitimation of particular ways of being in the world, for example in terms of identities and lifestyles. This chimes at least in part with arguments that social movement struggles for human rights should be seen as 'struggles for recognition' (Douzinas, 2000, Ch. 10).

Fourthly, historical evidence indicates that the nature of ideas of and claims to human rights have always been multifaceted and imbricated. This supports some recent arguments in the mainstream literature that dichotomous separations often made between different categories of rights (for example, between civil and political rights on the one hand and economic and social rights on the other, or between individual and collective rights) are untenable. It also casts doubt on the utility of thinking about human rights in terms of 'generations' and on those arguments that rely on the separation of notions of universality and particularity. This is not to say that there was never an emphasis on particular forms of rights claims in particular historical periods, rather that the separations often claimed in the mainstream literature are too crude and simplistic.

Fifthly, set alongside the arguments of many critics who point to the claimed universality of human rights as a major problem, a focus on social movement struggles for human rights indicates that a specific way of understanding universality could be endorsed in so far as it points to the ubiquity of oppressive power in the world. From this perspective, it is not particular lists or understandings of human rights that should be understood as universal. Instead, elements of the universalising trajectory of human rights thinking could be understood as signalling that oppressive power embedded politically, economically and culturally is a transhistorical and transcultural phenomenon. In contrast to this, the focus on social movements and human rights also suggests that it is in their particular instantiations (when they are institutionalised within a particular social order) that human rights can be exclusionary and take on an essentialist form. For example, in 1789, the French National Assembly consciously and explicitly excluded women from the Declaration of the Rights of Man and Citizen.

Sixthly, the focus on the relationship between social movements and human rights suggests that a major problem with much of the existing literature from both proponents and critics of human rights is that the various strands of this literature often contest and 'mirror' each other rather than properly connect to the historical and social reality of human rights. Despite their differences and apparent incompatibility, this literature shares a common characteristic, in that it tends to rely on a priori assumptions rather than engage in a full analysis of concrete historical and social praxis and processes.

While the above six points imply the necessity for incorporating an analysis of the relationship between social movements, human rights and power into theories of human rights, they also offer some (arguably controversial) pointers for how contemporary movement activists might orient themselves towards current and future praxis in respect of human rights. Firstly, and most fundamentally, activists should not assume that human rights and/or struggles for human rights can be simply or easily assessed as being either 'good' or 'bad'. A key issue for activists must be trying to discern how and when human rights claims and the institutionalisation they typically demand do, in fact, challenge relations and structures of power rather than threaten to, or actually, serve it. The considerable difficulties involved here are most manifest in what I have described as the paradox of institutionalisation but they are rooted in the complexity of the relationship between 'power to' and 'power over'.

Secondly, it follows from the above that the use of or demand for a particular form of concentrated power (e.g. state power) to constrain another form of concentrated power is fraught with difficulties and dangers. Given the long historical record of particular instantiations of human rights leading to exclusionary practices (for example in respect of 'lower classes', women, slaves and indigenous peoples) this needs to be carefully considered when activists call for human rights to be codified in the positive law of particular jurisdictions or incorporated into international public law.

Thirdly, a further issue (which raises the paradox of institutionalisation in another form) relates to the nature and organisational form of activism itself rather than specific formulations of human rights. Organisations arising out of social movements (for example large international non-governmental organisations) are themselves subject to strong dynamic tendencies towards professionalisation and institutionalisation. While these may be both difficult to avoid and perhaps necessary to facilitate effective engagement with institutional structures, there are real dangers that such organisations become thoroughly disconnected from their 'grassroots' and become incorporated and institutionalised to the extent that they too often serve only to reproduce existing relations and structures of power rather than challenge them (Eschle and Stammers, 2004). The roots of this organisational dilemma are also based in the complexities of the relationship between 'power to' and 'power over'.

The various points made above hopefully demonstrate the potential fertility of looking closely at the historical and contemporary relationships between social movements and human rights. Such study is likely to raise very difficult issues and problems for analysts and activists alike. Among these the problem of the analysis of power is bound to loom large. Yet the stakes could not be higher. If the history of human rights cannot be divorced from social movement struggles against power, can that also be made to be the future of human rights?

Further Reading

Douzinas, C. (2000) *The End of Human Rights*, Oxford: Hart Publishing.

Eschle, C. and Stammers, N. (2004) 'Taking Part: Social Movements, (I)NGOS and Global Change' in 29.3, *Alternatives: Global, Local, Political*, 333–372.

Stammers, N. (1999) 'Social Movements and the Social Construction of Human Rights' in 21.4, *Human Rights Quarterly*, 980–1008.

Stammers, N. (2004) 'The Emergence of Human Rights in the North: Towards Historical Re-evaluation' in Kabeer, N. (ed.)

Meanings and Expressions of Rights and Citizenship, London: Zed Books.

Contributor: Neil Stammers

SOCIAL RIGHTS

The term 'social rights', sometimes called 'socio-economic rights', refers to rights whose function it is to protect and to advance the enjoyment of basic human **NEEDS** and to ensure the material conditions for a life in dignity. The foundation of these rights in human rights law is found in the **UNIVERSAL DECLARATION OF HUMAN RIGHTS** (UDHR) Article 22: 'Everyone, as a member of society, has the right to social security and is entitled to realisation, through national effort and international cooperation and in accordance with the organisation and resources of each state, of the economic, social and cultural rights indispensable for his dignity and the free development of his personality.'

These rights have since been spelled out and the corresponding state obligations clarified in a number of global and regional human rights conventions. At the global level, the most important document is the **INTERNATIONAL COVENANT ON ECONOMIC, SOCIAL AND CULTURAL RIGHTS** (ICESCR), adopted by the United Nations General Assembly in 1966. The vast majority of existing states have ratified the covenant and are therefore bound by it. Provisions of relevance for social rights are also found in the **INTERNATIONAL CONVENTION ON THE ELIMINATION OF ALL FORMS OF DISCRIMINATION AGAINST WOMEN**, the **INTERNATIONAL CONVENTION ON THE ELIMINATION OF ALL FORMS OF RACIAL DISCRIMINATION**, the **INTERNATIONAL CONVENTION ON THE RIGHTS OF THE CHILD** and the International Convention on the Protection of the Rights of All Migrant Workers and Members of Their Families (See: **MIGRANT WORKERS' CONVENTION**). In the area of workers' rights, numerous conventions have been adopted by the International Labour Organisation (See: **LABOUR RIGHTS**).

Social rights are also extensively covered in regional instruments. Of special importance is the **EUROPEAN SOCIAL CHARTER**, adopted by the **COUNCIL OF EUROPE** in 1961 and revised in 1996, which contains very detailed provisions on social rights. The vast majority of European states are bound by the Social Charter though to varying degrees, since it is a framework convention making it possible for states to accept some but not all of the provisions. The Organisation of American States adopted in 1988 the 'Additional Protocol to the **AMERICAN CONVENTION ON HUMAN RIGHTS** in the area of Economic, Social and Cultural Rights' called 'the Protocol of San Salvador'. The **AFRICAN CHARTER ON HUMAN AND PEOPLES' RIGHTS** also contains several provisions concerning social rights.

Social rights fall in two categories: some spell out the needs that should be covered, the other deal with access to resources by which people can ensure their rights. In the first category we find the fundamental right of everyone to be free from hunger (See: **THE RIGHT TO FOOD AND WATER**) and the right to an adequate standard of living (See: **POVERTY AND HUMAN RIGHTS**), the right to **HEALTH** and the right to **EDUCATION**. In the other category we find the right to work and rights in work (See: **LABOUR RIGHTS**), the right to social security and the right to social protection of the family including maternity benefits and child benefits. The right to **PROPERTY**, while not in itself a social right, is also an important basis for the safeguarding of the needs that should be ensured.

In general terms, the most important needs to be covered are set out in the Universal Declaration of Human Rights Article 25: 'Everyone has the right to a standard of living adequate for the health and well-being of himself and of his family, including food, clothing, housing and medical care and necessary social services, and the right to security in the event of unemployment, sickness, disability, widowhood, old age or other lack of livelihood in circumstances beyond his control.'

Freedom from hunger is the most essential right and the only right which has been called 'fundamental' in international human rights law. It should be treated at the same level as **THE RIGHT TO LIFE** – indeed, serious hunger is a continuous **TORTURE** and one of the most widespread threats to life for millions of people, since many deadly diseases are associated with malnutrition.

The enjoyment of the right to food and to **HOUSING** is essential for a healthy and dignified life. These rights are set out in ICESCR Article 11 and their contents have been spelled out in considerable detail by the UN Committee on Economic, Social and Cultural Rights in its General Comments nos 4 and 7 on the right to housing and General Comment no. 12 on the right to food.

The right to the highest attainable standard of health is set out in ICESCR Article 12. Related provisions are found in the European Social Charter Articles 11 and 13. In order to ensure the enjoyment for all of this right, states have undertaken to take measures to reduce infant mortality, improve environmental and industrial hygiene, prevent, treat and control epidemic, endemic, occupational and other diseases and to create and maintain conditions which would assure to all medical services and medical attention in the event of sickness.

The right to education is both a social and a cultural right. It is set out in UDHR Article 26, in ICESCR Article 13 and in the Convention on the Rights of the Child Articles 28 and 29. States shall ensure that primary education is compulsory and available free to all and make secondary and vocational education generally available and accessible to all by every appropriate means.

The right to work and rights in work are set out in Articles 6, 7 and 8 of the ICESCR, in Articles 1 to 6 of the European Social Charter (revised), Articles 6, 7 and 8 of the Protocol of San Salvador, and special aspects are regulated in detail in many ILO conventions. The right to work does not mean a right to be given work, but the opportunity for everyone to secure the means for living a dignified and decent existence by work which she or he has freely chosen or accepted. The rights in work include a right to a decent remuneration, safe and healthy working conditions, equal pay for equal work (including between men and women), the right to rest and leisure and periodic holidays with pay. Much more detailed provisions can be found in the European Social Charter.

The right to social security is set out in ICESCR Article 9, in the European Social Charter Article 12, the San Salvador Protocol Article 9 and ILO Social Securi Standards) Convention (no. 102), a_ 1952. The essence of the right is the require ment that there shall be in existence within each state institutional arrangements for social security. These should cover medical care and some coverage in case of sickness, unemployment, old age, invalidity, employment injury, and should also include family benefit, maternity benefit and survivors' benefit. Motherhood and childhood are entitled to special care and assistance. All children, whether born in or out of wedlock, shall enjoy the same social protection.

Under Article 2 of the ICESCR, state parties are required to take steps to the maximum of their available resources to 'achieve progressively' the full realisation of the economic and social rights in that Covenant. This does not mean that the state in all or even in most respects has to be the provider of these rights. Fundamental to a realistic understanding of state obligations is that the individual her or himself is the active subject of all economic and social development. The individual is expected, whenever possible through his or her own efforts and by use of their own resources, to find ways to ensure the satisfaction of their needs, individually or in association with others. Use of resources, however, requires that the person has resources that can be used – typically land or other productive capital, or labour. Human rights impose three types or levels of obligations on state parties: the obligations to respect, to protect and to fulfil. States must, at the primary level, respect the resources owned by the individual, her or his freedom to find a job of preference and the freedom to take the necessary actions and use the necessary resources – alone or in association with others – to satisfy their needs. State obligations consist, at a secondary level, of, for example, the protection of the freedom of action and the use of resources against other, more assertive or aggressive subjects – more powerful economic interests, protection against fraud, against unethical behaviour in trade and contractual relations, against the marketing and dumping of hazardous or dangerous products. This protective function of the state is the most important aspect of state obligations also with regard to economic, social and cultural rights and it is similar to the role of the state as protector of civil and political rights.

At the tertiary level, the state has the obligations to fulfil the rights of everyone under economic, social and cultural rights, by way of facilitation or direct provision. The implementation of the obligation to facilitate takes many forms. For example, under the ICESCR (Article 11(2)), the state shall take measures to improve measures of production, conservation and distribution of food by making full use of technical and scientific knowledge and by developing or reforming agrarian systems.

The obligation to provide can consist in making available what is required to satisfy basic needs, such as food or resources which can be used for food (direct food aid or social security) when no other possibility exists, such as, for example: (1) when unemployment sets in (such as under recession); (2) for the disadvantaged, and the elderly; (3) during sudden situations of crisis or disaster (see below); and (4) for those who are marginalised (for example, due to structural transformations in the economy and production).

WEBSITES

Documents related to the implementation of the International Covenant on Economic, Social and Cultural Rights are found in www.unhchr.ch/tbs/doc.nsf, click CESCR – Committee on Economic, Social and Cultural Rights.
Documents related to the implementation of the European Social Charter by the European Committee on Social Rights are found in www.coe.int/T/E/Human_Rights/Esc/
In respect of national reports, it adopts 'conclusions'; in respect of collective complaints, it adopts 'decisions'.

Further Reading

Craven, Matthew (1993) *The International Covenant on Economic, Social and Cultural Rights*, Oxford: Clarendon Press.

Eide, Asbjørn, Krause, Catarina and Rosas, Allan (eds) (2001) *Economic, Social and Cultural Rights, a textbook*, 2nd edn, The Hague: Martinus Nijhoff Publishers.

Samuel, Lenia, (2002) *Fundamental Social Rights. Case law of the European Social Charter*, 2. edn, Strasbourg: Council of Europe Publishing.

Contributor: Asbjørn Eide

SUSTAINABLE DEVELOPMENT AND HUMAN RIGHTS

The idea of sustainable development can be traced back to 1972. Expressed simply, its central goal is to balance economic and social development without destroying the natural environment on which all human life ultimately relies. Moreover, sustainable development contains at its heart the idea not only of sustaining human life but of ensuring that human beings can lead a better quality of life. Sustainable development, thinking further, acknowledges that human quality of life is related to maintaining biodiversity on the planet, both flora and fauna. The pursuit of sustainable development is also concerned with enabling social, economic and environmental equity between humans alive today (or intra-generational equity) (See **ENVIRONMENTAL RIGHTS**). Finally, sustainable development is concerned with pursuing social, economic and environmental equity between those humans alive today and those yet to be born (or inter-generational equity). In other words, it promotes the idea that if we over-use natural resources, damage biodiversity and engage in gross pollution then generations to come will have a poorer quality of life than we enjoy today.

Sustainable development, then, relates to almost all areas of human activity. This makes it notoriously difficult to define in a way that appeals to disparate commentators. The most commonly recognised definition of sustainable development is the one given by the World Commission on Environment and Development in 1987 (more commonly known as the 'Brundtland' definition after the Norwegian Prime Minister who chaired this Commission on behalf of the UN). The Brundtland Commission's definition is of development which ' . . . meets the needs of the present without compromising the ability of future generations to meet their own needs'.

Despite disagreement over the definition, the United Nations has used sustainable development as a policy framework within which it tries to relate all of its other policy objectives to one another. The elevation of sustainable development to this role was first managed at the UN's Rio 'Earth Summit' in 1992, followed by New York's Earth Summit II in 1997 and Johannesburg's Earth Summit III in 2002. Taking their lead from the UN, more or less every country in the world has similarly used sustainable development as a policy framework.

The UN has continually repeated its view of the centrality of human rights to the success or otherwise of sustainable development. Inherent within sustainable development is the idea of humans living in a built and natural environment that is fit and safe for habitation; an economic environment that lifts them free from the grind of **POVERTY**; and, a socio-political environment that is just and free from tyranny and terror. Most recently, the international community paid special attention at Earth Summit III to human **HEALTH** rights and to human rights in Africa (See: **NEPAD**; **THE AFRICAN COURT AND COMMISSION**). The Summit concluded in more general terms that:

'Peace, security, stability and respect for human rights and fundamental freedoms, including the **RIGHT TO DEVELOPMENT**, as well as respect for cultural diversity, are essential for achieving sustainable development and ensuring that sustainable development benefits all.'

As a member of the UN the UK has fully supported international sustainable development policy, formulating its own national strategy 'A Better Quality of Life' and establishing seven key aims in relation to human communities: 'strengthening regional and local economies; meeting people's social needs – promoting better health; improving local surroundings . . . ensuring that development respects the character of our countryside; reducing crime and the fear of crime; addressing problems of poverty and social exclusion in the most deprived communities; making it easier for people to get involved in

their own communities; coordinating policies to bring these objectives together'. It is not only the UK government but also the devolved administrations for Scotland, Northern Ireland, Wales and London and all local authorities which are committed to the pursuit of sustainable development.

The planning system has been identified by the UK government as one of the main means by which sustainable development aims will be realised. This includes strategic planning for spatial and economic development; environmental mechanisms such as development, control in town and country and social mechanisms such as Community Planning, led by local authorities as a statutory requirement. Local authorities set out their own sustainable development strategies in Local Agenda 21 documents, which distil a local policy on sustainable development from the various planning mechanisms in place.

In all countries, planning shapes the places where people live and work and influences their abilities to meet their aspirations. As noted above, the planning systems in use in the UK to support social, economic and environmental development are seen as central to the government's pursuit of sustainable development. In the UK, the planning system is renowned for being stringent. Hence, any failings in the UK system which impinge upon human rights could almost certainly be experienced elsewhere. Although the figure overleaf is a simplification of a highly complex system, it does set out to demonstrate how sustainable development policies at national and local levels interact with planning for economic development and for environmental enhancement. It has not been possible within the figure to also map links to the Community Planning system.

With reference to the figure, in the Scottish context the devolved administration developed its own sustainable development strategy in 2002, entitled 'Meeting the Needs', to sit alongside the UK strategy. At the local authority level, structure plans (macro-level) and local plans are to be prepared in the context of sustainable development. Structure and local plans provide a statutory framework within which development control operates and contain policies for future development and land use in an area, covering a range of issues such as housing, transport,

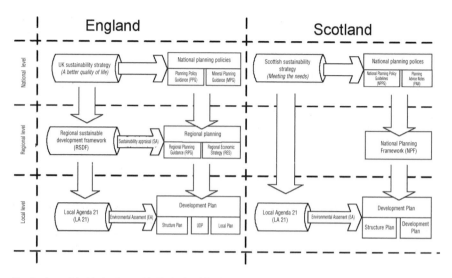

Planning for sustainable development in England and Scotland

employment, shopping, recreation and reservation of land for environmental protection, amenity and future economic development.

Despite the impressive array of capacity in the figure plus the Community Planning system, there are examples where these mechanisms are not promoting the development of UK communities in a sustainable manner. A high-profile example within Scotland is that of Greengairs and its environs. The problems experienced here are representative of problems that face human communities across the planet. Indeed, such problems are more widespread and often more acute in the developing world. Located in a coal-rich region, local communities in the Greengairs area suffered harsh social and economic consequences from the closure of most of the deep mines in the UK coalfield in the 1980s and 1990s. However, further indignities were to follow. Firstly, the expansion of open-cast mining, which generates few jobs and significant environmental harm as a result of the noise of heavy machines, lorries and blasting and the liberation of dust to the atmosphere. Once worked out, open-cast mines are required to be reinstated and one of the ways in which this can be achieved is by using them for landfill. This creates a number of further problems, including congestion and pollution on roads by yet more heavy lorries and the overwhelm-

ing stench of rotting waste in the summer. In the area as a whole there are now nine landfill sites and open-cast mines. The village of Greengairs is itself the location of two landfill sites (one the largest in Europe) and is in close proximity to Scotland's largest open-cast coal mine. All of the noise pollution, vibration, smell and dust emanating from the landfill and open-cast sites militate against the UN's goal of protecting human health rights and the right of every local resident as enshrined in the UK Human Rights Act 1998, 'to respect for his private and family life, his home and his correspondence'. It is assumed that respect for family homes would include the ability of people to be able to hang their laundry out to dry and to sit and relax in their gardens, neither of which can accomplished in a cloud of dust with constant noise and vibration and the stench of rotting garbage.

In recognition of the serious impact which the open-cast and landfill sites were having on residents in and around Greengairs, Scotland's First Minister pledged in 2002 that there would be no more landfill sites in the area, but in 2004 planning permission was granted for the creation of a new landfill, in the face of hostility and dismay on the part of local residents.

Although a particularly acute example, the case of Greengairs is not alone in illustrating a failure to implement a sustainable development agenda through planning systems. As noted earlier, the problems of this case are to be found replicated across the globe. For instance, the extreme examples from the 1980s of the Karin B (toxic waste in Nigeria) and Bhopal (siting of heavy industry in India) could not have occurred had stricter planning policies been formulated and implemented to protect human populations. The Greengairs case has been drawn from a country with a stringent planning system, yet even here four weaknesses in this system are restricting the ability of the government to meet its aims of 'making it easier for people to get involved in their own communities' and 'co-ordinating policies to bring these objectives together'. These same weaknesses are also restricting the ability of residents in Greengairs and environs to realise their statutory human rights.

Firstly, there is no 'third-party right of appeal' against planning decisions. Public agencies and developers can appeal against decisions, but residents in Greengairs could not directly challenge the permission for the latest landfill site in 2004.

Secondly, although the government wishes the planning system to promote sustainable development there is no central mechanism that allows for 360-degree assessment of sustainable development criteria, other than Local Agenda 21 documents, which have only advisory weight in regard to planning decisions.

Thirdly, the statutory Community Planning process is not fully integrated with economic and environmental planning, as can be seen from the figure and the text that relates to it. Thus, Community Planning can be considered as being somewhat in isolation from economic and environmental policies. The Government's aim to co-ordinate sustainable development via the planning system is not always working, highlighting a lack of 'joined-up' thinking in the public sector and demonstrating that it needs to be achieved to a larger extent.

Fourthly, development plans are not updated at predetermined regular intervals. The local plan covering Greengairs was published in 1995 and has not been updated subsequently. This allows problems to persist and can lead to a 'concentration' of certain activities such as open-cast mining and waste dis-

posal in certain areas, such as Greengairs. It is therefore easiest for those seeking to undertake landfill and open-cast mining to do so where there are existing permissions for such activities, rather than trying to get new permissions elsewhere (given the likely hostility that will be encountered). The end result is that those whose human rights are impinged upon continue to face a future of dust, noise vibration and obnoxious-smelling air.

With reference back to the UK government's other five aims for the sustainable development of human communities, it is hard to make much of a link between the Greengairs open-casting and landfill and crime. However, the case does not provide much evidence of progress in relation to the remaining four aims. As regards, 'ensuring that development respects the character of our countryside', see the accompanying photo, for a pictorial example of the countryside at Greengairs.

As regards the inter-linked aims of 'addressing problems of poverty and social exclusion' and 'strengthening regional and local economies', the achievement of both is hampered by the unpleasant nature of what has been done to the environment around Greengairs, which militates against investment in the area other than for more open-cast mining or landfill (both of which employ small numbers of staff in comparison with, for example, deep mining). Finally, the dust and noise pollution in particular directly contradict the UN and UK aim of 'promoting better health' and, taken together with the malodorous atmosphere, infringe everyone's 'right to respect for his private and family life, his home and his correspondence'.

* The authors wish to record their sincere thanks to Ann Coleman of the Greengairs

Environmental Forum for the information which she generously provided for this entry. Any errors however, belong to the authors. Photo © Glasgow Caledonian University.

Further Reading

Cullingworth, B. and Nadin, V. (2001) *Town and Country Planning in the UK*, 14th edn, London: Routledge.

Deputy Prime Minister (1999) *A Better Quality of Life: A Strategy for Sustainable Development for the United Kingdom*, Cm 4345, London: The Stationery Office.

McDowell, E. and McCormick, J. (eds) (1999) *Environment Scotland: Prospects for Sustainability*, Aldershot: Ashgate.

United Nations Environment Programme (2002) *World Summit on Sustainable Development: Plan of Implementation*, Nairobi: UNEP.

World Commission on Environment and Development (1987) *Our Common Future*, Oxford: Oxford University Press.

Contributors: David Silbergh, Liang Chen and Rubina Greenwood

TERRORISM AND HUMAN RIGHTS

The problem of subversive political violence, or terrorism as it is generally described, confronts the subject of human rights with a number of difficult challenges. First there is the nature of such violence. Occurring outside the mainstream of international armed conflict, and at the same time not being easily or properly described as part of a guerrilla or civil war, terrorism in most widely accepted definitions characteristically involves the taking of innocent lives in order either to communicate a political message or more effectively to engage in a low-level campaign of violence against an established political order. Shorn of the attributes of statehood, the perpetrators of such violent deeds have no

history of international relations or set of Westphalian ethics to fall back on to justify their actions; nor do they have the promise of future power which gives a veneer of proto-state legitimacy to even the most inflammatory of guerrilla leaders. The violence of the terrorist is invariably isolated, ahistorical and morally deplorable. In its dismissal of the integrity of the human person, and its willingness to use the individual as a means to an end, it is a shocking affront to human rights, a vicious and seemingly unfathomable rejection of the subject's core principles.

Second is the challenge posed by the reaction that terrorism stimulates in those nations and peoples that are subject to it. Political violence of this sort, unconnected with any wider civil strife, war or insurgency, is easier to realise in the freedom of a liberal democracy than in the stifling atmosphere of a repressive state. Trains need tracks, businesses need headquarters, the media needs stories, political leaders need to get re-elected, and all in a culture which has placed democracy, the rule of law and individual freedom and dignity – human rights in other words – at the very heart of its values. Such places are successful and prosperous, their citizens unused to the tragedy of daily life that is the lot of billions. The nature of liberal democracies is such that the grip that even low levels of terrorist violence can impose is out of all proportion to the harm that is actually caused. It would take a September 11 attack every week for ten years before even one-fifth of the population of New York City alone was killed, and similar points can be made about gun killings, suicide and even cancer deaths, but a sense of proportion is something that terrorists both do not possess for themselves and depend on others not having as well.

The ways in which these anxieties about terrorism are manifested in liberal democratic society produce the third challenge that the problem presents for our subject. The idea of human rights stands for the universality of our regard for our fellow human; it reaches behind the particulars of our identity to find the common ground of humanity that links us all. The reaction of democratic states to terrorism challenges the ethical basis behind such a project, or at very least undermines its social utility. When the nation itself is being attacked from afar by a band of rebels intent upon destruction, whose political programme hinges on the importance of human difference and whose leaders rage against the peoples of the West, it seems to many somewhat beside the point to persist in our pursuit of human solidarity. It is tempting for the West to allow itself to view terrorism as evidence of a battle of civilisations, in which certain humans count more than others and the people outside our parts of the world are different, not deserving of the sorts of things we deem essential for ourselves. This is a temptation to which it is essential not to succumb.

The fourth and largest challenge facing human rights is how to maintain a commitment to our subject while, on the one hand, not dismissing the terrorist threat out of hand and, on the other, not saying that a human rights approach allows a state to do anything it wants in order to survive. Proportionality may be a concept foreign to the terrorist and the counter-terrorist alike, but it is at the heart of human rights and provides a guide here as in so many other areas. In the face of a threat from terrorism, states cannot do everything they want in order to defeat such violence, but they can do everything that they should, everything that is necessary and effective to produce the outcome that the states and their leaders say they desire.

The discourse of human rights makes its contribution to the work of counter-terrorism in the following ways. First it recognises the danger that subversive violence poses to liberal democratic society, but recasts this as a threat to human security rather than a menace to a particular territory or sovereign space. In this way the false antonym between human rights and security is jettisoned, with the subject being reworked to embrace within its remit not only the individual freedoms of the few but also the right to life and security of the

The USA Patriot Act 2001, adopted in the aftermath of the attacks on the Pentagon and the World Trade Centre, makes extensive provision for legitimate electronic surveillance. There are similarities with the earlier Regulation of Investigatory Powers Act 2000 in the UK.

many. International human rights instruments which permit derogations in times of emergency can be seen in this light, and the various exceptions and limitations to rights that are to be found in most legally enforceable rights instruments can usefully be presented in this way, as mechanisms for protecting the integrity of the overall human rights picture rather than (as they might appear at first glance) a means for its subversion.

Second, the human rights perspective has been brought to bear on counter-terrorism in a practical as well as principled fashion. As the UNITED NATIONS Policy Working Group on the United Nations and Terrorism put it in its report published in 2002, '[t]he protection and promotion of human rights under the rule of law is essential in the prevention of terrorism' (UN Working Group on Terrorism, 2002: paragraph 26). This is not only because such an approach is right and any other method destroys the democratic credentials of the counter-terrorist actor, but also because terrorists 'exploit human rights violations to gain support for their cause' (ibid). As the Secretary General of the UN Kofi Annan said in a speech to the Security Council on 18 January 2002: '[w]hile we certainly need vigilance to prevent acts of terrorism, and firmness in condemning and punishing them, it will be self-defeating if we sacrifice other key priorities – such as human rights – in the process.' Other international bodies have made similar points, with the Committee of Ministers of the COUNCIL OF EUROPE in particular having made a valuable contribution through the guidelines on human rights and the fight against terrorism that it adopted on 11 July 2002. These recommendatory directives include a prohibition on 'any form of arbitrariness, as well as any discriminatory or racist treatment' (Committee of Ministers of the Council of Europe, 2002: Article II) and also contain an absolute ban on TORTURE, inhuman or degrading treatment or punishment 'in all circumstances' (Ibid: Article IV).

It follows that there is a particular, human rights-oriented approach to the problem of terrorism, one which recognises the affront to human rights that such political violence entails but which is also insistent that such crime be dealt with in a principled as well as an effective way. It is an approach that stresses the need to nurture and (increasingly) also to preserve the substance as well as the forms of democratic governance: a free and informed electorate is the best answer that it is possible to give to the political bullying of the violent subversive, while being also at the same time the soundest guarantor against serious human rights breaches at home (See: **DEMOCRACY AND HUMAN RIGHTS; THE RIGHT TO VOTE AND DEMOCRACY**). A human rights perspective on terrorism also emphasises, as the International Bar Association has recently done, the need not to succumb to the temptation to use the threat of terrorism to disregard international law (International Bar Association, 2003); indeed a confident human rights approach would argue that international law needs to be strengthened quickly if its integrity is to have a chance of being preserved.

If the world can show a strong commitment to democratic governance and the rule of law, then the task of nurturing human dignity is made that much easier, and the full set of values that underpin the human rights ideal will have every chance of emerging from the current war on terrorism not weakened but rather strengthened, forged in the heat of battle into something tougher and therefore more durable. But this outcome is not pre-ordained. Powerful elements in the West as well as in the rest of the world are not convinced that each of us deserves **EQUALITY** of esteem or that our political leaders should be drawn only from the winners of fair elections, or even that law should be a fetter on the governor as well as the governed. These fundamentalist forces, wherever they exist, need to be defeated, if the threat of terrorism is not to become the mechanism through which our commitment to democracy and human rights for all is effectively extinguished (Dworkin, 2003; Rorty, 2004).

Further Reading

Committee of Ministers of the Council of Europe (2002) *Guidelines on Human Rights and the Fight Against Terrorism*, Strasbourg: Council of Europe.

Dworkin, R. (2003) 'Terror and the Attack on Civil Liberties' in *New York Review of Books*, vol. 50, no. 17, 6 November.

International Bar Association Task Force Report (2003) *Global Principles on Suppressing Terrorism within an International Law Framework*, Washington DC.

Rorty, R. (2004) 'Post-Democracy' in *London Review of Books*, vol. 26, no. 7, 1 April.

United Nations (2002) *Report of the Policy Working Group on the United Nations and Terrorism*, United Nations, A/57/273-S/2002/875.

Contributor: Connor Gearty

TORTURE, FREEDOM FROM

In Europe torture was recognised from classical times to the Middle Ages as a lawful means of extracting confessions from certain subjects (for example slaves) under certain conditions (for example if there was already significant circumstantial evidence). Whatever may have been its use in practice, by the 19th century this de jure torture had been abolished in most if not all countries.

Nazi German political use of torture against its own citizens perceived as dissident or those of occupied territories made the world aware of the problems of de facto torture. Just as that regime's ruthless despotism created the context for human rights to move from the insulated realm of a state's domestic jurisdiction, so its brutality to those suspected of being a threat helped ensure that the right to be free from torture was recognised as a human right. Thus, in the simple words of Article 5 of the **UNIVERSAL DECLARATION OF HUMAN RIGHTS**: 'No one shall be subjected to torture or to cruel, inhuman, or degrading treatment or punishment.'

In 1973, Amnesty International launched its first worldwide campaign against torture, in which it was joined by numerous other non-governmental organisations (NGOs). That campaign, drawing on AI's experience of working on behalf of political prisoners, showed that torture was used in many countries, at least, as a response to political opposition, peaceful as well as violent. The campaign led to significant developments at the inter-governmental level, notably within the United Nations. These developments would first be confined to the area of standard-setting. Much as NGOs wanted international supervisory machinery to be established, the world was not then ready for that form of challenge to traditional notions of state sovereignty.

The 1973 session of the UN General Assembly adopted a modest text by which it rejected 'any form of torture and other cruel, inhuman or degrading treatment or punishment' (resolution 3059 (XXVIII)). Only two years later, it was to adopt the Declaration on the Protection of All Persons from Being Subjected to Torture and Other Cruel, Inhuman or Degrading Treatment or Punishment (resolution 3452 (XXX)). That same year it initiated a series of steps (resolution 3453 (XXX)) that would lead to the adoption of three further significant standard-setting instruments in the field of torture: the Code of Conduct for Law Enforcement Officials (resolution 34/169, 1979); the Principles of Medical Ethics relevant to the Role of Health Personnel, particularly Physicians, in the Protection of Prisoners and Detainees against Torture and other Cruel, Inhuman or Degrading Treatment or Punishment (resolution 37/194, 1982); and the Body of Principles for the Protection of All Persons under Any Form of Detention or Imprisonment (resolution 43/173, 1988). The first two of these were evidently addressed as guidance to personnel of two professions that could play an important role for ill in the perpetration of torture or for good in its prevention. The last, the Body of Principles, was aimed at states as such, its main contribution being to discourage practices of arbitrary detention, especially prolonged detention without access to or from the outside world, that were the fertile terrain for the weed of torture to flourish.

None of these instruments would, of themselves, establish legally binding rules. By 1977, the General Assembly confronted that dimension by initiating the drafting within the UN Commission on Human Rights of a Convention against Torture and Other Cruel, Inhuman or Degrading Treatment or Punishment. In 1984, the Assembly adopted the Convention on the basis of the draft prepared by the Commission (resolution 39/46).

It is evident that torture and cruel, inhuman or degrading treatment or punishment (hereafter 'ill-treatment') are prohibited by international law. Of course, the Convention Against Torture as such binds only the states that become parties to it. But other treaties also contain the prohibition. In the sphere of human rights they include (at the universal level) the **INTERNATIONAL COVENANT ON CIVIL AND POLITICAL RIGHTS** (Article 7) and (at the regional level) the **EUROPEAN CONVENTION ON HUMAN RIGHTS** (Article 3), the American Convention on Human Rights (Article 5) and the African Charter on Human and Peoples' Rights (Article 5) (See: **THE REGIONAL SYSTEM OF THE AMERICAS** and **AFRICAN COURT AND COMMISSION**). The prohibitions in all these instruments are formulated in such a way as to admit of no restrictions under any circumstances. Indeed, while all but the African Charter contemplate the possibility that some of the rights they contain may be suspendable in time of war or other emergency that threatens the life of the nation, the prohibition of torture and ill-treatment is already ringfenced against such suspension.

In addition, the international law of armed conflicts also prohibits at any time and in any place whatsoever the torture or inhuman or cruel treatment of persons in the hands of a party to an armed conflict, whether the conflict be international or non-international (the Geneva Conventions of 12 August 1949 and the Additional Protocols of 1977) (See: **HUMANITARIAN LAW AND HUMAN RIGHTS IN CONFLICT**). Most states of the world are parties to one or other of the CAT or the human rights treaties or both and virtually every state is a party to the Geneva Conventions.

As far as the few states that are not party to any of the human rights treaties or CAT, overwhelming international legal opinion holds that the prohibition of torture and ill-treatment is a rule of general international law binding on all states, regardless of treaty obligation (See: **CUSTOMARY LAW**). This view is sustained by the absolute nature of the rule as expressed in all the treaties (including those applicable to the extreme situation of armed conflict), by the consistent practice of international bodies called upon to apply the norm, by the fact that all states appear to claim that torture is illegal under their domestic law, and by the tendency of states to deny the practice rather than claim a right to engage in it.

It is in the interpretation of the norm, that is, what constitutes torture and ill-treatment, that the nature and scope of the rule can give rise to doubt. From a human rights perspective, torture may be understood as the infliction, under colour of state authority, of severe physical or mental pain or suffering on a person for such purposes as securing information or a confession (see CAT, Article 1). There is no authoritative definition of cruel or inhuman or degrading treatment. One approach (that of the **EUROPEAN COURT OF HUMAN RIGHTS**) is to see inhuman treatment as requiring less severe pain or suffering than torture and also not requiring the purposive element. Another, favoured by the present writer, would see cruel or inhuman treatment as involving the same degree of pain or suffering as torture, but without the purposive dimension. Degrading treatment would not demand the same threshold of suffering.

There is also uncertainty about what formal punishments may amount to torture or cruel, inhuman or degrading punishment. Imprisonment as such does not, though conditions may well make it so. Corporal punishment is generally understood to violate the prohibition but curiously, the **DEATH PENALTY** has not yet been acknowledged as doing so.

Since, despite its prohibition in national and international law, the practice of torture and ill-treatment persists in many states in most parts of the world, a focus of international normative efforts and case law has been to erect a buffer zone that would deny the opportunity to torture by promoting the accountability of those involved in carrying out detention and interrogation. For example, consistent with the approach of the Body of Principles, authoritative bodies are now typically treating incommunicado detention for more than a day or two as a violation of the prohibition of arbitrary detention and the **RIGHT TO LIBERTY** and security of the person. Indeed, if the incommunicado detention is sufficiently prolonged, it is itself being considered as a violation of the prohibition of torture and ill-treatment. Another prominent example of the buffer zone is the evolution of the notion, now reflected in CAT (Article 3), according to which the deportation of a person to a country where he or she runs a real risk of torture or ill-treatment would itself violate the principle.

By the 1980s the world was ready to engage in measures of specialised international monitoring and other action on (non-)compliance with the prohibition of torture and ill-treatment. Within the UN the process began with CAT. Under it, as with other UN human rights treaties, a Committee (the Committee Against Torture) was created. And, also following

Case study

Positive obligation to protect against torture

States can infringe the right of individuals to be free from torture even when the activity in question occurs outside the state.

The Human Rights Committee opined that Switzerland deporting Mutombo to Zaire could result in a violation of the International Covenant on Civil and Political Rights concerning torture, inhuman and degrading treatment or punishment. This has had a significant effect on other asylum cases. (Mutombo v Switzerland)

A deportation order of a man in the advanced stages of AIDS to his home in St. Kitts was deemed inhuman treatment by the European Court of Human Rights. This was due to the less advanced medical resources available there. (D v UK)

Complying with an extradition order of the USA was deemed to infringe international human rights law as there was a real risk that the extraditee would on conviction for multiple counts of murder be sentenced to death by gas asphyxiation. The Canadian Supreme Court ordered the extradition but the Human Rights Committee of the UN considered such a move would constitute cruel and inhuman treatment. (Ng v Canada)

The impact of such cases on asylum and extradition cases cannot be overlooked. It is particularly relevant in the current situation when deciding on the extradition of suspected terrorists.

other human rights treaties, the Committee was mandated to review periodically reports submitted by state parties, as well as consider interstate and individual petitions if the state(s) in question separately accepted these procedures. A novel power was that the Committee may of its own motion decide to investigate an apparent systematic practice of torture.

These procedures, of course, apply only to state parties to the Convention. It was not until 1985, in the wake of a renewed international campaign against torture by AI, that the UN Commission on Human Rights created the function of Special Rapporteur on the question of torture. This role involved taking up with governments apparently credible allegations of torture or similar ill-treatment (mainly from NGOs). Urgent cases would be the subject of electronic communication (urgent appeals) direct with the states' capitals. Fact-finding visits would be made to countries where there appeared to be an extensive problem. All of this was the subject of public reporting to the Commission on Human Rights.

As with most human rights monitoring procedures, the procedures under the CAT and those of the Special Rapporteur are essentially reactive. In the 1970s, as the result of an initiative of a retired Swiss banker, Jean-Jacques Gautier, himself inspired by the work of the International Committee of the Red Cross with which he had collaborated, there were moves to institutionalise at the intergovernmental level a preventive approach through a treaty obligation. An international body would as of right (unlike the ICRC) have access to any country accepting the treaty, and to all places of detention in the country; it would also be able to visit a country at very short notice and places of detention without notice. In addition, the body would (also unlike the ICRC) be able to announce publicly its findings if the country did not co-operate or seriously address the body's concerns. The expectation was that this method would encourage rather than shame states into improving the situation. Thanks to the persistent efforts of the Swiss Committee against Torture (an NGO formed by Gautier and now called the Association for the Prevention of Torture) and of the International Commission of Jurists, the project first saw

light in the form of the European Convention for the Prevention of Torture and Inhuman or Degrading Treatment or Punishment (1987). In 2002, the General Assembly adopted a protocol to the CAT establishing a similar system at the UN level. However, it does not provide explicitly for ad hoc visits to state parties. On the other hand, it does provide for national-level independent bodies to visit places of detention.

Finally, it should be appreciated that torture is more than a human rights violation; it is also a crime under international law. That means that perpetrators may and under some treaties (CAT; Geneva Conventions, in respect of international armed conflict) must be tried wherever they are found, unless extradited for trial elsewhere. They may also find themselves in the dock of an international criminal tribunal (See: **INTERNATIONAL CRIMINAL LAW AND THE REGIONAL TRIBUNALS**).

In three decades an impressive array of laws, standards and machinery has been created to prevent, expose and repress torture. NGOs played the role of engine of the whole enterprise. NGOs and official bodies may now be expected to co-operate to foster the political will necessary to make the prohibition of torture and ill-treatment a reality. This is especially imperative in the light of a response to the atrocities of 11 September 2001, whereby the unthinkable is being thought as a means to combat terrorism.

Further Reading

Amnesty International (1973) *Report on Torture.*

Amnesty International (1984) *Torture in the Eighties.*

Amnesty International (2003) *Combating Torture: A Manual for Action.*

Burgers, J. Herman and Danelius, Hans (1988) *The United Nations Convention Against Torture: Handbook on the Convention against Torture and other Inhuman or Degrading Treatment or Punishment,* The Hague: Brill,

Evans, Malcolm and Morgan, Rod (1998) *Preventing Torture: A study of the European Convention for the Prevention of Torture and Inhuman or Degrading Treatment or Punishment,* Oxford: Clarendon.

Langbein, John (1977) *Torture and the Law of Proof: Europe and England in the Ancien Regime*, Chicago University of Chicago Press.

Peters, Edward (1985) *Torture*, Oxford: Blackwell Press.

Rodley, Nigel (1999) *The Treatment of Prisoners under International Law*, 2nd edn, Oxford: Clarendon.

Ruthven, Malise (1978) *Torture – The Grand Conspiracy*, London: Weidenfield and Nicolson.

Contributor: Nigel Rodley

TREATY-BASED LAW

Treaties form the basis of most international human rights law. They are, in effect, contracts of international law, the most tangible proof of what states have agreed to, and are legally binding. Terminology varies – treaties, conventions, covenants, protocols, charters, even statutes – all essentially share the same features. Most treaties are written and governed by a comprehensive system of international law enshrined in the Vienna Convention on the Law of Treaties 1969 which addresses issues including the creation, interpretation, application and termination of treaties. Treaties can be bilateral (between two parties) or multilateral (involving many states). International human rights treaties are usually open multilateral instruments: any state can choose to sign up to the provisions at any time.

Treaties are frequently amended, often by protocols. Protocols are simply treaties addressing a specific issue and can be 'added on' to a principal treaty. They are usually optional so a state may be party to the main treaty but avoid obligations under any associated protocols. In the field of human rights, they frequently provide additional rights and freedoms. Examples of such protocols are the protocols on the abolition of the death penalty and the protocol on economic, social and cultural rights which supplement the **INTER-AMERICAN CONVENTION ON HUMAN RIGHTS** and the two protocols to the **UN CONVENTION ON THE RIGHTS OF THE CHILD** on children in armed conflict and on the sale of children, prostitution and pornography. Other protocols may provide an optional enforcement mechanism. For political reasons, the enforcement mechanism was left out of the main treaty. The First Optional Protocol to the **INTERNATIONAL COVENANT ON CIVIL AND POLITICAL RIGHTS** is such a protocol. It enshrines a system of individual petitions which many states elect not to sign up to. Within the African regional system, the protocol on establishing an **AFRICAN COURT ON HUMAN RIGHTS** was added to the **AFRICAN CHARTER ON HUMAN AND PEOPLES' RIGHTS** several years after the original treaty. The reason is simply that the system and political will had developed to the extent that it was feasible to establish a human rights' court.

States are legally bound only by those treaties they elect to sign up to. The treaty itself may be drafted by a number of states or by some other organisation. In the case of international and regional human rights treaties, the final text is normally discussed and even voted on in an international forum. The procedure for signing up to a treaty is essentially twofold. A state must usually sign and ratify an instrument before it is bound by it. Once the treaty is opened for signature, competent state representatives can indicate acquiescence to its terms by signing its. Such a simple signature may bind the state, but more commonly, states are required to ratify the signature. In other words, the state most formally confirm that it is bound by the treaty. This lapse of time allows the state to move from expressing its desire to be politically and morally bound to a treaty to confirming its willingness to be legally bound by it. The latter may require legal or political measures under

> 'International human rights law is best visualised as a network of different treaties whereby governments explicitly accept specific human rights obligations. The realm of the acceptable is delineated by minimum standards which should be in place worldwide; optimal standards vary in time and place.'
>
> Katarina Tomaševski, *Education Denied: costs and remedies*, Zed Books, 2003, p51

the national constitution. Once ratification occurs, a state is morally, politically and legally bound by the treaty. Following the doctrine of pacta sund servanda (essentially good faith), the state should thereafter ensure its actions conform to the standards set forth in the treaty.

Even following signature and ratification, the treaty may not be enforceable against a state because it has not entered into force. Treaties enter into force in accordance with the terms of the instrument itself. Some treaties require the agreement of all states in the drafting organisation. For example, the COUNCIL OF EUROPE's Protocol 11 to the EUROPEAN CONVENTION FOR THE PROTECTION OF HUMAN RIGHTS AND FUNDAMENTAL FREEDOMS dramatically changed the structure of the institutions involved in implementing human rights, removing the European Commission on Human Rights and developing a more complex and permanent court structure. This required the consent of all states currently party to the Convention before the changes could be effected. It would clearly have been untenable for some states to retain the Commission while others adopted the new streamlined court procedure.

Most treaties, however, enter into force after a certain number of states agree to be bound by the terms of the treaty. This is common with many international and regional human rights instruments. The 1989 UN Convention on the Rights of the Child, for example, entered into force on the 30th day following the date of deposit of the 20th instrument of ratification or accession (Article 49). This was achieved swiftly and that treaty remains one of the more universally accepted international human rights instruments. This position can be contrasted with the 1990 INTERNATIONAL CONVENTION ON THE PROTECTION OF THE RIGHTS OF ALL MIGRANT WORKERS which also required 20 ratifications. Although the convention was opened for signatures a year after the UN Convention on the Rights of the Child, it only entered into force in 2003, more than a decade later. Some instruments never achieve the minimum number of ratifications to enter into force – the Arab Charter on Human Rights is an example.

Even when a treaty enters into force, rati-fying states may enter RESERVATIONS OR DEROGATIONS, thereby limiting the extent of their legal obligation. With international human rights treaties, the result of reserva-tions can be a complex system of bilateral legal obligations. The operation of the CONVENTION ON THE ELIMINATION OF ALL FORMS OF DISCRIMINATION AGAINST WOMEN has been significantly affected by reservations.

When determining which international human rights and fundamental freedoms a specified individual can rely on against a spec-ified state, it is imperative that the status of the relevant treaties are examined. Is the treaty in force? Has the state ratified it? Has the state entered any valid reservations, declarations or derogations which may limit the liability of the state vis-a-vis the particular right or freedom?

Once a treaty has entered into force, new states can elect to join. They are required to sign and ratify the instrument in the normal way. Their active membership is notified to all other states currently party to the treaty. For ease of reference, all subsequent signatures and ratifications etc. are deposited with a cen-tral body, frequently the Secretary General of the United Nations.

Can a state revoke its treaty obligations? Most treaties permit states to sign up and opt out at will. Obviously there are political impli-cations but the legal position is clear. Human rights treaties, however, are often incontro-vertible – it is not technically possible for a state to change its mind and rescind its ratifi-cation. The nature of human rights demands that a state should increase not reduce the protection extended to its nationals. Denunciation undermines the universality of human rights and removes the state in ques-tion from the principal international monitor-ing mechanisms. Notably, the HUMAN RIGHTS COMMITTEE has opined that states may not opt out of the INTERNATIONAL COVENANT ON CIVIL AND POLITICAL RIGHTS. This followed an attempt by the Democratic People's Republic of Korea (North Korea) to withdraw in 1997. In the words of the Committee: once the people are accorded the protection of the rights under the Covenant, such protection devolves with territory and continues to belong to them, notwithstanding change in government of the state party, including dismemberment in more than one state or state succession or any subsequent action of the state party designed to divest them of the rights guaranteed by the Covenant (General Comment 26). Arguably the same could be said of other human rights treaties. Indeed, the AFRICAN CHARTER ON HUMAN AND PEOPLES RIGHTS does not permit denunciation. This appears not to have affected the willingness of states to ratify it.

Depending on the instrument, states becoming party to a treaty can be referred to as contracting states, high contracting parties, member states or even state parties.

Some principal international human rights treaties adopted under the auspices of the United Nations are:

- 1951 Convention Relating to the Status of Refugees and its 1967 Protocol.

- 1956 Supplementary Convention on the Abolition of Slavery, the Slave Trade and Institutions and Practices Similar to Slavery.

- 1966 CONVENTION ON THE ELIMINATION OF ALL FORMS OF RACIAL DISCRIMINATION.

- 1966 International Covenant on Civil and Political Rights and protocols.

- 1966 International Covenant on Economic, Social and Cultural Rights.

- 1989 Convention on the Elimination of all forms of Discrimination against Women.

- 1983 Convention against Torture and other Cruel Inhuman or Degrading Treatment or Punishment.

- 1989 UN Convention on the Rights of the Child and protocols.

- 1990 International Convention on the Protection of the Rights of all Migrant Workers.

Further Reading

Malanczuk, (2004) P. *Akehurst's Modern Introduction to International Law*, 8th revised edn, London: Routledge.

Sinclair, I. (1984) *The Vienna Convention on the Law of Treaties*, Manchester: Manchester University Press. Melland Schill Studies in International Law.

Contributor: Rhona K.M. Smith

TRUTH COMMISSIONS

There is near unanimity among scholars and practitioners that, in order to move forward, societies coming out of periods of violence must in some way examine, acknowledge and account for past violence committed by various groups. The end of military dictatorships and authoritarian governments in Latin America in the 1980s produced the field of transitional justice, which involves the attempts of newly democratic governments to establish a process to hold members of the former regime (as well as opposition groups) accountable for gross violations of human rights which occurred during their tenure. With the transition from authoritarianism to democracy first in Latin America and then in both Eastern Europe and Africa at the end of the cold war, families of victims of former regimes along with other survivors began to increase their demands for information about atrocities that had occurred under dictatorships. They wanted the truth about those periods to be uncovered and formally acknowledged, and they wanted those responsible for the atrocities to be held accountable.

One mechanism for producing and delivering this truth is a truth commission. Truth commissions have become a near-global phenomenon for delivering transitional justice to individual victims and for providing a common truth to society as a whole. At least 25 truth commissions have existed or currently exist in Latin America, Africa, Europe, South-East Asia, the Caribbean and the Far East. (For an up-to-date list of the status of truth commissions around the world, see the United States Institute of Peace's website: http://www.usip.org/library/truth.html#TC.) Additional commissions may well be formed in other countries as efforts to negotiate peaceful ends to ethnic conflicts slowly gain momentum. Even in the midst of war, human rights activists in places as varied as Afghanistan and Zimbabwe have begun to lay the groundwork for post-war justice and have begun planning new truth commissions. In the span of approximately 25 years, truth commissions have become an expected feature of post-war reconstruction and democratic transitions. While no two commissions are the same, the term 'truth commission' has come to refer generically to a particular type of transitional justice mechanism: one created in a post-conflict situation to examine past atrocities, issue findings of responsibility, and make future-oriented recommendations designed to foster and consolidate democracy and a human rights culture.

Although the mandate, goals, structure and function of each truth commission is context-specific, certain elements are generally considered necessary for a truth-telling mechanism to be considered a truth commission. Priscilla Hayner notes the following common features of truth commissions: they are institutions officially sanctioned by the state; they have temporary mandates (generally ranging from six months to two years); they focus on investigating patterns of abuse that occurred over a particular time period (as opposed to an inquiry into a specific event); they almost always focus on politically motivated repression; they are non-judicial (i.e. they do not have the power to prosecute); they are created during periods of political change in order to foster the transition to democracy; and they issue final reports that contain recommendations for future actions by the state to ensure that the transition is sustainable (Hayner, 2001, pp. 14–17).

Several assumptions underlie the call for the creation of truth commissions, as opposed to other transitional justice mechanisms such as trials and war crimes tribunals, in the aftermath of conflicts. The first assumption is that unless societies confront their histories of gross violations of human rights, future generations risk repeating those atrocities. In other words, when past abuses are left covered up, they will constantly be repeated until their causes are resolved. To ensure a future which does not reiterate the past, the atrocities of that past must be appropriately illuminated. The second underlying assumption is that one of the best ways for individual victims/survivors of human rights violations to move beyond their trauma and to heal past wounds is to uncover them and let them air. Paradoxically, Hayner argues, one of the best ways to forget is to remember. She notes, 'only by remembering, telling their story, and learning every last detail about what happened and who was responsible [are victims] able to begin to put the past behind them' (Hayner, 2001, p. 2). A final assumption held by proponents of truth commissions is that they are important mechanisms, especially through the issuing of recommendations, for fostering several crucial elements of sustainable peace, such as the rule of law and a strengthened judiciary. These assumptions have both individual and national dimensions; the healing of victims, for example, relates to individuals, while fostering the rule of law or preventing the recurrence of atrocities affects society as a whole.

The goals and functions of truth commissions tend to reflect these individual – and national-level assumptions. Hayner (2001, p. 2) lists five functions of truth commissions: to uncover the truth about past abuses, to respond to specific needs of victims, to contribute to justice and accountability, to outline institutional responsibility and recommend reforms, and to promote reconciliation. These underlying assumptions and basic goals were clearly evident in the South African Truth and Reconciliation Commission (TRC), which operated between 1995 and 1998 (although one important committee, the Amnesty Committee, did not conclude its work until 2003). In the history of truth commissions, the TRC is arguably the best known. It serves as a good example of the translation of assumptions and general goals into a specific institution, as well as an illustration of the various elements common to almost all truth commissions. The legislation which created the TRC listed four specific objectives. The first was to establish as complete a picture as possible of the causes, nature and extent of gross violations of human rights committed during the period between 1 March, 1960 and 10 May 1994 – in other words, to establish the truth. The second goal was to facilitate the granting of amnesty on the basis of full disclosure of acts associated with a political objective during the mandate period of the TRC investigation. (The TRC's high profile has led to a common misunderstanding that the granting of amnesty is a feature associated with most truth commissions. In reality, no other truth commission to date has had amnesty-granting powers.) The third goal of the TRC was to restore the human and civil dignity of victims by establishing and making known their fates and whereabouts, through giving them the opportunity to relate their own accounts and by recommending reparation measures. A final goal was to compile a report containing recommendations of measures to prevent future violations of human rights.

Several aspects of truth commissions have led to widespread debate. The first is the lack of clarity surrounding many concepts associated with the theory and practice of truth commissions. Two in particular which generate controversy are 'truth' and 'reconciliation'. In terms of 'truth', questions have been raised about whose truth is being told in final reports, as well as about the idea that a single type of truth is possible. Different scholars refer to different types of truth, including factual/forensic truth, narrative truth and structural truth. Finally, some find it helpful to distinguish between the terms 'knowledge' and 'acknowledgement', both of which speak to different goals of commissions. (Knowledge can help uncover the facts about the past, while acknowledgement can help restore the dignity of victims.) Likewise, no universally agreed upon definition of the concept of reconciliation exists. As a result, seldom are people talking about the same thing when using the term. Generally, one can infer two distinct usages of the term: individual reconciliation – which includes such actions as apology, repentance, forgiveness and healing – and national reconciliation – which is associated with such issues as tolerance, peaceful coexistence and conflict resolution. The existence of two understandings of reconciliation has consequences for the evaluation of truth commissions, as one's interpretation of the term will guide one's evaluation of a commission. Statements such as 'this truth commission did/did not foster reconciliation' are almost meaningless unless the sense in which the speaker is using the word is made clear.

A second area of controversy is the causal relationships often attributed to commissions. One frequently hears such claims as 'truth commissions are cathartic for victims and help them heal' or 'truth commissions lead to reconciliation'. In general, discussions of truth commissions tend to be highly aspirational, which results in insufficiently examined statements presented as empirical facts. Thus, the frequently repeated statement that truth commissions provide healing for victims ignores the fact that they sometimes exacerbate feelings of anger and pain. Similarly, the idea that truth is unequivocally linked to reconciliation is so taken for granted that often little attempt is made to determine whether it is in fact true. One scholar notes that, 'the thought that reconciliation requires truth is not very plausible as a general empirical rule' (Allen, 1999, p. 317). Such untested assumptions may result in unrealistically high expectations being placed on truth commission – expectations that, even under the best of circumstances, are unlikely to be met.

A final controversy is often referred to as the 'truth versus justice' debate, which posits that truth commissions are a second-best alternative to trials and that they undermine the rule of law because they fail to hold perpetrators legally accountable. Most scholars today, however, agree that truth commissions should rather be seen as parallel mechanisms to trials as opposed to replacements for them, as both types of institutions work towards the same ends, albeit using different means: justice and accountability.

Further Reading

Allen, Jonathan (1999) 'Balancing Justice and Social Unity: Political Theory and the Idea of a Truth and Reconciliation Commission', in *University of Toronto Law Journal*, vol. 49, no. 3, pp. 315–53.

Hayner, Priscilla B. (2001) *Unspeakable Truths: Confronting State Terror and Atrocity*, New York: Routledge.

Kritz, Neil (ed.) (1995) *Transitional Justice: How Emerging Democracies Reckon with Former Regimes*, Washington, DC: United States Institute of Peace.

Minow, Martha (1998) *Between Vengeance and Forgiveness: Facing History After Genocide and Mass Violence*, Boston, MA: Beacon Books.

Rotberg, Robert I. and Thompson, Dennis (eds) (2000) *Truth v. Justice: The Morality of Truth Commissions*, Princeton, NJ: Princeton University Press.

Contributor:　　　　　　　Tristan Anne Borer

UBUNTU AND HUMAN RIGHTS

Human rights need to preserve the dignity of all people. The modern human rights movement sought to internationalise the promotion of fundamental rights and freedoms. There is a growing need to ensure a more dynamic and culturally inclusive understanding of human rights. Ever since the **UNIVERSAL DECLARATION OF HUMAN RIGHTS** (UDHR) was adopted by the United Nations General Assembly on 10 December 1948 there has been an ongoing debate about whether the human rights standards were formulated, codified and adopted by appealing mainly to Western cultural and philosophical traditions. Does the absence of other cultural belief systems during the definition and drafting of the UDHR necessarily invalidate the universality of the current human rights discourse? Are these standards truly representative of a global consensus on notions of human dignity? Is the UDHR incomplete in its formulation? If there is indeed a Western bias in the human rights discourse then the current human rights paradigm is excluding lessons that can be learned from other traditions.

The current understanding and discourse of human rights, whether intentionally or unintentionally, tends to promote individualism. The notion of human obligations to other people tends to get marginalised. This is in contrast with what people in many non-Western cultures believe to be important. There is therefore a need for a more inclusive definition, of human rights by learning, borrowing and incorporating worldviews from other parts of the world. If the UDHR can be reinterpreted and reformulated by referring to different cultural perspectives, this would broaden the international respect and ultimately enhance human rights promotion and protection.

Even though African societies are not monolithic, most if not all societies on the continent have notions of human dignity that preceded the onslaught of slavery and colonialism. It is therefore regrettable that values and principles from African thought and belief systems were not included and recognised in the drafting of the UDHR. With the onset of colonialism there was an unspoken assumption that the traditions from these societies did not have any contributions to make to the human rights discourse. As a consequence, communities that were marginalised by colonising forces were not in a position to input and contribute towards the formulation of a global code of human rights. To remedy this situation, the indigenous, non-European/non-Western traditions of Asia, Africa, the Pacific and the Americas must be referred to in order to deconstruct the dominant Western discourse of human rights. Subsequently, a genuinely universal bundle of rights can be reconstructed which all human societies can claim as theirs.

In practical terms there are lessons that can be drawn from the African worldview know as 'ubuntu'. Ubuntu is an ancient African code of ethics, a cultural worldview that tries to capture the essence of what it means to be human. It emphasises the importance of hospitality, generosity, respect for all members of the community, and embraces the view that we all belong to one human family. This notion of ubuntu is found in diverse forms among the Bantu languages of east, central and southern Africa. In Southern Africa we find its clearest articulation among the Nguni group of languages. In terms of its definition, Desmond Tutu in his book *No Future Without Forgiveness* observes that 'ubuntu is very difficult to render into a Western language. It speaks to the very essence of being human. To give high praise to someone, we say "Yu, u nobuntu"; He or she has ubuntu, implying that the person is generous, hospitable, friendly, caring and compassionate and willing to share what he or she has. It also means that my humanity is caught up, is inextricably bound up, with that person. We belong in a bundle of life. We say, "A person is a person through other people" (in Xhosa "Ubuntu ungamntu ngabanye abantu" and in Zulu "Umuntu ngumuntu ngabanye")' (Tutu, 1999, 34–35).

I am human because I belong, I participate, I share. A person with ubuntu is open and available to others, affirming of others, does not feel threatened by the ability and goodness of others; for he or she has a proper self-assurance that comes with knowing that he or she belongs and is part of a greater whole. In fact, an 'ubuntian' is diminished when others are humiliated, diminished, tortured, oppressed or treated as if they were less than who they are. As a human being through other human beings it follows that what we do to others also impacts upon ourselves. As Tutu observes: 'In the process of dehumanising another, in inflicting untold harm and suffering, the perpetrator was inexorably being dehumanised as well.'

This notion of ubuntu sheds light on the importance of promoting human rights through the principles of reciprocity, inclusivity and a sense of shared destiny between peoples. Ubuntu provides a value system for giving and receiving forgiveness which in turn furthers human rights in war-affected societies and countries in transition from authoritarian regimes. It creates a rationale for letting go of the desire to revenge for past wrongs. It evokes an inspiration and suggests guidelines for societies and their governments on how to legislate and establish laws which will promote human rights. In short, it can culturally reinform and reconstruct our practical efforts to establish a more effective and relevant human rights regime in Africa and other parts of the world. It is to be noted that the principles found in ubuntu are not unique and exist in diverse forms in other cultures and traditions. Nevertheless, an ongoing reflection and reappraisal of this notion of ubuntu can serve to re-emphasise the essential unity of humanity and gradually endorse attitudes and values that uphold human rights, encourage the sharing of resources and cooperation in the resolution of our disputes.

Ubuntu societies maintained institutions which had at their core concern for human dignity of the individual in combination with an individual's obligation towards the community. Such institutions also served as mechanisms for maintaining law and order within a society. The wisdom of ubuntu lies in the recognition that a healthy community at peace with itself can only be built if the human dignity of all its members is safeguarded. With reference to the notion of I am because we are and a person being a person through other people, these ubuntu values can be drawn upon when obligations and solidarity need to be emphasised towards others.

A recognition of our 'ubuntuness' therefore is a call to 'internalise' these principles and put them into action, to practise politics with principle. Advancing an ubuntu perspective can facilitate the inclusion of an African voice in a dialogue on rights and responsibilities and contribute 'multiculturalisation' of the human rights movement. It will also allow the establishment of human rights standards which cannot be discredited because of the nature of their origins. All cultures have principles that can serve as a basis for re-emphasising collective human rights thereby reinforcing the notion that all human rights are indeed for all of us.

A rearticulation of human rights from an ubuntu perspective adds value to the human rights movement by placing more of an emphasis on the obligations that we have towards the 'other'. An appreciation of the ubuntu worldview can assist in developing the competence of human rights promoters as well as enhance and facilitate the appreciation and respect of human rights in Africa and other parts of the world.

Further Reading

Mutua, Makau (2002) *Human Rights: A Political and Cultural Critique*, Philadelphia: University of Pennsylvannia Press.

Odinkalu, Chidi Anselem (2003) 'Back to the Future: The Imperative of Prioritizing for the Protection of Human Rights in Africa' in 47, *Journal of African Law*, pp. 1–37.

Tutu, Desmond (1999) *No Future, Without Forgiveness*, London: Pinter.

Contributor: Tim Murithi

THE UNITED NATIONS HIGH COMMISSIONER FOR HUMAN RIGHTS

The High Commissioner for Human Rights (HCHR) is the principal official in the United Nations with responsibility for human rights and has the rank of Under Secretary General. The High Commissioner is answerable to the Secretary General and is appointed by the General Assembly for a four-year term that can be renewed once only. The position of

High Commissioner was established by resolution of the General Assembly in December 1993, marking the high point of post-cold war consensus on human rights and following up a proposal of the Vienna World Conference on Human Rights of the same year. The General Assembly resolution creating the post (GA Res.48/141) sets out an extensive job description for the position of High Commissioner. Over the first ten years of its existence the main challenge has been to establish a coherent programme with stable priorities from the vast range of responsibilities vested in the HCHR.

The High Commissioner heads an Office of the High Commissioner for Human Rights (OHCHR), which is a department of the United Nations Secretariat. Based in Geneva, it is housed in the former building of the League of Nations, the Palais Wilson. There is also a liaison office at United Nations Headquarters in New York. As of 1 October 2003, OHCHR had 564 staff distributed between Geneva (284), New York (9) and in country-level activities worldwide (271).

There have been four appointments as High Commissioner to date at the time of writing. Ayola Lasso, a career diplomat from Ecuador took up the position in April 1994. He was immediately faced with a priority not foreseen in the mandate, the need to deploy human rights personnel at country level following the outbreak of the genocide in Rwanda. The number of such 'field presences' or missions has multiplied since then. Ayola Lasso resigned in 1997 to become Foreign Minister in Ecuador and was replaced by Mary Robinson, former President of Ireland. She was High Commissioner until September 2002 and has exerted the most influence to date in shaping the role, in particular through her public campaigning profile and her efforts to implement one of Kofi Annan's 1997 reform proposals, the integration or 'mainstreaming' of human rights into the entire United Nations system. Sergio Vierra de Mello from Brazil was High Commissioner from September 2002 until August 2003. He was killed in an explosion in Baghdad while serving as the Special Representative of the Secretary General. Thereafter the serving Deputy High Commissioner, Bertrand Ramcharan, became acting High Commissioner. A new High Commissioner, Louise Arbour, former prosecutor at the ad hoc War Crimes Tribunal in The Hague and Canadian Supreme Court judge, took up the position in July 2004.

The mission statement of the OHCHR declares that its mandate is to promote and protect all human rights for all. In practice this goal is pursued through a range of activities which can be broken down as follows. Providing leadership for the global implementation of human rights is the first task of a High Commissioner. The official mandate speaks of acting to remove obstacles to human rights observance and engaging in dialogue with countries to ensure respect for human rights. It also expects a High Commissioner to encourage states to co-operate in building respect for international standards and to address their violation. Each High Commissioner has sought to play this essentially moral role of being the UN's principal human rights voice. It can be achieved through public statements alerting the world to actual or threatening human rights crises and calling in a public way on offending governments to end violations. It can be achieved by travelling to different countries including those where human rights are at risk, and meeting with different actors on the ground. It can be achieved by opening up dialogue with a government and seeking to assist through providing advice and expertise on protecting human rights. As part of this implementation strategy the High Commissioner has appointed regional advisers based in all world regions.

An internal dimension of the leadership function is the task of integrating human rights into other parts of the UN system. The High Commissioner for Human Rights was charged in 1997 with ensuring that human rights norms and standards were 'mainstreamed' into all UN activities including DEVELOPMENT and peacekeeping (See: HUMANITARIAN INTERVENTION). This goal has been of particular importance following the 11 September attacks in the United States in respect of the counter terrorism role of the Security Council (See: TERRORISM AND HUMAN RIGHTS). Several High Commissioners have addressed the Security Council and the Counter Terrorism Committee of the Council on the need to uphold the rule of law and human rights in the fight against terrorism.

The second main task is support for the UN human rights system. This represents the largest function of the High Commissioner and the OHCHR. It entails the management and co-ordination of the complex system that has grown up within the United Nations to promote and protect human rights. OHCHR provides research and secretariat services to a wide array of bodies that meet in Geneva during the year, in particular the Commission on Human Rights and its Sub-Commission and the treaty bodies (the monitoring committees of the core international human rights treaties). Support extends to the mechanisms and special procedures established by the Commission on Human Rights. These are the independent experts or special rapporteurs, special representatives and working groups charged with specific human rights protection and investigation mandates. The OHCHR secretariat is also responsible for the management and processing of the various individual complaint procedures over human rights violations. A further task is ensuring quick response to urgent appeals for protection. OHCHR dedicates two of its internal staff branches to these activities: the Treaty and Commission Branch and the Special Procedures Branch.

The third task, work in the field, has taken on rapidly increasing importance for the OHCHR. There were some 30 such country-based presences in 2003. Increasingly the OHCHR does not operate alone but within United Nations country teams (UNCTs). The nature of OCHR field presence varies from being part of UN peace missions in complex emergencies to technical assistance projects established with the agreement of governments. On the whole the work is largely the same in both contexts. The OHCHR provides advice on creating or strengthening national human rights protection systems including NATIONAL HUMAN RIGHTS INSTITUTIONS, ('capacity building'), encouraging ratification of international human rights treaties and assistance with HUMAN RIGHTS EDUCATION and training programmes. These activities, spread across every continent, are supported within OHCHR by a new Capacity Building and Field Operations Branch.

The fourth task is research on human rights priorities. This constitutes a further contribution of OHCHR mainly under mandates from the Commission on Human Rights and ECOSOC. A number of thematic priorities are pursued, added to and substituted over time. A staple focus has been on the Right to Development and the eradication of extreme POVERTY along with such ECONOMIC and SOCIAL RIGHTS as HEALTH, FOOD and EDUCATION. Another continuing priority is human rights education. Following the Durban World Conference on Racism, Racial Discrimination Xenophobia and related Intolerance of 2001, an Anti-Discrimination Unit has been given the task of coordinating the implementation of the Programme of Action adopted at the Conference. The remaining research themes at present are INDIGENOUS PEOPLES and MINORITIES, gender mainstreaming and WOMEN'S RIGHTS, HIV/AIDS, DISABILITY and trafficking, and a cluster of topics under the rubric of DEMOCRACY, development and human rights which include projects on the rule of law and the administration of justice. The outputs of research are provided to the Commission and Sub-Commission and can lead to education and training projects and advice on the integration of human rights into the programmes of other UN agencies. Publications on a wide range of human rights themes are also a significant contribution of OHCHR.

This array of activities in support of human rights costs money. The High Commissioner for Human Rights experiences the same financial constraints on what it can achieve as other parts of the United Nations. OHCHR works as with the rest of the UN on a biennial budget allocation. Its funds come from the regular budget and from individual donors. The regular budget total allocation from the UN for 2002–3 was $US 47.7 million, corresponding to 1.8 per cent of the total UN biennial budget of US$2.6 billion. Funding from the regular budget counted for only 34 per cent of annual expenditure in 2001, with 66 per cent or US $ 42.8 million coming from voluntary funds generated by appeal to UN member states. There are many concerns over this reliance on fundraising to run the UN's human rights programme. While there is a good spread of donor states and foundations, the OHCHR is reliant on too few large donors. The High Commissioner lobbies for a larger slice of the regular UN budget, arguing that budget share of less than 2 per cent for human rights is wrong, but with little prospect of success.

WEBSITE

www.ohchr.org The web site of the Office of the High Commissioner provides regularly updated news and information on the work of the High Commissioner and on all aspects of the United Nations and human rights.

Further Reading

Clapham, Andrew (2004) 'The High Commissioner for Human Rights' in Alston, P., *The United Nations and Human Rights*, 2nd edn, Oxford: Clarendon Press, chapter 15.

General Assembly Resolution 48/141 High Commissioner for the promotion and protection of all human rights, adopted on 20 December 1993.

Ramcharan, B. (2002) *The United Nations High Commissioner for Human Rights: the Challenges for International Protection*, Brill.

Contributor:　　　　　　　　Kevin Boyle

THE UNITED NATIONS SINCE THE UNIVERSAL DECLARATION OF HUMAN RIGHTS OF 1948

The United Nations is an intergovernmental organisation that emerged from the Second World War. It was, in fact, the successor to the League of Nations, which was widely considered to have been a failure. In a series of conferences during the Second World War, the allied powers prepared the outline of a new organisation which was meant to do the job that the League of Nations had failed to do: the preservation of international peace and security. These conferences culminated in a major meeting in San Francisco, where in June 1945 the representatives of 50 victorious states signed the United Nations Charter. The Charter entered into force on 24 October 1945. Fifty-nine years later, the organisation

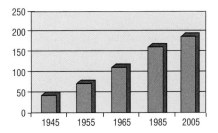

Growth in number of member states of the United Nations

still exists and has meanwhile grown to 191 members.

From the beginning, the issue of human rights has played an important role in the United Nations. In 1948, the General Assembly adopted the **UNIVERSAL DECLARATION OF HUMAN RIGHTS**, which in its preamble is named a 'common standard of achievement for all peoples and all nations'. Though not legally binding, it has become the foundation for establishing obligatory legal norms to govern international behaviour with regard to rights of individuals. More than 140 states have acceded to the two international covenants – on civil and political rights and on economic, social and cultural rights respectively – adopted in 1966 and based on the Declaration.

The Commission on Human Rights is the chief UN organ that deals with human rights. It meets annually for a five-week session in Geneva, and is composed of 53 states, elected for three-year terms by the Economic and Social Council. It has a broad mandate touching on any matter relating to human rights. The Commission carries out studies, prepares recommendations to governments, and drafts international instruments relating to human rights for ratification by governments. It investigates allegations of violations of human rights and receives and processes communications related to such violations. It has appointed 'thematic' rapporteurs on issues such as torture and summary or arbitrary executions and a working group on enforced or involuntary disappearances. Unique among UN-organs is the presence on the floor of representatives of non-governmental organisations which take an active part in the debates (albeit without a vote) and which may submit proposals for adoption by the Commission.

The Commission on Human Rights has been criticised for having among its members some notorious violators of human rights. For example, the 2004 term of the Commission included among its members China, Cuba, Congo, Ethiopia, Russia, Saudi Arabia, Sierra Leone and Sudan – countries whose governments have been cited for gross violations of human rights. These states, as well as non-member governments that attend the sessions of the Commission as observers, make frequent use of their 'right of reply' whenever they find themselves criticised for failing to live up to international human rights standards. It would, however, not be feasible and probably not even advisable to exclude such countries from the Commission: not feasible, as the members of the Commission are elected by the Economic and Social Council on a political and geographical basis; not advisable, as these countries in the Commission can be confronted with the norms they claim to adhere to – such confrontation has at times led to improvements in the situation.

In 1993, the General Assembly, acting on recommendations of the second World Conference on Human Rights, decided to establish a UN High Commissioner on Human Rights. This official has the principal responsibility for United Nations human rights activities and carries out the tasks assigned to him or her by the competent bodies of the United Nations. He/she coordinates all activities in the promotion and protection of human rights and heads the UN Centre for Human Rights, which in 1997 was joined with the secretariat of the High Commissioner to be known henceforth as Bureau of the High Commissioner. Former Ecuadorian diplomat José Ayalo Lasso and former Irish President Mary Robinson were the first holders of this position. Robinson's successor, the Brazilian diplomat SergioViera de Mello, was tragically killed in August 2003 while serving as United Nations representative in Iraq. Louise Arbour has taken up the mandate. The Office of the High Commissioner has established a number of 'field presences' all over the world. They are engaged in such matters as providing advice to governments to bring national laws and institutional practices in line with international human rights standards, developing human rights education, supporting human

rights institutions, legislative and policy reform, human rights training of policy and judicial officers, and building of human rights capacities in the field. Such field presences have been established for a great number of countries in Africa, Asia, Latin America and Eastern Europe, usually in the aftermath of the occurrence of major human rights violations.

Concern with violations of human rights and the international law of war led the Security Council in 1993 to create an international criminal tribunal, located in The Hague, to try persons accused of genocide and war crimes in former Yugoslavia. A number of former officials, including former Yugoslav President Slobodan Milosevic, have appeared before the Tribunal. Following this example, the Security Council in 1994 created a similar tribunal, located in Arusha, Tanzania, to try those accused of war crimes and genocide in Rwanda. In 1998, a Statute was adopted for an International Criminal Court, also to be located in The Hague. The Court will deal with the crime of genocide, crimes against humanity, war crimes and the crime of aggression (yet to be defined). The Statute entered into force on 1 July 2002. By February 2004 there were 139 states that had acceded to the Statute. However, major states, such as the United States, China, Israel, India and Pakistan have indicated that they do not intend to ratify the Statute.

The human rights activities of the United Nations have seen both successes and failures. The most positive result of the human rights programmes is undoubtedly the creation of international standards for the treatment of human beings all over the world. Common

'The United Nations inspires the hope of so many of the world's downtrodden. Every year thousands of individuals and groups appeal to UN bodies for help. On their behalf myriad non-governmental organisations attempt to place their cases on the international agenda. When national institutions fail, when governments are unresponsive, millions of the tortured, the repressed, the hungry, turn to the UN.'

(A.Bayefsky, 1996)

criteria now exist for judging whether human beings enjoy fundamental human rights. The United Nations can claim the accomplishment of making the norms more concrete so that it is possible to determine where and when they are violated. All governments accept human rights in principle, if not in practice. By paying at least lip-service to this idea, they also implicitly accept the assumption that a limited world community exists. Moreover, non-governmental organisations rely on these very norms to take governments to task and remind them of whatever moral or legal obligations they have assumed.

A second positive outcome can be demonstrated in the remarkable increase in information that UN bodies collect and distribute on the performance by states in the field of human rights. A vast reporting network includes the Commission on Human Rights, its special rapporteurs, various treaty bodies, some of the specialised agencies, the member states themselves in their national reports, various UN publications and more recently the activities of the High Commissioner for Human Rights. These efforts are again supplemented by extensive information gathering on the part of non-governmental organisations.

Both the process of creating norms and the monitoring of the performance of states have encouraged the active participation of non-governmental organisations, such as Amnesty International, the International Commission of Jurists and the various 'watch' committees. They constantly demand more effective enforcement and protection of human rights. They attempt to influence the United Nations directly through persuasion and indirectly through the member governments. Yet the performance of the United Nations in supervising and controlling the actual performance of states in the human rights field must be accounted as less positive than the formulation of standards. Even when violations of human rights can be pinpointed as to time and place, this does not necessarily ensure that UN bodies will deal with them in an objective manner. Some of the worst offenders in the field of human rights are members of the Commission on Human Rights, where their representatives make pious statements. Whether or not a case will be considered by a UN body depends more on political factors than on the nature of the alleged violations. The apartheid policies of South Africa (in the past) or human rights violations by the Israeli forces in the Occupied Territories have unfailingly figured highly on the agenda, while at the same time dramatic violations taking place in countries such as China or Russia (Chechnya) remain unchecked by UN action. In fact, complaints about violations of human rights often become the vehicle for presenting political points of view. It is not entirely without reason that some observers have accused the United Nations of applying double standards.

The United Nations can, moreover, neither effectively punish nor reward governments for their degree of compliance with human rights standards. The Security Council has the right to act only when it is convinced that a violation of human rights threatens international peace and security. It stated, however, in 1991, in resolution 688 relating to the repression of the Kurdish population in Iraq that 'the consequences (...) threaten international peace and security'. This was widely interpreted as linking human rights violations with possible action by the Security Council. Not all violations can in fact be clearly considered as endangering the peace. Furthermore, enforcement action under Chapter VII of the Charter may be too heavy an instrument to be appropriate and in any case, the powers that command the veto in the Council, have shown great reluctance to undertake sanctions. Voluntary sanctions remain an option, but these have never worked well. Finally, enforcement actions may bear more heavily on those who already suffer than on those who cause the difficulties.

Despite the difficulty of securing a high level of compliance with human rights standards, the importance of UN activities in this field should not be underestimated. The idea on which such work is based may take on a life of its own, just as did the French Declaration of the Rights of Man and the US Declaration of Independence. They matured over decades, slowly entered law and practice and eventually set actual limits on the behaviour of governments. The possibility of a similar development should not be excluded in the human rights standards within the framework of the United Nations.

Further Reading

Alston, Philip and Crawford, James (eds) (2000) *The Future of UN Human Rights Treaty Monitoring*, Cambridge: Cambridge University Press.

Baehr, Peter R. and Castermans, Monique (2003) *The Role of Human Rights in Foreign Policy*, Houndmills, Basingstoke: Palgrave Macmillan.

Bayefsky, Anne F. (ed.) (2000) *The UN Human Rights Treaty System in the 21st Century*, The Hague: Kluwer Law International.

Heyns, Cristof and Viljoen, Frans (2002) The Impact of the United Nations Human Rights Treaties on the Domestic Level, The Hague: Kluwer.

Katayanagi, Mari (2002) *Human Rights Functions of United Nations Peacekeeping Operations*, The Hague: Kluwer.

O'Flaherty, Michael (2002) *Human Rights and the UN: Practice Before the Treaty Bodies*, 2nd edn, London: Sweet & Maxwell.

Contributor: Peter R. Baehr

THE UNITED NATIONS SYSTEM OF HUMAN RIGHTS PROTECTION

The United Nations has, since its inception in 1945, pioneered international standard setting on human rights issues. Under its auspices, a number of human rights instruments have been adopted and a comprehensive monitoring system has been instituted with the aim of promoting compliance by states. A number of bodies are involved with human rights as the following diagram illustrates.

The principal UN institutions are the Security Council, the General Assembly and the International Court of Justice. These bodies were established in terms of the UN Charter which clearly explains their functions and powers. The Secretary General is also included as his offices are central to the successful functioning of the United Nations. The Security Council, which operates at the highest level, has primary responsibility for the maintenance of international peace and security. It comprises five permanent members (France, People's Republic of China, Russia, United Kingdom and United States of America) and a further ten members drawn from other states. A range of enforcement measures may be applied against states by the Security Council, ranging from diplomatic pressure through sanctions to military action. Given the principle of non-intervention in internal affairs of any state, the Security Council is most likely to be involved in human rights issues when friction caused by human rights threatens international peace. Examples of this include intervention in the former Yugoslavia in the 1990s. Given the failure to intervene timeously in Rwanda, it is possible that the Security Council will prove more willing to act in the future when evidence of gross violations of rights emerge, even if there is no inter-state element. In its early years, the Security Council spearheaded decolonisation, transforming the map of the world in barely 30 years. At the heart of decolonisation is a belief in SELF-DETERMINATION, one of the recognised fundamental rights. (Now with decolonisation almost complete, the scope of the right to self-determination is being explored in greater detail.)

The General Assembly comprises representatives of all member States of the United Nations. The Charter of the United Nations imbues it with responsibility in a number of areas including initiating studies and making

Judge Thomas Buergenthal
Professor Thomas Buergenthal was born in Slovakia though he spent his childhood in Poland and was a child survivor of Auschwitz and Sachsenhausen concentration camps during the Second World War. He proceeded to study law at New York University and Harvard Law Schools in the USA. Throughout his distinguished academic career he advocated the teaching of international human rights. He also accrued practical international human rights experience as the first US member of the UN Human Rights Committee and served 12 years as a judge of the Inter-American Court of Human Rights. In 2000, he was elected to the International Court of Justice for a nine-year term of office.

UN Human rights organisational Structure

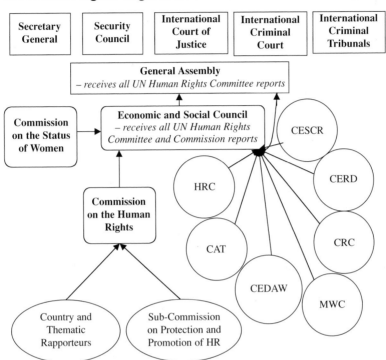

UN Human Rights Organisational Structure. © R.K.M. Smith

recommendations which promote the realisation of international human rights and fundamental freedoms. Probably the most significant success of the Assembly was the Proclamation of the **UNIVERSAL DECLARATION ON HUMAN RIGHTS** in 1948. In furtherance of the principles entrenched therein, the General Assembly has been instrumental in proclaiming a series of profile-raising international decades, not least that on human rights education. It has also instituted special investigations into areas of concern, for example reform of the UN Human Rights system. A number of resolutions on human rights issues have been adopted by the General Assembly. Although not legally binding, such resolutions have strong moral force, representing as they do the expressed will of the majority of the international community. Such mechanisms are sometimes termed 'soft law' by international lawyers.

The International Court of Justice is the principal Court of the UN system. However, it does not have competence to hear complaints from individuals. Its primary objective is as a venue for inter-state complaints. In a few occasions, this has overlapped with human rights issues – most notably in the proceedings brought by Croatia and Bosnia-Herzegovina against Yugoslavia concerning alleged violations of the Genocide Convention. The jurisdiction of the Court can be contrasted with the **INTERNATIONAL CRIMINAL COURT** which entered operation in July 2002. Individuals alleged to have been involved in war crimes could be brought to justice through this avenue. Obviously the crimes are serious infringement of human rights. Not all states have agreed to the terms proposed in the Statute of Rome.

As a figurehead of the United Nations, the Secretary General, at the time of writing currently Kofi Annan, can perform a valuable function raising the profile of human rights issues. Moreover, the current Secretary General has also been instrumental in introducing the current reform agenda for the United Nations and Human Rights.

In addition to these principal bodies, a number of other bodies were created under the auspices of the United Nations. The various councils and commissions with responsibility for human rights will be considered next. In each instance, the functions and powers of the body can be traced through to the UN Charter.

Turning to specific human rights bodies, the United Nations has one Council and two Commissions with particular responsibility for human rights. Thereafter, a number of lesser bodies are established with specific responsibility – most notably monitoring the compliance of contracting states with various human rights treaties. The Economic and Social Council has 54 individual members, elected by the General Assembly. It can initiate reports on a range of issues and make recommendations for, *inter alia*, the purpose of promoting respect for, and observance of, human rights and fundamental freedoms (Article 62, UN Charter). In general, the Council coordinates activities within its area of competence. For human rights, it thus receives reports from the Treaty monitoring bodies and from the Commissions. It also delegates areas for investigation to its Commissions and associated sub-bodies.

Two of the Council's Commissions impact on human rights: the Commission on the Status of Women and the Commission on Human Rights. Established in 1946, the Commission on the Status of Women has expanded from 15 to 45 members, imbued with responsibility preparing recommendations and reports to the Council on the pro-

motion of women's rights globally. The Commission on Human Rights, in contrast has a broader remit. Originally its goal was to draft the **UNIVERSAL DECLARATION OF HUMAN RIGHTS** (adopted 1948). Since then, its role has been redefined. Today, it has power not only to organise technical assistance for those states in need and appoint rapporteurs to investigate areas of concern, it also can action individual complaints. Should a pattern of systematic or gross violations of human rights emerge from studies, the Commission may investigate the matter further through a specific procedure (Resolution 1503(XLVIII) 1970). The investigation is carried out in private but the names of states involved are published: Vietnam and Zimbabwe are recent examples. Perhaps the greatest problem with the system is that the consent of the state concerned is required for a full investigation. However, as the United Nations is based on a principle of respect for the sovereignty of states, such a requirement is perhaps inevitable. Under the auspices of the Commission on Human Rights is the Sub-Commission on the Promotion and Protection of Human Rights, originally with a remit restricted to minority rights – a throwback to the system advocated by the League of Nations.

International human rights exists in its present form through a range of international treaties. Compliance with each of the principal UN treaties is monitored by a special committee. These committees only enjoy such powers and functions as are specified in the treaty concerned. In addition to these organs and bodies, a number of treaty-monitoring bodies have been established, essentially to oversee the implementation of specific treaties. For example, the **HUMAN RIGHTS COMMITTEE** was established to oversee the implementation of the International Covenant on Civil and Political Rights. All these committees, known as conventional mechanisms as they are established pursuant to specific instruments (the terms treaties and conventions can be used almost interchangeably), report to the Economic and Social Council and the General Assembly.

Finally, the 'public face' of international human rights in the UN is the High Commissioner for Human Rights. Just as the Secretary General is the figurehead of the

United Nations, the High Commissioner for Human Rights, an appointment at the level of Under-Secretary General, has primary responsibility for human rights activities. The Office of the UN HIGH COMMISSIONER FOR HUMAN RIGHTS was created to protect and promote human rights for all. Based in Geneva, the Office now coordinates and provides secretarial support for much of the UN's human rights activities. The fourth High Commissioner, Louise Arbour, assumed the post in summer 2004.

WEBSITES

www.ohchr.org – the Office of the High Commissioner of Human Rights

www.un.org – the United Nations

Further Reading

Murphy, S. and Buergenthal, T. (2002) *International Law in a Nutshell*, St. Paul, Minnesota: West Group/Thomson.

Shaw, M. (2003) *International Law*, 5th edn, Cambridge: Cambridge University Press.

United Nations fact sheets and information leaflets, available online.

Wallace, R. (2002) *International Law*, 4th edn, London:Sweet and Maxwell.

Contributor: Rhona K.M. Smith

THE UNIVERSAL DECLARATION OF HUMAN RIGHTS

The Universal Declaration of Human Rights may be the single most important human rights document in the world, although it was adopted over 50 years ago and is not a legally binding treaty. Initially adopted only as 'a common standard of achievement for all peoples and all nations', the Declaration today exerts a moral, political and legal influence far beyond the hopes of its drafters.

10 December, the anniversary of the adoption of the Universal Declaration on Human Rights, is now celebrated as Human Rights Day.

Formally, the Universal Declaration of Human Rights is only a resolution of the UN General Assembly, adopted on 10 December 1948, and it does not directly create binding legal obligations on states. Because it is not a treaty, it is not subject to 'ratification' by states (See: TREATY-BASED LAW). At the same time, it has contributed to the formation of the customary international law of human rights and the international legal system is replete with global and regional treaties based, in large measure, on the Declaration (See: CUSTOMARY INTERNATIONAL LAW). The Universal Declaration was the direct precursor to the two most comprehensive UN instruments in the field, THE COVENANT ON CIVIL AND POLITICAL RIGHTS AND THE COVENANT ON ECONOMIC, SOCIAL AND CULTURAL RIGHTS, each of which has been ratified by approximately 150 countries.

In addition, the Universal Declaration has served directly and indirectly as a model for many domestic constitutions, laws, regulations and policies that protect fundamental human rights. When governments, international organisations and non-governmental organisations appeal to countries to respect human rights, the Universal Declaration is often the touchstone for such appeals. The Declaration is a relatively short document, consisting of a Preamble and 30 articles. It created no institutions to oversee its implementation, but the Declaration and the UN Charter itself have given political legitimacy to the United Nations' actions in the field of human rights.

For those seeking to understand just what 'international human rights' are, the Universal Declaration offers the most authoritative summary. Its provisions have been supplemented by later texts that address the needs of particularly vulnerable groups (such as those protecting, for example, minorities, indigenous peoples, refugees, and people with disabilities), but the Universal Declaration sets forth almost all of the rights that are today widely recognised. The Universal Declaration includes the entire gamut of international human rights, which are often grouped into the categories of civil, political, ECONOMIC, SOCIAL and CULTURAL RIGHTS. One of the most basic rights is the right to equality and to be free from DISCRIMINATION (Articles 1, 2, 7) and the rights guaranteed in the Declaration are to be respected 'without distinction of any kind, such as race, colour, sex, language, religion, political or other opinion, national or social origin, property, birth or other status'. This does not prohibit reasonable and justifiable classifications based on some of these characteristics (e.g. a progressive tax system based on wealth or property), but the theme of **EQUALITY** runs throughout the document.

A number of so-called civil rights are proclaimed, all of which would be familiar to Anglo-American lawyers and most Europeans. These include the **RIGHT TO LIFE, LIBERTY** and security of person (Article 3); prohibitions against **SLAVERY, TORTURE** and other ill-treatment, and arbitrary arrest or detention (Articles 4, 5, 9); the right to a fair trial, including the presumption of innocence (Articles 10, 11); freedom from interference with privacy, family, home, or correspondence (Article 12); freedom of movement and the right to leave and return to one's country (Article 13); the right to seek asylum (Article 14); the right to a nationality (Article 15); **THE RIGHT TO MARRIAGE AND A FAMILY** (Article 16); the right to own **PROPERTY** (Article 17); and freedom of thought, conscience, **RELIGION**, opinion, **EXPRESSION**, assembly, and **ASSOCIATION** (Articles 18, 19, 20).

Article 21 sets forth political rights, including the right to take part in government and a requirement that government be based on the will of the people, as expressed in 'periodic and genuine elections ... by universal and equal suffrage'. It was understood by the drafters that these political rights could be limited to citizens or permanent residents of a country (although there is no requirement to do so); all other rights apply equally to everyone within a state's jurisdiction, whether citizen, resident, alien or visitor.

The next several articles deal with economic and social rights, which include the right to social security (Article 22); the right to work and free choice of employment, including 'just and favourable remuneration,' equal pay for equal work, and the right to form and join trade unions (Article 23); the right to rest and leisure, including limited working hours and periodic paid holidays (Article 24); the right to an adequate standard of living, including **FOOD**, clothing, housing, and medical care (Article 25); and the right to **EDUCATION** (Article 26).

The final substantive article, Article 27, proclaims the right of everyone to participate in the cultural life of the community and to have his or her interests resulting from any scientific, literary or artistic production protected.

Even this brief summary raises many questions of interpretation and scope, but the Universal Declaration is not a constitution or statute. It was designed to set out in fairly broad language 'a common understanding' of what human rights mean, not to codify them in detail. In addition, it is clear that most of the rights in the Declaration are not absolute and may be balanced against other legitimate interests of society. Article 29 of the Declaration recognises that everyone has (unspecified) duties to the community and that human rights may be limited in order to secure 'due recognition and respect for the rights and freedoms of others and of meeting the just requirements of morality, public order and the general welfare in a democratic society'. However, such limitations must be solely for one of these purposes and must be determined by law, not by administrative whim or autocratic fiat. The burden is on the government to demonstrate that any limitation does not unduly restrict the rights set forth in the Declaration.

The rights articulated in the Universal Declaration also reflect the different perspectives of the major political blocs of the time: the West was generally supportive of the civil and political rights set forth in Articles 1–21, while the Communist bloc and most developing countries emphasised the economic, social, and cultural rights in Articles 22–27. Of course, even these distinctions quickly became meaningless, if they were not already overdrawn in 1948. For example, even the most conservative capitalist believes in education and trade union rights, and no government today would openly reject providing some degree of social security protection to its citizens. Similarly, whatever the problems in practice, neither communist nor developing countries argued in favour of torture, slavery or unfair trials. It might be noted that, while no country voted against adoption of the Declaration in 1948, several communist bloc countries and Saudi Arabia did abstain from voting. Today, however, no state explicitly rejects the Declaration.

Human rights in general and the Universal Declaration of Human Rights, in particular, are sometimes criticised as being culturally biased, overly individualistic or simply too 'Western,' whatever that means. There can be no doubt that the inspiration for the Declaration may be found in 18th-century principles of individual freedom and 20th-century principles of liberal **DEMOCRACY**, and perhaps the most significant contributors to drafting the Declaration were Nobel Peace Prize laureate René Cassin (France), John Humphrey (Canada) and Eleanor Roosevelt (United States). However, the extremely wide acceptance of the Universal Declaration in subsequent decades by governments, non-governmental organisations and individuals throughout the world reinforces the notion that, whatever its beginnings, the Declaration had become truly universal by the dawn of the 21st century.

The Universal Declaration, like other human rights instruments, is not intended to remake societies into a mode that conforms precisely to 'liberal' or even 'democratic' societies in Europe or the Western hemisphere. It proclaims a set of individual rights and government obligations that are appropriate for modern states, but it does not require abandoning all of the moral, ethical, religious or philosophical norms that guide most people's lives. Human rights norms do not mandate a particular social order or how a country balances competing priorities or the particular degree of economic equality that a society deems appropriate.

Both the **UNIVERSALITY** and the flexibility of the Declaration's norms are evident in the concluding statement adopted by consensus at the UN's World Conference on Human Rights, which was held in Vienna in 1993. The conference, in which over 170 countries participated, proclaimed that '[a]ll human rights are universal, **INDIVISIBLE** and interdependent and interrelated. The international community must treat human rights globally in a fair and equal manner, on the same footing, and with the same emphasis. While the significance of national and regional particularities and various historical, cultural and religious backgrounds must be borne in mind, it is the duty of states, regardless of their political, economic and cultural systems, to promote and protect all human rights and fundamental freedoms.'

Further Reading

Glendon, Mary Ann (2002) *A World Made New: Eleanor Roosevelt and the Universal Declaration of Human Rights*, New York: Random House.

Hannum, Hurst (1995/96) 'The Status of the Universal Declaration of Human Rights in National and International Law', in *Georgia Journal of International and Comparative Law*, vol. 25, pp. 287–397.

Humphrey, John P. (1984) *Human Rights and the United Nations: A Great Adventure*, New York: Transnational Publishers.

Morsink, Johannes (1999) *The Universal Declaration of Human Rights: Origins, Drafting, and Intent*, Philadelphia: University of Pennsylvania Press.

Contributor: Hurst Hannum

UNIVERSALISM

Human rights universalism can be understood in at least three ways. First, it can refer to claims about the universal validity of or moral justification for human rights. Second, it can describe the status of human rights in international law. Finally, it can refer to the generality of human rights. These three forms of human rights universalism are interrelated in complex and sometimes contradictory ways.

Most theoretical discussion of human rights focuses on the deeply contentious debate over their validity. The debate primarily concerns what moral significance should attach to the origins of 'universal' human rights in the philosophy of Christian Europe and the Enlightenment. This debate pits universalists, who hold that human rights reflect timeless and absolute moral truths, against cultural relativists, who assert that moral truth or validity is an expression of the values and beliefs of a particular culture. Universalists maintain that some moral principles are valid regardless of when and where they originate. These principles have the status of metaphysical truth; human rights are universally valid because they derive from such principles. Among the claims and principles to which this transcendent status is sometimes ascribed are autonomy (See: **AUTONOMY AND HUMAN RIGHTS**), dignity, equality (See: **EQUALITY AND HUMAN RIGHTS**), human **CAPABILITIES**, human **NEEDS**, natural law and self-ownership (See: **LIBERTARIANISM AND HUMAN RIGHTS**). The primary difficulty with moral universalism lies in showing that some moral principle is in fact true. Despite numerous sophisticated attempts to provide a persuasive transcultural moral justification for human rights, profound disagreement persists about their philosophical foundations.

To relativists this intractability is unsurprising. On their view, cultures differ so widely in their moral norms and practices that no principles can be valid across all of them. Relativists do not typically reject the existence of moral truth; rather, they hold that truth or validity can be assessed only within the moral framework of a particular culture. Unlike universalists, then, relativists conceive the validity of a moral principle as closely related to its origins; that human rights originated in the West means that they must reflect distinctively Western values and beliefs. Whether human rights are valid in non-Western cultures is for relativists a question of whether the values and practices of those cultures include or can support human rights and in what form. The main difficulties with cultural relativism are that it presumes a high degree of homogeneity within cultures, a presumption belied by internal disagreement and contestation, and that it remains unclear why widespread acceptance of norms and practices alone should count as a moral justification for them.

This debate has reached a stalemate, with two unfortunate consequences. First, questions about human rights universalism are frequently treated as questions of moral validity, with other aspects of universalism suffering comparative neglect. Second, questions of moral validity have been reduced to questions of cultural and philosophical origins, with other possible sources of validity receiving little theoretical attention.

The legal universalism of human rights signifies their status as principles of international law, a topic covered extensively in this volume. Three aspects of legal universalism demand our attention here.

Positive international law is the body of law generated by agreements among states: treaties, conventions, etc. Positive laws bind the signatories of particular instruments; positive law is universal insofar as the instruments in question are acceded to by virtually all states. Human rights conventions are a form of positive law, some of which enjoy near-universal status by virtue of their ratification by most states (See: **TREATY-BASED LAW**). The legal concept of customary law traces to the Roman idea of *ius gentium*, the laws of the peoples with whom the Romans had contact. In the international context, this concept evolved to denote laws that were customary among nations; domestically, customary law retains its original connotation of traditional law – a guise in which frequent conflicts with human rights arise. Today, there are numerous recognised (and sometimes contested) sources of customary law, including the practice of states, national statutes, national and international judicial decisions, and the writings of respected and qualified persons. The **UNIVERSAL DECLARATION OF HUMAN RIGHTS,** which was approved by the United Nations General Assembly in a resolution and therefore lacks the status of positive international law, is increasingly recognised as an important source of customary law (See: **CUSTOMARY INTERNATIONAL LAW**).

A term difficult to translate, *ius cogens* refers to norms or principles of international law that cannot be abridged or set aside for any reason – such as the prohibitions on slavery and genocide. *Ius cogens* evolved in close connection with natural law (*ius naturale*), though the contemporary doctrine eschews this claim to divine or natural status, replacing it with a notion of 'general acceptability' in world opinion. On this basis some jurists and scholars argue that all basic human rights should be considered inviolable principles and included within *ius cogens*, though this position is controversial.

The evolving legal universalism of human rights is hampered by the constraints of the international system in matters of jurisdiction and enforcement. Despite growing acceptance of human rights as obligations binding upon all, whether and how third parties can enforce human rights law remains a contentious question, perhaps best exemplified by vociferous American objections to the nascent **INTERNATIONAL CRIMINAL COURT** and by the confusion attending the arrest of Augusto Pinochet in Britain on a Spanish warrant for crimes committed as dictator of Chile. Some states continue to resent discussion of their internal human rights records as an abrogation of their sovereignty – though few openly reject the legitimacy of human rights as legal and political concerns of citizens. Ironically, the recognition and acceptance of human rights has perhaps made them more salient and controversial in international politics, with often empty cold war rhetoric giving way to concrete questions concerning enforcement, intervention, and conditionality of political and economic assistance upon human rights performance.

Legal and moral universalism are analytically distinct but difficult to keep separate. It is generally recognised that legitimate positive law gives rise to moral duties and obligations, so the post-war explosion of positive human rights law would seem to provide the empirical foundation for a legally-based moral universalism. Moreover, the common norms and practices or 'generally accepted' principles underpinning arguments for customary law and *ius cogens* blur the line between empirical and normative claims, threatening to collapse the distinction between moral and legal universalism in these domains as well. To relativists and political realists, however, the evolving legal consensus is a product of ongoing Western hegemony, a form of moral imperialism signifying little about the free acceptance or moral acceptability of human rights.

An empirical claim concerns how things are; it is a claim about truth or falsity based on facts or states of affairs. For example, the claim that 'incidents of torture have increased under the rule of General X' is an empirical claim that can be verified or disproved by looking at the relevant data.

A normative claim concerns how things ought to be; it is a claim about what is right or wrong. For example, the claim that 'torture should not be permitted' is a normative claim expressing the view that torture is wrong.

A third form of human rights universalism refers to their generality. Generality is a formal characteristic of human rights; they are general or 'universal' in that they apply and are available to all. Everyone enjoys or can claim the same human rights; in this sense they embody a political ideal of equal freedom and dignity for all. The language of human rights is at the centre of modern discourses of freedom; rights are deeply tied up with the theory of and struggle for democracy in the modern era. Their generality explains their efficacy and political appeal: that everyone possesses the same (claim to) human rights demolishes arguments justifying political exclusion or subordination based on sex, race, class, gender, religion, ethnicity, nationality, political ideology or other status. Human rights have a levelling effect. Victims of tyranny and oppression have successfully invoked them in attacking patriarchy and aristocracy, combating colonialism and imperialism, resisting authoritarian rule and demanding recognition and inclusion in civil and political life.

The generality of human rights makes them attractive to groups and individuals struggling for emancipation. They provide a widely recognised source of moral and political arguments where local legal, political or cultural norms either support oppressive regimes or have been stifled by them – an established grounds for appeal outside any particular context. In short, human rights provide an ideological framework for emancipatory politics.

Appeals to human rights are often strenuously resisted by elites seeking to protect their status and privilege. Outright repression is commonplace. Additionally, elites frequently resort to relativist arguments against universality in portraying their opponents as enemies of the state or of the local culture or as dupes of foreign powers. These arguments often resonate because of the West's infamous historical misuse of 'universal' values in justifying racist colonial and imperial policies. Such attacks, along with the history that lends them credence, demonstrate the perils of conceiving human rights universalism solely in terms of their moral validity.

Human rights universalism does not require the discovery of incontrovertible philosophical foundations for rights. The legal universalism and widespread appeal and acceptance of human rights around the world indicate on what basis an alternative form of universalism might be established. The only way to achieve this universalism consistent with the demands of human rights is to build a cross-cultural political consensus through open, inclusive and respectful dialogue aimed at genuine understanding and motivated by a commitment to the equal freedom and dignity of all.

Further Reading

Baehr, Peter R. (1999) *Human Rights: Universality in Practice*, New York: St Martin's Press.

Donnelly, Jack (2003) *Universal Human Rights in Theory and Practice*, 2nd edn, Ithaca, NY: Cornell University Press.

Goodhart, Michael (2003) 'Origins and Universality in the Human Rights Debates: Cultural Essentialism and the Challenge of Globalization.' in *Human Rights Quarterly* 25 (4), pp. 935–64.

Perry, Michael J. (1997) 'Are Human Rights Universal? The Relativist Challenge and Related Matters.' in *Human Rights Quarterly* 19 (3), pp. 461–503.

Pollis, Adamantia (2000) 'A New Universalism' in *Human Rights: New Perspectives New Realities*, Pollis, Adamantia and Schwab, Peter (eds) Boulder, CO: Lynne Rienner.

Contributor: Michael Goodhart

UTILITARIANISM AND HUMAN RIGHTS

Utilitarianism comes in many forms and varieties. In its simplest form, utilitarianism states that those acts are right which produce the most utility. This principle's most famous form was expressed by Francis Hutcheson – 'That action is best which secures the greatest happiness of the greatest number' – and after him by Jeremy Bentham – 'It is the greatest happiness of the greatest number that is the measure of right and wrong.' Contemporary utilitarians tend to avoid the famous 'greatest happiness' slogan, for a variety of reasons. A typical formulation of simple act utilitarianism today would be 'the right action is the one that produces the most welfare'. The idea is that the only thing that matters to morality is consequences – specifically the consequences for welfare. The right action is the one that yields the most welfare, out of all the options open to the agent.

The potential incompatibility between utilitarianism and moral theories that regard human rights as 'trumps' is immediately apparent. For if ever a situation could come about in which the violation of a human right was the action that would produce the most welfare, utilitarianism demands that the right be violated. Examples of such situations abound both in imagined cases and in real life. Here is one real-life case. In what has become known as the 'Tuskegee syphilis experiment', four black men with syphilis had treatment withheld from them in order to study the progress of the disease. The men agreed to be examined and treated, but were not told what they were suffering from or informed of available treatments. This happened in Alabama, and lasted for 40 years, from 1932 until 1972. The relevant point here is that such a study would be justified, from a utilitarian point of view, if the knowledge gained from it produced an increase in general welfare that exceeded the decreased welfare of the men and their families (provided that the knowledge could not have been obtained in some other way). Indeed, when the study was made public by a whistle blower, the advisory panel set up to investigate it found that it was ethically unjustified because it yielded too little valuable information to outweigh the risk caused to the subjects (Tuskegee Syphilis Study Ad Hoc Advisory Panel (1973) Final Report, pp. 7–8). By implication, such risks might permissibly be imposed upon ignorant subjects, were the results sufficiently rewarding. That would be the utilitarian view.

Utilitarians, it seems, cannot believe in human rights. Certainly some utilitarians have accepted this conclusion. Most famously, Bentham dismisses the notion of natural human rights (as opposed to legal rights, with which he was quite happy), insisting that 'there are no such things as natural rights' and that the very phrase 'natural rights' is 'simple nonsense', even 'mischievous nonsense' and 'nonsense on stilts' (Bentham, 1843, pp. 501–2). Others have been less hostile. John Stuart Mill was perfectly prepared to speak of moral as opposed to legal rights. Indeed, he is at least as well known today for his 'harm principle' as he is for his utilitarianism. Mill says: 'The sole end for which mankind are warranted, individually or collectively, in interfering with the liberty of action of any of their number, is self-protection.' (Warnock, 1962, p. 135). In other words, harm to others is the only thing that justifies interference in someone's life. Mill appears to be claiming that individuals have a right to liberty, defeasible only by the need to prevent harm to other people. Harm to themselves, mere offence to others or being contrary to the popular will are not good enough reasons to prevent anyone from doing whatever they want to do. But Mill is a utilitarian. He believes that actions are good insofar as they tend to produce happiness for as many people as possible. The principle of utility is his fundamental position. One serious question for Mill is whether he can make the two principles consistent, since it seems that restrictions of people's liberty and interference with their lives might well be more productive of general happiness than allowing everyone to do whatever they liked that didn't harm others. Plato, after all, justifies the various offences against human rights in the Republic by saying that it is for the good of all the people that they are done. It's often been thought that a consistent utilitarian would have to take the same sort of view and hence that Mill's views on liberty are incompatible with his fundamental utilitarianism.

One reason for thinking this is that Mill's views on liberty are in opposition to any paternalism on the part of the rulers as well as opposed to any abuses of the citizenry. That is to say, Mill is opposed to any legal requirement that you do something or not do something for your own good. Although Mill is opposed to paternalism, he will be willing to countenance such laws and actions if they are going to prevent someone from doing something they don't know will hurt them. He says that it is permissible to stop someone forcibly from crossing a dangerous bridge if they don't know that it is dangerous. The reason for this, he says, is that you are not really stopping them from doing something which they wish to do: they wish to get to the other side, not plunge to their death. But if someone is knowingly doing something dangerous, the fact of its being dangerous is not good enough reason to prevent them. So legislation requiring the wearing of crash-helmets or banning the use of harmful substances would be illegitimate in his view, unless it could be shown that these measures were necessary for the safety of others as well. But it seems likely that happiness will be increased by some acts of paternalism. Just because people don't want to wear seatbelts doesn't mean that laws requiring them to won't increase happiness. If we subtract the negative results of such a law – inconvenience at worst – from the benefits – the saving of many lives – then it is clear that there will be a net gain in the amount of happiness that there is in the society.

If we are to understand how Mill can try to make his liberalism consistent with his moral theory, we need to know more about his brand of utilitarianism. On a plausible interpretation of Mill, he argues in utilitarianism for what has been called two-level utilitarianism. Utilitarianism faces a problem: that it is not productive of utility for everyone always to consider the likely benefits and costs of each and every act they perform. Utilitarianism therefore dictates that people not reason about what to do in an explicitly utilitarian way, at the everyday level. Rather, they would do better to follow certain secondary principles, enshrined in common morality, such as 'don't tell lies', 'don't steal', 'don't hurt others', and so on. These rules will occasionally prescribe actions which are not, in that particular case, most productive of utility, but the advantages of always following them outweighs these occasional instances. Mill can therefore be consistent in upholding the principle of liberty if he sees it as one of these secondary principles, the following of which will maximise happiness.

This suggests a strategy that can be employed to reconcile utilitarianism and human rights. Put simply, the strategy is to argue that more welfare will be produced if we all believe in human rights than if we do not. Thus, although welfare is the only thing that really matters in morality, we should accept the existence of human rights and act in ways indistinguishable from others who believe in human rights, precisely because our doing so will increase the amount of welfare in the world. This may be unsatisfactory to some people: it does not so much establish the existence of human rights as give us reason to act as though there are human rights. On the other hand, from the practical point of view, there is no difference. In addition, this approach would have the merits of providing a metaphysically economical grounding for human rights and a method for working out what they are.

Questions remain, including, most notably, whether the two-level strategy works at all. Several opponents have argued that it is inherently unstable, requiring us to think in a 'schizophrenic' fashion. Even if the strategy works, further argument is needed to justify the claim that respecting rights is more productive of utility than any alternative way of deciding what we ought to do.

Further Reading

Bentham, J. (1843) *The Works of Jeremy Bentham*, Edinburgh: William Tait.

Crisp, R. (1997) *Mill on Utilitarianism*, London: Routledge.

Jones, J.H. (1993) *Bad Blood: The Tuskegee Syphilis Experiment*, New York: Free Press.

Scarre, G. (1996) *Utilitarianism*, London: Routledge.

Warnock, M. (ed.) (1962) *Utilitarianism, On Liberty (and other essays by Mill, Bentham and John Austin)*, Glasgow: Collins.

Contributor: Iain Law

VIOLENCE AGAINST WOMEN – DOMESTIC VIOLENCE

According to the United Nations Declaration on the Elimination of Violence Against Women, 'violence against women means any act of gender-based violence that results in, or is likely to result in, physical, sexual or psychological harm or suffering to women, including threats of such acts, coercion or arbitrary deprivation of liberty, whether occurring in public or in private life'. Because violence against women has throughout history and throughout the world prevented women from enjoying the benefits of their other human rights and has been recognised as an obstacle to peace by the Security Council, it is today a priority on the agenda of the international community and organisations. Many campaigns have been dedicated to putting an end to this phenomenon; however, violence has not decreased and new forms keep appearing.

Violence suffered by women is multifaceted. It ranges from physical to psychological and economic forms to cover cases of trafficking (See: **FREEDOM FROM SLAVERY; THE MIGRANT WORKERS' CONVENTION**), forced sterilisation, sexual harassment and many more. Specific as well as general human rights instruments have been adopted to combat it, among them the United Nations **CONVENTION ON THE ELIMINATION OF DISCRIMINATION AGAINST WOMEN**. This convention does not specifically address violence against women but provisions against it can be drawn from its equality approach. Its Committee later adopted General Recommendation 19 on the issue. Two of the main specific mechanisms available today to combat violence against women are the Declaration on the Elimination of Violence Against Women, adopted by a General Assembly resolution following an ECOSOC recommendation, and the creation of a Special Rapporteur on violence against women, its causes and consequences. These initiatives resulted from the realisation, at the 1993 Vienna Conference on human rights, that there was a real void in international human rights law addressing this issue. These initiatives were most welcomed symbolically, in that they sent a clear message that violence against women would not be accepted any more. They also empowered women in undertaking action against it and facilitated the creation of other national specific mechanisms to address it. However, the main obstacle to sending a clear message to states on this issue consists of the fact that the Declaration on the Elimination of Violence Against Women is not a convention and is consequently not 'binding' on states; states are advised to take measures but not required to do so.

On the one hand, the feeling is of a missed opportunity, considering that many women, including the first Special Rapporteur on violence against women Radhika Coomaraswamy, were in favour of the adoption of a much stronger instrument under the form of an additional protocol to CEDAW specifically dedicated to the issue. On the other hand, the creation of the Special Rapporteur represents a real step forward symbolically and practically. The Special Rapporteur can indeed operate in a country regardless of that country having ratified a specific instrument. Neither does it require the exhaustion of all national remedies in order to be able to interfere, as is the case for international instruments. Lastly, building on the Declaration on the Elimination of Violence Against Women, the Beijing Platform for action provides for three strategic objectives dedicated to preventing and eliminating violence against women.

Limits to these instruments do exist and are quite often invoked. They are linked to the causes behind violence, causes that are rooted inter alia in the patriarchal nature of society, the historically disadvantaged position of women as well as the traditional perceptions of women's identities and roles in society and within the family. International instruments might appear to offer only a partial solution to the issue by not allowing for clearing all the legal, administrative, cultural and economical obstacles linked to fighting violence against women. Yet it is a necessary step that has resulted in empowering women, and women's organisations particularly, and in changing government approaches to the issue. The recognition of rape in a conflict situation as a crime of war is one of the proofs of this evolution.

Violence taking place within the family sphere, or domestic violence, is revealed to be of the most difficult and complex kind to combat. There are several reasons for this, including the cultural acceptance of the right of husbands to beat their wives, the legal doctrine of non-interference into private life, the private/public divide and the sacrosanct nature of the family. Studies have shown that women and girls are the predominant victims of this type of violence.

Legally, many arguments have been used to oppose the recognition of domestic violence as a human rights issue. The primary obstacle to such recognition lay in the traditional understanding of human rights law as covering only violations committed against individuals in the public sphere of life; the state was not to intervene in the private affairs of individuals, or so to say, in the private sphere of life, to which women were predominantly confined. Consequently, many violations committed against women have remained unpunished, unrecognised and sometimes tolerated. Failure to address violations that go beyond the classical realm of public life can be explained by the fact that only actions perpetrated by the state, or state-like actors, were condemnable under international human rights law. Feminist critiques have contributed to overcoming this limitation so as to allow for the recognition of state's failure to intervene with regard to actions committed by private actors, as a human rights violation (See: **FEMINIST CRITIQUES OF HUMAN RIGHTS**). The doctrine of responsibility par ricochet means that the state's systematic failure to intervene can be understood as acquiescence to such practices and can therefore be

Family Protection Project Management Team – Jordan

The project is a groundbreaking initiative in Jordanian society that has helped to lift the taboo on the subject of domestic violence, and promote open debate on issues of human rights, equity and gender. A team of seven men and five women, representing both governmental and non-governmental organisations, has been responsible for the development and implementation of the project, which takes a truly holistic, preventative and inclusive approach to tackling the root causes of domestic violence. The team has also developed a social justice partnership model to address domestic violence in other Arab and Islamic countries, and may provide a useful learning experience for other countries around the world. The team was awarded the 2003 United Nations Prize in the Field of Human Rights.

(From www.un.org/events/humanrights/awards.html)

sanctioned; this is because in the case of violence against women, 'the risk factor is being female', that is, a prohibited ground of discrimination. By suffering from domestic violence, women, as a group, also suffer violations of their most basic human rights such as life or dignity. Hence, the state's responsibility has been extended to non-state actors by recognising that states' failure to intervene to stop systematic human rights violations targeted at a specific group was to be considered a human rights violation. States can now be sanctioned for failing to act as well as failing to exercise due diligence when domestic violence takes place on their territory.

The complexity associated with combating domestic violence is also linked to the fact that the family is traditionally perceived as the central societal structure that is to be promoted and protected from external attacks. It is seen as an area of cooperation, care and peace, where men as well as women can have high aspirations. However, the private sphere of the home is also too often the arena of women's disempowerment and exploitation as well as the area of patriarchal and stereotypical practices. Societal, biological and economic inequalities are revealed more substantial in the home where it has up to now not been subject to scrutiny and was not expected to be challenged. Bringing domestic violence from 'the home to the transnational' is one of the tasks that the Special Rapporteur has endorsed and that is inevitable in making domestic violence a matter of concern for society as a whole.

Notwithstanding these evolutions, domestic violence is still perceived as less condemnable than other forms of abuse. Ways forward have been suggested to ensure more efficient responses to these violations. Human rights scholars and organisations have suggested that the recognition of domestic violence as a form of torture will ensure better visibility as well as a higher degree of moral and practical condemnation. The constitutive elements of torture, as defined by the United Nations Convention Against Torture, have been said to be applicable to the specific case of domestic violence. Such a qualification would enable the understanding that domestic violence is not a crime of lesser gravity than any form of violence inflicted by the state.

The recognition of domestic violence as a human rights issue will also have to be accompanied by complementary measures, essential to ensure the efficient treatment of cases. It will be necessary to integrate the way global factors like poverty contribute to increasing violence against women. Providing women with housing opportunities facilitated by better economic independence is a necessary condition to allow them to choose with whom they live and to enable them to leave their family home in cases of abuse. The creation of shelters for battered women is indispensable, too. There is also work to be done with law and police officials so as to ensure that they offer the appropriate assistance to women and reject any cultural exception sometimes applied to abuses. Women need to be able to rely on them from the moment a case of violation is uncovered or reported. If the role of police officials is of the utmost crucial nature, in their position of often first contact, it is also crucial to make all actors involved in fighting domestic violence understand the unacceptable nature of such violations. Domestic violence is to be treated and perceived as seriously as any other kind of violence inflicted outside the home or by public actors.

Further Reading

Amnesty International (2004) *It's in Our Hand, Stop Violence Against Women*, AI Index: ACT 77/001.

Cook, R.J. (ed.) (1994) *Human Rights, Women, National and International Perspectives*, Pennsylvania: University of Pennsylvania Press.

Subedi, S.P. (1997) 'Protection of Women Against Domestic Violence: The Response of International Law' in *European Human Rights Law Review*, issue 6, vol. 2, pp. 587–606.

Thomas, D.Q. and Beasley, M. E. (1993) 'Domestic Violence as a Human Rights Issue' in 15, *Human Rights Quarterly*, pp. 37–62.

Contributor: Audrey Guichon

VIOLENCE AGAINST WOMEN IN WAR TIME

Although wartime sexual violence affects both men and women, women are by far the more likely target and also face additional risks such as pregnancy. Often widespread and planned, sexual violence may be part of a genocidal strategy and includes rape, sexual mutilation, forced prostitution and forced pregnancy. Horrifically, women have been used in wars as a means of keeping troops happy and weakening the enemy by inflicting terror, destroying community values and pride. For many centuries, women were viewed as victors' spoils in armed conflict. In ancient Greece, as in many other societies, the victor in war gained the 'right to rape'; in the First World War the German army used sexual violence as a means of domination; and the extent of the mass rapes and sexual enslavements by Japanese soldiers in the Second World War is only now being acknowledged. But Allied forces were also accused of such crimes; in general it is the war crimes of the losing forces which are investigated after a war. Brothels were (and still are) maintained near military camps in the belief that this would improve morale and with varying levels of free choice for the women who worked there.

War glorifies violence of various kinds, but sexual violence in wartime has been a highly effective method of dehumanisation, domination and humiliation. It was only with the discovery of the scale of sexual atrocities committed during the war in the former Yugoslavia, and then in Rwanda, that the issue of wartime sex crime truly became a priority concern for the international community. That in Europe in the late 20th century detention centres had been set up for the explicit purpose of raping and violating women led to understandable outrage. International law and institutions struggled to provide justice for rape victims and to prevent impunity for their attackers. (See: **HUMANITARIAN LAW AND HUMAN RIGHTS IN CONFLICT** and **HUMAN RIGHTS BETWEEN WAR AND PEACE**.) Although sexual violence was committed on a huge scale in both Yugoslavia and Rwanda, charges have been brought against only a small proportion of suspects.

Rape in war has been a crime in customary law for centuries, but neither the Nuremberg nor Tokyo tribunals made any mention of sexual violence in their Charters (See: **INTERNATIONAL CRIMINAL LAW AND THE REGIONAL TRIBUNALS**). Not one charge of rape was brought at Nuremberg,

despite references to it in the evidence presented. Although some of the Tokyo tribunal trials did involve rape charges, not one victim was called as a witness. Sex crimes were often hidden behind generic charges, downplaying their gravity. The availability of evidence in such cases has always been a problem. Further, labels have often been applied to wartime sexual violence to 'de-crime' it. 'Comfort women' were called prostitutes, not the victims of sexual slavery that they were. The camps in which they were forcibly held were referred to as 'brothels', not rape camps. It was only after the full horror of the situation in the former Yugoslavia began to emerge that re-labelling of wartime rape occurred. It was finally perceived as the part of ethnic cleansing that it truly was, rather than an unfortunate, unavoidable and private matter.

The present international law on sexual violence is a mixture of conventions and case law. The Geneva Conventions of 1949 contain provisions which apply specifically to women and/or children. Some deal expressly with sexual violence, while others look to women in their capacity as mothers or 'special needs' prisoners. Even when the Conventions are explicitly addressing sexual violence as a crime, they do not seem to give it the priority it deserves. Sexual violence is not listed among the 'grave breaches' of the Conventions and Additional Protocol I and so, prima facie, it is not among the crimes for which states have a duty to seek out and try or extradite suspects. Most experts now agree that sexual violence is a grave breach of the Conventions by implication within explicit categories such as 'torture or inhuman treatment' or 'willfully causing great suffering or injury to body or health'. However, the need to do this by implication is telling; the international community was slow indeed to recognise and address the seriousness of wartime sexual violence, and to apply a label that reflects its significance for victims.

Perhaps even more telling is the language used in the conventions and protocols. Rape and sexual violence are 'attacks against the honour of women' or 'outrages upon human dignity'. The belief that a raped woman is dishonoured or loses her dignity should have no place in international humanitarian or criminal law. All crimes of sexual violence are crimes of violence, attacks upon the body;

violations of basic human rights, of personal self-determination and much else besides. Viewing them as attacks upon honour both trivialises crimes and depicts women as passive and in need of protection rather than concentrating on the attacker as being in need of punishment.

Rape is included as a crime against humanity in Article 5 of the International Criminal Tribunal for former Yugoslavia (ICTY) Statute and Article 3 of the International Criminal Tribunal for Rwanda (ICTR) Statute. The latter goes further, with Article 4 stating that there is jurisdiction over '…(e) Outrages upon personal dignity, in particular humiliating and degrading treatment, rape, enforced prostitution and any form of indecent assault…'

Thus, although there has been expansion in the scope of sexual violence in the statutory measures, there remains an unwelcome link between sexual violence and honour or dignity. Further, until the International Criminal Court Statute it has been through cases of the two tribunals that the real progress in the potential punishment of sexual violence in international criminal law has occurred, with each court interpreting the other offences under its Statute to include sexual violence by implication. One strength of ICTY, ICTR and now the ICC has been the extent to which their rules of procedure and evidence in the context of sexual violence cases far outstrip those of most domestic legal systems, including victim anonymity, limitations on consent defences and victims and witnesses units. Many of the factors that result in the extraordinarily high acquittal rate in national courts are deemed to be simply irrelevant or inadmissible, such as spurious consent defences and cross-examination of the victim as to her previous sexual experiences. When the factual situation is as extreme as that of war or internal armed conflict, behaviour of any party before the conflict is hardly relevant. In Rwanda, previously civil and even happy neighbours tortured and murdered each other. When the victims have undergone such great torment and pain, to allow further attacks on their dignity within the courtroom would be very difficult to justify.

After a long wait for the first conviction of rape in an international criminal tribunal, recognition of the importance of including sex-crime charges on indictments alongside more 'tried and tested' charges came first from judges, particularly female ones. ICTY judges have urged the prosecutor to think again and amend the charge list, having heard clear testimony from witnesses about rape camps (cf. Dragan Nikolic's decision, 20/11/1995). Guidelines on witness protection were developed by the Trial Chamber in Tadic (1996), the first international tribunal to hear direct evidence of rape. Key decisions of each tribunal have classified sexual violence as a substantive war crime with a clear and progressive definition of rape since adopted by the ICC Statute (Furundzija, ICTY, 1998); torture even when committed outside interrogation (Delalic, ICTY, 1998); genocide, again giving a progressive and welcomed definition to rape (Akayesu, ICTR, 1998); a violation of the victim's right to sexual autonomy and a crime against humanity, recognising sexual enslavement as such a crime (Kunarac, ICTY, 2001). The latter case notably involved charges only of sexual offences, without any precedent in an international tribunal. Therefore, ICTY and ICTR have been responsible for the most significant developments in criminalisation of sexual violence in international law. Sexual violence has been charged as violations of the laws or customs of war, genocide, crimes against humanity, grave breaches of the 1949 Geneva Conventions, and violations of common Article 3 of the 1949 Geneva Conventions and the 1977 Additional Protocols. Key and often revolutionary decisions of both tribunals provided blueprints for the new ICC rules on helping victims of crime – see Furundzija, Celebici – and contributed greatly towards the definitions of the ICC crimes encompassing or constituting sexual violence.

The ICC Statute in effect codifies both the significant ICTY and ICTR cases and many of women's international human rights. Although the Akayesu definition of rape came under attack in Prep Comms, it survived in a slightly narrower form (see Elements of Crimes). The ICC Prosecutor is under a duty to investigate crimes of sexual and gender violence (Article 54[1][b]). Article 8 specifically includes as war crimes in both internal and international armed conflict: … 'rape, sexual slavery, enforced prostitution, forced pregnancy … enforced sterilisation or any other form of sexual violence also constituting' either a grave breach or a violation of Common Article 3 of the Geneva Conventions. The same list qualifies as a crime against humanity (Article 7). The ICC Statute further builds upon the Rules of Procedure and Evidence developed by ICTY and ICTR judges; see Rule 70, Principles of Evidence in Cases of Sexual Violence, which contains a limitation of consent defences. Rules 85–98 also provide detailed measures for the protection of victims and witnesses going far beyond those guaranteed by the two prior Tribunals.

The ICC Statute fills in the gaps in international criminal law with regard to sexual violence other than rape and underlines their serious nature. Listing crimes of sexual violence as a separate category does not merely have symbolic importance; it also recognises that victims of such crimes suffer a special type of additional or aggravated harm. The Court could be an accountability mechanism for wartime sexual violence and advance gender equality more generally. The preparation of the ICC Statute provided a real opportunity for re-evaluation of the definitions of the crimes within the Court's jurisdiction, arguably with recognition that sexual or gender-based violence is just as serious as violence motivated by ethnic origin, race or religion. Having learned from the experiences of ICTY and ICTR, the Rome Statute's procedural provisions should also improve the experience of victims and other vulnerable witnesses.

But there is no room for complacency. The UN can do little on the ground when faced with armed fighting forces who show contempt for the rules and customs of international law and of war itself. However, it can do something about the under-reporting of wartime sexual violence, the identification of existing victims and the relocation of those in danger zones – and the resources and support made available when the International Criminal Court handles its first cases of sexual violence will be telling.

Further Reading

Chinkin (1994) 'Rape and Sexual Abuse of Women in International Law', 5 *EJIL* 326.

De Than, C. and Shorts (2003) *International Criminal Law and Human Rights*, Sweet & Maxwell, chapter 11.

Nowrojee (1996) 'Shattered Lives: Sexual Violence during the Rwandan Genocide and its Aftermath', in *New York Human Rights Watch*.

Koenig and Askin (2000) 'International Criminal Law and the International Criminal Court Statute: Crimes Against Women' in Koenig and Askin (eds), *Women and International Human Rights Law*, vol. 2.

Ryan, S. (1999) 'From the Furies of Nanking to the Eumenides of the International Criminal Court: the Evolution of Sexual Assaults as International Crimes' in *PACE International Law Review*, vol. XI, no. 2.

Contributor: Claire De Than

VOTE AND DEMOCRACY, THE RIGHT TO

Is the right to vote a human right? Since such a right is likely to be quite meaningless in the absence of democracy, it may be argued that the right to vote is necessarily a derivative right that depends upon the prior recognition of a right to democracy itself. In other words, the right to vote is available only if we first have a right to democracy. Can such a right be defended and justified as a human right?

At first glance, it would appear that the idea of democracy and the concept of human rights are addressing two quite different issues. Democracy, at least minimally, is a form of government, and therefore speaks to the question of how legitimate public power is constituted in a society. Human rights, on the other hand, are about the entitlements that individuals have, or should have, *qua* humans. The one is about the political organisation of a society, the other about the individual rights of its members. A closer examination will demonstrate that these are not unrelated, and indeed that democracy (and therefore the vote) and human rights are seriously incomplete without each other.

It is no accident that the earliest modern articulations of the democratic ideal are in fact contained in two documents that are about the natural rights of the individual. The

French Declaration of the Rights of Man and Citizen (1789) proclaimed the rights of personal liberty, freedom of thought and religion, security of property and political equality as the natural entitlements not merely of French citizens but of 'mankind' at large. In this, as in the American Declaration of Independence (1776), we encounter the idea that certain natural rights attach to the individual, which are inalienable and imprescriptible, and these include the rights to life, liberty and property. Underwriting this, however, is the more fundamental claim that a political community has, in an expression of its sovereign will, formulated and mandated such a charter, by which 'the people' claim the right to govern themselves. Democracy is a natural outgrowth of such a claim, for it expresses simultaneously two aspects of self-government: the first, that the members of a political community participate in the processes of collective decision-making in the polity; and the second, that the institutions they put in place to rule on their behalf will be accountable to, and controlled by, them.

The right to vote does not automatically

follow from the enunciation of the democratic principle. Ancient Athens, for instance, practised a form of democracy in which only a privileged few had the right to participate. Today, however, we acknowledge that restrictive citizenship, which excludes women or religious and racial minorities from the political community, undermines democracy. In the modern world too, not all were entitled to vote even when representative institutions had emerged in 19th-century Britain, and it was not until 1929 that women secured the right to vote, with universal adult suffrage being fully achieved only in 1948 when plural voting was abolished in favour of the principle of one-person one-vote. This is why two aspects of democracy are of particular importance: equality and universality.

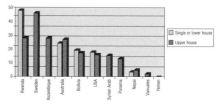

Equality of political representation between genders is still some way off. At the end of 2003, only 12 countries were headed by women. Graph shows percentage of women in national parliaments. (Statistics from the Inter-Parliamentary Union, www.ipu.org)

Aung Sung Suu Kyi © Associated Press, AP/Itsuo Inouye, Staff

The principle of equality is premised on the idea of individual autonomy, according to which individuals are autonomous beings, capable of rational thought and, therefore, of determining what is good for themselves. As such, all individuals should have an equal say in the determination of collective decisions that affect all of them equally. To the extent that democracy is premised on the principle of equality, it suggests that every citizen's vote should count for exactly the same as that of every other and that there should be no double-counting or special weight given to the vote of some citizens.

The principle of universality implies that the right to vote must be available to all adult citizens (because only adults are assumed to be politically competent) and that nobody should be excluded from the franchise on grounds of colour, sex or faith or indeed poverty or illiteracy. Together, these two conditions will ensure that the promise of democracy – as a guarantor of the right to participate on equal terms in the making of decisions that govern our lives – is fulfilled.

Democracy may be justified as having intrinsic or instrumental value. Valued instrumentally, democracy may be considered good because it fosters competition among political leaders and so gives us a better choice of leadership. Or it could be said that democracy is good because it makes everyone feel that they are a part of the decision-making process. Democracy may also be justified as a way of minimising the abuse of political power, by distributing it equally among citizens. Another instrumental justification for democracy is its role in human development, to the extent that it encourages people to take responsibility for their political lives.

The intrinsic value of democracy, as a good in and for itself, derives from its moral superiority as a way of giving effect to political equality. As a way of arriving at decisions among a group of persons, democracy is morally superior to any other way of arriving at decisions which are binding on all and which take everybody's interests into account. Even if citizens shared the same view of what constitutes the common good, they would surely hold different opinions of how to actually achieve that good. In such situations, democracy represents a fair moral compromise among people who live within the territory of the same state, but do not share a single conception of the good life.

In the Western world, democracy is frequently taken for granted and is assumed to be the natural and only way of constituting public power. This is a questionable assumption in many other parts of the world, even in countries that formally call themselves democracies, and there is a spirited debate in international human rights law about whether there is indeed a right to democratic governance. Many international instruments, beginning with the UN Charter and including the **UNIVERSAL DECLARATION OF HUMAN RIGHTS** (1948), the **INTERNATIONAL COVENANT ON CIVIL AND POLITICAL RIGHTS** (1976), as well as various other conventions of the **UNITED NATIONS** and the European Union, have accorded centrality to civil and political rights.

'The Electors shall meet in their respective states and vote by ballot for President and Vice-President, one of whom, at least, shall not be an inhabitant of the same state with themselves; they shall name in their ballots the person voted for as President, and in distinct ballots the person voted for as Vice-President, and they shall make distinct lists of all persons voted for as President, and of all persons voted for as Vice-President, and of the numbers of votes for each, which lists they shall sign and certify, and transmit sealed to the President of the Senate; – The President of the Senate shall, in presence of the Senate and House of Representatives, open all the certificates and the votes shall then be counted; – The person having the greatest number of votes for President shall be President, if such number be a majority of the whole number of Electors appointed; and if no person have such a majority, then from the persons having the highest numbers not exceeding three on the list of those voted for as President, the House of Representatives shall choose immediately, by ballot, the President. But in choosing the President, the voted shall be taken by states, the representation from each state having one vote; a quorum for this purpose shall consist of a member or members from two-thirds of the states, and a majority of all the states shall be necessary to a choice. The person having the greatest number of votes as Vice-President shall be Vice-President, if such number be a majority of the whole number of Electors appointed.'

(Amendment XII, 15 June 1804, to the Constitution of the United States of America)

In the European Union, indeed, democracy and human rights are necessary conditions that must be fulfilled by aspiring entrants. Though the voting booth is the focus of these rights, they also include the complementary rights to freedom of thought and opinion, speech and expression, and assembly and association: in other words, a comprehensive right to political participation.

Over the last decade and more, the United

Nations has been engaged in the observing and monitoring of elections, especially in states emerging from civil strife and conflict, such as Nicaragua, Cambodia and South Africa. Electoral assistance by UN agencies does imply a validation of governments that emerge from such electoral processes, thus endowing them with a legitimacy beyond that conferred by the electorate.

The thesis that there is a 'democratic entitlement' is, however, not without its difficulties. If democracy is indeed a good, should this be taken to imply that it is appropriate for the international community to force states to become democratic? In the pursuit of this objective, is it justifiable to use means/threats that are military, political or economic, and is such external interference not a violation of the sovereignty of the citizens of a particular state, precisely that which it is the avowed purpose of such interference to defend? Should the test of the legitimacy of a government be determined by its people or by the international community? Some have even argued that the project of democracy promotion by the international community and international NGOs is an attempt to impose a particular Western liberal-democratic vision of a desirable polity that is derived from the countries of the north.

It could also be argued that the endorsement of democracy by international law often amounts to little more than an endorsement of the shell of democracy, in the form of elections and party competition. The UN Human Development Report of 2002 estimated that the world is 'more democratic than ever before', with 140 countries having multiparty electoral systems. However, even in the minimal sense of being democratic, only 82 countries – representing 57 per cent of the world's population – are 'fully democratic'; 106 countries continue to place restrictions on civil and political freedoms.

Even as formal democracy is hard to achieve, political theorists advance a more exacting conception of democracy. Their dissatisfaction with the minimalist, procedural view of democracy, centred on the holding of elections, leads them to plead for a more robust and substantive notion of democracy that would recognise that, in the presence of background inequalities such as poverty and illiteracy, political rights are unlikely to be meaningful unless they are complemented by social and economic rights. On this view, the right to vote is not an adequate guarantee of democracy. It is a necessary, but arguably not a sufficient condition, for the realisation of the democratic ideal. As a human right, the right to vote needs to be embedded within a maximalist conception of human rights, including civil and political as well as social and economic rights. Only then will it be possible to achieve the necessary complementarity between democracy and human rights.

Further Reading

Beetham, David (1999) *Democracy and Human Rights*, Cambridge: Polity Press.

Fox, Gregory H. and Roth, Brad R. (eds) (2000) *Democratic Governance and International Law*, Cambridge: Cambridge University Press.

Ignatieff, Michael (2001) *Human Rights as Politics and Idolatry*, Princeton: Princeton University Press.

Przeworski, Adam (1999) 'Minimalist conception of democracy: a defense' in Shapiro, Ian and Hacker-Cordon, Casiano (eds) *Democracy's Value*, Cambridge: Cambridge University Press.

United Nations Development Programme (2002) *Human Development Report 2002: Deepening Democracy in a Fragmented World*, New York: Oxford University Press.

Contributor: Niraja Gopal Jayal

WOMEN'S RIGHTS

International human rights law regarding women is evolving through four overlapping strategies. Each is fluid, responding to the dynamics of women's lives and the human rights abuses as they emerge. For example, as evidence is gathered about how young girls are forced into child marriages, efforts are made to apply human rights to ensure that these marriages are prevented and that adolescent girls have meaningful alternatives to premature marriage through improved education and employment. Sometimes, different kinds of violations tend to predominate in certain regions. In Sub-Saharan Africa, for instance, women do not have the same access to or use of land that men enjoy. Moreover, as women's situations change, such as those of immigrant women, they are confronted with new forms of human rights violations.

As part of the first recent strategy of development of human rights law relating to women, states and non-state actors focus on the promotion of specific legal rights of women through the negotiation of specialised conventions, for instance concerning employment, trafficking in persons and violence against women. New international and regional conventions evolve, such as the 2000 Protocol to Prevent, Suppress and Punish Trafficking in Persons, especially Women and Children, supplementing the United Nations Convention against Transnational Organised Crime (See: **FREEDOM FROM SLAVERY** and **THE MIGRANT WORKER'S CONVENTION**). Each convention provides opportunities for debate and dialogue on one or more particular forms of violations of women's rights and has its own network of interested actors who work to ensure implementation of the convention.

The second strategy included sex as a legally prohibited ground of discrimination and works to implement the principle of sexual non-discrimination. This prohibition is included in the 1948 **UNIVERSAL DECLARATION OF HUMAN RIGHTS** and the international and regional human rights treaties designed to give legal effect to the Declaration (See: **THE INTERNATIONAL COVENANT ON CIVIL AND POLITICAL RIGHTS AND THE INTERNATIONAL COVENANT ON ECONOMIC SOCIAL AND CULTURAL RIGHTS**). The content and meaning of the prohibition of sex discrimination is expanding as these conventions are supplemented with protocols specific to women, such as the 2003 Protocol on the Rights of Women in Africa added to the African Charter on Human and Peoples' Rights, and as human rights tribunals apply these rights to remedy the particular forms of discrimination that women face (See: **INTERNATIONAL CRIMINAL LAW AND THE REGIONAL TRIBUNALS** and **VIOLENCE AGAINST WOMEN IN WAR TIME**).

Tribunals are recognising that some forms of discrimination are best remedied by ensuring that women's needs are treated according to their particularities, such as with respect to women's needs in reproduction. In other words, where there are legitimately recognised differences between men and women, they have to be treated according to their particular features. Courts have long recognised that similar cases have to be treated with regard to their similarities, such as in regard to women's equal pay for work of equal value, but that different cases justify treatment according to the differences, such as employment leave for maternity being longer than for paternity.

The third strategy in the development of international women's rights seeks to remedy the pervasive and structural nature of violations of women's rights, principally through the effective application of the 1979 **CONVENTION ON THE ELIMINATION OF ALL FORMS OF DISCRIMINATION AGAINST WOMEN**. The elimination of all forms of discrimination includes work on eliminating gender discrimination, meaning socially constructed discrimination, in contrast to sex discrimination, meaning exclusion on biological grounds, such as the exclusion of women from work on grounds of pregnancy or neglect of women's right to safety in pregnancy and childbirth. More recently, as insights have been gained into the intersections of different forms of discrimination, the reference to all forms of discrimination has been interpreted to mean multiple and overlapping forms of discrimination, such as sex and race, or sex and age discrimination (See: **CRITICAL RACE FEMINISM**). The content and meaning of the CEDAW Convention evolves as the Committee on the Elimination of Discrimination against Women (the CEDAW Committee) applies the Convention to specific forms of discrimination and develops General Recommendations to guide countries submitting the periodic reports the Convention requires.

For example, the CEDAW Committee's General Recommendation 25, adopted in 2004, addresses the need to adopt temporary special measures to achieve women's equality in fact, or *de facto* equality, also referred to as substantive equality or equality of result. This Recommendation explains that such measures are time-limited positive measures aimed 'to accelerate the improvement of the position of women to achieve their substantive equality with men, and to effect the structural, social and cultural changes necessary to correct past and current forms and effects of discrimination against women, as well as to provide them with compensation'. The Recommendation encourages states to consider adopting temporary special measures to accelerate the participation of women in political, economic, social, cultural and civil life, and the redistribution of power and resources necessary for such participation.

The fourth approach to the protection of women's rights seeks to integrate women's concerns into more generalised treaties such as on international trade, and, for example, the treaty establishing the **INTERNATIONAL CRIMINAL COURT**.

Unfortunately, all four approaches are characterised by a lack of state compliance in practice. The Preamble to the CEDAW Convention expressed the concern of state parties that 'despite these various instruments extensive discrimination against women continues to exist'. Many of the 177 States Parties to the CEDAW Convention have entered fundamental reservations to their acceptance of particular articles, which legally entitle them not to comply with those articles. Some states' reservations concern articles so central to the purpose of the Convention that there is doubt about whether those states can legally be considered parties at all (See: **DEROGATIONS AND RESERVATIONS**). In addition, many parties without such explicit reservations cannot be said to be implementing their commitments convincingly.

Explanations abound on why states do not comply with their obligations to respect and protect the human rights of women. One explanation is that human rights do not res-

Judge Rosalyn Higgins
Dame Rosalyn Higgins was the first female judge elected to the International Court of Justice. She studied in England and the USA then proceeded to combine international legal practice with academia. Among her many previous appointments, she served on the UN Human Rights Committee and the Tribunal for the International Centre for Settlement of Investment Disputes. She has published widely in Public International Law and International Human Rights.

onate with women, especially those who are not empowered or accustomed to hold their states or non-state actors accountable for neglect of their rights. From the perspective of some governments, their leaders and officers perceive that there is little political power to be gained by complying with human rights of women and in some countries political power might be lost by doing so. In contrast to the realist school of international law a more utopian school argues that governments comply with international law out of a sense of moral obligation and justice rather than simply out of self-interest. However, many governments that might comply with international law because of a sense of obligation and justice do not understand what obligations exist for the protection of women's rights.

A further explanation for states' lack of conformity with the CEDAW Convention to which they claim to subscribe is that reporting requirements do not provide sufficient incentives for compliance. States are obligated to report on a periodic basis on what they have done to bring their laws, policies and practices into compliance with the Convention. The CEDAW Committee makes note, in its Concluding Observations on each state report, of instances or patterns of non-compliance, but only has the power of persuasion to ensure compliance. The reporting requirement has now been strengthened by the adoption in 1999 of the Optional Protocol to the CEDAW Convention (the CEDAW Protocol) and its ratification by 60 states.

The CEDAW Protocol allows individuals from state parties to the CEDAW Convention that have ratified its Protocol to bring a communication in the form of a complaint to the CEDAW Committee, in order to seek redress for alleged violations of specific rights set forth in the Convention. The Protocol also allows the Committee to undertake inquiries when it receives reliable information indicating grave or systematic violations by a state party of the rights protected in the Convention. Unlike the complaints procedure, the inquiry procedure authorises the Committee to examine patterns of offending conduct culminating in grave or systematic violations rather than providing specific redress for individuals.

One of the CEDAW Protocol's greatest potentials lies in its ability to apply the principles of the CEDAW Convention to specific abuses affecting women, thereby developing the normative content of these principles. Moreover, the Protocol will provide women with a means of applying rights in areas that have not been sufficiently protected by other human rights conventions.

The CEDAW Protocol provides incentives for states to reform discriminatory laws and practices and to provide more effective avenues of redress for women at the domestic level. Individuals seeking redress must exhaust all reasonably available domestic remedies before the CEDAW Committee will admit their complaint. The author of the complaint must therefore make use of all available judicial and administrative avenues offering a reasonable prospect of redress. No obligation exists for a complainant to pursue remedies that are neither adequate nor effective. A significant contribution of this Protocol is to ensure that domestic remedies are available to and effective for women.

Beyond the formal mechanisms of enforcement of international human rights conventions relating to women are the less formal ways in which international human rights law influences or binds domestic constitutional practice with regard to women. Increasingly, norms of women's international human rights are applied in a variety of ways, such as to persuade judges to concretise or expand human rights or constitutional meanings in ways that are favourable to women.

WEBSITES

www.un.org/womenwatch/daw.htm

www.law-lib.utoronto.ca/diana.htm

Further Reading

Benedek, W., Kisaakye E., and Oberleitner, G. (eds) (2002) *Human Rights of Women International Instruments and African Experiences*, Zed Books.

Boerefijn, I. *et al.* (eds) (2003) *Temporary Special Measures – Accelerating de facto Equality of Women under Article 4(1) CEDAW*, Antwerp: Intersentia.

Knop, Karen (ed.) (2003) *Gender and Human Rights*, Oxford: Oxford University Press.

Contributors: Rebecca Cook and Simone Cusack

Afterword – globalisation with a human face: law, human rights and peace

The notion of 'globalisation' is often connected with the 20th century when the world, suppos-edly, became one big global village. It may seem to be paradoxical but at the same time con-temporary societies pay ever increasing attention to its atoms, to individuals who comprise it. However, we should be aware that discussions concerning the role of an individual in a state and subsequently in the international environment can be traced through several centuries and have their roots in a European value paradigm.

Throughout human history we have witnessed the mutual strugle between a tendency of power centres to consolidate and enlarge their domination over individuals and a tendency of societies to resist these endeavours and subject those in power to various forms of control. The notion of human and civil rights that gradually emerged from within this struggle has marked-ly developed since the Second World War.

While we stress the globalisation of values and benefits, we must, at the same time, acknowl-edge and pursue globalisation of equal opportunities and representation. In an ideal world globalisation of capital should be balanced by the globalisation of social justice. I am convinced that the United Nations' involvement in this area can be helpful or even crucial. Today the UN faces the need for closer cooperation between countries, promoting good governance and respect for human rights, sharing of benefits of globalisation, respect for cultural and religious diversity, involvement of other, non-state or non-governmental actors, such as civil societies, non-governmental organisations, the private sector: in brief – all stakeholders and therefore every citizen.

One of the most important sets of goals and targets that face the UN and the world com-munity are the Millenium Declaration Goals that attempt to address the most difficult problems affecting a majority of the world's population – POVERTY eradication, the fight against dis-eases, including HIV/AIDS, achieving universal primary EDUCATION and gender EQUALITY. Probably the most well-known commitment of the Millenium Summit was the ambitious task to halve the number of people living in extreme poverty by 2015. Whenever this will be achieved it will be an important step towards an environment much more conducive to respect for civil and political rights as well as SOCIAL, ECONOMIC and CULTURAL RIGHTS, and therefore for human rights in general.

Human rights or their violation are sometimes understood in a narrow sense, limited to physical abuse and violence. However, human rights include civil and political rights as well as economic, social and cultural rights, as I indicated above. Interconnection of civil and political rights and economic, social and cultural rights is a fact and each of these aspects of human rights is interrelated and cannot exist separately. People who are hungry or illiterate care very little for their empowerment of the right to vote and are not concerned about their potential power to bring about social change. On the other hand, people deprived of their right to vote can do very little to change their lives. It has to be welcomed that the UN human rights agenda includes civil and political rights as well as the right to adequate nourishment, the right to shel-ter, the right to live free from poverty, the right to HEALTH and life without HIV/AIDS, the right to education, to DEVELOPMENT, to equal treatment regardless of nationality, race or gender and the right to rebel against tyranny and abuse of the rule of law.

For the advancement of human rights it is important to involve other non-state and non-gov-ernmental actors as part of the concept of partnership. For example, an initiative of the

Secretary General Kofi Annan since January 1999 – the Global Compact – tries to reach the constituency of multinational companies and private businesses (See: **BUSINESS AND HUMAN RIGHTS**). The Global Compact asks them to embrace and enact, in their business operations, a set of core values in the areas of human rights, labour standards and the protection of the **ENVIRONMENT**. It is not a code of conduct and does not set legally binding arrangements. It is voluntary and designed as a learning forum. The Global Compact has also inspired many tangible projects, ranging from investment promotion in the least developed countries to human rights promotion in and around the workplace. Today more than 600 leading companies participate in the Global Compact. Kofi Annan's observation that 'if we cannot make globalisation work for all, in the end it will work for none.' has to be fully endorsed.

The United Nations Organisation plays an indispensable role not only in maintaining international peace and security but also in enhancing economic, developmental and humanitarian cooperation and promoting respect for human rights and fundamental freedoms. The United Nations was founded as a reaction to the atrocities and massive violations of basic human rights of the Second World War. Promoting and encouraging respect for rights and freedoms for all is, therefore, one of the main objectives embodied in the United Nations Charter. The preamble of the Charter contains a reaffirmation of 'faith in fundamental human rights, in the dignity and worth of the human person, in the equal rights of men and women and of nations large and small'. However, the general provisions of the Charter had to be substantiated through various General Assembly Resolutions and by international treaties. The most important among these instruments is the **UNIVERSAL DECLARATION OF HUMAN RIGHTS**, adopted by the General Assembly on 10 December 1948. Among the many international treaties that followed the Universal Declaration, I would emphasise the **INTERNATIONAL COVENANT ON CIVIL AND POLITICAL RIGHTS** and **INTERNATIONAL COVENANT ON ECONOMIC, SOCIAL AND CULTURAL RIGHTS**, both adopted in 1966 entering into force in 1976. These three documents together created the 'Bill of Human Rights'.

The United Nations also plays a pivotal role in the field of human rights by exercising general political pressure. Within the UN, the General Assembly and the Economic and Social Council can ask UN member states for information or reports on the status of human rights and fundamental freedoms in their respective countries. The state parties to the above mentioned human rights instruments are required to submit periodic reports on compliance with their obligations arising from each of the treaties. Expert bodies are established to consider these reports and to make recommendations in order to improve the promotion and protection of human rights.

However, it is necessary to underline again and again that the UN, as an intergovernmental organisation, can only reflect the political will of its members. In the absence of that will the UN is powerless and unable to prevent such great human tragedies as occurred in Rwanda or later in Srebrenica (See: **INTERNATIONAL CRIMINAL LAW AND THE REGIONAL TRIBUNALS**).

The United Nations can also offer technical cooperation in the field of human rights. States may receive technical assistance in the promotion and protection of human rights and in creating appropriate legislation. Such projects might include training courses for members of the armed forces, police forces or legal profession (See: **UNITED NATIONS HIGH COMMISSIONER FOR HUMAN RIGHTS**).

All UN actions, direct or indirect, can only be taken with the agreement of concerned member states and within the international law. In order to safeguard and defend basic human rights the United Nations seeks to use all available methods: anticipatory, preventive, curative, mitigatory and/or remedial. As an example of a direct action, the United Nations may provide protection by way of food, shelter and medical care to a population in distress from armed conflict. An indirect protection includes the creation of an international environment that is conducive to the realisation of human rights, as well as the elaboration of norms and standards, education, teaching, training, research and the dissemination of information and the provision of the advisory services in the field of human rights.

Depending on the political will of member states the United Nations should be able to help create, in time, an optimal socio-economic environment where people would be free of fear of hunger as well as free of fear of oppression and gross violation of their human rights, where the rule of law and justice – including social justice – will prevail. Within such an environment it would be easier to nip in the bud sources of tensions, conflicts, even wars and thus to effectively challenge feelings of powerlessness, frustration, anger and so on. It is obvious that these feelings, caused by a multitude of factors ranging from poverty to neglected and unsolved long-term political problems such as those in the Middle East, can provide fertile soil for radical, extremist or even terrorist behaviour (See: **TERRORISM AND HUMAN RIGHTS**).

As the President of the 57th Session of the General Assembly which ended in September 2003 I can fully endorse Secretary General Kofi Annan's recent assessment that that year was one of the most difficult in the history of the United Nations. I can testify that the war in Iraq directly or indirectly influenced all proceedings and discussions. UN diplomats discussed not just the alleged irrelevance of the UN but, in particular, how the notion of human rights was affected by the alleged main justification for the invasion of Iraq, that is the need to change the regime and export the US concept of **DEMOCRACY** and human rights.

Those who predicted the UN's demise because a majority on the Security Council refused to legitimise the invasion and to provide a fig leaf for the occupation of Iraq are disappointed. The UN's position has been vindicated. Today it is clear that there were no weapons of mass destruction nor any close cooperation between Saddam Hussein's secular regime and the fundamentalist terrorist organisation al-Qaeda, that is there was no smoke and no gun in Iraq and hence no legal excuse for the attack. It is clear that in March 2003 Iraq did not represent a grave, imminent and urgent threat and danger to the USA and the world. The Bush administration in the US has been slowly turning to the UN for help in extricating itself from the hole in the sand. The issue is one of legitimacy. No one, not even the handpicked members of the Iraqi Governing Council, want to be seen taking Iraqi 'sovereignty' as a gift from the coalition forces. They want the blessing of the United Nations, which because of its unique legitimacy is able to take away the stigma of quislinghood from any new Iraqi regime. There has not been any UN resolution that, even retrospectively, authorises or legalises the US and British invasion or occupation.

The uneasy relationship between the USA and the UN reflects an international system where one single nation possesses an unprecedented military and economic power, a nation so powerful that it can almost afford to ignore the entire international order – almost, but not entirely. The USA still needs the legitimacy and existence of a world order that only the United Nations can provide. On the other hand, the absence of the United States in the UN Organisation's activities would substantially hold back the entire institution and jeopardise many of its crucial programmes in the developing countries. The UN, in order to be effective, has to reflect the real world in which the USA is almost as indispensable as it thinks it is. If the UN did not reflect this reality, it would be out of touch with it and thus unable to influence it.

The case of Iraq illustrates the fact that preventive wars were projected from the US military doctrine into practice too hastily and probably without much consideration of the consequences and of the possibility that other countries may follow the US example and apply it in their own regions. It seems to me that the notion of preventive wars simply served the US need for its unilateralist decision to be backed by some theoretical justification. This new theory presents a great danger to multilateralism and in fact to the whole philosophy on which the UN rests. I agree with Kofi Annan's warning that preventive wars carried out unilaterally or in ad hoc coalitions, without any mandate from the Security Council of the UN, can lead to unilateral use of force outside international law and based on very questionable justifications. This would lead to a lawless jungle where only the will of the strongest prevails. The main victims will be human rights, peace and stability. Pope John Paul II pointedly argued that peace and international law are closely connected: the law is on the side of peace. To prefer the law of power against the power of law will lead to lawlessness and injustice.

A unilateral war – a war in which a country attacks another when it has not been itself attacked – must be undertaken only when the country's national survival is clearly at stake or under circumstances where the international community is so threatened that a strong power such as the US must save it from an enormous menace. Iraq clearly did not meet either of those tests. At the same time I would, of course, unhesitatingly agree that Iraq and the world are better off without Saddam Hussein.

I have spent more than two decades actively supporting Czech and other East and Central European human rights movements in their struggle against the authoritarian communist regimes. I remained a committed defender of human rights everywhere even after the fall of the Iron Curtain. As a Foreign Minister I tried to pursue an ethical foreign policy, though I do not claim to have been always 100 per cent successful. I, therefore, unhesitatingly supported Kofi Annan's endeavours to initiate a serious discussion on how we should best respond to threats of genocide or massive violations of human rights. The use of force should be considered only as the last resort and always in a multilateral context legitimised by the UN.

I fully understand that a 'regime change' may be sometimes desirable but that concept is not anchored in any international legal instrument. At least not yet. The process of setting of international human rights standards and its codification is obviously still developing and besides the UN member states, many international organisations and agencies, as well as non-governmental organisations, are participating in it. An important step towards the international protection of human rights and fundamental freedoms is a broad ratification of pertinent international treaties followed by implementation of those obligations by domestic legislation. This may help to accelerate the process of international law evolution that may, in time, even place at its very centre the need for human rights and dignity of individuals to be fully respected at almost all costs.

However, today the international law still recognises the 17th-century Westphalian principle of sovereignty of nation-states. The opponents of this status quo argue that it does not adequately incorporate the San Francisco Principles of individual human rights as proposed at the inauguration of the UN. The argument goes on to suggest that in the 21st century, sovereignty has become a 'responsibility to protect' rather than a right to rule with impunity. Supporters of this view state that undemocratic states that systematically abuse basic human rights open themselves up to the military intervention by democratic states in the name of protecting the fundamental human rights of sovereign citizens. The Westphalian order ended, allegedly, during the period that began with the attacks on 11 September 2001 and ended with the second Gulf War. The removal of illegitimate regimes that perpetrate gross abuses of human rights is – the argument goes on – the logical conclusion of the new international ethic based on a humanitarian universalism. The ideology of human rights has to, we are told, overrule the principle of sovereignty and that means that the current international law dominated by the inviolability of state sovereignty has to be either ignored or changed.

I have lived in an undemocratic country where we could not remove the ruling dictators alone and only by using democratic means. So I do find the above argument to a certain extent attractive and logical. However, I have to reiterate that international law, as it exists at any given time, has to be always fully respected and observed. This conviction of mine was only further strengthened by my experience as the President of the 57th session of the UN General Assembly, that is during the Iraq war. I have read that there are at least 43 undemocratic governments ruling a third of the world's population. Most of the ruled are among the world's poorest people with little personal security and fewer human rights. In the absence of clear rules and criteria who will, for example, decide which country is so grossly undemocratic that its government should be removed by force? Whose human rights are more important than others? Who will decide to justify a war during which many of these poor and oppressed citizens will die?

The idea that a regime change is justified by a gross violation of human rights in a given country assumes a kind of globalisation of justice. However, such a globalisation of justice requires a proper institutional framework which is not consistent with attempts to bypass the United Nations or the rejection of the **INTERNATIONAL CRIMINAL COURT**. Without such an institutional background and the full support of the international community, even a well-intentioned decision to invade can resemble an old-fashioned imperial decision. The notion of sovereignty is evolving, as is the notion of human rights. With increasing globalisation sovereignty is more and more limited, occasionally shared with others within more or less integrated groups of states but at the same time it is clear that within the foreseeable future sovereignty will not disappear and will continue to be cherished by many nation-states. Until this situation changes a regime change to facilitate an implementation of human rights has to be subjected to consensual rules of international law.

Jan Kavan

Further Reading

Dunne, Tim (1999) *Human Rights in Global Politics,* Cambridge: Cambridge University.

Forsythe, David P. (2000) *Human Rights in International Relations,* Cambridge: Cambridge University Press.

The Czech Republic's Presidency of the 57th Session of the United Nations General Assembly (10 Sept 2002–15 Sept 2003), New York, 2003.

UNDPI, (2001) *Basic Facts About the United Nations.*

Williams, Ian (2003) *Three Cheers for the UN,* Dissent, New York.

Williams, Ian (2004) 'Hole in the Sand', in *LA WEEKLY,* March.

INDEX